Incidents of Travel in Yucatan

Volumes I & II

JOHN LLOYD STEPHENS
FREDERICK CATHERWOOD, ILLUSTRATOR

NEW YORK

High above the heads of the crowd, catching the eye
on first entering the church, was the figure of Santiago,
or Saint James, on horseback, holy in the eyes of all
who saw it, and famed for its power of working miracles,
healing the sick, curing the fever and ague, insuring to
prospective parents a boy or girl as desired, bringing back
a lost cow or goat, healing a cut of the machete, or relieving
from any other calamity incident to an Indian's lot.

—from Chapter IX

Incidents of Travel in Yucatan

Volume I

CONTENTS

CHAPTER I

CHAPTER II

CHAPTER III

CHAPTER IV

CHAPTER V

CHAPTER VI

CHAPTER VII

CHAPTER VIII

CHAPTER IX

CHAPTER X

CHAPTER XI

CHAPTER XII

CHAPTER XVI

CHAPTER XVII

APPENDIX

LIST OF ILLUSTRATIONS

xiii

CHAPTER I

Embarcation.—Fellow-passengers.—A Gale at Sea.—Arrival at Sisal.—
Ornithological Specimens.—Merida.—Fête of San Cristoval.—The Lottery.—
A Scene of Confusion.—Principle of the Game.—Passion for Gambling.—A
deformèd Indian.

The reader of my "Incidents of Travel in Central America, Chiapas, and Yucatan," may remember that the researches of Mr. Catherwood and myself in the last-mentioned country were abruptly terminated by the illness of the former. During our short sojourn in Yucatan, we received vague, but, at the same time, reliable intelligence of the existence of numerous and extensive cities, desolate and in ruins, which induced us to believe that the country presented a greater field for antiquarian research and discoveries than any we had yet visited. Under these circumstances, it was a severe hardship that we were compelled to leave it, and our only consolation in doing so was the hope of being able to return, prepared to make a thorough exploration of this unknown and mysterious region. In about a year we found ourselves in a condition to do so; and on Monday, the ninth of October, we put to sea on board the bark Tennessee, Scholefield master, for Sisal, the port from which we had sailed on our return to the United States.

The Tennessee was a down-Easter of two hundred and sixty tons burden, turned out apparently from one of those great factories where ships are built by the mile and chopped off to order, but stout, strong, well manned and equipped.

Her cargo was assorted for the Yucatan market, and consisted of a heavy stratum of iron at the bottom; midway were miscellanies, among which were cotton, muskets, and two hundred barrels of turpentine; and on top, within reach of the hatches, were six hundred kegs of gunpowder.

We had a valuable addition to our party in Dr. Cabot, of Boston, who accompanied us as an amateur, particularly as an

1

ornithologist. Besides him, our only fellow-passenger was Mr. Camerden, who went out as supercargo.

The first morning out we woke with an extraordinary odour of turpentine, giving us apprehensions that a barrel had sprung a leak, which, by means of the cotton, might use up our gunpowder before it came to the hands of its consignee. This odour, however, was traced to a marking-pot, which quieted our apprehensions.

On the evening of the fourth day we had a severe thunderstorm. This was an old acquaintance of ours in the tropics, but one which at that time we were not disposed to welcome very cordially. Peals of thunder broke and crashed close over our heads, lightning flashed across the dark vault of the heavens, lighting up the surface of the water, and making fearfully visible our little vessel, tossing and pitching, a mere speck in immensity; and at times an angry ray darted toward the horizon, as if expressly to ignite our gunpowder. We discussed, though rather disjointedly, the doctrine of conductors and non-conductors, and advised the captain to put a few links of a chain cable round the mainmast, and carry the end of it over the side. We had some consolation in thinking that six hundred kegs were no worse than sixty, and that six would do our business; but, in fact, at the moment, we were very much of opinion that lightning and gunpowder were the only dangers of the sea. The night, however, wore through, and morning brought with it the usual, and, unhappily, almost the only change in those who go down to the sea in ships—forgetfulness of past danger.

On the evening of the seventeenth we passed, with a gentle breeze, the narrow passage known as the Hole in the Wall, and before morning we were lying broadside to the wind, and almost flying before it. The gale was terrific; nothing could stand upright to windward, and the sea was portentous. The captain sat under the quarter rail, watching the compass, and turning anxiously to the misty quarter of the heavens from which the winds seemed let loose. At breakfast large drops of sweat stood on his forehead; and though at first unwilling to admit it even to himself, we discovered that we were really in danger. We were driving, as fast as the wind could send us, upon the range of sunken rocks known as Abaco reef. Directly under our lee was the worst part of the whole reef, marked on the chart "Dangerous rocky shore." Unless the gale abated or the wind hauled, in eight or ten hours we must strike. I must confess I saw but little hope of a change, and this rocky reef was but a few feet under water, and twenty miles distant from terra firma. If the vessel struck, she must go to pieces; nothing made by man's hands could stand against the fury of the sea, and every moment we were nearer destruction. We sat with the chart before us, looking at it as a sentenced convict might look at an advertisement of the time fixed for his execution. The sunken rocks seemed to stand out horribly on the paper; and though every glance at the sea told us that with daylight no human strength could prevail against it, it added to our uncomfortable feelings to know that it would be nearly night when the crisis arrived. We had but one consolation—there were no women or children on board. All were able-bodied men, capable of doing all that men could do in a struggle for life. But, fortunately for the reader of these pages, to say nothing of the relief to ourselves, at one o'clock the wind veered; we got on a little canvass; the good ship struggled for her life; by degrees she turned her back upon danger, and at night we were again on our way rejoicing.

On the twenty-seventh we furled sails off the port of Sisal. Five vessels were at anchor, an extraordinary circumstance for Sisal, and fortunate for us, because otherwise, as our captain had never been there before, though carefully looking for it, we might not have been able to find it. Our anchorage ground was on the open coast, two or three miles from land, at which distance it was necessary to keep, lest we should be driven ashore in case of a norther. Captain Scholefield, in fact, before he had discharged his cargo, was obliged to slip his cables and put to sea, and did not get back to his anchorage ground in nine days.

It was only four o'clock in the afternoon, but, by the regulations of the port, no passenger could land until the vessel had been visited by the health and custom-house officers. We looked out till dark, and long after the moon rose, but no notice whatever was taken of us, and, with no very amiable feelings toward the lazy officials, we turned in again on board.

In the morning, when we went on deck, we saw anchored under our stern the brig Lucinda, in which we had thought of taking passage; she had sailed from New-York four days after we did, and arrived during the night.

Very soon we saw coming off toward us the separate canoas of the health and custom-house officers. We were boarded by a very little man with a very big mustache, who was seasick before he mounted the deck, and in a few minutes betook himself to a berth. The preliminaries, however, were soon settled, and we went ashore. All disposition we might have had to complain the night before ceased on landing. Our former visit was not forgotten. The account of it had been translated and published, and, as soon as the object of our return was known, every facility was given us, and all our trunks, boxes, and multifarious luggage were passed without examination by the custom-house officers.

The little town of Sisal had not increased either in houses or inhabitants, and did not present any additional inducements to remain in it. The same afternoon we sent off our luggage in a carreta for Merida, and the next morning started in calezas ourselves.

From the suburbs of the town the plain was inundated, and for more than a mile our horses were above their knees in water. When we passed before, this ground was dry, parched, and cracking open. It was now the last of the rainy season, and the great body of water, without any stream by which to pass off, was drying up under a scorching sun, to leave the earth infected with malaria.

We had arrived in the fulness of tropical vegetation; the stunted trees along the road were in their deepest green, and Dr. Cabot opened to us a new source of interest and beauty. In order to begin business at once, he rode in the first caleza alone, and before he had gone far, we saw the barrel of his gun protrude on one side, and a bird fall. He had seen at Sisal, egretes, pelicans, and ducks which were rare in collections at home, and an oscillated wild turkey, which alone he thought worth the voyage to that place; and now, our attention being particularly directed to the subject, in some places the shrubs and bushes seemed brilliant with the plumage and vocal with the notes of birds. On the road he saw four different species which are entirely unknown in the United States, and six others which are found only in Louisiana and Florida, of most of which he procured specimens.

We stopped at Huncuma during the heat of the day; at dark reached Merida, and once more rode up to the house of Doña Micaela. Coming directly from home, we were not so much excited as when we reached it after a toilsome and comfortless journey in Central America; but even now it would ill become me to depreciate it, for the donna had read the account of my former visit to Merida, and she said, with an emphasis that covered all the rest, that the dates of arrival and departure as therein mentioned corresponded exactly with the entries in her book.

We had arrived at Merida at an opportune moment. As on

the occasion of our first visit, it was again a season of fiesta. The fête of San Cristoval, an observance of nine days, was then drawing to its close, and that evening a grand *function* was to be performed in the church dedicated to that saint. We had no time to lose, and, after a hasty supper, under the guidance of an Indian lad belonging to the house, we set out for the church. Very soon we were in the main street leading to it, along which, as it seemed, the whole population of Merida was moving to the fête. In every house a lantern hung from the balconied windows, or a long candle stood under a glass shade, to light them on their way. At the head of the street was a large plaza, on one side of which stood the church, with its great front brilliantly illuminated, and on the platform and steps, and all the open square before it, was a great moving mass of men, women, and children, mostly Indians, dressed in white.

We worked our way up to the door, and found the church within a blaze of light. Two rows of high candlesticks, with wax candles eight or ten feet high, extended the whole length from the door to the altar. On each side hung innumerable lamps, dotting the whole space from the floor to the ceiling; and back at the extreme end, standing on an elevated platform, was an altar thirty feet high, rich with silver ornaments and vases of flowers, and hung with innumerable lamps brilliantly burning. Priests in glittering vestments were officiating before it, music was swelling through the corridor and arches, and the floor of the immense church was covered with women on their knees, dressed in white, with white shawls over their heads. Through the entire body of the church not a man was to be seen. Near us was a bevy of young girls, beautifully dressed, with dark eyes, and their hair adorned with flowers, sustaining, though I was now a year older and colder, my previous impressions of the beauty of the ladies of Merida.

The chant died away, and as the women rose from their knees, their appearance was like the lifting of a white cloud, or spirits of air rising to a purer world; but, as they turned toward the door, the horizon became dusky with Indian faces, and half way up a spot rose above the rest, black as a thunder-cloud. The whole front ranks were Indians, except a towering African, whose face, in the cloud of white around, shone like the last touch of Day and Martin's best.

We waited till the last passed out, and, leaving the empty church blazing with light, with rockets, fireworks, drums, and violins all working away together on the steps, we followed the crowd.

Turning along the left side of the plaza, we entered an illuminated street, at the foot of which, and across it, hung a gigantic cross, also brilliantly illuminated, and apparently stopping the way. Coming as we did directly from the church, it seemed to have some immediate connexion with the ceremonies we had just beheld; but the crowd stopped short of the cross, opposite a large house, also brilliantly illuminated. The door of this house, like that of the church, was open to all who chose to enter, or rather, at ʳhat moment, to all who could force their way through. Waiting the motion of the mass before us, and pressed by those behind, slowly, and with great labour, we worked our way into the sala. This was a large room extending along the whole front of the house, hot to suffocation, and crowded, or rather jammed, with men and women, or gentlemen and ladies, or by whatever other names they may be pleased to be called, clamorous and noisy as Bedlam let loose. For some time it was impossible for us to form any idea of what was going on. By degrees we were carried lengthwise through the sala, at every step getting elbowed, stamped upon, and occasionally the rim of a straw hat across the nose, or the puff of a paper cigar in the eyes. Very soon our faces were trickling with tears, which there was no friendly hand to wipe away, our own being pinned down to our sides.

On each side of the sala was a rude table, occupying its whole length, made of two rough boards, and supporting candles stuck in little tin receivers, about two feet apart. Along the tables were benches of the same rough materials, with men and women, whites, Mestizoes, and Indians, all sitting together, as close as the solidity and resistance of human flesh would permit, and seemingly closer than was sufferable. Every person at the table had before him or her a paper about a foot square, covered with figures in rows, and a small pile of grains of corn, and by its side a thumping stick some eighteen inches long, and one in diameter; while, amid all the noise, hubbub, and confusion, the eyes of all at the tables were bent constantly upon the papers before them. In that hot place, they seemed like a host of necromancers and witches, some of the latter young and extremely pretty, practising the black art.

By degrees we were passed out into the corridor, and here we were brought to a dead stand. Within arm's length was an imp of a boy, apparently the ringleader in this nocturnal orgy,

who stood on a platform, rattling a bag of balls, and whose un-
intermitted screeching, singsong cries had throughout risen
shrill and distinct above every other sound. At that moment the
noise and uproar were carried to the highest. The whole house
seemed rising against the boy, and he, single-handed, or rather
single-tongued, was doing battle with the whole, sending forth
a clear stream of vocal power, which for a while bore its way
triumphantly through the whole troubled waters, till, finding
himself overpowered by the immense majority, with a tone that
set the whole mass in a roar, and showed his democratic principles, he cried out, "Vox populi est vox Dei!" and submitted.

Along the corridor, and in the whole area of the patio, or
courtyard, were tables, and benches, and papers, and grains of
corn, and ponderous sticks, the same as in the sala, and men and
women sitting as close together. The passages were choked up,
and over the heads of those sitting at the tables, all within reach
were bending their eyes earnestly upon the mysterious papers.
They were grayheads, boys and girls, and little children; fathers
and mothers; husbands and wives; masters and servants; men
high in office, muleteers, and bull-fighters; señoras and señoritas,
with jewels around their necks and roses in their hair, and
Indian women, worth only the slight covering they had on;
beauty and deformity; the best and the vilest in Merida; perhaps, in all, two thousand persons; and this great multitude,
many of whom we had seen but a few minutes before on their
knees in the church, and among them the fair bevy of girls who
had stood by us on the steps, were now assembled in a public
gambling-house! a beautiful spectacle for a stranger the first
night of his arrival in the capital!

But the devil is not so black as he is painted. I do not mean
to offer any apology for gambling, in Yucatan, as in all the rest
of Mexico, the bane and scourge of all ranks of society; but Merida is, in a small way, a city of my love, and I would fain raise
this great mass of people from the gulf into which I have just
plunged them: at least, I would lift their heads a little above
water.

The game which they were engaged in playing is called La
Loteria, or the Lottery. It is a favourite amusement throughout
all the Mexican provinces, and extends to every village in Yucatan. It is authorized by the government, and, as was formerly
the case to a pernicious extent with the lotteries in our own
country, is used as an instrument to raise money, either for the
use of the government itself, or for other purposes which are

considered deserving. The principle of the game, or the scheme, consists of different combinations of numbers, from one to ninety, which are written on papers, nine rows on each side, with five figures in each row. As ninety figures admit of combinations to an almost indefinite extent, any number of papers can be issued, each containing a different series of combinations. These papers are stamped by the government, and sold at a real, or twelve and a half cents each. Every player purchases one of these papers, and fastens it to the table before him with a wafer. A purse is then made up, each player putting in a certain sum, which is collected by a boy in a hat. The boy with the bag of balls then announces, or rather sings out, the amount of the purse, and rattling his bag of balls, draws out one, and sings the number drawn. Every player marks on his paper with a grain of corn the number called off, and the one who is first able to mark five numbers in a row wins the purse. This he announces by rapping on the table with the stick, and standing up in his place. The boy sings over again the numbers drawn, and if, on comparison, all is found right, delivers the purse. The game is then ended, and another begins. Sometimes mistakes occur, and it was a mistake that led to the extraordinary clamour and confusion we had found on reaching the neighbourhood of the boy.

The amount played for will give some idea of the character of the game. Before commencing, the boy called out that the stake should in no case exceed two reals. This, however, was considered too high, and it was fixed by general consent at a medio, or six and a quarter cents. The largest amount proclaimed by the boy was twenty-seven dollars and three reals, which, divided among four hundred and thirty-eight players, did not make very heavy gambling. In fact, an old gentleman near whom I was standing told me it was a small affair, and not worth learning; but he added that there was a place in the neighbourhood where they played monté for doubloons. The whole amount circulated during the evening fell far short of what is often exchanged at a small party in a private drawing-room at home, and among those who would not relish the imputation of being accounted gamblers. In fact, it is perhaps but just to say that this great concourse of people was not brought together by the spirit of gambling. The people of Merida are fond of amusements, and in the absence of theatres and other public entertainments, the loteria is a great gathering-place, where persons of all ages and classes go to meet acquaintances. Rich and poor, great and small, meet under the same roof on a footing of perfect equality; good feeling is cultivated among all without any forgetting their place. Whole families go thither together; young people procure seats near each other, and play at more desperate games than the loteria, where hearts, or at least hands, are at stake, and perhaps that night some bold player, in losing his medios, drew a richer prize than the large purse of twenty-seven dollars and three reals. In fact, the loteria is considered merely an accessory to the pleasures of social intercourse; and, instead of gaming, it might be called a grand *conversacione,* but not very select; at least such was our conclusion; and there was something to make us rather uncharitable, for the place was hot enough to justify an application to it of the name bestowed in common parlance on the gambling-houses of London and Paris.

At about eleven o'clock we left. On our way down the street we passed the open door of a house in which were tables piled with gold and silver, and men around playing what, in the opinion of my old adviser of the loteria, was a game worth learning. We returned to the house, and found, what in our haste to be at the fiesta we had paid no attention to, that Doña Micaela could give us but one room, and that a small one, and near the door. As we expected to remain some days in Merida, we determined the next morning to take a house and go to housekeeping. While arranging ourselves for the night, we heard a loud, unnatural noise at the door, and, going out, found rolling over the pavement the Cerberus of the mansion, an old Indian miserably deformed, with his legs drawn up, his back down, his neck and head thrust forward, and his eyes starting from their sockets; he was entertaining himself with an outrageous soliloquy in the Maya tongue, and at our appearance he pitched his voice higher than before. Signs and threats had no effect. Secure in his deformity, he seemed to feel a malicious pleasure that he had it in his power to annoy us. We gave up, and while he continued rolling out tremendous Maya, we fell asleep. So passed our first night in Merida.

CHAPTER II

Early the next morning the carreta arrived
with our luggage, and, to avoid the trouble of loading and un-
loading, we directed it to remain at the door, and set out
immediately to look for a house. We had not much time, and,
consequently, but little choice; but, with the help of Doña
Micaela, in half an hour we found one that answered our purpose. We returned and started the carreta; an Indian followed,
carrying on his head a table, and on the top of it a washhand-
basin; another with three chairs, all Doña Micaela's, and we
closed the procession.

Our house was in the street of the Flamingo. Like most of
the houses in Merida, it was built of stone, and had one story;
the front was about thirty feet, and had a sala covering the
whole, about twenty feet in depth. The ceiling was perhaps
eighteen feet high, and the walls had wooden knobs for fastening hammocks. Behind the sala was a broad corridor, opening
on a courtyard, at one side of which was a sleeping-room,
and at the back of that a comeder or eating-room. The floors
were all of hard cement. The courtyard was about thirty feet
square, with high stone walls, and a well in the centre. Next,
running across the lot, was a kitchen, with a sleeping-room for
servants, and back of that another courtyard, forty feet deep,
with stone walls fifteen feet high; and in order that my inquiring fellow-citizens may form some idea of the comparative
value of real estate in Merida and New York, I mention that
the rent was four dollars per month, which for three persons

we did not consider extravagant. We had our own travelling beds, the table, washhand-basin, and chairs set up, and before breakfast our house was furnished.

In the mean time the fiesta of San Cristoval was going on. Grand mass was over, and the next ceremony in order was a *corrida de toros,* or bull-fight, to commence at ten o'clock.

The Plaza de Toros, or, in English, the bull-ring, was in the square of the church of San Cristoval. The enclosure or place for spectators occupied nearly the whole of the square, a strange and very original structure, which in its principles would astonish a European architect. It was a gigantic circular scaffold, perhaps fifteen hundred feet in circumference, capable of containing four or five thousand persons, erected and held together without the use of a single nail, being made of rude poles, just as they were cut in the woods, and tied together with withes. The interior was enclosed by long poles, crossing and interlacing each other, leaving only an opening for the door, and was divided in like manner by poles into boxes. The whole formed a gigantic frame of rustic lattice-work, admirably adapted for that hot climate, as it admitted a free circulation of air. The top was covered with an arbour made of the leaves of the American palm. The whole structure was simple and curious. Every Indian could assist in building it, and when the fiesta was over it could be torn down, and the materials used for firewood.

The corrida had begun when we arrived on the ground, and the place was already thronged. There was a great choice of seats, as one side was exposed to the full blaze of the sun. Over the doors were written Palco No. 1, Palco No. 2, &c., and each box had a separate proprietor, who stood in the doorway, with a little rickety step-ladder of three or four steps, inviting customers. One of them undertook to provide for us, and for two reals apiece we were conducted to front seats. It was, if possible, hotter than at the loteria, and in the movement and confusion of passing us to our seats, the great scaffold trembled, and seemed actually swaying to and fro under its living load.

The spectators were of all classes, colours, and ages, from gray heads to children asleep in their mother's arms; and next to me was a half-blooded maternal head of a family, with the key of her house in her hand, her children tucked in between the legs of her neighbours, or under their chairs. At the feet of those sitting on the front seats was a row of boys and girls, with their little heads poked through the railing, and all around hung down a variegated fringe-work of black and white legs. Opposite, and on the top of the scaffold, was a band of music, the leader of which wore a shining black mask, caricaturing a negro.

A bull was in the ring, two barbed darts trimmed with blue and yellow paper were hanging from his flanks, and his neck was pierced with wounds, from which ran down streams of blood. The picadores stood aloof with bloody spears in their hands; a mounted dragoon was master of ceremonies, and there were, besides, eight or ten vaqueros, or cattletenders, from the neighbouring haciendas, hard riders, and brought up to deal with cattle that run wild in the woods. These were dressed in pink-coloured shirt and trousers, and wore small hats of straw platted thick, with low round crowns, and narrow brims turned up at the side. Their saddles had large leathern flaps, covering half the body of the horse, and each had a lazo, or coil of rope, in his hand, and a pair of enormous iron spurs, perhaps six inches long, and weighing two or three pounds, which, contrasted with their small horses, gave a sort of Bombastes Furioso character to their appearance. By the order of the dragoon, these vaqueros, striking their coils of rope against the large flaps of their saddles, started the bull, and, chasing him round the ring, with a few throws of the lazo caught him by the horns and dragged him to a post at one side of the ring, where, riding off with the rope, they hauled his head down to the ground close against the post. Keeping it down in that position, some of the others passed a rope twice round his body just behind the fore legs, and, securing it on the back, passed it under his tail, and returning it, crossed it with the coils around his body. Two or three men on each side then hauled upon the rope, which cut into and compressed the bull's chest, and by its tightness under the tail almost lifted his hind legs from off the ground. This was to excite and madden him. The poor animal bellowed, threw himself on the ground, and kicked and struggled to get rid of the brutal tie. From the place where we sat we had in full view the front of the church of San Cristoval, and over the door we read in large characters, *"Hic est domus Dei—hic est portus cœli."* "This is the house of God—this is the gate of heaven."

But they had yet another goad for the bull. Watching narrowly that the ropes around his horns did not get loose, they fixed upon his back the figure of a soldier in a cocked hat, seated in a saddle. This excited a great laugh among the spectators. We learned that both the saddle and the figure of the soldier were made of wood, paper, and gunpowder, composing a formidable piece of fireworks. When this was fairly secured, all fell back, and the picadores, mounted, and with their spears poised, took their places in the ring. The band, perhaps in compliment to us, and to remind us of home, struck up the beautiful *national* melody of "Jim Crow." A villanous-looking fellow set off large and furiously-whizzing rockets within a few feet of the bull; another fired in the heel the figure of the soldier on his back; the spectators shouted, the rope was slipped, and the bull let loose.

His first dash was perfectly furious. Bounding forward and throwing up his hind legs, maddened by the shouts of the crowd, and the whizzing and explosion, fire and smoke of the engine of torture on his back, he dashed blindly at every picador, receiving thrust after thrust with the spear, until, amid the loud laughter and shouts of the spectators, the powder burned out, and the poor beast, with gaping wounds, and blood streaming from them, turned and ran, bellowed for escape at the gate of entrance, and then crawled around the wall of the ring, looking up to the spectators, and with imploring eyes seemed pleading to the mild faces of the women for mercy.

In a few minutes he was lazoed and dragged off, and he had hardly disappeared when another was led in, the manner of whose introduction seemed more barbarous and brutal than any of the torments inflicted on the former. It was by a rope two or three hundred feet long, passed through the fleshy part of the bull's nose, and secured at both ends to the vaquero's saddle. In this way he was hauled through the streets and into the ring. Another vaquero followed, with a lazo over the horns, to hold the bull back, and keep him from rushing upon his leader. In the centre of the ring the leader loosed one end of the rope, and, riding on, dragged it trailing on the ground its whole length, perhaps a hundred yards, through the bull's nose, leaving a crust of dirt on one side as it came out bloody on the other. The bull, held back by the rope over his horns, stood with his neck outstretched; and when the end of the rope passed through, he licked his gory nose, pawed the ground, and bellowed.

He was then lazoed, dragged up to the post, girt with the rope around his body like the other, and then, amid bursts of music, rockets, and shouts, again let loose. The chulos went at him, flaring before him with the left hand red and yellow ponchas, and holding in the right darts containing fireworks, and ornamented with yellow paper cut into slips. These they thrust into his neck and flanks. The current of air accelerated the ignition of the fire; and when the fireworks exploded, the paper still rattled about his ears. The picadores then mounted their horses; but, after a few thrusts of the spear, the bull flinched, and the spectators, indignant that he did not show more fight, cried out, *"Saca esa vaca!"* "Take out that *cow!"*

The next was hauled on in the same way by a rope through the nose. He was girt with the rope, tortured with darts, speared by the picadores on horseback, and, as he did not show good fight, they dismounted and attacked him on foot. This is considered the most dangerous contest both for man and beast. The picadores formed in front of him, each with a black or yellow poncha in his left hand, and poising his spear with the right. They stood with their legs extended and knees bent, so as to keep a firm foothold, changing position by a spring forward or backward, on one side or the other, to meet the movement of the bull's head. The object was to strike between the horns into the back of the neck. Two or three struck him fairly with a cutting, heavy sound, and drew out their spears reeking with blood. One man misdirected his blow; the bull threw up his neck with the long handle of the spear standing upright in it, and rushing upon the picador, hurled him to the ground, and passed over his body, seeming to strike him with all four of his hoofs. The man never moved, but lay on his back, with his arms outstretched, apparently dead. The bull moved on with the handle of the spear still standing up in his neck, a terror to all in the ring. The vaqueros went in pursuit of him with the lazos, and, chasing him round, the spear fell out, and they caught him. In the mean time, the fallen man was picked up by some of his companions, and carried off, doubled up, and apparently cured forever of bull-fighting. We heard afterward that he only had some of his ribs broken.

He was hardly out of sight when the accident was forgotten; the bull was again assaulted, worried out, and dragged off. Others followed, making eight in all. At twelve o'clock the church bells rang and the fight ended, but, as we were dispersing, we were reminded that another would begin at four o'clock in the afternoon.

At four we were again in our places. Our special reason for following up this sport so closely was because we were advised that in the morning common people only attended, but that in the afternoon all the *gente decente,* or upper classes, of Merida would be present. I am happy to say, however, that this was not true, and the only sensible difference that we noticed was, that it was more crowded and hotter, and that the price of admission was double.

This was the last corrida of the fiesta, and some of the best bulls had been kept in reserve. The first that was dragged on was received with acclamations, as having distinguished himself before during the fiesta; but he bore an ugly mark for a favourite of the people, having been dragged by the nose till the cartilage was completely torn out by the rope.

The next would have been worthy of the best bull-fights of Old Spain, when the cavalier, at the glance of his lady's eye, leaped into the ring to play the matador with his sword. He was a large black bull, without any particular marks of ferocity about him; but a man who sat in our box, and for whose judgment I had conceived a great respect, lighted a new straw cigar, and pronounced him *"muy bravo."* There was no bellowing, blustering, or bravado about him, but he showed a calmness and self-possession which indicated a consciousness of strength. The picadores attacked him on horseback, and, like the Noir Faineant, or Sluggish Knight, in the lists at Ashby, for a time he contented himself with merely repelling the attacks of his assailants; but suddenly, as if a little vexed, he laid his head low, looked up at the spears pointed at his neck, and, shutting his eyes, rushed upon a picador on one side, struck his horse in the belly with his horns, lifted him off his feet, and brought horse and rider headlong to the ground. The horse fell upon the rider, rolled completely over him, with his heels in the air, and rose with one of the rider's feet entangled in the stirrup. For an instant he stood like a breathing statue, with nostrils wide and ears thrown back, wild with fright; and then, catching sight of the bull, he sprang clear of the ground, and dashed off at full speed around the ring, dragging after him the luckless picador. Around he went, senseless and helpless, his whole body grimed with dirt, and with no more life in it, apparently, than in a mere log of wood. At every bound it seemed as if the horse must strike his hind hoofs into his forehead. A cold shudder ran through the spectators. The man was a favourite; he had friends and relatives present, and everybody knew his name. A deep murmur of *"El Pobre"* burst from every bosom. I felt actually lifted from my seat, and the president of the Life and Trust would not have given a policy upon him for any premium. The picadores looked on aghast; the bull was roaming loose in the ring, perhaps the only indifferent spectator. My own feelings were roused against his companions, who, after what seemed an age of the rack, keeping a special good lookout upon the bull, at length started in pursuit with lazos, caught the horse around the neck, and brought him up headlong. The picadores extricated their fallen companion, and carried him out. His face was so begrimed with dirt that not a feature was visible; but, as he was borne across the ring, he opened his eyes, and they seemed starting from his head with terror.

He was hardly out of the ring when a hoarse cry ran through the spectators, "*a pie! a pie!*" "on foot! on foot!" The picadores dismounted and attacked the bull fiercely on foot, flourishing their ponchas. Almost at the first thrust he rushed upon one of his adversaries, tumbled him down, passed over his body and walked on without even turning round to look at him. He too was picked up and carried off.

The attack was renewed, and the bull became roused. In a few moments he brought another picador to the ground, and, carried on by his own impetus, passed over the body, but, with a violent effort, recovered himself, and turned short round upon his prostrate prey, glared over him for a moment with a low bellow, almost a howl, and, raising his fore feet a little from the ground, so as to give full force to the blow, thrust both horns into the stomach of the fallen picador. Happily, the points were sawed off; and, furious at not being able to gore and toss him, he got one horn under the picador's sash, lifted him, and dashed him back violently upon the ground. Accustomed as the spectators were to scenes of this kind, there was a universal burst of horror. Not a man moved to save him. It would, perhaps, be unjust to brand them as cowards, for, brutal and degrading as their tie was, they doubtless had a feeling of companionship; but, at all events, not a man attempted to save him, and the bull, after glaring over him, smelling and pawing him for a moment, to all a moment of intense excitement, turned away and left him.

This man, too, was carried off. The sympathy of the spectators had for a while kept them hushed; but, as soon as the man was out of sight, all their pent-up feelings broke out in indignation against the bull, and there was a universal cry, in which the soft tones of women mingled with the hoarse voices of the men, "*Matálo! matálo!*" "Kill him! kill him!" The picadores stood aghast. Three of their companions had been struck down and carried off the field; the bull, pierced in several places, with blood streaming from him, but fresh as when he began, and fiercer, was roaming round the ring, and they held back, evidently afraid to attack him. The spectators showered upon them the opprobrious name of *"cobardes! cobardes!"* "cowards! cowards!" The dragoon enforced obedience to their voice, and, fortifying themselves with a strong draught of agua ardiente, they once more faced the bull, poised their spears before him, but with faint hands and trembling hearts, and finally, without a single thrust, amid the contemptuous shouts of the crowd, fell back, and left the bull master of the field.

Others were let in, and it was almost dark when the last fight ended. With the last bull the ring was opened to the boys, who, amid roars of laughter, pulled, hauled, and hustled him till he could hardly stand, and, amid the solemn tones of the vesper bell, the bull-fight in honour of San Cristoval ended.

Modern laws, we are told, have done much to abate the danger and ferocity of bull-fights. The horns of the bull are sawed off, so that he cannot gore, and spears are not allowed of more than a certain length, so that the bull cannot be killed by a direct blow; but, in my opinion, it would be really better for effect upon moral character that a bullfight should be, as it once was, a battle for life between man and beast, for then it was an exhibition of skill and daring, around which were sometimes thrown the graces of chivalry. The danger to which the man exposed himself, to a certain extent atoned for the barbarities inflicted on the bull. Here for eight days bulls with blunted horns had been stabbed, mangled, and tortured; many, no doubt, died of their wounds, or were killed because they could not recover; and that day we had seen four men struck down and carried off, two of whom had narrowly escaped with their lives, if, indeed, they ever recovered. After the immediate excitement of the danger, the men were less objects of commiseration than the beasts, but the whole showed the still bloody effects of this modified system of bull-fighting. Men go into all places without shame, though not without reproach, but I am happy in being able to say that none of what are called the higher classes of the ladies of Merida were present. Still there were many whose young and gentle faces did not convey the idea that they could find pleasure in scenes of blood, even though but the blood of brutes.

In the evening we took another hot-bath at the loteria, and the next day was Sunday, the last day of the fiesta, which opened in the morning with grand mass in the church of San

Cristoval. The great church, the paintings and altars, the burning of incense, the music, the imposing ceremonies of the altar, and the kneeling figures, inspired, as they always do, if not a religious, at least a solemn feeling; and, as on the occasion of grand mass in the Cathedral on my first visit to Merida, among the kneeling figures of the women my eyes rested upon one with a black mantle over her head, a prayer-book in her hand, and an Indian woman by her side, whose face exhibited a purity and intellectual softness which it was easy for the imagination to invest with all those attributes that make woman perfect. Whether she was maid, wife, or widow, I never learned.

At four o'clock in the afternoon we set out for the procession and paseo. The intense heat of the day was over, there was shade in the streets, and a fresh evening breeze. The streets through which the procession was to pass were adorned with branches, and at the corners were large collections of them, forming groves of green. The balconies of the windows were hung with silk curtains and banners, and in the doorways and along the walks sat rows of ladies simply but beautifully dressed, without hats, their hair adorned with flowers, and their necks with jewels. Near the church of San Cristoval we were arrested by the crowd, and waited till the procession came up.

It was headed by three priests, all richly dressed, one supporting a large silver cross ten feet high, and each of the others bearing a tall silver candlestick. They were followed by an Indian band, a motley group, the leaders of which were three Indians, one supporting the head and another the foot of a large violoncello. Next came a party of Indians, bearing on their shoulders a barrow supporting a large silver cross. At the foot of the cross sat the figure of Mary Magdalen, large as life, dressed in red. Over her head was a blue silk mantilla, with a broad gold border, and across her lap the figure of the dead Christ. The barrow was ornamented with large glass shades, under which candles were burning, and garlands and wreaths of flowers. This constituted the whole of the ceremonial part of the procession, and it was followed by a large concourse of Indians, men and women, dressed in white, all carrying in their hands long lighted candles.

When the crowd had passed by we strolled to the Alameda. This is the great place of promenade and paseo in Merida. It consists of a broad paved avenue, with a line of stone seats on each side, and beyond, on both sides, are carriage roads, shaded by rows of trees. In full sight, and giving a picturesque beauty to the scene, rises the Castillo, a ruined fortress, with battlements of dark gray stone, and the spires of the old Franciscan church rising inside, romantic in its appearance, and identified with the history of the Spanish conquest. Regularly every Sunday there is a paseo around the castle and along the Alameda, and this day, on account of the fête, it was one of the best and gayest of the year.

The most striking feature, the life and beauty of the paseo, were the calesas. Except one or two gigs, and a black, square box-wagon, which occasionally shame the paseo, the calesa is the only wheeled carriage in Merida. The body is somewhat like that of an oldfashioned gig, only much larger, and resting on the shaft a little in front of the wheels. It is painted red, with light and fancifully coloured curtains for the sun, drawn by one horse, with a boy riding him—simple, fanciful, and peculiar to Yucatan. Each calesa had two, and sometimes three ladies, in the latter case the prettiest sitting in the middle and a little in front, all without hats or veils, but their hair beautifully arranged and trimmed with flowers. Though exposed to the gaze of thousands, they had no boldness of manner or appearance, but, on the contrary, an air of modesty and simplicity, and all had a mild and gentle expression. Indeed, as they rode alone and unattended through the great mass of pedestrians, it seemed as if their very gentleness was a protection and shield from insult. We sat down on one of the stone benches in the Alameda, with the young, and gay, and beautiful of Merida. Strangers had not been there to laugh at and break up their good old customs. It was a little nook almost unknown to the rest of the world, and independent of it, enjoying what is so rarely found in this equalizing age, a sort of primitive or Knickerbocker state. The great charm was the air of contentment that reigned over the whole. If the young ladies in the calesas had occupied the most brilliant equipages in Hyde Park, they could not have seemed happier; and in their way, not less attractive were the great crowds of Mestizas and Indian women, some of the former being extremely pretty, and all having the same mild and gentle expression; they wore a picturesque costume of white, with a red border around the neck and skirt, and of that extraordinary cleanness which I had remarked as the characteristic of the poorest in Merida. For an hour, one continued stream of calesas, with ladies, and Mestizas, and Indian women, passed us without any noise, or confusion, or tumult, but in all there was such an air of quiet enjoyment that we felt sad as night came on;

and, as the sun sank behind the ruins of the castillo, we thought that there were few places in the world where it went down upon a prettier or happier scene.

The crowning ceremonies of the fiesta were a display of fireworks in the square of the church, followed by a concert and ball. The former was for the people, the latter for a select few. This, by-the-way, could hardly be considered very select, as, upon the application of our landlady, all our household received tickets.

The entertainment was given by an association of young men called *La Sociedad Philharmonica*. It was the second of a series proposed to be given on alternate Sundays, and already those who look coldly upon the efforts of enterprising young men were predicting that it would not hold out long, which prediction was unfortunately verified. It was given in a house situated on a street running off from the Plaza, one of the few in the city that had two stories, and which would be considered respectable among what are called palazzos in Italy. The entrance was into an entresol paved with stone, and the ascent by a broad flight of stone steps. The concert room was the sala. At one end was a platform, with instruments for the performers and amateurs, and two rows of chairs were arranged in parallel lines, opposite each other, the whole length of the room. When we entered, one row was occupied entirely by ladies, while that opposite was vacant. We approached it, but, fortunately, before exposing our ignorance of Merida etiquette, it occurred to us that these also were intended for ladies, and we moved on to a corner which afforded a longitudinal view of one line and an oblique view of the other. As different parties arrived, after leaving shawls, &c., at the door, a gentleman entered, leading the lady by the hand, which seemed much more graceful and gallant than our fashion of hitching her on his arm, particularly when there were two ladies. Leading her to a seat, he left her, and retired to the corridor, or the embrasure of a window. This continued till the whole line of chairs was filled up, and we were crowded out of our corner for our betters, so that the room presented a *coup d'œil* of ladies only. Here they sat, not to be touched, handled, or spoken to, but only to be looked at, which, long before the concert was over, some were tired of doing, and I think I am safe in saying that the faces of some of the ladies lighted up when the concert was done, and the gentlemen were invited to take partners for a waltz.

For the first time in my life, I saw beauty in a waltz. It

was not the furious whirl of the French waltz, stirring up the blood, making men perspire and young ladies look red, but a slow, gentle, and graceful movement, apparently inducing a languid, dreaming, and delightful state of being. The music, too, instead of bursting with a deafening crash, stole on the ear so gently, that, though every note was heard clearly and distinctly, it made no noise; and as the feet of the dancers fell to the gentle cadence, it seemed as if the imagination was only touched by the sound. Every face wore an expression of pure and refined enjoyment—an enjoyment derived rather from sentiment than from excited animal spirits. There were not the show and glitter of the ballroom in Europe or at home, but there were beauty of personal appearance, taste in dress, and propriety and simplicity of manners. At eleven o'clock the ball broke up; and if the loteria was objectionable, and the bull-fight brutal, the paseo and baglio redeemed them, and left on our minds a pleasing impression of the fête of San Cristoval.

One fiesta was hardly ended when another began. On Monday was the great fête of Todos Santos. Grand mass was said in all the churches, and in every family prayers were offered up for the souls of the dead; and, besides the usual ceremonies of the Catholic Church throughout the world, there is one peculiar to Yucatan, derived from the customs of the Indians, and called Mukbipoyo. On this day every Indian, according to his means, purchases and burns a certain number of consecrated candles, in honour of his deceased relatives, and in memory of each member of his family who has died within the year. Besides this, they bake in the earth a pie consisting of a paste of Indian corn, stuffed with pork and fowls, and seasoned with chili, and during the day every good Yucateco eats nothing but this. In the interior, where the Indians are less civilized, they religiously place a portion of this composition out of doors, under a tree, or in some retired place, for their deceased friends to eat, and they say that the portion thus set apart is always eaten, which induces the belief that the dead may be enticed back by appealing to the same appetites which govern when living; but this is sometimes accounted for by malicious and skeptical persons, who say that in every neighborhood there are other Indians, poorer than those who can afford to regale their deceased relatives, and these consider it no sin, in a matter of this kind, to step between the living and the dead.

We have reason to remember this fête from one untoward circumstance. A friendly neighbour, who, besides visiting us frequently with his wife and daughter, was in the habit of sending us fruit and dulces more than we could eat, this day, on the top of a large, undisposed-of present, sent us a huge piece of mukbipoyo. It was as hard as an oak plank, and as thick as six of them; and having already overtasked ourselves to reduce the pile on the table, when this came, in a fit of desperation we took it out into the courtyard and buried it. There it would have remained till this day but for a malicious dog which accompanied them on their next visit; he passed into the courtyard, rooted it up, and, while we were pointing to the empty platters as our acknowledgment of their kindness, this villanous dog sneaked through the sala and out at the front door with the pie in his mouth, apparently grown bigger since it was buried.

The fêtes were now ended, and we were not sorry, for now, for the first time, we had a prospect of having our clothes washed. Ever since our arrival, our linen, &c., accumulated during the voyage, had stood in gaping bundles, imploring us to do something for them, but during the continuance of the fiestas not a lavandera in Merida could be found to take in washing.

CHAPTER III

I trust the reader has not forgotten our old
friend Don Simon Peon, to whom, of course, our first visit
was made. We were received by himself and his mother, the Doña
Joaquina, with the same kindness as on the former occasion,
and in a greater degree. They immediately offered all in their
power to further the objects of our visit, and to the last day of
our residence in the country we continued to feel the benefit of
their friendly assistance. For the present, the sala of the Doña
Joaquina was every evening the rendezvous of her large and
respectable family connexion; there we were in the habit of
visiting at all times, and had reason to believe that we were
always welcome guests.

Among the first of Don Simon's good offices was a presenta-
tion to the governor of the state. This gentleman, by reason of
the peculiar political position of Yucatan, occupied at that time
a prominent and important position; but, before introducing
him to the reader, it may not be amiss to give a brief account of
the country of which he is the official head.

It may be remembered that Columbus, in his first three
voyages, did not reach the Continent of America. On his fourth,
final, and ill-fated expedition, "after sixty days of tempestuous
weather, without seeing sun or stars," he discovered a small
island, called by the Indians Guanaja, supposed to be that now
laid down on some maps as the island of Bonaca. While on
shore at this island, we saw coming from the west a canoe of
large size, filled with Indians, who appeared to be a more

civilized people than any the Spaniards had yet encountered. In return to the inquiries of the Spaniards for gold, they pointed toward the west, and endeavoured to persuade them to steer in that direction.

"Well would it have been for Columbus," says Mr. Irving, "had he followed their advice. Within a day or two he would have arrived at Yucatan; the discovery of Mexico and the other opulent countries of New Spain would have necessarily followed. The Southern Ocean would have been disclosed to him, and a succession of splendid discoveries would have shed fresh glory on his declining age, instead of its sinking amid gloom, neglect, and disappointment."

Four years afterward, in the year 1506, Juan Dias de Solis, in company with Vincent Yañez Pinzon, one of the companions of Columbus on his last voyage, held the same course to the island of Guanaja, and then, steering to the west, discovered the east coast of the province now known by the name of Yucatan, and sailed along it some distance, without, however, prosecuting the discovery.

On the eighth of February, 1517, Francisco Hernandez de Cordova, a rich hidalgo of Cuba, with three vessels of good burden and one hundred and ten soldiers, set sail from the port now known as St. Jago de Cuba, on a voyage of discovery. Doubling St. Anton, now called Cape St. Antonio, and sailing at hazard toward the west, at the end of twenty-one days they saw land which had never been seen before by Europeans.

On the fourth of March, while making arrangements to land, they saw coming to the ships five large canoes, with oars and sails, some of them containing fifty Indians; and on signals of invitation being made, above thirty came on board the captain's vessel. The next day the chief returned with twelve large canoes and numerous Indians, and invited the Spaniards to his town, promising them food, and whatever was necessary. The words he used were *Conèx cotoch*, which, in the language of the Indians of the present day, means, "Come to our town." Not understanding the meaning, and supposing it was the name of the place, the Spaniards called it Point or Cape Cotoche, which name it still bears.

The Spaniards accepted the invitation, but, seeing the shore lined with Indians, landed in their own boats, and carried with them fifteen crossbows and ten muskets.

After halting a little while, they set out, the chief leading the way; and, passing by a thick wood, at a signal from the chief a great body of Indians in ambush rushed out, poured upon them a shower of arrows, which at the first discharge wounded fifteen, and then fell upon them with their lances; but the swords, crossbows, and firearms of the Spaniards struck them with such terror that they fled precipitately leaving seventeen of their number slain.

The Spaniards returned to their ships, and continued toward the west, always keeping in sight of land. In fifteen days they discovered a large town, with an inlet which seemed to be a river. They went ashore for water, and were about returning, when some fifty Indians came toward them, dressed in good mantas of cotton, and invited them to their town. After some hesitation, the Spaniards went with them, and arrived at some large stone houses like those they had seen at Cape Cotoche, on the walls of which were figures of serpents and other idols. These were their temples, and about one of the altars were drops of fresh blood, which they afterward learned was the blood of Indians, sacrificed for the destruction of the strangers.

Hostile preparations of a formidable character were soon apparent, and the Spaniards, fearing to encounter such a multitude, retired to the shore, and embarked with their water-casks. This place was called Kimpech, and at this day it is known by the name of Campeachy.

Continuing westwardly, they came opposite a town about a league from the coast, which was called Potonchan or Champoton. Being again in distress for water, they went ashore all together, and well armed. They found some wells, filled their casks, and were about putting them into the boats, when large bodies of warlike Indians came upon them from the town, armed with bows and arrows, lances, shields, double-handed swords, slings, and stones, their faces painted white, black, and red, and their heads adorned with plumes of feathers. The Spaniards were unable to embark their water-casks, and, as it was now nearly night, they determined to remain on shore. At daylight great bodies of warriors, with colours flying, advanced upon them from all sides. The fight lasted more than half an hour; fifty Spaniards were killed; and Cordova, seeing that it was impossible to drive back such a multitude, formed the rest into a compact body and cut his way to the boats. The Indians followed close at their heels, even pursuing them into the water. In the confusion, so many of the Spaniards ran to the boats together that they came near sinking them; but, hanging to the boats, half wading and half swimming, they reached the small vessel, which came up to their assistance. Fifty-seven of their companions were killed, and five more died of their wounds. There was but one soldier who escaped unwounded; all the rest had two, three, or four, and the captain, Hernandez de Cordova, had twelve arrow wounds. In the old Spanish charts this place is called the Bay "de Mala Pelea," or "of the bad fight."

This great disaster determined them to return to Cuba. So many sailors were wounded that they could not man the three vessels, in consequence of which they burned the smaller one, and, dividing the crew between the other two, set sail. To add to their calamity, they had been obliged to leave behind their water-casks, and they came to such extremities with thirst, that their tongues and lips cracked open. On the coast of Florida they procured water, and when it was brought alongside one soldier threw himself from the ship into the boat, and, seizing an earthen jar, drank till he swelled and died.

After this the vessel of the captain sprung a leak, but by great exertions at the pumps they kept her from sinking, and brought her into Puerto Carenas, which is now the port of Havana. Three more soldiers died of their wounds; the rest dispersed, and the captain, Hernandez de Cordova, died ten days after his arrival. Such was the disastrous end of the first expedition to Yucatan.

In the same year, 1517, another expedition was set on foot. Four vessels were fitted out, two hundred and forty companions enrolled themselves, and Juan de Grijalva, "a hopeful young man and well-behaved," was named captain-in-chief.

On the sixth of April, 1518, the armament sailed from the port of Matanzas for Yucatan. Doubling Cape San Antonio, and forced by the currents farther down than its predecessor, they discovered the Island of Cozumel.

Crossing over, and sailing along the coast, they came in sight of Potonchan, and entered the Bay of Mala Pelea, memorable for the disastrous repulse of the Spaniards. The Indians, exulting in their former victory, charged upon them before they landed, and fought them in the water; but the Spaniards made such slaughter that the Indians fled and abandoned the town. The victory, however, cost them dear. Three soldiers were killed, more than seventy wounded, and Juan de Grijalva was hurt by three arrows, one of which knocked out two of his teeth.

Embarking again, and continuing toward the west, in three days they saw the mouth of a very broad river, which, as Yucatan was then supposed to be an island, they thought to be its boundary, and called the Boca de Terminos. At Tobasco they first heard the famous name of Mexico; and after sailing on to Culua, now known as San Juan de Ulloa, the fortress of Vera Cruz, and some distance beyond along the coast, Grijalva returned to Cuba to add new fuel to the fire of adventure and discovery.

Another expedition was got up on a grand scale. Ten ships were fitted out, and it is creditable to the fame of Juan de Grijalva that all his old companions wished him for their chief; but, by a concurrence of circumstances, this office was conferred upon Hernando Cortez, then alcalde of Santiago de Cuba, a man comparatively unknown, but destined to be distinguished among the daring soldiers of that day as the Great Captain, and to build up a name almost overshadowing that of the discoverer of America.

The full particulars of all these expeditions form part and parcel of the history of Yucatan; but to present them in detail would occupy too large a portion of this work; and, besides, they form part of the great chain of events which led to the conquest of Mexico, the history of which, by the gifted author of Ferdinand and Isabella, it is hoped, will soon adorn the annals of literature.

Among the principal captains in the expeditions both of Grijalva and Cortez was Don Francisco Montejo, a gentleman of Seville. After the arrival of Cortez in Mexico, and while he was prosecuting his conquests in the interior, twice it was considered necessary to send commissioners to Spain, and on both occasions Don Francisco Montejo was nominated, the first time with one other, and the last time alone. On his second visit, besides receiving a confirmation of former grants and privileges, and a new coat of arms, as an acknowledgment of his distinguished services rendered to the crown in the expeditions of Grijalva and Cortez, he obtained from the king a grant for the pacification and conquest of the islands (as it is expressed) of Yucatan and Cozumel, which countries, amid the stirring scenes and golden prospects of the conquest of Mexico, had been entirely overlooked.

This grant bears date the eighth day of December, 1526, and, among other things, stipulated,

That the said Don Francisco de Montejo should have license and power to conquer and people the said islands of Yucatan and Cozumel:

That he should set out within one year from the date of the instrument:

That he should be governor and captain-general for life:

That he should be adelantado for life, and on his death the office should descend to his heirs and successors forever.

Ten square leagues of land and four per cent. of all the profit or advantage to be derived from all the lands discovered and peopled were given to himself, his heirs and successors forever.

Those who should join the expedition under him were for the first three years to pay only the one tenth part of the gold of the mines, the fourth year a ninth part, and the per centage should go on increasing till it reached a fifth part.

They should be exempted from export duty upon the articles they carried with them, provided they were not taken for barter or sale.

They were allowed portions of land, and, after living on them four years complete, were to be at liberty to sell them and use them as their own.

Also to take rebellious Indians for slaves, and to take and buy Indians held by the caciques as slaves, under the regulations of the council of the Indies. The tithes or tenth parts were granted to be expended in churches and ornaments, and things necessary for divine worship.

The last provision, which may seem rather illiberal, if not libellous, was, that no lawyers or attorneys should go into those lands from the kingdom of Spain, nor from any other part, on account of the litigation and controversies that would follow them.

Don Francisco Montejo, now adelantado, is described as "of the middle stature, of a cheerful countenance, and gay disposition. At the time of his arrival here (in Mexico) he was about thirty-five years of age. He was fitter for business than war, and of a liberal turn, expending more than he received;" in which latter qualification for a great enterprise he could perhaps find his match at the present day.

The adelantado incurred great expenses in the purchase of arms, ammunition, horses, and provisions; and, selling an estate, which yielded him two thousand ducats of rent, he fitted out four vessels at his own expense, and embarked in them four hundred Spaniards, under an agreement for a certain share of the advantages of the expedition.

In the year 1527 (the month is not known) the armament

sailed from Seville, and, touching at the islands for supplies, it was remarked, as a circumstance of bad omen, that the adelantado had not on board two priests, which, under a general provision, every captain, officer, or subject who had license to discover and people islands or terra firma within the limits of the King of Spain, was bound to carry with him.

The fleet stopped at the island of Cozumel, where the adelantado had great difficulty in communicating with the Indians from want of an interpreter. Taking on board one of them as a guide, the fleet crossed over to the continent, and came to anchor off the coast. All the Spaniards went on shore, and, as the first act, with the solemnities usual in the new conquests, took formal possession of the country in the name of the king. Gonzalo Nieto planted the royal standard, and cried out, in a loud voice, "España! España! viva España!"

Leaving the sailors on board to take care of the vessel, the Spaniards landed their arms, ammunition, horses, and provisions, and, remaining here a few days to rest, from the excessive heat some became sick. The Indians knew that the Spaniards had established themselves in New Spain, and were determined to resist this invasion with all their strength; but, for the moment, they avoided any hostile demonstrations.

As yet the adelantado had only touched along the coast, and knew nothing of the interior. Experiencing great difficulty from the want of an interpreter, he commenced his march along the coast under the guidance of the Indian from Cozumel. The country was well peopled, and, without committing any violence upon the inhabitants, or suffering any injury from them, the Spaniards proceeded from town to town until they arrived at Conil. At this place, the Indians being apparently friendly, the Spaniards were thrown off their guard; and on one occasion, an Indian, who came to pay a visit, snatched a hanger from a little negro slave, and attempted to kill the adelantado. The latter drew his sword to defend himself, but the soldiers rushed forward and killed the Indian on the spot.

The adelantado now determined to march from Conil to the province of Choaca, and from this time they began to experience the dreadful hardships they were doomed to suffer in subduing Yucatan. There were no roads; the country was stony, and overgrown with thick woods. Fatigued with the difficulties of their march, the heat, and want of water, they arrived at Choaca, and found it deserted: the inhabitants had gone to join other Indians who were gathering for war. No one appeared to whom they could give notice of their pacific intentions, and the tidings that an Indian had been killed had gone before them.

Setting out again, still under the guidance of the Cozumel Indian, they reached a town named Aké. Here they found themselves confronted by a great multitude of Indians, who had lain in ambush, concealed in the woods.

These Indians were armed with quivers of arrows, sticks burned at the ends, lances pointed with sharp flints, and two-handed swords of very hard wood. They had flutes, and large sea-shells for trumpets, and turtle-shells which they struck with deers' horns. Their bodies were naked, except around the loins, and stained all over with earth of different colours, and they wore stone rings in their ears and noses.

The Spaniards were astonished at seeing such strange figures, and the noise that they made with the turtle-shells and horns, accompanied by a shout of voices, seemed to make the hills quake. The adelantado encouraged the Spaniards by relating his experience of war with the Indians, and a fearful battle commenced, which lasted all that day. Night came to put an end to the slaughter, but the Indians remained on the ground. The Spaniards had time to rest and bind up their wounds, but kept watch all night, with the dismal prospect of being destroyed on the next day.

At daylight the battle began again, and continued fiercely till midday, when the Indians began to give way. The Spaniards, encouraged by hope of victory, pressed them till they turned and fled, hiding themselves in the woods; but, ignorant of the ground, and worn out with constant fighting, the victors could only make themselves masters of the field. In this battle more than twelve hundred Indians were killed.

In the beginning of the year 1528, the adelantado determined again, by slow marches, to reconnoiter the country; and, having discovered the warlike character of the inhabitants, to avoid as much as possible all conflict with them. With this resolution, they set out from Aké in the direction of Chichen Itza, where, by kindness and conciliation, they got together some Indians, and built houses of wood and poles covered with palm leaves.

Here the adelantado made one unfortunate and fatal movement. Disheartened by not seeing any signs of gold, and learning from the Indians that the glittering metal was to be found in the province of Ba Khalal, the adelantado determined to send the Captain Davila to found in that province a town of Spaniards. Davila set out with fifty foot-soldiers and sixteen horsemen, and from the time of this separation difficulties and dangers accumulated upon both. All efforts to communicate with each other proved abortive. After many battles, perils, and sufferings, those in Chichen Itza saw themselves reduced to the wretched alternative of dying by hunger or by the hands of the Indians. An immense multitude of the latter having assembled for their destruction, the Spaniards left their fortifications, and went out on the plain to meet them. The most severe battle ever known in wars with the Indians took place. Great slaughter was made among them, but a hundred and fifty Spaniards were killed; nearly all the rest were wounded, and, worn down with fatigue, the survivors retreated to the fortifications. The Indians did not follow them, or, worn out as they were, they would have perished miserably to a man. At night the Spaniards escaped. From the meager and unsatisfactory notices of these events that have come down to us, it is not known with accuracy by what route they reached the coast; but the next that we hear of them is at Campeachy.

The fortunes of Davila were no better. Arrived at the province of Ba Khalal, he sent a message to the Lord of Chemecal to inquire about gold, and requesting a supply of provisions; the fierce answer of the cacique was, that he would send fowls on spears, and Indian corn on arrows. With forty men and five horses left, Davila struggled back to the coast, and, two years after their unfortunate separation, he joined the adelantado in Campeachy.

Their courage was still unbroken. Roused by the arrival of Davila, the adelantado determined to make another attempt to penetrate the country. For this purpose he again sent off Davila with fifty men, himself remaining in Campeachy with but forty soldiers and ten horsemen. As soon as the Indians discovered his small force, an immense multitude gathered round the camp. Hearing a tumult, the adelantado went out on horseback, and, riding toward a group assembled on a little hill, cried out, endeavouring to pacify them; but the Indians, turning in the direction of the voice, and recognising the adelantado, surrounded him, laid hands upon the reins of his horse, and tried to wrest from him his lance. The adelantado spurred his horse, and extricated himself for a moment, but so many Indians came up that they held his horse fast by the feet, took away his lance, and endeavoured to carry him off alive, intending, as they afterward said, to sacrifice him to their gods. Blas Gonzales was the only soldier near him, who, seeing his danger, threw himself on horseback, cleared a way through the Indians with his lance, and, with others who came up at the moment, rescued the adelantado. Both himself and the brave Gonzales were severely wounded, and the horse of the latter died of his wounds.

About this time the fame of the discovery of Peru reached these unlucky conquerors, and, taking advantage of the opportunity afforded by their proximity to the coast, many of the soldiers deserted. To follow up the conquest of Yucatan, it was indispensable to recruit his forces, and for this purpose the adelantado determined on going to New Spain.

He had previously sent information to the king of his misfortunes, and the king had despatched a royal parchment to the audiencia of Mexico, setting forth the services of the adelantado, the labours and losses he had sustained, and charging them to give him assistance in all that related to the conquest of Yucatan. With this favour and his rents in New Spain, he got together some soldiers, and bought vessels, arms, and other munitions of war, to prosecute his conquest. Unluckily, as Tobasco belonged to his government, and the Indians of that province, who had been subdued by Cortez, had revolted, he considered it advisable first to reduce them. The vessels sailed from Vera Cruz, and, stopping at Tobasco with a portion of his recruits, he sent on the vessels with the rest, under the command of his son, to prosecute the conquest in Yucatan.

But the adelantado found it much more difficult than he expected to reduce the Indians of Tobasco; and while he was engaged in it, the Spaniards in Campeachy, instead of being able to penetrate into the country, were undergoing great sufferings. The Indians cut off their supplies of provisions, and, being short of sustenance, nearly all became ill. They were obliged to make constant sorties to procure food, and it was necessary to let the horses go loose, though at the risk of their being killed. They were reduced so low that but five soldiers remained to watch over and provide for the rest. Finding it impossible to hold out any longer, they determined to abandon the place. Gonzales Nieto, who first planted the royal standard on the shores of Yucatan, was the last to leave it, and in the year 1535 not a single Spaniard remained in the country.

It was now notorious that the adelantado had not fulfilled the order to carry with him priests, and, by many of the daring but devout spirits of that day, his want of success in Yucatan was ascribed to this cause. The viceroy of Mexico, in the exercise of the discretion allowed under a rescript from the queen, determined forthwith to send priests, who should conquer the country by converting the Indians to Christianity.

The venerable Franciscan friar, Jacobo de Festera, although superior and prelate of the rich province of Mexico, zealous, says the historian, for the conversion of souls, and desirous to reduce the whole world to the knowledge of the true God, offered himself for this spiritual conquest, expecting many hardships, and doubtful of the result. Four persons of the same order were assigned as his companions; and, attended by some friendly Mexicans who had been converted to Christianity, on the eighth of March they arrived at Champoton, famed for the "mala pelea," or bad fight, of the Spaniards.

The Mexicans went before them to give notice of their coming, and to say that they came in the spirit of peace, few in number, and without arms, caring only for the salvation of souls, and to make known to the people the true God, whom they ought to worship. The lords of Champoton received the Mexican messengers amicably, and, satisfied that they could run but little risk, allowed the missionaries to enter their country. Regardless of the concerns of this world, says the historian, and irreproachable in their lives, they prevailed upon the Indians to listen to their preaching, and in a few days enjoyed the fruit of their labours. This fruit, he adds, "was not so great as if they had had interpreters familiar with the idiom; but the divine grace and the earnestness of these ministers were so powerful that, after forty days' communication, the lords brought voluntarily all their idols, and delivered them to the priests to be burned;" and, as the best proof of their sincerity, they brought their children, whom, says the Bishop Las Casas, they cherished more than the light of their eyes, to be indoctrinated and taught. Every day they became more attached to the padres, built them houses to live in, and a temple for worship; and one thing occurred which had never happened before. Twelve or fifteen lords, with great territories and many vassals, with the consent of their people, voluntarily acknowledged the dominion of the King of Castile. This agreement, under their signs and attested by the monks, the bishop says he had in his possession.

At this time, when, from such great beginnings, the conversion of the whole kingdom of Yucatan seemed almost certain, there happened (to use, as near as possible, the language of the historian) the greatest disaster that the devil, greedy of souls, could desire. Eighteen horsemen and twelve foot-soldiers, fugitives from New Spain, entered the country from some quarter, bringing with them loads of idols, which they had carried off from other provinces. The captain called to him a lord of that part of the country by which he entered, and told him to take the idols and distribute them throughout the country, selling each one for an Indian man or woman to serve as a slave, and adding, that if the lord refused to do so, he would immediately make war upon them. The lord commanded his vassals to take these idols and worship them, and in return to give him Indian men and women to be delivered to the Spaniards. The Indians, from fear and respect to the command of their lord, obeyed. Whoever had two children gave one, and whoever had three gave two.

In the mean time, seeing that, after they had given up their gods to be burned, these Spaniards brought others to sell, the whole country broke out in indignation against the monks, whom they accused of deceiving them. The monks endeavoured to appease them, and, seeking out the thirty Spaniards, represented to them the great evil they were doing, and required them to leave the country; but the Spaniards refused, and consummated their wickedness by telling the Indians that the priests themselves had induced them to come into the country. The Indians were now roused beyond all forbearance, and determined to murder the priests, who, having notice of this intention, escaped at night. Very soon, however, the Indians repented, and, remembering the purity of their lives, and satisfied of their innocence, they sent after the monks fifty leagues, and begged them to return. The monks, zealous only for their souls, forgave them and returned; but, finding that the Spaniards would not leave the country, and that they were constantly aggrieving the Indians, and especially that they could not preach in peace, nor without continual dread, they determined to leave the country and return to Mexico. Thus Yucatan remained without the light and help of the doctrine, and the miserable Indians in the darkness of ignorance.

Such is the account of the mission of these monks given by the old Spanish historians, but the cautious reader of the present day will hardly credit that these good priests, "ignorant of the language, and without interpreters who understood the idiom," could in forty days bring the Indians to throw their idols at their feet; and still less, that this warlike people, who had made such fierce resistance to Cordova, Grijalva, Cortez, and the adelantado, would all at once turn cravens before thirty vagabond Spaniards; but says the historian, these are secrets of Divine justice; perhaps for their many sins they did not deserve that at that time the word should be preached to them.

We return now to the adelantado, whom we left at Tobasco. Severe wars with the Indians, want of arms and provisions, and, above all, desertions instigated by the fame of Peruvian riches, had left him at a low ebb. In this situation he was joined by Captain Gonzalo Nieto and the small band which had been compelled to evacuate Yucatan, and by the presence of these old companions his spirits were again roused.

But the pacification of Tobasco was much more difficult than was supposed. By communication with the Spaniards, the Indians had lost their fears of them. The country was bad for carrying on war, particularly with cavalry, on account of the marshes and pools; their provisions were again cut off; many of the soldiers went away disgusted, and others, from the great humidity and heat, sickened and died.

While they were in this extremity, the Captain Diego de Contreras, with no fixed destination, and ready to embark in any of the great enterprises which at that time attracted the adventurous soldier, arrived at the port. He had with him a vessel of his own, with provisions and other necessaries, his son, and twenty Spaniards. The adelantado represented to him the great service he might render the king, and by promises of reward induced him to remain. With this assistance he was enabled to sustain himself in Tobasco until, having received additional reenforcements, he effected the pacification of the whole of that country.

The adelantado now made preparations to return to Yucatan. Champoton was selected as the place of disembarcation. According to some of the historians, he did not himself embark on this expedition, but sent his son. It seems more certain, however, that he went in person as commander-in-chief of the armada, and leaving his son, Don Francisco de Montejo, in command of the soldiers, returned to Tobasco, as being nearer to Mexico, from which country he expected to receive and send on more recruits and necessaries. The Spaniards landed some time in the year 1537, and again planted the royal standard in Yucatan. The Indians allowed them to land without noise or opposition, but they were only lying in wait for an opportunity to destroy them. In a few days a great multitude assembled, and at midnight they crept silently up the paths and roads which led to the camp of the Spaniards, seized one of the sentinels, and killed him; but the noise awoke the Spaniards, who, wondering less at the attack than at its being made by night, rushed to their arms. Ignorant as they were of the ground, in the darkness all was confusion. On the east, west, and south they heard the clamour and outcries of the Indians. Nevertheless, they made great efforts, and the Indians, finding their men falling, and hearing the groans of the wounded and dying, relaxed in the fury of their attack, and at length retreated. The Spaniards did not pursue them, but remained in the camp, keeping watch till daylight, when they collected and buried the bodies of their own dead.

For some days the Indians did not make any hostile demonstrations, but they kept away or concealed as much as possible all supplies of provisions. The Spaniards were much straitened, and obliged to sustain themselves by catching fish along the shores. On one occasion two Spaniards, who had straggled to some distance from the camp, fell into the hands of the Indians, who carried them away alive, sacrificed them to their idols, and feasted upon their bodies.

During this time the Indians were forming a great league of all the caciques in the country, and gathered in immense numbers at Champoton. As soon as all the confederates were assembled, they attacked with a horrible noise the camp of the Spaniards, who could not successfully contend against such a multitude. Many Indians fell, but they counted as well lost a thousand of their own number for the life of one Spaniard. There was no hope but in flight, and the Spaniards retreated to the shore. The Indians pursued them, heaping insults upon them, entered their camp, loaded themselves with the clothing and other things, which in the hurry of retreat they had been obliged to leave behind, put on their dresses, and from the shore mocked and scoffed at them, pointing with their fingers, taunting them with cowardice, and crying out, "Where is the courage of the Spaniards?" The latter, hearing from their boats these insults, resolved that death and fame were better than life and ignominy, and, wounded and worn out as they were, took up their arms and returned to the shore. Another fierce battle ensued; and the Indians, dismayed by the resolution with which these vanquished men again made front against them, retired slowly, leaving the Spaniards masters of the field. The Spaniards cared for no more, content to recover the ground they had lost.

From this time the Indians determined not to give battle again, and the great multitude, brought together from different places, dispersed, and returned to their homes. The Spaniards remained more at their ease. The Indians, seeing that they could not be driven out of the country, and did not intend to leave it, contracted a sort of friendship with them, but they were not able to make any advances into the interior. On every attempt they were so badly received that they were compelled to return to their camp in Champoton, which was, in fact, their only refuge.

As Champoton was on the coast, which now began to be somewhat known, vessels occasionally touched there, from which the poor Spaniards relieved some of their necessities. Occasionally a new companion remained, but their numbers still diminished, many, seeing the delay and the little fruit derived from their labours, abandoning the expedition. The time came when there were only nineteen Spaniards in Champoton, the names of some of whom are still preserved, and they affirm in their judicial declaration, that in this critical situation they owed their preservation to the prudence and good management of Don Francisco Montejo, the son of the adelantado.

Again they were relieved, and again their force dwindled away. The fame of the riches of Peru was in every mouth. The poverty of Yucatan was notorious. There were no mines; there was but little encouragement for others to join the expedition, and those in Champoton were discouraged. Struggling with continual hardships and dangers, they made no advance toward the conquest of the country; all who could, endeavoured to get away, some going in canoes, others by land, as occasion offered. In order to confer upon some means of bettering the condition of things, it was necessary for the son of the adelantado to visit his father at Tobasco, and he set out, leaving the soldiers at Champoton under the command of his cousin, a third Don Francisco.

During his absence matters became worse. The people continued going away, and Don Francisco knew that if they lost Champoton, which had cost them so much, all was lost. Consulting with a few who were most desirous of persevering in the enterprise, he brought together those who were suspected of meditating desertion, and told them to go at once, and leave the rest to their fate. The poor soldiers, embarrassed, and ashamed at being confronted with companions whom they intended to desert, determined to remain.

But the succour so earnestly hoped for was delayed. All the expedition which the son of the adelantado could make was not sufficient for those who remained in Champoton. They had been nearly three years without making any advances or any impression upon the country. Despairing of its conquest, and unable to exist in the straits in which they found themselves, they talked openly of disbanding, and going where fortune might lead them. The captain did all that he could to encourage them, but in vain. All had their luggage and ship-stores ready to embark, and nothing was talked of but leaving the country.

The exertions of the captain induced them to take better counsel, and they agreed not to execute their resolution hastily, but, to save themselves from injurious imputations, first to send notice of their intention to the adelantado. Juan de Contreras was sent with the despatches, who gave the adelantado, besides, a full account of the desperate condition in which they remained at Champoton.

His intelligence gave the adelantado much anxiety. All his resources were exhausted; he had been unable to procure the succour necessary, and he knew that if the Spaniards abandoned Champoton, it would be impossible to prosecute the conquest of Yucatan. Aware of their necessities, when the news arrived, he had some Spaniards collected to go to their assistance, and now, by gifts and promises, he made some additions; and while waiting until these could be got ready, despatched Alonzo Rosado, one of the new recruits, to give notice of the succour at hand.

It does not appear whether the adelantado went to Champoton in person, but vessels arrived carrying soldiers, provisions, clothing, and arms, and toward the end of the year 1539 his son returned, with twenty horsemen, from New Spain. The drooping spirits of the Spaniards were revived, and again they conceived hopes of achieving the conquest of the country.

About this time, too, the adelantado, grieving over the common misfortune of himself and those who had been constant and enduring, but doubting his own fortune, and confiding in the valour of his son Don Francisco, determined to put into the hands of the latter the pacification of Yucatan. He was at that time settled in the government of Chiapas, to which place he summoned his son, and by a formal act substituted him in all the powers given to himself by the king. The act of substitution is creditable alike to the head and heart of the adelantado. It begins with an injunction "that he should strive that the people under his charge should live and be as true Christians, separating themselves from vices and public sins, not permitting them to speak ill of God, nor his blessed mother, nor the saints;" and it concludes with the words, "because I know that you are a person who will know how to do it well, putting first God our Lord, and the service of his majesty, and the good of the country, and the execution of justice."

Within a month from the time when he was called away by his father, Don Francisco returned to Champoton with all the provisions necessary for prosecuting, on his own accout, the conquest of Yucatan. From this time the door of better fortune seemed opened to the Spaniards.

Don Francisco determined forthwith to undertake the march to Campeachy. At a short distance from Champoton they encountered a large body of Indians, routed them, and, determined not to make any retrograde movement, encamped upon the spot.

From this place the Indians, mortified and incensed at their defeat, erected fortifications along the whole line of march. The Spaniards could not advance without encountering walls, trenches, and embankments, vigorously defended. All these they gained in succession; and so great was the slaughter of the Indians, that at times their dead bodies obstructed the battle, and the Spaniards were obliged to pass over the dead to fight with the living. In one day they had three battles, in which the Spaniards were almost worn out with fighting.

Here, again, the history fails, and it does not appear how they were received in Campeachy; but it is manifest from other authorities that in the year 1540 they founded a city under the name of San Francisco de Campeche.

Remaining in this place till things were settled, Don Francisco, in pursuance of his father's instructions, determined on descending to the province of Quepech, and founding a city in the Indian town of Tihoo. Knowing that delay was dangerous, he sent forward the Captain Francisco de Montejo, his cousin, with fifty-seven men. He himself remained in Campeachy to receive and organize the soldiers, who, stimulated by the tidings of his improving fortunes, were every day coming in from his father.

Don Francisco set out for Tihoo, and in all the accounts there is a uniform correspondence in regard to the many dangers they encountered on that journey from the smallness of their numbers, the great multitudes of warlike Indians, and the strong walls and other defences which they found at every step to obstruct their progress. The Indians concealed the wells and ponds, and as there were no streams or fountains, they were perishing with thirst. Provisions were cut off, and they had war, thirst, and hunger on their path. The roads were mere narrow passes, with thick woods on both sides, encumbered with the dead bodies of

men and animals, and their sufferings from want of water and
provisions were almost beyond endurance.

Arriving at a town called Pokboc, they pitched and fortified
their camp, with the intention of making a halt, but at night
they were roused by finding the camp on fire. All ran to arms,
thinking less of the fire than of the Indians, and in darkness and
silence waited to discover the quarter whence the attack would
come; but hearing no noise, and relieved from the apprehension
of enemies, they attempted to extinguish the flames. By this time,
however, the whole camp, and almost everything that they had,
were burned up. But they were not dismayed. The captain gave
notice of this misfortune to his cousin in Campeachy, and resumed his march. In the year 1540 he arrived at Tihoo.

In a few days he was joined by forty other Spaniards, who
were sent on by Don Francisco Montejo, and at this time some
Indians came to them and said, "What are you doing here, Spaniards? more Indians are coming against you, more than there are
hairs on the skin of a deer." The Spaniards answered that they
would go out to seek them; and, leaving the guard in the camp,
the Captain Don Francisco Montejo immediately set out, came
upon them at a place five leagues distant, and attacked them
with such vigour, that, though they at first defended themselves
bravely, the Spaniards gained upon them, and killing many, the
rest became disheartened and took to flight.

In the mean time the son of the adelantado arrived from
Campeachy; and being now all united, and the Indians at first
withholding all supplies, they very soon began to suffer from
want of provisions. While in this condition, unexpectedly a
great cacique from the interior came to them voluntarily (the
circumstances will appear hereafter) and made submission. Some
neighbouring caciques of Tihoo, either moved by this example,
or finding that, after so many years of war, they could not prevail against the Spaniards, also submitted. Encouraged by the
friendship of these caciques, and believing that they might count
upon their succour until they had finished the subjection of the
country, the Spaniards determined to found a city on the site occupied by Tihoo; but in the mean time a terrific storm was
gathering over their heads. All the Indians from the east of Tihoo were drawing together; and in the month of June, toward
the evening of the feast of Barnaby the apostle, an immense body,
varying, according to manuscript accounts, from forty to seventy
thousand, came down upon the small band of a little more than
two hundred then in Tihoo. The following day they attacked the

Spanish camp on all sides. The most terrible battle the Spaniards had ever encountered ensued. "Divine power," says the pious historian, "works more than human valour. What were so few Catholics against so many infidels?" The battle lasted the greater part of the day. Many Indians were killed, but immediately others took their places, for they were so many that they were like the leaves on the trees. The arquebuses and crossbows made great havoc, and the horsemen carried destruction wherever they moved, cutting down the fugitives, trampling under foot the wounded and dying. Piles of dead bodies stopped the Spaniards in their pursuit. The Indians were completely routed, and for a great distance the ground was covered with their dead.

The fame of the Spaniards rose higher than before, and the Indians never rallied again for a general battle. All this year the invaders were occupied in drawing to them and conciliating the neighbouring caciques, and on the sixth of January, 1542, they founded, with all legal formalities, on the site of the Indian town of Tihoo, the "very loyal and noble" city of Merida.

Here I shall leave them; and I make no apology for presenting this history. It was forty years since a straggling canoe at the island of Guanaja first gave intelligence of the existence of such a country as Yucatan, and sixteen since Don Francisco Montejo received the royal authority to conquer and people it. During that time Cortez had driven Montezuma from the throne of Mexico, and Pizarro had seized the sceptre of the Peruvian Incas. In the glory of these conquests Yucatan was unnoticed, and has been to this day. The ancient historians refer to it briefly and but seldom. The only separate account of it is that of Cogolludo, a native historian.

The work of this author was published in the year 1658. It is voluminous, confused, and ill-digested, and might almost be called a history of the Franciscan Friars, to which order he belonged. It is from this work principally that, with no small labour, I have gathered the events subsequent to the grant made by the king to Don Francisco Montejo; it is the only work that purports to give an account of those events, and as it has never been translated, and is scarcely known out of Yucatan, and even in that country is almost out of print, it must at least be new to the reader.

CHAPTER IV

From the time of the conquest, Yucatan existed as a distinct captain-generalcy, not connected with Guatimala, nor subject to the viceroy of Mexico. So it continued down to the Mexican revolution. The independence of Yucatan followed that of Mexico without any struggle, and actually by default of the mother-country in not attempting to keep it in subjection.

Separated from Spain, in an evil hour Yucatan sent commissioners to Mexico to deliberate upon forming a government; and on the return of these commissioners, and on their report, she gave up her independent position, and entered into the Mexican confederation as one of the states of that republic. Ever since she had been suffering from this unhappy connexion, and, a short time before our former visit, a revolution broke out all over the country; in the successful progress of which, during that visit, the last Mexican garrison was driven out of Yucatan. The state assumed the rights of sovereignty, asserting its independent powers, at the same time not disconnecting itself entirely from Mexico, but declaring itself still a component part of that republic upon certain conditions. The declaration of its independence was still a moot question. The assembly had passed a bill to that effect, but the senate had not yet acted upon it, and its fate in that body was considered doubtful. In the mean time, a commissioner had been sent to Texas, and two days after our arrival at Merida the Texan schooner of war San Antonio arrived at Sisal, bringing a proposition for Yucatan to pay $8000 per month toward the support of the Texan navy, and for the Texan vessels to remain upon the coast of Yucatan and protect it against invasion by Mexico. This proposition was accepted immediately, and negotiations were pending for farther co-operation in procuring a recognition of their mutual independence. Thus, while shrinking from an open declaration of independence, Yucatan was widening the breach, and committing an offence which Mexico could never forgive, by an alliance with a people whom that government, or rather Santa Ana, regarded as the worst of rebels, and whom he was bent upon exerting the whole power of the country in an effort to reconquer. Such was the disjointed and false position in which Yucatan stood at the time of our presentation to the governor.

Our visit to him was made at his private residence, which was one befitting his station as a private gentleman, and not unworthy of his public character. His reception-room was in the sala or parlour of his house, in the centre of which, after the fashion of Merida, three or four large chairs covered with morocco were placed facing each other.

Don Santiago Mendez was about fifty years of age, tall and thin, with a fine intellectual face, and of very gentlemanly appearance and deportment. Free from internal wars, and saved by her geographical position from the sanguinary conflicts common in the other Mexican states, Yucatan has had no school for soldiers; there are no military chieftains and no prepossessions for military glory. Don Santiago Mendez was a merchant, until within a few years, at the head of a respectable commercial house in Campeachy. He was so respected for uprightness and integrity, that in the unsettled state of affairs he was agreed upon by the two opposite parties as the best person in the state to place at the head of the government. His popularity, however, was now somewhat on the wane, and his position was neither easy nor enviable. From a quiet life and occupations, he found himself all at once in the front rank of a wide-spread rebellion. An invasion from Mexico was constantly apprehended, and should it prove successful, while others would escape by reason of their insignificance, his head would be sure to fall. The two great parties, one in favour of keeping open the door of reconciliation with Mexico, and the other for immediate and absolute separation, were both urging him to carry out their views. The governor shrank from the hazard of extremes, was vacillating, undecided, and unequal to the emergency. In the mean time, the enthusiasm which led to the revolution, and which might have achieved independence, was wearing away. Dissatisfaction and discontent prevailed. Both parties blamed the governor, and he did not know himself to which he belonged.

There was nothing equivocal, however, in his reception of us. He knew the object of our return to the country, and offered us all the facilities the government could bestow. Whatever was to be the fate of Yucatan, it was fortunate for us that it was then free from the dominion of Mexico, and repudiated entirely the jealous policy which threw impediments in the way of strangers seeking to explore the antiquities of the country; and it was also fortunate, that on my former visit Yucatan had impressed me favourably; for, had it been otherwise, my situation might have been made uncomfortable, and the two journals of Merida, the "Commercial Bulletin" and the "Nineteenth Century," instead of giving us a cordial welcome, and bespeaking favour for us, might have advised us to return home by the same vessel that brought us out.

Our only business in Merida was to make inquiries about ruins and arrangements for our journey into the interior, but in the mean time we had no lack of other occupation.

The house of the Doña Micaela was the rendezvous of all strangers in Merida, and a few days after our arrival there was an unprecedented gathering. There were Mr. Auchincloss and his son, Mr. Tredwell, Mr. Northrop, Mr. Gleason, and Mr. Robinson, formerly United States consul at Tampico, who had come out passengers by the Lucinda, all citizens of the United States; and, besides these, the arrival of the schooner of war San Antonio, from Texas, brought among us a citizen of the world, or, at least, of a great part of it. Mr. George Fisher, as appeared by his various papers of naturalization, was "natural de la ciudad y fortaleza de Belgrada en la provincia de Servia del Imperio Ottomano," or a "native of the city and fortress of Belgrade, in the province of Servia, in the Ottoman Empire." His Sclavonic name was Ribar, which in the German language means a Fischer, and at school in Austria it was so translated, from which in the United States it became modified to Fisher. At seventeen he embarked in a revolution to throw off the yoke of the sultan, but the attempt was crushed, and forty thousand Sclavonians, men, women, and children, were driven across the Danube, and took refuge in the Austrian territory. The Austrian government, not liking the presence of so many revolutionists within its borders, authorized the organizing of a Sclavonic legion. Mr. Fisher entered it, made a campaign in Italy, and, at the end of the year, in the interior of the country, where there was no danger of their disseminating revolutionary notions, the legion was disbanded. After expeditions of various kinds along the Danube, in Turkey, to Adrianople, and along the Adriatic, he traded back, most of the way on foot, until he reached Hamburgh, where, in 1815, he embarked for Philadelphia. Hence he crossed over to the Ohio River, and in the State of Mississippi, by five years' residence, and abjuring all other allegiance, became a citizen of the United States. Mexico obtained her independence, and he moved on to that country, becoming, by due process of law, a Mexican citizen. Here he established a newspaper, which, during the presidency of Santa Ana, became so conspicuous for its liberal opinions, that one fine morning an officer waited upon him with a paper containing permission for him to leave the country "por el tiempo necesario," which being translated, meant, not to return very soon. With this he "sloped" for Texas, and became a citizen of that young republic. It was strange in that remote and secluded place to meet one from a region still more distant and even less known, speaking every language in Europe, familiar with every part of it, with the history of every reigning family, the territoral limits of every prince, and at the same time a citizen of so many republics.

His last allegiance was uppermost; his feelings were all Texan, and he gave us many interesting particulars touching the condition and prospects of that country. He was, of course, soon at home in the politics of Yucatan, and he had some little personal interest in watching them closely; for, should Santa Ana regain the ascendancy, the climate would be altogether too warm for him. He had saddle and bridle, sword and pistols—all that he needed except a horse—hanging up in his room, and at a moment's notice he was ready to mount and ride.

Our meeting with this gentleman added much to the interest of our time in Merida. In the evening, when we had settled the affairs of Yucatan, we made an excursion into Illyria or the interior of Turkey. He was as familiar with the little towns in those countries as with those in Mexico. His knowledge of persons and places, derived from actual observation, was most extensive; in short, his whole life had been a chapter of incidents and adventures; and these were not yet ended. He had a new field opened to him in Yucatan. We parted with him in Merida, and the next that we heard of him was of his being in a situation quite as strange as any he had ever been in before. Yet there was nothing reckless, restless, or unsettled about him; he was perfectly fixed and methodical in all his notions and modes of action; in Wall-street he would be considered a staid, regular, quiet, middle-aged man, and he was systematic enough in his habits to be head director of the Bank of England.

I must not omit to mention, among those whom we were in the habit of seeing every day, another old acquaintance, of the Spanish Hotel in Fulton-street, Don Vicente Calera, who, at the time of our former visit, was still travelling in the United States. In the mean time he had returned, married, and was again domesticated in his native city.

Under his escort we traversed Merida in every direction, and visited all the public buildings and institutions.

The population of Merida is probably about twenty-three thousand. Two tables are published in the Appendix; but both purport to give the population of the district, and neither that of the city alone. The city stands on a great plain, on a surface of limestone rock, and the temperature and climate are very uniform. During the thirteen days that we were in Merida the thermometer varied but nine degrees; and, according to a table of observations kept for many years by the much-esteemed Cura Villamil, it appears that during the year beginning on the first of September, 1841, which included the whole time that we were in the country, the greatest variation was but twenty-three degrees. By the kindness of the cura, I have been furnished with a copy of this table, from which I extract the observations for the days that we passed in Merida. The entire table is published in the Appendix. The observations were made by a Fahrenheit thermometer kept in the open air and in the shade, and noted at six in the morning, midday, and six in the afternoon.

	6 A.M.	12 M.	6 P.M.
Oct. 30	78	81	81
" 31	81	82	82
Nov. 1	82	83	82
" 2	80	82	81
" 3	78	80	80
" 4	80	77	77
" 5	77	78	78
" 6	74	77	76
" 7	74	76	76
" 8	75	78	78
" 9	75	78	78
" 10	74	79	79
" 11	76	79	79

I may remark, however, that in the interior of the country we found a much greater variation than any noted in the table published in the Appendix.

The general aspect of the city is Moorish, as it was built at a time when the Moorish style prevailed in Spanish architecture. The houses are large, generally of stone, and one story in height, with balconies to the windows and large courtyards. In the centre of the city stands the plaza major, a square of about six hundred feet. The whole of the east side is occupied by the cathedral and the bishop's palace. On the west stand the house of the municipality and that of the Doña Joaquina Peon. On the north is the palace of the government, and on the south a building which on our first visit arrested our attention the moment we entered the plaza. It is distinguished by a rich sculptured façade of curious design and workmanship. In it is a stone with this inscription:

> Esta obra mando hacerla el
> Adelantado D. Francisco de Montejo
> Año de MDXLIX.

> The Adelantado Don Francisco Montejo caused this to be made in the year 1549.

The subject represents two knights in armour, with visors, breastplates, and helmets, standing upon the shoulders of crushed naked figures, probably intended to represent the conquering Spaniard trampling upon the Indian. Mr. Catherwood attempted to make a drawing of it, and, to avoid the heat of the sun, went into the plaza at daylight for that purpose; but he was so annoyed by the crowd that he was obliged to give it up. There is reason to believe that it is a combination of Spanish and Indian art. The design is certainly Spanish, but as, at that early period of the conquest, but five years after the foundation of Merida, Spaniards were but few, and each man considered himself a conqueror, probably there were none who practised the mechanic arts. The execution was no doubt the work of Indians; and perhaps the carving was done with their own instruments, and not those furnished them by the Spaniards.

The history of the erection of this building would be interesting and instructive; and, with the hope of learning something about it, I proposed to examine thoroughly the archives of the cabildo; but I was advised that all the early archives were lost, or in such confusion that it would be a Herculean labour to ex-

plore them, and I saw that it would consume more time than I
should be able to devote to it.

Besides the inscription on the stone, the only information
that exists in regard to this building is a statement in Cogolludo,
that the façade cost fourteen thousand dollars. It is now the
property of Don Simon Peon, and is occupied by his family. It
has been lately repaired, and some of the beams are no doubt
the same which held up the roof over the adelantado.

Eight streets lead from the plaza, two in the direction of
each cardinal point. In every street, at the distance of a few
squares, is a gate, now dismantled, and beyond are the barrios,
or suburbs.

The streets are distinguished in a manner peculiar to
Yucatan. In the angle of the corner house, and on the top, stands
a painted wooden figure of an elephant, a bull, a flamingo, or
some other visible object, and the street is called by the name
of this object. On one corner there is the figure of an old woman
with large spectacles on her nose, and the street is called la Calle
de la Vieja, or the Street of the Old Woman. That in which we
lived had on the corner house a flamingo, and was called the
Street of the Flamingo; and the reason of the streets being named
in this way gives some idea of the character of the people. The
great mass of the inhabitants, universally the Indians, cannot
read. Printed signs would be of no use, but every Indian knows
the sign of an elephant, a bull, or a flamingo.

In the front wall of a house in a street running north from
the plaza, and also in a corner house near the square of the Alameda, are sculptured figures from the ruins of ancient buildings,
of which Mr. Catherwood made drawings, but, in the multiplicity of other subjects, we do not think it worth while to present them to the reader.

The great distinguishing feature of Merida, as of all the
cities of Spanish America, is in its churches. The great Cathedral;
the parish church and convent of San Cristoval; the church of
the Jesuits; the church and convent of the Mejorada; the chapels
of San Juan Bautista; of Our Lady of Candelaria; of the Santa
Lucia and the Virgin, and the convent de las monjas, or the
nunnery, with its church and enclosures occupying two whole
squares, are all interesting in their history. Some are of good
style in architecture, and rich in ornaments; but there is one
other, not yet mentioned, which I regard as the most interesting
and remarkable edifice in Merida. It is the old Franciscan convent. It stands on an eminence in the eastern part of the city,

and is enclosed by a high wall, with turrets, forming what is now called the Castillo. These walls and turrets are still erect, but within is ruin irretrievable.

In 1820 the new constitution obtained by the patriots in Spain reached the colonies, and on the 30th of May Don Juan Rivas Vertiz, then Gefe Politico, and now living in Merida, a fine memorial of the olden time, published it in the plaza. The church sustained the old order of things, and the Franciscan friars, confident in their hold upon the feelings of the populace, endeavoured to put down this demonstration of liberal feeling. A mob gathered in the plaza; friars appeared among them, urging them on; field-pieces were brought out, the mob dispersed, and Don Juan Rivas marched to the Franciscan convent, opened the doors, drove out the monks, above 300 in number, at the point of the bayonet, and gave up the building to destruction. The superior and some of the brothers became seculars or regular priests; others turned to worldly pursuits; and of this once powerful order, but eleven are now left who wear the garb of the Franciscan monks.

It was in company with one of these that I paid my last visit to this convent. We entered by the great portal of the castle wall into an overgrown courtyard. In front was the convent, with its large corridors and two great churches, the walls of all three standing, but without doors or windows. The roof of one of the churches had fallen, and the broad glare of day was streaming into the interior. We entered the other—the oldest, and identified with the times of the conquerors. Near the door was a blacksmith's forge. A Mestizo was blowing at the bellows, hauling out a red-hot bar of iron, and hammering it into spikes. All along the floor were half-naked Indians and brawny Mestizoes, hewing timber, driving nails, and carrying on the business of making gun-carriages for artillery. The altars were thrown down and the walls defaced; half way up were painted on them, in coarse and staring red characters (in Spanish,) "First squadron," "Second squadron;" and at the head of the church, under a golden gloria, were the words "Comp'y Light Infantry." The church had been occupied as barracks, and these were the places where they stacked their arms. As we passed through, the workmen stared at my companion, or rather at the long blue gown, the cord around his waist, and the cross dangling from it—the garb of his scattered order. It was the first time he had visited the place since the expulsion of the monks. To me it was mournful to behold the destruction and desecration of this noble build-

ing; what, then, must it have been to him? In the floor of the
church near the altar and in the sacristia were open vaults, but
the bones of the monks had been thrown out and scattered on
the floor. Some of these were the bones of his earliest friends. We
passed into the refectory, and he pointed out the position of the
long table at which the brotherhood took their meals, and the
stone fountain at which they performed their ablutions. His old
companions in their long blue gowns rose up before him, now
scattered forever, and their home a desolation and ruin.

But this convent contains one memorial far more interesting
than any connected with its own ruin; one that carries the be-
holder back through centuries of time, and tells the story of a
greater and a sadder fall.

In one of the lower cloisters going out from the north, and
under the principal dormitory, are two parallel corridors. The
outer one faces the principal patio, and this corridor has that
peculiar arch so often referred to in my previous volumes, two
sides rising to meet each other, and covered, when within about
a foot of forming an apex, by a flat layer of stones. There can be
no mistake about the character of this arch; it cannot for a moment be supposed that the Spaniards constructed anything so different from their known rules of architecture; and beyond doubt
it formed part of one of those mysterious buildings which have
given rise to so much speculation; the construction of which has
been ascribed to the most ancient people in the Old World, and
to races lost, perished, and unknown.

I am happy thus early in these pages to have an opportunity
of recurring to the opinion expressed in my former volumes, in
regard to the builders of the ancient American cities.

The conclusion to which I came was, that "there are not sufficient grounds for belief in the great antiquity that has been
ascribed to these ruins;" "that we are not warranted in going
back to any ancient nation of the Old World for the builders of
these cities; that they are not the works of people who have
passed away, and whose history is lost; but that there are strong
reasons to believe them the creation of the same races who inhabited the country at the time of the Spanish conquest, or of
some not very distant progenitors."

This opinion was not given lightly, nor without due consideration. It was adverse to my feelings, which would fain have
thrown around the ruins the interest of mystery and hoary age;
and even now, though gratified at knowing that my opinion has
been fully sustained, I would be willing to abandon it, and

involve the reader and myself in doubt, did circumstances warrant me in so doing; but I am obliged to say that subsequent investigations have fortified and confirmed my previous conclusions, and, in fact, have made conviction what before was mere matter of opinion.

When I wrote the account of my former journey, the greatest difficulty attending the consideration of this subject was the absence of all historical record concerning the places visited. Copan had some history, but it was obscure, uncertain, and unsatisfactory. Quirigua, Palenque, and Uxmal had none whatever; but a ray of historic light beams upon the solitary arch in the ruined convent of Merida.

In the account of the conquest of Yucatan by Cogolludo it is stated, that on the arrival of the Spaniards at the Indian town of Tihoo, on the site of which, it will be remembered, Merida now stands, they found many cerros hechos a mano, *i. e.*, hills made by hand, or artificial mounds, and that on one of these mounds the Spaniards encamped.

This mound, it is stated, stood on the ground now occupied by the plaza major. East of it was another large mound, and the Spaniards laid the foundation of the city between these two, because, as it is assigned, the stones in them were a great convenience in building, and economized the labour of the Indians. These mounds were so large, it is added, that with the stones the Spaniards built all the edifices in the city, so that the ground which forms the plaza major remained nearly or quite level. The buildings erected are specified, and it is added that there was abundance of material for other edifices which the Spaniards wished to erect.

Other mounds are mentioned as obstructing the laying out of streets according to the plan proposed, and there is one circumstance which bears directly upon this point, and, in my opinion, is conclusive.

In the history of the construction of the Franciscan convent, which was founded in the year 1547, five years after the arrival of the Spaniards in Tihoo, it is expressly stated that it was built upon a small artifical mound, one of the many that were then in the place, on which mound, it is added, were *some ancient buildings*. Now we must either suppose that the Spaniards razed these buildings to the ground, and then constructed this strange arch themselves, which supposition is, I think, utterly untenable, or that this corridor formed part of the ancient buildings which, according to the historical account, stood on this artificial mound, and that for some purpose or other the monks incorporated it with their convent.

There is but one way to overthrow this latter conclusion, and that is by contending that these mounds were all ruined, and this building too, at the time when it was made to form part of the convent; but then we are reduced to the necessity of supposing that a great town, the fame of which reached the Spaniards at Campeachy, and which made a desperate and bloody resistance to their occupation of it, was a mere gathering of hordes around the ruined buildings of another race; and, besides, it is a matter of primary importance to note that these artificial mounds are mentioned, not in the course of describing the Indian town, for no description whatever is attempted, but merely incidentally, as affording conveniences to the Spaniards in furnishing materials for building the city, or as causing obstructions in the laying out of streets regularly and according to the plan proposed. The mound on which the convent stands would perhaps not have been mentioned at all but for the circumstance that the Padre Cogolludo was a Franciscan friar, and the mention of it enabled him to pay a tribute to the memory of the blessed father Luis de Villpando, then superior of the convent, and to show the great estimation in which he was held, for he says that the adelantado had fixed upon this mound for the site of one of his fortresses, but on the application of the superior he yielded it to him readily for the site of the convent; and, more than all this, even in the incidental way in which these mounds are referred to, there is one circumstance which shows clearly that they were not at that time disused and in ruins, but, on the contrary, were then in the actual use and occupation of the Indians; for Cogolludo mentions particularly and with much detail one that completely obstructed the running of a particular street, which, he says, was called El grande de los Kues, adoratorio que era de los idolos. Now the word "Kues," in the Maya language, as spoken by the Indians of Yucatan at the present day, means their ancient places of worship, and the word "adoratorio," as defined in the Spanish dictionary, is the name given by the Spaniards to the temples of idols in America. So that when the historian describes this mound as El grande de los Kues el adora-, torio de los idolos, he means to say that it was the great one, or the greatest among the places of worship of the Indians, or the temples of their idols.

It is called the "great one" of their places of worship, in contradistinction to the smaller ones around, among which was that now occupied by the Franciscan convent. In my opinion, the solitary arch found in this convent is very strong, if not conclusive, evidence that all the ruined buildings scattered over Yucatan were erected by the very Indians who occupied the country at the time of the Spanish conquest, or, to fall back upon my old ground, that they were the work "of the same race of people," or "their not very distant progenitors."

Who these races were, whence they came, or who were their progenitors, I did not undertake to say, nor do I now.

CHAPTER V

But the reader must not suppose that our only business in Merida was the investigation of antiquities; we had other operations in hand which gave us plenty of employment. We had taken with us a Daguerreotype apparatus, of which but one specimen had ever before appeared in Yucatan. Great improvements had been since made in the instrument, and we had reason to believe that ours was one of the best; and having received assurances that we might do a large business in that line, we were induced to set up as ladies' Daguerreotype portrait takers. It was a new line for us, and rather venturesome, but not worse than for the editor of a newspaper to turn captain of a steamboat; and, besides, it was not like banking—we could not injure any one by a failure.

Having made trials upon ourselves until we were tired of the subjects, and with satisfactory results, we considered ourselves sufficiently advanced to begin; and as we intended to practice for the love of the art, and not for lucre, we held that we had a right to select our subjects. Accordingly, we had but to signify our wishes, and the next morning put our house in order for the reception of our fair visiters. We cleared everything out of the hammock, took the washhand basin off the chair, and threw odds and ends into one corner; and as the sun was pouring its rays warmly and brightly into our door, it was farther lighted up by the entry of three young ladies, with their respective papas and mammas. We had great difficulty in finding them all seats, and were obliged to put the two mammas into the hammock together. The young ladies were dressed in their prettiest costume, with earrings and chains, and their hair adorned with flowers. All were pretty, and one was much more than pretty; not in the style of Spanish beauty, with dark eyes and hair, but a delicate and dangerous blonde, simple, natural, and unaffected, beautiful without knowing it, and really because she could not help it. Her name, too, was poetry itself. I am bound to single her out, for, late on the evening of our departure from Merida, she sent us a large cake, measuring about three feet in circumference by six inches deep, which, by-the-way, everything being packed up, I smothered into a pair of saddle-bags, and spoiled some of my scanty stock of wearing apparel.

The ceremonies of the reception over, we made immediate preparations to begin. Much form and circumstance were necessary in settling preliminaries; and as we were in no hurry to get rid of our subjects, we had more formalities than usual to go through with.

Our first subject was the lady of the poetical name. It was necessary to hold a consultation upon her costume, whether the colours were pretty and such as would be brought out well or not; whether a scarf around the neck was advisable; whether the hair was well arranged, the rose becoming, and in the best position; then to change it, and consider the effect of the change, and to say and do many other things which may suggest themselves to the reader's imagination, and all which gave rise to many profound remarks in regard to artistical effect, and occupied much time.

The lady being arrayed to the best advantage, it was necessary to seat her with reference to a right adjustment of light and shade; to examine carefully the falling of the light upon her face; then to consult whether it was better to take a front or a side view; to look at the face carefully in both positions; and, finally, it was necessary to secure the head in the right position; that it should be neither too high nor too low; too much on one side nor on the other; and as this required great nicety, it was sometimes actually indispensable to turn the beautiful little head with our own hands, which, however, was a very innocent way of turning a young lady's head.

Next it was necessary to get the young lady into focus—that is, to get her into the box, which, in short, means, to get a reflec-

tion of her face on the glass in the camera obscura at that one
particular point of view which presented it better than any
other; and when this was obtained, the miniature likeness of the
object was so faithfully reflected, that, as artists carried away by
enthusiasm, we were obliged to call in the papas and mammas,
who pronounced it beautiful—to which dictum we were in courtesy obliged to respond.

The plate was now cleaned, put into the box, and the light
shut off. Now came a trying time for the young lady. She must
neither open her lips nor roll her eyes for one minute and thirty
seconds by the watch. This eternity at length ended, and the
plate was taken out.

So far our course had been before the wind. Every new formality had but increased our importance in the eyes of our fair
visiters and their respectable companions. Mr. Catherwood retired to the adjoining room to put the plate in the mercury
bath, while we, not knowing what the result might be, a little
fearful, and neither wishing to rob another of the honour he
might be justly entitled to, nor to be dragged down by another's
failure, thought best to have it distinctly understood that Mr.
Catherwood was the maestro, and that we were merely amateurs.
At the same time, on Mr. Catherwood's account, I took occasion
to suggest that the process was so complicated, and its success
depended upon such a variety of minute circumstances, it seemed
really wonderful that it ever turned out well. The plate might
not be good, or not well cleaned; or the chemicals might not be
of the best; or the plate might be left too long in the iodine box,
or taken out too soon; or left too long in the bromine box, or
taken out too soon; or a ray of light might strike it on putting it
into the camera or in taking it out; or it might be left too long
in the camera or taken out too soon; or too long in the mercury
bath or taken out too soon; and even though all these processes
were right and regular, there might be some other fault of omis-
sion or commission which we were not aware of; besides which,
climate and atmosphere had great influence, and might render
all of no avail. These little suggestions we considered necessary
to prevent too great a disappointment in case of failure; and perhaps our fair visiters were somewhat surprised at our audacity in
undertaking at all such a doubtful experiment, and using them
as instruments. The result, however, was enough to induce us
never again to adopt prudential measures, for the young lady's
image was stamped upon the plate, and made a picture which

enchanted her and satisfied the critical judgment of her friends and admirers.

Our experiments upon the other ladies were equally successful, and the morning glided away in this pleasant occupation.

We continued practising a few days longer; and as all our good results were extensively shown, and the poor ones we took care to keep out of sight, our reputation increased, and we had abundance of applications.

In this state of things we requested some friends to whom we were under many obligations, to be permitted to wait upon them at their houses. On receiving their assent, the next morning at nine o'clock Mr. C. in a caleza, with all the complicated apparatus packed around him, drove up to their door. I followed on foot. It was our intention to go through the whole family, uncles, aunts, grandchildren, down to Indian servants, as many as would sit; but man is born to disappointment. I spare the reader the recital of our misfortunes that day. It would be too distressing. Suffice it to say that we tried plate after plate, sitting after sitting, varying light, time, and other points of the process; but it was all in vain. The stubborn instrument seemed bent upon confounding us; and, covering our confusion as well as we could, we gathered up our Daguerreotype and carried ourselves off. What was the cause of our complete discomfiture we never ascertained, but we resolved to give up business as ladies' Daguerreotype portrait takers.

There was one interesting incident connected with our short career of practice. Among the portraits put forth was one of a lady, which came to the knowledge of a gentleman particularly interested in the fair original. This gentleman had never taken any especial notice of us before, but now he called upon us, and very naturally the conversation turned upon that art of which we were then professors. The portrait of this lady was mentioned, and by the time he had finished his third straw cigar, he unburdened himself of the special object of his visit, which was to procure a portrait of her for himself. This seemed natural enough, and we assented, provided he would get her to sit; but he did not wish either her or her friends to know anything about it. This *was* a difficulty. It was not very easy to take it by stealth. However strong an impression a young lady may make by a glance upon some substances, she can do nothing upon a silver plate. Here she requires the aid of iodine, bromine, and mercury. But the young man was fertile in expedients. He said that we could easily make some excuse, promising her something more

perfect, and in making two or three impressions, could slip one
away for him. This was by no means a bad suggestion, at least so
far as he was concerned, but we had some qualms of conscience.
While we were deliberating, a matter was introduced which perhaps lay as near Doctor Cabot's heart as the young lady did that
of our friend. That was a pointer or setter dog for hunting, of
which the doctor was in great want. The gentlemen said he had
one—the only one in Merida—and he would give it for the portrait. It was rather an odd proposition, but to offer a dog for
his mistress's portrait was very different from offering his mistress's portrait for a dog. It was clear that the young man was in
a bad way; he would lay down his life, give up smoking, part
with his dog or commit any other extravagance. The case was
touching. The doctor was really interested; and, after all, what
harm could it do? The doctor and I went to look at the dog, but
it turned out to be a mere pup, entirely unbroken, and what the
result might have been I do not know, but all farther negotiations were broken off by the result of our out-of-door practice
and disgust for the business.

There is no immediate connexion between taking Daguerreotype portraits and the practice of surgery, but circumstances
bring close together things entirely dissimilar in themselves, and
we went from one to the other. Secluded as Merida is, and seldom visited by strangers, the fame of new discoveries in science
is slow in reaching it, and the new operation of Mons. Guerin
for the cure of strabismus had not been heard of. In private
intercourse we had spoken of this operation, and, in order to
make it known, and extend its benefits, Doctor Cabot had offered to perform it in Merida. The Merida people have generally fine eyes, but, either because our attention was particularly
directed to it, or that it is really the case, there seemed to be
more squinting eyes, or biscos, as they are called, than are usually seen in any one town, and in Merida, as in some other places,
this is not esteemed a beauty; but, either from want of confidence in a stranger, or a cheap estimation of the qualifications of
a medico who asked no pay for his services, the doctor's phil-
anthropic purposes were not appreciated. At least, no one cared
to be the first; and as the doctor had no sample of his skill with
him, no subject offered.

We had fixed the day for our departure; and the evening
but one before, a direct overture was made to the doctor to perform the operation. The subject was a boy, and the application
in his behalf was made by a gentleman who formed one of a

circle in which we were in the habit of visiting, and whom we were all happy to have it in our power to serve.

The time was fixed at ten o'clock the next day. After breakfast our sala was put in order for the reception of company, and the doctor for the first time looked to his instruments. He had some misgivings. They were of very fine workmanship, made in Paris, most sensitive to the influence of the atmosphere, and in that climate it was almost impossible to preserve anything metallic from rust. The doctor had packed the case among his clothing in the middle of his trunk, and had taken every possible precaution, but, as usual upon such occasions, the most important instrument had rusted at the point, and in that state was utterly useless. There was no cutler in the place, nor any other person competent to touch it. Mr. Catherwood, however, brought out an old razor hone, and between them they worked off the rust.

At ten o'clock the doctor's subject made his appearance. He was the son of a widow lady of very respectable family, about fourteen years old, but small of stature, and presenting even to the most casual glance the stamp of a little gentleman. He had large black eyes, but, unluckily, their expression was very much injured by an inward squint. With the light heart of boyhood, however, he seemed indifferent to his personal appearance, and came, as he said, because his mother told him to do so. His handsome person, and modest and engaging manners, gave us immediately a strong interest in his favour. He was accompanied by the gentleman who had spoken of bringing him, Dr. Bado, a Guatimalian educated in Paris, the oldest and principal physician of Merida, and by several friends of the family, whom we did not know.

Preparations were commenced immediately. The first movement was to bring out a long table near the window; then to spread upon it a mattress and pillow, and upon these to spread the boy. Until the actual moment of operating, the precise character of this new business had not presented itself to my mind, and altogether it opened by no means so favourably as Daguerreotype practice.

Not aiming to be technical, but desiring to give the reader the benefit of such scraps of learning as I pick up in my travels, modern science has discovered that the eye is retained in its orbit by six muscles, which pull it up and down, inward and outward, and that the undue contraction of either of these muscles produces that obliquity called squinting, which was once supposed to proceed from convulsions in childhood, or other un-

known causes. The cure discovered is the cutting of the contracted muscle, by means of which the eye falls immediately into
its proper place. This muscle lies under the surface; and, as it is
necessary to pass through a membrane of the eye, the cutting
cannot be done with a broadaxe or a handsaw. In fact, it requires a knowledge of the anatomy of the eye, manual dexterity,
fine instruments, and Mr. Catherwood, and myself for assistants.

Our patient remained perfectly quiet, with his little hands
folded across his breast; but while the knife was cutting through
the muscle he gave one groan, so piteous and heart-rending, that
it sent into the next room all who were not immediately engaged.
But before the sound of the groan had died away the operation
was over, and the boy rose with his eye bleeding, but perfectly
straight. A bandage was tied over it, and, with a few directions
for its treatment, amid the congratulations and praises of all
present, and wearing the same smile with which he had entered,
the little fellow walked off to his mother.

The news of this wonder spread rapidly, and before night
Dr. Cabot had numerous and pressing applications, among which
was one from a gentleman whom we were all desirous to oblige,
and who had this defect in both eyes.

On his account we determined to postpone our departure
another day; and, in furtherance of his original purpose, Dr.
Cabot mentioned that he would perform the operation upon all
who chose to offer. We certainly took no trouble to spread this
notice, but the next morning, when we returned from breakfast,
there was a gathering of squint-eyed boys around the door, who,
with their friends and backers, made a formidable appearance,
and almost obstructed our entrance. As soon as the door opened
there was a rush inside; and as some of these slanting eyes might
not be able to distinguish between meum and tuum, we were
obliged to help their proprietors out into the street again.

At ten o'clock the big table was drawn up to the window,
and the mattress and pillow were spread upon it, but there was
such a gathering around the window that we had to hang up a
sheet before it. Invitations had been given to Dr. Bado and Dr.
Munoz, and all physicians who chose to come, and having met
the governor in the evening, I had asked him to be present.
These all honoured us with their company, together with a
number of self-invited persons, who had introduced themselves,
and could not well be turned out, making quite a crowded room.

The first who presented himself was a stout lad about nineteen or twenty, whom we had never seen or heard of before. Who

he was or where he came from we did not know, but he was a
bisco of the worst kind, and seemed able-bodied enough to undergo anything in the way of surgery. As soon as the doctor began
to cut the muscle, however, our strapping patient gave signs of
restlessness; and all at once, with an actual bellow, he jerked his
head on one side, carried away the doctor's hook, and shut his
eye upon it with a sort of lockjaw grip, as if determined it should
never be drawn out. How my hook got out I have no idea; fortunately, the doctor let his go, or the lad's eye would have been
scratched out. As it was, there he sat with the bandage slipped
above one eye, and the other closed upon the hook, the handle
of which stood out straight. Probably at that moment he would
have been willing to sacrifice pride of personal appearance, keep
his squint, and go through life with his eye shut, the hook in it,
and the handle sticking out; but the instrument was too valuable
to be lost. And it was interesting and instructive to notice the
difference between the equanimity of one who had a hook in his
eye, and that of lookers-on who had not. All the spectators up-
braided him with his cowardice and want of heart, and after a
round of reproof to which he could make no answer, he opened
his eye and let out the hook. But he had made a bad business of
it. A few seconds longer, and the operation would have been
completed. As it was, the whole work had to be repeated. As the
muscle was again lifted under the knife, I thought I saw a glare
in the eyeball that gave token of another fling of the head, but
the lad was fairly browbeaten into quiet; and, to the great satisfaction of all, with a double share of blackness and blood, and
with very little sympathy from any one, but with his eye straight,
he descended from the table. Outside he was received with a loud
shout by the boys, and we never heard of him again.

The room was now full of people, and, being already disgusted with the practice of surgery, I sincerely hoped that this
exhibition would cure all others of a wish to undergo the operation, but a little Mestizo boy, about ten years old, who had been
present all the time, crept through the crowd, and, reaching the
table, squinted up at us without speaking, his crisscross expression telling us very plainly what he wanted. He had on the usual
Mestizo dress of cotton shirt and drawers and straw hat, and
seemed so young, simple, and innocent, that we did not consider
him capable of judging for himself. We told him he must not be
operated on, but he answered, in a decided though modest tone,
"Yo quiero, yo quiero," "I wish it, I wish it." We inquired if
there was any one present who had any authority over him, and

a man whom we had not noticed before, dressed, like him, in shirt and drawers, stepped forward and said he was the boy's father; he had brought him there himself on purpose, and begged Doctor Cabot to proceed. By his father's directions, the little fellow attempted to climb up on the table, but his legs were too short, and he had to be lifted up. His eye was bandaged, and his head placed upon the pillow. He folded his hands across his breast, turned his eye, did in all things exactly as he was directed, and in half a minute the operation was finished. I do not believe that he changed his position a hair's breadth or moved a muscle. It was an extraordinary instance of fortitude. The spectators were all admiration, and, amid universal congratulation, he was lifted from the table, his eye bound up, and, without a word, but with the spirit of a little hero, he took his father's hand and went away.

At this time, amid a press of applicants, a gentleman came to inform us that a young lady was waiting her turn. This gave us an excuse for clearing the room, and we requested all except the medical gentlemen and the immediate friends to favour us with their absence. Such was the strange curiosity these people had for seeing a most disagreeable spectacle, that they were very slow in going away, and some slipped into the other rooms and the yard, but we ferreted them out, and got the room somewhat to ourselves.

The young lady was accompanied by her mother. She was full of hesitation and fears, anxious to be relieved, but doubting her ability to endure the pain, and the moment she saw the instruments, her courage entirely forsook her. Doctor Cabot discouraged all who had any distrust of their own fortitude, and, to my mingled joy and regret, she went away.

The next in order was the gentleman on whose account we had postponed our departure. He was the oldest general in the Mexican service, but for two years an exile in Merida. By the late revolution, which placed Santa Ana in power, his party was uppermost; and he had strong claims upon our good feelings, for, in a former expatriation from Mexico, he had served as volunteer aid to General Jackson at the battle of New-Orleans. This gentleman had an inward squint in both eyes, which, however, instead of being a defect, gave character to his face; but his sight was injured by it, and this Doctor Cabot thought might be improved. The first eye was cut quickly and successfully, and while the bloody orb was rolling in its socket, the same operation was performed on the other. In this, however, fearing that the eye might be drawn too far in the opposite direction, the doctor had not thought it advisable to cut the muscle entirely through, and, on examining it, he was not satisfied with the appearance. The general again laid his head upon the pillow, and the operation was repeated, making three times in rapid succession. Altogether, it was a trying thing, and I felt immensely happy when it was over. With his eyes all right and both bandaged, we carried him to a caleza in waiting, where, to the great amusement of the vagabond boys, he took his seat on the footboard, with his back to the horse, and it was some time before we could get him right.

In the mean time the young lady had returned with her mother. She could not bear to lose the opportunity, and though unable to make up her mind to undergo the operation, she could not keep away. She was about eighteen, of lively imagination, picturing pleasure or pain in the strongest colours, and with a smile ever ready to chase away the tear. At one moment she roused herself to the effort, and the next, calling herself coward, fell into her mother's arms, while her mother cheered and encouraged her, representing to her, with that confidence allowed before medical men, the advantage it would give her in the eyes of our sex. Her eyes were large, full, and round, and with the tear glistening in them, the defect was hardly visible; in fact, all that they wanted was to be made to roll in the right direction.

I have given the reader a faint picture of Daguerreotype practice with young ladies, but this was altogether another thing, and it was very different from having to deal with boys or men. It is easy enough to spread out a boy upon a table, but not so with a young lady; so, too, it is easy enough to tie a bandage around a boy's head, but vastly different among combs and curls, and long hair done up behind. As the principal assistant of Doctor Cabot, this complicated business devolved upon me; and having, with the help of her mother, accomplished it, I laid her head upon the pillow as carefully as if it had been my own property. In all the previous cases I had found it necessary, in order to steady my hand, to lean my elbow on the table, and my wrist on the forehead of the patient. I did the same with her, and, if I know myself, I never gazed into any eyes as I did into that young lady's one eye in particular. When the doctor drew out the instrument, I certainly could have taken her in my arms, but her imagination had been too powerful; her eyes closed, a slight shudder seized her, and she fainted. That passed off, and she rose with her eyes all right. A young gentleman was in attendance to escort her to her home, and the smile had again returned to her cheek as he told her that now her lover would not know her.

This case had occupied a great deal of time; the doctor's labours were doubled by the want of regular surgical aid, he was fatigued with the excitement, and I was worn out; my head was actually swimming with visions of bleeding and mutilated eyes, and I almost felt doubtful about my own. The repetition of the operations had not accustomed me to them; indeed, the last was more painful to me than the first, and I felt willing to abandon forever the practice of surgery. Doctor Cabot had explained the modus operandi fully to the medical gentlemen, had offered to procure them instruments, and considering the thing fairly introduced into the country, we determined to stop. But this was not so easy; the crowd out of doors had their opinion on the subject; the biscos considered that we were treating them outrageously, and became as clamorous as a mob in a western city about to administer Lynch law. One would not be kept back. He was a strapping youth, with cast enough in his eye to carry everything before him, and had probably been taunted all his life by merciless schoolboys. Forcing himself inside, with his hands in his pockets, he said that he had the money to pay for it, and would not be put off. We were obliged to apologize, and, with a little wish to bring him down, gave him some hope that he should be attended to on our return to Merida.

The news of these successes flew like wild-fire, and a great sensation was created throughout the city. All the evening Doctor Cabot was besieged with applications, and I could but think how fleeting is this world's fame! At first my arrival in the country had been fairly trumpeted in the newspapers; for a little while Mr. Catherwood had thrown me in the shade with the Daguerreotype, and now all our glories were swallowed up by Doctor Cabot's cure of strabismus. Nevertheless, his fame was reflected upon us. All the afternoon squint-eyed boys were passing up and down the street, throwing slanting glances in at the door, and toward evening, as Mr. Catherwood and I were walking to the plaza, we were hailed by some vagabond urchins with the obstreperous shout, "There go the men who cure the biscos."

CHAPTER VI

On Thursday, the twelfth day of November, we rose for our departure from Merida. The plan of our route, and all the arrangements for our journey, were made by our friend Don Simon Peon. Early in the morning our luggage was sent forward on the backs of mules and Indians, and we had only to take leave of our friends. Our landlord refused to receive the four dollars due to him for rent. The pleasure of our society, he said, was compensation enough, and between friends house-rent was not to be thought of. We bade him an affectionate farewell, and in all probability "we ne'er shall see his like again," at least in this matter of house-rent. We breakfasted for the last time with our countrymen, including Mr. Fisher and Captain M'Kinley, who had arrived that morning direct from New-York, at the house of the Doña Micaela, and, attended by the good wishes of all for our safety and success, mounted for our journey into the interior.

It was our intention to resume our explorations at Uxmal, the point where we were interrupted by the illness of Mr. Catherwood. We had received intelligence, however, of the ruins of Mayapan, an ancient city which had never been visited, about eight leagues distant from Merida, and but a few leagues aside from the road, by the haciendas, to Uxmal. The accounts which we could obtain were meager, and it was represented as completely in ruins; but, in fulfillment of the purpose we at that time entertained of going to every place of which we heard any account whatever, we determined to visit this on our way to Uxmal. It was for Mayapan, therefore, that we were now setting out.

Our saddles, bridles, holsters, and pistols, being entirely different from the mountings of horsemen in that country, attracted all eyes as we rode through the streets. A friend accompanied us beyond the suburbs, and put us into a straight road, which led, without turning, to the end of our day's journey. Instead of the ominous warnings we were accustomed to receive in Central America, his parting words were, that there was no danger of robbers, or of any other interruptions.

Under these favourable circumstances, in good health and spirits, with recommendations from the government to its officers in different sections of the country, and through the newspapers to the hospitality of citizens in the interior, we set out on our journey. We had before us a new and unexplored region, in which we might expect to find new scenes every day. There was but one drawback. We had no servant or attendant of any kind, our friends having been disappointed in procuring those which were expected. This, however, did not give us much uneasiness.

The day was overcast, which saved us from the scorching sun, that otherwise, at this hour, would have molested us. The road was straight, level, stony, and uninteresting. On both sides were low, thick woods, so that there was no view except that of the road before us; and already, in the beginning of our journey, we felt that, if we were safe from the confusion and danger which had attended us in Central America, we had lost, too, the mountains, valleys, volcanoes, rivers, and all the wild and magnificent scenery that gave a charm to the country in spite of the difficulties and dangers by which travelling was there attended.

I would remark that no map of Yucatan at all to be depended on has ever been published. The Doña Joaquina Peon had one in manuscript, which she was so kind as to place at our disposal, but with notice that it was not correct; and, in order to keep a record of our own track from the time we left Merida until we returned to it, we took the bearings of the roads, noted the number of hours on each day's journey, and the pace of our horses, and at some places Mr. Catherwood took an observation for latitude. From these memoranda our map is prepared. It is correct so far as regards our route, but does not fix accurately the location of places which we did not visit.

At the distance of a league we passed a fine cattle hacienda, and at twenty minutes past one reached Timucui, a small village five leagues from Merida. This village consisted of a few Indian huts, built around a large open square, and on one side was a sort of shed for a casa real. It had no church or cura, and already we experienced a difficulty which we did not expect to encounter so soon. The population consisted entirely of Indians, who in general throughout the country speak nothing but the Maya; there was not a white man in the place, nor any one who could speak in any tongue that we could comprehend. Fortunately, a muleteer from the interior, on his way to Merida, had stopped to bait his mules under the shade of a large tree, and was swinging in a hammock in the casa real. He was surprised at our undertaking alone a journey into the interior, seeing that we were brought to a stand at the first village from the capital; but, finding us somewhat rational in other respects, he assisted us in procuring ramon leaves and water for the horses. His life had been passed in driving mules from a region of country called the Sierra, to the capital; but he had heard strange stories about foreign countries, and, among others, that in El Norte a man could earn a dollar a day by his labour; but he was comforted when he learned that a real in his country was worth more to him than a dollar would be in ours; and as he interpreted to his nearly naked companions, crouching in the shade, nothing touched them so nearly as the idea of cold and frost, and spending a great portion of the day's earnings for fuel to keep from freezing.

At three o'clock we left the hamlet, and at a little after four we saw the towers of the church of Tekoh. In the suburbs of this village we passed the campo santo, a large enclosure with high stone walls; over the gateway of which, and in niches along the top of the wall, was a row of human skulls. Inside the enclosure, at the farthest extremity, was a pile of skulls and bones, which, according to a custom of the Indians observed from time immemorial, had been dug up from the graves and thrown into this shallow pit, a grim and ghastly charnel-house.

The village consisted of a long, straight street, with houses or huts almost hidden by foliage, and inhabited exclusively by Indians. We rode up to the plaza without meeting a single person. At one side of the plaza, on a high stone platform, stood a gigantic church, with two lofty towers, and in front and on each side was a broad flight of stone steps. Crossing the plaza we saw an Indian woman, to whom we uttered the word *convento*, and, following the direction of her hand, rode up to the house of the cura. It was in the rear of the church, and enclosed by a large wall. The gate was closed, but we opened it without knocking. The convent stood on the same platform with the church, and had a high flight of stone steps. A number of Indian servants ran out to the corridor, to stare at such strange-looking persons, and we understood that the padre was not at home; but we were too well pleased with the appearance of things to think of going elsewhere. We tied our horses in the yard, ascended the steps, and strolled through the corridor of the convent and along the platform of the church, overlooking the village.

Before the door of the church lay the body of a child on a bier. There was no coffin, but the body was wrapped in a tinsel dress of paper of different colours, in which red and gold were predominant; and amid this finery worms several inches long were issuing from its nostrils, curling and twisting over its face: a piteous and revolting spectacle, showing the miserable lot of the children of the poor in these Indian villages.

In a few minutes the ministro, or assistant of the cura, joined us, from whom we learned that the cura was preparing to bury this child, and as soon as it was over, would come to receive us. In the mean time, under his escort, we ascended to the top of the church.

The ascent was by a large stone staircase within one of the towers. The top commanded a view of a great plain, covered by an almost boundless forest, extending on one side to the sea, and on the other to the sierra which crosses the peninsula of Yucatan, and runs back to the great traversing range in Guatimala, broken only by a high mound, which at three leagues' distance towered above the plain, a mourning monument of the ruins of Mayapan, the capital of the fallen kingdom of Maya.

On our return we found the cura, Don José Canuta Vela, waiting to receive us; he had been notified of our coming, and had expected us the day before. His curacy consisted of nearly two thousand souls, and, except his ministro, we did not see a white man among this population. He was under thirty, born and bred in Merida, and in manners and attainments apparently out of place in such a position; but his feelings and sympathies were identified with the people under his charge. The convent was a great stone building, with walls several feet thick, and in size corresponded with the church. Being so near Merida, it was more than ordinarily well supplied with comforts; and, among other things, the cura had a small collection of books, which, for that country, constituted quite a library.

He relieved us of all difficulty arising from the want of an interpreter, and, sending for the Indian alcaldes, made immediate arrangements to forward our luggage, and to accompany us himself the next day to the ruins of Mayapan. We had again made a beginning with the padres, and this beginning, in heartiness of welcome and goodness of cheer, corresponded with all that we had before received at their hands. We had the choice of cot or hammock for the night, and at breakfast a group of Indian musicians were seated under the corridor, who continued making a noise, which they called la musica, till we mounted to depart.

The cura accompanied us, mounted on one of the best horses we had seen in the country; and as it was a rare thing for him to absent himself a day from his parochial duties, he set out as for a holy-day excursion, worrying our poor nags, as well as ourselves, to keep up with him.

The road upon which we entered turned off abruptly from the camino real. This royal road itself, like most of the others which bore that name, would not be considered, in other countries, as indicating a very advanced state of internal improvement, but the one into which we now struck was much rougher and more stony, entirely new, and in some places still unfinished. It had been but lately opened, and the reason of its being opened at all illustrates one striking feature in the character of the Indians. The village to which it leads was under the pastoral charge of our friendly companion, and was formerly reached by a road, or rather path, so circuitous and difficult that, on account of his other duties, he was obliged to give notice that he would be compelled to give it up. To prevent this calamity, all the Indians, in a body, turned out and made this new road, being a straight cut through the woods, two leagues in length.

The padre took a lively interest in the zeal lately awakened for exploring the antiquities of the country, and told us that this particular region abounded with traces of the ancient inhabitants. At a short distance from the camino real we came to a line of fallen stones, forming what appeared to be the remains of a wall which crossed the road, and ran off into the forest on both sides, traversing, he said, the country for a great distance in both directions.

A short distance beyond, we turned off to a large hollow basin perfectly dry, which he called an aguada, and said it was an artificial formation, excavated and walled around, and had been used by the ancients as a reservoir for water. At the time, we did not agree with him, but considered the basin a natural formation, though, from what we saw afterward, we are induced to believe that his account may have been correct.

At ten o'clock we reached the small village of Telchaquillo, containing a population of six hundred souls, and these, again, were all Indians. It was they who had made the road we had travelled over, and the church was under our friend's pastoral charge. We rode to the convent, and dismounted. Immediately the bell of the church tolled, to give notice of his arrival, that all who wished to confess or get married, who had sick to be visited, children to be baptized, or dead to be buried, might apply to him, and have their wants attended to.

The village consisted entirely of huts, or casas de paja. The church had been commenced on a large scale, under the direction of a former cura, who afterward became dissatisfied with the people, and discontinued the building. One end was covered over, and fitted up rudely as a chapel; beyond were two high walls, but roofless.

In the square of this little village was a great senote, or subterraneous well, which supplied all the inhabitants with water. At a distance the square seemed level and unbroken; but women walking across it with cantaros or water-jars suddenly disappeared, and others seemed to rise out of the earth. On a nearer approach, we found a great orifice or opening in the rocky surface, like the mouth of a cave. The descent was by irregular steps cut and worn in the rocks. Over head was an immense rocky roof, and at a distance of perhaps five hundred feet from the mouth was a large basin or reservoir of water. Directly over the water the roof was perhaps sixty feet high; and there was an opening above which threw down a strong body of light. The water had no current, and its source was a mystery. During the rainy season it rises a little, but never falls below a certain point, and at all times it is the only source of supply to the inhabitants. Women, with their water-jars, were constantly ascending and descending; swallows were darting through the cave in every direction, and the whole formed a wild, picturesque, and romantic scene.

At this village we found waiting for us the major domo of the hacienda of San Joaquin, on which stand the ruins of Mayapan. Leaving the senote, we mounted and followed him.

At the distance of half a mile he stopped near a great cave that had lately been discovered, and which, he said, had no end.

Tying our horses to the bushes, we turned off to visit it. The major domo cut a path a short distance into the woods, following which we came to a large hollow, overgrown with trees, and, descending, entered a great cavern with a lofty roof, and gigantic passages branching off in different directions, and running no one knew whither. The cave had been discovered by the major domo and some vaqueros while in pursuit of robbers who had stolen a bull; and no robber's cave in romantic story could equal it in wildness. The major domo said he had entered it with ten men, and had passed four hours in exploration without finding any end. The cave, its roof, base, and passages, were an immense fossil formation. Marine shells were conglomerated together in solid masses, many of them perfect, showing a geological structure which indicated that the whole country, or, at least, that portion of it, had been once, and probably at no very remote period, overflowed by the sea.

We could have passed a day with much satisfaction in rambling through this cave, but, remaining only a few minutes, and taking away some curious and interesting specimens, we remounted, and very soon reached mounds of earth, fragments of sculptured stones, broken walls, and fallen buildings, indicating that we were once more treading upon the sepulchre of an aboriginal city.

At eleven o'clock we came to a clearing, in which was situated the hacienda of San Joaquin. The building was a mere rancho, erected only for the residence of a mayoral, a person inferior to a major domo; but there was a fine clearing around it, and the situation was wild and beautiful. In the cattle-yard were noble trees. In the platform of the well were sculptured stones taken from the ancient buildings; it was shaded by the spreading branches of a fine ramon or tropical oak, with a foliage of vivid green; and crowning the top, and apparently growing out of it, were the long pale leaves of the cocoanut.

The hacienda, or rather rancho, of San Joaquin, on which the ruins of Mayapan lie scattered, is ten leagues south from Merida. It forms part of the great hacienda of Xcanchakan, the property of Don José Maria Meneses, the venerable cura of San Cristoval, formerly provesor of the Church of Yucatan. We had made the acquaintance of this gentleman at the house of his friend Señor Rejon, secretary of state, and he had sent instructions to his major domo, the same who had met us at the last village, to place at our command all the disposable force of the hacienda.

The ruins of Mayapan cover a great plain, which was at that time so overgrown that hardly any object was visible until we were close upon it, and the undergrowth was so thick that it was difficult to work our way through it. Our's was the first visit to examine these ruins. For ages they had been unnoticed, almost unknown, and left to struggle with rank tropical vegetation; and the major domo, who lived on the principal hacienda, and had not seen them in twenty-three years, was more familiar with them than any other person we could find. He told us that within a circumference of three miles, ruins were found, and that a strong wall once encompassed the city, the remains of which might still be traced through the woods.

Fig. 1

At a short distance from the hacienda, but invisible on account of the trees, rises the high mound which we had seen at three leagues' distance, from the top of the church at Tekoh, and which is represented in Figure 1. It is sixty feet high, and one hundred feet square at the base; and, like the mounds at Palenque and Uxmal, it is an artificial structure, built up solid from the plain. Though seen from a great distance above the tops of the trees, the whole field was so overgrown that it was scarcely visible until we reached its foot; and the mound itself, though retaining the symmetry of its original proportions, was also so overgrown that it appeared a mere wooded hill, but peculiar in its regularity of shape. Four grand staircases, each twenty-five feet wide, ascended to an esplanade within six feet of the top. This esplanade was six feet in width, and on each side was a smaller staircase leading to the top. These staircases are in a ruinous condition; the steps are almost entirely gone, and we climbed up by means of fallen stones and trees growing out of its sides. As we ascended, we scared away a cow, for the wild cattle roaming on these wooded wastes pasture on its sides, and ascend to the top.

The summit was a plain stone platform, fifteen feet square. It had no structure upon it, nor were there vestiges of any. Probably it was the great mound of sacrifice, on which the priests, in the sight of the assembled people, cut out the hearts of human victims. The view commanded from the top was a great desolate plain, with here and there another ruined mound rising above the trees, and far in the distance could be discerned the towers of the church at Tekoh.

Around the base of this mound, and throughout the woods, wherever we moved, were strewed sculptured stones. Most of them were square, carved on the face, and having a long stone tenon or stem at the back; doubtless they had been fixed in the wall, so as to form part of some ornament, or combination of ornaments, in the façade, in all respects the same as at Uxmal.

Besides these, there were other and more curious remains. These were representations of human figures, or of animals, with hideous features and expressions, in producing which the skill of the artist seems to have been expended. The sculpture of these figures was rude, the stones were timeworn, and many were half buried in the earth. Figure 2 represents two of them. One is four, and the other three feet high. The full length seems intended to represent a warrior with a shield. The arms are broken off, and to my mind they conveyed a lively idea of the figures or idols which Bernal Dias met with on the coast, containing hideous faces of demons. Probably, broken and half buried as they lie, they were once objects of adoration and worship, and now exist as mute and melancholy memorials of ancient paganism.

At a short distance from the base of the mound was an open-

FIG. 2

ing in the earth, forming another of those extraordinary caves
before presented to the reader. The cura, the major domo, and
the Indians called it a senote, and said that it had supplied the
inhabitants of the old city with water. The entrance was by a
broken, yawning mouth, steep, and requiring some care in the
descent. At the first resting-place, the mouth opened into an extensive subterraneous chamber, with a high roof, and passages
branching off in every direction. In different places were remains
of fires and the bones of animals, showing that it had at times
been the place of refuge or residence of men. In the entrance of
one of the passages we found a sculptured idol, which excited us
with the hope of discovering some altar or sepulchre, or perhaps
mummied figures. With this hope, we sent the Indians to procure torches; and while Mr. Catherwood was making some
sketches, Doctor Cabot and myself passed an hour in exploring
the recesses of the cave. In many places the roof had fallen, and
the passages were choked up. We followed several of them with
much toil and disappointment, and at length fell into one, low
and narrow, along which it was necessary to crawl on the hands
and feet, and where, from the flame and smoke of the torches, it
was desperately hot. We at length came to a body of water, which,
on thrusting the hand into it, we found to be incrusted with a

thin coat of sulphate of lime, that had formed on the top of the water, but decomposed on being brought into the air.

Leaving the cave or senote, we continued rambling among the ruins. The mounds were all of the same general character, and the buildings had entirely disappeared on all except one; but this was different from any we had at that time seen, though we afterward found others like it.

FIG. 3

It stood on a ruined mound about thirty feet high. What the shape of the mound had been it was difficult to make out, but the building was circular. Figure 3 represents this edifice, with the mound on which it stands. The exterior is of plain stone, ten feet high to the top of the lower cornice, and fourteen more to that of the upper one. The door faces the west, and over it is a lintel of stone. The outer wall is five feet thick; the door opens into a circular passage three feet wide, and in the centre is a cylindrical solid mass of stone, without any doorway or opening of any kind. The whole diameter of the building is twenty-five feet, so that, deducting the double width of the wall and passage, this centre mass must be nine feet in thickness. The walls had four or five coats of stucco, and there were remains of painting, in which red, yellow, blue, and white were distinctly visible.

On the southwest side of the building, and on a terrace projecting from the side of the mound, was a double row of columns eight feet apart, of which only eight remained, though probably, from the fragments around, there had been more, and, by clearing away the trees, more might have been found still standing. In our hurried visit to Uxmal, we had seen objects which we supposed might have been intended for columns, but were not sure; and though we afterward saw many, we considered these the first decided columns we had seen. They were two feet and a half in diameter, and consisted of five round stones, eight or ten inches thick, laid one upon another. They had no capitals, and what particular connexion they had with the building did not appear.

So far, although the fragments of sculpture were of the same general character as at Uxmal, we had not found any edifice sufficiently entire to enable us to identify that peculiar arch which we had found in all the ruined buildings of this country; but it was not wanting. At some distance from this place, and on the other side of the hacienda, were long ranges of mounds. These had once been buildings, the tops of which had fallen, and almost buried the structures. At the end was a doorway, encumbered and half filled with rubbish, crawling through which, we stood upright in apartments exactly similar to those at Uxmal, with the arch formed of stones overlapping, and a flat stone covering the top. The apartments were ruder and narrower, but they were of precisely the same character with all the others we had seen.

The day was now nearly spent; with the heat and labour we were exceedingly fatigued, and the Indians insisted that we had seen all the principal remains. The place was so overgrown with trees that it would have taken a long time to clear them away, and for the present at least it was out of the question. Besides, the only result we could promise ourselves was the bringing to light of fragments and single pieces of buried sculpture. Of one thing, however, we had no doubt: the ruins of this city were of the same general character with those at Uxmal, erected by the same builders, probably of older date, and suffering more from the corrosion of the elements, or they had been visited more harshly by the destroying hand of man.

Fortunately, at this place again we have a ray of historic light. According to the best accounts, the region of country now called Yucatan was known to the natives, at the time of the Spanish invasion, by the name of Maya, and before that time it had never been known by any other. The name of Yucatan was given to it by the Spaniards. It is entirely arbitrary and accidental, and its origin is not known with certainty. It is supposed by some to be derived from the plant known in the islands by the name of *Yuca,* and *tal* or *thale,* the heap of earth in which this plant grows; but more generally it is derived from certain words supposed to have been spoken by the natives in answer to a question asked by the Spaniards on their first arrival. The supposed question is, "What is the name of this country?" or, "How is this country called?" and the conjectured answer, "I do not understand those words," or, "I do not understand your words," either of which expressions, in the language of the natives, has some resemblance in pronunciation to the word Yucatan. But whatever was its origin, the natives have never recognised the name, and to this day, among themselves, they speak of their country only under its ancient name of Maya. No native ever calls himself a Yucateco, but always a Macegual, or native of the land of Maya.

One language, called the Maya, extended throughout the whole peninsula; and though the Spaniards found the country parcelled into different governments, under various names and having different caciques, hostile to each other, at an earlier period of its history the whole land of Maya was united under one head or supreme lord. This great chief or king had for the seat of his monarchy a very populous city called Mayapan, and had under him many other lords and caciques, who were bound to pay him tribute of cotton clothes, fowls, cacao, and gum or resin for incense; to serve him in wars, and day and night in the temples of the idols, at festivals and ceremonies. These lords, too, had under them cities and many vassals. Becoming proud and ambitious, and unwilling to brook a superior, they rebelled against the power of the supreme lord, united all their forces, and besieged and destroyed the city of Mayapan. This destruction took place in the year of our Lord 1420, about one hundred years, or, according to Herrera, about seventy years, before the arrival of the Spaniards in Yucatan; and, according to the computation of the ages of the Indians, two hundred and seventy years from the foundation of the city. The account of all the details is confused and indistinct; but the existence of a principal city called Mayapan, and its destruction by war at about the time indicated, are mentioned by every historian. This city was occupied by the same race of people who inhabited the country at the time of the conquest, and its site is identified as that which has just been presented to the reader, retaining, through all changes and in its ruins, its ancient name of Mayapan.

CHAPTER VII

The interest of our day at Mayapan came near being marred by an unlucky accident. Just as we were leaving the ruins a messenger came to inform us that one of our pistols had shot an Indian. These pistols had never shown any particular antipathy to Indians, and had never shot one before; but, hurrying back to the hacienda, we found the poor fellow with two of his fingers nearly shot off. The ball had passed through his shirt, making two holes in it, fortunately without hitting his body. The Indians said that the pistol had gone off itself while they were only looking at it. We felt sure that this was not exactly the case, knowing that pistols are not free agents, and laid the blame upon them; but it was a great satisfaction that the accident was no worse, and also that Doctor Cabot was at hand to dress the wound. The Indian seemed to think less of it than we did.

It was late when we left the hacienda. Our road was a mere bridle-path through a wilderness. At some distance we crossed a broken range of stones, rising on each side to a wall, which the major domo said was the line of wall that encompassed the ancient city.

It was nearly dark when we reached the stately hacienda of Xcanchakan, one of the three finest in Yucatan, and containing nearly seven hundred souls. Plate I represents the front of this hacienda. The house is perhaps one of the best in the country, and being within one day's ride of the capital, and accessible by calesa, it is a favourite residence of its venerable proprietor. The

79

Plate I

Rolph.

Catherwood.

HACIENDA OF XCANCHAKAN

whole condition of the hacienda showed that it was often subject to the master's eye, and the character of that master may be judged of from the fact that his major domo, the same who was attendant upon us, had been with him twenty-six years.

I have given the reader some idea of a hacienda in Yucatan, with its cattle-yard, its great tanks of water and other accessories. All these were upon a large and substantial scale, equal to any we had seen; and there was one little refinement in their arrangement, which, though not, perhaps, intended for that purpose, could not fail to strike the eye of a stranger. The passage to the well was across the corridor, and, sitting quietly in the shade, the proprietor could see every day, passing and repassing, all the women and girls belonging to the estate.

Our friend the cura of Tekoh was still with us, and the Indians of the hacienda were within his curacy. Again immediately upon our arrival the bell of the church was tolled to announce his arrival to the sick, those who wished to confess, marry, or be baptized. This over, it struck the solemn note of the *oracion,* or vesper prayers. All rose, and, with uncovered heads stood silent till the last note died away, all, according to the beautiful injunction of the Catholic Church, breathing an inward prayer. Then they bade each other a *buenas noches,* each kissed the cura's hand, and then, with his petata, or straw hat, in his hand, came to us, bowing respectfully, and wishing each of us also the good night.

The cura still considered us on his hands, and, in order to entertain us, requested the major domo to get up a dance of the Indians. Very soon we heard the sound of the violins and the Indian drum. This latter consists of a hollow log about three feet long, with a piece of parchment stretched over the end, on which an Indian, holding it under his left arm, beats with his right hand. It is the same instrument known to the inhabitants at the time of the conquest by the name of *tunkul* and is the favourite now. Going out into the back corridor, we saw the musicians sitting at one end, before the door of the chapel; on one side of the corridor were the women, and on the other the men. For some time there was no dancing, until, at length, at the instance of the cura, the major domo gave his directions, and a young man stood up in the middle of the corridor. Another, with a pocket-handkerchief in his hand having a knot tied in one end, walked along the line of women, threw the handkerchief at one, and then returned to his seat. This was considered a challenge or invitation; but, with a proper prudery, as if to show that she was not to be had for the asking, she waited some minutes, then rose, and slowly taking the shawl from her head, placed herself opposite the young man, at a distance of about ten feet, and commenced dancing. The dance was called the toros, or the bull. The movements were slow; occasionally the performers crossed over and changed places, and when the time ended the lady walked deliberately off, which either brought the young man to a standstill, or he went on dancing, as he liked. The manager or master of ceremonies, who was called the *bastonero*, again walked along the line, and touched another lady in the same way with the handkerchief. She again, after waiting a moment, removed her shawl and took her place on the floor; and in this way the dance continued, the dancing man being always the same, and taking the partner provided for him. Afterward the dance was changed to a Spanish one, in which, instead of castanets, the dancers from time to time snapped their fingers. This was more lively, and seemed to please them better than their own, but throughout there was nothing national or characteristic.

Early in the morning we were roused by loud bursts of music in the church. The cura was giving them the benefit of his accidental visit by an early mass. After this we heard music of a different kind. It was the lash on the back of an Indian. Looking out into the corridor, we saw the poor fellow on his knees on the pavement, with his arms clasped around the legs of another Indian, so as to present his back fair to the lash. At every blow he rose on one knee, and sent forth a piercing cry. He seemed struggling to restrain it, but it burst from him in spite of all his efforts. His whole bearing showed the subdued character of the present Indians, and with the last stripe the expression of his face seemed that of thankfulness for not getting more. Without uttering a word, he crept to the major domo, took his hand, kissed it, and walked away. No sense of degradation crossed his mind. Indeed, so humbled is this once fierce people, that they have a proverb of their own, "Los Indios no oigan si no por las nalgas"—"The Indians cannot hear except through their backs," and the cura related to us a fact which indicates an abasement of character perhaps never found in any other people. In a village not far distant, the name of which I have lost, they have a fiesta with a scenic representation called Shtol. The scene is laid at the time of the conquest. The Indians of the village gather within a large place enclosed by poles, and are supposed to be brought together by an invasion of the Spaniards. An old man rises and exhorts them to defend their country; if need be, to die for it.

The Indians are roused, but in the midst of his exhortations a stranger enters in the dress of a Spaniard and armed with a musket. The sight of this stranger throws them all into consternation; he fires the musket, and they fall to the ground. He binds the chief, carries him off captive, and the play is ended.

After breakfast the cura left us to return to his village, and we set out to continue our journey to Uxmal. Our luggage was sent off by Indians of the hacienda, and the major domo accompanied us on horseback. Our road was by a bridle path over the same stony country, through thick woods. The whole way it lay through the lands of the provisor, all wild, waste, and desolate, and showing the fatal effects of accumulation in the hands of large landed proprietors. In two hours we saw rising before us the gate

FIG. 4

of the hacienda of Mucuyché (Figure 4). To the astonishment of the gaping Indians, the doctor, as he wheeled his horse, shot a hawk that was hovering over the pinnacle of the gateway, and we rode up to the house.

I trust the reader has not forgotten this fine hacienda. It was the same to which, on our former visit, we had been borne on the shoulders of Indians, and in which we had taken a bath in a senote, never to be forgotten. We were once more on the hands of our old friend Don Simon Peon. The whole hacienda, horses, mules, and Indians, were at our disposal. It was but ten o'clock, and we intended to continue our journey to Uxmal, but first we resolved upon another bath in the senote. My first impression of the beauty of this fancy bathing place did not deceive me, and the first glance satisfied me that I incurred no risk in introducing to it a stranger. A light cloud of almost imperceptible dust, ascribed to the dripping of the waters of the rainy season, or

FIG. 5. Senote.

perhaps made visible by the rays of the midday sun, rested on the surface, but underneath were the same crystal fluid and the same clear bottom. Very soon we were in the water, and before we came out we resolved to postpone our journey till the next day, for the sake of an evening bath.

As the reader is now on ground which I trust he has travelled before, I shall merely state that the next day we rode on to the hacienda of San José, where we stopped to make some preparations, and on the fifteenth, at eleven o'clock, we reached the hacienda of Uxmal.

It stood in its suit of sombre gray, with cattle-yard, large trees, and tanks, the same as when we left it, but there were no friends of old to welcome us: the Delmonico major domo had gone to Tobasco, and the other had been obliged to leave on account of illness. The mayoral remembered us, but we did not know him; and we determined to pass on and take up our abode immediately in the ruins. Stopping but a few minutes, to give directions about the luggage, we mounted again, and in ten minutes, emerging from the woods, came out upon the open field in which, grand and lofty as when we saw it before, stood the House of the Dwarf; but the first glance showed us that a year had made great changes. The sides of the lofty structure, then bare and naked, were now covered with high grass, bushes, and weeds, and on the top were bushes and young trees twenty feet high. The House of the Nuns was almost smothered, and the whole field was covered with a rank growth of grass and weeds, over which we could barely look as we rode through. The foundations, terraces, and tops of the buildings were overgrown, weeds and vines were rioting and creeping on the façades, and mounds, terraces, and ruins were a mass of destroying verdure. A strong and vigorous nature was struggling for mastery over art, wrapping the city in its suffocating enbraces, and burying it from sight. It seemed as if the grave was closing over a friend, and we had arrived barely in time to take our farewell.

Amid this mass of desolation, grand and stately as when we left it, stood the Casa del Gobernador, but with all its terraces covered, and separated from us by a mass of impenetrable verdure.

On the left of the field was an overgrown milpa, along the edge of which a path led in front of this building. Following this path, we turned the corner of the terrace, and on the farthest side dismounted, and tied our horses. The grass and weeds were above our heads, and we could see nothing. The mayoral broke a way through them, and we reached the foot of the terrace. Working our way over the stones with much toil, we reached the top of the highest terrace. Here, too, the grass and weeds were of the same rank growth. We moved directly to the wall at the east end, and entered the first open door. Here the mayoral wished us to take up our abode; but we knew the localities better than he did, and, creeping along the front as close to the wall as possible, cutting some of the bushes, and tearing apart and trampling down others, we reached the centre apartment. Here we stopped. Swarms of bats, roused by our approach, fluttered and flew through the long chamber, and passed out at the doors.

The appearance of things was not very promising for a place of residence. There were two salas, each sixty feet long; that in front had three large doors, opening upon the encumbered terrace, and the other had no windows and but one door. In both there was an extreme sensation of closeness and dampness, with an unpleasant smell, and in the back room was a large accumulation of dirt and rubbish. Outside, high grass and weeds were growing into the very doorway. We could not move a step, and all view was completely cut off. After the extreme heat of the sun out of doors, we were in a profuse perspiration from climbing up the terrace, and the dank atmosphere induced a feeling of chilliness which made us reflect seriously upon what we had not sufficiently regarded before.

Throughout Yucatan "el campo," or the country, is considered unhealthy in the rainy season. We had arrived in Yucatan counting upon the benefit of the whole dry season, which generally begins in November and lasts till May; but this year the rains had continued longer than usual, and they were not yet over. The proprietors of haciendas were still cautious about visiting them, and confined themselves to the villages and towns. Among all the haciendas, Uxmal had a reputation pre-eminent for its unhealthiness. Every person who had ever been at work among the ruins had been obliged by sickness to leave them. Mr. Catherwood had had sad experience, and this unhealthiness was not confined to strangers. The Indians suffered every season from fevers; many of them were at that time ill, and the major domo had been obliged to go away. All this we had been advised of in Merida, and had been urged to postpone our visit; but as this would have interfered materially with our plan, and as we had with us a "medico" who could cure "biscos," we determined to risk it. On the spot, however, perceiving the dampness of the apartments and the rankness of vegetation, we felt that we had been imprudent; but it was too late to draw back, even if we had wished to do so. We agreed that we were better on this high terrace than at the hacienda, which stood low, and had around it great tanks of water, mantled with green, and wearing a very fever-and-aguish aspect. We therefore set to work immediately to make the best of our condition.

The mayoral left us to take the horses back to the hacienda, and give directions about the luggage, and we had only a little Indian boy to help us. Him we employed to clear with his machete a space before the principal doorway, and in order to change as quickly as possible the damp, unwholesome atmosphere within, we undertook to kindle a fire ourselves. For this purpose we made a large collection of leaves and brush, which we placed in one corner of the back corridor, and, laying stones at the bottom, built up a pile several feet high, and set fire to it. The blaze crept through the pile, burning the light combustible stuff, and went out. We kindled it again, and the result was the same. Several times we thought we had succeeded, but the dampness of the place and of the materials baffled our efforts, and extinguished the flame. We exhausted all our odd scraps of paper and other availables, and were left with barely a spark of fire to begin anew. The only combustible we had left was gunpowder, of which we made what the boys call a squib, by wetting a quantity of it, and this, done up in a ball, we ignited under the pile. It did not answer fully, but gave us encouragement, and we made a larger ball of the same, which we ignited with a slow match. It blew our pile to atoms, and scattered the materials in all directions. Our ingenuity had now been taxed to the uttermost, and our resources were exhausted. In extremity we called in the boy.

He had, in the mean time, been more successful; for, continuing the work at which we had set him, with characteristic indifference taking no notice of our endeavours, he had cleared a space of several yards around the door. This admitted a sunbeam, which, like the presence of a good spirit, gladdened and cheered all within its reach. We intimated to him by signs that we wanted a fire, and, without paying any respect to what we had done, he began in his own way, with a scrap of cotton, which he picked up from the ground, and, lighting it, blew it gently in his folded hands till it was all ignited. He then laid it on the floor, and, throwing aside all the material we had been using, looked around carefully, and gathered up some little sticks, not larger than matches, which he laid against the ignited cotton, with one point on the ground and the other touching the fire. Then kneeling down, he encircled the nascent fire with his two hands, and blew gently on it, with his mouth so close as almost to touch it. A slight smoke rose above the palms of his hands, and in a few minutes he stopped blowing. Placing the little sticks carefully together, so that all their points touched the fire, he went about picking up others a little larger than the first, and laying them in order one by one. With the circumference of his hands a little extended, he again began blowing gently; the smoke rose a little stronger than before. From time to time he gently changed the position of the sticks, and resumed his blowing. At length he stopped, but whether in despair or satisfied with the result seemed doubtful. He had a few little sticks with a languishing fire at one end, which might be extinguished by dropping a few tears over it. We had not only gone beyond this, but had raised a large flame, which had afterward died away. Still there was a steadiness, an assurance in his manner that seemed to say he knew what he was about. At all events, we had nothing to do but watch him. Making a collection of larger sticks, and again arranging them in the same way as before, taking care not to put them so close together as to smother the fire, with a circumference too large for the space of his hands, but of materials so light as easily to be thrown into confusion, he again commenced blowing, so gently as not to disturb a single stick, and yet to the full power that the arrangement would bear. The wood seemed to feel the influence of his cherishing care, and a full body of smoke rose up to gladden us, and bring tears into his eyes. With the same imperturbable industry, unconscious of our admiration, he went on again, having now got up to sticks as large as the finger. These he coaxed along with many tears, and at the next size he saved his own wind and used his petata, or straw hat. A gentle blaze rose in the whole centre of the pile; still he coaxed it along, and by degrees brought on sticks as large as his arm, which, by a gentle waving of his hat, in a few minutes were all ignited. Our uncertainty was at an end. The whole pile was in a blaze, and all four of us went busily to work gathering fuel. There was no necessity for dry wood; we cut down bushes, and carried them in green; all burned together; the flames extended, and the heat became so great that we could not approach to throw on more. In our satisfaction with the result we did not stop to read the moral of the lesson taught us by the Indian boy. The flames were fast rectifying the damp, unwholesome atmosphere, and inducing more warm and genial sensations. Very soon, however, this bettering of our house's condition drove us out of doors. The smoke rolled through the long apartment, and, curling along the roof, passed into the front sala, where, dividing, it rushed through the doors in three dense bodies, and rolled up the front of the palace. We sat down outside, and watched it as it rolled away.

While this was going on, the mayoral crawled along the same path by which we had ascended, and told us that the luggage had arrived. How it could be got to us seemed a problem. The slight clearing on the upper terrace gave us a view of the lower one, which was an unbroken mass of bushes and weeds ten or twelve feet high. Perhaps half an hour elapsed, when we saw a single Indian ascend the platform of the second terrace, with his machete slowly working his way toward us. Very soon the top of a long box was seen rising above the same terrace, apparently tottering and falling back, but rising again and coming on steadily, with an Indian under it, visible from time to time through the bushes. Toward the foot of the terrace on which we were it disappeared, and after a few minutes rose to the top. Holding on with both hands to the strap across his forehead, with every nerve strung, and the veins of his forehead swelled almost to bursting, his face and his whole body dripping with sweat, he laid his load at our feet. A long line followed; staggering, panting, and trembling, they took the loads from their backs, and deposited them at the door. They had carried these loads three leagues, or nine miles, and we paid them eighteen and three quarter cents, being at the rate of a *medio,* or six and a quarter cents, per league. We gave them a medio extra for bringing the things up the terrace, and the poor fellows were thankful and happy.

In the mean time the fire was still burning, and the smoke rushing out. We set the Indians at work on the terrace with their machetes, and as the smoke rolled away we directed them to sweep out the apartments. For brooms they had merely to cut a handful of bushes, and to shovel out the dirt they had their hands. This over, we had our luggage carried in, set up our beds in the back sala, and swung our hammocks in the front. At nightfall the Indians left us, and we were again alone in the palace of unknown kings.

We had reached the first point of our journey; we were once more at the ruins of Uxmal. It was nearly two years since we originally set out in search of American ruins, and more than a year since we were driven from this place. The freshness and enthusiasm with which we had first come upon the ruins of an American city had perhaps gone, but our feelings were not blunted, and all the regret which we had felt in being obliged to leave was more than counterbalanced by the satisfaction of returning.

It was in this spirit that, as evening came on, we swung in our hammocks and puffed away all troubles. The bats, retiring to their nightly haunt, seemed startled by the blaze of our fire. Owls and other birds of darkness sent up their discordant cries from the woods, and as the evening waned we found ourselves debating warmly the great question of excitement at home, whether M'Leod ought to be hanged or not.

As a measure of precaution, and in order to have the full benefit of a medical man's company, we began immediately upon a course of preventive treatment, by way of putting ourselves on the vantage ground against fever. As we were all in perfect health, Dr. Cabot thought such a course could not hurt us. This over, we threw more wood upon the pile and went to bed.

Up to this time our course had been before the wind. Our journey from Merida had again been a sort of triumphal procession. We had been passed from hacienda to hacienda, till we fell into the hospitable hands of Don Simon Peon, and we were now in absolute possession of the ruins of Uxmal. But very soon we found that we had to encounter troubles from which neither Don Simon, nor the government, nor recommendations to the hospitality of citizens of the interior, could afford us protection. Early in the evening a few straggling moschetoes had given us notice of the existence of these free and independent citizens of Yucatan; but while we were swinging in our hammocks and the fire burned brightly, they had not troubled us much. Our heads, however, were hardly upon our pillows, before the whole population seemed to know exactly where they could have us, and, dividing into three swarms, came upon us as if determined to lift us up and eject us bodily from the premises. The flame and volumes of smoke which had rolled through the building, in ridding us of the damp, unwholesome atmosphere, seemed only to have started these torments from their cracks and crevices, and filled them with thirst for vengeance or for blood. I spare the reader farther details of our first night at Uxmal, but we all agreed that another such would drive us forever from the ruins.

CHAPTER VIII

Morning brought with it other perplexities. We
had no servant, and wanted breakfast, and altogether our prospects were not good. We did not expect to find the hacienda so
entirely destitute of persons with whom we could communicate.
The mayoral was the only one who spoke a word of Spanish,
and he had the business of the hacienda to attend to. He had received special orders from his master to do everything in his
power to serve us, but the power of his master had limits. He
could not make the Indians, who knew only the Maya, speak
Spanish. Besides this, the power of the master was otherwise re-
stricted. In fact, except as regards certain obligations which they
owed, the Indians were their own masters, and, what was worse
for us, their own mistresses, for one of our greatest wants was a
woman to cook, make tortillas, and perform those numerous domestic offices without which no household can go on well. The
mayoral had given us no hope of being able to procure one; but
in the midst of our anxieties, and while we were preparing breakfast for ourselves, we perceived him coming across the terrace,
followed by a train of Indians, and closing the procession was
a woman, at that time really a welcome visiter. The mayoral said
that the evening before, on his return to the hacienda, he had
gone round to all the huts, and proposed to woman after woman,
promising liberal pay and good treatment, but they all refused

until he came to this one, and with her he had been obliged to stipulate that she should not remain at the ruins in the night, but should return home every evening. This was a great drawback, as we wanted to breakfast early, but we had no choice, and were glad to get her upon her own terms.

She was taller than most of the Indian women, and her complexion was somewhat darker. Her dress fitted more closely to her body, and she had more of it. Her character was unimpeached, her bearing would have kept presumption at a distance, and, as an additional safeguard, she had with her a little grandson, named José, whose complexion indicated that the descending line of her house had no antipathies to the white race. Her age might be a little over fifty, and her name was Chaipa Chi.

The preliminaries being settled, we immediately installed her as *chef de cuisine,* without assistants, and sent off the mayoral to direct the Indians in some clearings which we wished made immediately. The first essay of Chaipa Chi was in boiling eggs, which, according to the custom of the country, she boiled *para beber,* or to drink; that is, by breaking a small hole in the shell, into which a stick is inserted to mix together the white and yolk; the egg is to be disposed of through this hole in the primitive way which nature indicates to the new-born babe. This did not suit us, and we wished the process of cooking to be continued a little longer, but Chaipa Chi was impenetrable to hints or signs. We were obliged to stand over her, and, but for the name of the thing, we might as well have cooked them ourselves. This over, we gave up, and left our dinner to the mercies of our chef.

Before we were in a condition to begin an examination and exploration of the ruins, we had a serious business before us in making the necessary clearings. These were not required for picturesque effect; indeed, overgrown as the ruins were, they addressed themselves more powerfully to the imagination than if the whole field and every stone lay bare; but facilities of moving from place to place were indispensable, and for this purpose we determined first to clear the terrace of the Casa del Gobernador, and cut roads from ruin to ruin, until we had a complete line of communication; and that we might know exactly our whereabout, Mr. Catherwood took an observation, by which he found the latitude of Uxmal to be 20° 27′ 30″ N.

Our Indians made a good beginning, and by the afternoon we had the upper terrace cleared. Toward evening they all left us, including Chaipa Chi, and at night, while the moon was glimmering mournfully over the ruins, we had a stroll along the whole front of the Casa del Gobernador.

We were in no hurry to retire, and when we did so it was with some misgivings. Besides a little general attention to what was going on out of doors, the principle business of the day had been to prepare our moscheto-nets, and for this we grudged no time, labour, or ingenuity; but our success was complete. Throughout the whole long apartment there was a continued singing and whizzing, lower or louder as the musicians came near or retired, furious at being defrauded of their prey, but they could not touch us. Our satisfaction went beyond that of the mere prospect for the night, for we felt sure of rest after labour, and of being able to maintain our ground.

The next day we made a valuable addition to our household. Among the Indians who came out to work was a lad who spoke Spanish. He was the puniest, lankest, and leanest of any we had seen on the hacienda, and his single garment was the dirtiest. His name was Bernaldo. He was but fifteen, and he was already experiencing the vicissitudes of fortune. His education had been neglected; and for confounding some technical distinctions in the laws of property, he was banished from a hacienda near Merida to the deserts of Uxmal. We were in such straits for want of an interpreter, and, except during the short visit of the mayoral, so entirely destitute, that we overlooked entirely Bernaldo's moral weakness, withdrew him from the workmen, and led him to the sala of the palace, where, in the course of conveying some instructions to Chaipa Chi, he showed such an interest in the subject that Doctor Cabot immediately undertook to give him a lesson in cookery. In his first essay he was so apt that we forthwith inducted him as ruler over the three stones that composed our kitchen fireplace, with all the privileges and emoluments of sipping and tasting, and left Chaipa Chi to bestow all her energies upon the business that her soul loved, the making of tortillas.

Being now domesticated, I shall introduce the reader without preface to the ruins of Uxmal. In the account of my former visit I endeavoured to give a brief description of these ruins. Hurried away, however, without plans or drawings, it was impossible to present any definite idea of their character. Plate II represents the plan of this ancient city, as indicated by the remaining edifices. The ranges were all taken with the compass, and the distances measured, and the dimensions of the buildings and their

Plate II

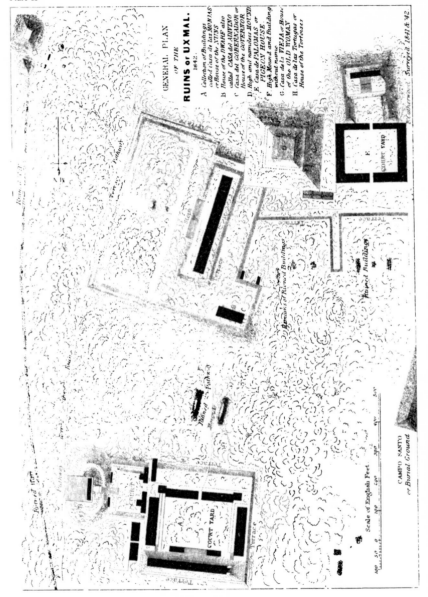

GENERAL PLAN
OF THE
RUINS OF UXMAL.
1842.

A Collection of Buildings called Casa de las MONJAS or House of the NUNS
B House of the DWARF also called CASA del ADIVINO
C Casa del GOBERNADOR or House of the GOVERNOR
D High and narrow MOUND
E Casa de PALOMAS or PIGEON HOUSE
F High Mound and Building without rooms
G Casa de la VIEJA or House of the OLD WOMAN
H Casa de las Tortugas or House of the Tortoises

Surveyed 1841 & '42.

COURT YARD

COURT YARD

Remains of Ruined Buildings

Ruined Buildings

Scale of English Feet.

100 50 0 100 200 300 400 500

CAMPO SANTO
or Burial Ground

distances from each other can be ascertained by means of the scale at the foot of the plate.

The first ruin which I shall present is that in which we lived, called the Casa del Gobernador. The engraving which forms the frontispiece of this volume represents its front, with the three great terraces on which it stands. This front is three hundred and twenty-two feet long. Large as the engraving is, it can serve only to give some idea of the general effect; the detail of ornament cannot be shown.

The edifice is represented as it exists now, without any attempt at restoration, and the reader will perceive that over two of the doorways the façade has fallen. Don Simon Peon told us that in the year 1825 this fallen part was still in its place, and the whole front almost entire. The fragments now lie as they fell, forming, as appears in the engraving, a great mass of mortar, rude and sculptured stones, all imbedded together, which had never been disturbed until we dug into it for the purpose of disinterring and bringing to light some of the fallen ornaments.

This building was constructed entirely of stone. Up to the cornice, which runs round it the whole length and on all four of its sides, the façade presents a smooth surface; above is one solid mass of rich, complicated, and elaborately sculptured ornaments, forming a sort of arabesque.

The grandest ornament, which imparts a richness to the whole façade, is over the centre doorway. Around the head of the principal figure are rows of characters, which, in our first hurried visit, we did not notice as essentially different from the other incomprehensible subjects sculptured on the façade; but we now discovered that these characters were hieroglyphics. We had ladders made, by means of which Mr. Catherwood climbed up and made accurate drawings of them. They differ somewhat from the hieroglyphics before presented, and are more rich, elaborate, and complicated, but the general character is the same. From their conspicuous position, they no doubt contain some important meaning: probably they were intended as a record of the construction of the building, the time when and the people by whom it was built.

The full drawing of this rich and curious ornament cannot be presented with any effect on the scale adapted to these pages. All the other doorways have over them striking, imposing, and even elegant decorations, varying sometimes in the details, but corresponding in general character and effect with that represented in the accompanying engravings.

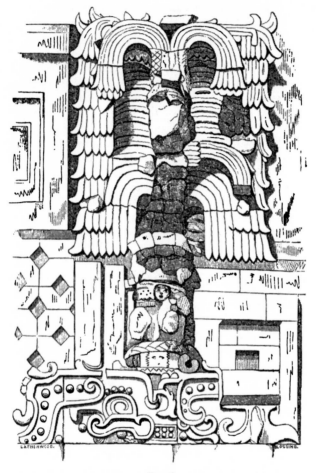

FIG. 6

Figure 6 represents the part immediately over the doorway. It shows the remaining portion of a figure seated on a
kind of throne. This throne was formerly supported by a rich
ornament, still forming part of similar designs over other doorways in this building. The head-dress is lofty, and from it proceed enormous plumes of feathers, dividing at the top, and falling symmetrically on each side, until they touch the ornament on
which the feet of the statue rest. Each figure was perhaps the
portrait of some cacique, warrior, prophet, or priest, distinguished in the history of this unknown people.

Plate III represents that part of the ornament immediately above the preceding; it occupies the whole portion of the wall from the top of the head-dress to the cornice along the top of the building. This ornament or combination appears on all parts of the edifice, and throughout the ruins is more frequently seen than any other. In the engraving the centre presents a long, flat, smooth surface. This indicates a projecting ornament, which cannot be exhibited in a front view; but, as seen in profile, consists of a stone projecting from the face of the wall, as shown in Figure 7; and the reader must suppose this stone projecting in order clearly to understand the character of the ornament last presented. It measures one foot seven inches in length from the stem by which it is fixed in the wall to the end of the curve, and resembles somewhat an elephant's trunk, which name has, perhaps not inaptly, been given to it by Waldeck, though it is not probable that as such the sculptor intended it, for the elephant was unknown on the Continent of America.

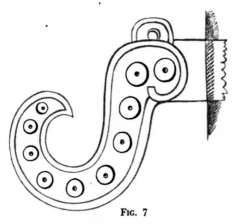

FIG. 7

This projecting stone appears with this combination all over the façade and at the corners; and throughout all the buildings it is met with, sometimes in a reversed position, oftener than any other design in Uxmal. It is a singular fact, that though entirely out of reach, the ends of nearly all of them have been broken off; and among the many remains in every part of the walls throughout the whole ruins, there are but three that now exist entire. Perhaps they were wantonly broken by the Spaniards; though at this day the Indians believe these old buildings are haunted, and that all the monefatos or ornaments are animated, and walk at

Plate III

Ornament of the Casa del Gobernador.   Uxmal.

night. In the daytime, it is believed, they can do no harm, and for ages the Indians have been in the habit of breaking and disfiguring them with the machete, believing that by so doing they quiet their wandering spirits.

The combination of the last two engravings is probably intended to represent a hideous human face; the eyes and teeth appear in the first, and the projecting stone is perhaps intended for the nose or snout. It occupies a space in breadth equal to about five feet of the wall. To present the whole façade on the same scale would require an engraving sixty-four times as long as this. The reader will perceive how utterly unprofitable it would be to attempt a verbal description of such a façade, and the lines in the engraving show that, as I remarked in my former account, there is no tablet or single stone representing separately and by itself an entire subject, but every ornament or combination is made up of separate stones, each of which had carved on it part of the subject, and was then set in its place in the wall. Each stone by itself is an unmeaning fractional portion, but, placed by the side of others, makes part of a whole, which without it would be incomplete. Perhaps it may with propriety be called a species of sculptured mosaic; and I have no doubt that all these ornaments have a symbolical meaning; that each stone is part of a history, allegory, or fable.

The rear elevation of the Casa del Gobernador is a solid wall, without any doorways or openings of any kind. Like the front, above the cornice it was ornamented throughout its whole length with sculptured stone. The subjects, however, were less complicated, and the sculpture less gorgeous and elaborate; and on this side, too, a part of the façade has fallen.

The two ends are thirty-nine feet each. Figure 8 represents the southern end. It has but one doorway, and of this, too, the sculptured subjects were more simple.

The roof is flat, and had been covered with cement; but the whole is now overgrown with grass and bushes.

Such is the exterior of the Casa del Gobernador. To go into any description of details would extend these pages to an indefinite length. Its distinguishing features are, that it was long, low, and narrow; below the cornice plain, and above ornamented with sculpture all around. Mr. Catherwood made minute architectural drawings of the whole, and has in his possession the materials for erecting a building exactly like it; and I would remark that, as on our former expedition, he made all his drawings with the camera lucida, for the purpose of obtaining the utmost ac-

Fig. 8

curacy of proportion and detail. Besides which, we had with us a
Daguerreotype apparatus, the best that could be procured in
New-York, with which, immediately on our arrival at Uxmal, Mr.
Catherwood began taking views; but the results were not sufficiently perfect to suit his ideas. At times the projecting cornices
and ornaments threw parts of the subject in shade, while others
were in broad sunshine; so that, while parts were brought out
well, other parts required pencil drawings to supply their defects.
They gave a general idea of the character of the buildings, but
would not do to put into the hands of the engraver without copy-
ing the views on paper, and introducing the defective parts,
which would require more labour than that of making at once
complete original drawings. He therefore completed everything
with his pencil and camera lucida, while Doctor Cabot and myself took up the Daguerreotype; and, in order to ensure the utmost accuracy, the Daguerreotype views were placed with the
drawings in the hands of the engravers for their guidance.

50 40 80 20 10 0   50   100   150 *Feet*

FIG. 9

The ground plan of the Casa del Gobernador is represented in Figure 9. It has eleven doorways in front and one at each end. The doors are all gone, and the wooden lintels over them have fallen. The interior is divided longitudinally by a wall into two corridors, and these again, by cross walls or partitions, into oblong rooms. Every pair of these rooms, the front and back, communicate by a doorway exactly opposite a corresponding doorway in front.

The principal apartments in the centre, with three doorways opening upon the terrace, are sixty feet long. The one in front is eleven feet six inches wide, and the inner one thirteen feet. The former is twenty-three feet high to the top of the arch, and the other twenty-two feet. The latter has but one door of entrance from the front room, and except this it has no door or aperture of any kind, so that at the ends it is dark and damp, as is the case with all the inner rooms. In these two apartments we took up our abode.

The walls are constructed of square, smooth blocks of stone, and on each side of the doorway are the remains of stone rings fixed in the walls with shafts, which no doubt had some connexion with the support of the doors. The floors were of cement, in some places hard, but, by long exposure, broken, and now crumbling under the feet.

The ceiling forms a triangular arch, as at Palenque, without the keystone. The support is made by stones overlapping, and bevilled so as to present a smooth surface, and within about a foot of the point of contact covered by a layer of flat stones. Across the arch were beams of wood, the ends built in the wall on each side, which had probably been used for the support of the arch while the building was in progress.

For the rest, I refer to the plan, mentioning only one circumstance. In working out the plan on the spot, it was found that the back wall, throughout its whole length of two hundred and seventy feet, was nine feet thick, which was nearly equal to the width of the front apartment. Such thickness was not necessary for the support of the building, and, supposing it might contain some hidden passages, we determined to make a breach through the wall, and to do this in the centre apartment.

I must confess that I felt some repugnance to this work of demolition, but one stone had already been picked out by an Indian to serve for mashing maize upon; and as this was likely to be done at any time when another might be wanted, I got over my scruples.

Over the cavity left in the mortar by the removal of the stone were two conspicuous marks, which afterward stared us in the face in all the ruined buildings of the country. They were the prints of a red hand with the thumb and fingers extended, not drawn or painted, but stamped by the living hand, the pressure of the palm upon the stone. He who made it had stood before it alive as we did, and pressed his hand, moistened with red paint, hard against the stone. The seams and creases of the palm were clear and distinct in the impression. There was something lifelike about it that waked exciting thoughts, and almost presented the images of the departed inhabitants hovering about the building. And there was one striking feature about these hands; they were exceedingly small. Either of our own spread over and completely hid them; and this was interesting from the fact that we had ourselves remarked, and heard remarked by others, the smallness of the hands and feet as a striking feature in the physical conformation of the Indians at the present day.

The stones with this red hand upon them were the first that fell as we commenced our breach into the wall. There were two crowbars on the hacienda, and working nearly two days, the Indians made a hole between six and seven feet deep, but throughout the wall was solid, and consisted of large stones imbedded in mortar, almost as hard as rock. The reason of this immense back wall, where everything else had a certain degree of fitness and conformity, we did not discover, and we had this huge hole staring us reproachfully in the face during all the remainder of our residence.

A few words more, and I have done with this building. In the south end apartment, the façade of which has been presented, we found the sculptured beam of hieroglyphics which had so much interested us on our former visit. In some of the inner apartments the lintels were still in their places over the doorways, and some were lying on the floor sound and solid, which better condition was no doubt owing to their being more sheltered than those over the outer doorway. This was the only sculptured beam in Uxmal, and at that time it was the only piece of carved wood we had seen. We considered it interesting, as indicating a degree of proficiency in an art of which, in all our previous explorations, we had not discovered any evidence, except, perhaps, at Ocosingo, where we found a beam, not carved, but which had evidently been reduced to shape by sharp instruments of metal. This time I determined not to let the precious beam escape me. It was ten feet long, one foot nine inches broad, and ten inches thick, of Sapote wood, enormously heavy and unwieldly. To keep the sculptured side from being chafed and broken, I had it covered with costal or hemp bagging, and stuffed with dry grass to the thickness of six inches. It left Uxmal on the shoulders of ten Indians, after many vicissitudes reached this city uninjured, and was deposited in Mr. Catherwood's Panorama. I had referred to it as being in the National Museum at Washington, whither I intended to send it as soon as a collection of large sculptured stones, which I was obliged to leave behind, should arrive; but on the burning of that building, in the general conflagration of Jerusalem and Thebes, this part of Uxmal was consumed, and with it other beams afterward discovered, much more curious and interesting; as also the whole collection of vases, figures, idols, and other relics gathered upon this journey. The collecting, packing, and transporting of these things had given me more trouble and annoyance than any other circumstance in our journey, and their loss cannot be replaced; for, being first on the ground, and having all at my choice, I of course selected only those objects which were most curious and valuable; and if I were to go over the whole ground again, I could not find others equal to them. I had the melancholy satisfaction of seeing their ashes exactly as the fire had left them. We seemed doomed to be in the midst of ruins; but in all our explorations there was none so touching as this.

Next to the great building of the Casa del Gobernador, and hardly less extraordinary and imposing in character, are the three great terraces which hold it aloft, and give it its grandeur of position; all of them artificial, and built up from the level of the plain.

The lowest of these terraces is three feet high, fifteen feet broad, and five hundred and seventy-five feet long; the second is twenty feet high, two hundred and fifty feet wide, and five hundred and forty-five feet in length; and the third, on which the building stands, is nineteen feet high, thirty feet broad, and three hundred and sixty feet in front. They were all supported by substantial stone walls; that of the second terrace is still in a good state of preservation, and at the corners the stones which support it are still in their places, with their outer surfaces rounded, instead of presenting sharp angles.

The platform of this terrace is a noble terra plana, five hundred and forty-five feet long and two hundred and fifty feet wide, and, from the remains still visible upon it, once contained structures and ornaments of various kinds, the character of which it is now difficult to make out. On our first arrival the whole was covered with a rank growth of bushes and weeds ten or twelve feet high, on clearing which away these remains were brought to light.

Along the south end there is an oblong structure about three feet high, two hundred long, and fifteen feet wide, at the foot of which there is a range of pedestals and fragments of columns about five feet high and eighteen inches in diameter. There are no remains of a roof or of any other structure connected with them.

Near the centre of the platform, at a distance of eighty feet from the foot of the steps, is a square enclosure, consisting of two layers of stones, in which stands, in an oblique position, as if falling, or perhaps, as if an effort had been made to throw it down, a large round stone, measuring eight feet above the ground and five feet in diameter. This stone is striking for its uncouth and irregular proportions, and wants conformity with the regularity and symmetry of all around. From its conspicuous position, it doubtless had some important use, and, in connexion with other monuments found at this place, induces the belief that it was connected with the ceremonial rites of an ancient worship known to have existed among all Eastern nations. The Indians call this stone the Picote, or whipping-post.

At a distance of sixty feet in a right line beyond this was a rude circular mound, about six feet high. We had used it as a position from which to take a Daguerreotype view of the front of the building, and, at the instance of the Cura Carillo, who came to pay us a visit, we determined to open it. It was a mere mass of earth and stones; and, on digging down to the depth of three or four feet, a sculptured monument was discovered, which is represented in Figure 10. It was found standing on its feet, in the position represented in the engraving. It is carved out of a single block of stone, and measures three feet two inches in length and two feet in height. It seems intended to represent a doube-headed cat or lynx, and is entire with the exception of one foot, which is a little broken. The sculpture is rude. It was too

FIG. 10

heavy to carry away. We had it raised to the side of the mound
for Mr. Catherwood to draw, and probably it remains there still.
The *picote*, or great stone, before referred to, appears in Figure
10 in the distance.

Why this monument had been consigned to the strange
place in which it was discovered we were at a loss to conjecture.
This could never have been its original destination. It had been
formally and deliberately buried. In my opinion, there is but one
way of accounting for it. It had been one of the many idols worshipped by the people of Uxmal; and the probability is, that
when the inhabitants abandoned the city they buried it, that it

might not be desecrated; or else the Spaniards, when they drove out the inhabitants and depopulated the city, in order to destroy all the reverential feeings of the Indians toward it, followed the example of Cortez at Cholula, and threw down and buried the idols.

At a distance of 130 feet from this mound was a square stone structure, six feet high and twenty feet at the base, in which we made an excavation, and discovered two sculptured heads, no doubt intended as portraits.

From the centre of this great platform a grand staircase 130 feet broad, which once contained 35 steps, rises to the third terrace, on which the building stands; besides this there is no staircase connected with either of the three terraces, and the only ascent to the platform of the second is by an inclined plane 100 feet broad, at the south end of the building, which makes it necessary for all approaching from the north to pass the whole length of the lower terrace, and, ascending by the inclined plane, go back to reach the steps. The probability is, that the labour of this was not regarded by the ancient inhabitants, and that all visiters or residents in the building passed in and out on the shoulders of Indians in coches, as the rich do now.

There remains to be noticed one important building on the grand platform of the second terrace. It stands at the northwest corner, and is represented in Plate IV. It is called the Casa de las Tortugas, or the House of the Turtles, which name was given to it by a neighbouring cura, from a bead or row of turtles which goes round the cornice, indicated in the engraving.

This building is 94 feet in front and 34 feet deep, and in size and ornaments contrasts strikingly with the Casa del Gobernador. It wants the rich and gorgeous decoration of the former, but is distinguished for its justness and beauty of proportions, and its chasteness and simplicity of ornament. Throughout there is nothing that borders on the unintelligible or grotesque, nothing that can shock a fastidious architectural taste; but, unhappily, it is fast going to decay. On our first visit Mr. Catherwood and myself climbed to the roof, and selected it as a good position from which to make a panoramic sketch of the whole field of ruins. It was then trembling and tottering, and within the year the whole of the centre part had fallen in. In front the centre of the wall is gone, and in the rear the wooden lintel, pressed down and broken in two, still supports the superincumbent mass, but it gave us a nervous feeling to pass under it. The interior is filled up with the ruins of the fallen roof.

Plate IV

U X M A L.
Front of the Casa de Las Tortugas.

This building, too, has the same peculiar feature, want of convenient access. It has no communication, at least by steps or any visible means, with the Casa del Gobernador, nor were there any steps leading to the terrace below. It stands isolated and alone, seeming to mourn over its own desolate and ruinous condition. With a few more returns of the rainy season it will be a mass of ruins, and perhaps on the whole continent of America there will be no such monument of the purity and simplicity of aboriginal art.

Such is a brief description of the Casa del Gobernador, with its three great terraces, and the buildings and structures upon the grand platform of the second. From the place which we had fixed upon as our residence, and the constant necessity of ascending and descending the terraces, it was with these that we became the soonest familiar. The reader will be able to form some idea of the subjects that engaged our attention, and the strange spectacle that we had constantly before our eyes.

CHAPTER IX

Having made such advances in the clearing that Mr. Catherwood had abundance of occupation, on Thursday, the 18th of November, I set out, under the guidance of the mayoral, on an excursion to meet Don Simon Peon at the fair of Jalacho, and visit some ruins on another hacienda of his in that neighbourhood. We started at half past six, our course being west by north. At ten minutes past seven we crossed a *serrania*, or range of hills, about a hundred and fifty feet high, and came down upon an extensive savanna of low, flat land, a mere canebrake. The road was the worst I had found in the country, being simply a wet and very muddy path for mules and horses to the fair. My horse sunk up to his saddle-girths, and it was with great exertion that he dragged himself through. Every moment I had fear of his rolling over in the mud, and in some places I was strongly reminded of the *malos pasos* in Central America. Occasionally the branches were barely high enough to allow mules to pass, and then I was obliged to dismount, and trudge through the mud on foot. At eight o'clock we came to an open savanna, and saw a high mound with ruins on the top, bearing south, about a mile distant. It was called, as the mayoral said, Senuisacal. I was strongly tempted to turn aside and examine it, but, on account of the thickness of the cane-brake and the mud, it would have been impossible to reach it, and the mayoral said that it was entirely in ruins.

In half an hour we came into a clear and open country, and at ten we entered the camino real for Jalacho, a broad and open road, passable for calesas. Up to this time we had not seen a single habitation or met a human being, and now the road was literally thronged with people moving on to the fair, with whose clean garments my mud-stained clothes contrasted very unfavourably. There were Indians, Mestizoes, and white people on horseback, muleback, and on foot, men, women, and children, many carrying on their backs things to sell, in petaquillas, or long baskets of straw; whole families, sometimes half a village moving in company; and I fell in behind a woman perched on a loaded horse, with a child in her arms, and a little fellow behind, his legs stretched out nearly straight to span the horse's flanks, and both arms clasping her substantial body to keep himself from slipping off. We passed parties sitting in the shade to rest or eat, and families lying down by the roadside to sleep, without any fear of molestation from the rest.

At half past eleven we reached the village of Becal, conspicuous, like all the others, for a large plaza and church with two towers. In the suburbs the mayoral and I interchanged sentiments about breakfast, and, after making a circle in the plaza, he struck off direct for the house of the cura. I do not think the cura could have been expecting me, but if so, he could not have provided a better breakfast, or at shorter notice. Besides the breakfast, the cura told me of ruins on his hacienda which he had never visited, but which he promised to have cleared away, and be ready to show me on my return. Circumstances occurred to prevent my returning by the same road, but the cura, having had the ruins cleared away, visited them himself, and I afterward heard that I had lost something by not seeing them. I took leave of him with the buoyancy of old times, breakfast secured, and a prospect of another ruined city.

In an hour I reached Jalacho, where I met Don Simon and two of his brothers, with whom I was not yet acquainted; Don Lorenzo, who had a hacienda in that neighbourhood, and Don Alonzo, then living in Campeachy, who was educated in New-York, and spoke English remarkably well.

The village of Jalacho lies on the main road from Merida to Campeachy, and, next to that of Yzamal, its fair is the greatest in Yucatan, while in some respects it is more curious. It is not attended by large merchants with foreign goods, nor by the better classes from Merida, but it is resorted to by all the Indians from the haciendas and villages. It is inferior in one respect: gambling is not carried on upon so large a scale as at Yzamal.

The time was when all countries had their periodical fairs; but the changed and improved condition of the world has almost abolished this feature of ancient times. Increased facilities of communication with foreign countries and different parts of the same country make opportunties for buying and selling an everyday thing; and at this day, in general throughout Europe, for all articles of necessity, and even of luxury, every man has, as it were, a fair every day at his own door. But the countries in America subject to the Spanish dominion have felt less sensibly, perhaps, than any others in the world, the onward impulse of the last two centuries, and in them many usages and customs derived from Europe, but there long since fallen into oblivion, are still in full force. Among them is this of holding fairs, of which, though several took place during the time of my journey in Central America, I had no opportunity of seeing any.

The fair of Jalacho was an observance of eight days, but the first two or three were marked only by the arrival of scattering parties, and the business of securing places to live in and to display wares. The great gathering or high change did not begin till Thursday, which was the day of my arrival, and then it was computed that there were assembled in the village ten thousand persons.

Of all this crowd the plaza was the grand point of concentration. Along the houses fronting it was a range of tables set out with looking-glasses in frames of red paper, rings and necklaces, cotton, and toys and trinkets for the Indians. On the opposite side of the street, along the square of the church, were rustic arbours, occupied by venders having similar commodities spread before them. The plaza was partitioned, and at regular intervals was a merchant, whose shop was a rude stick fixed upright in the ground, and having another crosswise at the top, covered with leaves and twigs, thus forming a sort of umbrella, to protect its sitting occupant from the sun. These were the merchants of dulces and other eatables. This part of the fair was constantly crowded, and perhaps nine tenths were Indians from the pueblos and haciendas around. Don Simon Peon told me that he had entered on his books a hundred and fifty *criados*, or servants, who had applied to him for money, and he did not know how many more were present.

It may be supposed that the church was not uninterested

in this great gathering. In fact, it was the fête of Santiago, and among the Indians this fiesta was identified with the fair. The doors of the church were constantly open, the interior was thronged with Indians, and a crowd continually pressing to the altar. In the doorway was a large table covered with candles and small figures of arms and legs in wax, which the Indians purchased as they entered at a medio apiece, for offerings to the saint. Near the altar, on the left, sat an unshaved ministro, with a table before him, on which was a silver waiter, covered with medios, reales, and two shilling pieces, showing to the backward what others had done, and inviting them to do the same. The candles purchased at the door had been duly blessed, and as the Indians went up with them, a strapping negro, with linen particularly dirty, received and lighted them at one burning on the altar, whence with his black hands he passed them on to a rusty white assistant, who arranged them upon a table, and, even before the backs of the offerers were turned, puffed out the light, and took the candles to be smoothed over, and resold at the door for another medio each.

High above the heads of the crowd, catching the eye on first entering the church, was the figure of Santiago, or Saint James, on horseback, holy in the eyes of all who saw it, and famed for its power of working miracles, healing the sick, curing the fever and ague, insuring to prospective parents a boy or girl as desired, bringing back a lost cow or goat, healing a cut of the machete, or relieving from any other calamity incident to an Indian's lot. The fore feet of the horse were raised in the air, and the saint wore a black cocked hat, with a broad gold band, a short mantle of scarlet velvet, having a broad gold edging round the cape and skirts, green velvet trousers, with a wide gold stripe down the sides, and boots and spurs. All the time I stood there, and every time I went into the church, men, women, and children were pressing forward, struggling with each other to kiss the foot of the saint. The simple Indian, as the first act of devotion, led up his whole family to do this act of obeisance. The mother lifted her sucking child, and pressed its lips, warm from her breast, against the foot of the bedizened statue.

In the afternoon commenced the first bull-fight. The *toreadores*, or bull-fighters, all lived at the house opposite ours, and from it the procession started. It was headed by a wrinkled, squint-eyed, bandy-legged Indian, carrying under his arm the old Indian drum, and dancing grotesquely to his own music;

then followed the band, and then the gallant picadores, a cut-throat looking set of scoundrels, who, imagining themselves the admiration, were the contempt of the crowd.

The Plaza de Toros was on óne side of the square of the plaza, and, like that in the square of the church of San Cristoval, was constructed of poles and vines, upright, intwining and inter-laced, tottering and yielding under pressure, and yet holding to-gether firmly. In the centre was a pole, on the top of which flour-ished the Mexican eagle, with outspread wings, holding in his beak a scroll with the appropriate motto, "Viva la Republica de Yucatan," and strings extended like radii to different parts of the boxes, wrapped with cut and scolloped papers fluttering in the wind. On one side of the ring was a pole with a wooden beam, from which hung, by strings fastened to the crown of an old straw hat, two figures stuffed with straw, with grotesque masks and ludicrous dresses. One was very narrow in the should-ers and very broad below, and his trousers were buttoned be-hind.

The toros, fallen into disrepute in the capital, is still the favourite and national amusement in the pueblos. The animal tied to the post when we entered was from the hacienda of the senote, which was famed for the ferocity of its bulls. The pica-dores, too, were fiercer than those in the capital, and the con-tests were more sanguinary and fatal. Several times the bulls were struck down, and two, reeking with blood, were dragged off by the horns, dead; and this was in the presence of women, and greeted with their smiles and approbation: a disgusting and degrading spectacle, but as yet having too strong a hold upon popular feeling to be easily set aside. The entertainment was got up at the expense of the village, and all who could find a place had liberty to enter.

This over, there was an interval for business, and partic-ularly for visiting the horse-market, or rather a particular sec tion to which dealers sent their horses to be exhibited. I was more interested in this than any other branch of commerce carried on at the fair, as I wished to purchase horses for our journey. There were plenty of them, though, as in all other sec-tions of the country, but few fine ones. Prices varied from ten dollars to two hundred, the value depending, not upon bone, blood, or muscle, but upon training and paces. The young hacienda horses, with nothing but the trot, or trotones, as they were called, were worth from ten dollars to twenty-five, but as they excelled in pace or easiness of movement their value increased. No one pretends to ride a trotting horse in Yucatan, for he who does labours under the imputation of not being able to purchase a pacer. The finest horses in the country in appearance are those imported; but the Yucatan horses, though small, are remarkably hardy, require no care, and endure an extraordinary degree of fatigue.

Night came on, and the plaza was alive with people and brilliant with lights. On one side, opposite the church, along the corridors of the houses and in front of them, were rows of tables, with cards and dice, which were very soon crowded with players, whites and Mestizoes; but the great scene of attraction was the gathering of Indians in the centre of the plaza. It was the hour of supper, and the small merchants had abundant custom for their eatables. Turkeys which had stood tied by one leg all day, inviting people to come and eat them, were now ready, of which for a medio two men had a liberal allowance; and I remarked, what I had heard of, but had not seen before, that grains of cacao circulated among the Indians as money. Every merchant or vender of eatables, the most of whom were women, had on the table a pile of these grains, which they were constantly counting and exchanging with the Indians. There is no copper money in Yucatan, nor any coin whatever under a medio, or six and a quarter cents, and this deficiency is supplied by these grains of cacao. The medio is divided into twenty parts, generally of five grains each, but the number is increased or decreased according to the quantity of the article in the market, and its real value. As the earnings of the Indians are small, and the articles they purchase are the mere necessaries of life, which are very cheap, these grains of cacao, or fractional parts of a medio, are the coin in most common use among them. The currency has always a real value, and is regulated by the quantity of cacao in the market, and the only inconvenience, economically speaking, that it has, is the loss of a certain public wealth by the destruction of the cacao, as in the case of bank notes. But these grains had an interest independent of all questions of political economy, for they indicate or illustrate a page in the history of this unknown and mysterious people. When the Spaniards first made their way into the interior of Yucatan, they found no circulating medium, either of gold, or silver, or any other species of metal, but only grains of cacao; and it seemed a strange circumstance, that while the manners and customs of the Indians have undergone an immense change, while their cities have been destroyed, their religion dishonoured, their princes swept away, and their whole government modified by foreign laws, no experiment has yet been made upon their currency.

In the midst of this strange scene, there was a stir at one end of the plaza, and an object presented itself that at once turned my thoughts and feelings homeward. It was a post-coach, from a Troy factory, exactly like those seen on every road in our country, but it had on the panel of the door "La Diligencia Campechana." It was one of the line of diligences between Campeachy and Merida, and just arrived from the former place. It came up on a run, drawn by wild, uncombed horses, not yet broken to the bit, and with their breasts galled and raw from the pressure of the collar. It had nine inside, and had an aspect so familiar that, as the door opened, I expected to see acquaintances get out; but all spoke a foreign tongue, and instead of being welcomed to supper or bed by an officious landlord and waiter, all inquired anxiously where they could get something to eat and a place to sleep in.

Leaving them to do as well as they could, we went to the baile or ball. In front of the quartel was a rustic arbour, enclosed by a temporary railing, with benches and chairs arranged around the sides, and the centre cleared for dancing. Until I saw them collected together, I did not suppose that so many white persons were present at the fair, and, like the men at the gambling-table, and the Indians in the plaza, these seeemed to forget that there was any other party present than themselves. In this obliviousness I sympathized, and slipping into an easy arm-chair, from the time of my drag through the mud in the morning I had not so quiet and comfortable a moment, in which condition I remained until awakened by Don Simon.

The next day was a repetition of the same scenes. In the afternoon, at the bull-fight, I fell into conversation with a gentleman who sat next to me, and who gave me information of some antiquities in Maxcanú, a village four leagues distant. That I might take this place on my return to Uxmal, it was advisable to visit the ruins on Don Simon's hacienda the next day. Don Simon could not go with me until after the fair, and amid the great concourse of Indians it was difficult to find one who could serve as a guide.

It was not till eleven o'clock the next day that I was able to set out, and I had as a guide a major domo of another hacienda, who, being, as I imagined, vexed at being obliged to leave the fiesta, and determined to get me off his hands as soon as possible, set out at a swinging trot. The sun was scorching, the road broad, straight, and stony, and without a particle of shade, but in forty minutes, both considerably heated, we reached the hacienda of Sijoh, two leagues distant.

This hacienda belonged to a brother of Don Simon, then resident in Vera Cruz, and was under the latter's charge. Here my guide passed me over into the hands of an Indian, and rode back as fast as he could to the fair. The Indian mounted another horse, and, continuing a short distance on the same road through the lands of the hacienda, we turned off to the right, and in five minutes saw in the woods to our left, near the road, a high mound of ruins of that distinctive character once so strange, but now so familiar to me, proclaiming the existence of another unknown, nameless, desolate, and ruined city.

We continued on to another mound nearer than the first, where we dismounted and tied our horses to the bushes. This mound was a solid mass of masonry, about thirty feet high, and nearly square. The stones were large, one at the corner measuring six feet in length by three in width, and the sides were covered with thorns and briers. On the south side was a range of steps still in good condition, each fifteen inches high, and in general three feet long. On the other sides the stones rose in a pyramidal form, but without steps. On the top was a stone building, with its wall as high as the cornice standing. Above this the façade had fallen, but the mass of stone and mortar which formed the roof remained, and within the apartment was precisely like the interior of the buildings at Uxmal, having the same distinctive arch. There were no remains of sculpture, but the base of the mound was encumbered with fallen stones, among which were some about three feet long, dug out so as to form a sort of trough, the same as we had seen at Uxmal, where they were called pilas or fountains.

Leaving this, we returned through the woods to the mound we had first seen. This was perhaps sixty feet high, and was a mere mass of fallen stone. Whatever it might have been, its features were entirely lost, and but for the structure I had just seen, and the waste of ruins in other parts of the country, it might have seemed doubtful whether it had ever been formed according to any plan or rules of art. The mass of stone was so solid that no vegetation could take root upon it; its sides were bare and bleached, and the pieces, on being disturbed, slid down with a metallic sound like the ringing of iron. In climbing up I received a blow from a sliding stone, which nearly carried me back to the bottom, for the moment completely disabled me, and from which I did not entirely recover until some time afterward.

From the top of this mound I saw two others of nearly the same height, and, taking their direction with the compass, I descended and directed my steps toward them. The whole ground was covered with trees and a thick undergrowth of brush and thorn-bushes. My Indian had gone to lead the horses round to another road. I had no machete, and though the mounds were not far distant, I was excessively scratched and torn in getting to them. They were all ruined, so that they barely preserved their form. Passing between these, I saw beyond three others, forming three angles of a patio or square; and in this patio, rising above the thorn-bushes and briers, were huge stones, which, on being first discovered, suddenly and unexpectedly, actually startled me. At a distance they reminded me of the monuments of Copan, but they were even more extraordinary and incomprehensible. They were uncouth in shape, and rough as they came from the quarry. Four of them were flat; the largest was fourteen feet high, and measured toward the top four feet in width, and one and a half in thickness. The top was broader than the bottom, and it stood in a leaning posture, as if its foundation had been loosened. The others were still more irregular in shape, and it seemed as if the people who erected them had just looked out for the largest stones they could lay their hands on, tall or short, thick or thin, square or round, without regard to anything except bulk. They had no beauty or fitness of design or proportion, and there were no characters upon them. But in that desolation and solitude they were strange and striking, and, like unlettered headstones in a churchyard, seemed to mark the graves of unknown dead.

On one of the mounds, looking down upon this patio, was a long building, with its front wall fallen, and leaving the whole interior exposed to view. I climbed up to it, but saw only the remains of the same narrow corridor and arch, and on the wall were prints of the red hand. The whole country was so overgrown that it was impossible to form any idea of what its extent had been, but one thing was certain, a large city had once stood here, and what its name was no man knew.

At this time my visit was merely intended as preliminary, for the purpose of judging whether there were any subjects for Mr. Catherwood's pencil, and it was now about one o'clock. The heat was intense, and sweating and covered with briers and burrs, which stuck to every part of my clothes, I came out into the open road, where my Indian was waiting for me with the horses. We mounted immediately, and continued on a gallop to the hacienda of Tankuché, two leagues distant.

This hacienda was a favourite with Don Simon, as he had created it out of the wilderness, and the entire road from the village he had made himself. It was a good logwood country, and here he had erected machinery for extracting the dye. In general, it was the most busy place of all his haciendas, but this day it seemed as if a desolating scourge had swept over it. The huts of the Indians were closed and locked up; no barebodied children were playing around them, and the large gate was locked. We tied our horses by one of the panels, and, ascending by a flight of stone steps, entered the lane and walked up to the house. Every door was locked, and not a person in sight. Moving on to the high stone structure forming the platform of the well, I saw a little boy, dressed in a straw hat, dozing on an old horse, which was creeping round with the well-beam, drawing in broken buckets a slow stream of water, for which no one came. At sight of me he rose from the neck of his horse, and tried to stop him, but the old animal seemed so used to going round that he could not stop, and the little fellow looked as if he expected to be going till some one came to take him off. All had gone to the fiesta, and were now swelling the great crowd I had left in the village. It was an immense change from the thronged fair to the solitude of this desolate hacienda. I sat down under a large seybo tree overshadowing the well, and ate a roll of bread and an orange, after which I strolled back to the gate, and, to my surprise, found only one horse. My guide had mounted his and returned to his hacienda. I walked into the factory, returned to the well, and attempted speech with the boy, but the old horse started forward and carried him away from me; I lay down on the platform of the well; the creaking of the beam served as a sort of lullaby, and I had made such progress that I was not very eager to be interrupted, when an Indian lad arrived, who had been hunted up by my missing guide, and directed to show me the ruins. This fact, however, he would not have been able to communicate, but, fortunately, he was accompanied by an Indian who spoke Spanish. The latter was an intelligent, middle-aged man, of highly respectable appearance, but Don Simon told me he was the worst fellow on the hacienda. He was desperately in love with a girl who did not live on the estate, and he was in the habit of running away to visit her, and of being brought back with his arms tied behind him; as a punishment for a late offence of this kind, he had been prohibited from going to the fiesta. Through him I had an understanding with my new guide, and set out again.

In five minutes after leaving the hacienda, we passed between two mounds of ruins, and, from time to time having glimpses of other vestiges in the woods, in twenty minutes we came to a mound about thirty feet high, on the top of which was a ruined building. Here we dismounted, tied our horses, and ascended the mound. The whole of the front wall had fallen, together with the front half of the arch; the interior chamber was filled with dirt and rubbish nearly up to the cornice, and the arch of the back wall was the only part above ground; but this, instead of being of smooth stones, like all the others we had seen in Yucatan, was plastered and covered with paintings, the colours of which were still bright and fresh. The principal colours were red, green, yellow, and blue, and at first the lines and figures seemed so distinct, that I thought I could make out the subjects. The apartment being filled up with dirt, I stood above the objects, and it was only by sitting, or rather lying down, that I could examine them. One subject at first sight struck me as being a representation of the mask found at Palenque. I was extremely desirous to get this off entire, but found, by experiments upon other parts of the plaster with the machete, that it would be impossible to do so, and left it untouched.

In the interest of the work, I did not discover that thousands of garrapatas were crawling over me. These insects are the scourge of Yucatan, and altogether they were a more constant source of annoyance and suffering than any we encountered in the country. I had seen something of them in Central America, but at a different season, when the hot sun had killed off the immensity of their numbers, and those left had attained such a size that a single one could easily be seen and picked off. These, in colour, size, and numbers, were like grains of sand. They disperse themselves all over the body, get into the seams of the clothes, and, like the insect known among us as the tick, bury themselves in the flesh, causing an irritation that is almost intolerable. The only way to get rid of them effectually is by changing all the clothes. In Uxmal we had not been troubled with them, for they are said to breed only in those woods where cattle pasture, and the grounds about Uxmal had been used as a milpa, or plantation of corn. It was the first time I had ever had them upon me in such profusion, and their presence dis-

turbed most materially the equanimity with which I examined
the paintings. In fact, I did not remain long on the ground.

It is particularly unfortunate that, while so many apartments have remained free, this most curious and interesting one
has become filled up. It is probable that the walls, as well as the
arch, are plastered and painted. It would have cost a week's labour to clear it out, and my impression was, that, in consequence
of the dirt having been piled up against the walls for an unknown length of time, through a long succession of rainy seasons,
the colours were so completely effaced that nothing would have
been discovered to compensate for the labour.

It was now nearly dark. My day's work had been a severe
one. I was tired and covered with garrapatas, but the next day
was Sunday, the last of the fiesta, and I determined on returning
to the village that night. There was a brilliant moonlight, and,
hurrying on, at eleven o'clock I saw, at the end of a long straight
road, the illuminated front of the church of Jalacho. Very soon,
amid the shining lights and congregated thousands, I forgot
desolations and ruins, and my sympathies once more moved
with the living. I passed by the tables of the gamblers, worked
my way through the plaza and through a crowd of Indians, who
fell back in deference to the colour of my skin, and, unexpectedly to my friends, presented myself at the baile. This time I
had no disposition to sleep. For the last night of the fiesta the
neighbouring villages had sent forth their all; the ball was larger
and gayer of whites and those in whose veins white blood ran,
while outside, leaning upon the railing, looking in, but not
presuming to enter, were close files of Indians, and beyond, in
the plaza, was a dense mass of them—natives of the land and
lords of the soil, that strange people in whose ruined cities I had
just been wandering, submitting quietly to the dominion of
strangers, bound down and trained to the most abject submission, and looking up to the white man as a superior being.
Could these be the descendants of that fierce people who had
made such bloody resistance to the Spanish conquerors?

At eleven o'clock the ball broke up, and fireworks were let
off from the balustrade of the church. These ended with the
national piece of El Castillo, and at twelve o'clock, when we
went away, the plaza was as full of Indians as at midday. At no
time since my arrival in the country had I been so struck with
the peculiar constitution of things in Yucatan. Originally portioned out as slaves, the Indians remain as servants. Veneration
for masters is the first lesson they learn, and these masters, the

descendants of the terrible conquerors, in centuries of uninterrupted peace have lost all the fierceness of their ancestors. Gentle, and averse to labour themselves, they impose no heavy burdens upon the Indians, but understand and humour their ways, and the two races move on harmoniously together, with nothing to apprehend from each other, forming a simple, primitive, and almost patriarchal state of society; and so strong is the sense of personal security, that, notwithstanding the crowds of strangers, and although every day Don Simon had sat with doors open and piles of money on the table, so little apprehension was there of robbery, that we slept without a door or window locked.

CHAPTER X

The next day was Sunday. The church was thronged for grand mass; candles were burned, and offerings were made to the amount of many medios, and at nine o'clock the bells tolled for the procession, the crowning scene of the fiesta. The church was emptied of its votaries, and the plaza was alive with people hurrying to take a place in the procession, or to see it pass. I climbed up into the Plaza de Toros, and had a whole box to myself.

The space along the side of the bull-ring was thronged; and first came a long procession of Indians with lighted candles; then the ministro with the large silver salver, and money upon it, presenting it on either side to receive additional offerings. As it passed, a woman walked up and put upon it two reales, probably her all. Then came, borne on a barrow above the heads of the crowd, the figure which had attracted so much veneration in the church, Santiago on horseback, with his scarlet and embroidered mantle and green velvet pantaloons bordered with gold. This was followed by the cura, a fat, yellow-looking half-breed, with his two dirty-faced assistants. Directly under me the procession stopped, and the priests, turning toward the figure of the saint, set up a chant. This over, the figure moved on, and stopping from time to time, continued to work its way around the church, until finally it was restored to its place on the altar. So ended the fair of Jalacho and the fête of Santiago, the second which I had seen since my arrival in the country, and both exhibiting the powerful influence of the ceremonials of the church over the minds of the Indians. Throughout the state, this class of the inhabitants pays annually a tax of twelve reales per head for the support of the cura; and it was said on the ground that the Indians at this fiesta had paid eight hundred dollars for salves, five hundred for aves, and six hundred for masses, which, if true, was an enormous sum out of their small earnings.

But the fiesta was over, and almost immediately the crowd was in motion, preparing to set out for home. At three o'clock every street was lined with people, some less and others more heavily laden than they came, and some carrying home the respectable head of a family in a state of brutal intoxication; and here I particularly remarked, what I had frequently observed before, that among all the intoxication of the Indians, it was a rare thing to see a woman in that state; it was really an interesting spectacle to see these poor women, with their children around them, supporting and conducting homeward their intoxicated husbands.

At four o'clock I set off with Don Lorenzo Peon, a brother of Don Simon, for Maxcanú. Our mode of conveyance, much used in Yucatan, but new to me, was called a caricoché. It was a long wagon, on two large wheels, covered with cotton cloth as a protection against the sun, and on the bottom was stretched a broad mattress, on which two persons could recline at full length. If they would sit up, it was large enough for three or four. It was drawn by one horse, with a driver riding as postillion, and another horse followed to change. The road was broad, even, and level. It was the camino real between Merida and Campeachy, and would pass in any country for a fair carriage-road. All along we passed parties of Indians returning from the fair. In an hour we came in sight of the sierra which traverses at that point the whole peninsula of Yucatan from east to west. The sight of hills was cheering, and with the reflection of the setting sun upon them, they presented almost the first fine scenery I had encountered in the country. In an hour and ten minutes we reached Maxcanú, twelve miles distant, being by far the greatest speed at which I ever travelled in Yucatan.

The hacienda of Don Lorenzo was in this neighbourhood, and he had a large house in the village, at which we stopped. My object in coming to this place was to visit La Cueva de Maxcanú, or the Cave of Maxcanú. In the evening, when notice was given of my intention, half the village was ready to join me, but in the morning my volunteers were not forthcoming, and I was reduced to the men procured for me by Don Lorenzo. From the time consumed in getting the men together and procuring torches, cord, &c., I did not get off till after nine o'clock. Our direction was due east till we reached the sierra, ascending which through a passage overgrown with woods, at eleven o'clock we arrived at the mouth, or rather door, of the cueva, about a league distant from the village.

I had before heard so much of caves, and had been so often disappointed, that I did not expect much from this; but the first view satisfied me in regard to the main point, viz., that it was not a natural cave, and that, as had been represented to me, it was hecha à mano, or made by hand.

La Cueva de Maxcanú, or the Cave of Maxcanú, has in that region a marvellous and mystical reputation. It is called by the Indians Satun Sat, which means in Spanish El Laberinto or El Perdedero, the Labyrinth, or place in which one may be lost. Notwithstanding its wonderful reputation, and a name which alone, in any other country, would induce a thorough exploration, it is a singular fact, and exhibits more strikingly than anything I can mention the indifference of the people of all classes to the antiquities of the country, that up to the time of my arrival at the door, this Laberinto had never been examined. My friend Don Lorenzo Peon would give me every facility for exploring it except joining me himself. Several persons had penetrated to some distance with a string held outside, but had turned back, and the universal belief was, that it contained passages without number and without end.

Under these circumstances, I certainly felt some degree of excitement as I stood in the doorway. The very name called up those stupendous works in Crete and on the shores of the Mœritic Lake which are now almost discredited as fabulous.

My retinue consisted of eight men, who considered themselves in my employ, besides three or four supernumeraries, and all together formed a crowd around the door. Except the mayoral of Uxmal, I had never seen one of them before, and as I considered it important to have a reliable man outside, I stationed him at the door with a ball of twine. I tied one end round my left wrist, and told one of the men to light a torch and follow me, but he refused absolutely, and all the rest, one after the other, did the same. They were all ready enough to hold the string; and I was curious to know, and had a conference with them on the interesting point, whether they expected any pay for their services in standing out of doors. One expected pay for showing me the place, others for carrying water, another for taking care of the horses, and so on, but I terminated the matter abruptly by declaring that I should not pay one of them a medio; and, ordering them all away from the door, which they were smothering, and a little infected with one of their apprehensions of starting some wild beast, which might be making his lair in the recesses of the cave, I entered with a candle in one hand and a pistol in the other.

The entrance faces the west. The mouth was filled up with rubbish, scrambling over which, I stood in a narrow passage or gallery, constructed, like all the apartments above ground, with smooth walls and triangular arched ceiling. This passage was about four feet wide, and seven feet high to the top of the arch. It ran due east, and at the distance of six or eight yards opened into another, or rather was stopped by another crossing it, and running north and south. I took first that on the right hand, running south. At the distance of a few yards, on the right side of the wall, I found a door, filled up, and at the distance of thirty-five feet the passage ended, and a door opened at right angles on the left into another gallery running due east. Following this, at the distance of thirteen feet I found another gallery on the left, running north, and beyond it, at the end, still another, also on the left, and running north, four yards long, and then walled up, with only an opening in it about a foot square.

Turning back, I entered the gallery which I had passed, and which ran north eight or ten yards; at the end was a doorway on the right, opening into a gallery that ran east. At the end of this were six steps, each one foot high and two wide, leading to another gallery, which ran north twelve yards. At the end there came another gallery on the left, which ran west ten yards, and at the end of this another on the right, running north about sixty feet. This passage was walled up at the north end, and at the distance of five yards from this end another doorway led into a passage running to the east. At the distance of four yards a gallery crossed this at right angles, running north and south, forty-five feet long, and walled up at both ends; and three or four yards farther on another gallery crossed it, also running north and south. This last was walled up at the south, and on the north led to still another gallery, which ran east, three yards long. This was stopped by another gallery crossing it, running to the south three yards, when it was walled up, and to the north eight yards, when it turned to the west.

In utter ignorance of the ground, I found myself turning and doubling along these dark and narrow passages, which seemed really to have no end, and justly to entitle the place to its name of El Laberinto.

I was not entirely free from the apprehension of starting some wild animal, and moved slowly and very cautiously. In the mean time, in turning the corners, my twine would be entangled, and the Indians, moved by the probability of getting no pay, entered to clear it, and by degrees all came up with me in a body. I got a glimpse of their torches behind me just as I was turning into a new passage, and at the moment I was startled by a noise which sent me back rather quickly, and completely routed them. It proceeded from a rushing of bats, and, having a sort of horror of these beastly birds, this was an ugly place to meet them in, for the passage was so low, and there was so little room for a flight over head, that in walking upright there was great danger of their striking the face. It was necessary to move with the head bent down, and protecting the lights from the flapping of their wings. Nevertheless, every step was exciting, and called up recollections of the Pyramids and tombs of Egypt, and I could not but believe that these dark and intricate passages would introduce me to some large saloon, or perhaps some royal sepulchre. Belzoni, and the tomb of Cephrenes and its alabaster sarcophagus, were floating through my brain, when all at once I found the passage choked up and effectually stopped. The ceiling had fallen in, crushed by a great mass of superincumbent earth, and farther progress was utterly impossible.

I was not prepared for this abrupt termination. The walls and ceiling were so solid and in such good condition that the possibility of such a result had not occurred to me. I was sure of going on to the end and discovering something, and I was arrested without knowing any better than when I entered to what point these passages led, or for what purposes they had been constructed. My first impulse was, not to turn back, but to begin immediately and dig a way through; but the impossibility of accomplishing anything in this way soon presented itself. For the Indians to carry out the earth on their backs through all these passages would be a never-ending work; besides, I had no idea how far the destruction extended, and, for the present at least, nothing could be done.

In a spirit of utter disappointment, I pointed out to the Indians the mass of earth that, as it were, maliciously cut off all my hopes, and told them to put an end to their lying stories about the Laberinto and its having no end; and in my disappointment I began to feel most sensibly the excessive heat and closeness of the place, which I had hardly perceived before, and which now became almost insufferable from the smoke of the torches and the Indians choking the narrow passage.

All that I could do, and that was very unsatisfactory, was to find out the plan of this subterraneous structure. I had with me a pocket compass, and, notwithstanding the heat and smoke, and the little help that the Indians afforded me, under all annoyances, and with the sweat dropping on my memorandum book, I measured back to the door.

I remained outside a few moments for fresh air, and entered again to explore the passage which branched off to the left of the door. I had just gone far enough to have my hopes revived by the prospect of some satisfactory result, when again I found the passage choked up by the falling in and burial of the arch.

I measured and took the bearings of this too. From the excessive heat and annoyance, this plan may not be very correct, and therefore I do not present it. The description will enable the reader to form some general idea of the character of the structure.

In exploring that part to the left of the door, I made an important discovery. In the walls of one of the passages was a hole eight inches square, which admitted light, and looking through it, I saw some plump and dusky legs, which clearly did not belong to the antiguos, and which I easily recognised as those of my worthy attendants.

Having heard the place spoken of as a subterraneous construction, and seeing, when I reached the ground, a half-buried door with a mass of overgrown earth above it, it had not occurred to me to think otherwise; but on examining outside, I found that what I had taken for an irregular natural formation, like a hill-side, was a pyramidal mound of the same general character with all the rest we had seen in the country. Making the Indians clear away some thorn-bushes, with the help of the branches of a tree growing near I climbed up it. On the top were the ruins of a building, the same as all the others. The door of El Laberinto, instead of opening into a hill-side, opened into this mound, and, as near as I could judge from the ruins along the base, was ten feet high, and the Laberinto, instead of being subterraneous, or, rather, under the surface of the earth, was in the body of this mound. Heretofore it had been our impression that these mounds were solid and compact masses of stone and earth, without any chambers or structures of any kind, and the discovery of this gave rise to the exciting idea that all the great mounds scattered over the country contained secret, unknown, and hidden chambers, presenting an immense field for exploration and discovery, and, ruined as the buildings on their summits were, perhaps the only source left for acquiring knowledge of the people by whom the cities were constructed.

I was really at a loss to know what to do. I was almost tempted to abandon everything else, send word to my companions, and not leave the spot till I had pulled down the whole mound, and discovered every secret it contained; but it was not a work to be undertaken in a hurry, and I determined to leave it for a future occasion. Unfortunately, in the multiplicity of other occupations in distant regions of the country, I never had an opportunity of returning to this mound. It remains with all its mystery around it, worthy the enterprise of some future explorer, and I cannot but indulge the hope that the time is not far distant when its mystery will be removed and all that is hidden brought to light.

In the account which I had received of this Labyrinth, no mention had been made of any ruins, and probably, when on the ground, I should have heard nothing of them, but from the top of this mound I saw two others, both of which, with a good deal of labour, I reached under the guidance of the Indians, crossing a patch of beans and milpa. I ascended them both. On the top of one was a building eighty or a hundred feet long. The front wall had fallen, and left exposed the inner part of the back wall, with half the arch, as it were, supporting itself in the air. The Indians then led me to a fourth mound, and told me that there were others in the woods, but all in the same ruinous condition; and, considering the excessive heat and the desperate toil of clambering, I did not think it worth while to visit them. I saw no sculptured stones, except those I have before mentioned, dug out like troughs, and called *pilas*, though the Indians persisted in saying that there were such all over, but they did not know exactly where to find them.

At three o'clock I resumed my journey toward Uxmal. For a short distance the road lay along the ridge of the sierra, a mere bed of rock, on which the horse's hoofs clattered and rang at every step. Coming out upon the brow of the sierra, we had one of those grand views which everywhere present themselves from this mountain range; an immense wooded plain, in this place broken only by a small spot like a square on a chessboard, the clearing of the hacienda of Santa Cruz. We descended the sierra, and at the foot of it struck the camino real.

About an hour before dark, and a league before reaching the village of Opocheque, I saw on the left, near the road, a high mound, with an edifice on its top, which at that distance, as seen through the trees, seemed almost entire. It stood in a cornfield. I was not looking out for anything of the kind, and but for the clearing made for the milpa, I could not have seen it at all. I threw the bridle of my horse to the major domo, and made for it, but it was not very easy of access. The field, according to the fashion of the country, was enclosed by a fence, which consisted of all the brush and briers collected on the clearing, six or eight feet high and as many wide, affording a sufficient barrier against wild cattle. In attempting to cross this, I broke through, sinking almost to my neck in the middle, and was considerably torn by thorns before I got over into the milpa.

The mound stood on one side of the milpa, isolated, and of the building upon it, the lower part, to the cornice, was standing. Above the cornice the outer wall had fallen, but the roof remained, and within all was entire. There was no view from the top; beyond the milpa all was forest, and what lay buried in it I had no means of ascertaining. The place was silent and desolate; there was no one of whom I could ask any questions. I never heard of these ruins till I saw them from the back of my horse, and I could never learn by what name they are called.

At half past six we reached the village of Opocheque. In the centre of the plaza was a large fountain, at which women were drawing water, and on one side was a Mestizo family, with two men playing the guitar. We stopped for a cup of water, and then, pushing on by a bright moonlight, at nine o'clock reached the village of Moona, which the reader of my former volumes may remember was the first stage of our journey on leaving Uxmal for home.

Early the next morning we resumed our course. Immediately behind the village we crossed the sierra, the same broken and stony range, commanding on both sides the same grand view of a boundless wooded plain. In an hour we saw at a distance on our left the high mound of ruins visible from the House of the Dwarf, known under the Indian name of Xcoch. About five miles before arriving at Uxmal, I saw on the right another high mound. The intervening space was covered with trees and thorn-bushes, but I reached it without dismounting. On the top were two buildings about eighteen feet each, with the upper part of the outer walls fallen. Of both, the inner part was entire.

At twelve o'clock I reached Uxmal. The extent of my journey had been thirteen leagues, or thirty-nine miles; for though I had varied my route in returning, I had not increased the distance, and I had seen seven different places of ruins, memorials of cities which had been and had passed away, and such memorials as no cities built by the Spaniards in that country would present.

The ruins of Uxmal presented themselves to me as a home, and I looked upon them with more interest than before. I had found the wrecks of cities scattered more numerously than I expected, but they were all so shattered that no voice of instruction issued from them; here they still stood, tottering and crumbling, but living memorials, more worthy than ever of investigation and study, and as I then thought, not knowing what others more distant, of which we had heard, might prove, perhaps the only existing vestiges that could transmit to posterity the image of an American city.

As I approached, I saw on the terrace our beds, with moscheto-nets fluttering in the wind, and trunks and boxes all turned out of doors, having very much the appearance of a forcible ejectment or ouster for non-payment of rent; but on arriving I found that my companions were *moving*. In the great sala, with its three doors, they had found themselves too much exposed to the heavy dews and night air, and they were about removing to a smaller apartment, being that next to the last on the south wing, which had but one door, and could more easily be kept dry by a fire. They were then engaged in cleaning house, and at the moment of my arrival I was called in to consult whether the rooms should undergo another sweeping. After some deliberation, it was decided in the affirmative, and about two bushels more of dirt were carried out, which discouraged us from carrying the process of cleaning any farther.

During my absence an addition had been made to our household in a servant forwarded from Merida by the active kindness of the Doña Joaquina Peon. He was a dark Mestizo named Albino, short and thick, and so near being squint-eyed that at the first glance I thought him a subject for Doctor Cabot to practise on. Bernaldo was still on hand, as also Chaipa Chi, the former under the doctor's instructions, as chef de cuisine, and Chaipa still devoting all her energies to the business in which she shone, the making of tortillas.

In the afternoon we were comfortably settled in our new quarters. We continued the precaution of kindling a fire in one corner, to drive away malaria, and at night we had a bonfire out of doors. The grass and bushes which had been cut down on the terrace, parched and dried by the hot sun, were ready for the fire; the flames lighted up the façade of the great palace, and when they died away, the full moon broke upon it, mellowing its rents and fissures, and presenting a scene mournfully beautiful.

CHAPTER XI

Superintending Indians.—The Storm El Norte.—Arrival of Don Simon.—
Subterraneous Chambers.—Discovery of broken Pottery and a Terra Cotta
Vase.—Great Number of these Chambers.—Their probable Uses.—Harvest
of the Maize Crop.—Practical Views.—System of Agriculture in Yucatan.—
Planting of Corn.—A primitive Threshing Machine.—News from Home.—
More Practice in Surgery.—A rude Bedstead.—A Leg Patient.—An Arm
Patient.—Increasing Sickness on the Hacienda.—Death of an Indian Woman.
—A Campo Santo.—Digging a Grave.—An Indian Funeral.

The next day I resumed my occupation of superintending the Indians. It was, perhaps, the hardest labour I
had in that country to look on and see them work, and it was
necessary to be with them all the time; for if not watched, they
would not work at all.

The next day opened with a drizzling rain, the beginning
of the prevailing storm of the country, called El Norte. This
storm, we were told, rarely occurred at this season, and the
mayoral said that after it was over, the regular dry season would
certainly set in. The thermometer fell to fifty-two, and to our
feelings the change was much for the better. In fact, we had
begun to feel a degree of lassitude, the effect of the excessive
heat, and this change restored and reinvigorated us.

This day, too, with the beginning of the storm, Don Simon
arrived from Jalacho, according to promise, to pay us a visit. He
was not in the habit of visiting Uxmal at this season, and though
less fearful than other members of his family, he was not without apprehensions on account of the health of the place. In
fact, he had suffered much himself from an illness contracted
there. At the hacienda he found the mayoral, who had just returned with me from Jalacho, ill with calentura or fever. This,
with the cold and rain of the Norther, did not tend to restore
his equanimity. We insisted on his becoming our guest, but
agreed to let him off at night on account of the moschetoes. His

visit was a fortunate circumstance for us; his knowledge of localities, and his disposition to forward our views, gave us great facilities in our exploration of the ruins, and at the same time our presence and co-operation induced him to satisfy his own curiosity in regard to some things which had not yet been examined.

Throughout the ruins circular holes were found at different places in the ground, opening into chambers underneath, which had never been examined, and the character of which was entirely unknown. We had noticed them, at the time of our former visit, on the platform of the great terrace; and though this platform was now entirely overgrown, and many of them were hidden from sight, in opening a path to communicate with the hacienda we had laid bare two. The mayoral had lately discovered another at some distance outside the wall, so perfect at the mouth, and apparently so deep on sounding it with a stone, that Don Simon wished to explore it.

The next morning he came to the ruins with Indians, ropes, and candles, and we began immediately with one of those on the platform before the Casa del Gobernador. The opening was a circular hole, eighteen inches in diameter. The throat consisted of five layers of stones, a yard deep, to a stratum of solid rock. As it was all dark beneath, before descending, in order to guard against the effects of impure air, we let down a candle, which soon touched bottom. The only way of descending was to tie a rope around the body, and be lowered by the Indians. In this way I was let down, and almost before my head had passed through the hole my feet touched the top of a heap of rubbish, high directly under the hole, and falling off at the sides. Clambering down it, I found myself in a round chamber, so filled with rubbish that I could not stand upright. With a candle in my hand, I crawled all round on my hands and knees. The chamber was in the shape of a dome, and had been coated with plaster, most of which had fallen, and now encumbered the ground. The depth could not be ascertained without clearing out the interior. In groping about I found pieces of broken pottery, and a vase of terra cotta, about one foot in diameter, of good workmanship, and having upon it a coat of enamel, which, though not worn off, had lost some of its brightness. It had three feet, each about an inch high, one of which is broken. In other respects it was entire.

The discovery of this vase was encouraging. Not one of these places had ever been explored. Neither Don Simon nor any of the Indians knew anything about them, and, entering them now for the first time, we were excited by the hope that we had discovered a rich mine of curious and interesting fabrics wrought by the inhabitants of this ruined city. Besides this, we had already ascertained one point in regard to which we were doubtful before. This great terrace was not entirely artificial. The substratum was of natural rock, and showed that advantage had been taken of a natural elevation, so far as it went, and by this means some portion of the immense labour of constructing the terrace had been saved.

On the same terrace, directly at the foot of the steps, was another opening of the same kind, and, on clearing around, we found near by a circular stone about six inches in thickness, which fitted the hole, and no doubt had served as a cover. This hole was filled up with dirt to within two feet of the mouth, and setting some Indians at work to clear it out, we passed on in search of another.

Descending the terrace, and passing behind the high and nameless mound which towers between the Casa del Gobernador and Casa de Palomos, the Indians cleared away some bushes, and brought us to another opening, but a few feet from the path we had cut through, entirely hidden from view until the clearing was made. The mouth was similar to that of the first; the throat about a yard deep, and the Indians lowered me down, without any obstruction, to the bottom.

The Indians looked upon our entering these places as senseless and foolhardy, and, besides imaginary dangers, they talked of snakes, scorpions, and hornets, the last of which, from the experience we had had of them in different parts of the ruins, were really objects of fear; for a swarm of them coming upon a man in such a place, would almost murder him before he could be hauled out.

It did not, however, require much time to explore this vault. It was clear of rubbish, perfect and entire in all its parts, without any symptoms of decay, and to all appearances, after the lapse of unknown years, fit for the uses to which it was originally applied. Like the one on the terrace, it was dome-shaped, and the sides fell in a little toward the bottom, like a well-made haystack. The height was ten feet and six inches directly under the mouth, and it was seventeen feet six inches in diameter. The walls and ceiling were plastered, still in a good state of preservation, and the floor was of hard mortar. Don Simon and Dr. Cabot were lowered down, and we examined every part thoroughly.

Leaving this, we went on to a third, which was exactly the same, except that it was a little smaller, being only five yards in diameter.

The fourth was the one which had just been discovered, and which had excited the curiosity of the mayoral. It was a few feet outside of a wall which, as Don Simon said, might be traced through the woods, broken and ruined, until it met and enclosed within its circle the whole of the principal buildings. The mouth was covered with cement, and in the throat was a large stone filling it up, which the mayoral, on discovering it, had thrown in to prevent horses or cattle from falling through. A rope was passed under the stone, and it was hauled out. The throat was smaller than any of the others, and hardly large enough to pass the body of a man. In shape and finish it was exactly the same as the others, with perhaps a slight shade of difference in the dimensions. The smallness of this mouth was, to my mind, strong proof that these subterraneous chambers had never been intended for any purposes which required men to descend into them. I was really at a loss how to get out. The Indians had no mechanical help of any kind, but were obliged to stand over the hole and hoist by dead pull, making, as I had found before, a jerking, irregular movement. The throat was so small that there was no play for the arms, to enable me to raise myself up by the rope, and the stones around the mouth were insecure and tottering. I was obliged to trust to them, and they involuntarily knocked my head against the stones, let down upon me a shower of dirt, and gave me such a severe rasping that I had no disposition at that time to descend another. In fact, they too were tired out, and it was a business in which, on our own account at least, it would not do to overtask them.

We were extremely disappointed in not finding any more vases or relics of any kind. We could not account for the one found in the chamber under the terrace, and were obliged to suppose that it had been thrown in or got there by accident.

These subterraneous chambers are scattered over the whole ground covered by the ruined city. There was one in the cattle-yard before the hacienda, and the Indians were constantly discovering them at greater distances. Dr. Cabot found them continually in his hunting excursions, and once, in breaking through bushes in search of a bird, fell into one, and narrowly escaped a serious injury; indeed, there were so many of them, and in places where they were so little to be expected, that they made rambling out of the cleared paths dangerous, and to the last day of our visit we were constantly finding new ones.

That they were constructed for some specific purpose, had some definite object, and that that object was uniform, there was no doubt, but what it was, in our ignorance of the habits of the people, it was difficult to say. Don Simon thought that the cement was not hard enough to hold water, and hence that they were not intended as cisterns or reservoirs, but for granaries or store-houses of maize, which, from our earliest knowledge of the aborigines down to the present day, has been the staff of life to the inhabitants. In this opinion, however, we did not concur, and from what we saw afterward, believe that they were intended as cisterns, and had furnished, in part at least, a supply of water to the people of the ruined city.

We returned to our apartments to dine, and in the afternoon accompanied Don Simon to see the harvest of the maize crop. The great field in front of the Casa del Gobernador was planted with corn, and on the way we learned a fact which may be interesting to agriculturists in the neighbourhood of those numerous cities throughout our country which, being of premature growth, are destined to become ruins. The debris of ruined cities fertilize and enrich land. Don Simon told us that the ground about Uxmal was excellent for milpas or corn-fields. He had never had a better crop of maize than that of the last year; indeed, it was so good that he had planted a part of the same land a second time, which is a thing unprecedented under their system of agriculture; and Don Simon had another practical view of the value of these ruins, which would have done for the meridian of our own city. Pointing to the great buildings, he said that if he had Uxmal on the banks of the Mississippi, it would be an immense fortune, for there was stone enough to pave every street in New-Orleans, without sending to the North for it, as it was necessary to do; but, not to be outdone in sensible views of things, we suggested that if he had it on the banks of the Mississippi, easy of access, preserved from the rank vegetation which is now hurrying it to destruction, it would stand like Herculaneum and Pompeii, a place of pilgrimage for the curious; and that it would be a much better operation to put a fence around it and charge for admission, than to sell the stone for paving streets.

By this time we had reached the foot of the terrace, and a few steps brought us into the corn-field. The system of agriculture in Yucatan is rather primitive. Besides hemp and sugar, which the Indians seldom attempt to raise on their own account, the principal products of the country are corn, beans, and calabazas, like our pumpkins and squashes, camotes, which are perhaps the parent of our Carolina potatoes, and chili or pepper, of which last an inordinate quantity is consumed, both by the Indians and Spaniards. Indian corn, however, is the great staple, and the cultivation of this probably differs but little now from the system followed by the Indians before the conquest. In the dry season, generally in the months of January and February, a place is selected in the woods, from which the trees are cut down and burned. In May or June the corn is planted. This is done by making little holes in the ground with a pointed stick, putting in a few grains of corn and covering them over. Once in the ground, it is left to take care of itself, and if it will not grow, it is considered that the land is not worth having. The corn has a fair start with the weeds, and they keep pace amicably together. The hoe, plough, and harrow are entirely unknown; indeed, in general neither of the last two could be used, on account of the stony face of the country: the machete is the only instrument employed.

The milpa around the ruins of Uxmal had been more than usually neglected; the crop turned out badly, but such as it was, the Indians from three of Don Simon's adjoining haciendas, according to their obligation to the master, were engaged in getting it in. They were distributed in different parts of the field; and of those we came upon first, I counted a small group of fifty-three. As we drew near, all stopped working, approached Don Simon, bowed respectfully to him, and then to us as his friends. The corn had been gathered, and these men were engaged in threshing it out. A space was cleared of about a hundred feet square, and along the border of it was a line of small hammocks hanging on stakes fixed in the ground, in which the Indians slept during the whole time of the harvest, each with a little fire underneath to warm him in the cool night air, and drive away the moschetoes.

Don Simon threw himself into one of the hammocks, and held out one of his legs, which was covered with burrs and briers. These men were free and independent electors of the State of Yucatan; but one of them took in his hand Don Simon's foot, picked off the burrs, pulled off the shoe, cleaned the stocking, and restoring the shoe, laid the foot back carefully in the hammock, and then took up the other. It was all done as a matter of course, and no one bestowed a thought upon it except ourselves.

On one side of the clearing was a great pile or small mountain of corn in the ear, ready to be threshed, and near by was the threshing machine, which certainly could not be considered an infringement of any Yankee patent right. It was a rude scaffold about eighteen or twenty feet square, made of four untrimmed upright posts for corners, with poles lashed to them horizontally three or four feet from the ground, and across these was a layer of sticks, about an inch thick, side by side; the whole might have served as a rude model of the first bedstead ever made.

The parallel sticks served as a threshing floor, on which was spread a thick layer of corn. On each side a rude ladder of two or three rounds rested against the floor, and on each of these ladders stood a nearly naked Indian, with a long pole in his hand, beating the corn. The grains fell through, and at each corner under the floor was a man with a brush made of bushes, sweeping off the cobs. The shelled corn was afterward taken up in baskets and carried to the hacienda. The whole process would have surprised a Genesee farmer; but perhaps, where labour was so little costly, it answered as well as the best threshing machine that could be invented.

The next day we had another welcome visiter in our fellow-passenger, Mr. Camerden, who was just from Campeachy, where he had seen New-York papers to the third of November. Knowing our deep interest in the affairs of our country, and postponing his own curiosity about the ruins, he hastened to communicate to us the result of the city elections, viz., a contest in the sixth ward and entire uncertainty which party was uppermost.

Unfortunately, Mr. Camerden, not being in very good health at the time, was also infected with apprehensions about Uxmal, and as El Norte still continued, the coldness and rain made him uneasy in a place of such bad reputation. Having no ill feelings against him and no spare moscheto-net, we did not ask him to remain at night, and he accompanied Don Simon to the hacienda to sleep.

The next day Doctor Cabot had a professional engagement at the hacienda. In both my expeditions into that region of country our medical department was incomplete. On the former occasion we had a medicine-chest, but no doctor, and this time we had a doctor, but no medicine-chest. This necessary appendage had been accidentally left on board the ship, and did not come to our hands till some time afterward. We had only a small stock purchased in Merida, and on this account, as well as because it interfered with his other pursuits, the doctor had avoided entering into general practice. He was willing to attend to cases that might be cured by a single operation, but the principle diseases were fevers, which could not be cut out with a knife. The day before, however, a young Indian came to the ruins on an errand to Don Simon, who had a leg swollen with varicose veins. He had a mild expression, meek and submissive manners, and was what Don Simon called, in speaking of his best servants, muy docil, or very docile. He stood at that time in an interesting position, being about to be married. Don Simon had had him at Merida six months, under the care of a physician, but without any good result, and the young man was taking his chance for better or worse, almost with the certainty of becoming in a few years disabled, and a mass of corruption. Doctor Cabot undertook to perform an operation, for which purpose it was necessary to go to the hacienda; and, that we might return with Mr. Camerden, we all went there to breakfast.

Under the corridor was an old Indian leaning against a pillar, with his arms folded across his breast, and before him a row of little Indian girls, all, too, with arms folded, to whom he was teaching the formal part of the church service, giving out a few words, which they all repeated after him. As we entered the corridor, he came up to us, bowed, and kissed our hands, and all the little girls did the same.

Don Simon had breakfast ready for us, but we found some deficiencies. The haciendas of that country never have any surplus furniture, being only visited by the master once or twice a year, and then only for a few days, when he brings with him whatever he requires for his personal comfort. Uxmal was like the rest, and at that moment it was worse off, for we had stripped it of almost every movable to enlarge our accommodations at the ruins. Our greatest difficulty was about seats. All contrived to be provided for, however, except Don Simon, who finally, as it was an extreme case, went into the church and brought out the great confessional chair.

Breakfast over, the doctor's patient was brought forward. He was not consulted on the subject of the operation, and had no wish of his own about it, but did as his master ordered him. At the moment of beginning, Doctor Cabot asked for a bed. He had not thought of asking for it before, supposing it would be ready at a moment's notice; but he might almost as well have asked for a steamboat or a locomotive engine. Who ever thought of wanting a bed at Uxmal? was the general feeling of the Indians. They were all born in hammocks, and expected to die in them, and who wanted a bed when he could get a hammock? A bed, however (which means a bedstead), was indispensable, and the Indians dispersed in search, returning, after a long absence, with tidings that they had heard of one on the hacienda, but it had been taken apart, and the pieces were in use for other purposes. They were sent off again, and at length we received notice that the bed was coming, and presently it appeared advancing through the gate of the cattle-yard in the shape of a bundle of poles on the shoulder of an Indian. For purposes of immediate use, they might as well have been on the tree that produced them, but, after a while, they were put together, and made a bedstead that would have astonished a city cabinet-maker.

In the mean time the patient was looking on, perhaps with somewhat the feeling of a man superintending the making of his own coffin. The disease was in his right leg, which was almost as thick as his body, covered with ulcers, and the distended veins stood out like whipcords. Doctor Cabot considered it necessary to cut two veins. The Indian stood up, resting the whole weight of his body on the diseased leg, so as to bring them out to the fullest, and supporting himself by leaning with his hands on a bench. One vein was cut, the wound bound up, and then the operation was performed on the other by thrusting a stout pin into the flesh under the vein, and bringing it out on the other side, then winding a thread round the protruding head and point, and leaving the pin to cut its way through the vein and fester out. The leg was then bound tight, and the Indian laid upon the bed. During the whole time not a muscle of his face moved, and, except at the moment when the pin was thrust under the vein, when his hand contracted on the bench, it could not have been told that he was undergoing an operation of any kind.

This over, we set out on our return with Mr. Camerden to the ruins, but hardly left the gate of the cattle-yard, when we met an Indian with his arm in a sling, coming in search of Doctor Cabot. A death-warrant seemed written in his face. His little wife, a girl about fourteen years old, soon to become a mother, was trotting beside him, and his case showed how, in those countries, human life is the sport of accident and ignorance. A few days before, by some awkwardness, he had given his left arm a severe cut near the elbow with a machete. To stop the bleeding, his wife had tied one string as tightly as possible around the wrist, and another in the hollow of the arm, and so it had remained three days. The treatment had been pretty effectual in stopping the bleeding, and it had very nearly stopped the circulation of his blood forever. The hand was shrunken to nothing, and seemed withered; the part of the arm between the two ligatures was swollen enormously, and the seat of the wound was a mass of corruption. Doctor Cabot took off the fastenings, and endeavoured to teach her to restore the circulation by friction, or rubbing the arm with the palm of the hand, but she had no more idea of the circulation of the blood than of the revolution of the planets.

The wound, on being probed, gave out a foul and pestilential discharge, and, when that was cleared away, out poured a stream of arterial blood. The man had cut an arterial vein. Doctor Cabot had no instruments with him with which to take it up, and, grasping the arm with a strong pressure on the vein, so as to stop the flow of blood, he transferred the arm to me, fixing my fingers upon the vein, and requesting me to hold it in that position while he ran to the ruins for his instruments. This was by no means pleasant. If I lost the right pressure, the man might bleed to death; and, having no regular diploma warranting people to die on my hands, not willing to run the risk of any accident, and knowing the imperturbable character of the Indians, I got the arm transferred to one of them, with a warning that the man's life depended upon him. Doctor Cabot was gone more than half an hour, and during all that time, while the patient's head was falling on his shoulder with fainting fits, the Indian looked directly in his face, and held up the arm with a fixedness of attitude that would have served as a model for a sculptor. I do not believe that, for a single moment, the position of the arm varied a hair's breadth.

Doctor Cabot dressed the wound, and the Indian was sent away, with an even chance, as the doctor considered, for life or death. The next that we heard of him, however, he was at work in the fields; certainly, but for the accidental visit of Doctor Cabot, he would have been in his grave.

After this there were some delicate cases among the women of the hacienda; and these multifarious occupations consumed the whole of the morning, which we had intended to devote to Mr. Camerden and the ruins. It was a cold and cheerless day; the

Norther was increasing in force, and he saw malaria and sickness all around him. In the afternoon he left us to return to New-York by the same vessel which had brought us out. Unfortunately, he carried away with him the seeds of a dangerous illness, from which he did not recover in many months.

The next day Don Simon left us, and we were again alone. Sickness was increasing on the hacienda, and two days afterward we received notice that Doctor Cabot's leg patient was ill with fever, and also that a woman had died that day of the same disease, and was to be buried the next morning. We ordered horses to be sent up to the ruins, and early in the morning Dr. Cabot and myself rode to the hacienda, he to visit his patient, and I to attend the funeral, in the expectation that such an event, on a retired hacienda, without any priest or religious cere-monies, would disclose some usage or custom illustrative of the ancient Indian character. Leaving my horse in the cattle-yard, in company with the mayoral I walked to the campo santo. This was a clearing in the woods at a short distance from the house, square, and enclosed by a rude stone fence. It had been conse-crated with the ceremonies of the church, and was intended as a burial-place for all who died on the estate; a rude place, befitting the rude and simple people for whom it was designed. When we entered we saw a grave half dug, which had been abandoned on account of the stones, and some Indians were then occupied in digging another.

Only one part of the cemetery had been used as a burial-place, and this was indicated by little wooden crosses, one planted at the head of each grave. In this part of the cemetery was a stone enclosure about four feet high, and the same in diameter, which was intended as a sort of charnel-house, and was then filled with skulls and bones, whitening in the sun. I moved to this place, and began examining the skulls.

The Indians, in digging the grave, used a crowbar and ma-chete, and scooped out the loose earth with their hands. As the work proceeded, I heard the crowbar enter something with a cracking, tearing sound: it had passed through a human skull. One of the Indians dug it out with his hands, and, after they had all examined and commented upon it, handed it to the may-oral, who gave it to me. They all knew whose skull it was. It was that of a woman who had been born and brought up, and who had died among them, and whom they had buried only the last dry season, but little more than a year before. The skull was laid upon the pile, and the Indians picked out the arms and legs, and all the smaller bones. Below the ribs, from the back downward, the flesh had not decayed, but dried up and adhered to the bones, which, all hanging together, they lifted out and laid upon the pile. All this was done decently and with respect.

As I stood by the enclosure of bones, I took up different skulls, and found that they were all known and identified. The campo santo had been opened but about five years, and every skull had once sat upon the shoulders of an acquaintance.

The graves were all on one side, and on the other no dead had been buried. I suggested to the mayoral, that by beginning on the farther side, and burying in order, every corpse would have time to decay and become dust before its place was wanted for another, which he seemed to think a good idea, and communicated it to the Indians, who stopped their work, looked at him and at me, and then went on digging. I added, that in a few years the bones of the friend they were about burying, and his own, and those of all the rest of them, would be pulled and handled like those on the pile, which, also, he communicated to them, and with the same effect. In the mean time I had overhauled the skulls, and placed on the top two which I ascertained to be those of full-blooded Indians, intending to appropriate and carry them off at the first convenient opportunity.

The Indians worked as slowly as if each was digging his own grave, and at length the husband of the deceased came out, apparently to hurry them. He was bare-headed, had long black hair hanging down over his eyes, and, dressed in a clean blue flannel shirt, he seemed what he really was, one of the most respectable men on the hacienda. Sitting down by the side of the grave, he took two sticks which were there for that purpose, with one of which he measured the length, and with the other the breadth. This, to say the least of it, was cool, and the expression of his face was of that stolid and unbending kind, that no idea could be formed of his feelings; but it was not too much to suppose that a man in the early prime of life, who had fulfilled well all the duties of his station, must feel some emotion in measuring the grave of one who had been his companion when the labours of the day were over, and who was the mother of his children.

The grave was not large enough, and he took his seat at the foot, and waited while the Indians enlarged it, from time to time suggesting an improvement. In the mean time Doctor Cabot arrived on the ground with his gun, and one of the gravediggers pointed out a flock of parrots flying over. They were too

far off to kill, but as the Indians were always astonished at seeing a shot on the wing, and all seemed anxious to have him
shoot, he fired, and knocked out some feathers. The Indians
laughed, watched the feathers as they fell into the graveyard,
and then resumed their work. At length the husband again took
the sticks, measured the grave, and finding all right, returned to
the house. The Indians picked up a rude barrow made of two
long poles with crosspieces, which had been thrown down by the
side of the last corpse it had carried, and went off for the dead
body. They were gone so long that we thought they wished to
wear out our patience, and told the mayoral to go and hurry
them; but presently we heard a shuffling of feet, and the sound
of female voices, heralding a tumultuous procession of women.
On reaching the fence of the cemetery they all stopped, and, seeing us, would not come in, except one old Beelzebub, who
climbed over, walked directly to the foot of the grave, leaned
down, and, looking into it, made some exclamation which set
all the women outside laughing. This so incensed the old woman
that she picked up a handful of stones, and began pelting them
right and left, at which they all scattered with great confusion
and laughter, and in the midst of this, the corpse, attended by
an irregular crowd of men, women, and children, made its
appearance.

The barrow was lifted over the fence and laid down beside
the grave. The body had no coffin, but was wrapped from head
to foot in a blue cotton shawl with a yellow border. The head
was uncovered, and the feet stuck out, and had on a pair of
leather shoes and white cotton stockings, probably a present
from her husband on his return from some visit to Merida,
which the poor woman had never worn in life, and which he
thought he was doing her honour by placing in her grave.

The Indians passed ropes under the body; the husband himself supported the head, and so it was lowered into the grave.
The figure was tall, and the face was that of a woman about
twenty-three or twenty-four years old. The expression was painful, indicating that in the final struggle the spirit had been reluctant to leave its mortal tenement. There was but one present
who shed tears, and that was the old mother of the deceased,
who doubtless had expected this daughter to lay her own head
in the grave. She held by the hand a bright-eyed girl, who looked
on with wonder, happily unconscious that her best friend on
earth was to be laid under the sod. The shawl was opened, and
showed a white cotton dress under it; the arms, which were

folded across the breast for the convenience of carrying the body, were laid down by the sides, and the shawl was again wrapped round. The husband himself arranged the head, placed under it a cotton cloth for a pillow, and composed it for its final rest as carefully as if a pebble or a stone could hurt it. He brushed a handful of earth over the face; the Indians filled up the grave, and all went away. No romance hangs over such a burial scene, but it was not unnatural to follow in imagination the widowed Indian to his desolate hut.

We had been disappointed in not seeing any relic of Indian customs, and, as it was now eleven o'clock and we had not breakfasted, we did not consider ourselves particularly indemnified for our trouble.

CHAPTER XII

In the account of my former visit to the ruins of Uxmal, I mentioned the fact that this city was entirely destitute of apparent means for obtaining water. Within the whole circumference there is no well, stream, or fountain, and nothing which bears the appearance of having been used for supplying or obtaining water, except the subterraneous chambers before referred to; which, supposing them to have been intended for that purpose, would probably not have been sufficient, however numerous, to supply the wants of so large a population.

All the water required for our own use we were obliged to procure from the hacienda. We felt the inconvenience of this during the whole of our residence at the ruins, and very often, in spite of all our care to keep a supply on hand, we came in, after hard work in the sun, and, parched with thirst, were obliged to wait till we could send an Indian to the hacienda, a distance, going and returning, of three miles.

Very soon after our arrival our attention and inquiries were directed particularly to this subject, and we were not long in satisfying ourselves that the principal supply had been drawn from aguadas, or ponds, in the neighbourhood. These aguadas are now neglected and overgrown, and perhaps, to a certain extent, are the cause of the unhealthiness of Uxmal. The principal of them we saw first from the top of the House of the Dwarf,

Fig. 11

bearing west, and perhaps a mile and a half distant. We visited it under the guidance of the mayoral, with some Indians to clear the way. The whole intervening space was overgrown with woods, the ground was low and muddy, and, as the rains still continued, the aguada was at that time a fine sheet of water. It was completely imbosomed among trees, still and desolate, with tracks of deer on its banks; a few ducks were swimming on its surface, and a kingfisher was sitting on the bough of an over-hanging tree, watching for his prey. The mayoral told us that this aguada was connected with another more to the south, and that they continued, one after the other, to a great distance; to use his own expression, which, however, I did not understand literally, there were a hundred of them.

The general opinion with regard to these aguadas is the same with that expressed by the cura of Tekoh respecting that near Mayapan; viz., that they were "hechas á mano," artificial formations or excavations made by the ancient inhabitants as reservoirs for holding water. The mayoral told us that in the dry season, when the water was low, the remains of stone embankments were still visible in several places. As yet we were incredulous as to their being at all artificial, but we had no

difficulty in believing that they had furnished the inhabitants
of Uxmal with water. The distance, from what will be seen hereafter, in that dry and destitute country amounts to but little.

At the time of our first visit to it, however, this aguada
had in our eyes a more direct and personal interest. From
the difficulty of procuring water at the ruins, we were obliged
to economize in the use of it, while, from the excessive heat
and toil of working among the ruins, covered with dust and
scratched with briers, there was nothing we longed for so
much as the refreshment of a bath, and it was no unimportant
part of our business at the aguada to examine whether it would
answer as a bathing-place. The result was more satisfactory than
we expected. The place was actually inviting. We selected a
little cove shaded by a large tree growing almost out of the
water, had a convenient space cleared around it, a good path
cut all the way through the woods to the terrace of the Casa del
Gobernador, and on the first of December we consecrated it by
our first bath. The mayoral, shrunken and shattered by fever
and ague, stood by protesting against it, and warning us of the
consequences; but we had attained the only thing necessary for
our comfort at Uxmal, and in the height of our satisfaction had
no apprehensions for the result.

Up to this time our manner of living at the ruins had been
very uniform, and our means abundant. All that was on the
hacienda belonging to the master was ours, as were also the
services of the Indians, so far as he had a right to command
them. The property of the master consisted of cattle, horses,
mules, and corn, of which only the last could be counted as provisions. Some of the Indians had a few fowls, pigs, and turkeys
of their own, which they were in general willing to sell, and
every morning those who came out to work brought with them
water, fowls, eggs, lard, green beans, and milk. Occasionally we
had a haunch of venison, and Doctor Cabot added to our larder
several kinds of ducks, wild turkeys, chachalachas, quails, pigeons, doves, parrots, jays, and other smaller birds. Besides these,
we received from time to time a present from the Doña Joaquina
or Don Simon, and altogether our living was better than we had
ever known in exploring ruins. Latterly, however, on account of
the thickness of the woods, Doctor Cabot had become disgusted
with sporting; having no dog, it was sometimes impossible to
find one bird out of six, and he confined his shooting to birds
which he wanted for dissection. At this time, too, we received

intelligence that the fowls at the hacienda were running short, and the eggs gave out altogether.

There was no time to be lost, and we forthwith despatched Albino with an Indian to the village of Moona, twelve miles distant, who returned with a back-load of eggs, beans, rice, and sugar, and again the sun went down upon us in the midst of plenty. A pig arrived from Don Simon, sent from another hacienda, the cooking of which enlisted the warmest sympathies of all our heads of departments, Albino, Bernaldo, and Chaipa Chi. They had their own way of doing it, national, and derived from their forefathers, being the same way in which those respectable people cooked men and women, as Bernal Dias says, "dressing the bodies in their manner, which is by a sort of oven made with heated stones, which are put under ground." They made an excavation on the terrace, kindled a large fire in it, and kept it burning until the pit was heated like an oven. Two clean stones were laid in the bottom, the pig (not alive) was laid upon them, and covered over with leaves and bushes, packed down with stones so close as barely to leave vent to the fire, and allow an escape for the smoke.

While this bake was going on I set out on a business close at hand, but which, in the pressure of other matters, I had postponed from day to day. On a line with the back of the Casa del Gobernador rises the high and nameless mound represented in the frontispiece, forming one of the grandest and most imposing structures among all the ruins of Uxmal. It was at that time covered with trees and a thick growth of herbage, which gave a gloominess to its grandeur of proportions, and, but for its regularity, and a single belt of sculptured stones barely visible at the top, it would have passed for a wooded and grass-grown hill. Taking some Indians with me, I ascended this mound, and began clearing it for Mr. Catherwood to draw. I found that its vast sides were all incased with stone, in some places richly ornamented, but completely hidden from view by the foliage.

The height of this mound was sixty-five feet, and it measured at the base three hundred feet on one side and two hundred on the other. On the top was a great platform of solid stone, three feet high and seventy-five feet square, and about fifteen feet from the top was a narrow terrace running on all four of the sides. The walls of the platform were of smooth stone, and the corners had sculptured ornaments. The area consisted entirely of loose rough stones, and there are no remains or other indications of any building. The great structure seemed raised only for the purpose of holding aloft this platform. Probably it had been the scene of grand religious ceremonies, and stained with the blood of human victims offered up in sight of the assembled people. Near as it was, it was the first time I had ascended this mound. It commanded a full view of every building. The day was overcast, the wind swept mournfully over the desolate city, and since my arrival I had not felt so deeply the solemnity and sublimity of these mysterious ruins.

Around the top of the mound was a border of sculptured stone ten or twelve feet high. The principal ornament was the Grecque, and in following it round, and clearing away the trees and bushes, on the west side, opposite the courtyard of the Casa de Palomos, my attention was arrested by an ornament, the lower part of which was buried in rubbish fallen from above. It was about the centre of this side of the mound, and from its position, and the character of the ornament, I was immediately impressed with the idea that it was over a doorway, and that underneath was an entrance to an apartment in the mound. The Indians had cleared beyond it, and passed on, but I called them back, and set them to excavating the earth and rubbish that buried the lower part of the ornament. It was an awkward place to work in: the side of the mound was steep, and the stones composing the ornament were insecure and tottering. The Indians, as usual, worked as if they had their lifetime for the job. They were at all times tedious and trying, but now, to my impatient eagerness, more painfully so than ever. Urging them, as well as I could, and actually making them comprehend my idea, I got them to work four long hours without any intermission, until they reached the cornice. The ornament proved to be the same hideous face, with the teeth standing out, before presented, varying somewhat in detail, and upon a grander scale. Throwing up the dirt upon the other side of them, the Indians had made a great pile outside, and stood in a deep hole against the face of the ornament. At this depth the stones seemed hanging loosely over their heads, and the Indians intimated that it was dangerous to continue digging, but by this time my impatience was beyond control. I had from time to time assisted in the work, and, urging them to continue, I threw myself into the hole, and commenced digging with all my strength. The stones went rolling and crashing down the side of the mound, striking against roots and tearing off branches. The perspiration rolled from me in a stream, but I was so completely carried away by the idea that had taken possession of me, so sure of entering some chamber that had been closed for ages, that I stopped at nothing; and with all this I considered myself cool and calm, and with great method resolved, as soon as I reached the doorway, to stop and send for Mr. Catherwood and Doctor Cabot, that we might all enter together, and make a formal note of everything exactly as it was found; but I was doomed to a worse disappointment than at El Laberinto de Maxcanú. Before getting below the cornice I thrust the machete through the earth, and found no opening, but a solid stone wall. The ground of my hope was gone, but still I kept the Indians digging, unconsciously, and without any object. In the interest of the moment I was not aware that the clouds had disappeared, and that I had been working in this deep hole, without a breath of air, under the full blaze of a vertical sun. The disappointment and reaction after the high excitement, co-operating with the fatigue and heat, prostrated all my strength. I felt a heaviness and depression, and was actually sick at heart, so that, calling off the Indians, I was fain to give over and return to our quarters. In descending the mound my limbs could scarcely support me. My strength and elasticity were gone. With great difficulty I dragged myself to our apartments. My thirst was unquenchable. I threw myself into my hammock, and in a few moments a fiery fever was upon me. Our household was thrown into consternation. Disease had stalked all around us, but it was the first time it had knocked at our door.

On the third day, while in the midst of a violent attack, a gentleman arrived whose visit I had expected, and had looked forward to with great interest. It was the cura Carillo of Ticul, a village seven leagues distant. A week after our arrival at the ruins, the mayoral had received a letter from him, asking whether a visit would be acceptable to us. We had heard of him as a person who took more interest in the antiquities of the country than almost any other, and who possessed more knowledge on the subject. He had been in the habit of coming to Uxmal alone to wander among the ruins, and we had contemplated an excusion to Ticul on purpose to make his acquaintance. We were, therefore, most happy to receive his overture, and advised him that we should anxiously expect his visit. His first words to me were, that it was necessary for me to leave the place and go with him to Ticul. I was extremely reluctant to do so, but it was considered advisable by all. He would not consent to my going alone, or with his servant, and the next morning, instead of a pleasant visit to the ruins, he found himself trotting

home with a sick man at his heels. In consequence of some mis-
understanding, no coché was in readiness, and I set out on
horseback. It was my interval day, and at the moment the bare
absence of pain was a positively pleasant sensation. In this
humour, in the beginning of our ride, I listened with much interest to the cura's exposition of different points and localities,
but by degrees my attention flagged, and finally my whole soul
was fixed on the sierra, which stood out before us at a distance
of two leagues from San José. Twice before I had crossed that
sierra, and had looked upon it almost with delight, as relieving
the monotony of constant plains, but now it was a horrible
prospect. My pains increased as we advanced, and I dismounted
at the hacienda in a state impossible to be described. The
mayoral was away, the doors were all locked, and I lay down
on some bags in the corridor. Rest tranquillized me. There was
but one Indian to be found, and he told the cura that there
were none to make a coché. Those in the neighbourhood were
sick, and the others were at work more than a league away. It
was impossible to continue on horseback, and, fortunately, the
mayoral came, who changed the whole face of things and in a
few minutes had men engaged in making a coché. The cura
went on before to prepare for my reception. In an hour my
coché was ready, and at five o'clock I crawled in. My carriers
were loth to start, but, once under way, they took it in good part,
and set off on a trot. Changing shoulders frequently, they never
stopped till they carried me into Ticul, three leagues or nine
miles distant, and laid me down on the floor of the convent. The
cura was waiting to receive me. Albino had arrived with my
catre, which was already set up, and in a few minutes I was in
bed. The bells were ringing for a village fiesta, rockets and fireworks were whizzing and exploding, and from a distance the
shrill voice of a boy screeching out the numbers of the loteria
pierced my ears. The sounds were murderous, but the kindness of the cura, and the satisfaction of being away from an
infected atmosphere, were so grateful that I fell asleep.

For three days I did not leave my bed; but on the fourth I
breathed the air from the balcony of the convent. It was fresh,
pure, balmy, and invigorating.

In the afternoon of the next day I set out with the cura
for a stroll. We had gone but a short distance, when an Indian
came running after us to inform us that another of the cabal-
leros had arrived sick from the ruins. We hurried back, and
found Doctor Cabot lying in a coché on the floor of the corridor

at the door of the convent. He crawled out labouring under a violent fever, increased by the motion and fatigue of his ride, and I was startled by the extraordinary change a few days had made in his appearance. His face was flushed, his eyes were wild, his figure lank; and he had not strength to support himself, but pitched against me, who could barely keep myself up, and both nearly came down together. He had been attacked the day after I left, and the fever had been upon him, with but little intermission, ever since. All night, and all the two ensuing days, it continued rising and decreasing, but never leaving him. It was attended with constant restlessness and delirium, so that he was hardly in bed before he was up again, pitching about the room.

The next day Mr. Catherwood forwarded Albino, who, with two attacks, was shaken and sweated into a dingy-looking white man. Mr. Catherwood wrote that he was entirely alone at the ruins, and should hold out as long as he could against fever and ghosts, but with the first attack should come up and join us.

Our situation and prospects were now gloomy. If Mr. Catherwood was taken ill, work was at an end, and perhaps the whole object of our expedition frustrated; but the poor cura was more to be pitied than any of us. His unlucky visit to Uxmal had brought upon him three infermos, with the prospect every day of a fourth. His convent was turned into a hospital; but the more claims we made upon him, the more he exerted himself to serve us. I could not but smile, when speaking to Doctor Cabot of his kindness, as the latter, rolling and tossing with fever, replied, that if the cura had any squint-eyed friends, he could cure them.

The cura watched the doctor carefully, but without venturing to offer advice to a medico who could cure biscos, but the third day he alarmed me by the remark that the expression of the doctor's face was *fatál*. In Spanish this only means very bad, but it had always in my ears an uncomfortable sound. The cura added that there were certain indices of this disease which were mortal, but, happily, these had not yet exhibited themselves in the doctor. The bare suggestion, however, alarmed me. I inquired of the cura about the mode of treatment in the country, and whether he could not prescribe for him. Doctor Cabot had never seen anything of this disease, particularly as affected by climate. Besides, he was *hors de combat* on account of the absence of our medicine-chest, and in such constant pain and delirium that he was in no condition to prescribe for himself.

The cura was the temporal as well as spiritual physician of the village; there were daily applications to him for medicine, and he was constantly visiting the sick. Doctor Cabot was willing to put himself entirely into his hands, and he administered a preparation which I mention for the benefit of future travellers who may be caught without a medicine-chest. It was a simple decoction of the rind of the sour orange flavoured with cinnamon and lemon-juice, of which he administered a tumblerful warm every two hours. At the second draught the doctor was thrown into a profuse perspiration. For the first time since his attack the fever left him, and he had an unbroken sleep. On waking, copious draughts of tamarind water were given; when the fever came on again the decoction was repeated, with tamarind water in the intervals. The effect of this treatment was particularly happy, and it is desirable for strangers to know it, for the sour orange is found in every part of the country, and from what we saw of it then and afterward, it is, perhaps, a better remedy for fever in that climate than any known in foreign pharmacy.

The village of Ticul, to which we were thus accidentally driven, was worthy of the visit, once in his life, of a citizen of New-York. The first time I looked upon it from the balcony of the convent, it struck me as the perfect picture of stillness and repose. The plaza was overgrown with grass; a few mules, with their fore feet hoppled, were pasturing upon it, and at long intervals a single horseman crossed it. The balcony of the convent was on a level with the tops of the houses, and the view was of a great plain, with houses of one story, flat roofs, high garden walls, above which orange, lemon, and plantain trees were growing, and, after the loud ringing of the matin and vesper bell was over, the only noise was the singing of birds. All business or visiting was done early in the morning or toward evening; and through the rest of the day, during the heat, the inhabitants were within doors, and it might almost have passed for a deserted village.

Like all the Spanish villages, it was laid out with its plaza and streets running at right angles, and was distinguished among the villages of Yucatan for its casas de piedra, or stone houses. These were on the plaza and streets adjoining; and back, extending more than a mile each way, were the huts of the Indians. These huts were generally plastered, enclosed by stone fences, and imbowered among trees, or, rather, overgrown and concealed by weeds. The population was about five thousand, of which about three hundred families were vecinos, or white people, and the rest Indians. Fresh meat can be procured every day; the tienda grande, or large store of Guzman, would not disgrace Merida. The bread is better than at the capital. Altogether, for appearance, society, and conveniences of living, it is perhaps the best village in Yucatan, and famous for its bull-fights and the beauty of its Mestiza women.

The church and convent occupy the whole of one side of the plaza. Both were built by the Franciscan monks, and they are among the grandest of those gigantic buildings with which that powerful order marked its entrance into the country. They stand on a stone platform about four feet high and several hundred feet in front. The church was large and sombre, and adorned with rude monuments and figures calculated to inspire the Indians with reverence and awe. In one place, in a niche in the wall, was a funeral urn, painted black, with a white streak around the top, which contains the ashes of a lady of the village. Under it was a monument with this inscription:

¡Hombres!
He aqui el termino de nuestros afanes;
La muerte, tierra, nada.

En esta urna reposan los restos de Dña Loretta Lara,
Muger caritativa, y esposa fiel, madre tierna,
prudente y virtuosa.

¡Mortales!
Al Senor dirigamos por ella nuestras preces.
Falleció
El 29 de Novembre del año 1830, á los 44 de su edad.

¡O Man!
Behold the end of our troubles—
Death, Earth, Nothing.

In this urn repose the remains of Dña Loretta Lara,
A charitable woman, faithful wife, and tender mother,
prudent and virtuous.

¡Mortals!
To the Lord let us direct our prayers for her.
She died
The 29th of November, in the year 1830, aged 44.

One of the altars was decorated with human skulls and cross-bones, and in the rear of the church was a great charnel-house. It was enclosed by a high stone wall, and was filled with a collection of skulls and bones, which, after the flesh had decayed, had been dug up from the graves in the cemetery of the church.

The convent is connected with the church by a spacious corridor. It is a gigantic structure, built entirely of stone, with massive walls, and four hundred feet in length. The entrance is under a noble portico, with high stone pillars, from which ascends a broad stone staircase to a spacious corridor twenty feet wide. This corridor runs through the whole length of the building, with a stone pavement, and is lighted in two places by a dome. On each side are cloisters, once occupied by a numerous body of Franciscan friars. The first two and principal of these cloisters on the left are occupied by the cura, and were our home. Another is occupied by one of his ministros, and in the fourth was an old Indian making cigars. The rest on this side are unoccupied, and on the right, facing the great garden of the convent, all the cloisters are untenanted, dismantled, and desolate; the doors and windows are broken, and grass and weeds are growing out of the floors. The garden had once been in harmony with the grandeur and style of the convent, and now shares its fortunes. Its wells and fountains, parterres and beds of flowers, are all there, but neglected and running to waste, weeds, oranges, and lemons growing wildly together, and our horses were turned into it loose, as into a pasture.

Associated in my mind with this ruined convent, so as almost to form part of the building, is our host, the pride and love of the village, the cura Carillo. He was past forty, tall and thin, with an open, animated, and intelligent countenance, manly, and at the same time mild, and belonged to the once powerful order of Franciscan friars, now reduced in this region to himself and a few companions. After the destruction of the convent at Merida, and the scattering of the friars, his friends procured for him the necessary papers to enable him to secularize, but he would not abandon the brotherhood in its waning fortunes, and still wore the long blue gown, the cord, and cross of the Franciscan monks. By the regulations of his order, all the receipts of his curacy belonged to the brotherhood, deducting only forty dollars per month for himself. With this pittance, he could live and extend hospitality to strangers. His friends urged him to secularize, engaging to procure for him a better curacy, but he steadily refused; he never expected to be rich, and did not wish to be; he had enough for his wants, and did not desire more. He was content with his village and with the people; he was the friend of everybody, and everybody was his friend; in short, for a man not indolent, but, on the contrary, unusually active both in mind and body, he was, without affectation or parade, more entirely contented with his lot than any man I ever knew. The quiet and seclusion of his village did not afford sufficient employment for his active mind, but, fortunately for science and for me, and strangely enough as it was considered, he had turned his attention to the antiquities of the country. He could neither go far from home, nor be absent long, but he had visited every place within his reach, and was literally an enthusiast in the pursuit. His friends smiled at this folly, but, in consideration of his many good qualities, excused it. There was no man in the country whom we were so well pleased to meet, and as it was a rare thing for him to associate with persons who took the slightest interest in his hobby, he mourned that he could not throw up all his business and accompany us in our exploration of the ruins.

It is worthy of remark, that even to a man so alive to all subjects of antiquarian interest, the history of the building of this convent is entirely unknown. In the pavement of the great corridor, in the galleries, walls, and roof, both of the church and convent, are stones from ancient buildings, and no doubt both were constructed with materials furnished by the ruined edifices of another race, but when, or how, or under what circumstances, is unknown. On the roof the cura had discovered, in a situation which would hardly have attracted any eyes but his own, a square stone, having roughly engraved on it this inscription:

26
Marzo,
1625.

Perhaps this had reference to the date of the construction, and if so, it is the only known record that exists in relation to it; and the thought almost unavoidably occurs, that where such obscurity exists in regard to a building constructed by the Spaniards but little more than two hundred years ago, how much darker must be the cloud that hangs over the ruined cities of the aborigines, erected, if not ruined, before the conquest.

During the first days of my convalescence I had a quiet and almost mournful interest in wandering about this venerable convent. I passed, too, some interesting hours in looking over the archives. The books had a time-worn aspect, with parchment covers, tattered and worm-eaten. In some places the ink had faded, and the writing was illegible. They were the records of the early monks, written by their own hands, and contained a register of baptisms and marriages, including, perhaps, the first Indian who assented to these Christian rites. It was my hope to find in these archives some notice, however slight, of the circumstances under which the early fathers set up the standard of the cross in this Indian town, but the first book has no preamble or introduction of any kind, commencing abruptly with the entry of a marriage.

This entry bears date in 1588, but forty or fifty years after the Spaniards established themselves in Merida. This is thirty-eight years anterior to the date on the stone before referred to, but it is reasonable to suppose that the convent was not built until some time after the beginning of the archives. The monks doubtless commenced keeping a register of baptisms and marriages as soon as there were any to record, but as they were distinguished for policy and prudence as well as zeal, it is not likely that they undertook the erection of this gigantic building until they had been settled in the country long enough to understand thoroughly its population and resources, for these buildings had not only to be erected, but to be kept up, and their ministers supported by the resources of the district. Besides, the great churches and convents found in all parts of Spanish America were not built by means of funds sent from Spain, but by the labour of the Indians themselves, after they were completely subdued and compelled to work for the Spaniards, or, more generally, after they had embraced Christianity, when they voluntarily erected buildings for the new worship and its ministers. It is not probable that either of these events occurred in this interior village so early as 1588.

These first entries are of the marriage, or rather marriages, of two widowers and two widows—X. Diego Chuc with Maria Hu, and Zpo-Bot with Cata Keul. In running over the archives, it appeared, I found, that there was in those days an unusual number of widowers and widows disposed to marry again, and, in fact, that the business of this kind was in a great measure confined to them; but probably, as the relation of husband and wife was not very clearly defined among the Indians, these candidates for Christian matrimony had only parted from former companions, and, through the charity or modesty of the monks, were called widowers and widows.

The first baptisms are on the twentieth of November, 1594, when considerable business seems to have been done. There are four entries on that day, and, in looking over the pages, from my acquaintance with the family I was struck with the name of Mel Chi, probably an ancestor of our Chaipa Chi. This Mel seems to have been one of the pillars of the padres, and a standing godfather for Indian babies.

There was no instruction to be derived from these archives, but the handwriting of the monks, and the marks of the Indians, seemed almost to make me a participator in the wild and romantic scenes of the conquest; at all events, they were proof that, forty or fifty years after the conquest, the Indians were abandoning their ancient usages and customs, adopting the rites and ceremonies of the Catholic Church, and having their children baptized with Spanish names.

CHAPTER XIII

It was fortunate for the particular objects of our expedition that, go where we would in this country, the monuments of its ancient inhabitants were before our eyes. Near the village of Ticul, almost in the suburbs, are the ruins of another ancient and unknown city. From the time of our arrival the memorials of it had been staring us in the face. The cura had some sculptured stones of new and exceedingly pretty design; and heads, vases, and other relics, found in excavating the ruins, were fixed in the fronts of houses as ornaments. My first stroll with the cura was to these ruins.

At the end of a long street leading out beyond the campo santo we turned to the right by a narrow path, overgrown with bushes covered with wild flowers, and on which birds of beautiful plumage were sitting, but so infested with garrapatas that we had to keep brushing them off continually with the bough of a tree.

This path led us to the hacienda of San Francisco, the property of a gentleman of the village, who had reared the walls of a large building, but had never finished it. There were fine shade trees, and the appearance of the place was rural and picturesque, but it was unhealthy. The deep green foliage was impregnated with the seeds of death. The proprietor never visited it except in the daytime, and the Indians who worked on the milpas returned to the village at night.

A short distance in the rear of the hacienda were the ruins

of another city, desolate and overgrown, having no name except that of the hacienda on which they stand. At this time a great part of the city was completely hidden by the thick foliage of the trees. Near by, however, several mounds were in full sight, dilapidated, and having fragments of walls on the top. We ascended the highest, which commanded a magnificent view of the great wooded plain, and at a distance the towers of the church of Ticul rising darkly above. The cura told me that in the dry season, when the trees were bare of foliage, he had counted from this point thirty-six mounds, every one of which had once held aloft a building or temple, and not one now remained entire. In the great waste of ruins it was impossible to form any idea of what the place had been, except from its vastness and the specimens of sculptured stone seen in the village, but beyond doubt it was of the same character as Uxmal, and erected by the same people. Its vicinity to the village had made its destruction more complete. For generations it had served as a mere quarry to furnish the inhabitants with building-stone. The present proprietor was then excavating and selling, and he lamented to me that the piedra labrada, or worked stone, was nearly exhausted, and his profit from this source cut off.

A few words toward identifying these ruins. The plan for reducing Yucatan was to send a small number of Spaniards, who were called *vecinos* (the name still used to designate the white population), into the Indian towns and villages where it was thought advisable to make settlements. We have clear and authentic accounts of the existence of a large Indian town called Ticul, certainly in the same neighbourhood where the Spanish village of that name now stands. It must have been either on the site now occupied by the latter, or on that occupied by the ruins of San Francisco. Supposing the first supposition to be correct, not a single vestige of the Indian city remains. Now it is incontestible that the Spaniards found in the Indian towns of Yucatan, mounds, temples, and other large buildings of stone. If those on the hacienda of San Francisco are of older date, and the work of races who have passed away, as vast remains of them still exist, though subject to the same destroying causes, why has every trace of the stone buildings in the Indian city disappeared?

And it appears in every page of the history of the Spanish conquest, that the Spaniards never attempted to occupy the houses and villages of the Indians as they stood. Their habits of life were inconsistent with such occupation, and, besides, their policy was to desolate and destroy them, and build up others after their own style and manner. It is not likely that at the early epoch at which they are known to have gone to Ticul, with their small numbers, they would have undertaken to demolish the whole Indian town, and build their own upon its ruins. The probability is, that they planted their own village on the border, and erected their church as an antagonist and rival to the heathen temples; the monks, with all the imposing ceremonies of the Catholic Church, battled with the Indian priests; and, gradually overthrowing the power of the caciques, or putting them to death, they depopulated the old town, and drew the Indians to their own village. It is my belief that the ruins on the hacienda of San Francisco are those of the aboriginal city of Ticul.

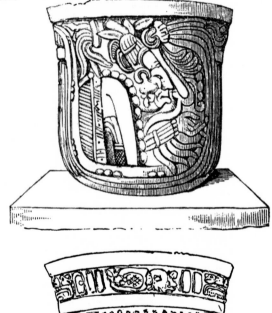

FIG. 12.   Front and back of Ticul vase.

From the great destruction of the buildings, I thought it unprofitable to attempt any exploration of these ruins, especially considering the insalubrity of the place and our own crippled state. In the excavations constantly going on, objects of interest were from time to time discovered, one of which, a vase, was fortunately only loaned to us to make a drawing of, or it would have shared the fate of the others, and been burned up by *that* fire. Figure 12 represents two sides of the vase; on one side is a border of hieroglyphics, with sunken lines running to the bottom, and on the other the reader will observe that the face portrayed bears a strong resemblance to those of the sculptured and stuccoed figures at Palenque: the headdress, too, is a plume of feathers, and the hand is held out in the same stiff position. The vase is four and a half inches high, and five inches in diameter. It is of admirable workmanship, and realizes the account given by Herrera of the markets at the Mexican city of Tlascala. "There were goldsmiths, feather-men, barbers, baths, and *as good earthenware as in Spain.*"

It was not yet considered safe for me to return to Uxmal, and the sight of these vases induced me to devote a few days to excavating among the ruins. The cura took upon himself the whole burden of making arrangements, and early in the morning we were on the ground with Indians. Amid the great waste of ruins it was difficult to know what to do or where to begin. In Egypt, the labours of discoverers have given some light to subsequent explorers, but here all was dark. My great desire was to discover an ancient sepulchre, which we had sought in vain among the ruins of Uxmal. These were not to be looked for in the large mounds, or, at all events, it was a work of too much labour to attempt opening one of them. At length, after a careful examination, the cura selected one, upon which we began.

It was a square stone structure, with sides four feet high, and the top was rounded over with earth and stones bedded in it. It stood in a small milpa, or corn-field, midway between two high mounds, which had evidently been important structures, and from its position seemed to have some direct connexion with them. Unlike most of the ruined structures around, it was entire, with every stone in its place, and probably had not been disturbed since the earth and stones had been packed down on the top.

The Indians commenced picking out the stones and clearing away the earth with their hands. Fortunately, they had a crowbar, an instrument unknown in Central America, but indispensable here on account of the stony nature of the soil, and for the first and only time in the country I had no trouble in superintending the work. The cura gave them directions in their own language, and under his eye they worked actively.

Nevertheless, the process was unavoidably slow. In digging down, they found the inner side of the outer wall, and the whole interior was loose earth and stones, with some layers of large flat stones, the whole very rough. In the mean time the sun was beating upon us with prodigious force, and some of the people of the village, among others the proprietor of the hacienda, came down to look on and have an inward smile at our folly. The cura had read a Spanish translation of the Antiquary, and said that we were surrounded by Edie Ochiltrees, though he himself, with his tall, thin figure and long gown, presented a lively image of that renowned mendicant. We continued the work six hours, and the whole appearance of things was so rude that we began to despair of success, when, on prying up a large flat stone, we saw underneath a skull. The reader may imagine our satisfaction. We made the Indians throw away crowbar and machete, and work with their hands. I was exceedingly anxious to get the skeleton out entire, but it was impossible to do so. It had no covering or envelope of any kind; the earth was thrown upon it as in a common grave, and as this was removed it all fell to pieces. It was in a sitting posture, with its face toward the setting sun. The knees were bent against the stomach, the arms doubled from the elbow, and the hands clasping the neck or supporting the head. The skull was unfortunately broken, but the facial bone was entire, with the jaws and teeth, and the enamel on the latter still bright, but when the skull was handed up many of them fell out. The Indians picked up every bone and tooth, and handed them to me. It was strangely interesting, with the ruined structures towering above us, after a lapse of unknown ages, to bring to light these buried bones. Whose were they? The Indians were excited, and conversed in low tones. The cura interpreted what they said; and the burden of it was, "They are the bones of our kinsman," and "What will our kinsman say at our dragging forth his bones?" But for the cura they would have covered them up and left the sepulchre.

In collecting the bones, one of the Indians picked up a small white object, which would have escaped any but an Indian's eye. It was made of deer's horn, about two inches long, sharp at the point, with an eye at the other end. They all called it a needle, and the reason of their immediate and unhesitating opinion was the fact that the Indians of the present day use needles of the same material, two of which the cura procured for me on our return to the convent. One of the Indians, who had acquired some confidence by gossiping with the cura, jocosely said that the skeleton was either that of a woman or a tailor.

The position of this skeleton was not in the centre of the sepulchre, but on one side, and on the other side of it was a very large rough stone or rock firmly imbedded in the earth, which it would have taken a long time to excavate with our instruments. In digging round it and on the other side, at some little distance from the skeleton we found a large vase of rude pottery, resembling very much the cantaro used by the Indians now as a water-jar. It had a rough flat stone lying over the mouth, so as to exclude the earth, on removing which we found, to our great disappointment, that it was entirely empty, except some little hard black flakes, which were thrown out and buried before the vase was taken up. It had a small hole worn in one side of the bottom, through which liquid or pulverized substances could have escaped. It may have contained water or the heart of the skeleton. This vase was got out entire, and is now ashes.

One idea presented itself to my mind with more force than it had ever possessed before, and that was the utter impossibility of ascribing these ruins to Egyptian builders. The magnificent tombs of the kings at Thebes rose up before me. It was on their tombs that the Egyptians lavished their skill, industry, and wealth, and no people, brought up in Egyptian schools, descended from Egyptians, or deriving their lessons from them, would ever have constructed in so conspicuous a place so rude a sepulchre. Besides this, the fact of finding these bones in so good a state of preservation, at a distance of only three or four feet from the surface of the earth, completely destroys all idea of the extreme antiquity of these buildings; and again there was the universal and unhesitating exclamation of the Indians, "They are the bones of our kinsman."

But whosesoever they were, little did the pious friends who placed them there ever imagine the fate to which they were destined. I had them carried to the convent, thence to Uxmal, and thence I bore them away forever from the bones of their kindred. In their rough journeys on the backs of mules and Indians they were so crumbled and broken that in a court of law their ancient proprietor would not be able to identify them, and they left me one night in a pocket-handkerchief to be carried to Doctor S. G. Morton of Philadelphia.

Known by the research he has bestowed upon the physical features of the aboriginal American races, and particularly by his late work entitled "Crania Americana," which is acknowledged, in the annual address of the president of the Royal Geographical Society of London, as "a welcome offering to the lovers of comparative physiology," this gentleman, in a communication on that subject, for which I here acknowledge my obligations, says that this skeleton, dilapidated as it is, has afforded him some valuable facts, and has been a subject of some interesting reflections.

The purport of his opinion is as follows: In the first place, the needle did not deceive the Indian who picked it up in the grave. The bones are those of a female. Her height did not exceed five feet three or four inches. The teeth are perfect, and not appreciably worn, while the *epiphyses*, those infallible indications of the growing state, have just become consolidated, and mark the completion of adult age.

The bones of the hands and feet are remarkably small and delicately proportioned, which observation applies also to the entire skeleton. The skull was crushed into many pieces, but, by a cautious manipulation, Doctor Morton succeeded in reconstructing the posterior and lateral portions. The occiput is remarkably flat and vertical, while the lateral or parietal diameter measures no less than five inches and eight tenths.

A chemical examination of some fragments of the bones proves them to be almost destitute of animal matter, which, in the perfect osseous structure, constitutes about thirty-three parts in the hundred.

On the upper part of the left tibia there is a swelling of the bone, called, in surgical language, a *node*, an inch and a half in length, and more than half an inch above the natural surface. This morbid condition may have resulted from a variety of causes, but possesses greater interest on account of its extreme infrequency among the primitive Indian population of the country.

On a late visit to Boston I had the satisfaction of examining a small and extremely interesting collection of mummied bodies in the possession of Mr. John H. Blake, of that city, dug up by himself from an ancient cemetery in Peru. This cemetery lies on the shore of the Bay of Chacota, near Arica, in latitude 18° 20' south. It covers a large tract of ground. The graves are all of a circular form, from two to four feet in diameter, and from four to five feet deep. In one of them Mr. Blake found the mummies of a man, a woman, a child twelve or fourteen years old, and an infant. They were all closely wrapped in woollen garments of various colours and degrees of fineness, secured by needles of thorn thrust through the cloth. The skeletons are saturated with some bituminous substance, and are all in a remarkable state of preservation. The woollen cloths, too, are well preserved, which no doubt is accounted for, in a great degree, by the extreme dryness of the soil and atmosphere of that part of Peru.

Mr. Blake visited many other cemeteries between the Andes and the Pacific Ocean as far south as Chili, all of which possess the same general features with those found in the elevated valleys of the Peruvian Andes. No record or tradition exists in regard to these cemeteries, but woollen cloths similar to those found by Mr. Blake are woven at this day, and probably in the same manner, by the Indians of Peru; and in the eastern part of Bolivia, to the southward of the place where these mummies were discovered, he found, on the most barren portion of the Desert of Atacama, a few Indians, who, probably from the difficulty of access to their place of abode, have been less influenced by the Spaniards, and for this reason retain more of their primitive customs, and their dress at this day resembles closely that which envelops the bodies in his possession, both in the texture and the form.

Doctor Morton says that these mummies from Peru have the same peculiarities in the form of the skull, the same delicacy of the bones, and the same remarkable smallness of the hands and feet, with that found in the sepulchre at San Francisco. He says, too, from an examination of nearly four hundred skulls of individuals belonging to older nations of Mexico and Peru, and of skulls dug from the mounds of our western country, that he finds them all formed on the same model, and conforming in a remarkable manner to that brought from San Francisco; and that this cranium has the same *type* of physical conformation which has been bestowed with amazing uniformity upon all the tribes on our continent, from Canada to Patagonia, and from the Atlantic to the Pacific Ocean. He adds, that it affords additional support to the opinion which he has always entertained, that, notwithstanding some slight variation in physical conformation, and others of a much more remarkable character in intellectual attainments, all the aboriginal Americans of all known epochs belong to the same great and distinctive race.

If this opinion is correct, and I believe it—if this skeleton does present the same *type* of physical conformation with all the tribes of our continent—then, indeed, do these crumbling bones declare, as with a voice from the grave, that we cannot go back to any ancient nation of the Old World for the builders of these cities; they are not the works of people who have passed away, and whose history is lost, but of the same great *race* which, changed, miserable, and degraded, still clings around their ruins.

To return to the ruins of San Francisco. We devoted two days more to excavating, but did not make any farther discoveries.

Among the ruins were circular holes in the ground like those at Uxmal. The mouth of one was broken and enlarged, and I descended by a ladder into a dome-shaped chamber, precisely the same as at Uxmal, but a little larger. At Uxmal the character of these was mere matter of conjecture; but at this short distance, the Indians had specific notions in regard to their objects and uses, and called them chultunes, or wells. In all directions, too, were seen the oblong stones hollowed out like troughs, which at Uxmal were called pilas, or fountains, but here the Indians called them hólcas or piedras de molir, stones for grinding, which they said were used by the ancients to mash corn upon; and the proprietor showed us a round stone like a bread roller, which they called kabtum, brazo de piedra, or arm of stone, used, as they said, for mashing the corn. The different names they assigned in different places to the same thing, and the different uses ascribed to it, show, with many other facts, the utter absence of all traditionary knowledge among the Indians; and this is perhaps the greatest difficulty we have to encounter in ascribing to their ancestors the building of these cities.

The last day we returned from the ruins earlier than usual, and stopped at the campo santo. In front stood a noble seybo tree. I had been anxious to learn something of the growth of this tree, but had never had an opportunity of doing it before. The cura told me that it was then twenty-three years old. There could be no doubt or mistake on this point. Its age was as well known as his own, or that of any other person in the village. Figure 13 represents this tree. The trunk at the distance of five feet from the ground measured 17½ feet in circumference, and its great branches afforded on all sides a magnificent shade. We had found trees like it growing on the tops of the ruined structures at Copan and Palenque, and many had for that reason ascribed to the buildings a very great antiquity. This tree completely removed all doubts which I might have entertained, and confirmed me in the opinion I had before expressed, that no correct judgment could be formed of the anti-

Fig. 13. Seybo Tree.

quity of these buildings from the size of the trees growing upon
them. Remarkable as I considered this tree at that time, I afterward saw larger ones, in more favourable situations, not so old.

The campo santo was enclosed by a high stone wall. The
interior had some degree of plan and arrangement, and in some
places were tombs, built above ground, belonging to families in
the village, hung with withered wreaths and votive offerings.
The population tributary to it was about five thousand; it had
been opened but five years, and already it presented a ghastly
spectacle. There were many new-made graves, and on several of
the vaults were a skull and small collection of bones in a box or
tied up in a napkin, being the remains of one buried within and
taken out to make room for another corpse. On one of them
were the skull and bones of a lady of the village, in a basket; an
old acquaintance of the cura, who had died within two years.
Among the bones was a pair of white satin shoes, which she had
perhaps worn in the dance, and with which on her feet she had
been buried.

At one corner of the cemetery was a walled enclosure, about

twenty feet high and thirty square, within which was the charnel-house of the cemetery. A flight of stone steps led to the top
of the wall, and on the platform of the steps and along the wall
were skulls and bones, some in boxes and baskets, and some tied
up in cotton cloths, soon to be thrown upon the common pile,
but as yet having labels with the names written on them, to
make known yet a little while longer the individuals to whom
they had once belonged. Within the enclosure the earth was
covered several feet deep with the promiscuous and undistinguishable bones of rich and poor, high and low, men, women, and
children, Spaniards, Mestizoes, and Indians, all mingled together
as they happened to fall. Among them were fragments of bright-
coloured dresses, and the long hair of women still clinging to the
skull. Of all the sad mementoes declaring the end to which all
that is bright and beautiful in this world is doomed, none ever
touched me so affectingly as this—the ornament and crowning
charm of woman, the peculiar subject of her taste and daily care,
loose, dishevelled, and twining among dry and mouldering
bones.

We left the campo santo, and walked up the long street of
the village, the quiet, contented character of the people impressing itself more strongly than ever upon my mind. The Indians
were sitting in the yards, shrouded by cocoanut and orange trees,
weaving hammocks and platting palm leaves for hats; the children were playing naked in the road, and the Mestiza women
were sitting in the doorways sewing. The news of our digging
up the bones had created a sensation. All wanted to know what
the day's work had produced, and all rose up as the cura passed;
the Indians came to kiss his hand, and, as he remarked, except
when the crop of maize was short, all were happy. In a place of
such bustle and confusion as our own city, it is impossible to
imagine the quiet of this village.

CHAPTER XIV

The next day was Sunday, which I passed in making preparations for returning to Uxmal. I had, however, some distraction. In the morning the quiet of the village was a little disturbed by intelligence of a revolution in Tekax, a town nine leagues distant. Our sojourn in the country had been so quiet that it seemed unnatural, and a small revolution was necessary to make me feel at home. The insurgents had deposed the alcalde, appointed their own authorities, and laid contributions upon the inhabitants, and the news was that they intended marching three hundred men against Merida, to extort an acknowledgment of independence. Ticul lay in their line of march, but as it was considered very uncertain whether they would carry this doughty purpose into execution, I determined not to change my plan.

Doctor Cabot's presence in the village was, of course, generally known, and though it was rather prejudicial to his reputation as a medical man to be ill himself, he did not fail to have patients. His fame as a curer of biscos had reached this place, but, fortunately for his quiet, there was only one squinter among the inhabitants, though his was violent enough for a whole village. In the afternoon this man applied for relief. Doctor Cabot told him that his hand was not yet steady enough to perform the

operation, and that I was going away the next day; but this by
no means satisfied him. It happened, however, that a gentleman
present, who was consulting the doctor on some ailment of his
own, mentioned incidentally that one of the doctor's patients at
Merida had lost the eye, though he added that the loss was not
ascribed to the operation, but to subsequent bad treatment. This
story, as we afterward learned, was entirely without foundation,
but it had its effect upon the bisco, who rolled his eye toward
the door so violently that the rest of him followed, and he never
came near the doctor again. His only operation that day was
upon the wife of the proprietor of San Francisco, whose head
he laid open, and took out a hideous wen.

I have mentioned the extraordinary stillness of this place.
Every night, however, since my arrival, this stillness had been
broken by the canting, singing tones of a boy calling out the
numbers of the loteria. Preparations were making for a village
fête in February; the ground was already marked out in front of
the convent for the Plaza de Toros, and the loteria was adopted
as the means of raising money to pay the expenses. I had not yet
attended, and on the last night of my stay in Ticul I determined
to go. It was held in the corridor of the audiencia, along which
hung branches of palm leaves to protect the lights. It was Sunday evening, and, consequently, the attendance was more numerous than usual. At the entrance sat the boy, whose voice is even
now ringing in my ears, rattling a bag of balls, drawing them
out, and calling off the numbers. Along the corridor was a rough
table with a row of candles in the centre, and benches on each
side were occupied by the villagers, without distinction of persons, with papers and grains of corn before them, the same as at
Merida. The largest sum called off was twenty-nine reals. One
real was deducted from every dollar for the particular object of
the lottery, and the fund which the boy had obtained by such a
potent use of his voice then amounted to sixty-three dollars.
There were several performers giving out somewhat equivocal
music, without which nothing in that country could go on long,
and occasionally two reals were drawn from the purse for them.
All entered who pleased. There was no regulation of dress or
etiquette, but much quiet courtesy of manner, and it was regarded a mere converzatione, or place for passing the evening.
I remained about an hour. As we crossed the plaza, the moon
lighted up the venerable front of the convent, and for the last
time I slept within its walls.

The next morning I bade farewell to the cura, with an

understanding, that as soon as Doctor Cabot was able to return, the good padre would accompany him to finish his interrupted visit to us at Uxmal. My time at Ticul had not been lost. Besides exploring the ruins of San Francisco, I had received accounts of others from the cura, which promised to add greatly to the interest of our expedition.

That I might take a passing view of one of these places on my return to Uxmal, I determined to go back by a different road, across the sierra, which rises a short distance from the village of Ticul. The ascent was steep, broken, and stony. The whole range was a mass of limestone rock, with a few stunted trees, but not enough to afford shade, and white under the reflection of the sun. In an hour I reached the top of the sierra, Looking back, my last view of the plain presented, high above everything else, the church and convent which I had left. I was an hour crossing the sierra, and on the other side my first view of the great plain took in the church of Nohcacab, standing like a colossus in the wilderness, the only token to indicate the presence of man. Descending to the plain, I saw nothing but trees, until, when close upon the village, the great church again rose before me, towering above the houses, and the only object visible.

The village was under the pastoral charge of the cura of Ticul, and in the suburbs I met his ministro on horseback, waiting, according to the directions of the former, to escort me to the ruins of Nohpat. At a league's distance we turned off from the main road, and, following a narrow path leading to some milpas, in fifteen minutes we saw towering before us lofty but shattered buildings, the relics of another ruined city. I saw at a glance that it would be indispensable for Mr. Catherwood to visit them. Nevertheless, I passed three hours on the ground, toiling in the hot sun, and at four o'clock, with strong apprehensions of another attack of fever, I mounted to continue my journey.

A little before dark I emerged from the woods, and saw Mr. Catherwood standing on the platform of the Casa del Gobernador, the sole tenant of the ruins of Uxmal. His Indians had finished their day's work, Bernaldo and Chaipa Chi had gone, and since Doctor Cabot left he had slept alone in our quarters. He had a feeling of security from the tranquil state of the country, the harmless character of the Indians, their superstitions in regard to the ruins, and a spring pistol with a cord across the door, which could not fail to bring down any one who might attempt to enter at night.

It had happened most fortunately for our operations that Mr. Catherwood had held out. Without any resources or anything to occupy him except work, he had accomplished an enormous deal, and from being so much better provided with the comforts of living than at any former time while exploring ruins, he had continued in good health and spirits.

At dark the Indian arrived with my luggage, sweating at every pore, having carried it twenty-one miles, for which I paid him three shillings and sixpence. As he was going away we gave him a roll of bread, and he asked by signs if he was to carry it to the cura. Being made to comprehend that he was to eat it himself, he sat down and commenced immediately, having probably never eaten so much bread before in his life. We then gave him half a cup of Habanero, some plantains and a cigar, and, as the dew was heavy, told him to sit by the fire. When he had finished these we repeated the portion, and he seemed hardly to believe his good fortune real, but he had an idea that he was well off, and either from being a stranger, and free from the apprehensions felt by the Indians at Uxmal, or else from a fancy he had taken to us, he asked for a costal, a piece of hemp bagging, to sleep upon. We gave him one, and he lay down by the fire; for a while he endeavoured to protect his naked body against the moschetoes, and kept up a continued slapping, lighter or heavier according to the aggravation, changed his position, and tried the back corridor, but it was all in vain; and, finally, with a sad attempt at a smile, he asked for another drink of Habanero and a cigar, and went away.

On the twenty-fourth of December Doctor Cabot returned from Ticul, bringing back with him Albino, who was still in a rueful plight. Unfortunately, the cura Carillo was unwell, and unable to accompany him, but had promised to follow in a few days. On Christmas eve we were all once more together, and Christmas Day, in spite of ourselves, was a holyday. No Indians came out to work. Chaipa Chi, who had moved regularly as the sun, for the first time failed. We had, however, as visiters, a number of women from the village of Moona. From the top of the House of the Dwarf we saw them moving toward that of the Nuns, and went down to receive them. The only males who accompanied them were a lad about fourteen attending his newly-married wife, and the husband of the woman I had seen buried, who either had not the spirit for joining in the festivities at the hacienda, or was putting himself in the way of repairing his loss.

Unable to do anything at the ruins, I walked down to the hacienda to see one of our horses which had a sore back. The hacienda was deserted, but the sound of violins led me to the place where the Indians were congregated. Preparations were making on a large scale for the evening feast. The place looked like a butcher's shambles, for they had cut up what had once composed eight turkeys, two hogs, and I do not know how many fowls. The women were all busy; Chaipa Chi was lady-patroness, and up to her elbows in tortillas.

I walked on to the campo santo, for the purpose of carrying away two skulls which I had selected and laid aside on the charnel pile at the time of the funeral. I had taken some precautions, for the news of the carrying off the bones from San Francisco had created some excitement among the Indians all over the country; and as I had to pass a long row of huts, I had procured two calabazas, or gourds, for drinking cups, which I carried in a pocket-handkerchief, and intended to throw away in the grave-yard, and substitute the skulls. On reaching the pile, however, I found that other hands had been upon it. The skulls I had selected had been displaced and mingled with the others, so that I could not identify them. I examined the whole heap, but could recognise only the huge skull of an African and that of the woman I had seen dug up. The latter was the skull of a full-blooded Indian, but it had been damaged by the crowbar; besides, I had seen all her bones and her very flesh taken piece-meal out of the grave; I had heard so much of her that she seemed an acquaintance, and I had some qualms of conscience about carrying her skull away. In fact, alone in the stillness and silence of the place, something of a superstitious feeling came over me about disturbing the bones of the dead and robbing a graveyard. I should nevertheless, perhaps, have taken up two skulls at random, but, to increase my wavering feeling, I saw two Indian women peeping at me through the trees, and, not wishing to run the risk of creating a disturbance on the ha-cienda, I left the graveyard with empty hands. The mayoral after-ward told me that it was fortunate I had done so, for that if I had carried any away, it would have caused an excitement among the Indians, and perhaps led to mishchief.

The account of our residence at Uxmal is now drawing to a close, and it is time to bring before the reader the remainder of the ruins; but before doing so I shall make one remark in re-gard to the work of Mr. Waldeck, which was published in folio at Paris in 1835, and, except my own hurried notice, is the only account that has ever been published of the ruins at Uxmal. I had this work with me on our last visit. It will be found that our plans and drawings differ materially from his, but Mr. Waldeck was not an architectural draughtsman, and he complains that his drawings were taken from him by the Mexican government. I differ from him, too, in the statement of some facts, and almost entirely in opinions and conclusions; but these things occur of course, and the next person who visits these ruins will perhaps differ in many respects from both of us. It is proper to say, moreover, that Mr. Waldeck had much greater difficulties to encounter than we, for at the time of his visit the ground had not been cleared for a milpa, and the whole field was overgrown with trees; besides, he is justly entitled to the full credit of being the first stranger who visited these ruins, and brought them to the notice of the public.

To return. I have already mentioned the Casa del Gobernador and the Casa de las Tortugas, or House of the Turtles, the latter of which stands on the grand platform of the second terrace of the Casa del Gobernador, at the northwest corner.

Descending from this building, and on a line with the doorway of the Casa de las Monjas, going north, at the distance of two hundred and forty feet are two ruined edifices facing each other, and seventy feet apart, as laid down on the general plan of the ruins. Each is one hundred and twenty-eight feet long, and thirty feet deep, and, so far as they can be made out, they appear to have been exactly alike in plan and ornament. The sides facing each other were embellished with sculpture, and there remain on both the fragments of entwined colossal serpents, which ran the whole length of the walls.

In the centre of each façade, at points directly opposite each other, are the fragments of a great stone ring. Each of these rings was four feet in diameter, and secured in the wall by a stone tenon of corresponding dimensions. They appear to have been broken wilfully; of each, the part nearest the stem still projects from the wall, and the outer surface is covered with sculptured characters. We made excavations among the ruins along the base of the walls, in hope of discovering the missing parts of these rings, but without success.

These structures have no doorways or openings of any kind, either on the sides or at the ends. In the belief that they must have interior chambers, we made a breach in the wall of the one on the east to the depth of eight or ten feet, but we found only rough stones, hanging so loosely together as to make it dangerous for the Indians to work in the holes, and they were obliged to discontinue.

This excavation, however, carried us through nearly one third of the structure, and satisfied us that these great parallel edifices did not contain any interior apartments, but that each consisted merely of four great walls, filled up with a solid mass of stones. It was our opinion that they had been built expressly with reference to the two great rings facing each other in the façades, and that the space between was intended for the celebration of some public games, in which opinion we were afterward confirmed.

Passing between these buildings, and continuing in the same direction, we reach the front of the Casa de las Monjas, or House of the Nuns.

This building is quadrangular, with a courtyard in the centre. It stands on the highest of three terraces. The lowest is three feet high and twenty feet wide; the second, twelve feet high and forty-five feet wide; and the third, four feet high and five feet wide, extending the whole length of the front of the building.

The front is two hundred and seventy-nine feet long, and above the cornice, from one end to the other, it is ornamented with sculpture. In the centre is a gateway ten feet eight inches wide, spanned by the triangular arch, and leading to the courtyard. On each side of this gateway are four doorways with wooden lintels, opening to apartments averaging twenty-four feet long, ten feet wide, and seventeen feet high to the top of the arch, but having no communication with each other.

The building that forms the right or eastern side of the quadrangle is one hundred and fifty-eight feet long; that on the left is one hundred and seventy-three feet long, and the range opposite or at the end of the quadrangle measures two hundred and sixty-four feet.

These three ranges of buildings have no doorways outside, but the exterior of each is a dead wall, and above the cornice all are ornamented with the same rich and elaborate sculpture. On the exterior of the range last mentioned, the designs are simple, and among them are two rude, naked figures, which have been considered as indicating the existence of that same Eastern worship before referred to among the people of Uxmal.

Such is the exterior of this building. Passing through the arched gateway, we enter a noble courtyard, with four great façades looking down upon it, each ornamented from one end

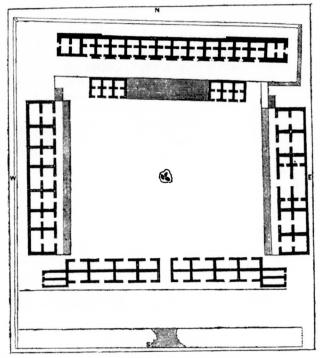

FIG. 14.   Plan of the Courtyard.

to the other with the richest and most intricate carving known
in the art of the builders of Uxmal; presenting a scene of
strange magnificence, surpassing any that is now to be seen
among its ruins. This courtyard is two hundred and fourteen
feet wide, and two hundred and fifty-eight feet deep. At the
time of our first entrance it was overgrown with bushes and
grass, quails started up from under our feet, and, with a whirring
flight, passed over the tops of the buildings. Whenever we went
to it, we started flocks of these birds, and throughout the whole
of our residence at Uxmal they were the only disturbers of its
silence and desolation.

Among my many causes of regret for the small scale on
which I am obliged to present these drawings, none is stronger
than the consequent inability to present, with all their detail of
ornament, the four great façades fronting this courtyard. There
is but one alleviating circumstance; which is, that the side most
richly ornamented is so ruined that, under any circumstances, it
could not be presented entire.

This façade is on the left of the visiter entering the courtyard. It is one hundred and seventy-three feet long, and is distinguished by two colossal serpents entwined, running through and encompassing nearly all the ornaments throughout its whole length. Plates V and VI represent the only parts remaining.

Plate V exhibits that portion of the façade toward the north end of the building. The tail of one serpent is held up nearly over the head of the other, and has an ornament upon it like a turban, with a plume of feathers. The marks on the extremity of the tail are probably intended to indicate a rattlesnake, with which species of serpent the country abounds. The lower serpent has its monstrous jaws wide open, and within them is a human head, the face of which is distinctly visible on the stone, and appears faintly in the drawing. From the ruin to which all was hurrying, Don Simon cared only to preserve this serpent's head. He said that we might tear out and carry away every other ornament, but this he intended to build into the wall of a house in Merida as a memorial of Uxmal.

Plate VI represents the two entwined serpents enclosing and running through the ornaments over a doorway. The principal feature in the ornament enclosed is the figure of a human being, standing, but much mutilated. The bodies of the serpents, according to the representations of the same design in other parts of the sculpture, are covered with feathers.

Plates V and VI represent about one fifth of the whole façade; the other four fifths were enriched with the same mass of sculptured ornaments, and toward the south end the head and tail of the serpents corresponded in design and position with the portion still existing at the other. Had it been our fortune to reach this place a few years sooner, we might have seen the whole entire. Don Simon told us that in 1835 the whole front stood, and the two serpents were seen encircling every ornament in the building. In its ruins it presents a lively idea of the "large and very well constructed buildings of lime and stone" which Bernal Dias saw on landing at Campeachy, "with figures of serpents and of idols painted on the walls."

At the end of the courtyard, and fronting the gate of entrance, is the façade of a lofty building, two hundred and sixty-four feet long, standing on a terrace twenty feet high. The ascent is by a grand but ruined staircase, ninety-five feet wide, flanked on each side by a building with sculptured front, and having three doorways, each leading to apartments within.

The height of this building to the upper cornice is twenty-

Plate V

Graham

Catherwood.

PORTION OF WESTERN BUILDING. MONJAS. UXMAL.

Plate VI

PORTION OF THE WESTERN RANGE OF BUILDING, MONJAS, UXMAL.

Plate VII

F. Catherwood

Jordan & Halpin

VIEW FROM LA CASA DE LAS MONJAS, UXMAL, LOOKING SOUTH.

five feet. It has thirteen doorways, over each of which rose a perpendicular wall ten feet wide and seventeen feet high above the cornice, making the whole height forty-two feet from the ground. These lofty structures were no doubt erected to give grandeur and effect to the building, and at a distance they appear to be turrets, but only four of them now remain. The whole great façade, including the turrets, is crowded with complicated and elaborate sculpture, among which are human figures rudely executed: two are represented as playing on musical instruments, one being not unlike a small harp, and the other in the nature of a guitar; a third is in a sitting posture, with his hands across his breast, and tied by cords, the ends of which pass over his shoulders. Of the rest there is nothing which stands out distinct and intelligible like the serpent, and the whole, loaded as it is with ornament, conveys the idea of vastness and magnificence rather than that of taste and refinement.

This building has one curious feature. It is erected over, and completely encloses, a smaller one of older date. The doorways, walls, and wooden lintels of the latter are all seen, and where the outer building is fallen, the ornamented cornice of the inner one is visible.

From the platform of the steps of this building, looking across the courtyard, a grand view presents itself, embracing all the principal buildings that now tower above the plain, except the House of the Dwarf. Plate VII represents this view. In the foreground is the inner façade of the front range of the Monjas, with a portion of the range on each side of the courtyard. To the left, in the distance, appears the Casa de la Vieja, or of the Old Woman, and, rising grandly above the front of the Monjas, are the House of the Turtles, that of the Governor, and the Casa de Palomos, or the House of the Pigeons.

The last of the four sides of the courtyard, standing on the right of the entrance, is represented in Plate VIII. It is the most entire of any, and, in fact, wants but little more than its wooden lintels, and some stones which have been picked out of the façade below the cornice, to make it perfect. It is, too, the most chaste and simple in design and ornament, and it was always refreshing to turn from the gorgeous and elaborate masses on the other façades to this curious and pleasing combination.

The ornament over the centre doorway is the most important, the most complicated and elaborate, and of that marked and peculiar style which characterizes the highest efforts of these ancient builders. The ornaments over the other doorways are

Plate VIII

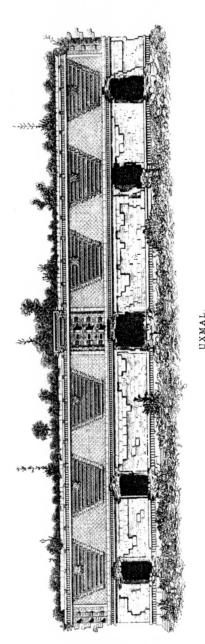

J.R. Cambrak.

UXMAL.

EASTERN RANGE OF BUILDING, MONJAS.

Warwood.

less striking, more simple, and more pleasing. In all of them there is in the centre a masked face with the tongue hanging out, surmounted by an elaborate headdress; between the horizontal bars is a range of diamond-shaped ornaments, in which the remains of red paint are still distinctly visible, and at each end of these bars is a serpent's head, with the mouth wide open.

Plate IX represents the southeast corner of this building. The angle exhibits the great face before presented, with the stone curving upward at the projecting end. On each side is a succession of compartments, alternately plain, and presenting the form of diamond lattice-work. In both there is an agreeable succession of plain and ornamented, and, in fact, it would be difficult, in arranging four sides facing a courtyard, to have more variety, and at the same time more harmony of ornament. All these façades were painted; the traces of the colour are still visible, and the reader may imagine what the effect must have been when all this building was entire, and according to its supposed design, in its now desolate doorways stood noble Maya maidens, like the vestal virgins of the Romans, to cherish and keep alive the sacred fire buring in the temples.

I omit a description of the apartments opening upon this courtyard. We made plans of all of them, but they are generally much alike, except in the dimensions. The number in all is eighty-eight.

In the range last presented, however, there is one suite different from all the rest. The entrance to this suite is by the centre and principal doorway, and Plate X represents the interior. It consists of two parallel chambers, each thirty-three feet long and thirteen wide; and at each end of both chambers is a doorway communicating with other chambers nine feet long and thirteen wide. The doorways of all these are ornamented with sculpture, and they are the only ornaments found in the interior of any buildings in Uxmal. The whole suite consists of six rooms; and there is a convenience in the arrangements not unsuited to the habits of what we call civilized life; opening as they do upon this noble courtyard, in the dry season, with nothing to apprehend from vegetation and damp, they would be by far the most comfortable residence for any future explorer of the ruins of Uxmal; and every time I went to them I regretted that we could not avail ourselves of the facilities they offered.

With these few words I take leave of the Casa de las Monjas, remarking only that in the centre is the fragment of a large stone like that on the terrace of the Casa del Gobernador, called

Plate IX

Catherwood Del   Prudhomme Sc

SOUTH EAST ANGLE OF MONJAS, UXMAL

Plate X

the Picote, and also that, induced by the account of Waldeck that the whole was once paved with sculptured turtles, I passed a morning digging all over the courtyard below the slight accumulation of earth, and found nothing of the kind. The substratum consisted of rude stones, no doubt once serving as a foundation for a floor of cement, which, from long exposure to the rainy seasons, has now entirely disappeared.

At the back of the last-mentioned range of the Monjas is another, or rather there are several ranges of buildings, standing lower than the House of the Nuns, in irregular order, and much ruined.

To the first portion of these we gave the name of the House of the Birds, from the circumstance of its being ornamented on

FIG. 15

the exterior with representations of feathers and birds rudely sculptured. Figure 15 represents a part of these ornaments.

The remaining portion consists of some very large rooms, among which are two fifty-three feet long, fourteen wide, and about twenty high, being the largest, or at least the widest in Uxmal. In one of them are the remains of painting well preserved, and in the other is an arch, which approaches nearer to the principle of the keystone than any we had yet met with in our whole exploration of ruins. It is very similar to the earliest arches, if they may be so called, of the Etruscans and Greeks, as seen at Arpino in the kingdom of Naples, and Tiryns in Greece. (See engravings in the Appendix.)

From this range of buildings we descend to the House of the Dwarf, also known by the name of la Casa del Adivino, or the House of the Diviner, from its overlooking the whole city, and enabling its occupant to be cognizant of all that was passing around him.

The courtyard of this building is one hundred and thirty-five feet by eighty-five. It is bounded by ranges of mounds from twenty-five to thirty feet thick, now covered with a rank growth of herbage, but which, perhaps, once formed ranges of buildings. In the centre is a large circular stone, like those seen in the other courtyards, called the Picote.

Plate XI represents the west front of this building, with the mound on which it stands. The base is so ruined and encumbered with fallen stones that it is difficult to ascertain its precise dimensions, but, according to our measurement, it is two hundred and thirty-five feet long, and one hundred and fifty-five wide. Its height is eighty-eight feet, and to the top of the building it is one hundred and five feet. Though diminishing as it rises, its shape is not exactly pyramidal, but its ends are rounded. It is encased with stone, and apparently solid from the plain.

A great part of the front presented in the engraving has fallen, and now lies a mass of ruins at the foot of the mound. Along the base, or rather about twenty feet up the mound, and probably once reached by a staircase, now ruined, is a range of curious apartments, nearly choked up with rubbish, and with the sapote beams still in their places over the door.

At the height of sixty feet is a solid projecting platform, on which stands a building loaded with ornaments more rich, elaborate, and carefully executed, than those of any other edifice in Uxmal. A great doorway opens upon the platform. The sapote

Plate XI

M. Osborne

WEST FRONT OF THE HOUSE OF THE DWARF
UXMAL.

Plate XII

beams are still in their places, and the interior is divided into two apartments; the outer one fifteen feet wide, seven feet deep, and nineteen feet high, and the inner one twelve feet wide, four feet deep, and eleven feet high. Both are entirely plain, without ornament of any kind, and have no communication with any part of the mound.

The steps or other means of communication with this building are all gone, and at the time of our visit we were at a loss to know how it had been reached; but, from what we saw afterward, we are induced to believe that a grand staircase upon a different plan from any yet met with, and supported by a triangular arch, led from the ground to the door of the building, which, if still in existence, would give extraordinary grandeur to this great mound.

The crowning structure is a long and narrow building, measuring seventy-two feet in front, and but twelve feet deep.

The front is much ruined, but even in its decay presents the most elegant and tasteful arrangement of ornaments to be seen in Uxmal, of which no idea could be given in any but a large engraving. The emblems of life and death appear on the wall in close juxta-position, confirming the belief in the existence of that worship practised by the Egyptians and all other Eastern nations, and before referred to as prevalent among the people of Uxmal.

The interior is divided into three apartments, that in the centre being twenty-four feet by seven, and those on each side nineteen feet by seven. They have no communication with each other; two have their doors opening to the east and one to the west.

A narrow platform five feet wide projects from all the four sides of the building. The northern end is decayed, and part of the eastern front, and to this front ascends a grand staircase one hundred and two feet high, seventy feet wide, and containing ninety steps.

Plate XII represents this front. The steps are very narrow, and the staircase steep; and after we had cleared away the trees, and there were no branches to assist us in climbing, the ascent and descent were difficult and dangerous. The padre Cogolludo, the historian referred to, says that he once ascended these steps, and "that when he attempted to descend he repented; his sight failed him, and he was in some danger." He adds, that in the apartments of the building, which he calls "small chapels," were the "idols," and that there they made sacrifices of men, women, and children. Beyond doubt this lofty building was a great Teocalis, "El grande de los Kues," the great temple of idols worshipped by the people of Uxmal, consecrated by their most mysterious rites, the holiest of their holy places. "The High Priest had in his Hand a large, broad, and sharp Knife made of Flint. Another Priest carried a wooden collar wrought like a snake. The persons to be sacrificed were conducted one by one up the Steps, stark naked, and as soon as laid on the Stone, had the Collar put upon their Necks, and the four priests took hold of the hands and feet. Then the high Priest with wonderful Dexterity ripped up the Breast, tore out the Heart, reeking, with his Hands, and showed it to the Sun, offering him the Heart and Steam that came from it. Then he turned to the Idol, and threw it in his face, which done, he kicked the body down the steps, and it never stopped till it came to the bottom, because they were *very upright;*" and "one who had been a Priest, and had been converted, said that when they tore out the Heart of the wretched Person sacrificed, it did beat so strongly that he took it up from the Ground three or four times till it cooled by Degrees, and then he threw the Body, still moving, down the Steps." In all the long catalogue of superstitious rites that darkens the page of man's history, I cannot imagine a picture more horribly exciting than that of the Indian priest, with his white dress and long hair clotted with gore, performing his murderous sacrifices at this lofty height, in full view of the people throughout the whole extent of the city.

From the top of this mound we pass over the Casa del Gobernador to the grand structure marked on the general plan as the Casa de Palomos, or the House of the Pigeons, the front of which is represented in Plate XIII. It is two hundred and forty feet long; the front is much ruined, the apartments are filled, and along the centre of the roof, running longitudinally, is a range of structures built in a pyramidal form, like the fronts of some of the old Dutch houses that still remain among us, but grander and more massive. These are nine in number, built of stone, about three feet thick, and have small oblong openings through them. These openings give them somewhat the appearance of pigeon-houses, and from this the name of the building is derived. All had once been covered with figures and ornaments in stucco, portions of which still remain. The view presented is in profile, as the full front could not be exhibited on this scale.

In the centre of this building is an archway ten feet wide,

Plate XIII

UXMAL.
Casa de los Palomos.

which leads into a courtyard one hundred and eighty feet long and one hundred and fifty feet deep. In the centre of the courtyard, and thrown down, is the same large stone so often mentioned. On the right is a range of ruined buildings, on the left a similar range, and rising behind it the high mound represented in the frontispiece; and in front, at the end of the courtyard, is a range of ruined buildings, with another archway in the centre. Crossing the courtyard, and passing through this archway, we ascend a flight of steps, now ruined, and reach another courtyard, one hundred feet long by eighty-five deep. On each side of this courtyard, too, is a range of ruined buildings, and at the other end is a great Teocalis, two hundred feet in length, one hundred and twenty deep, and about fifty feet high. A broad staircase leads to the top, on which stands a long narrow building, one hundred feet by twenty, divided into three apartments.

There was a mournful interest about this great pile of ruins. Entering under the great archway, crossing two noble courtyards, with ruined buildings on each side, and ascending the great staircase to the building on the top, gave a stronger impression of departed greatness than anything else in this desolate city. It commanded a view of every other building, and stood apart in lonely grandeur, seldom disturbed by human footsteps. On going up to it once Mr. Catherwood started a deer, and at another time a wild hog.

At the northeast angle of this building is a vast range of high, ruined terraces, facing east and west, nearly eight hundred feet long at the base, and called the Campo Santo. On one of these is a building of two stories, with some remains of sculpture, and in a deep and overgrown valley at the foot, the Indians say, was the burial-place of this ancient city; but, though searching for it ourselves, and offering a reward to them for the discovery, we never found in it a sepulchre.

Besides these there was the Casa de la Vieja, or the House of the Old Woman, standing in ruins. Once, when the wind was high, I saw the remains of the front wall bending before its force. It is four or five hundred feet from the Casa del Gobernador, and has its name from a mutilated statue of an old woman lying before it.

Near by are other monuments lying on the ground, overgrown and half buried (referred to in the Appendix), which were pointed out to us by the Indians on our first visit. North of this there is a circular mound of ruins, probably of a circular building like that of Mayapan. A wall which was said to encompass the city is laid down on the plan so far as it can be traced; and beyond this, for a great distance in every direction, the ground is strewed with ruins; but with this brief description I close. I might extend it indefinitely, but I have compressed it within the smallest possible limits. We made plans of every building and drawings of every sculptured stone, and this place alone might furnish materials for larger volumes than these; but I have so many and such vast remains to present that I am obliged to avoid details as much as possible. These it is my hope at some future day to present with a minuteness that shall satisfy the most craving antiquary, but I trust that what I have done will give the reader some definite idea of the ruins of Uxmal. Perhaps, as we did, he will imagine the scene that must have been presented when all these buildings were entire, occupied by people in costumes strange and fanciful as the ornaments on their buildings, and possessing all those minor arts which must have been coexistent with architecture and sculpture, and which the imperishable stone has survived.

The historic light which beamed upon us at Merida and Mayapan does not reach this place; it is not mentioned in any record of the conquest. The cloud again gathers, but even through it a star appears.

The padre Cogolludo says, that on the memorable occasion when his sight failed as he was going down the steps of the great Teocalis, he found in one of the apartments, or, as he calls it, one of the chapels, offerings of cacao and marks of copal, used by the Indians as incense, *burned there but a short time before;* an evidence, he says, *of some superstition or idolatry recently committed by the Indians of that place.* He piously adds, "God help those poor Indians, for the devil deceives them very easily."

While in Merida I procured from Don Simon Peon the title papers to this estate. They were truly a formidable pile, compared with which the papers in a protracted chancery or ejectment suit would seem a billet-doux, and, unfortunately, a great portion of them was in the Maya language; but there was one folio volume in Spanish, and in this was the first formal conveyance ever made of these lands by the Spanish government. It bears date the twelfth day of May, 1673, and is entitled a testimonial of royal favour made to the Regidor Don Lorenzo de Evia, of four leagues of land (desde los edificios de Uxmal) from the buildings of Uxmal to the south, one to the east, another to the west, and another to the north, for his distinguished merits and services therein expressed. The preamble sets forth that the Regidor Don Lorenzo de Evia, by a writing that he presented to his majesty, made a narrative showing that at sixteen leagues from Merida, and three from the sierra of the village of Ticul, were certain meadows and places named Uxmalchecaxek, Tzemchan - Cemin - Curea - Kusultzac, Exmuue-Hixmon-nec, uncultivated and belonging to the crown, which the Indians could not profit by for tillage and sowing, and which could only serve for horned cattle; that the said regidor had a wife and children whom it was necessary for him to maintain for the service of the king in a manner conforming to his office, and that he wished to stock the said places and meadows with horned cattle, and praying a grant of them for that purpose in the name of his majesty, since no injury could result to any third person, but, *"on the contrary, very great service to God our Lord, because with that establishment it would prevent the Indians in those places from worshipping the devil in the ancient buildings which are there, having in them their idols, to which they burn copal, and performing other detestable sacrifices, as they are doing every day notoriously and publicly."*

Following this is a later instrument, dated the third of December, 1687, the preamble of which recites the petition of the Captain Lorenzo de Evia, setting forth the grant above referred to, and that an Indian named Juan Can had importuned him with a claim of right to the said lands on account of his being a descendant of the ancient Indians, to whom they belonged; that the Indian had exhibited some confused papers and maps, and that, although it was not possible for him to justify the right that he claimed, to avoid litigation, he, the said Don Lorenzo de Evia, agreed to give him seventy-four dollars for the price and value of the said land. The petition introduces the deed of consent, or quit-claim, of Juan Can, executed with all the formalities required in the case of Indians (the original of which appears among the other title papers), and prays a confirmation of his former grant, and to be put in real and corporeal possession. The instrument confirms the former grant, and prescribes the formal mode of obtaining possession.

Under the deed of confirmation appears the deed of livery of seisin, beginning, "In the place called the edifices of Uxmal and its lands, the third day of the month of January, 1688," &c., &c., and concluding with these words: "In virtue of the power and authority which by the same title is given to me by the said governor, complying with its terms, I took by the hand the said Lorenzo de Evia, and he walked with me all over Uxmal and its buildings, *opened and shut some doors* that had several rooms, cut within the space some trees, picked up fallen stones and threw them down, drew water from one of the aguadas of the said place of Uxmal, and performed other acts of possession."

The reader will perceive that we have here two distinct, independent witnesses testifying that, one hundred and forty years after the foundation of Merida, the buildings of Uxmal were regarded with reverence by the Indians; that they formed the nucleus of a dispersed and scattered population, and were resorted to for the observance of religious rites at a distance from the eyes of the Spaniards. Cogolludo saw in the House of the Dwarf the "marks of copal recently burned," "the evidence of some idolatry recently committed;" and the private title papers of Don Simon, never intended to illustrate any point in history, besides showing incidentally that it was the policy of the government, and "doing God service," to break up the Indian customs, and drive the natives away from their consecrated buildings, are proofs, which would be good evidence in a court of law, that the Indians were, at the time referred to, openly and notoriously worshipping El Demonio, and performing other detestable sacrifices in these ancient buildings. Can it be supposed that edifices in which they were thus worshipping, and to which they were clinging with such tenacity as to require to be driven away, were the buildings of another race, or did they cling to them because they were adapted to the forms and ceremonies received from their fathers, and because they were the same in which their fathers had worshipped? In my mind there is but little question as to the fair interpretation to be put upon these acts, and I may add that, according to the deed of the notary, but one hundred and fifty-four years ago the ruined buildings of Uxmal had "doors" which could be "opened" and "shut."

CHAPTER XV

The reader, perhaps, is now anxious to hurry away from Uxmal, but he cannot be more anxious to do so than we were. We had finished our work, had resolved on the day for our departure, and had determined to devote the intermediate time to getting out of the wall and collecting together some ornaments for removal, and, having got the Indians fairly at work, we set about making some farewell Daguerreotype views. While working the camera under a blazing sun in the courtyard of the Monjas, I received a note from Mr. Catherwood advising me that his time had come, that he had a chill, and was then in bed. Presently a heavy rain came down, from which I took refuge in a damp apartment, where I was obliged to remain so long that I became perfectly chilled. On my return, I had a severe relapse, and in the evening Dr. Cabot, depressed by the state of things, and out of pure sympathy, joined us. Our servants went away, we were all three pinned to our beds together, and determined forthwith to leave Uxmal.

The next day it rained again, and we passed the hours in packing up, always a disagreeable operation, and then painfully so. The next day we departed, perhaps forever, from the Casa del Gobernador.

As we descended the steps, Mr. C. suggested that it was New-year's Day. It was the first time this fact had presented itself; it called up scenes strikingly contrasted with our own miserable condition, and for the moment we would have been glad to be at home. Our cochés were in readiness at the foot of the terrace, and we crawled in; the Indians raised us upon their shoulders, and we were in motion from Uxmal. There was no danger of our incurring the penalty of Lot's wife; we never looked back; all the interest we had felt in the place was gone, and we only wanted to get away. Silent and desolate as we found them, we left the ruins of Uxmal, again to be overgrown with trees, to crumble and fall, and perhaps, in a few generations, to become, like others scattered over the country, mere shapeless and name-less mounds.

Our housekeeping and household were again broken up. Albino and Bernaldo followed us, and as we passed along the edge of the milpa, half hidden among the cornstalks was the stately figure of Chaipa Chi. She seemed to be regarding us with a mournful gaze. Alas! poor Chaipa Chi, the white man's friend! never again will she make tortillas for the Ingleses in Uxmal! A month afterward she was borne to the campo santo of the ha-cienda. The sun and rain are beating upon her grave. Her bones will soon bleach on the rude charnel pile, and her skull may perhaps one day, by the hands of some unscrupulous traveller, be conveyed to Doctor S. G. Morton of Philadelphia.

Our departure from Uxmal was such a complete rout, that it really had in it something of the ludicrous, but we were not in condition to enjoy it at the time. Notwithstanding the com-paratively easy movement of the coché, both Mr. C. and I suf-fered excessively, for, being made of poles hastily tied together, the vehicle yielded under the irregular steps of the carriers. At the distance of two leagues they laid us down under a large seybo tree, opposite the hacienda of Chetulish, part of the do-main of Uxmal. As if in mockery of us, the Indians were all out of doors in holyday dresses, celebrating the opening of the new year. We remained a short time for our carriers to rest, and in two hours we reached the village of Nohcacab, and were laid down at the door of the casa real. When we crawled out, the miserable Indians who had borne us on their shoulders were happy compared with us.

The arrival of three Ingleses was an event without precedent in the history of the village. There was a general curiosity to see us, increased by knowledge of the extraordinary and unaccountable purpose for which we were visiting the country. The circumstance of its being a fête day had drawn together into the plaza all the people of the village, and an unusual concourse of Indians from the suburbs, most of whom gathered round our door, and those who dared came inside to gaze upon us as we lay in our hammocks. These adventurous persons were only such as were particularly intoxicated, which number, however, included on that day a large portion of the respectable community of Nohcacab. They seemed to have just enough of reason left, or rather of instinct, to know that they might offend by intruding upon white men, and made up for it by exceeding submissiveness of manner and good nature.

We were at first excessively annoyed by the number of visiters and the noise of the Indians without, who kept up a contineud beating on the tunkul, or Indian drum; but by degrees our pains left us, and, with the comfortable reflection that we had escaped from the pernicious atmosphere of Uxmal, toward evening we were again on our feet.

The casa real is the public building in every village, provided by the royal government for the audienzia and other public offices, and, like the cabildo of Central America, is intended to contain apartments for travellers. In the village of Nohcacab, however, the arrival of strangers was so rare an occurrence that no apartment was assigned expressly for their accommodation. That given to us was the principal room of the building, used for the great occasions of the village, and during the week it was occupied as a public schoolroom; but, fortunately for us, being Newyear's Day, the boys had holyday.

It was about forty feet long and twenty-five wide. The furniture consisted of a very high table and some very low chairs, and in honour of the day the doors were trimmed with branches of cocoanut tree. The walls were whitewashed, and at one end was an eagle holding in his beak a coiled serpent, tearing it also with his claws. Under this were some indescribable figures, and a sword, gun, and cannon, altogether warlike emblems for the peaceful village which had never heard the sound of hostile trumpet. On one side of the eagle's beak was a scroll with the words "Sala Consistorial Republicana, Año 1828." The other had contained the words "El Systema Central," but on the triumph of the Federal party the brush had been drawn over it, and nothing was substituted in its place, so that it was all ready to be restored in case the Central party returned to power. On the wall hung a paper containing a "notice to the public" in

Spanish and the Maya language, that his Excellency the Governor of the State had allowed to this village the establishment of a school of first letters for teaching children to read, write, count, and the doctrines of the holy Catholic religion; that fathers and other heads of families should send their children to it, and that, being endowed by the public funds, it should not cost a medio real to any one. It was addressed to vecinos, or white people, indigenos, or Indians, and other classes, meaning Mestizoes.

On one side of this principal room was the quartel, with the garrison, which consisted of seven soldiers, militia, three or four of whom were down with fever and ague. On the other was the prison with its grated door, and one gentleman in misfortune looking through the grating.

This building occupied all one side of the plaza. The village was the only one I had seen that gave any indications of "improvement;" and certainly I had not seen any that needed it more. The plaza was the poorest in appearance, and at that time was worse than usual. It had been laid out on a hillside, and the improvement then going on was making it level. There was a great pile of earth thrown up in the centre, and the houses on one side had their foundations laid bare, so that they could only be entered by means of ladders; and it was satisfactory to learn that the alcaldes who had planned the improvement had got themselves into as much trouble as our aldermen sometimes do in laying out new streets.

From the door of the casa real two striking objects were in sight, one of which, grand in proportions and loftily situated, was the great church I had seen from the top of the sierra in coming from Ticul; the other was the noria, or well. This was an oblong enclosure with high stone walls, and a roof of palm leaves at one end, under which a mule was going round continually with a beam, drawing water into a large oblong basin cemented, from which the women of the village were filling their water-jars.

In our stroll out of doors our Indian carriers espied us, and came staggering toward us in a body, giving us to understand that they were overjoyed at seeing us, and congratulating us upon our recovery. They had not had a fair start with the Indians of the village, but they had been expeditious, and, by making good use of their time and the money we paid them, were as thoroughly intoxicated as the best in Nohcacab. Still they were good-natured as children, and, as usual, each one concluded his little speech with begging a medio.

The North American Indian is by drinking made insolent, ferocious, and brutal, and with a knife in his hand he is always a dangerous character; but the Indians of Yucatan when intoxicated are only more docile and submissive. All wear machetes, but they never use them to do harm.

We endeavoured to persuade our bearers to return to the hacienda before their money was all spent, and at length, giving us to understand that it was in obedience to us, they went away. We watched them as they reeled down the road, which they seemed to find hardly wide enough for one abreast, turning to look back and make us another reverence, and at length, when out of our reach, they all stopped, sat down in the road, and again took to their bottles.

We had arrived at Nohcacab at an interesting and exciting moment. The village had just gone through the agony of a contested election. During the administration of the last alcalde, various important causes, among which were the improvements in the plaza, had roused the feelings of the whole community, and a strong notion prevailed, particularly among the aspirants to office, that the republic was in danger unless the alcaldes were changed. This feeling extended through all classes, and, through the interposition of Providence, as it was considered by the successful party, the alcaldes were changed, and the republic saved.

Fig. 16

The municipal elections of Nohcacab are, perhaps, more important than those of any other village in the state. The reader is aware of the great scarcity of water in Yucatan; that there are no rivers, streams, or fountains, and, except in the neighbourhood of aguadas, no water but what is obtained from wells. Nohcacab has three public wells, and it has a population of about six thousand entirely dependant upon them. Two of these wells are called norias, being larger and more considerable structures, in which the water is drawn by mules, and the third is simply a poso, or well, having merely a cross-beam over the mouth, at which each comer draws with his own bucket and rope. For leagues around there is no water except that furnished by these wells. All the Indians have their huts or places of residence in the village, within reach of the wells; and when they go to work on their milpas, which are sometimes several miles distant, they are obliged to carry a supply with them. Every woman who goes to the noria for a cantaro of water carries a handful of corn, which she drops in a place provided for that purpose: this tribute is intended for the maintenance of the mules, and we paid two cents for the drinking of each of our horses.

The custody and preservation of these wells are an important part of the administration of the village government. Thirty Indians are elected every year, who are called alcaldes of the wells, and whose business it is to keep them in good order, and the tanks constantly supplied with water. They receive no pay, but are exempted from certain obligations and services, which makes the office desirable; and no small object of the political struggle through which the village had passed, was to change the alcaldes of the wells. Buried among the ruins of Uxmal, the news of this important election had not reached us.

Though practically enduring, in some respects, the appendages of an aristocratic government, the Indians who carried us on their shoulders, and our loads on their backs, have as good votes as their masters; and it was painful to have lost the opportunity of seeing the democratic principle in operation among the only true and real *native American* party; the spectacle being, as we were told, in the case of the hacienda Indians, one of exceeding impressiveness, not to say sublimity. These, being criados, or servants, in debt to their masters and their bodies mortgaged, go up to the village unanimous in opinion and purpose, without partiality or prejudice, either in favour of or against particular men or measures; they have no bank questions, nor questions of internal improvement, to consider; no angry discussions about the talents, private characters, or public services of candidates; and, above all, they are free from the degrading imputation of man worship, for in general they have not the least idea for whom they are voting. All they have to do is to put into a box a little piece of paper given to them by the master or major domo, for which they are to have a holyday. The only danger is that, in the confusion of greeting acquaintances, they may get their papers changed; and when this happens, they are almost invariably found soon after committing some offence against hacienda discipline, for which these independent electors are pretty sure to get flogged by the major domo.

In the villages the indifference to political distinctions, and the discrimination of the public in rewarding unobtrusive merit, are no less worthy of admiration, for Indian alcaldes are frequently elected without being aware that they have been held up for the suffrages of their fellow-citizens; they pass the day of election on the ground, and go home without knowing anything about it. The night before their term is to commence the retiring functionaries go round the village and catch these unconscious favourites of the people, put them into the cabildo, and keep them together all night, that they may be at hand in the morning to receive the staves and take the oath of office.

These little peculiarities were told to us as facts, and of such a population I can believe them to be true. At all events, the term of the incumbent officers was just expiring; the next morning the grand ceremony of the inauguration was to take place, and the Indians going out of office were actively engaged in hunting up their successors and bringing them together in the cabildo. Before retiring we went in with the padrecito to look at them. Most of them had been brought in, but some were still wanting. They were sitting round a large table, on which lay the record of their election; and, to beguile the tediousness of their honourable imprisonment, they had instruments by them, called musical, which kept up a terrible noise all night. Whatever were the circumstances of their election, their confinement for the night was, no doubt, a wise precaution, to ensure their being sober in the morning.

When we opened our door the next day, the whole village was in commotion, preparatory to the august ceremony of installing the new alcaldes. The Indians had slept off the debauch of the Newyear, and in clean dresses thronged the plaza; the great steps ascending to the church and the platform in front were filled with Indian women dressed in white, and near the door was a group of ladies, with mantas and veils, and the costume of the señoras in the capital. The morning air was fresh and invigorating; there were no threatening clouds in the sky, and the sun was pouring its early beams upon the scene of rejoicing. It was a great triumph of principle, and the humble mules which trod their daily circle with the beam of the noria, had red ribands round their necks, hung with half dollar and two shilling pieces, in token of rejoicing at the change of the alcaldes of the wells.

At seven o'clock the old alcaldes took their seats for the last time, and administered the oath of office to their successors, after which a procession formed for the church. The padrecito led the way, accompanied by the new alcaldes. They were dressed in black body-coats and black hats, which, as we had not seen such things since we left Merida, among the white dresses and straw hats around seemed a strange costume. Then followed the Indian officials, each with his staff of office, and the rest of the crowd in the plaza. Grand mass was said, after which the padrecito sprinkled the new alcaldes with holy water, and withdrew into his room in the convent to take chocolate. We followed him, and about the same time the whole body of new officers entered. The white alcaldes all came up and shook hands with us, and while the padrecito was raising his chocolate to his lips, the Indians went one by one and kissed his hand without disturbing his use of it. During this time he asked us what we thought of the muchachas, or girls of the village, whether they would compare with those of our country, and, still sipping his chocolate, made an address to the Indians, telling them that, although they were great in respect to the other Indians, yet in respect to the principal alcaldes they were but small men; and, after much other good advice, he concluded by telling them that they were to execute the laws and obey their superiors.

At nine o'clock we returned to our quarters, where, either by reason of our exertion, or from the regular course of the disease, we all had a recurrence of fever, and were obliged to betake ourselves to our hammocks. While in this condition the padrecito came in with a letter he had just received from Ticul, bringing intelligence that the cura had passed a fatál night, and was then dying. His ministro had written to us at the ruins, advising us of his continued indisposition and inability to join us, but, until our arrival at Nohcacab, we had no intimation that his illness was considered dangerous. The intelligence was sudden and most afflicting. It was so short a time since we had parted with him to meet again at Uxmal, his kindness was so fresh in our recollection, that we would have gone to him immediately, but we were fastened to our hammocks.

His illness had created a great sensation among the Indians of Ticul. They said that he was going to die, and that it was a visitation of God for digging up the bones in San Francisco; this rumour became wilder as it spread, and was not confined to the Indians. An intelligent Mestizo lad belonging to the village came over with the report, which he repeated to gaping listeners, that the poor cura lay on his back with his hands clasped on his breast, crying out, in a deep, sepulchral voice, every ten minutes by the watch, "Devuelve esos huesos." "Restore those bones."

We heard that he had with him accidentally an English physician, though we could not make any English of the name. Our fever might leave us in a few hours, and with the desperate hope that we might arrive in time for Doctor Cabot's skill to be of some use to him, or, if not, to bid him a last farewell, we requested the padrecito to procure cochés and Indians by two o'clock in the afternoon.

Two fête days in succession were rather too much for the Indians of Nohcacab. In about an hour one of the new alcaldes came to tell us that, in celebrating the choice of their new officers, the independent electors had all become so tipsy that competent men could be found for only one coché. Perhaps it would have been difficult for the alcaldes to know whether their immediate condition was really the fruit of that day's celebration or a holding over from Newyear's Day, but the effect was the same so far as we were concerned.

The alcaldes and the padrecito, however, appreciated our motives, and knew it was utterly impossible for us to go on horseback, so that, with great exertions, by two o'clock the requisite number came reeling and staggering into the room. We were still in our hammocks, uncertain whether it would be possible to go at all, and their appearance did not encourage us, for they seemed unable to carry themselves on their feet, much less us on their shoulders. However, we got them out of the room, and told them to get the cochés ready. At three o'clock we crawled into the vehicles, and in the mean time our carriers had taken another drink. It seemed foolhardy to trust ourselves to such men, particularly as we had to cross the sierra, the most dangerous road in the country; but the alcaldes said they were hombres de bien, men of good character and conduct; that they would be sober before the first league was passed; and with this encouragement we started. The sun was still scorching hot, and came in directly upon the back of my head. My carriers set off on a full run, which they continued for perhaps a mile, when they moderated their pace, and, talking and laughing all the time, toward evening they set me down on the ground. I scrambled out of the coché; the freshness of the evening air was reviving, and we waited till Doctor Cabot came up. He had had a much worse time than I, his carriers happening to be more intoxicated.

It was nearly dark when we reached the foot of the sierra, and, as we ascended, the clouds threatened rain. Before, it had been an object to leave the coché as open and airy as possible, on account of the heat, but now it was a greater object to avoid getting wet, and I had everything fastened down on the sides. On the top of the sierra the rain came on, and the Indians hurried down as fast as the darkness and the ruggedness of the road would permit. This road required care on horseback and by daylight; but as the Indians were now sober, and I had great confidence in their sureness of foot, I had no apprehensions, when all at once I felt the coché going over, and pinned in as I was, unable to help myself, with a frightful crash it came down on its side. My fear was that it would go over a precipice; but the Indians on the upper side held on, and I got out with considerable celerity. The rain was pouring, and it was so dark that I could see nothing. My shoulder and side were bruised, but, fortunately, none of the Indians were missing, and they all gathered round, apparently more frightened than I was hurt. If the accident had been worse, I could not have blamed them; for in such darkness, and on such a road, it was a wonder how they could get along at all. We righted the coché, arranged things as well as we could, and in due season I was set down at the door of the convent. I stumbled up the steps and knocked at the door, but the good cura was not there to welcome me. Perhaps we had arrived too late, and all was over. At the extreme end of the long corridor I saw a ray of light, and, groping my way toward it, entered a cloister, in which a number of Indians were busily employed making fireworks. The cura had been taken to the house of his sister-in-law, and we sent one of them over to give notice of our arrival. Very soon we saw a lantern crossing the plaza, and recognised the long gown of the padre Brizeño, whose letter to the padrecito had been the occasion of our coming. It had been written early in the morning, when there was no hope; but within the last six hours a favourable change had taken place, and the crisis had passed. Perhaps no two men were ever more glad than the doctor and myself at finding their journey bootless. Doctor Cabot was even more relieved than I; for, besides the apprehension that we might arrive too late, or barely in time to be present at the cura's death, the doctor had that of finding him under the hands of one from whom it would be necessary to extricate him, and still his interference might not be effectual.

As a matter of professional etiquette, Doctor Cabot proposed to call upon the English physician. His house was shut up, and he was already in his hammock, being himself suffering from calentura, for which he had just taken a warm bath; but before the door was opened we were satisfied that he was really an Ingles. It seemed a strange thing to meet, in this little village in the interior of Yucatan, one speaking our own language, but the circuitous road by which he had reached it was not less strange.

Doctor Fasnet, or Fasnach as he was called, was a small man, considerably upward of fifty. Thirty years before he had emigrated to Jamaica, and, after wandering among the West India Islands, had gone over to the continent; and there was hardly a country in Spanish America in which he had not practised the healing art. With an uncontrollable antipathy to revolutions, it had been his lot to pass the greater part of his life in countries most rife with them. After running before them in Colombia, Peru, Chili, and Central America, where he had prescribed for Carrera when the latter was pursuing his honest calling as a pig-driver, unluckily he found himself in Salama when Carrera came upon it with twelve hundred Indians, and the cry of death to the whites. With a garrison of but thirty soldiers and sixty citizens capable of bearing arms, Doctor Fasnach was fain to undertake the defence; but, fortunately, Carrera drew off his Indians, and Doctor Fasnet drew off himself, came into Yucatan, and happened to settle in Tekax, the only town in the state that could get up a revolution. He was flying from it, and on his way to Merida, when he was arrested by the cura's illness. The doctor's long residence in tropical countries had made him familiar with their diseases, but his course of treatment would not be considered legitimate by regular practitioners. The cura's illness was cholera morbus, attended with excessive swelling and inflammation of the stomach and intestines. To reduce these, Doctor F. had a sheep killed at the door, and the stomach of the patient covered with flesh warm from the animal, which in a very few minutes became tainted and was taken off, and a new layer applied; and this was continued till eight sheep had been killed and applied, and the inflammation subsided.

From the house of Doctor Fasnet we went to the cura. The change which two weeks had made in his appearance was appalling. Naturally thin, his agonizing pains had frightfully reduced him, and as he lay extended on a cot with a sheet over him, he seemed more dead than living. He was barely able, by the feeble pressure of his shrunken hand, to show that he appreciated our visit, and to say that he had never expected to see us again; but the happy faces of those around him spoke more than words. It was actually rejoicing as over one snatched from the grave.

The next morning we visited him again. His sunken eyes lighted up as he inquired about our excavations at Uxmal, and a smile played upon his lips as he alluded to the superstition of the Indians about digging up the bones in San Francisco. Our visit seemed to give him so much satisfaction, that, though we could not talk with him, we remained at the house nearly all day, and the next day we returned to Nohcacab on horseback. Our visit to Ticul had recruited us greatly, and we found Mr. Catherwood equally improved. A few days' rest had done wonders for us all, and we determined immediately to resume our occupations.

On leaving Uxmal we had directed our steps toward Nohcacab, not from any attractions in the place itself, but on account of the ruins which we had heard of as existing in that neighbourhood; and, after ascertaining their position, we considered that they could be visited to the best advantage by making this place our head-quarters. We had the prospect of being detained there some time, and, as the casa real was low, damp, and noisy, and, moreover, our apartment was wanted for the schoolroom, by the advice of the padrecito we determined to abandon it, and take up our abode in the convent.

This was a long stone building in the rear of the church, standing on the same high table-land, overlooking the village, and removed from its annoyances and bustle. In the part immediately adjoining the church were two large and convenient apartments, except that, quick in detecting all which could bring on a recurrence of fever and ague, we noticed on one side puddles of water and green mould, from the constant shade of the great wall of the church, and on the door of one of the rooms was written, "Here died Don José Trufique: may his soul rest in peace."

In these rooms we established ouselves. On one side of us we had the padrecito, who was always gay and lively, and on the other six or eight Indian sacristans, or sextons, who were always drunk. Before the door was a broad high platform, running all round the church, and a little beyond it was a walled enclosure for our horses. Opposite the door of the sacristia was a thatched cocina, or kitchen, in which these Indian church ministers cooked and Albino and Bernaldo slept.

It is ascertained by historical accounts, that at the time of the conquest an Indian town existed in this immediate neighbourhood, bearing the name of Nohcacab. This name is compounded of three Maya words, signifying literally the great place of good land; and from the numerous and extraordinary ruins scattered around, there is reason to believe that it was the heart of a rich, and what was once an immensely populous country. In the suburbs are numerous and large mounds, grand enough to excite astonishment, but even more fallen and overgrown than those of San Francisco, and, in fact, almost inaccessible.

The village stands in the same relative position to these ruins that Ticul does to the ruins of San Francisco, and, like that, in my opinion it stands on the offskirts of the old Indian town, or rather it occupies part of the very site, for in the village itself, within the enclosures of some of the Indians, are the remains of mounds exactly like those in the suburbs. In making excavations in the plaza, vases and vessels of pottery are continually brought to light, and in the street wall of the house where the padrecito's mother lived is a sculptured head dug up fifteen years ago.

The whole of this region is retired and comparatively unknown. The village is without the line of all the present main roads; it does not lie on the way to any place of general resort, and is not worth stopping at on its own account. Notwithstanding the commencement of improvements, it was the most backward and thoroughly Indian of any village we had visited. Merida was too far off for the Indians to think of; but few of the vecinos ever reached it, and Ticul was their capital. Everything that was deficient in the village they told us was to be had at Ticul, and the sexton, who went over once a week for the holy wafer, was always charged with some errand for us.

The first place which we proposed visiting was the ruins of Xcoch, and in the very beginning of our researches in this neighbourhood we found that we were upon entirely new ground. The attention of the people had never been turned to the subject of the ruins in the neighbourhood. Xcoch was but a league distant, and, besides the ruins of buildings, it contained an ancient poso, or well, of mysterious and marvellous reputation, the fame of which was in everybody's mouth. This well was said to be a vast subterraneous structure, adorned with sculptured figures, an immense table of polished stone, and a plaza with columns supporting a vaulted roof, and it was said to have a subterraneous road, which led to the village of Mani, twenty-seven miles distant.

Notwithstanding this wondrous reputation and the publicity of the details, and although within three miles of Nohcacab, the intelligence we received was so vague and uncertain that we were at a loss how to make our arrangements for exploring the well. Not a white man in the place had ever entered it, though several had looked in at the mouth, who said that the wind had taken away their breath, and they had not ventured to go in. Its fame rested entirely upon the accounts of the Indians, which, coming to us through interpreters, were very confused. By the active kindness of the padrecito and his brother, the new alcalde Segunda, two men were brought to us who were considered most familiar with the place, and they said that it would be impossible to enter it except by employing several men one or two days in making ladders, and, at all events, they said it would be useless to attempt the descent after the sun had crossed the meridian; and to this all our friends and counsellors, who knew nothing about it, assented. Knowing, however, their dilatory manner of doing business, we engaged them to be on the ground at daylight. In the mean time we got together all the spare ropes in the village, including one from the noria, and at eight o'clock the next morning we set out.

For a league we followed the camino real, at which distance we saw a little opening on the left, where one of our Indians was waiting for us. Following him by a narrow path just opened, we again found ourselves among ruins, and soon reached the foot of the high mound which towered above the plain, itself conspicuous from the House of the Dwarf at Uxmal, and which is represented in Figure 17. The ground in this neighbourhood was open, and there were the remains of several buildings, but all prostrate and in utter ruin.

The great cerro stands alone, the only one that now rises above the plain. The sides are all fallen, though in some places

FIG. 17

the remains of steps are visible. On the south side, about half
way up, there is a large tree, which facilitates the ascent to the
top. The height is about eighty or ninety feet. One corner of a
building is all that is left; the rest of the top is level and overgrown with grass. The view commanded an immense wooded
plain, and, rising above it, toward the southeast the great church
of Nohcacab, and on the west the ruined buildings of Uxmal.

Returning in the same direction, we entered a thick grove,
in which we dismounted and tied our horses. It was the finest
grove we had seen in the country, and within it was a great
circular cavity or opening in the earth, twenty or thirty feet deep,
with trees and bushes growing out of the bottom and sides, and
rising above the level of the plain. It was a wild-looking place,
and had a fanciful, mysterious, and almost fearful appearance;
for while in the grove all was close and sultry, and without a
breath of air, and every leaf was still, within this cavity the
branches and leaves were violently agitated, as if shaken by an
invisible hand.

This cavity was the entrance to the poso, or well, and its
appearance was wild enough to bear out the wildest accounts we
had heard of it. We descended to the bottom. At one corner was

a rude natural opening in a great mass of limestone rock, low and narrow, through which rushed constantly a powerful current of wind, agitating the branches and leaves in the area without. This was the mouth of the well, and on our first attempting to enter it the rush of wind was so strong that it made us fall back gasping for breath, confirming the accounts we had heard in Nohcacab. Our Indians had for torches long strips of the castor-oil plant, which the wind only ignited more thoroughly, and with these they led the way. It was one of the marvels told us of this place, that it was impossible to enter after twelve o'clock. This hour was already past; we had not made the preparations which were said to be necessary, and, without knowing how far we should be able to continue, we followed our guides, other Indians coming after us with coils of rope.

The entrance was about three feet high and four or five wide. It was so low that we were obliged to crawl on our hands and feet, and descended at an angle of about fifteen degrees in a northerly direction. The wind, collecting in the recesses of the cave, rushed through this passage with such force that we could scarcely breathe; and as we all had in us the seeds of fever and ague, we very much doubted the propriety of going on, but curiosity was stronger than discretion, and we proceeded. In the floor of the passage was a single track, worn two or three inches deep by long-continued treading of feet, and the roof was incrusted with a coat of smoke from the flaring torches. The labour of crawling through this passage with the body bent, and against the rush of cold air, made a rather severe beginning, and, probably, if we had undertaken the enterprise alone we should have turned back.

At the distance of a hundred and fifty or two hundred feet the passage enlarged to an irregular cavern, forty or fifty feet wide and ten or fifteen high. We no longer felt the rush of cold wind, and the temperature was sensibly warmer. The sides and roof were of rough, broken stone, and through the centre ran the same worn path. From this passage others branched off to the right and left, and in passing along it, at one place the Indians held their torches down to a block of sculptured stone. We had, of course, already satisfied ourselves that the cave or passage, whatever it might lead to, was the work of nature, and had given up all expectation of seeing the great monuments of art which had been described to us; but the sight of this block encouraged us with the hope that the accounts might have some foundation. Very soon, however, our hopes on this head were materially abated, if not destroyed, by reaching what the Indians had described as a mesa, or table. This had been a great item in all the accounts, and was described as made by hand and highly polished. It was simply a huge block of rude stone, the top of which happened to be smooth, but entirely in a state of nature. Beyond this we passed into a large opening of an irregular circular form, being what had been described to us as a plaza. Here the Indians stopped and flared their torches. It was a great vaulted chamber of stone, with a high roof supported by enormous stalactite pillars, which were what the Indians had called the columns, and though entirely different from what we had expected, the effect under the torchlight, and heightened by the wild figures of the Indians, was grand, and almost repaid us for all our trouble. This plaza lay at one side of the regular path, and we remained in it some minutes to refresh ourselves, for the closeness of the passage and the heat and smoke were becoming almost intolerable.

Farther on we climbed up a high, broken piece of rock, and descended again by a low, narrow opening, through which we were obliged to crawl, and which, from its own closeness, and the heat and smoke of the torches, and the labour of crawling through it, was so hot that we were panting with exhaustion and thirst. This brought us to a rugged, perpendicular hole, three or four feet in diameter, with steps barely large enough for a foothold, worn in the rock. We descended with some difficulty, and at the foot came out upon a ledge of rock, which ran up on the right to a great height, while on the left was a deep, yawning chasm. A few rude logs were laid along the edge of this chasm, which, with a pole for a railing, served as a bridge, and, with the torchlight thrown into the abyss below, made a wild crossing-place; the passage then turned to the right, contracting to about three feet in height and the same in width, and descending rapidly. We were again obliged to betake ourselves to crawling, and again the heat became insufferable. Indeed, we went on with some apprehensions. To faint in one of those narrow passages, so far removed from a breath of air, would be almost to die there. As to carrying a man out, it was impossible for either of us to do more than drag himself along, and I believe that there could have been no help from the Indians.

This passage continued fifty or sixty feet, when it doubled on itself, still contracted as before, and still rapidly descending. It then enlarged to a rather spacious cavern, and took a south-west direction, after which there was another perpendicular hole, leading, by means of a rude and rickety ladder, to a steep, low, crooked, and crawling passage, descending until it opened into a large broken chamber, at one end of which was a deep hole or basin of water.

This account may not be perfectly accurate in all the details, but it is not exaggerated. Probably some of the turnings and windings, ascents and descents, are omitted; and the truest and most faithful description that could be given of it would be really the most extraordinary.

The water was in a deep, stony basin, running under a shelf of overhanging rock, with a pole laid across on one side, over which the Indians leaned to dip it up with their calabashes; and this alone, if we had wanted other proof, was confirmation that the place had been used as a well.

But at the moment it was a matter of very little consequence to us whether any living being had ever drunk from it before; the sight of it was more welcome to us than gold or rubies. We were dripping with sweat, black with smoke, and perishing with thirst. It lay before us in its stony basin, clear and inviting, but it was completely out of reach; the basin was so deep that we could not reach the water with our hands, and we had no vessel of any kind to dip it out with. In our entire ignorance of the character of the place, we had not made any provision, and the Indians had only brought what they were told to bring. I crawled down on one side, and dipped up a little with one hand; but it was a scanty supply, and with this water before us we were compelled to go away with our thirst unsatisfied. Fortunately, however, after crawling back through the first narrow passage, we found some fragments of a broken water-jar, with which the Indians returned and brought us enough to cool our tongues.

In going down we had scarcely noticed anything except the wild path before us; but, having now some knowledge of the place, the labour was not so great, and we inquired for the passage which the Indians had told us led to Mani. On reaching it, we turned off, and, after following it a short distance, found it completely stopped by a natural closing of the rock. From the best information we could get, although all said the passage led to Mani, we were satisfied that the Indians had never attempted to explore it. It did not lead to the water, nor out of the cave, and our guides had never entered it before. We advised them for the future to omit this and some other particulars in their stories about the well; but probably, except from the padrecito, and others to whom we communicated what we saw, the next travellers will hear the same accounts that we did.

As we advanced, we remained a little while in the cooler atmosphere before exposing ourselves to the rush of cold air toward the mouth, and in an hour and a half from the time of entering, we emerged into the outer air.

As a mere cave, this was extraordinary; but as a well or watering-place for an ancient city, it was past belief, except for the proofs under our own eyes. Around it were the ruins of a city without any other visible means of supply, and, what rarely happened, with the Indians it was matter of traditionary knowledge. They say that it was not discovered by them; it was used by their fathers; they did not know when it began to be used. They ascribe it to that remote people whom they refer to as the antiguos.

And a strong circumstance to induce the belief that it was once used by the inhabitants of a populous city, is the deep track worn in the rock. For ages the region around has been desolate, or occupied only by a few Indians during the time of working in the milpas. Their straggling footsteps would never have made that deep track. It could only have been made by the constant and long-continued tread of thousands. It must have been made by the population of a city.

In the grove surrounding the entrance we found some water collected in the hollow of a stone, with which we slaked our thirst and made a partial ablution; and it was somewhat extraordinary that, though we were barely recovered from illness, had exerted ourselves greatly, and been exposed to rapid alternations of heat and cold, we never experienced any bad effects from it.

On our return to the village we found that an unfortunate accident had occurred during our absence; a child had been run away with by a horse, thrown off, and killed. In the evening, in company with the alcalde, the brother of the padrecito, we went to the velorio, or watching. It was an extremely dark night, and we stumbled along a stony and broken street till we reached the house of mourning. Before the door were a crowd of people, and a large card-table, at which all who could find a place were seated playing cards. At the moment of our arrival, the whole company was convulsed with laughter at some good thing which one of them had uttered, and which was repeated for our benefit; a strange scene at the threshold of a house of mourning. We entered the house, which was crowded with women, and hammocks were vacated for our use, these being in all cases the seat of honour. The house, like most of those in the village, consisted of a single room rounded at each end. The floor was of earth, and the roof thatched with long leaves of the guano. From the cross-poles hung a few small hammocks, and in the middle of the room stood a table, on which lay the body of the child. It had on the same clothes which it wore when the accident happened, torn and stained with blood. At one side of the face the skin was scratched off from being dragged on the ground; the skull was cracked; and there was a deep gash under the ear, from which the blood was still oozing. On each side of the head was a lighted candle. It was a white child, three years old, and that morning had been playing about the house. The mother, a woman of uncommonly tall and muscular frame, was applying rags to stanch the flow of blood. She had set out that morning with all her family for Campeachy, with the intention of removing to that place. An Indian woman went before on horseback, carrying this child and another. In the suburbs of the village the horse took fright and ran away, throwing them all off; the servant and one child escaped unhurt; but this one was dragged some distance, and in two hours died of its wounds. The women were quiet and grave, but outside there was a continual laughing, jesting, and uproar, which, with the dead child before our eyes, seemed rude and heartless. While this was going on, we heard the gay voice of the padrecito, just arrived, contributing largely to the jest, and presently he came in, went up to the child, and, addressing himself to us, lifted up the head, showed us the wounds, told what he had done for it, and said that if the doctor had been there it might have been saved, or if it had been a man, but, being so young, its bones were very tender; then he lighted a straw cigar, threw himself into a hammock, and, looking around, asked us, in a tone of voice that was intended for the whole company, what we thought of the girls.

This ceremony of el velorio is always observed when there is death in a family. It is intended, as the padrecito told us, para divertirse, or to amuse and distract the family, and keep them from going to sleep. At twelve o'clock chocolate is served round, and again at daybreak; but in some respects the ceremony is different in the case of grown persons and that of children. In the latter, as they believe that a child is without sin, and that God takes it immediately to himself, the death is a subject of rejoicing, and the night is passed in card-playing, jesting, and story-telling. But in the case of grown persons, as they are not so sure what becomes of the spirit, they have no jesting or story-telling, and only play cards. All this may seem unfeeling, but we must not judge others by rules known only to ourselves. Whatever the ways of hiding or expressing it, the stream of natural affection runs deep in every bosom.

The mother of the child shed no tears, but as she stood by its head, stanching its wounds from time to time, she did not seem to be rejoicing over its death. The padrecito told us that she was poor, but a very respectable woman. We inquired about the other members of her family, and especially her husband. The padrecito said she had none, nor was she a widow; and, unfortunately for his standard of respectability, when we asked who was the father of the child, he answered laughingly, "Quien sabe?" "Who knows?" At ten o'clock he lighted a long bundle of sticks at one of the candles burning at the head of the child, and we went away.

CHAPTER XVI

The next day we set out for another ruined city. It lay on the road to Uxmal, and was the same which I had visited on my first return from Ticul, known by the name of Nohpat. At the distance of a league we turned off from the main road to the left, and, following a narrow milpa path, in fifteen minutes reached the field of ruins. One mound rose high above the rest, holding aloft a ruined building, as shown in Fig-

FIG. 18

ure 18. At the foot of this we dismounted and tied our horses. It was one hundred and fifty feet high on the slope, and about two hundred and fifty feet long at the base. At the top, the mound, with the building upon it, had separated and fallen apart, and while one side still supported part of the edifice, the other presented the appearance of a mountain slide.

Cocome, our guide, told us that the separation had happened only with the floods of the last rainy season. We ascended on the fallen side, and, reaching the top, found, descending on the south side, a gigantic staircase, overgrown, but with the great stone steps still in their places, and almost entire. The ruined building on the top consisted of a single corridor, but three feet five inches wide, and, with the ruins of Nohpat at our feet, we looked out upon a great desolate plain, studded with overgrown mounds, of which we took the bearings and names as known to the Indians; toward the west by north, startling by the grandeur of the buildings and their height above the plain, with no decay visible, and at this distance seeming perfect as a living city, were the ruins of Uxmal. Fronting us was the great Casa del Gobernador, apparently so near that we almost looked into its open doors, and could have distinguished a man moving on the terrace; and yet, for the first two weeks of our residence at Uxmal, we did not know of the existence of this place, and, wanting the clearings that had been made at Uxmal, no part of it was visible from the terraces or buildings there.

FIG. 19

Descending the mound, we passed around by the side of the staircase, and rose upon an elevated platform, in the centre of which was a huge and rude round stone, like that called the picote in the courtyards at Uxmal. At the base of the steps was a large flat stone, having sculptured upon it a colossal human figure in bas-relief, which is represented in Figure 19. The stone measures eleven feet four inches in length, and three feet ten in breadth, and lies on its back, broken in two in the middle. Probably it once stood erect at the base of the steps, but, thrown down and broken, has lain for ages with its face to the sky, exposed to the floods of the rainy season. The sculpture is rude and worn, and the lines were difficult to make out. The Indians said that it was the figure of a king of the antiguos, and no doubt it was intended as a portrait of some lord or cacique.

At a short distance to the southeast of the courtyard was another platform or terrace, about twenty feet high and two hundred feet square, on two sides of which were ranges of buildings standing at right angles to each other. One of them had two stories, and trees growing out of the walls and on the top, forming the most picturesque ruins we had seen in the country. As we approached it Doctor Cabot was climbing up a tree at the corner to get on the roof in pursuit of a bird, and, in doing so, started a gigantic lizard, which went bounding among the trees and along the cornice till he buried himself in a large fissure in the front.

Beyond this was another terrace, having on it ruined buildings overgrown with trees. Mr. Catherwood was tempted to sketch them merely on account of their pictureque effect, and while we were on the ground they seemed to us the most touching and interesting of any we had seen; but as they contribute nothing to illustrate the architecture and art of these unknown people, we do not present them.

Leaving this neighbourhood, and passing by many ruined buildings and mounds, at the distance of six or seven hundred feet we reached an open place, forming the most curious and interesting part of this field of ruins. It was in the vicinity of three mounds, lines drawn from which to each other would form a right angle, and in the open space were some sculptured monuments, shattered, fallen, and some of them half buried. Strange heads and bodies lay broken and scattered, so that at first we did not discover their connexion; but, by examining carefully, we found two fragments, which, from the shape of the broken surfaces, seemed to be parts of one block, one of them representing a huge head, and the other a huger body. The latter we set up in its proper position, and with some difficulty, by means of poles, and ropes which the Indians took from their sandals, we got the other part on the top, and fitted in its place, as it had once stood. Figure 20 represents this monument. It was a solid block of stone, measuring four feet three inches high,

Fig. 20

and one foot six inches thick, and represents a human figure in a crouching posture, with the face, having a hideous expression, turned over the shoulder, almost behind. The headdress is a representation of the head of a wild beast, the ears, eyes, teeth, and jaws being easily distinguishable. The sculpture is rude, and the whole appearance uncouth and ugly. Probably it was one of the idols worshipped by the people of this ancient city.

There were others of the same general character, of which the sculpture was more defaced and worn; and, besides these, there were monuments of a different character, half buried, and dispersed without apparent order, but which evidently had an

Fig. 21

adaptation to each other; after some examination, we made out what we considered the arrangement in which they had stood, and had them set up according to our combination. Figure 21 represents these stones. They vary from one foot four inches to one foot ten inches in length.

Each stone is two feet three inches high. The subject is the skull and cross-bones. The sculpture is in bas-relief, and the carving good, and still clear and distinct. Probably this was the holy place of the city, where the idols or deities were presented to the people with the emblems of death around them.

The ruins lie on the common lands of the village of Noh-cacab, at least so say the alcaldes of that place, but Don Simon Peon claims that they are within the old boundaries of the hacienda of Uxmal, and the settling of the question is not worth the expense of a survey. The name Nohpat is compounded of two Maya words, which signify a great lord or señor, and this is all the information I was able to collect about this ancient city. If we had met with it on our former journey we should have planted ourselves, and given it a thorough exploration. The mounds and vestiges of buildings were perhaps as numerous as those of Uxmal, but they were all ruined. The day was like the finest of October at home, and, as a relief from the heat of the sun, there was a constant and refreshing breeze. The country was open, or studded with trees barely enough to adorn the landscape, and give picturesque beauty to the ruins. It was cut up by numerous paths, and covered with grass like a fine piece of upland at home, and for the first and only time in the country we found pleasure in a mere ramble over fields. Bernaldo came out from the village with a loaded Indian at the precise moment when we wanted dinner, and altogether it was one of the most agreeable and satisfactory days that we passed among the relics of the antiguos.

The next day, being the eighth of January, we set out for the ruins of Kabah. Our direction was south, on the camino real to Bolonchen. The descent from the great rocky table on which the convent stands was on this side rough, broken, and precipitous. We passed through a long street having on each side thatched

FIG. 22

huts, occupied exclusively by Indians. Some had a picturesque appearance, and Figure 22 represents one of them. At the end of the street, as well as at the ends of the three other principal streets, which run toward the cardinal points, were a small chapel and altar, at which the inhabitants of the village might offer up prayers on leaving it, and thanks for their safe return. Beyond, the road was stony, bordered on both sides by scrubby trees and bushes: but as we advanced we passed through an open country, adorned with large forest trees. At the distance of two leagues we turned off by a milpa path on the left, and very soon found ourselves among trees, bushes, and a thick, overgrown foliage, which, after the fine open field of Nohpat, we regarded as among the vicissitudes of our fortunes. Beyond we saw through an opening a lofty mound, overgrown, and having upon it the ruins of a building like the House of the Dwarf, towering above every other object, and proclaiming the site of another lost and deserted city. Moving on, again, through openings in the trees, we had a glimpse of a great stone edifice, with its front apparently entire. We had hardly expressed our admiration before we saw another, and at a few horses' length a third. Three great buildings at once, with façades which, at that distance, and by the imperfect glimpses we had of them, showed no imperfection, and seemed entire. We were taken by surprise. Our astonishment and wonder were again roused; and we were almost as much excited as if this was the first ruined city we had seen.

Our guides cut a path for us, and with great difficulty we went on till we found ourselves at the foot of an overgrown terrace in front of the nearest building. Here we stopped; the Indians cleared a place for our horses, we secured them, and, climbing up a fallen wall of the terrace, out of which large trees were growing, came out upon the platform, and before us was a building with its walls entire, its front more fallen, but the remains showing that it had once been more richly decorated than any at Uxmal. We crossed the terrace, walked up the steps, and entering its open doors, ranged through every apartment. Then we descended the back terrace, and rose upon a high mound, having a great stone staircase different from anything we had seen, and, groping our way among the trees, passed on to the next; and the third presented a façade almost entire, with trees growing before it and on the top, as if nature and ruin had combined to produce their most picturesque effect. On the way we had glimpses of other buildings, separated from us by a thick growth of underwood; and after a hard but most interesting morning's work, we returned to the first building.

Since we first set out in search of ruins we had not been taken so much by surprise. During the whole time of our residence at Uxmal, and until my forced visit to Ticul, and fortunate intimacy with the cura Carillo, I had not even heard of the existence of such a place. It was absolutely unknown; and the Indians who guided us having conducted us to these buildings, of all the rest seemed as ignorant as ourselves. They told us, in fact, that these were all; but we could not believe them; we felt confident that more lay buried in the woods, and, tempted by the variety and novelty of what we saw, we determined not to go away until we had discovered all. So far, since we began at Nohcacab, we had "done up" a city a day, but we had now a great field of labour before us, and we saw at once that it was to be attended with many difficulties.

There was no rancho, and no habitation of any kind nearer than the village. The buildings themselves offered good shelter; with the necessary clearings they could be made extremely agreeable, and on many considerations it was advisable again to take up our abode among the ruins; but this arrangement was not without its dangers. The season of El Norte seemed to have no end; every day there was rain; the foliage was so thick that the hot sun could not dry the moisture before another rain came, and the whole country was enveloped in a damp, unwholesome atmosphere. Besides, unluckily for us, it was a season of great abundance in the village; the corn crop had been good; the Indians had plenty to eat, and did not care to work. Already we had found difficulty in hiring them; it would require constant urging and our continual presence to secure them from day to day. As to getting them to remain with us, it was out of the question. We determined, therefore, to continue our residence at the convent, and go out to the ruins every day.

Late in the afternoon we returned to the village, and in the evening had a levee of visiters. The sensation we had created in the village had gone on increasing, and the Indians were really indisposed to work for us at all. The arrival of a stranger even from Merida or Campeachy was an extraordinary event, and no Ingleses had ever been seen there before. The circumstance that we had come to work among the ruins was wonderful, incomprehensible. Within the memory of the oldest Indians these remains had never been disturbed. The account of the digging up of the bones in San Francisco had reached them, and they had much conversation with each other and with the padrecito about us. It was a strange thing, they said, that men with strange faces, and a language they could not understand, had come among them to disinter their ruined cities; and, simple as their ancestors when the Spaniards first came among them, they said that the end of the world was nigh.

It was late the next day when we reached the ruins. We could not set out before the Indians, for they might disappoint us altogether, and we could do nothing until they came, but, once on the ground, we soon had them at work. On both sides we watched each other closely, though from somewhat different motives: they from utter inability to comprehend our plans and purposes, and we from the fear that we should get no work out of them. If one of us spoke, they all stopped to listen; if we moved, they stopped to gaze upon us. Mr. Catherwood's drawing materials, tripod, sextant, and compass were very suspicious, and occasionally Doctor Cabot filled up the measure of their astonishment by bringing down a bird as it flew through the air. By the time they were fairly broken in to know what they had to do, it was necessary to return to the village.

The same labour was repeated the next day with a new set of men; but, by continual supervision and urging, we managed to get considerable work done. Albino was a valuable auxiliary; indeed, without him I could hardly have got on at all. We had not fairly discovered his intelligence until we left Uxmal. There all had a beaten track to move in, but on the road little things were constantly occurring in which he showed an ingenuity and a fertility of resource that saved us from many annoyances. He had been a soldier, and at the siege of Campeachy had received a sabre-cut in a fleshy part of the body, which rather intimated that he was moving in an opposite direction when the sabre overtook him. Having received neither pay for his services nor pension for his wound, he was a little disgusted with patriotism and fighting for his country. He was by trade a blacksmith, which business, on the recommendation of Doña Joaquina Peon, he had given up to enter our service. His usefulness and capacity were first clearly brought out at Kabah. Knowing the character of the Indians, speaking their language, and being but a few degrees removed from them by blood, he could get out of them twice as much work as I could. Him, too, they could ask questions about us, and lighten labour by the indulgence of social humour, and very soon I had only to give instructions as to what work was to be done, and leave the whole management of it to him. This doubled our effective force, as we could work with two sets of Indians in different places at the same time, and gave Albino a much greater value than that of a common servant. He had one bad habit, which was that of getting the fever and ague. This he was constantly falling into, and, with all our efforts, we could never break him of it, but, unluckily, we never set him a good example. In the mean time Bernaldo sustained his culinary reputation; and, avoiding the bad habit of Albino and his masters, while all the rest of us were lank as the village dogs of that country, his cheeks seemed always ready to burst open.

While we were working at the ruins, the people in the village were losing no time. On the eleventh began the fiesta of Corpus Alma, a festival of nine days' observance in honour of Santo Cristo del Amor. Its opening was announced by the ringing of church bells and firing of rockets, which, fortunately, as we were away at the ruins, we avoided hearing; but in the evening came the procession and the baile, to which we were formally invited by a committee, consisting of the padrecito, the alcalde, and a much more important person than either, styled El Patron del Santo, or the Patron of the Saint.

I have mentioned that Nohcacab was the most backward and thoroughly Indian of any village we had visited. With this strongly-marked Indian character, its church government is somewhat peculiar, and differs, I believe, from that of all the other villages. Besides smaller saints, the favourites of individuals, it has nine principal ones, who have been selected as special objects of veneration: San Mateo, the patron, and Santa Barbara, the patroness of the village; Nuestra Señora de la Concepcion; Nuestra Señora del Rosario; El Señor del Transfigùracion; El Señor de Misericordia; San Antonio, the patron of souls, and El Santo Cristo del Amor. Each of these saints, while acting as patron in general, is also under the special care of a patron in particular.

The process of putting a saint under patronage is peculiar. Among the images distributed around the walls of the church, whenever one is observed to attract particular attention, as, for instance, if Indians are found frequently kneeling before it, and making offerings, the padre requires of the cacique twelve Indians to serve and take care of the saint, who are called mayoles. These are furnished according to the requisition, and they elect a head, but not from their own number, who is called the patron, and to them is intrusted the guardianship of the saint. The

padre, in his robes of office, administers an oath, which is sancti-
fied by sprinkling them with holy water. The patron is sworn to
watch over the interests of the saint, to take care of all the
candles and other offerings presented to him, and to see that
his fête is properly observed; and the mayoles are sworn to obey
the orders of the patron in all things touching the custody and
service of the saint. One of these saints, to whom a patron had
been assigned, was called El Santo Cristo del Amor, the addition
having reference to the love of the Saviour in laying down his
life for man. The circumstance of the Saviour being reverenced
as a saint was as new to us as that of a saint having a patron. It
was the fiesta of this saint which was now celebrated, and to
which we were formally invited. We accepted the invitation, but,
having had a hard day's work, we were taking supper rather
leisurely, when the patron came in a hurry to tell us that the
procession was ready, and the saint was only waiting for us. Not
wishing to put him to this inconvenience, we hurried through
our meal, and proceeded to the church.

The procession had formed in the body of the church, and
at the head of it, in the doorway, were Indians bearing the cross.
Upon our arrival it began to move with a loud chant, and under
the direction of the patron. Next to the cross were four Indians,
bearing on a barrow the figure of the saint, being that of the
Saviour on the cross, about a foot high, and fastened against a
broad wooden back with a canopy overhead, and a small look-
ing-glass on each side. This was followed by the patron and his
mayoles, the padrecito and ourselves, the vecinos, or white people of the village, and a long train of Indian men and women,
bareheaded, in white dresses, and all bearing long lighted candles. Moving down the great steps of the church with a loud
chant, and the cross and the figure of the saint conspicuous
under the light of hundreds of candles, the coup d'œil of the
procession was solemn and imposing. Its march was toward the
house of the patron, and, on turning up the street that led to it,
we noticed a rope stretched along it for perhaps a hundred
yards, and presently a piece of fireworks was set off, called by
them the idas, or goers, and known by pyrotechnists among us
as flying pigeons. The flaming ball whizzed along the rope backward and forward, scattering fire on the heads of the people
underneath, and threw the whole procession into confusion and
laughter. The saint was hurried into a place of security, and the
people filed off on each side of the rope, out of reach of the
sparks. The idas went off with universal applause, and showed

that the custody of the saint had not been placed in unworthy hands. This over, the chant was resumed, and the procession moved on till it reached the house of the patron, at the door of which the padrecito chanted a salve, and then the saint was borne within. The house consisted of a single long room, having at one end a temporary altar, adorned with flowers, and at the other a table, on which were spread dulces, bread, cheese, and various compound mixtures both for eating and drinking.

The saint was set up on the altar, and in a few minutes the patron led the way, through a door opposite that by which we had entered, into an oblong enclosure about one hundred feet long and forty wide, having an arbour of palm leaves overhead. The floor was of hard earth, and seats were arranged around the sides. All the vecinos followed, and we, as strangers and attendants of the padrecito and his family, were conducted to the principal places, being a row of large wooden arm-chairs, two of which were occupied by the padrecito's mother and sister. Very soon all the seats were occupied by whites and Mestiza women, and the whole enclosure, with the exception of a small space for dancing, was filled up with Indian servants and children sitting on the ground.

Preparations were immediately made for dancing, and the ball was opened by the patron of the saint. This patron was not very saintly in his appearance, but really a most respectable man in his deportment and character, and in his youth had been the best bull-fighter the village had ever produced.

He began with the dance called the toros. The brother of the padrecito acted as master of the ceremonies, and with a pocket-handkerchief called out the ladies one after the other, until every dancing lady present had had her turn.

He then took the patron's place, the patron acting as Bastonero in his stead, and called out again every lady who chose to dance. It was a *bal champêtre,* in which no costume was required, and the brother of the padrecito, who had opened upon us, as alcalde elect, with a black dress-coat, white pantaloons, and fur hat, danced in shirt, drawers, straw hat, and sandals, pieces of leather on the soles of his feet, with cords wound round nearly up to the calf of the leg.

When he had finished we were solicited to take his place, which, however, though with some difficulty, we avoided.

I have not yet mentioned, what is a subject of remark throughout Yucatan, and was particularly manifest at this ball, the great apparent excess of female population. This excess was said to be estimated at the rate of two to one; but although it was an interesting subject, and I was seeking for statistical information which was said to exist, I could not obtain any authentic information in regard to it. I have no doubt, however, that there are many more than one woman to one man, which the men say makes Yucatan a great country to live in. Perhaps this is one reason why the standard of morality is not very high, and without wishing to reflect upon our friends in Nohcacab, as this was a public ball, I cannot help mentioning that one of the most personally attractive and lady-like looking women at the ball was the amiga of a married man, whose wife had left him; the best dressed and most distinguished young lady was the daughter of the padre who died in one of our rooms, and who, strictly speaking, ought never to have had any daughters; and in instances so numerous as not to be noticed by the people, husbands without wives and wives without husbands were mingling unrestrainedly together. Many of the white people could not speak Spanish, and the conversation was almost exclusively in the Maya language.

It was the first time we had appeared in society, and we were really great lions—in fact, equal to an entire menagerie. Whenever we moved, all eyes were turned upon us; when we spoke, all were silent; and when we spoke with each other in English, all laughed. In the interlude for refreshments, they had seen us eat, and all that they wanted was to see us dance. The padrecito told us we should be obliged to come out. A dance was introduced called Saca el suyo, or "take out your own," which brought us all out. The patron then called out the mother of the padrecito, a heavy old lady, whose dancing days were long since over, but she went through her part convulsed with laughter, and then called out her son, the padrecito, who, to the great merriment of the whole company, tried to avoid the challenge, but, once started, showed himself decidedly the best dancer at the ball. At eleven o'clock the ball broke up with great good humour; the vecinos lighted their torches, and all went home in a body, filing off at different streets. The Indians remained to take their places, and pass the night in the ball-room, dancing in honour of the saint.

Every evening, besides numerous visiters, we had the baile for recreation. When we did not go, Albino did. His intelligence and position as our head man gave him a degree of consequence, and admitted him within the arbour, where he completely eclipsed his masters, and was considered the best dancer in the place except the padrecito.

CHAPTER XVII

In the mean time we continued our work at Kabah, and, during all our intercourse with the Indians, we were constantly inquiring for other places of ruins. In this we were greatly assisted by the padrecito; indeed, but for him, and the channels of information opened to us through him, some places which are presented in these pages would perhaps never have been discovered. He had always eight Indian sextons, selected from the most respectable of the inhabitants, to take care of the church, who, when not wanted to assist at masses, salves, or funerals, were constantly lounging about our door, always tipsy, and glad to be called in. These sextons knew every Indian in the village, and the region in which he had his milpa, or cornfield; and through them we were continually making inquiries. All the ruins scattered about the country are known to the Indians under the general name of "Xlap-pahk," which means in Spanish "paredes viejas," and in English "old walls." The information we obtained was in general so confused that we were unable to form any idea of the extent or character of the ruins. We could establish no standard of comparison, as those who told us of one place were, perhaps, not familiar with any other, so that it was necessary to see all; and we had one perplexity, the magnitude of which can hardly be conceived, in the extraordinary ignorance of all the people, whites and Indians, in regard to the geography of their own immediate neighbourhood. A place they had never visited, though but a few leagues distant, they knew nothing about, and, from the extreme difficulty of ascertaining the juxtaposition of places, it was hard to arrange the plan of a route so as to embrace several. To some I made preliminary visits; those from which I expected most turned out not worth the trouble of going to, while others, from which I expected but little, proved extremely interesting. Almost every evening, on returning to the convent, the padrecito hurried into our room, with the greeting, "buenas noticias! otras ruinas!" "good news! more ruins!" and at one time these noticias came in so fast that I sent Albino on a two days' excursion to "do" some preliminary visits, who returned with a report justifying my opinion of his judgment, and a bruised leg from climbing over a mound, which disabled him for some days.

As these pages will be sufficiently burdened, I shall omit all the preliminary visits, and present the long line of ruined cities in the order in which we visited them for the purposes of exploration. Chichen was the only place we heard of in Merida, and the only place we knew of with absolute certainty before we embarked for Yucatan; but we found that a vast field of research lay between us and it, and, not to delay the reader, I proceed at once to the ruins of Kabah.

Plate XIV represents the plan of the buildings of this city. It is not made from actual measurements, for this would have required clearings which, from the difficulty of procuring Indians, it would have been impossible to make; but the bearings were taken with the compass from the top of the great teocalis, and the distances are laid down according to our best judgment with the eye.

On this plan the reader will see a road marked "Camino Real to Bolonchen," and on the left a path marked "Path to Milpa." Following this path toward the field of ruins, the teocalis is the first object that meets his eye, grand, picturesque, ruined, and covered with trees, like the House of the Dwarf at Uxmal, towering above every other object on the plain. It is about one hundred and eighty feet square at the base, and rises in a pyramidal form to the height of eighty feet. At the foot is a range of ruined apartments. The steps are all fallen, and the sides present a surface of loose stones, difficult to climb, except on one side, where the ascent is rendered practicable by the aid

Plate XIV

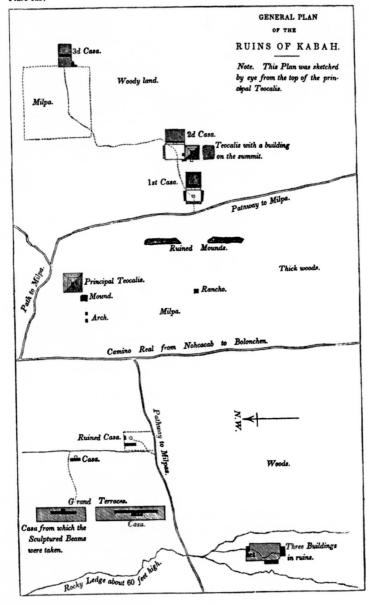

of trees. The top presents a grand view. I ascended it for the first time toward evening, when the sun was about setting, and the ruined buildings were casting lengthened shadows over the plain. At the north, south, and east the view was bounded by a range of hills. In part of the field of ruins was a clearing, in which stood a deserted rancho, and the only indication that we were in the vicinity of man was the distant church in the village of Nohcacab.

Leaving this mound, again taking the milpa path, and following it to the distance of three or four hundred yards, we reach the foot of a terrace twenty feet high, the edge of which is overgrown with trees; ascending this, we stand on a platform two hundred feet in width by one hundred and forty-two feet deep, and facing us is the building represented in Plate XV. On the right of the platform, as we approach this building, is a high range of structures, ruined and overgrown with trees, with an immense back wall built on the outer line of the platform, perpendicular to the bottom of the terrace. On the left is another range of ruined buildings, not so grand as those on the right, and in the centre of the platform is a stone enclosure twenty-seven feet square and seven feet high, like that surrounding the picote at Uxmal; but the layer of stones around the base was sculptured, and, on examination, we found a continuous line of hieroglyphics. Mr. Catherwood made drawings of these as they lay scattered about, but, as I cannot present them in the order in which they stood, they are omitted altogether.

In the centre of the platform is a range of stone steps forty feet wide and twenty in number, leading to an upper terrace, on which stands the building. This building is one hundred and fifty-one feet in front, and the moment we saw it we were struck with the extraordinary richness and ornament of its façade. In all the buildings of Uxmal, without a single exception, up to the cornice which runs over the doorway the façades are of plain stone; but this was ornamented from the very foundation, two layers under the lower cornice, to the top.

The reader will observe that a great part of this façade has fallen; toward the north end, however, a portion of about twenty-five feet remains, which, though not itself entire, shows the gorgeousness of decoration with which this façade was once adorned. Plate XVI represents this part, exactly as it stands, with the cornice over the top fallen.

The ornaments are of the same character with those at Uxmal, alike complicated and incomprehensible, and from the

Plate XV

K A B A H.
Front of the 1st Casa.

fact that every part of the façade was ornamented with sculpture, even to the portion now buried under the lower cornice, the whole must have presented a greater appearance of richness than any building at Uxmal. The cornice running over the doorways, tried by the severest rules of art recognised among us, would embellish the architecture of any known era, and, amid a mass of barbarism, of rude and uncouth conceptions, it stands as an offering by American builders worthy of the acceptance of a polished people.

The lintels of the doorways were of wood; these are all fallen, and of all the ornaments which decorated them not one now remains. No doubt they corresponded in beauty of sculpture with the rest of the façade. The whole now lies a mass of rubbish and ruin at the foot of the wall.

On the top is a structure which, at a distance, as seen indistinctly through the trees, had the appearance of a second story, and, as we approached, it reminded us of the towering structures on the top of some of the ruined buildings at Palenque.

The access to this structure was by no means easy. There was no staircase or other visible means of communication, either within or without the building, but in the rear the wall and roof had fallen, and made in some places high mounds reaching nearly to the top. Climbing up these tottering fabrics was not free from danger. Parts which appeared substantial had not the security of buildings constructed according to true principles of art; at times it was impossible to discover the supporting power, and the disorderly masses seemed held up by an invisible hand. While we were clearing off the trees upon the roof, a shower came up suddenly, and, as we were hurrying to descend and take refuge in one of the apartments below, a stone on the edge of the cornice gave way and carried me down with it. By great good fortune, underneath was a mound of ruins which reached nearly to the roof, and saved me from a fall that would have been most serious, if not fatal, in its consequences. The expression on the face of an Indian attendant as he saw me going was probably a faint reflection of my own.

The structure on the top of this building is about fifteen feet high and four feet thick, and extends over the back wall of the front range of apartments, the whole length of the edifice. In many places it has fallen, but we were now more struck than when at a distance with its general resemblance to the ruined structures on the top of some of the buildings at Palenque. The

Plate XVI

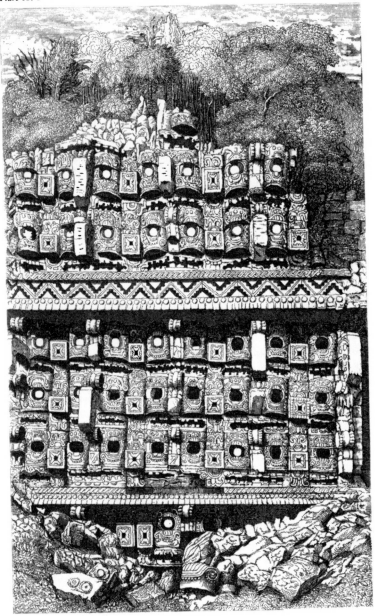

KABAH

Detail of Ornament 1st Casa

Plate XVII

E. Catherwood

H. Adlard

KABAH.

Interior of Centre Room 1st Casa.

latter were stuccoed; this was of cut stone, and more chaste and simple. It could not have been intended for any use as part of the edifice; the only purpose we could ascribe to it was that of *ornament*, as it improved the appearance of the building seen from a distance, and set it off with great effect on near approach.

I have said that we were somewhat excited by the first view of the façade of this building. Ascending the steps and standing in the doorway of the centre apartment, we broke out into an exclamation of surprise and admiration. At Uxmal there was no variety; the interiors of all the apartments were the same. Here we were presented with a scene entirely new. Plate XVII represents the interior of this apartment. It consists of two parallel chambers, the one in front being twenty-seven feet long and ten feet six inches wide, and the other of the same length, but a few inches narrower, communicating by a door in the centre. The inner room is raised two feet eight inches higher than the front, and the ascent is by two stone steps carved out of a single block of stone, the lower one being in the form of a scroll. The sides of the steps are ornamented with sculpture, as is also the wall under the doorway. The whole design is graceful and pretty, and, as a mere matter of taste, the effect is extremely good. Here, on the first day of our arrival, we spread out our provisions, and ate to the memory of the former tenant. His own domains could not furnish us with water, and we were supplied from the wells of Nohcacab.

In the engraving but one doorway appears on each side of the centre, the front wall at the two ends having fallen. On both sides of this centre doorway were two other doorways opening into apartments. Each apartment contains two chambers, with the back one raised, but there are no steps, and the only ornament is a row of small pilasters about two feet high under the door, and running the whole length of the room.

Such is a brief description of the façade and front apartments, and these formed not more than one third of the building. At the rear and under the same roof were two ranges of apartments of the same dimensions with those just described, and having a rectangular area in front. The whole edifice formed nearly a square, and though having less front, with a great solid mass, nearly as thick as one of the corridors, for the centre wall, it covered nearly as many square feet as the Casa del Gobernador, and probably, from its lavishness of ornament, contained more sculptured stone. The rest of the building, however, was in a much more ruinous condition than that presented.

Plate XVIII

At both ends the wall had fallen, and the whole of the other front, with the roof, and the ruins filled up the apartments so that it was extremely difficult to make out the plan.

The whole of the terrace on this latter side is overgrown with trees, some of which have taken root among the fragments, and are growing out of the interior of the chambers.

Plate XVIII will give some idea of the manner in which the rankness of tropical vegetation is hurrying to destruction these interesting remains. The tree is called the alamo, or elm, the leaves of which, with those of the ramon, form in that country the principal fodder for horses. Springing up beside the front wall, its fibres crept into cracks and crevices, and became shoots and branches, which, as the trunk rose, in struggling to rise with it, unsettled and overturned the wall, and still grew, carrying up large stones fast locked in their embraces, which they now hold aloft in the air. At the same time, its roots have girded the foundation wall, and form the only support of what is left. The great branches overshadowing the whole cannot be exhibited in the plate, and no sketch can convey a true idea of the ruthless gripe in which these gnarled and twisted roots encircle sculptured stones.

Such is a brief description of the first building at Kabah. To many of these structures the Indians have given names stupid, senseless, and unmeaning, having no reference to history or tradition. This one they call Xcocpoop, which means in Spanish petato doblado, or a straw hat doubled up; the name having reference to the crushed and flattened condition of the façade and the prostration of the rear wall of the building.

Descending the corner of the back terrace, at the distance of a few paces rises a broken and overgrown mound, on which stands a ruined building, called by the Indians the cocina, or kitchen, because, as they said, it had chimneys to let out smoke. According to their accounts, it must have contained something curious; and it was peculiarly unfortunate that we had not reached it one year sooner, for then it stood entire. During the last rainy season some muleteers from Merida, scouring the country in search of maize, were overtaken by the afternoon's rain, and took shelter under its roof, turning their mules out to graze among the ruins. During the night the building fell, but, fortunately, the muleteers escaped unhurt, and, leaving their mules behind them, in the darkness and rain made the best of their way to Nohcacab, reporting that El Demonio was among the ruins of Kabah.

On the left of this mound is a staircase leading down to the area of Casa No. 2, and on the right is a grand and majestic pile of buildings, having no name assigned to it, and which, perhaps, when entire, was the most imposing structure at Kabah. It measured at the base one hundred and forty-seven feet on one side and one hundred and six on the other, and consisted of three distinct stories or ranges, one on the roof of the other, the second smaller than the first, and the third smaller than the second, having on each side a broad platform in front. Along the base on all four of the sides was a continuous range of apartments, with the doorways supported by pillars, and on the side fronting the rear of Casa No. 1 was another new and interesting feature.

This was a gigantic stone staircase, rising to the roof, on which stood the second range of apartments. This staircase was not a solid mass, resting against the wall of the mound, but was supported by the half of a triangular arch springing from the ground, and resting against the wall so as to leave a passage under the staircase. This staircase was interesting not only for its own grandeur and the novelty of its construction, but as explaining what had before been unintelligible in regard to the principal staircase in the House of the Dwarf at Uxmal.

The steps of this staircase are nearly all fallen, and the ascent is as on an inclined plane. The buildings on the top are ruined, and many of the doorways so encumbered that there was barely room to crawl into them. On one occasion, while clearing around this so as to make a plan, rain came on, and I was obliged to crawl into one with all the Indians, and remain in the dark, breathing a damp and unwholesome atmosphere, pent up and almost stifled, for more than an hour.

The doorways of the ranges on the north side of this mound opened upon the area of Casa No. 2. The platform of this area is one hundred and seventy feet long, one hundred and ten broad, and is elevated ten feet from the ground. It had been planted with corn, and required little clearing. Plate XIX represents the front of this building, and the picote, or great stone found thrown down in all the courtyards and areas, is exhibited on one side in the engraving. The edifice stands upon an upper terrace; forming a breastwork for which, and running the whole length, one hundred and sixty-four feet, is a range of apartments, with their doors opening upon the area. The front wall and the roof of this range have nearly all fallen.

A ruined staircase rises from the centre of the platform to

KABAH.
Front of Casa N.º 2.

Plate XX

KABAH.
3ra Casa.

the roof of this range, which forms the platform in front of the principal building.

This staircase, like that last mentioned, is supported by the half of a triangular arch, precisely like the other already mentioned. The whole front was ornamented with sculpture, and the ornaments best preserved are over the doorway of the centre apartment, which, being underneath the staircase, cannot be exhibited in the engraving.

The principal building, it will be seen, has pillars in two of its doorways. At this place, for the first time, we met with pillars used legitimately, according to the rules of known architecture, as a support, and they added greatly to the interest which the other novelties here disclosed to us presented. These pillars, however, were but six feet high, rude and unpolished, with square blocks of stone for capitals and pedestals. They wanted the architectural majesty and grandeur which in other styles is always connected with the presence of pillars, but they were not out of proportion, and, in fact, were adapted to the lowness of the building. The lintels over the doors are of stone.

Leaving this building, and crossing an overgrown and wooded plain, at the distance of about three hundred and fifty yards we reach the terrace of Casa No. 3. The platform of this terrace, too, had been planted with corn, and was easily cleared. Plate XX represents the front of the edifice, which, when we first came upon it, was so beautifully shrouded by trees that it was painful to be obliged to disturb them, and we spared every branch that did not obstruct the view. While Mr. Catherwood was making his drawing, rain came on, and, as he might not be able to get his camera lucida in position again, he continued his work, with the protection of an India-rubber cloak and an Indian holding an umbrella over the stand. The rain was of that sudden and violent character often met with in tropical climates, and in a few minutes flooded the whole ground. The washing of the water from the upper terrace appears in the engraving.

This building is called by the Indians la Casa de la Justicia. It is one hundred and thirteen feet long. There are five apartments, each twenty feet long and nine wide, and all perfectly plain. The front is plain, except the pillars in the wall between the doorways indicated in the engraving; and above, in front, at the end, and on the back are rows of small pillars, forming a simple and not inelegant ornament.

Besides these, there are on this side of the camino real the remains of other buildings, but all in a ruinous condition, and

Fig. 23

there is one monument, perhaps more curious and interesting than any that has been presented. It is a lonely arch, of the same form with all the rest, having a span of fourteen feet. It stands on a ruined mound, disconnected from every other structure, in solitary grandeur. Darkness rests upon its history, but in that desolation and solitude, among the ruins around, it stood like the proud memorial of a Roman triumph. Perhaps, like the arch of Titus, which at this day spans the Sacred Way at Rome, it was erected to commemorate a victory over enemies.

These were all the principal remains on this side of the camino real; they were all to which our Indian guides conducted us, and, excepting two mentioned hereafter, they were all of which, up to that time, any knowledge existed; but on the other side of the camino real, shrouded by trees, were the trembling and tottering skeletons of buildings which had once been grander than these.

From the top of the great teocalis we had our first glimpses of these edifices. Following the camino real to a point about in a range with the triumphal arch, there is a narrow path which leads to two buildings enclosed by a fence for a milpa. They are small, and but little ornamented. They stand at right angles to each other, and in front of them is a patio, in which is a large broken orifice, like the mouth of a cave, with a tree growing near the edge of it. My first visit to this place was marked by a brilliant exploit on the part of my horse. On dismounting, Mr. Catherwood found shade for his horse, Doctor Cabot got his into one of the buildings, and I tied mine to this tree, giving him fifteen or twenty feet of halter as a range for pasture. Here we left them, but on our return in the evening my horse was missing, and, as we supposed, stolen; but before we reached the tree I saw the halter still attached to it, and knew that an Indian would be much more likely to steal the halter and leave the horse than *vice versa*. The halter was drawn down into the mouth of the cave, and looking over the edge, I saw the horse hanging at the other end, with just rope enough, by stretching his head and neck, to keep a foothold at one side of the cave. One of his sides was scratched and grimed with dirt, and it seemed as if every bone in his body must be broken, but on getting him out we found that, except some scarifications of the skin, he was not at all hurt; in fact, he was quite the reverse, and never moved better than on our return to the village.

Beyond these buildings, none of the Indians knew of any ruins. Striking directly from them in a westerly direction through a thick piece of woods, without being able to see anything, but from observation taken from the top of the teocalis, and passing a small ruined building with a staircase leading to the roof, we reached a great terrace, perhaps eight hundred feet long and one hundred feet wide. This terrace, besides being overgrown with trees, was covered with thorn-bushes, and the maguey plant, or Agave Americana, with points as sharp as needles, which made it impossible to move without cutting the way at every step.

Two buildings stood upon this overgrown terrace. The first was two hundred and seventeen feet long, having seven doorways in front, all opening to single apartments except the centre one, which had two apartments, each thirty feet long. In the rear were other apartments, with doorways opening upon a courtyard, and from the centre a range of buildings ran at right angles, terminating in a large ruined mound. The wall of the whole of this great pile had been more ornamented than either of the buildings before presented except the first, but, unfortunately, it was more dilapidated. The doorways had wooden lintels, most of which have fallen.

To the north of this building is another, one hundred and forty-two feet in front and thirty-one feet deep, with double corridors communicating, and a gigantic staircase in the centre leading to the roof, on which are the ruins of another building. The doors of two centre apartments open under the arch of this great staircase. In that on the right we again found the prints of the red hand; not a single print, or two, or three, as in other places, but the whole wall was covered with them, bright and distinct as if but newly made.

All the lintels over the doorways are of wood, and all are still in their places, mostly sound and solid. The doorways were encumbered with rubbish and ruins. That nearest the staircase was filled up to within three feet of the lintel; and, in crawling under on his back, to measure the apartment, Mr. Catherwood's eye was arrested by a sculptured lintel, which, on examination, he considered the most interesting memorial we had found in Yucatan. On my return that day from a visit to three more ruined cities entirely unknown before, he claimed this lintel as equal in interest and value to all of them together. The next day I saw them, and determined immediately, at any trouble or cost, to carry them home with me; but this was no easy matter. Our operations created much discussion in the village. The general belief was that we were searching for gold. No one could believe that we were expending money in such a business without being sure of getting it back again; and remembering the fate of my castings at Palenque, I was afraid to have it known that there was anything worth carrying away.

To get them out by our own efforts, however, was impossible; and, after conferring with the padrecito, we procured a good set of men, and went down with crowbars for the purpose of working them out of the wall. Doctor Cabot, who had been confined to the village for several days by illness, turned out on this great occasion.

The lintel consisted of two beams, and the outer one was split in two lengthwise. They lapped over the doorway about a foot at each end, and were as firmly secured as any stones in the building, having been built in when the wall was constructed. Fortunately, we had two crowbars, and the doorway being filled up with earth both inside and out, the men were enabled to stand above the beam, and use the crowbars to advantage. They began inside, and in about two hours cleared the lintel directly over the doorway, but the ends were still firmly secured. The beams were about ten feet long, and to keep the whole wall from falling and crushing them, it was necessary to knock away the stones over the centre, and make an arch in proportion to the base. The wall was four feet thick over the doorway, increasing in thickness with the receding of the inner arch, and the whole was a solid mass, the mortar being nearly as hard as the stone. As the breach was enlarged it became dangerous to stand near it; the crowbar had to be thrown aside, and the men cut down small trees, which they used as a sort of battering-ram, striking at the mortar and small stones used for filling up, on loosening which the larger stones fell. To save the beams, we constructed an inclined plane two or three feet above them, resting against the inner wall, which caught the stones and carried them off. As the breach increased it became really dangerous to work under it, and one of the men refused to do so any longer. The beams were almost within my grasp, but if the ragged mass above should fall, it would certainly bury the beams and the men too, either of which would be disagreeable. Fortunately, we had the best set of assistants that ever came out to us from Nohcacab, and their pride was enlisted in the cause. At length, almost against hope, having broken a rude arch almost to the roof, the inner beam was got out uninjured. Still the others were not safe, but, with great labour, anxiety, and good fortune, the whole three at length lay before us, with their sculptured faces uppermost. We did no more work that day; we had hardly changed our positions, but, from the excitement and anxiety, it was one of the most trying times we had in the country.

The next day, knowing the difficulty and risk that must attend their transportation, we had the beams set up for Mr. Catherwood to draw.

Plate XXI represents this lintel, indicated in the engraving as three pieces of wood, but originally consisting of only two, that on which the figure is carved being split through the middle by some unequal pressure of the great superincumbent wall. The top of the outer part was worm-eaten and decayed, probably from the trickling of water, which, following some channel in the ornaments, touched only this part; all the rest was sound and solid.

The subject is a human figure standing upon a serpent. The face was scratched, worn, and obliterated, the headdress was a plume of feathers, and the general character of the figure and ornaments was the same with that of the figures found on the

Plate XXI

F. Catherwood.

KABAH
Carved Beam of Sapote Wood

walls at Palenque. It was the first subject we had discovered
bearing such a striking resemblance in details, and connecting
so closely together the builders of these distant cities.

But the great interest of this lintel was the carving. The
beam covered with hieroglyphics at Uxmal was faded and worn.
This was still in excellent preservation; the lines were clear and
distinct; and the cutting, under any test, and without any reference to the people by whom it was executed, would be considered as indicating great skill and proficiency in the art of
carving on wood. The consciousness that the only way to give
a true idea of the character of this carving was the production of
the beams themselves, determined me to spare neither labour
nor expense to have them transported to this city; and when we
had finished our whole exploration, we were satisfied that these
were the most interesting specimens the country afforded. I had
the sculptured sides packed in dry grass and covered with hemp
bagging, and intended to pass them through the village without
stopping, but the Indians engaged for that purpose left them
two days on the ground exposed to heavy rain, and I was obliged
to have them brought to the convent, where the grass was taken
out and dried. The first morning one or two hundred Indians at
work at the noria came up in a body to look at them. It was
several days before I could get them away, but, to my great relief, they at length left the village on the shoulders of Indians,
and I brought them with me safely to this city. The reader an-
ticipates my conclusion, and if he have but a shade of sympathy
with the writer, he mourns over the melancholy fate that overtook them but a short time after their arrival.

The accidental discovery of these sculptured beams, and in
a position where we had no reason to look for such things, induced us to be more careful than ever in our examination of
every part of the building. The lintel over the corresponding
doorway on the other side of the staircase was still in its place,
and in good condition, but perfectly plain, and there was no
other sculptured lintel among all the ruins of Kabah. Why this
particular doorway was so distinguished it is impossible to say.
The character of this sculpture added to the interest and wonder
of all that was connected with the exploration of these American
ruins. There is no account of the existence of iron or steel
among the aborigines on this continent. The general and well-
grounded belief is, that the inhabitants had no knowledge whatever of these metals. How, then, could they carve wood, and that
of the hardest kind?

In that large canoe which first made known to Columbus the existence of this great continent, among other fabrics of the country from which they came, the Spaniards remarked hatchets of copper, as it is expressed, for "hewing wood." Bernal Dias, in his account of the first voyage of the Spaniards along the coast of Guacaulco, in the Empire of Mexico, says, "It was a Custom of the Indians of this Province *invariably* to carry small Hatchets of Copper, very bright, and the wooden Handles of which were highly painted, as intended both for Defence and Ornament. These were supposed by us to be Gold, and were, of Course, eagerly purchased, *insomuch that within three days we had amongst us procured above six hundred,* and were, while under the Mistake, as well pleased with our Bargain as the Indians with their green Beads." And in that collection of interesting relics from Peru before referred to, in the possession of Mr. Blake of Boston—the existence of which, by-the-way, from the unobtrusive character of its owner, is hardly known to his neighbours in his own city—in that collection are several copper knives, one of which is alloyed with a small portion of tin, and sufficiently hard to cut wood. In other cemeteries in the same district, Mr. Blake found several copper instruments resembling modern chisels, which, it is not improbable, were designed for carving wood. In my opinion, the carving of these beams was done with the copper instruments known to have existed among the aboriginal inhabitants, and it is not necessary to suppose, without and even against all evidence, that at some remote period of time the use of iron and steel was known on this continent, and that the knowledge had become lost among the latter inhabitants.

From the great terrace a large structure is seen at a distance indistinctly through the trees, and, pointing it out to an Indian, I set out with him to examine it. Descending among the trees, we soon lost sight of it entirely, but, pursuing the direction, the Indian cutting a way with his machete, we came upon a building, which, however, I discovered, was not the one we were in search of. It was about ninety feet in front, the walls were cracked, and all along the base the ground was strewed with sculptured stones, the carving of which was equal to any we had seen. Before reaching the door I crawled through a fissure in the wall into an apartment, at one end of which, in the arch, I saw an enormous hornet's nest; and in turning to take a hasty leave, saw at the opposite end a large ornament in stucco, having also a hornet's nest attached to it, painted, the colours being still bright and vivid, and surprising me as much as the sculptured beams. A great part had fallen, and it had the appearance of having been wantonly destroyed. Figure 24 represents this fragment. The ornament, when entire, appears to have been intended to represent two large eagles facing each other; on each side are seen drooping plumes of feathers. The opposite end of the arch, where hung the hornet's nest, had marks of stucco in the same form, and probably once contained a corresponding ornament.

Fig. 24

Beyond this was the great building which we had set out to find. The front was still standing, in some places, particularly on the corner, richly ornamented; but the back part was a heap of ruins. In the centre was a gigantic staircase leading to the top, on which there was another building with two ranges of apartments, the outer one fallen, the inner one entire.

In descending on the other side over a mass of ruins, I found at one corner a deep hole, which apparently led into a cave, but, crawling down, I found that it conducted to the buried door of a chamber on a new and curious plan. It had a raised platform about four feet high, and in each of the inner corners was a rounded vacant place, about large enough for a man to stand in; part of the back wall was covered with prints of the red hand. They seemed so fresh, and the seams and creases were so distinct, that I made several attempts with the machete to get one print off entire, but the plaster was so hard that every effort failed.

Beyond this was another building, so unpretending in its appearance compared with the first, that, but for the uncertainty in regard to what might be found in every part of these ruins, I should hardly have noticed it. This building had but one doorway, which was nearly choked up; but on passing into it I noticed sculptured on the jambs, nearly buried, a protruding corner of a plume of feathers. This I immediately supposed to be a headdress, and that below was a sculptured human figure. This, again, was entirely new. The jambs of all the doors we had hitherto seen were plain. By closer inspection I found on the opposite jamb a corresponding stone, but entirely buried. The top stone of both was missing, but I found them near by, and determined immediately to excavate the parts that were buried, and carry the whole away; but it was a more difficult business than that of getting out the beams. A solid mound of earth descended from the outside to the back wall of the apartment, choking the doorway to within a few feet of the top. To clear the whole doorway was out of the question, for the Indians had only their hands with which to scoop out the accumulated mass. The only way was to dig down beside each stone, then separate it from the wall with the crowbar, and pry it out. I was engaged in this work two entire days, and on the second the Indians wanted to abandon it. They had dug down nearly to the bottom, and one man in the hole refused to work any longer. To keep them together and not lose another day, I was obliged to labour myself; and late in the afternoon we got out the stones, with poles for levers, lifted them over the mound, and set them up against the back wall.

Plates XXII and XXIII represent these two jambs as they stood facing each other in the doorway. Each consists of two separate stones, as indicated in the engravings. In each the upper stone is one foot five inches high, and the lower one four feet six inches, and both are two feet three inches wide. The subject consists of two figures, one standing, and the other kneeling before him. Both have unnatural and grotesque faces, probably containing some symbolical meaning. The headdress is a lofty plume of feathers, falling to the heels of the standing figure; and under his feet is a row of hieroglyphics.

While toiling to bring to light these buried stones, I little thought that I was raising up another witness to speak for the builders of these ruined cities. The reader will notice in Plate

Plate XXII

F Catherwood A Jones

KABAH.

Figure on jamb of Doorway.

Place XXIII

F.Catherwood.

A.Jones.

KABAH.

Figure on jamb of Doorway

XXII a weapon in the hands of the kneeling figure. In that same large canoe before referred to, Herrera says, the Indians had "Swords made of Wood, having a Gutter in the fore Part, in which were sharp-edged Flints, strongly fixed with a sort of Bitumen and Thread." The same weapon is described in every account of the aboriginal weapons; it is seen in every museum of Indian curiosities, and it is in use at this day among the Indians of the South Sea Islands. The sword borne by the figure represented in the engraving is precisely of the kind described by Herrera. I was not searching for testimony to establish any opinion or theory. There was interest enough in exploring these ruins without attempting to do so, and this witness rose unbidden.

In lifting these stones out of the holes and setting them up against the walls, I had been obliged to assist myself, and almost the moment it was finished I found that the fatigue and excitement had been too much for me. My bones ached; a chill crept over me; I looked around for a soft stone to lie down upon; but the place was cold and damp, and rain was threatening. I saddled my horse, and when I mounted I could barely keep my seat. I had no spurs; my horse seemed to know my condition, and went on a slow walk, nibbling at every bush. The fever came on, and I was obliged to dismount and lie down under a bush; but the garrapatas drove me away. At length I reached the village, and this was my last visit to Kabah; but I have already finished a description of its ruins. Doubtless more lie buried in the woods, and the next visiter, beginning where we left off, if he be at all imbued with interest in this subject, will push his investigations much farther. We were groping in the dark. Since the hour of their desolation and wo came upon them, these buildings had remained unknown. Except the cura Carillo, who first informed us of them, perhaps no white man had wandered through their silent chambers. We were the first to throw open the portals of their grave, and they are now for the first time presented to the public.

But I can do little more than state the naked fáct of their existence. The cloud which hangs over their history is much darker than that resting over the ruins of Uxmal. I can only say of them that they lie on the common lands of the village of Nohcacab. Perhaps they have been known to the Indians from time immemorial; but, as the padrecito told us, until the opening of the camino real to Bolonchen they were utterly unknown to the white inhabitants. This road passed through the ancient city, and discovered the great buildings, overgrown, and in some places towering above the tops of the trees. The discovery, however, created not the slightest sensation; the intelligence of it had never reached the capital; and though, ever since the discovery, the great edifices were visible to all who passed along the road, not a white man in the village had ever turned aside to look at them, except the padrecito, who, on the first day of our visit, rode in, but without dismounting, in order to make a report to us. The Indians say of them, as of all the other ruins, that they are the works of the antiguos; but the traditionary character of the city is that of a great place, superior to the other Xlap-pahk scattered over the country, coequal and coexistent with Uxmal; and there is a tradition of a great paved way, made of pure white stone, called in the Maya language Sacbé, leading from Kabah to Uxmal, on which the lords of those places sent messengers to and fro, bearing letters written on the leaves and bark of trees.

At the time of my attack, Mr. Catherwood, Doctor Cabot, and Albino were all down with fever. I had a recurrence the next day, but on the third I was able to move about. The spectacle around was gloomy for sick men. From the long continuance of the rainy season our rooms in the convent were damp, and corn which we kept in one corner for the horses had swelled and sprouted.

Death was all around us. Anciently this country was so healthy that Torquemada says, "Men die of pure old age, for there are none of those infirmities that exist in other lands; and if there are slight infirmities, the heat destroys them, and so there is no need of a physician there;" but the times are much better for physicians now, and Doctor Cabot, if he had been able to attend to it, might have entered into an extensive gratuitous practice. Adjoining the front of the church, and connecting with the convent, was a great charnel-house, along the wall of which was a row of skulls. At the top of a pillar forming the abutment of the wall of the staircase was a large vase piled full, and the cross was surmounted with them. Within the enclosure was a promiscuous assemblage of skulls and bones several feet deep. Along the wall, hanging by cords, were the bones and skulls of individuals in boxes and baskets, or tied up in cloths, with names written upon them, and, as at Ticul, there were the fragments of dresses, while some of the skulls had still adhering to them the long black hair of women.

The floor of the church was interspersed with long patches

FIG. 25

of cement, which covered graves, and near one of the altars was
a box with a glass case, within which were the bones of a woman,
the wife of a lively old gentleman whom we were in the habit of
seeing every day. They were clean and bright as if polished, with
the skull and cross-bones in front, the legs and arms laid on the
bottom, and the ribs disposed regularly in order, one above the
other, as in life, having been so arranged by the husband himself; a strange attention, as it seemed, to a deceased wife. At the
side of the case was a black board, containing a poetical inscription (in Spanish) written by him.

> "Stop, mortal!
> Look at yourself in this mirror,
> And in its pale reflection
> Behold your end!
> This eclipsed crystal
> Had splendour and brilliancy;
> But the dreadful blow
> Of a fatal destiny
> Fell upon Manuela Carillo.

Born in Nohcacab in the year 1789, married at the same village to Victoriano Machado in 1808, and died on the first of August, 1833, after a union of 25 years, and in the forty-fourth of her age.
He implores your pious prayers."

The widowed husband wrote several stanzas more, but could not get them on the black board; and made copies for private distribution, one of which is in my hands.

Near this were the bones of a brother of our friend the cura of Ticul and those of a child, and in the choir of the church, in the embrazure of a large window, were rows of skulls, all labelled on the forehead, and containing startling inscriptions. I took up one, and staring me in the face were the words, "Soy Pedro Moreno: un Ave Maria y un Padre nuestro por Dios, hermano." "I am Peter Moreno: an Ave Maria and Paternoster for God's sake, brother." Another said, "I am Apolono Balche: a Paternoster and an Ave Maria for God's sake, brother." This was an old schoolmaster of the padrecito, who had died but two years before.

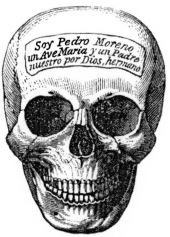

FIG. 26

The padrecito handed me another, which said, "I am Bartola Arana: a Paternoster," &c. This was the skull of a Spanish lady whom he had known, young and beautiful, but it could not be distinguished from that of the oldest and ugliest Indian woman. "I am Anizetta Bib," was that of a pretty young Indian girl whom he had married, and who died but a year afterward. I took them all up one by one; the padrecito knew them all; one was young, another old; one rich, another poor; one ugly, and another beautiful; but here they were all alike. Every skull bore the name of its owner, and all begged a prayer.

One said, "I am Richard Joseph de la Merced Truxeque and Arana, who died the twenty-ninth of April of the year 1838, and I am enjoying the kingdom of God forever." This was the skull of a child, which, dying without sin, had ascended to heaven, and needed not the prayers of man.

In one corner was a mourning box, painted black, with a white border, containing the skull of an uncle of the padrecito. On it was written in Spanish, "In this box is enclosed the skull of Friar Vicente Ortigon, who died in the village of Cuhul in the year 1820. I beseech thee, pious and charitable reader, to intercede with God for his soul, repeating an Ave Maria and a Paternoster, that he may be released from purgatory, if he should be there, and may go to enjoy the kingdom of heaven. Whoever the reader may be, God will reward his charity. 26th of July, 1837." The writing bore the name of Juana Hernandez, the mother of the deceased, an old lady then living in the house of the mother of the padrecito.

Accustomed as we were to hold sacred the bones of the dead, the slightest memorial of a departed friend accidentally presented to view bringing with it a shade of sadness, such an exhibition grated harshly upon the feelings. I asked the padrecito why these skulls were not permitted to rest in peace, and he answered, what is perhaps but too true, that in the grave they are forgotten; but when dug up and placed in sight with labels on them, they remind the living of their former existence, of their uncertain state—that their souls may be in purgatory—and appeal to their friends, as with voices from the grave, to pray for them, and have masses said for their souls. It is for this reason, and not from any feeling of wantonness or disrespect, that the skulls of the dead are thus exposed all over the country. On the second of November, at the celebration of the fête in commemoration *de los fieles difuntos,* all these skulls are brought together and put into the túmulo, a sort of bier hung with black and lighted by blessed candles, and grand mass is said for their souls.

In the afternoon the padrecito passed our door in his robes, and, looking in, as he usually did, said, "Voy á buscar un muerto," "I am going for a corpse." The platform of the church was the campo santo; every day the grave-digger was at his work, and soon after the padrecito left us we heard the chant herald--ing the funeral procession. I went out, and saw it coming up the steps, the padrecito leading it and chanting the funeral service. The corpse was brought into the church, and, the service over, it was borne to the grave. The sacristans were so intoxicated that they let it fall in with its neck twisted. The padrecito sprinkled it with holy water, and, the chant over, went away. The Indians around the grave looked at me with an expression of face I could not understand. They had told the padrecito that we had brought death into the village. In a spirit of conciliation I smiled at a woman near me, and she answered with a laugh. I carried my smile slowly around the whole circle; as my eyes met theirs, all burst into a laugh, and while the body lay uncovered and distorted in the grave I went away. With these people death is merely one of the accidents of life. "Voy á descansar," "I am going to rest," "Mis trabajos son acabados," "My labours are ended," are the words of the Indian as he lies down to die; but to the stranger in that country death is the king of terrors.

In the mean time pleasure was treading lightly upon the heels of death. The fiesta of Santo Cristo del Amor was still going on, and it was to conclude the next day with a baile de dia, or ball by daylight, at the place where it began, in the house of the patron. We were busy in making preparations for our departure from Nohcacab, and, though strongly solicited, I was the only one of our party able to attend. Early in the morning the saint was in its place at one end of the room, the altar was adorned with fresh flowers, and the arbour for dancing was covered with palm leaves to protect it from the sun. Under a shed in the yard was a crowd of Indian women making tortillas, and preparing dishes of various kinds for a general village feast. At twelve o'clock the ball began, a little before two the padrecito disappeared from my side, and soon after the ball broke up, and all moved toward the house. When I entered, the padrecito was in his robes before the image of the saint, singing a salve. The Indian sexton was perfuming it with incense, and the dancers were all on their knees before it, each with a lighted candle in her hand. This over, came the procession de las velas, or of the candles. The cross led the way; then the figure of the saint, a drunken Indian sexton perfuming it with incense. The padrecito, in taking his place behind it, took my arm and carried me along; the patron of the saint supported me on the other side. We were the only men in the procession. An irregular troop of women followed, all in their ball dresses, and bearing long lighted candles. Moving on to the church, we restored the saint to his altar, and set up the candles in rough wooden tripods, to be ready for grand mass the next morning. At this time a discharge of rockets was heard without, and going out, I saw another strange procession. We had all the women; this was composed entirely of men, and might have passed for a jubilee over the downfall of temperance. Nearly all were more than half intoxicated; and I noticed that some who had kept sober during the whole of the fiesta were overtaken at last. The procession was preceded by files of them in couples, each carrying two plates, for the purpose of receiving some of the dishes provided by the bounty of the patron. Next came, borne on barrows on the shoulders of Indians, two long, ugly boxes, the emblems of the custody and property of the saint, one of them being filled with wax received as offerings, ropes for the fireworks, and other property belonging to the saint, which were about being carried to the house of the person now entitled to their custody; and the other had contained these things, and was to remain with its present keeper as a sort of holy heirloom. Behind these, also on the shoulders of Indians, were two men, sitting side by side in large arm-chairs, with scarfs around their necks, and holding on desperately to the arms of the chairs, with an expression of face that seemed to indicate a consciousness that their elevation above their fellow-citizens was precarious, and of uncertain duration, for their Indian carriers were reeling and staggering under their load and agua ardiente. These were the hermanos de la misa, or brothers of the mass, the last incumbent of the office of the keeper of the box and his successor, to whom it was to be delivered over. Moving on with uproarious noise and confusion, they were set down under the corridor of the quartel.

In the mean time our procession of women from the church had arrived, the musicians took their places under the corridor, and preparations were immediately made for another dance. Cocom, who had acted as our guide to Nohpat, and had repaired the locks and keys of our boxes, was master of ceremonies; and the first dance over, two Mestiza girls commenced a song. The whole village seemed given up to the pleasure of the moment; there were features to offend the sight and taste, but there were pretty women prettily dressed; in all there was an air of abandonment and freedom from care that enlisted sympathetic feelings; and as the padrecito and myself returned to the convent, the chorus reached us on the steps, soft and sweet from the blending of women's voices, and seeming to spring from the bottom of every heart,

"Que bonito es el mundo;
  Lastima es que yo me muera."

"How beautiful is the world;
  It is a pity that I must die."

APPENDIX

APPENDIX. VOL. I.

THERMOMETRICAL OBSERVATIONS.

TEMPERATURE of Merida, according to observations taken by the cura Don Eusebio Villamil, for one year, beginning on the 1st of September, 1841, and ending on the 31st of August, 1842. The observations were taken with a Fahrenheit thermometer at six in the morning, midday, and six in the evening. The thermometer stood in the shade, in an apartment well ventilated.

SEPTEMBER, 1842.

Days.	Morn.	Noon.	Even.
1,	80°	84°	84°
2,	80	84	83
3,	60	84	83
4,	80	84	82
5,	80	84	83
6,	81	85	84
7,	81	84	82
8,	81	86	85
9,	81	85	84
10,	82	85	85
11,	83	85	84
12,	82	85	84
13,	82	85	85
14,	82	86	85
15,	82	86	85
16,	83	86	85
17,	83	85	84
18,	83	85	84
19,	83	85	84
20,	84	86	85
21,	84	86	86
22,	84	86	84
23,	84	86	86
24,	84	85	83
25,	80	84	83
26,	80	85	83
27,	81	85	83
28,	82	85	84
29,	82	86	86
30,	83	86	85

OCTOBER.

Days.	Morn.	Noon.	Even.
1,	83°	86°	85°
2,	83	86	85
3,	83	85	83
4,	81	84	82
5,	81	84	83
6,	81	84	82

Days.	Morn.	Noon.	Even.
7,	81°	84°	82°
8,	81	84	82
9,	80	84	82
10,	80	84	83
11,	80	85	84
12,	82	85	84
13,	80	84	84
14,	80	84	84
15,	81	84	84
16,	81	84	83
17,	80	83	83
18,	81	83	83
19,	81	84	84
20,	82	83	81
21,	80	81	80
22,	78	80	78
23,	76	78	78
24,	76	78	78
25,	76	76	76
26,	74	76	76
27,	74	78	78
28,	76	80	79
29,	77	81	80
30,	78	81	81
31,	81	82	82

NOVEMBER.

Days.	Morn.	Noon.	Even.
1,	82°	83°	82°
2,	80	82	81
3,	78	80	80
4,	80	77	77
5,	77	78	78
6,	74	77	76
7,	74	76	76
8,	75	78	78
9,	75	78	78
10,	74	79	79
11,	76	79	79
12,	77	80	80

Days.	Morn.	Noon.	Even.
13,	77°	80°	80°
14,	80	80	80
15,	78	79	79
16,	74	78	78
17,	74	78	78
18,	72	77	77
19,	73	79	79
20,	75	79	79
21,	78	82	82
22,	80	83	82
23,	80	84	83
24,	79	82	82
25,	80	83	83
26,	79	82	80
27,	79	78	78
28,	78	76	75
29,	73	73	74
30,	73	74	74

DECEMBER.

Days.	Morn.	Noon.	Even.
1,	72°	74°	74°
2,	73	77	77
3,	73	79	79
4,	78	79	79
5,	75	76	75
6,	72	74	74
7,	72	74	74
8,	71	74	74
9,	70	74	74
10,	74	78	78
11,	76	78	78
12,	74	77	77
13,	74	78	77
14,	73	78	78
15,	75	79	79
16,	76	78	77
17,	75	75	75
18,	71	74	74
19,	65	73	75

Days.	Morn.	Noon.	Even.
20,	68°	74°	74°
21,	70	76	76
22,	72	88	78
23,	74	78	78
24,	76	77	77
25,	75	77	76
26,	75	78	77
27,	74	79	78
28,	76	79	78
29,	76	78	78
30,	76	77	76
31,	76	78	78

JANUARY, 1842.

Days.	Morn.	Noon.	Even.
1,	75°	78°	77°
2,	75	77	77
3,	76	76	76
4,	74	78	77
5,	74	78	78
6,	74	78	78
7,	74	78	78
8,	74	78	77
9,	74	77	76
10,	74	77	76
11,	73	78	77
12,	74	78	77
13,	74	77	76
14,	73	78	77
15,	74	77	76
16,	74	76	76
17,	73	76	75
18,	73	76	75
19,	70	76	76
20,	73	76	76
21,	72	72	72
22,	70	72	72
23,	68	72	72
24,	68	73	72
25,	69	74	74
26,	72	78	77
27,	73	76	76
28,	73	76	77
29,	74	78	78
30,	74	79	79
31,	74	80	80

FEBRUARY.

Days.	Morn.	Noon.	Even.
1,	75°	78°	78°
2,	74	80	80
3,	76	81	81
4,	76	80	79
5,	77	80	79
6,	76	80	80
7,	76	80	80
8,	76	74	74
9,	73	74	74
10,	71°	76°	76°
11,	74	79	78
12,	74	80	79
13,	76	80	79
14,	77	80	79
15,	77	80	80
16,	78	76	76
17,	72	76	76
18,	75	79	79
19,	76	79	78
20,	77	80	80
21,	78	76	75
22,	73	74	74
23,	70	74	72
24,	69	78	76
25,	71	77	77
26,	74	78	78
27,	76	81	81
28,	77	81	81

MARCH.

Days.	Morn.	Noon.	Even.
1,	78°	82°	82°
2,	78	83	82
3,	78	83	82
4,	78	83	82
5,	78	84	84
6,	78	84	84
7,	78	85	84
8,	78	84	82
9,	77	82	84
10,	76	84	84
11,	78	84	84
12,	78	84	83
13,	76	84	83
14,	79	84	81
15,	78	84	81
16,	78	81	80
17,	77	82	80
18,	76	83	82
19,	76	81	81
20,	76	81	80
21,	75	80	80
22,	76	81	80
23,	76	82	81
24,	74	82	81
25,	76	82	81
26,	76	84	80
27,	76	80	75
28,	76	82	80
29,	76	82	82
30,	78	83	82
31,	78	83	82

APRIL.

Days.	Morn.	Noon.	Even.
1,	78°	83°	80°
2,	76	80	82
3,	77°	83°	82°
4,	78	84	84
5,	78	84	84
6,	79	86	84
7,	79	84	84
8,	79	84	84
9,	81	85	84
10,	77	84	83
11,	79	85	84
12,	78	85	83
13,	78	84	83
14,	77	84	83
15,	79	84	83
16,	80	85	84
17,	81	84	84
18,	80	84	84
19,	79	83	82
20,	78	84	82
21,	78	84	83
22,	79	83	82
23,	77	83	82
24,	78	84	84
25,	80	85	85
26,	81	86	85
27,	84	83	82
28,	80	83	82
29,	78	84	84
30,	78	83	83

MAY.

Days.	Morn.	Noon.	Even.
1,	79°	84°	84°
2,	81	86	86
3,	82	87	86
4,	83	86	83
5,	82	84	84
6,	80	82	82
7,	79	81	80
8,	78	81	80
9,	78	81	81
10,	76	83	81
11,	78	84	82
12,	78	84	83
13,	80	85	83
14,	80	85	83
15,	79	85	84
16,	79	84	84
17,	79	85	85
18,	79	86	86
19,	80	86	86
20,	81	86	85
21,	82	86	85
22,	82	86	85
23,	82	86	86
24,	81	86	86
25,	82	86	85
26,	82	84	82

Days.	Morn.	Noon.	Even.	Days.	Morn.	Noon.	Even.	Days.	Morn.	Noon.	Even.
27,	82°	83°	81°	28,	82°	88°	85°	30,	83°	88°	86°
28,	80	84	80	29,	82	86	85	31,	83	87	86
29,	80	83	80	30,	82	88	85				
30,	80	83	81						AUGUST.		
31,	80	84	83					1,	83°	88°	86°
					JULY.			2,	82	87	86
				1,	83°	86°	84°	3,	84	87	86
	JUNE.			2,	83	86	84	4,	84	87	86
1,	79°	84°	84°	3,	82	86	84	5,	83	87	86
2,	80	86	85	4,	82	86	85	6,	82	86	85
3,	81	86	85	5,	82	86	83	7,	82	86	86
4,	82	86	85	6,	81	86	86	8,	82	87	86
5,	83	86	86	7,	82	88	86	9,	83	88	86
6,	84	87	85	8,	82	86	85	10,	83	88	87
7,	82	86	85	9,	81	86	85	11,	84	88	82
8,	83	87	85	10,	81	84	82	12,	82	86	86
9,	83	86	85	11,	80	82	81	13,	83	86	86
10,	83	86	83	12,	78	82	82	14,	82	87	85
11,	81	86	85	13,	80	84	83	15,	83	86	83
12,	82	86	85	14,	79	86	85	16,	82	86	83
13,	84	86	86	15,	82	87	85	17,	81	85	84
14,	84	87	86	16,	82	86	86	18,	81	86	85
15,	85	88	88	17,	82	86	86	19,	80	86	84
16,	85	88	84	18,	81	85	83	20,	82	86	86
17,	84	87	86	19,	81	85	83	21,	82	86	86
18,	84	88	88	20,	81	85	82	22,	82	86	84
19,	84	88	88	21,	80	85	82	23,	81	86	86
20,	84	88	87	22,	80	85	82	24,	82	86	86
21,	84	88	87	23,	80	85	82	25,	83	87	86
22,	83	88	88	24,	81	86	85	26,	84	87	86
23,	82	88	86	25,	82	87	85	27,	82	87	86
24,	82	89	86	26,	81	86	84	28,	80	85	85
25,	83	88	86	27,	82	87	86	29,	80	85	85
26,	82	88	86	28,	83	87	86	30,	81	86	86
27,	82	88	86	29,	83	86	86	31,	82	86	86

TABLE OF STATISTICS OF YUCATAN.

Districts	Principal Places	Parishes	Villages annexed	Distance from the Capital—the Leagues	Population	PRODUCTIONS
Capital	Mérida	4	5		37,801	Horned cattle, horses, mules, tallow, jerked beef, leather, salt, gypsum, hemp, raw and manufactured, straw hats, guitars, cigars, and extract of logwood.
Campeachy	City of Campeachy .	2	"	36	19,600	Salt, logwood, rice, sugar, and marble of good quality.
Lerma	Village of Lerma .	3	8	37	10,567	Logwood, timber, rice, and fish oil.
Valladolid	City of Valladolid .	11	17	36	63,161	Cotton, sugar, starch, gum copal, tobacco, cochineal, saffron, vanilla, cotton fabrics, yarns, &c., wax, honey, castor oil, horned cattle, hogs, and skins.
Coast	City of Izamal .	16	27	15	78,846	Horned cattle, horses, mules, tallow, jerked beef, castor oil, hides, wax, honey, timber, indigo, hemp, raw and manufactured, straw cigars, barilla, and salt.
The Upper Highlands .	City of Tekax .	9	7	25	60,776	Horned cattle, horses, mules, hogs, sheep, skins, sugar, molasses, timber, rice, tobacco, in the leaf and manufactured, spirits, arrow-root, straw hats, cotton lace, ochre, flints, and grindstones.
The Lower Highlands .	Village of Teabo .	8	5	17	42,188	Horned cattle, horses, mules, hogs, sheep, skins, tallow, dried beef, hemp, raw and manufactured, and cotton lace.
The Upper Royal Road .	Town of Jequelchakan	6	11	26	54,447	Cattle, horses, mules, skins, tallow, dried beef, logwood, tobacco, sugar, and rum.
The Lower Royal Road .	Village of Maxcanú .	5	7	14	41,726	Horned cattle, horses, mules, oil of palma Cristi, tobacco, hemp, and fine straw hats.
The Upper "Beneficios" .	Village of Ichmul .	7	15	39	66,680	Sugar, molasses, rum, tobacco of good quality, rice, laces, pepper, gum copal, sarsaparilla, hats, hammocks, ebony, barilla, gypsum, and skins.
The Lower "Beneficios" .	Village of Sotuta .	6	16	22	49,443	Horned cattle, horses, mules, hogs, skins, tallow, and dried beef.
Tizimin	Village of Tizimin .	7	18	41	37,168	Tortoise-shell, skins, timber, logwood, India-rubber, incense, tobacco, achiote (a substitute for saffron, and a very rich dye), starch from the yuca, cotton, wax, honey, molasses, sugar, rum, castor oil, salt, amber, vanilla, hogs, cochineal.
Island of Cármen . .	Town of Cármen .	2	1	80	4,364	Logwood.
Sciba-playa . . .	Village of Seiba-playa .	3	6	42	8,183	Timber, rice, logwood, and salt.
Bacalar	Town of Bacalar .	2	"	88	3,986	Logwood, valuable timber, sugar of inferior quality, tobacco of the best description, rum. a fine species of hemp, known under the name of *pita*, resin, India-rubber, gum copal, pimento, sarsaparilla, vanilla, and gypsum.
Total	15	91	143		578,939	

POPULATION OF YUCATAN.

STATEMENT showing the number of inhabitants in the five departments into which the state is divided, distinguishing the sexes; taken from the census made by order of the government on the 8th of April, 1841.

Departments.	Men.	Women.	Total.
Merida . .	48,606	58,663	107,269
Izamal . .	32,915	37,933	70,848
Tekax . .	58,127	64,697	122,824
Valladolid .	45,353	46,926	92,279
Campeachy	39,017	40,639	79,656
			472,876

NOTE.—"This census is probably not very exact, because, having continually the fear of new contributions, and detesting military service, every one reduces as far as possible the number of his family in the lists prepared for the census. It appears to me that the total population of Yucatan may be fixed at 525,000 souls."—P. DE R.

"The best information I have been enabled to obtain goes to show that the population of the state cannot fall short of 600,000 souls."—J. B. JR.

SYSTEM ADOPTED BY THE ANCIENT BUILDERS OF YUCATAN IN COVERING THEIR ROOMS WITH STONE ROOFS.

THE engraving No. 1 represents the arch referred to in the description of the Monjas at Uxmal; and as the stones are not quite horizontal, but stand nearly at right angles to the line of the arch, it shows how near an approach was made to the real principle on which the arch is constructed.

Throughout every part of Central America, Chiapas, and Yucatan, the same method is to be traced with slight modifications. The stones forming the side walls are made to overlap each other until the walls almost meet above, and then the narrow ceilings are covered with a layer of flat stones. In every case the stones were laid in horizontal layers, the principle of constructing arches, as understood by us, being unknown to the aboriginal builders. This readily accounts for the extreme narrowness of all their rooms, the widest not exceeding twenty feet, and the width more frequently being only from six to ten feet. In a few cases the covering stone is wanting, and the two sides meet so as to form a sharp angle. At Palenque the builders did not cut the edges of the stones, so as to form an even surface, their practice differing in this respect from that adopted in Yucatan, where in every instance the sides of the arch are made perfectly straight, or have a slight curve, with the inner surfaces smooth.

It may now be interesting to inquire if any similarity exists between the American method and those observed among the nations of antiquity in

No. 1.

Europe and Asia. A true arch is formed of a series of wedge-like stones
or of bricks, supporting each other, and all bound firmly together by the
pressure of the centre one upon them, which latter is therefore distinguished by the name of keystone.

It would seem that the arch, as thus defined, and as used by the Romans,
was not known to the Greeks in the early periods of their history, otherwise a language so copious as theirs, and of such ready application, would
not have wanted a name properly Greek by which to distinguish it.　The

use of both arches and vaults appears, however, to have existed in Greece previous to the Roman conquest, though not to have been in general practice. And the former made use of a contrivance, even before the Trojan war, by which they were enabled to gain all the advantages of our archway in making corridors or hollow galleries, and which, in appearance, resembled the pointed arch, such as is now termed Gothic. This was effected by cutting away the superincumbent stones at an angle of about 45° with the horizon.

Of the different forms and curves of arches now in use, the only one adopted by the Romans was the semicircle; and the use of this constitutes one leading distinction between Greek and Roman architecture, for by its application the Romans were enabled to execute works of far bolder construction than those of the Greeks: to erect bridges and aquæducts, and the most durable and massive structures of brick. On the antiquity of the arch among the Egyptians, Mr. Wilkinson has the following remarks: "There is reason to believe that some of the chambers in the pavilion of Remeses III., at Medeenet Haboo, were arched with stone, since the devices on the upper part of their walls show that the fallen roofs had this form. At Saggara, a stone arch still exists of the time of the second Psamaticus, and, consequently, erected six hundred years before our era; nor can any one, who sees the style of its construction, for one moment doubt that the Egyptians had been long accustomed to the erection of stone vaults. It is highly probable that the small quantity of wood in Egypt, and the consequent expense of this kind of roofing, led to the invention of the arch. It was evidently used in their tombs as early as the commencement of the eighteenth dynasty, or about the year 1540 B.C.; and, judging from some of the drawings at Beni Hassan, it seems to have been known in the time of the first Osirtasen, whom I suppose to have been contemporary with Joseph."—*Manners and Customs of the Anc. Egyptians*, vol. ii., p. 116, 117, 1st series.

The entrance to the great Pyramid at Gizeh is somewhat similar in form to the arches found in Yucatan; it consists of two immense granite stones of immense size, meeting in a point and forming a sharp angle.

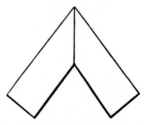

Of the accompanying plates, No. 2 represents the arches in the walls of Tiryns, copied from Sir W. Gell's Argolis; No. 3, an arch (called Cyclo-

No. 2.

No. 3.

pean) at Arpino, in the Neapolitan Territory; No. 4, the most common

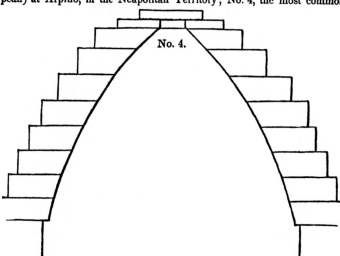

No. 4.

form of arch used by the ancient American builders. A striking resemblance will doubtless be observed, indeed, they may almost be considered identical; and it may be added, that at Medeenet Haboo, which forms a part of the ancient Egyptian Thebes, a similar contrivance was observed by Mr. Catherwood. From this it will appear that the true principles of the arch were not understood by the ancient Egyptians, Greeks, or Etruscans, or by the American builders. It might be supposed that a coincidence of this strongly-marked character would go far to establish an ancient connexion between all these people; but, without denying that such may have been the case, the probabilities are greatly the other way.

This most simple mode of covering over a void space with stone, when single blocks of sufficient size could not be employed, would suggest itself to the most barbarous as well as to the most refined people. Indeed, in a mound lately opened in the Ohio Valley, two circular chambers were discovered, and are still preserved, the walls being made of logs, and the roofs formed by overlapping stones rising to a point, on precisely the same plan as the Treasury of Atreus at Mycenæ, and the chamber at Orchomenus, built by Minyas, king of Bœotia. No inference as to common origin or international communication can with safety be drawn from such coincidences, or from any supposed coincidence between the pyramidal structures of this Continent and those of Egypt, for no agreement exists, except that both are called pyramids.

In the Egyptian Pyramids the sides are of equal lengths, and, with one exception (Saccara), composed of straight lines, which is not the case with any pyramid of the American Continent. The sides are never equal, are frequently composed of curves and straight lines, and in no instance form a sharp apex.

————

VESTIGIA PHALLICÆ RELIGIONIS PROUT QUIBUSDAM MONUMENTIS AMERICANIS INDICANTUR.—(*Vid. tom.* i., *pag.* 181.)

Hæc monumenta ex undecim Phallis constant, omnibus plus minusve fractis, undique dispersis, atque solo semiobrutis, duorum circiter vel trium pedum mensuram habentibus. Non ea nosmetipsi reperimus neque illis hanc Phallicam naturam attribuimus; nobis autem, has regiones ante pererrantibus, hæc eadem monumenta Indi ostenderunt, quodam nomine appellantes lingua ipsorum eandem vim habente, ac supra dedimus. Quibus auditis, hæc Phallicæ religionis, his etiam in terris, vestigia putanda esse tunc primum judicavimus. Monumenta attamen de quibus huc usque locuti sumus, non, ut bene sciunt eruditi, libidinem denotant, sed potius, quod memoria dignissimum, nostra etiam continente vis genitalis cultum, omnibus pæne antiquis Europæ Asiæque nationibus communem, per symbola nota olim viguisse. Quam autem cognationem hic Phallorum cultus his populis cum Americæ aboriginibus indicare videatur, non nostrum est, qui visa tantum vel audita litteris mandamus, his paginis exponere.

————

ANCIENT CHRONOLOGY OF YUCATAN; OR, A TRUE EXPOSITION OF THE METHOD USED BY THE INDIANS FOR COMPUTING TIME.—*Translated from the Manuscript of Don Juan Pio Perez, Gefe Politico of Peto, Yucatan.*

1°. *Origin of the Period of 13 Days (triadecateridas).*

THE inhabitants of this peninsula, which, at the time of the arrival of the Spaniards, was called *Mayapan*, and by its first inhabitants or settlers *Chacnouitan*, divided time by calculating it almost in the same manner as their ancestors the Tulteques, differing only in the particular arrangement of their great ages (siglos).

The period of 13 days, resulting from their first chronological combinations, afterward became their sacred number, to which, introducing it ingeniously in their reckonings, they made all those divisions subordinate which they devised to adjust their calendar to the solar course; so that the days, years, and ages were counted by periods of thirteen numbers.

It is very probable that the Indians, before they had corrected their computation, used the lunations (neomenias) to regulate the annual course of the sun, counting (señalando) 26 days for each lunation; which is a little more or less than the time during which the moon is seen above the horizon in each of its revolutions; dividing this period into two of 13 days, which served them as weeks, giving to the first the first 13 days during which the new moon is seen till it is full; and to the second, the other thirteen, during which the moon is decreasing until it cannot be seen by the naked eye.

In the lapse of time, and by constant observations, they obtained a better knowledge of the solar course, perceiving that the 26 days, or two periods of 13 days, did not give a complete lunation, and that the year could not be regulated exactly by lunations, inasmuch as the solar revolutions do not coincide with those of the moon, except at long intervals. Adding this knowledge to more correct principles and data, they finally constructed their calendar in accordance with the course of the principal luminary, preserving always their periods of 13 days, not in order to make them agree with the apparent course of the moon, but to use them as weeks, and for their chronological divisions.

2°. *The Weeks.*

It must not be supposed that the weeks of the ancient Indians were similar to ours, that is to say, that they were the revolution of a period of days, each having a particular name: they were only the revolution or successive repetition of thirteen numbers applied in arithmetical progression to the twenty days of the month. The year being composed of 28 weeks and one additional day or number, the course of the years, on account of that excess, followed the arithmetical progression of the thirteen weekly numbers; so that if a year commenced with the number 1, the next would commence with number 2, and so on to the close of the 13 years, which formed an indiction, or week of years, as will be explained hereafter.

3°. *The Month.*

"Month" is called in the Yucateco language "U," which means also "the moon;" and this corroborates the presumption that the Indians went on from the computation of lunations to determine the course of the sun, calling the months "moons." But in some manuscripts, the name of *Uinal* in the singular and *Uinalob* in the plural is given to the eighteen months which compose the year; applying this comprehensive term to the series, and to each one of the particular names assigned to the twenty days that composed the month.

The day was called *Kin*, "the sun;" and the particular names by which the 20 days composing the month were designated are stated in the following table, in which they are divided into sets of five, for the better understanding of the subsequent explanations.

1st.	2d.	3d.	4th.
Kan.	Muluc.	Gix (Hix).	Ca-uac.
Chicchan.	Oc.	Men.	Ajau (Ahau).
Quimí (Cimí).	Chuen.	Quib (Cib).	Ymix.
Manik.	Eb.	Caban.	Yk.
Lamat.	Been.	Edznab.	Akbal.

As those names corresponded in number with the days of the month, it followed that, the name of the first day of the year being known, the names of the first days of all the successive months were equally known; and they were distinguished from each other only by adding the number of the week to which they respectively belonged. But the week consisting of thirteen days, the month necessarily consisted of a week and seven days; so that if the month began with the first number of a week, it ended with the seventh number of the week ensuing.

[In order to know the number of the week corresponding with the first day of each month respectively, it is necessary only to know the number of the week with which the year begins, and to add successively seven, but subtracting thirteen whenever the sum of this addition exceeds thirteen, which gives the following series for the first days of the eighteen months: 1, 8, 2 (15–13), 9, 3 (16–13), 10, 4, 11, 5, 12, 6, 13, 7, 1, 8, 2, 9, 3, supposing the first day of the year to be the first day of the week, and generally taking for the first number of the series the number of the week by which the year begins.]

4°. *The Year.*

To this day the Indians call the year *Jaab* or *Haab*, and, while heathens, they commenced it on the 16th of July. It is worthy of notice that their progenitors, having sought to make it begin from the precise day on which the sun returns to the zenith of this peninsula on his way to the southern regions, but being destitute of instruments for their astronomical observations, and guided only by the naked eye, erred only forty-eight hours in advance. That small difference proves that they endeavoured to determine, with the utmost attainable correctness, the day on which the luminary passed the most culminating point of our sphere, and that they were not ignorant of the use of the gnomon in the most tempestuous days of the rainy season.

They divided the year into 18 months, as follows:

> 1st, Pop, beginning on the 16th of July.
> 2d, U66, beginning on the 5th of August.
> 3d, Zip, beginning on the 25th of August.
> 4th, Zodz, beginning on the 14th of September.
> 5th, Zeec, beginning on the 4th of October.
> 6th, Xul, beginning on the 24th of October.
> 7th, Dze-yaxkin, beginning on the 13th of November.
> 8th, Mol, beginning on the 3d of December.
> 9th, Dchen, beginning on the 23d of December.
> 10th, Yaax, beginning on the 12th of January.
> 11th, Zac, beginning on the 1st of February.
> 12th, Quej, beginning on the 21st of February.
> 13th, Mac, beginning on the 13th of March.
> 14th, Kankin, beginning on the 2d of April.

15th, Moan, beginning on the 22d of April.
16th, Pax, beginning on the 12th of May.
17th, Kayab, beginning on the 1st of June.
18th, Cumkú, beginning on the 21st of June.

As the 18 months of 20 days each contained but 360 days, and the common year consists of 365, five supplementary days were added at the end of each year, which made part of no month, and which, for that reason, they called "days without name," *xona kaba kin.* They called them also *uayab* or *uayeb Jaab;* which may be interpreted two different ways. The word *uayab* may be derived from *uay,* which means "bed" or "chamber," presuming that the Indians believed the year to rest during those days; or *uayab* may equally be derived from another signification of *uay,* viz., to be destroyed, wounded, corroded by the caustic juice of plants, or with ley and other strong liquids. And on this account the Indians feared those days, believing them to be unfortunate, and to carry danger of sudden deaths, plagues, and other misfortunes. For this reason these five days were assigned for the celebration of the feast of the god *Mam,* "grandfather." On the first day they carried him about, and feasted him with great magnificence; on the second they diminished the solemnity; on the third they brought him down from the altar and placed him in the middle of the temple; on the fourth they put him at the threshold or door; and on the fifth, or last day, the ceremony of taking leave (or dismissal) took place, that the new year might commence on the following day, which is the first of the month *Pop,* corresponding with the 16th of July, as appears by the preceding table. The description of the god *Mam* may be seen in Cogolludo.

The division of the year into 18 months of 20 days would have given only the sum of 360 days; and the first day of the year falling on *Kan,* the last would have fallen on *Akbal,* so as to begin again the next year with the same *Kan,* making all the years alike. But as, in order to complete the year, they added five days, the result was that the year which commenced in *Kan* ended in *Lamat,* the last of the first series of five days; the ensuing year commenced in *Muluc,* the first of the second series of five days; the third commenced in *Gix,* the first of the third series; and the fourth in Cauac (the first ending in *Akbal*), the last of the fourth series of five days; so that the fifth year again began with *Kan.* It has also been stated that the year consisted of 28 weeks of 13 days each, and of one additional day; so that, if the year commenced with the number one of the week, it ended with the same number, and the ensuing year began with number two; and so on through the thirteen numbers of the week, thus forming, with the four initial days, the week of years, or indiction, of which we shall speak hereafter.

The following is the order of the twenty days in each of the 18 months composing the years formed by the four initial days, together with the intercalary or complementary days.

Year beginning with the day *Kan.*	Year beginning with the day *Muluc.*	Year of Gix.	Year of Cauac.
Kan.	Muluc.	Gix.	Cauac.
Chicchan.	Oc.	Men.	Ajau.
Quimí.	Chuen.	Quib.	Ymix.
Manik.	Eb.	Caban.	Yk.
Lamat.	Ben.	Edznab.	Akbal.
Muluc.	Gix.	Cauac.	Kan.
Oc.	Men.	Ajau.	Chicchan.
Chuen.	Quib.	Ymix.	Quimí.
Eb.	Caban.	Yk.	Manik.
Ben.	Edznab.	Akbal.	Lamat.
Gix.	Cauac.	Kan.	Muluc.
Men.	Ajau.	Chicchan.	Oc.
Quib.	Ymix.	Quimí.	Chuen.
Caban.	Yk.	Manik.	Eb.
Edznab.	Akbal.	Lamat.	Ben.
Cauac.	Kan.	Muluc.	Gix.
Ajau.	Chicchan.	Oc.	Men.
Ymix.	Quimí.	Chuen.	Quib.
Yk.	Manik.	Eb.	Caban.
Akbal.	Lamat.	Ben.	Edznab.
Intercalary days.	*Intercalary days.*	*Intercalary days.*	*Intercalary days.*
Kan.	Muluc.	Gix.	Cauac.
Chicchan.	Oc.	Men.	Ajau.
Quimí.	Chuen.	Quib.	Ymix.
Manik.	Eb.	Caban.	Yk.
Lamat.	Ben.	Edznab.	Akbal.

5°. *The Bissextile.*

The connexion between the days or numbers of the week which designate the beginning of the year, and the four initial or first days of the series of five, is so intimate that it is very difficult to intercalate an additional day for the bissextile, without disturbing that correlative order of the initials which is constantly followed in the denomination of the years, and forms their indictions, or weeks. But as the bissextile is necessary to complete the solar course, and as I have not any certain knowledge of the manner in which the Indians effected that addition, I will exhibit the method adopted by the Mexicans, their computation being very analogous to that of Yucatan, which in its origin probably emanated from Mexico.

Veyta asserts, in ch. x. of his "Historia Antigua de Mexico," that the bissextile was made by adding at the end either of the 18 months or of the five supplementary days, a day which was marked with the same hieroglyphic as the one preceding, but with a different number of the week, viz., with the succeeding number. But in each way that numerical order by which the years follow each other till they form the week of years, is disturbed; since the fifth year would thus be designated by the number 6 instead cf 5, and the regular order of the years 4 to 6 be thereby interrupted. These interruptions, recurring every fourth year, would render it impossible to preserve that continuous harmony (on which rests the whole system of the Indian computation) between the numbers of the week which designate the ending year and its successor, as shown in the uniform succession of the four initial days.

In order to prevent that inconvenience, it is necessary to suppose that the Indians, whether they intercalated the additional day at the end of the 18 months or after the five supplementary days, did not only give to it the same number and hieroglyphic as to the day immediately preceding, but also designated it by some peculiar sign or number, in order that it might not be confounded with any other.

In a treatise published by Akerman, the opinion is expressed that the Indians, at the end of their cycle of 52 years, added a week of days in lieu of the bissextile days which had been neglected. This method has not the defect of disturbing the numerical order of the years, but that of deranging the series of the four initial days, which, as has been stated, gives designation to the years. It will be seen by the table of indictions, that each cycle consists of four complete weeks of years, formed by series of each one of the four initial signs, each week of years commencing with number one and ending with number thirteen; consequently, if, at the end of each cycle, a week of days be added, the first day of the ensuing year would be the 14th in the series of the 20 days of the month (instead of being the 1st, 6th, 11th, or 16th), thus abandoning the regular series of the four initial days, and substituting others, changing them again at each new cycle.

6°. *Katun, or Cycle.*

The Indians made (painted) a small wheel, in which they placed the four hieroglyphics of the initial days, *Kan* in the east, *Muluc* in the north, *Gix* in the west, and *Cauac* in the south, to be counted in that order. Some suppose that when the fourth year was accomplished, and *Kan* was again in order, a *Katun*, or lustre of four years, was completed; others, that three revolutions of the wheel, with its four signs, were reckoned, with one (sign) more, which made 13 years, and that this completed the *Katun*; others, again, that the four complete weeks of years, or indictions, constituted the *Katun*; and this is probable. Besides the small wheel aforesaid, they made another great wheel, which they also called *buk xoc*, and in which they placed three revolutions of the four signs of the small wheel, making 12 signs; beginning to count by the first *Kan*, and continuing to reckon all until the fourth naming of the same Kan, which was included, thus making thirteen years, and forming one indiction, or week (of years); the second reckoning began with *Muluc*, ending in the same, which formed the next thirteen; and so on, till they came to Cauac, which formed a Katun.

7°. *Of the Indiction and Cycle of 52 Years, or Katun.*

As in the preceding explanations sufficient idea has been given of what constituted the indiction and the cycle of 52 years, called by the Indians *Katun*, the facts are briefly recapitulated here, that the reader may not be fatigued hereafter with new explanations.

1st. The name of indiction is given to each one of the four weeks of years composing the cycle of 52 years.

2d. The American week was formed by the course of 13 numbers, applied indiscriminately to the 20 days of the month.

3d. It has been explained, that as the year was formed of 28 weeks and one day, by this overplus the years succeeded each other, following the correlative order of their numbers up to 13, in order to form a week, or indiction; for if the year had been composed of exactly 28 weeks, the numbers of the new years would never have formed a correlative week, because they would have commenced with the number 1, and finished with 13; by the other method, one year begins with the first, and terminates in the same; the second year commences with the number 2, and also finishes with it; and so on successively, until the 13 are completed.

4th. It has also been explained that the Indians, seeing that 18 months of 20 days did not make up the sum of 365, in order to complete them added five days more; resulting from this, the 20 days were divided into four portions, and the first of each of these, being *Kan, Muluc, Gix,* and *Cauac,* became initials, forming in turn the beginning of the years by courses of four years, every fifth year commencing again with Kan. But as the weeks were composed of 13 numbers, there were in each week three revolutions of the four initials and one initial more, by this excess of one causing each initial to have its own week: thus the indiction, or week, which began with *Kan* concluded also with the same *Kan;* so that the next indiction might commence with *Muluc,* the second initial, and in its turn conclude with the same *Muluc;* and so on continually, until each one of the initials had formed its own indiction, or week, and given to it its name, the whole composing 52 years, which is the sum of the four weeks of 13 years each, as may be seen in the following table.

Order of the years in the cycle of 52, *divided into four indictions, or weeks of years; and as the year* 1841 *happens to be the first of one of these cycles, it is taken as the starting-point.*

1st Indiction.		2d Indiction.		3d Indiction.		4th Indiction.	
1841,	1. Kan.	1854,	1. Muluc.	1867,	1. Gix.	1880,	1. Cauac.
1842,	2. Muluc.	1855,	2. Gix.	1868,	2. Cauac.	1881,	2. Kan.
&c.	3. Gix.	&c.	3. Cauac.	&c.	3. Kan.	&c.	3. Muluc.
	4. Cauac.		4. Kan.		4. Muluc.		4. Gix.
	5. Kan.		5. Muluc.		5. Gix.		5. Cauac.
	6. Muluc.		6. Gix.		6. Cauac.		6. Kan.
	7. Gix.		7. Cauac.		7. Kan.		7. Muluc.
	8. Cauac.		8. Kan.		8. Muluc.		8. Gix.
	9. Kan.		9. Muluc.		9. Gix.		9. Cauac.
	10. Muluc.		10. Gix.		10. Cauac.		10. Kan.
	11. Gix.		11. Cauac.		11. Kan.		11. Muluc.
	12. Cauac.		12. Kan.		12. Muluc.		12. Gix.
	13. Kan.		13. Muluc.		13. Gix.	1892,	13. Cauac.

This period of 52 years was called by the Indians *Katun*, and at its conclusion great feasts were celebrated, and a monument was raised, on which a large stone was placed crosswise, as is signified by the word *Kat-tun*, for a memento and record of the cycles, or *Katunes*, that had elapsed. It should be observed, that until the completion of this period, the initial days of the years did not again fall upon the same numbers of the week; for which reason, by merely citing them, it was at once known what year of that cycle was arrived at; being aided in this by the wheel or table on which the years were engraved in hieroglyphics.

8°. *Of the great Cycle of* 312 *Years, or Ajau Katunes.*

Besides the cycle of 52 years, or *Katun*, there was another great cycle peculiar to the Yucatecos, who referred to its periods for dating their principal epochs and the most notable events of their history. It contained 13 periods of 24 years each, making together 312 years. Each period, or *Ajau Katun*, was divided into two parts; the first of 20 years, which was included in a square, and therefore called *amaytun, lamayte,* or *lamaytun;* and the other of four years, which formed, as it were, a pedestal for the first, and was called *chek oc Katun*, or *lath oc Katun*, which means "stool" or "pedestal." They considered those four years as intercalated; therefore believed them to be unfortunate, and called them *u yail Jaab*, as they did the five supplementary days of the year, to which they likened them.

From this separation of the first 20 years from the last four, arose the erroneous belief that the *Ajaus* consisted only of 20 years, an error into which almost all have fallen who have written on the subject; but if they had counted the years which compose a period, and noted the positive declarations of the manuscripts that the *Ajaues* consisted of 24 years divided as above stated, they would not have misled their readers on this point.

It is incontrovertible that those periods, epochs, or ages, took the name

of *Ajau Katun*, because they began to be counted from the day *Ajau*, which
was the second day of those years that began in Cauac; but as these days
and numbers were taken from years which had run their course, the periods of 24 years could never have an arithmetical order, but succeeded each
other according to the numbers 13, 11, 9, 7, 5, 3, 1, 12, 10, 8, 6, 4, 2. As
the Indians established the number 13 as the first, it is probable that some
remarkable event had happened in that year, because, when the Spaniards
came to this peninsula, the Indians reckoned then the 8th as the 1st, that
being the date at which their ancestors came to settle it; and an Indian
writer proposed that they should abandon that order also, and begin counting from the 11th, solely because the conquest had happened in that. Now
if the 13 *Ajau Katun* began on a second day of the year, it must be that
year which began on 12 *Cauac*, and the 12th of the indiction. The 11 *Ajau*
would commence in the year of 10 *Cauac*, which happens after a period of
24 years, and so on with the rest; taking notice that after that lapse of
years we come to the respective number marked in the course of the Ajaues,
which is placed first; proving that they consist of 24, and not, as some
have believed, of 20 years.

*Series of the years completed in two Ajau Katunes, having their beginning in
the year of our Lord 1488, in which the 13th Ajau commences on the 2d day
of the year 12 Cauac, being the 12th of the first indiction.*

A.D.	13th Ajau.		A.D.	13th Ajau.		A.D.	11th Ajau.		A.D.	11th Ajau.	
1488	12. Cauac		1500	11. Cauac		1512	10. Cauac		1524	9. Cauac	
1489	13. Kan		1501	12. Kan		1513	11. Kan		1525	10. Kan	
1490	1. Muluc		1502	13. Muluc		1514	12. Muluc		1526	11. Muluc	
1491	2. Gix		1503	1. Gix		1515	13. Gix		1527	12. Gix	
1492	3. Cauac		1504	2. Cauac		1516	1. Cauac		1528	13. Cauac	
1493	4. Kan		1505	3. Kan		1517	2. Kan		1529	1. Kan	
1494	5. Muluc		1506	4. Muluc		1518	3. Muluc		1530	2. Muluc	
1495	6. Gix		1507	5. Gix		1519	4. Gix		1531	3. Gix	
1496	7. Cauac		1508	6. Cauac		1520	5. Cauac		1532	4. Cauac	
1497	8. Kan		1509	7. Kan		1521	6. Kan.		1533	5. Kan	
1498	9. Muluc		1510	8. Muluc		1522	7. Muluc		1534	6. Muluc	
1499	10. Gix		1511	9. Gix		1523	8. Gix		1535	7. Gix	

The fundamental point of departure from which to adjust the Ajaus with
the years of the Christian era, to count the periods or cycles which have
elapsed, and to make the years quoted by the Indians in their histories
agree with the same era, is the year of our Lord 1392, which, according to
all sources of information, confirmed by the testimony of Don Cosme de
Burgos, one of the conquerors, and a writer (but whose observations have
been lost), was the year in which fell the 7 *Cauac*, giving in its second day
the commencement of 8 Ajau; and from this, as from a root, all that preceded and have followed it are adjusted according to the table of them
which has been given; and as this agrees with all the series that have been
found, it is highly probable that it is the correct one.

"At the end of each Ajau Katun, or period of 24 years," says a manuscript, "great feasts were celebrated in honour of the god thereof, and a statue of the god was put up, with letters and inscriptions." It must be supposed that these were expressed by means of signs or hieroglyphics.

The use of this cycle was of very great advantage and importance, because when, for example, the 8th Ajau was referred to in their histories in describing some event which it was necessary to distinguish from others, the 8th Ajau was established as a distinct date, and it was understood that the 312 years had elapsed, which made up the whole Katun, in order to return to the same number; this was more clear, if the writer explained that a *uudz Kalun* had elapsed, which is the sum total of the thirteen Katunes, or the great cycle. They had various modes of quoting the *Ajaues*, as by saying generally the beginning, middle, or end of such an Ajau, or by mentioning the years of the Katun which had elapsed, without stating the month or day of the year, or by specifying all the particulars of the epoch, the year, month, and day. Such is the passage in which is noticed the death of a certain, without doubt very notable, *Ajpula*. It is said that he died in the 6th year of 13 Ajau, when the first day of the year was 4 Kan at the east end of the wheel, in the day of 9 Ymix, 18th of the month Zip. This date being so circumstantial, we will trace it out, that it may serve as an example.

Looking at the series of years which belong to the 13 Ajau, and which we have given above, it will be seen that 12 Cauac falls in the year 1488, the second day of that year being, therefore, the beginning of the 13th Ajau; that the year 1493 is the sixth from the beginning of the said Ajau, and that its first day is designated as 4 Kan, which is the title of that year, "18th of the month Zip." As this month begins on the 25th of August, the 18th corresponds with the 11th of September. Let us see now whether this 18th day falls on 9 Ymix. The first month of that year commenced with 4 Kan, since 4 Kan designates that year (see the rule given in treating of the months). We find the numbers (of the week) annexed to the first days of the following months by successively adding 7 to each month, &c. (or, which is the same thing, by the rule *buk xoc*). The number of the 1st day of the 1st month being in this case 4, the number of the 1st day of the 2d month will be 4+7=11, and that of the 1st day of the 3d month, viz., of Zip, will be 11+7—13=5. That month begins, therefore, in that year, with 5 Kan, and the following days are,

Days of Aug.	Zip.	Days of the Week.	Days of Sept.	Zip.	Days of the Week.	Days of Sept.	Zip.	Days of the Week.
25	1	5. Kan.	1	8	12. Chuen.	8	15	6. Edznab.
26	2	6. Chicchan.	2	9	13. Eb.	9	16	7. Cauac.
27	3	7. Quimí.	3	10	1. Ben.	10	17	8. Ajau.
28	4	8. Manik.	4	11	2. Gix.	11	18	9. Ymix.
29	5	9. Lamac.	5	12	3. Men.			
30	6	10. Muluc.	6	13	4. Quin.			
31	7	11. Oc.	7	14	5. Caban.			

Thus the 11th of September was the 18th of Zip, which does fall on 9 Ymix, and accords with the date given in the MS. This date appears, therefore, to have been very correct.

Of the Origin of this Cycle.

The origin and use of this species of age, epoch, or cycle, and (the time) when it commenced, are not known. Neither the Mexican nor Toltecan authors, nor those who corrected the chronological system for the computation of time, ever used it, nor had their writers any knowledge of its existence. The few and incomplete manuscripts which exist in this peninsula make no mention of it; so that there is neither record nor even conjecture to guide us, unless there be something on the subject in the work written by Don Cristobal Antonio Xiu, son of the King of Mani, by order of the then government, which, according to the padre Cogolludo, existed in his time, and some allege to be even yet extant.

It appears only that the Chevalier Boturini had some knowledge, though imperfect, of that mode of reckoning time; inasmuch as Don Mariano Veytia, in the second chapter of his "Historia Antigua de Mexico," transcribes literally the explanation which Boturini gives at page 122 of the work which he published under the title of "Idea of a New History of North America," and says, "that the Mexican Indians, when they reckoned in their calendar the first sign of their indiction under number 1, as, for instance, Ce Tecpatl (1 Tecpatl), it was understood that it was (so placed) only one time in every four cycles, because they spoke then of the initial characters of each cycle; and thus, according to the contrivance of their painted wheels, Ce Tecpatl was but once the commencement of the four cycles" [meaning—began a cycle but once in four cycles. But the fact is not so: both in the Mexican and the Yucatec calendar, every cycle of 52 years begins with the same initial character of the year]; "for which reason, any character of those initial signs placed in their history means that four Indian cycles of 52 years each have elapsed, which makes 208 years before they can again occur as initial, because, in this way, no account is taken of characters which are in the body of the four cycles; and though the same characters are found there, they have not the same value."

Veytia affirms that he did not find any similar explanation, or anything alluding to the system of Boturini, in any of the ancient monuments which he had collected or examined, or mentioned by any Indian historian, not even in order to designate the epochs of the most remarkable events. But I believe that, in answer to this remark of Veytia, it may be said that Boturini, as Veytia states elsewhere, had examined the calendars used in old times by the Indians of Oaxacac, Chiapas, and Soconusco, and these being similar to that of the Yucatecos, it is not unreasonable to suppose that they, like the Yucatecos, computed by cycles greater than the Mexicans employed; and that Boturini took from them the idea, though confused and incorrect, of our Ajaus, or great cycles. This incorrectness might arise either from his not understanding the mechanism of their mode of computing, owing to the defective explanation given by the Indians, or from the manuscripts which Boturini had before him being mutilated, or, finally, from the possible fact that the Indians in those provinces had a particular custom of counting by cycles of four indictions, or of 208 years, which, notwithstanding the difference observed in their calculation, and the number of years which it produces, have a great analogy with the Yucateco cycles of 312 years. The only thing for which Boturini may be censured, if the Mexicans had no knowledge of that cycle, and did not use it, was the ascribing of it to them as being in common use for the computation of the greater periods of time.

The great similarity between the names of the days in the calendar of Oajaca, Chiapas, and Soconusco, and those of the Yucatecos, has been mentioned, and appears clearly by comparing the latter with those of the said provinces, which Veytia has transcribed in his history, chap. xi., at the end.

Days of the Oajaquian Month.		Days of the Yucateco Month.	
1. Votan.	11. Ben.	1. Kan.	11. Hix or Gix.
2. Ghanan.	12. Hix.	2. Chicchan.	12. Men.
3. Abagh.	13. Tzinkin.	3. Quimí.	13. Quib.
4. Tox.	14. Chabin.	4. Manik.	14. Caban.
5. Moxic.	15. Chue or Chic.	5. Lamat.	15. Edznab.
6. Lambat.	16. Chinax.	6. Muluc.	16. Cauac.
7. Molo or Mulu.	17. Cahogh.	7. Oc.	17. Ajau.
8. Elah or Elab.	18. Aghual.	8. Chuen.	18. Ymix.
9. Batz.	19. Mox.	9. Eb.	19. Yk.
10. Enoh or Enob.	20. Ygh.	10. Ben.	20. Akbal.

Oajacan Ghanan, *gh* being pronounced as *k*, is the same with the Yucateco *Kan* or *Kanan* (yellow); Molo or Mulu, *Muluc;* Chue, *Chuen;* Aghual, *Akbal* or *Akual;* Ygk, *Yk;* Lambat, *Lamat;* Ben and Hix, *Be-en* and *Gix* or *Hix*. These analogies, and the fact that some of the Yucateco names have no known signification, induce the belief that both calendars had a common origin, with only such alterations as the priests made on account of particular events or for other reasons; which alterations our Indians adopted, leaving the other signs unchanged, either because they were accustomed to them, or because their signification, now forgotten, was then known.

The Indians of Yucatan had yet another species of cycle; but as the method followed by them in using it cannot be found, nor any example by which an idea of its nature might be imagined, I shall only copy what is literally said of it in a manuscript, viz.: "There was another number, which they called *Ua Katun,* and which served them as a key to find the Katunes. According to the order of its march, it falls on the days of the *Uayeb jaab,* and revolves to the end of certain years: Katunes 13, 9, 5, 1, 10, 6, 2, 11, 7, 3, 12, 8, 4."

[N.B. Uayeb jaab is one of the names given to the five supplementary days of the year, and also to the last four years of the Ajau of 24 years.]

Series of Ajaues, from the beginning of the vulgar era to the present year, and those following until the end of the cycle. It is formed of three columns: the first containing the years of the Christian era; the second, the years of the indiction in which the Ajaues commenced, on their second day; and the third, the succession of these Ajaues. (The vulgar era began in the year 7 Kan, which was the 2d of 7 Ajau, that commenced the second day of the year of the indiction 6 Cauac).

Years of our Lord.	Years of the Indiction.	Ajaues that began in them.	Years of our Lord.	Years of the Indiction.	Ajaues that began in them.
24	4. Cauac.	5. Ajau.	984	2. Cauac.	3. Ajau.
48	2. Cauac.	3. Ajau.	1008	13. Cauac.	1. Ajau.
72	13. Cauac.	1. Ajau.	1032	11. Cauac.	12. Ajau.
96	11. Cauac.	12. Ajau.	1056	9. Cauac.	10. Ajau.
120	9. Cauac.	10. Ajau.	1080	7. Cauac.	8. Ajau.
144	7. Cauac.	8. Ajau.	1104	5. Cauac.	6. Ajau.
168	5. Cauac.	6. Ajau.	1128	3. Cauac.	4. Ajau.
192	3. Cauac.	4. Ajau.	1152	1. Cauac.	2. Ajau.
216	1. Cauac.	2. Ajau.	*1176	*12. Cauac.	*13. Ajau.
*240	*12. Cauac.	*13. Ajau.	1200	10. Cauac.	11. Ajau.
264	10. Cauac.	11. Ajau.	1224	8. Cauac.	9. Ajau.
288	8. Cauac.	9. Ajau.	1248	6. Cauac.	7. Ajau.
312	6. Cauac.	7. Ajau.	1272	4. Cauac.	5. Ajau.
336	4. Cauac.	5. Ajau.	1296	2. Cauac.	3. Ajau.
360	2. Cauac.	3. Ajau.	1320	13. Cauac.	1. Ajau.
384	13. Cauac.	1. Ajau.	1344	11. Cauac.	12. Ajau.
408	11. Cauac.	12. Ajau.	1368	9. Cauac.	10. Ajau.
432	9. Cauac.	10. Ajau.	1392	7. Cauac.	8. Ajau.
456	7. Cauac.	8. Ajau.	1416	5. Cauac.	6. Ajau.
480	5. Cauac.	6. Ajau.	1440	3. Cauac.	4. Ajau.
504	3. Cauac.	4. Ajau.	1464	1. Cauac.	2. Ajau.
528	1. Cauac.	2. Ajau.	*1488	*12. Cauac.	*13. Ajau.
*552	*12. Cauac.	*13. Ajau.	1512	10. Cauac.	11. Ajau.
576	10. Cauac.	11. Ajau.	1536	8. Cauac.	9. Ajau.
600	8. Cauac.	9. Ajau.	1560	6. Cauac.	7. Ajau.
624	6. Cauac.	7. Ajau.	1584	4. Cauac.	5. Ajau.
648	4. Cauac.	5. Ajau.	1608	2. Cauac.	3. Ajau.
672	2. Cauac.	3. Ajau.	1632	13. Cauac.	1. Ajau.
696	13. Cauac.	1. Ajau.	1656	11. Cauac.	12. Ajau.
720	11. Cauac.	12. Ajau.	1680	9. Cauac.	10. Ajau.
744	9. Cauac.	10. Ajau.	1704	7. Cauac.	8. Ajau.
768	7. Cauac.	8. Ajau.	1728	5. Cauac.	6. Ajau.
792	5. Cauac.	6. Ajau.	1752	3. Cauac.	4. Ajau.
816	3. Cauac.	4. Ajau.	1776	1. Cauac.	2. Ajau.
840	1. Cauac.	2. Ajau.	*1800	*12. Cauac.	*13. Ajau.
*864	*12. Cauac.	*13. Ajau.	1824	10. Cauac.	11. Ajau.
888	10. Cauac.	11. Ajau.	1848	8. Cauac.	9. Ajau.
912	8. Cauac.	9. Ajau.	1872	6. Cauac.	7. Ajau.
936	6. Cauac.	7. Ajau.	1896	4. Cauac.	5. Ajau.
960	4. Cauac.	5. Ajau.			

From the preceding series it is manifest that from the birth of Christ until the beginning of this cycle, have elapsed 6 great cycles, one epoch, and 17 (years) of another; the first epoch of the first cycle requiring a year, as has been stated.

Since this exposition was written, I have had an opportunity of seeing the work, above quoted, of Chevalier Boturini, in which, speaking of the Toltec Indians, he says:

After their peregrination through Asia, they reached the Continent (America), and penetrated to Hutchuetlapallan, the first city of New Spain, in which their wise men convened 130 and some years before the birth of Christ; and seeing that the civil did not agree with the astronomical year, and that the equinoctial days were altered, they determined to add in every four years one day, in order to recover the hours which were (annually) lost. And it is supposed that they effected it by counting one of the symbols of the last month of the year twice (as the Romans did with their bissextile days), without disturbing their order, because adding or taking away (a symbol) would destroy their perpetual system; and thus they made the commencement of the civil year to agree with the vernal equinox, which was the principal and governing part of the year.

He adds, that although the intercalated day had not a place in the order of the symbols of the days of the year, but was thrust in, as it were, like an interloper, still it gave a name (or character) to the bissextile year, having most solemn feasts reserved to it, which, even in the third age, were sanctioned by the emperor or king of those provinces; and they were held in honour of the god *Xinteuctli*, "lord of the year," with great preparation of viands and sumptuous dances, in which the lords alone danced and sang; and for this reason they were called "the songs and dances of the lords." In the same bissextile year was held the solemn ceremony of piercing the ears of the girls and young men, it being reserved for the high-priest to execute that function, assisted by godfathers and godmothers.

In the 27th paragraph of the observations he says, that there was in the third age another mode of intercalating, applied only to the ritual calendar, and that, in order not to disturb either the perpetual order of the fixed feasts, or of the sixteen movable feasts, which circulated among the symbols of the days of the year, by (or for the sake of) counting twice the symbol of the last month of the bissextile year, which caused them much anxiety on account of the displeasure of their gods, it was held better to reserve the 13 bissextile days for the end of the cycle of 52 years; which (days) are distinguished in their wheels or tables by thirteen ciphers, (painted) blue or of some other colour; and they belonged neither to any month nor any year, nor had they particular or individual symbols, like the other days. It was with them as if there were no such days, nor were they dedicated to any of their gods, on which account they were reputed "unfortunate." The whole of those 13 days was a time of penitence and fasting, for fear that the world should come to an end; nor did they eat any warm food, as the fire was extinguished through the whole land till the new cycle began, when the ceremony of the new fire was celebrated.

But as all these were matters relating only to rites and sacrifices (not to the true computation of time), this mode of intercalating had no application to the natural year, because it would have greatly deranged the solstices, equinoxes, and beginnings of the years; and the fact is abundantly proved by the circumstance that the days thus intercalated (at the end of the cycle) had none of the symbols belonging to the days of the year, and the ritual calendar accounted them bissextiles at the end of each cycle, in imitation, though by a different order, of the civil bissextiles, which (as being more accurate) were more proper for the regulation of public affairs.

AN ALMANAC, ADJUSTED ACCORDING TO THE CHRONOLOGICAL CALCULATION OF THE ANCIENT INDIANS OF YUCATAN, FOR THE YEARS 1841 AND 1842, BY DON JUAN PIO PEREZ.

Observations.—The notes or remarks *utz, yutz kin*, a lucky day, *lob, u lob kin*, an unlucky day, signify that the Indians had their days of good and of ill fortune, like some of the nations of ancient Europe; although it is easily perceived that the number of their days of ill fortune is excessive, still they are the same found by me in three ancient almanacs which I have examined, and found to agree very nearly. I have applied them to the number, not the name, of the day, because the announcements of rain, of planting, &c., must, in my opinion, belong to the fixed days of the month, and not to the names of particular days; as these each year are changed, and turn upon the four primaries, *Kan, Muluc, Gix*, and *Cauac*, chiefs of the year. In another place, however, I have seen it laid down as a rule that the days *Chicchan, Cimi* or *Kimi, Oc, Men, Ahau*, and *Akbal*, are the days of rest in the month; and this appears probable, as I see no reason why there should be so great an excess of days of ill fortune. In the almanacs cited above, this order was not observed, either from ignorance or excessive superstition.

Thus the days on which the burner takes his fire, kindles it, gives it free scope, and extinguishes it, are subject to the 3d, 4th, 10th, and 11th of the days *Chicchan, Oc, Men*, and *Ahau;* as they say, for example, that on the 3d Chicchan the burner takes his fire, on the 10th Chicchan he begins, the 4th Chicchan he gives it scope, and the 11th Chicchan he extinguishes it; the same may be said of Oc, Men, and Ahau; from which we see that these epochs are movable, as the days 3, 4, 10, and 11 do not always fall on the same days of the month, but only according to the combination of the weekly numbers with the days referred to.

It may be asked, who is this burner that takes his fire, kindles it, permits it to destroy, and extinguishes it? To this I cannot reply, as I have been unable to find an explanation of the mystery; perhaps the days specified might be days of sacrifice, or some other act of superstition.

1st INDIAN MONTH, "POP," OF THE YEAR 1 KAN.

	Pop.		July.
1. Kan.	1	Hun Kan, utz licil u cutal, Pop (good, as the beginning of Pop).	
2. Chicchan.	2	Ca Chicchan, utz u tial pakal (good for planting).	16
3. Quimí.	3	Ox Quimí, lob kin (an unlucky day).	17
4. Manik.	4	Can Manik, utz u tial pakal (good for planting).	18
5. Lamat.	5	Ho Lamat, utz kin (a good day).	19
6. Muluc.	6	Uac Muluc, utz kin (6 Muluc; a good day).	20
7. Oc.	7	Uuc Oc, utz u tial ahguehob (good for hunting; for the settlers).	21
8. Chuen.	8	Uaxxac Chuen, yutz kin, kal ikal u chibal tok (good day; without wind).	22
9. Eb.	9	Bolon Eb, u lob kin (9 Eb; a bad day).	23
10. Been.	10	Lahun Been, yutz kin (10 Been; a good day).	24
11. Hix.	11	Buluc Hix, yutz kin (11 Hix; a good day).	25
12. Men.	12	Lahca Men, yutz kin (12 Men; a good day).	26
13. Quib.	13	Oxlahun Quib, u lob kin (13 Quib; an unlucky day).	27
1. Caban.	14	Hun Caban, u lob kin (1 Caban; an unlucky day).	28
2. Edznab.	15	Ca Edznab, yutz kin, licil u zihil ahmiatz yetel ahdzib hunob (good day; in which are born writers and wise men).	29
3. Cauac.	16	Ox Cauac, yutz kin (a good day).	30
4. Ahau.	17	Can Ahau, yutz kin ti almehenob; yalcab u kak ahtoc (a good day for the nobles; the burner gives the fire scope).	31
5. Ymix.	18	Ho Ymix, u lob kin (a bad day).	Aug. 1
6. Yk.	19	Uac Yk, u lob kin (an unlucky day).	2
7. Akbal.	20	Uuc Akbal, yutz kin (a good day).	3
			4

UO, 2D INDIAN MONTH.

	Uo.		August.
8. Kan.	1	Uaxxac Kan, u lob kin licil u cutal Uo (a bad day, as the root of Uo).	
9. Chicchan.	2	Bolon Chicchan, u lob kin (an unlucky day).	5
10. Quimí.	3	Lahun Quimí, u lob kin (an unlucky day).	6
11. Manik.	4	Buluc Manik, u lob kin (an unlucky day).	7
12. Lamat.	5	Lahca Lamat, u lob kin (an unlucky day).	8
13. Muluc.	6	Oxlahun Muluc, u lob kin (an unlucky day).	9
			10

UO, 2D INDIAN MONTH (Continued).

Uo.		August.
7	1, Oc, u lob kin, cimil hoppol kin (a bad day; death in the five following).	11
8	2, Chuen, u lob kin (an unlucky day).	12
9	3, Eb, u lob kin, chetun cimil yani (a bad day; sudden deaths).	13
10	4, Been, u lob kin, u ɔoc cimil (an unlucky day; sudden deaths).	14
11	5, Hix, u lob kin (an unfortunate day).	15
12	6, Men, u lob kin (an unfortunate day).	16
13	7, Quib, u lob kin (an unfortunate day).	17
14	8. Caban, u lob kin (an unfortunate day).	18
15	9, Edznab, u lob kin, cimil yani (a bad day; death is here).	19
16	10, Cauac, u lob kin (an unlucky day).	20
17	11, Ahau, lob, u tup kak ahtoc (bad; the burner puts out the fire).	21
18	12, Ymix, u lob kin (an unfortunate day).	22
19	13, Yk, u lob kin (an unfortunate day).	23
20	1, Akbal, au yutz kin (a lucky day).	24

ZIP, 3D INDIAN MONTH.

Zip.		August.
1	2, Kan, yutz kin, licil u cutal Zip (a good day; the root of Zip).	25
2	3, Chicchan, lob, u cha kak ahtoc (bad; the burner takes the fire).	26
3	4, Quimí, yutz kin, u kin takal u kab balam (a good day; one in which the hands are laid on the tiger).	27
4	5, Manik, u lob kin (an unlucky day).	28
5	6, Lamat, u lob kin.	29
6	7, Muluc, u lob kin.	30
7	8, Oc, u lob kin.	31
8	9, Chuen, u lob kin.	Sept. 1
9	10, Eb, u lob kin.	2
10	11, Ben, u lob kin.	3
11	12, Hix, utz kin (a good day).	4
12	13, Men, utz u zihil ahau (good; the king is born).	5
13	1, Quib, utz kin.	6
14	2, Caban, yutz kin.	7
15	3, Edznab, yutz kin.	8
16	4, Cauac, yutz kin.	9
17	5, Ahau, yutz kin.	10
18	6, Ymix, yutz kin, haahal telá (a good day; there is rain).	11
19	7, Yk, yutz kin, haahal telá (a good day; there is rain).	12
20	8, Akbal, yutz.	13

ZODZ, 4TH INDIAN MONTH.

Zodz.		Sept.
1	9, Kan, utz u zian ku, u kin chac licil u cutal zoɔ (good; church day, of rain, &c.).	14
2	10, Chicchan, u lob kin, u hoppol u kak ahtoc (a bad day; the fire begins).	15

ZODZ, 4TH INDIAN MONTH (Continued).

Zodz.		Sept.
3	11, Quimí, u lob kin, u kin u nichco hun ahau, coh u nich (a bad day).	16
4	12, Manik, u lob kin (a bad day).	17
5	13, Lamat, yutz kin.	18
6	1, Muluc, yutz kin.	19
7	2, Oc, yutz kin.	20
8	3, Chuen, yutz kin.	21
9	4, Eb, lob kin, licil u zihil ahau (bad; the king is born).	22
10	5, Ben, lob kin.	23
11	6, Hix, utz u tial Ahcabnalob licil u pakal cab (good for the bee-hunters; in it the swarms are hived).	24
12	7, Men, utz.	25
13	8, Quib, yutz kin.	26
14	9, Caban, u yutz kin.	27
15	10, Edznab, u yutz kin.	28
16	11, Cauac, u yutz kin.	29
17	12, Ahau, lob u kukumtok chapahal yani (bad; the plume of infirmities).	30
18	13, Ymix, lob kin.	Oct. 1
19	1, Yk, utz kin, u zian chac (good; a day of rain).	2
20	2, Akbal, u lob kin.	3

ZEC, 5TH INDIAN MONTH.

Zec.		October.
1	3, Kan, utz u zian chac licil u cutal zec (good; beginning of Zec; rain).	4
2	4, Chicchan, lob u yalcab u kak ahtoc (bad; the burner gives the fire scope).	5
3	5, Quimí, lob u lubul u koch mehen palalob; chapahal yani (bad; the tax on children falls due; there is sickness).	6
4	6, Manik, lob.	7
5	7, Lamat, u lob kin.	8
6	8, Muluc, u lob kin.	9
7	9, Oc, u yutz kin, zut ti kaax xinxinbal (good for walking, &c.).	10
8	10, Chuen, u lob kin.	11
9	11, Eb, u lob kin.	12
10	12, Been, u lob kin.	13
11	13, Hix, u lob kin.	14
12	1, Men, u lob kin.	15
13	2, Quib, u lob kin, kalal hub, cinil yani (an unlucky day; the snail retreats to his shell, or is sawn open; death is in the day).	16
14	3, Caban, yutz kin.	17
15	4, Edznab, lob, u hokol chacmitan tac metnal ti kin ti akab (bad; hunger is loosed from hell by day and night).	18
16	5, Cauac, u lob kin.	19
17	6, Ahau, u lob kin.	20
18	7, Ymix, u lob kin.	21
19	8, Yk, u lob kin.	22
20	9, Akbal, u lob kin.	23

XUL, 6TH INDIAN MONTH.

Xul.		October.
1	10, Kan, lob, u zian chac licil u cutal Xul (bad; rain; beginning of Xul).	24
2	11, Chicchan, utz u tup kak ahtoc, u ca kin haí (good; second day of rain; the burner extinguishes the fire).	25
3	12, Quimí, lob kin.	26
4	13, Manik, u lob kin.	27
5	1, Lamat, utz u yalcab muyal (good; the clouds fly).	28
6	2, Muluc, lob u lubul u koch mehenob yetel akkinob licil u ppixichob (bad; day of watching; the tax of the sons and priests falls due).	29
7	3, Oc, lob u cha kak ahtoc (bad; the burner takes fire).	30
8	4, Chuen, lob kin.	31
9	5, Eb, u lob kin.	Nov. 1
10	6, Been, u lob kin.	2
11	7, Hix, lob kin, u lubul u koch almehenob ppixich yani (bad; a day of watching; of taxes from the nobles).	3
12	8, Men, u lob kin.	4
13	9, Quib, u lob kin.	5
14	10, Caban, u lob kin.	6
15	11, Edznab, u lob kin.	7
16	12, Cauac, u lob kin, u mupptun cizin lae (a bad day, and of attacks from the devil).	8
17	13, Ahau, u lob kin.	9
18	1, Ymix, u lob kin.	10
19	2, Yk, u lob kin.	11
20	3, Akbal, u lob kin.	12

DZEYAXKIN, 7TH INDIAN MONTH.

Dzeyaxkin.		Nov.
1	4, Kan, u lob kin, licil u cutal Teyaxkin (bad day; beginning of Dzeyaxkin).	13
2	5, Chicchan, u lob kin.	14
3	6, Quimí, u lob kin.	15
4	7, Manik, lob, utz u pec chaci u kin haí, u zut muyal nocoycaan chalbaku (bad; thunder, rain, clouds, &c.)	16
5	8, Lamat, u lob kin.	17
6	9, Muluc, lob u kaalal hub u yail kin, u chibal, hub yani (bad; the snail's horn is closed; a bad day on it, a snail will bite).	18
7	10, Oc, lob kin, u hoppol u kak ahtoc (bad; the burner begins).	19
8	11, Chuen, u lob kin.	20
9	12, Eb, u lob kin.	21
10	13, Been, u lob kin.	22
11	1, Hix, yutz kin.	23
12	2, Men, yutz kin.	24
13	3, Quib, u lob kin, yoc uah payambe (bad; beginning of bread).	25
14	4, Caban, u lob kin, ceel yani (bad; there are agues).	26
15	5, Edznab, u lob kin.	27
16	6, Cauac, u lob kin.	28
17	7, Ahau, u lob kin.	29
18	8, Ymix, u lob kin.	30
19	9, Yk, utz u hoppol haí (good; the rain begins).	Dec. 1
20	10, Akbal, utz kin.	2

MOL, 8TH INDIAN MONTH.

Mol.		Dec.
1	11, Kan, u lob kin, licil u cutal Mol (a bad day; the beginning of Mol).	3
2	12, Chicchan, u lob kin.	4
3	13, Quimí, u lob kin.	5
4	1, Manik, utz.	6
5	2, Lamat, u lob kin.	7
6	3, Muluc, u lob kin.	8
7	4, Oc, yutz kin u yalcab u kak ahtoc (a good day; the burner gives scope to the fire).	9
8	5, Chuen, yutz kin.	10
9	6, Eb, u lob kin.	11
10	7, Been, yutz kin.	12
11	8, Hix, u lob kin.	13
12	9, Men, u lob kin.	14
13	10, Quib, yutz kin u kin noh uah (a day of abundance).	15
14	11, Caban, yutz kin.	16
15	12, Edznab, u lob kin, u Chaalba ku (a bad day for the church).	17
16	13, Cauac, yutz kin licil, u kokol u yik hub u kin ha (good; the horn sounds well; rain).	18
17	1, Ahau, u lob kin.	19
18	2, Ymix, u lob kin, u coi kinal ahau ku (bad; a day lessened by the King of the Temple, God).	20
19	3, Yk, u lob kin.	21
20	4, Akbal, u lob kin, u coi kinal ahau ku (an unlucky day; lessened by the King God, or King of the Temple).	22

CHEN, 9TH INDIAN MONTH.

Chen.		Dec.
1	5, Kan, lob (utz) licil u cutal Chen (bad or good; beginning of Chen).	23
2	6, Chicchan, u lob kin (utz).	24
3	7, Quimí, yutz kin.	25
4	8, Manik, lob kin.	26
5	9, Lamat, u lob kin.	27
6	10, Muluc, u lob kin.	28
7	11, Oc, utz, u tup kak ahtoc (good; the burner puts out the fire).	29
8	12, Chuen, yutz kin.	30
9	13, Eb, yutz kin.	31
10	1, Been, yutz kin.	1842 Jan. 1
11	2, Hix, yutz kin.	2
12	3, Men, utz u cha kak ahtoc (good; the burner takes his fire).	3
13	4, Quib utz.	4
14	5, Caban, lob licil u cimil uinicob u xulti (bad; the end of man).	5
15	6, Edznab, u lob kin.	6
16	7, Cauac, utz kin, u tial kabnal (good for the bee-hunter).	7
17	8, Ahau, yutz kin.	8
18	9, Ymix, yutz kin.	9
19	10, Yk, yutz kin.	10
20	11, Akbal, yutz kin.	11

YAX, 10TH INDIAN MONTH.

Yax.		January.
1	12, Kan, lob licil u cutal Yax (bad ; beginning of Yax).	12
2	13, Chicchan, lob u kukumtok chapahal yani (an unfortunate day ; plume of maladies).	13
3	1, Quimí, lob kin.	14
4	2, Manik, utz u xul kaxal haí (end of rains).	15
5	3, Lamat, u lob kin.	16
8	4, Muluc, utz u zian chaac (day of rain).	17
7	5, Oc, licil u kalal u koch mehen palal (the taxing of children is ended).	
8	6, Chuen, u lob kin.	18
9	7, Eb, yutz kin.	19
10	8, Been, yutz kin.	20
11	9, Hix, u lob kin.	21
12	10, Men, utz u hoppol u kak ahtoc, utz ti cucut, ti kaax u tial ahcehob (a good day ; the fire of the burner begins ; good for the body, for the forests, and the deer).	22
13	11, Quib, u lob kin.	23
14	12, Caban, u lob kin.	24
15	13, Edznab, u lob kin.	25
16	1, Cauac, u lob kin.	26
17	2, Ahau, u lob kin.	27
18	3, Ymix, u lob kin, u kin kal be hub (bad ; the horn does not sound).	28
19	4, Yk, yutz kin.	29
20	5, Akbal, lob u kin, u hokol chacmitan choctal metnal chetun cimil yani (bad ; hunger stalks abroad ; death is here).	30
		31

ZAC, 11TH INDIAN MONTH.

Zac.		February
1	6, Kan, lob licil u cutal Zac (bad ; the commencement of Zac).	1
2	7, Chicchan, lob kin.	2
3	8, Quimí, u lob kin.	3
4	9, Manik, u lob kin.	4
5	10, Lamat, u lob kin.	5
6	11, Muluc, utz cu pec chaaci, hâ yani (good ; thunder and rain).	
7	12, Oc, yutz kin.	6
8	13, Chuen, u lob kin.	7
9	1, Eb, lob kin.	8
10	2, Been, yutz kin.	9
11	3, Hix, u lob kin.	10
12	4, Men, u lob kin, u yalcab a kak ahtoc, u lubul u koch ahkin ppixich (a bad day ; the burner gives scope to the fire ; taxation of the priests).	11
13	5, Quib, u lob kin chapahal chocuil.	12
14	6, Caban, u lob kin.	13
15	7, Edznab, u lob kin.	14
16	8, Cauac, u lob kin ti ppix ich.	15
17	9, Ahau, u lob kin, u lubul u koch al mehenob (bad ; the days of the contribution of the nobles are completed).	16
18	10, Ymix, u lob kin (utz).	17
19	11, Yk, u lob kin.	18
20	12, Akbal, u lob kin, u nup cizin telae (bad ; insidious attacks of the arch-fiend).	19
		20

QUEJ, 12TH INDIAN MONTH.

Quej.		February
1	13, Kan, u lob kin.	21
2	1, Chicchan, u lob kin.	22
3	2, Quimí, u lob kin u thalal u koch ahkulelob (day of lawyers).	23
4	3, Manik, yutz kin u thalal u koch ahaulil uincob (a day of service, or binding on the kings of men).	24
5	4, Lamat, u lob kin.	25
6	5, Muluc, u lob kin.	26
7	6, Oc, u lob kin.	27
8	7, Chuen, u lob kin.	28
9	8, Eb, yutz kin, u kin pec chaac (good; it thunders).	Mar. 1
10	9, Been, u lob kin.	2
11	10, Hix, lob kin u kalaal hub.	3
12	11, Men, u lob kin, u tup kak ahtoc (bad; the burner puts out the fire).	4
13	12, Quib, u lob kin.	5
14	13, Caban, u lob kin.	6
15	1, Edznab, u lob kin, uchac u pec chaaci (bad; it may thunder).	7
16	2, Cauac, u lob kin.	8
17	3, Ahau, u lob kin, u cha kak ahtoc (bad; the burner handles the fire).	9
18	4, Ymix, utz, yoc uil payambe, ti u kaxal ha: chikin chaac (good; abundance).	10
19	5, Yk, u lob kin; ceel xan u yoc uil (bad; agues; and day of plenty).	11
20	6, Akbal, lob chac ceeli (utz) (bad; fevers).	12

MAC, 13TH INDIAN MONTH.

Mac.		March.
1	7, Kan, u lob kin, licil u cutal Mac (bad; beginning of Mac).	13
2	8, Chicchan, u lob kin.	14
3	9, Quimí, u lob kin.	15
4	10, Manik, utz, u hoppol haí (good; the beginning of rain).	16
5	11, Lamat, yutz kin.	17
6	12, Muluc, yutz kin.	18
7	13, Oc, u lob kin.	19
8	1, Chuen, u lob kin.	20
9	2, Eb, yutz kin.	21
10	3, Been, u lob kin, licil u pec chikin chac (bad; westerly rains).	22
11	4, Hix, u lob kin.	23
12	5, Men, u lob kin.	24
13	6, Quib, u lob kin.	25
14	7, Caban, u lob kin.	26
15	8, Edznab, utz yoc uil (sign of abundance).	27
16	9, Cauac, utz kin.	28
17	10, Ahau, utz u hoppol u kak ahtoc, yoc uil (the burner lights his fire; harvest day).	29
18	11, Ymix, utz u yoc uil.	30
19	12, Yk, yutz kin.	31
20	13, Akbal, utz u chaalba ku (u zian ku) (church day).	Apr. 1

KANKIN, 14TH INDIAN MONTH.

Kankin.		April.
1	1, Kan, lob, licil u cutal Kankin (bad; the root of Kankin).	2
2	2, Chicchan, lob u hokol u yik hub, u kin ha (an unlucky day; day of rain; the horn sounds).	3
3	3, Quimí, yutz kin.	4
4	4, Manik, yutz kin.	5
5	5, Lamat, yutz kin.	6
6	6, Muluc, yutz kin.	7
7	7, Oc, yutz kin.	8
8	8, Chuen, utz, licil u lubul hâ hach kaam (heavy rains).	9
9	9, Eb, lob ca cha u kin haí (day of rain).	10
10	10, Been, u lob kin.	11
11	11, Hix, yutz kin.	12
12	12, Men, yutz kin.	13
13	13, Quib, yutz kin.	14
14	1, Caban, yutz kin.	15
15	2, Edznab, yutz kin.	16
16	3, Cauac, yutz kin.	17
17	4, Ahau, utz u yalcab u kak ahtoc (licil u zihil cabnal) (good; the bee-hunter is born; the burner gives scope to the fire).	18
18	5, Ymix, u lob kin.	19
19	6, Yk, u lob kin.	20
20	7, Akbal, u lob kin.	21

MOAN, 15TH INDIAN MONTH.

Moan.		April.
1	8, Kan, lob, licil u cutal Moan (bad; the root of Moan.)	22
2	9, Chicchan, u lob kin.	23
3	10, Quimí, u lob kin.	24
4	11, Manik, u lob kin.	25
5	12, Lamat, u lob kin.	26
6	13, Muluc, yutz kin, chac ikal (good; a hurricane).	27
7	1, Oc, u lob kin.	38
8	2, Chuen, u lob kin, u nuptun cizin oxppel kin ca uchuc ppixich chabtan kini (bad; a day of temptation; three days of watching).	29
9	3, Eb, lob hun chabtan oxppel akab u ppixichlae, u cappel u kinil nuptun cizin ca ppixichnac uinic baix tu yoxppel kinil xan (bad; a day of temptation; three days of watching),	30
10	4, Been, yutz u kin u haí (rain).	May 1
11	5, Hix, u lob kin.	2
12	6, Men, u lob kin.	3
13	7, Quib, u lob kin zutob ti kax (bad for travellers).	4
14	8, Caban, lob, u tabal u keban yahanlil cabob (an unlucky day; the sins of the king are proved).	5
15	9, Edznab, u lob kin.	6
16	10, Cauac, u lob kin ximxinbal ti kax (bad for those who walk).	7
17	11, Ahau, u tup kak ahtoc, lob pazal cehob (the burner puts out the fire).	8
18	12, Ymix, u lob kin ti kuku uincob (bad for the sacrificers).	9
19	13, Yk, utz ti yahanlil cabob (good for the queen bees).	10
20	1, Akbal, utz u kin haí (a good day of rain).	11

PAX, 16TH INDIAN MONTH.

Pax.		May.
1	2, Kan, lob, ti batabob licil u cutal Pax (bad for the caciques; the beginning of Pax).	
2	3, Chicchan, lob u cha kak ahtoc iktan yol uinici (bad; the burner puts out the fire).	12
3	4, Quimí, u lob kin, licil u ppixichob (bad; a day of watching).	13
4	5, Manik, u lob kin, cup ikal (bad; a great and suffocating heat).	14
5	6, Lamat, u lob kin.	15
6	7, Muluc, u lob kin.	16
7	8, Oc, yutz kin.	17
8	9, Chuen, yutz kin.	18
9	10, Eb, yutz kin u xocol yoc kin (the days of the sun are reckoned).	19
10	11, Been, u lob kin.	20
11	12, Hix, u lob kin.	21
12	13, Men, yutz kin.	22
13	1, Quib, u lob kin.	23
14	2, Caban, u lob kin.	24
15	3, Edznab, lob, u lubul haf tu kuch haabil Muluc u cappel yoc uil) bad; year of Muluc; second day of planting).	25
16	4, Cauac, yutz kin.	26
17	5, Ahau, yutz kin.	27
18	6, Ymix, yutz kin.	28
19	7, Yk, yutz kin, u hoppol haf (it rains).	29
20	8, Akbal, u lob kin.	30
		31

KAYAB, 17TH INDIAN MONTH.

Kayab.		June.
1	9, Kan, lob, licil u cutal kayab (bad; the beginning of Kayab).	
2	10, Chicchan, lob, u hoppol u kak ahtoc (the burner begins).	1
3	11, Quimí, u lob kin.	2
4	12, Manik, u lob kin.	3
5	13, Lamat, u lob kin.	4
6	1, Muluc, yutz kin.	5
7	2, Oc, u lob kin.	6
8	3, Chuen, u lob kin.	7
9	4, Eb, yutz u kin noh haf (heavy rains).	8
10	5, Been, u lob kin.	9
11	6, Hix, u lob kin.	10
12	7, Men, u lob kin.	11
13	8, Quib, u lob kin.	12
14	9, Caban, u lob kin.	13
15	10, Edznab, u lob kin thol caan chaac (bad; from all parts).	14
16	11, Cauac, u lob kin, mankin ha (daily rains).	15
17	12, Ahau, u lob kin.	16
18	13, Ymix, yutz kin.	17
19	1, Yk, yutz kin.	18
20	2, Akbal, yutz kin.	19
		20

39

CUMKU, 18TH INDIAN MONTH.

Cumkú.		June.
1	3, Kan, utz, ñicil u cutal Cumkú (good; beginning of Cumkú).	21
2	4, Chicchan, lob kin, yalcab u kak ahtoc (bad; the burner gives scope to the fire).	22
3	5, Quimí, u lob kin.	23
4	6, Manik, u lob kin.	24
5	7, Lamat, u lob kin.	25
6	8, Muluc, utz u zian ku (a day to attend the temple).	26
7	9, Oc, yutz kin.	27
8	10, Chuen, u lob kin.	28
9	11, Eb, u lob kin.	29
10	12, Been, yutz kin.	30
11	13, Hix, u lob kin.	July 1
12	1, Men, u lob kin.	2
13	2, Quib, u lob kin.	3
14	3, Caban, utz u kin balam haabil.	4
15	4, Edznab, utz ppixichnebal ppolom (the traders watch).	5
16	5, Cauac, u lob kin.	6
17	6, Ahau, u lob kin.	7
18	7, Ymix, utz u payalte lae ɔac uinabal uli.	8
19	8, Yk, u lob kin.	9
20	9, Akbal, u lob kin.	10

" XMA KABA KIN," OR INTERCALARY DAYS.

		July.
1	10, Kan, yutz kin, u nay eb haab, xma kaba kin ca culac u chun haab poop (cradle of the year, &c.).	11
2	11, Chicchan, u lob kin, u tup kak ahtoc (the burner puts out the fire).	12
3	12, Quimí, u lob kin.	13
4	13, Manik, utz u tial sabal ziil (to make presents).	14
5	1, Lamat, yutz kin.	15

The next year would commence with 2 Muluc, the following one with 3 Hix, the fourth year with 4 Cauac, the fifth with 5 Kan; and so on continually, until the completion of the 13 numbers of the week of years, which commences with the day Kan; after which the weeks of Muluc, Hix, and Cauac follow, in such manner that, after the lapse of 52 years, the week of years again begins with 1 Kan, as in the preceding almanac. Respecting the bissextile, I have already manifested my opinion in the chronology of the Indians.

The translation of the names of the months and days is not as easy as it would appear, because some are not at present in use, and others, again, from the different meanings attached to them, and from the want of their true pronunciation, cannot be correctly understood; however, be this as it may, I shall endeavour to decipher them as nearly as possible, and according to the present state of the language, beginning with the months.

1. Pop, mat of cane. 2. Uo, frog. 3. Zip, a tree. 4. Zodz, a bat. 5. Zec, obsolete. 6. Xul, end or conclusion. 7. Dzeyaxkin; I know not its signification, although the meaning of *yaxkin* is summer. 8. Mol, to reunite. 9.

Chen, a well. 10. Yax, first, or Yaax, green or blue, though, as the following month is *Zac*, white, I believe this should be Yaax. 11. Zac, white. 12. Quez, a deer. 13. Mac, a lid or cover. 14. Kankin, yellow sun, perhaps because in this month of April the atmosphere is charged with smoke; owing to the woods being cut down and burned, the light of the sun is darkened, and at 5 P.M. it appears red and throws but little light. 15. Moan, antiquated, and its signification forgotten. 16. Pax, any instrument of music. 17. Kayab, singing. 18. Cumkú, a thunder-clap, or noise like the report of a cannon, which is heard in the woods while the marshes are drying, or from some other cause. Uayebhaab, Xma kaba kin, which signifies bed, or chamber of the year, or days without name, were the appellations given to the intercalary days, as they appertained to no month to which a name was given.

Translation of the 20 Days.

1. Kan, string or yarn of twisted hemp; it also means anything yellow, or fruit and timber proper for cutting. 2. Chicchan, obsolete; if it is Chichan, it signifies small or little. 3. Quimí, or Cimí, death or dead. 4. Manik, obsolete, but if the word may be divided, it would signify wind that passes; for *Man* is to pass, to buy, and *ik* is wind. 5. Lamat, obsolete, not understood. 6. Muluc, obsolete; although, should it be the primitive of *mulucbal*, it will signify reunion. 7. Oc, that which may be held in the palm of the hand. 8. Chuen, disused; some say it is equivalent to board. 9. Eb, ladder. 10. Been, obsolete. 11. Hix, not used, although, combined with others, it signifies roughness, as in Hixcay, rasp, Hihixci, rough. 12. Men, builder. 12. Quib, or Cib, wax or gum copal. 14. Caban, obsolete. 15. Edznab, obsolete. 16. Cauac, disused, although it appears to be the word *cacau*. 17. Ahau, king, or period of 24 years; the day in which this period commenced, and therefore they called it Ahau Katun. 18. Ymix, obsolete; although it appears to be the same as Yxim, corn or maize. 19. Yk, wind. 20. Akbal, word disused and unknown.

This is the signification given to those days.

Peto, 14th *April*, 1842.

Incidents of Travel in Yucatan

Volume II

CONTENTS

CHAPTER I

CHAPTER II

CHAPTER III

CHAPTER IV

CHAPTER V

CHAPTER VI

CHAPTER VII

CHAPTER VIII

Contents

ix

CHAPTER XII

CHAPTER XIII

CHAPTER XIV

CHAPTER XV

No Vestiges of a Spanish Town at Uxmal.—Churches erected
by the Spaniards in all their Settlements.—No Indications of
a Church at Uxmal—Conclusions.—Suspicions of the People.—
Church and Convent.—Extensive View from the Top of the

CHAPTER XVI

Departure from Mani.—Ornithology of Yucatan.—Discoveries of
Doctor Cabot.—Village of Tixmeach.—Peto.—Church and Convent.
—News from Home.—Don Pio Perez.—Indian Almanac.—A Frag-
ment of Maya Manuscript.—Journey resumed.—Taihxiu.—Yaxcala.
—Pisté.—Arrival at Chichen.—First Sight of the Ruins.—The Haci-
enda.—A strange Reception.—Lodgings.—Situation of the Ruins.—
Mr. Burke.—Magnificent Appearance of the Ruins.—Derivation of
the Word Chichen.—Senotes.—Different from those before pre-

CHAPTER XVII

Plan of the Ruins.—An Edifice called Akatzeeb.—Doorways.—
Apartments.—Circular Mass of Masonry.—Mysterious Chamber.—
Sculptured Stone Tablet.—Majestic Pile of Building called the
Monjas.—Hieroglyphics.—Rich Ornaments.—Doorways, Chambers,
&c.—Remains of Painting.—The Eglesia, or Church.—Ornaments
on the Façade.—Cartouches in Plaster.—Circular Edifice called the
Caracol.—Apartment.—Staircase, having on each Side entwined
Serpents. — Gigantic Head. — Doorways. — Paintings. — Building
called Chichanchob.—Ornaments.—Row of Hieroglyphics.—An-
other Building.—Vestiges of Mounds and ruined Buildings.—
Extraordinary Edifice, to which the Name Gymnasium or Ten-
nis-court is given.—Ornamented Columns.—Sculptured Figures in
Bas-relief.—Massive Stone Rings, with entwined Serpents.—In-
dian Sports.—Two Ranges of Buildings.—Procession of Tigers.—
Sculptured Columns—Figures in Bas-relief.—Richly-carved Lintel.
—Paintings.—The Castillo.—Staircase.—Colossal Serpents' Heads.
—Doorways.—Carved Lintels.—Jambs ornamented with Sculp-
tured Figures.—Corridors.—Apartments.—Square Pillars, covered
with Sculptured Figures.—Rows of Columns.—Occupation and
Abandonment of Chichen by the Spaniards.—First Discovery of

CHAPTER XVIII

Departure from Chichen.—Village of Kaua.—Cuncunul.—Arrival
at Valladolid.—An Accident.—Appearance of the City.—Don
Pedro Baranda's Cotton Factory.—A Countryman.—Mexican
Revolution.—The Indians as Soldiers.—Adventures of a Demonio.
—Character of the People.—Gamecocks.—Difficulty of obtaining

CHAPTER XXII

CHAPTER XXIII

CHAPTER XXIV

CHAPTER XXV

APPENDIX

LIST OF ILLUSTRATIONS

CHAPTER I

On the twenty-fourth of January we left Nohcacab. It was a great relief to bid farewell to this place, and the only regret attending our departure was the reflection that we should be obliged to return. The kindness and attentions of the padrecito and his brother, and, indeed, of all the villagers, had been unremitted, but the fatigue of riding twelve miles every day over the same ground, and the difficulty of procuring Indians to work, were a constant source of annoyance; besides which, we had a feeling that operated during the whole of our journey: wherever we were taken ill we became disgusted with the place, and were anxious to leave it.

We were setting out on a tour which, according to the plan laid out, embraced a circuit of ruins, and required us to revisit Nohcacab, although our return would be only to make it a point of departure in another direction.

In consequence of this plan we left behind all our heavy luggage, and carried with us only the Daguerreotype apparatus, hammocks, one large box containing our tin table service, a candlestick, bread, chocolate, coffee, and sugar, and a few changes

1

of clothing in pestaquillas. Besides Albino and Bernaldo we had
a puny lad of about fifteen, named Barnaby, a much smaller
pattern than either of the others, and all three together were
hardly equal in bulk to one fairly developed man.

We were all provided with good horses for the road. Mr.
Catherwood had one on which he could make a sketch without
dismounting; Dr. Cabot could shoot from the back of his. Mine
could, on an emergency, be pushed into a hard day's journey for
a preliminary visit. Albino rode a hard-mouthed, wilful beast,
which shook him constantly like a fit of the fever and ague, and
which we distinguished by the name of the trotter. Bernaldo
asked for a horse, because Albino had one, but, instead of riding,
he had to put a strap across his forehead and carry his own luggage on his back.

We were about entering a region little or not at all frequented by white men, and occupied entirely by Indians. Our
road lay through the ruins of Kabah, a league beyond which we
reached the rancho of Chack. This was a large habitation of
Indians, under the jurisdiction of the village of Nohcacab. There
was not a white man in the place, and as we rode through, the
women snatched up their children, and ran from us like startled
deer. I rode up to a hut into which I saw a woman enter, and,
stopping at the fence, merely from curiosity, took out a cigar,
and, making use of some of the few Maya words we had picked
up, asked for a light, but the door remained shut. I dismounted,
and before I had tied my horse the woman rushed out and disappeared among the bushes. In one part of the rancho was a casa
real, being a long thatched hut with a large square before it,
protected by an arbour of leaves, and on one side was a magnificent seybo tree, throwing its shade to a great distance round.

On leaving this rancho we saw at a distance on the left a
high ruined building standing alone amid a great intervening
growth of woods, and apparently inaccessible. Beyond, and at the
distance of four leagues from Nohcacab, we reached the rancho
of Schawill, which was our first stopping-place, on account of the
ruins of Zayi in its immediate neighbourhood. This place also
was inhabited exclusively by Indians, rancho being the name
given to a settlement not of sufficient importance to constitute
a village. The casa real, like that at Chack, was a large hut, with
mud walls and a thatched roof. It had an open place in front
about a hundred feet square, enclosed by a fence made of poles,
and shaded by an arbour of palm leaves. Around the hut were
large seybo trees. The casa real is erected in every rancho of

Indians expressly for the reception of the cura on his occasional or perhaps barely possible visits, but it is occupied also by small dealers from the villages, who sometimes find their way to these ranchos to buy up hogs, maize, and fowls. The hut, when swept out, and comparatively clear of fleas, made a large and comfortable apartment, and furnished ample swinging room for six hammocks, being the number requisite for our whole retinue.

This place was under the parochial charge of our friend the cura of Ticul, who, however, owing to the multiplicity of his other occupations, had visited it but once. The padrecito had sent notice of our coming, and had charged the people to be in readiness to receive us. Immediately on our arrival, therefore, Indians were at hand to procure ramon for the horses, but there was no water. The rancho had no well, and was entirely dependant on that of Chack, three miles distant. For two reals, however, the Indians undertook to procure us four cantaros, one for each horse, which would serve for the night. In the evening we had a formal visit from the alcalde and his alguazils, and half the village besides.

Although we had been some time in the country, we regarded this as really the beginning of our travels; and though the scenes we had met with already were not much like any we had ever encountered before, our first day's journey introduced us to some that were entirely new. The Indians assembled under the arbour, where they, with great formality, offered us seats, and the alcalde told us that the rancho was poor, but they would do all they could to serve us. Neither he nor any other in the place spoke a word of Spanish, and our communications were through Albino. We opened the interview by remonstrating against the charge of two reals for watering our horses, but the excuse was satisfactory enough. In the rainy season they had sources of supply in the neighbourhood, and these were perhaps as primitive as in any other section of the habitable world, being simply deposites of rain-water in the holes and hollows of rocks, which were called sartenejas. From the rocky nature of the country, these are very numerous; during the rainy season they are replenished as fast as they are exhausted, and at the time of our visit, owing to the long continuance of the rains, they furnished a sufficient supply for domestic use, but the people were not able to keep horses or cows, or cattle of any kind, the only animals they had being hogs. In the dry season this source of supply failed them; the holes in the rocks were dry, and they were obliged to send to the rancho of Chack, the well of which

they represented as being half a mile under ground, and so steep
that it was reached only by descending nine different staircases.

This account saved them from all imputation of churlish-
ness in not giving our horses water. It seemed strange that any
community should be willing to live where this article of primary necessity was so difficult to be obtained, and we asked them
why they did not break up their settlement and go elsewhere;
but this idea seemed never to have occurred to them; they said
their fathers had lived there before them, and the land around
was good for milpas. In fact, they were a peculiar people, and
I never before regretted so much my ignorance of the Maya
language. They are under the civil jurisdiction of the village of
Nohcacab, but the right of soil is their own by inheritance. They
consider themselves better off than in the villages, where the
people are subject to certain municipal regulations and duties,
or than on the haciendas, where they would be under the control
of masters.

Their community consists of a hundred labradores, or working men; their lands are held and wrought in common, and the
products are shared by all. Their food is prepared at one hut,
and every family sends for its portion, which explained a singular spectacle we had seen on our arrival; a procession of women
and children, each carrying an earthen bowl containing a quantity of smoking hot broth, all coming down the same road, and
dispersing among the different huts. Every member belonging to
the community, down to the smallest pappoose, contributed in
turn a hog. From our ignorance of the language, and the number of other and more pressing matters claiming our attention,
we could not learn all the details of their internal economy, but
it seemed to approximate that improved state of association
which is sometimes heard of among us; and as theirs has existed
for an unknown length of time, and can no longer be considered
merely experimental, Owen or Fourier might perhaps take lessons from them with advantage.

They differ from professed reformers in one important particular—they seek no converts. No stranger is allowed, upon any
consideration, to enter their community; every member must
marry within the rancho, and no such thing as a marriage out
of it had ever occurred. They said it was impossible; it could
not happen. They were in the habit of going to the villages to
attend the festivals; and when we suggested a supposable case of
a young man or woman falling in love with some village Indian,
they said it might happen; there was no law against it; but none

could *marry* out of the rancho. This was a thing so little apprehended that the punishment for it was not defined in their penal
code; but being questioned, after some consultation they said
that the offender, whether man or woman, would be expelled.
We remarked that in their small community constant intermar-
riages must make them all relatives, which they said was the case
since the reduction of their numbers by the cholera. They were,
in fact, all kinsfolk, but it was allowable for kinsfolk to marry
except in the relationship of brothers and sisters. They were very
strict in attendance upon the ceremonies of the Church, and
had just finished the celebration of the carnival two weeks in
advance of the regular time; but when we corrected their chronology, they said they could celebrate it over again.

Early in the morning we set out for the ruins of Zayi, or
Salli. At a short distance from the rancho we saw in an overgrown milpa on our left the ruins of a mound and building, so
far destroyed that they are not worth presenting.

After proceeding a mile and a half we saw at some distance
before us a great tree-covered mound, which astonished us by its
vast dimensions, and, but for our Indian assistants, would have
frightened us by the size of the trees growing upon it. The woods
commenced from the roadside. Our guides cut a path, and, clearing the branches overhead, we followed on horseback, dismounting at the foot of the Casa Grande. It was by this name that the
Indians called the immense pile of white stone buildings, which,
buried in the depths of a great forest, added new desolation to
the waste by which they were surrounded. We tied our horses,
and worked our way along the front. The trees were so close that
we could take in but a small portion of it at once. If we had encountered these woods at Kabah, where we had such difficulties
in procuring Indians, we should have despaired of being able to
accomplish anything, but, fortunately so far, where our labours
were great we had at hand the means of performing them.

We were at no loss what to do, our great object now being
to economize time. Without waiting to explore the rest of the
ground, we set the Indians at work, and in a few minutes the
stillness of ages was broken by the sharp ringing of the axe and
the crash of falling trees. With a strong force of Indians, we were
able, in the course of the day, to lay bare the whole of the front.

Dr. Cabot did not arrive on the ground till late in the day,
and, coming upon it suddenly from the woods, when there were
no trees to obstruct the view, and its three great ranges and im-

mense proportions were visible at once, considered it the grandest spectacle he had seen in the country.

Plate I represents the front of this building. The view was taken from a mound, at the distance of about five hundred feet, overgrown and having upon it a ruined edifice. In clearing away the trees and undergrowth to this mound we discovered a pila, or stone, hollowed out, and filled with rain-water, which was a great acquisition to us while working at these ruins.

The plate represents so much of the building as now remains and can be presented in a drawing. It has three stories or ranges, and in the centre is a grand staircase thirty-two feet wide, rising to the platform of the highest terrace. This staircase, however, is in a ruinous condition, and, in fact, a mere mound, and all that part of the building on the right had fallen, and was so dilapidated that no intelligible drawing could be made of it; we did not even clear away the trees. The engraving represents all that part which remains, being the half of the building on the left of the staircase.

The lowest of the three ranges is two hundred and sixty-five feet in front and one hundred and twenty in depth. It had sixteen doorways, opening into apartments of two chambers each. The whole front wall has fallen; the interiors are filled with fragments and rubbish, and the ground in front was so encumbered with the branches of fallen trees, even after they had been chopped into pieces and beaten down with poles, that, at the distance necessary for making a drawing, but a small portion of the interior could be seen. The two ends of this range have each six doorways, and the rear has ten, all opening into apartments, but in general they are in a ruinous condition.

The range of buildings on the second terrace was two hundred and twenty feet in length and sixty feet in depth, and had four doorways on each side of the grand staircase. Those on the left, which are all that remain, have two columns in each doorway, each column being six feet six inches high, roughly made, with square capitals, like Doric, but wanting the grandeur pertaining to all known remains of this ancient order. Filling up the spaces between the doorways are four small columns curiously ornamented, close together, and sunk in the wall. Between the first and second and third and fourth doorways a small staircase leads to the terrace of the third range. The platform of this terrace is thirty feet in front and twenty-five in the rear. The building is one hundred and fifty feet long by eighteen feet

Plate I

F. Catherwood

ZAYI.

deep, and has seven doorways opening into as many apartments. The lintels over the doorways are of stone.

The exterior of the third and highest range was plain; that of the two other ranges had been elaborately ornamented; and, in order to give some idea of their character, I present in Plate II a portion of the façade of the second range. Among designs common in other places is the figure of a man supporting himself on his hands, with his legs expanded in a curious rather than delicate attitude, of which a small portion appears on the right of the engraving; and again we have the "large and very well constructed buildings of lime and stone" which Bernal Dias saw at Campeachy, "with figures of *serpents* and of idols painted on the walls."

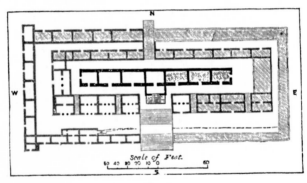

Fɪɢ. 1

Figure 1 represents the ground plan of the three ranges, and gives the dimensions of the terraces. The platforms are wider in front than in the rear; the apartments vary from twenty-three to ten feet, and the north side of the second range has a curious and unaccountable feature. It is called the Casa Cerrada, or closed house, having ten doorways, all of which are blocked up inside with stone and mortar. Like the well at Xcoch, it had a mysterious reputation in the village of Nohcacab, and all believed that it contained hidden treasure. Indeed, so strong was this belief, that the alcalde Segundo, who had never visited these ruins, resolved to take advantage of our presence; and, according to agreement in the village, came down with crowbars to assist us in breaking into the closed apartments and discovering the precious hoard. The first sight of these closed-up doorways gave us a strong desire to make the attempt; but on moving along we found that the Indians had been beforehand with us. In front of

Plate II

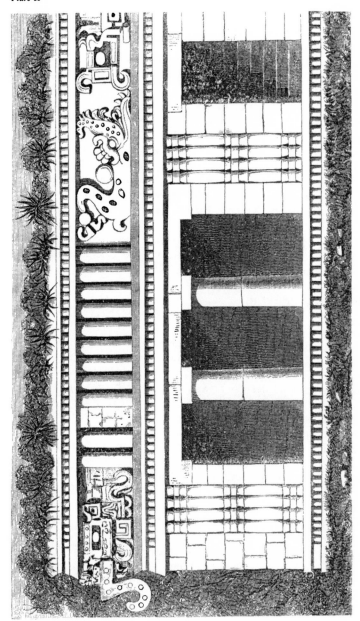

several were piles of stones, which they had worked out from the doorways, and under the lintels were holes, through which we were able to crawl inside; and here we found ourselves in apartments finished with walls and ceilings like all the others, but filled up (except so far as they had been emptied by the Indians) with solid masses of mortar and stone. There were ten of these apartments in all, 220 feet long and ten feet deep, which being thus filled up, made the whole building a solid mass; and the strangest feature was that the filling up of the apartments must have been simultaneous with the erection of the buildings, for, as the filling-in rose above the tops of the doorways, the men who performed it never could have entered to their work through the doors. It must have been done as the walls were built, and the ceiling must have closed over a solid mass. Why this was so constructed it was impossible to say, unless the solid mass was required for the support of the upper terrace and building; and if this was the case, it would seem to have been much easier to erect a solid structure at once, without any division into apartments.

The top of this building commanded a grand view, no longer of a dead plain, but of undulating woodlands. Toward the northwest, crowning the highest hill, was a lofty mound, covered with trees, which, to our now practised eyes, it was manifest shrouded a building, either existing or in ruins. The whole intervening space was thick wood and underbrush, and the Indians said the mound was inaccessible. I selected three of the best, and told them that we must reach it; but they really did not know how to make the attempt, and set out on a continuation of the road by which we had reached the ruins, and which led us rather from than to the mound. On the way we met another Indian, who turned back with us, and a little beyond, taking his range, he cut through the woods to another path, following which a short distance, he again struck through the woods, and, all cutting together, we reached the foot of a stony hill covered with the gigantic maguey, or Agave Americana, its long thorny points piercing and tearing all that touched them. Climbing up this hill with great toil, we reached the wall of a terrace, and, climbing this, found ourselves at the foot of the building.

It was in a ruinous condition, and did not repay us for the labour; but over the door was a sculptured head with a face of good expression and workmanship. In one of the apartments was a high projection running along the wall; in another a raised platform about a foot high; and on the walls of this apartment was the print of the red hand. The doorway commanded an extensive view of rolling woodland, which, with its livery of deep green, ought to have conveyed a sensation of gladness, but, perhaps from its desolation and stillness, it induced rather a feeling of melancholy. There was but one opening in the forest, being that made by us, disclosing the Casa Grande, with the figures of a few Indians still continuing their clearings on the top.

In front of the Casa Grande, at the distance of five hundred yards, and also visible from the top, is another structure, strikingly different from any we had seen, more strange and inexplicable, and having at a distance the appearance of a New-England factory.

Fig. 2

Figure 2 represents this building. It stands on a terrace, and may be considered as consisting of two separate structures, one above the other. The lower one, in its general features, resembled all the rest. It was forty feet front, low, and having a flat roof, and in the centre was an archway running

through the building. The front is fallen, and the whole so
ruined that nothing but the archway appears in the engraving.
Along the middle of the roof, unsupported, and entirely independent of everything else, rises a perpendicular wall to the
height of perhaps thirty feet. It is of stone, about two feet
thick, and has oblong openings through it about four feet long
and six inches wide, like small windows. It had been covered with stucco, which had fallen off, and left the face of rough
stone and mortar; and on the other side were fragments of stuccoed figures and ornaments. An Indian appears before it in the
act of killing a snake, with which all the woods of Yucatan
abound. Since we began our exploration of American ruins we
had not met with anything more inexplicable than this great
perpendicular wall. It seemed built merely to puzzle posterity.

These were the only buildings in this immediate neighbourhood which had survived the wasting of the elements; but, inquiring among the Indians, one of them undertook to guide me
to another, which he said was still in good preservation. Our
direction was south-southwest from the Casa Grande; and at the
distance of about a mile, the whole intermediate region being
desolate and overgrown, we reached a terrace, the area of which
far exceeded anything we had seen in the country. We crossed
it from north to south, and in this direction it must have been
fifteen hundred feet in length, and probably was quite as much
in the other direction; but it was so rough, broken, and overgrown, that we did not attempt to measure it.

On this great platform was the building of which the Indian had told us; I had it cleared, and Mr. Catherwood drew it
the next day, as it appears in Plate III. It measures one hundred
and seventeen feet in front, and eighty-four feet deep, and contains sixteen apartments, of which those in front, five in number,
are best preserved. That in the centre has three doorways. It is
twenty-seven feet six inches long, by only seven feet six inches
wide, and communicates by a single doorway with a back room
eighteen feet long and five feet six inches wide. This room is
raised two feet six inches above the one in front, and has steps
to ascend. Along the bottom of the front room, as high as the
sill of the door, is a row of small columns, thirty-eight in number, attached to the wall.

In several places the great platform is strewed with ruins,
and probably other buildings lie buried in the woods, but without guides or any clew whatever, we did not attempt to look for
them.

Plate III

Catherwood

Graham

ZAYI

Such, so far as we were able to discover them, are the ruins of Zayi, the name of which, to the time of our visit, had never been uttered among civilized men, and, but for the notoriety connected with our movements, would probably be unknown at this day in the capital of Yucatan. Our first accounts of them were from the cura Carillo, who, on the occasion of his only visit to this part of his curacy, passed a great portion of his time among them.

It was strange and almost incredible that, with these extraordinary monuments before their eyes, the Indians never bestowed upon them one passing thought. The question, who built them? never by any accident crossed their minds. The great name of Montezuma, which had gone beyond them to the Indians of Honduras, had never reached their ears, and to all our questions we received the same dull answer which first met us at Copan, "Quien sabe?" "Who knows?" They had the same superstitious feelings as the Indians of Uxmal; they believed that the ancient buildings were haunted, and, as in the remote region of Santa Cruz del Quiché, they said that on Good Friday of every year music was heard sounding among the ruins.

There was but one thing connected with the old city that interested them at all, and that was the subject of a well. They supposed that somewhere among these ruins, overgrown and lost, existed the fountain which had supplied the ancient inhabitants with water; and, believing that by the use of our instruments its site could be discovered, they offered to cut down all the trees throughout the whole region covered by the ruins.

CHAPTER II

The next morning, while Mr. Catherwood was engaged in drawing the building represented in the last engraving, Dr. Cabot and myself set out to visit the one which we had passed in coming from the rancho of Chack.

In the suburbs of the rancho we turned off to the right by a path, which we followed for some distance on horseback, when it changed its direction, and we dismounted. From this place our guides cut a path through the woods, and we came out upon a large field of táje, being long stems growing close together, eight or ten feet high, straight, and about half an inch thick, having a yellow flower on the top, which is a favourite food for horses. The stems, tied up in bundles three or four inches thick, are used for torches. On one side of this field we saw the high building before referred to, and on the other side was a second not visible before. A bird which the doctor wished to procure lighted on a tree growing upon the latter, and we went to it, but found nothing of particular interest, and struck across the field of táje for the former. This táje was as bad as the woods to walk through, for it grew so high as to exclude every breath of

15

air, and was not high enough to be any protection against the sun.

The building stood on the top of a stony hill, on a terrace still firm and substantial. It consisted of two stories, the roof of the lower one forming the platform in front of the upper, and had a staircase, which was broken and ruined. The upper building had a large apartment in the centre, and a smaller one on each side, much encumbered with rubbish, from one of which we were driven by a hornet's nest, and in another a young vulture, with a hissing noise, flapped its plumeless wings and hopped out of the door.

The terrace commanded a picturesque view of wooded hills, and at a distance the Casa Grande, and the high wall before presented. They were perhaps three or four miles distant. All the intermediate space was overgrown. The Indians had traversed it in all directions in the dry season, when there was no foliage to hide the view, and they said that in all this space there were no vestiges of buildings. Close together as we had found the remains of ancient habitations, it seemed hardly possible that distinct and independent cities had existed with but such a little space between, and yet it was harder to imagine that one city had embraced within its limits these distant buildings, the extreme ones being four miles apart, and that the whole intermediate region of desolation had once swarmed with a teeming and active population.

Leaving this, we toiled back to our horses, and, returning to the road, passed through the rancho, about a mile beyond which we reached the pozo, or well, the accounts of which we had heard on our first arrival.

Near the mouth were some noble seybo trees, throwing their great branches far and wide, under which groups of Indians were arranging their calabashes and torches, preparing to descend; others, just out, were wiping their sweating bodies. At one moment an Indian disappeared, and at the next another rose up out of the earth. We noticed that there were no women, who, throughout Yucatan, are the drawers of water, and always seen around a well, but we were told that no woman ever enters the well of Chack; all the water for the rancho was procured by the men, which alone indicated that the well was of an extraordinary character. We had brought with us a ball of twine, and made immediate preparations to descend, reducing our dress as near as possible to that of the Indians.

Our first movement was down a hole by a perpendicular

ladder, at the foot of which we were fairly entered into a great cavern. Our guides preceded us with bundles of táje lighted for torches, and we came to a second descent almost perpendicular, which we achieved by a ladder laid flat against the rock. Beyond this we moved on a short distance, still following our guides, and still descending, when we saw their torches disappearing, and reached a wild hole, which also we descended by a long rough ladder. At the foot of this the rock was damp and slippery, and there was barely room enough to pass around it, and get upon another ladder down the same hole, now more contracted, and so small that, with the arms akimbo, the elbows almost touched on each side. At this time our Indians were out of sight; and in total darkness, feeling our way by the rounds of the ladder, we cried out to them, and were answered by distant voices directly underneath. Looking down, we saw their torches like moving balls of fire, apparently at an interminable distance below us.

At the foot of this ladder there was a rude platform as a resting-place, made to enable those ascending and descending to pass each other. A group of naked Indians, panting and sweating under the load of their calabashes, were waiting till we vacated the ladder above; and even in this wild hole, with loads on their backs, straps binding their foreheads, and panting from fatigue and heat, they held down their torches, and rendered obeisance to the blood of the white man. Descending the next ladder, both above and below us were torches gleaming in the darkness. We had still another ladder to descend, and the whole perpendicular depth of this hole was perhaps two hundred feet.

From the foot of this ladder there was an opening to the right, and from it we soon entered a low, narrow passage, through which we crawled on our hands and knees. With the toil and the smoke of the torches the heat was almost beyond endurance. The passage enlarged and again contracted, descending steeply, and so low that the shoulders almost touched the roof. This opened upon a great chasm at one side, and beyond we came to another perpendicular hole, which we descended by steps cut in the rock. From this there was another low, crawling passage, and, almost stifled with heat and smoke, we came out into a small opening, in which was a basin of water, being the well. The place was crowded with Indians filling their calabashes, and they started at the sight of our smoky white faces as if El Demonio had descended among them. It was, doubtless,

the first time that the feet of a white man had ever reached this
well.

On returning we measured the distance, Doctor Cabot going before with a line of about a hundred feet, in the wild and
broken passages being soon out of sight, and sometimes out of
hearing. I followed, with an Indian winding up the line, while
I made notes. I had two Indians with long bundles of lighted
sticks, who, whenever I stopped to write, either held them so
far off as to be of no use, or else thrust them into my face, blinding
the eyes with smoke and scorching the skin. I was dripping as
if in a vapour-bath; my face and hands were black with smoke
and incrusted with dirt; large drops of sweat fell upon my book,
which, with the dirt from my hands, matted the leaves together,
so that my notes are almost useless. They were, no doubt, imperfect, but I do not believe that, with the most accurate details,
it is possible to convey a true idea of the character of this cave,
with its deep holes and passages through a bed of solid rock, and
the strange scene presented by the Indians, with torches and
calabashes, unmurmuring and uncomplaining, at their daily
task of seeking, deep in the bowels of the earth, one of the great
elements of life.

The distance, as we traversed it, with its ladders, ascents and
descents, winding and crawling passages, seemed a full half
league, as represented by the Indians. By measurement it was
not quite fifteen hundred feet, which is about equal to the
length of the Park fronting on Broadway. The perpendicular
depth to the water I am not able to give, but some idea may be
formed of these passages from the fact that the Indians did not
carry their calabashes on their shoulders, because, with the body
bent, they would strike against the roof or roll over the head;
but the straps across the forehead were let out so long that the
calabashes rested below the hips, and in crawling on the hands
and feet their loads did not rise above the line of the back.

And this well was not, as at Xcoch, the occasional resort of
a straggling Indian, nor the mere traditional watering-place of
an ancient city. It was the regular and only supply of a living
population. The whole rancho of Chack was entirely dependant
upon it, and in the dry season the rancho of Schawill, three
miles distant.

The patient industry of such a people may well be supposed
to have reared the immense mounds and the great stone structures scattered all over the country. We consumed a calabash of
water in washing and quenching our thirst, and as we rode back

to the rancho of Schawill, came to the conclusion that an admission into the community of this exclusive people was no great privilege, when it would entail upon the applicant, for six months in the year, a daily descent into this subterraneous well.

We arrived at the rancho in good season. Mr. Catherwood had finished his drawing, and Bernaldo was ready with his dinner. We had nothing to detain us, ordered carriers forthwith for our luggage, and at half past two we were in the saddle again in search of ruined cities.

The reader has some idea of the caminos reales of this country, and they were all like English turnpikes compared with that upon which we entered on leaving this rancho. In fact, it was a mere path through the woods, the branches of the trees being trimmed away to a height barely sufficient to admit of an Indian passing under with a load of maize on his back. We were advised that it would be very difficult to get through on horseback, and were obliged to keep dodging the head and bending the body to avoid the branches, and at times we were brought to a stand by some overhanging arm of a tree, and obliged to dismount.

At the distance of two leagues we reached the rancho of Sannacté, the Indians of which were the wildest people in appearance we had yet seen. As we rode through, the women ran away and hid themselves, and the men crouched on the ground bareheaded, with long black hair hanging over their eyes, gazing at us in stupid astonishment. The same scarcity of water still continued. The rancho was entirely destitute; it had no pozo or well of any kind, either ancient or modern, and the inhabitants procured their whole supply from the village of Sabachshé, two leagues, or six miles, distant! This supply, too, was brought daily on the backs of Indians; but again in this arid and destitute region was still another evidence of ancient population— another desolate and ruined city.

Beyond the outskirts of the rancho was a large clearing for a milpa, within which, naked and exposed to full view, were two ancient buildings. The milpa was enclosed by a fence, and was overgrown with táje. We tied our horses to the stems of the táje, and, leaving them eating the flowers, followed a path which led between the two buildings. Figure 3 represents the one on the left. It stands on a terrace, still strong and substantial, and, fortunately, clear of trees, though many were growing on the top. It has five apartments; the façade above the cornice is fallen, and between the doorways are fragments of small columns

FIG. 3

set in the wall. On the other side of the milpa was another edifice, holding aloft a high wall, like that we had seen at Zayi,
extraordinary in its appearance and incomprehensible in its
uses and purposes. From the tact and facility we had now acquired, a short time sufficed for our examination of this place,
and, with one more added to our list of ruined cities, we
mounted, and resumed our journey.

At half past five we reached the rancho of Sabachshé, lying
on the camino real from Ticul to Bolonchen, and inhabited
entirely by Indians. The casa real stood on an elevation in an
open place; it was thatched with palm leaves, had mud walls,
and an arbour before it, and a table and benches within. Altogether, it was better in appearance and furniture than the others
we had encountered, which, as we afterward learned, was owing
to the circumstance that, besides its regular uses, it was intended
for the residence of the mistress on her annual visits to the rancho. But much more interesting and important was the fact, that
this rancho was distinguished by a well, the sight of which was
more grateful to us than that of the best hotel to the traveller

in a civilized country. We were scratched with thorns, and smarting with garrapata bites, and looked forward to the refreshment of a bath. Very soon our horses had the benefit of it, the bath being in that country, where the currycomb and brush are entirely unknown, the only external refreshment these animals ever get. The well was built by the present owner, and formerly the inhabitants were dependant entirely upon the well at Tabi, six miles distant! Besides its real value, it presented a curious and lively spectacle. A group of Indian women was around it. It had no rope or fixtures of any kind for raising water, but across the mouth was a round beam laid upon two posts, over which the women were letting down and hoisting up little bark buckets. Every woman brought with her and carried away her own bucket and rope, the latter coiled up and laid on the top of her head, with the end hanging down behind, and the coil forming a sort of headdress.

Near the well was the hut of the alcalde, enclosed by a rude fence, and within were dogs, hogs, turkeys, and fowls, which all barked, grunted, gobbled, and cackled together as we entered. The yard was shaded by orange-trees loaded with ripe and unusually large fruit. Under one of them was a row of twenty or thirty wild boars' jaws and tusks, trophies of the chase, and memorials attesting the usefulness of the barking dogs. The noise brought the alcalde to the door, a heavy and infirm old man, apparently rich, and suffering from the high living indicated by his hogs and poultry; but he received us with meekness and humility. We negotiated forthwith for the purchase of some oranges, and bought thirty for a medio, stipulating that they should all be the largest and best on the trees; after which, supporting himself by his cane, he hobbled on to the casa real, had it swept out, and assigned Indians to attend upon us. If he wanted alacrity himself, he infused it into his people, and made up for all deficiencies by unqualified personal deference and respect. It was a fine evening, and we spread our supper-table under the arbour. The old alcalde remained with us, and a group of Indians sat on the steps, not like the proud and independent race of Schawill, but acknowledging themselves criados, or servants, bound to obey the orders of their mistress. La señora was, in their eyes, a miniature print of Queen Victoria, but skill in the use of figures may arrive at the value of at least this part of her possessions. There were fifty-five labradores, or labouring men, under an obligation to plant and harvest ten micates of maize for her benefit. Each micate produces ten cargas, or loads, making in all five hundred and fifty, which, at three reals per carga, gives as the revenue this lady comes regularly to collect, about two hundred dollars per annum; but this gives more power than lands or money to any amount in our country could give; and the labradores being all free and independent electors, fifty-five votes could always be calculated upon in an emergency for the side of principle and la señora.

Having made our arrangements for the next day, we went into the hut and shut the door. Some time afterward the old alcalde sent in to ask permission to go home, as he was very sleepy, which we graciously granted, and, by his direction, three or four Indians swung their little hammocks under the arbour, to be at hand in case we should need anything. During the night we found it extremely cold, and, with the little covering we had brought, could hardly keep ourselves comfortable.

Early in the morning we found a large gathering round the house to escort us to the ruins. In the suburbs of the rancho we turned off to the left, and passed among the huts of the Indians, almost smothered by weeds, and having at the doors rude boxes of earth set up on posts, for vegetables to grow in out of the reach of the hogs.

Crossing the fence of the last hut, we entered a thick growth of trees. As if instinctively, every Indian drew his machete, and in a few minutes they cut a path to the foot of a small building, not rich in ornament, but tasteful, having some shades of difference from any we had seen, overgrown by trees, and beautifully picturesque. On one corner of the roof a vulture had built her nest, and, scared away at our approach, hovered over our heads, looking down upon us as if amazed. We gave directions, all the Indians fell to work, and in a few minutes the small terrace in front was cleared. I had not expected so many Indians, and, not knowing what occasion I might have for their services, told them that I did not need so great a number, and should only pay those whom I had engaged. All stopped, and when the purport of my words was explained to them, said that made no difference; they immediately set to work again, and the machetes fell with a rapidity unparalleled in our experience. In half an hour space enough was cleared for Mr. Catherwood to set up his camera lucida. The same alertness was shown in preparing a place for him to stand in, and half a dozen stood ready to hold an umbrella for his protection against the sun.

Plate IV represents the front of the building. Its design is tasteful and even elegant, and when perfect it must have pre-

Plate IV

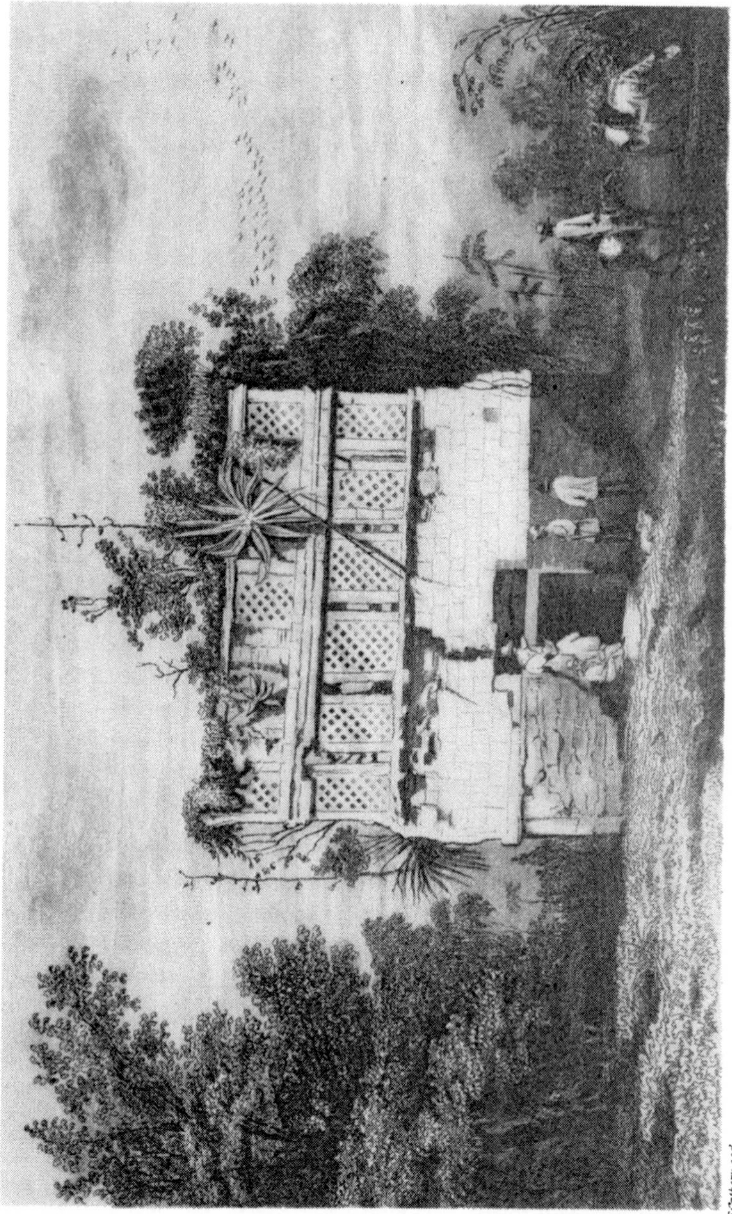

F. Catherwood

A. Halbert.

SABACHTSCHE

sented a fine appearance. It has a single doorway, opening into a chamber twenty-five feet long by ten wide. Above the door is a portion of plain masonry, and over this a cornice supporting twelve small pilasters, having between them the diamond ornament, then a massive cornice, with pilasters and diamond work, surmounted by another cornice, making in all four cornices; an arrangement we had not previously met with.

While Mr. Catherwood was making his drawing, the Indians stood around under the shade of the trees, looking at him quietly and respectfully, and making observations to each other. They were a fine-looking race. Some of them, one tall old man particularly, had noble Roman faces, and they seemed to have more respectability of appearance and character than was consistent with the condition of men not wearing pantaloons. All at once an enormous iguana, or lizard, doubled the corner of the building, ran along the front, and plunged into a crevice over the door, burying his whole body, but leaving the long tail out. Among these unsophisticated people this reptile is a table delicacy, and here was a supper provided for some of them. Machetes flew out, and, cutting down a sapling with a crotch in it, they rested it against the wall, and, standing in the crotch, pulled upon the tail; but the animal held on with his feet as if a part of the building. All the Indians, one after the other, had a pull at the tail, but could not make him budge. At length two of them contrived to get hold together, and, while pulling with all their strength, the tail came off by the roots, a foot and half long in their hands. The animal was now more out of their reach than before, his whole body being hidden in the wall; but he could not escape. The Indians picked away the mortar with their machetes, and enlarged the hole until they got his hind legs clear, when, griping the body above the legs, they again hauled; but, though he had only the fore legs to hold on with, they could not tear him out. They the untied the ropes of their sandals, and, fastening them above the hind legs, and pulling till the long body seemed parting like the tail, they at length dragged him out. They secured him by a gripe under the fore part of the body, cracked his spine, and broke the bones of his fore legs so that he could not run; pried his jaws open, fastened them apart with a sharp stick so that he could not bite, and then put him away in the shade. This refined cruelty was to avoid the necessity of killing him immediately, for if killed, in that hot climate he would soon be unfit for food; but, mutilated and mangled as he was, he could be kept alive till night.

This over, we moved on in a body, carrying the iguana, to the next building, which was situated in a different direction, about a quarter of a mile distant, and completely buried in woods. It was seventy-five feet long, and had three doorways, leading to the same number of apartments. A great part of the front had fallen; Plate V represents that which remains. With some slight difference in the detail of ornament, the character is the same as in all the other buildings, and the general effect pleasing. Growing on the roof are two maguey plants, Agave Americana, in our latitude called the century plant, but under the hot sun of the tropics blooming every four or five years. There are four species of this plant in Yucatan: the maguey, from which is produced the pulqué, a beverage common in all the Mexican provinces, which, taken in excess, produces intoxication; the henneken, which produces the article known in our markets as Sisal hemp; the sabila, with which the Indian women wean children, covering the breast with the leaf, which is very bitter to the taste; and the peta, having leaves twice as large as the last, from which a very fine white hemp is made. These plants, in some or all of their varieties, were found in the neighbourhood of all the ruins, forming around them a pointed and thorny wall, which we were obliged to cut through to reach the buildings.

While Mr. C. was engaged in drawing this structure, the Indians told us of two others half a league distant. I selected two of them for guides, and, with the same alacrity which they had shown in everything else, nine volunteered to accompany me. We had a good path nearly all the way, until the Indians pointed out a white object seen indistinctly through the trees, again uttering, with strong gutturals, the familiar sound of "Xlappahk," or old walls. In a few minutes they cut a path to it. The building was larger than the last, having the front ornamented in the same way, much fallen, though still presenting an interesting spectacle. As it was not much overgrown, we set to work and cleared it, and left it for another, in regard to which I formed some curious expectations, for the Indians described it as *very new*. It lay on the same path, to the left in returning to the rancho, and separated from us by a great field of táje, through which we were obliged to cut a path for several hundred yards to the foot of the terrace. The walls were entire and very massive; but climbing up it, I found only a small building, consisting of but two apartments, the front much fallen, and the doors filled up, but no sign or token distinguishing it as *newer*

Plate V

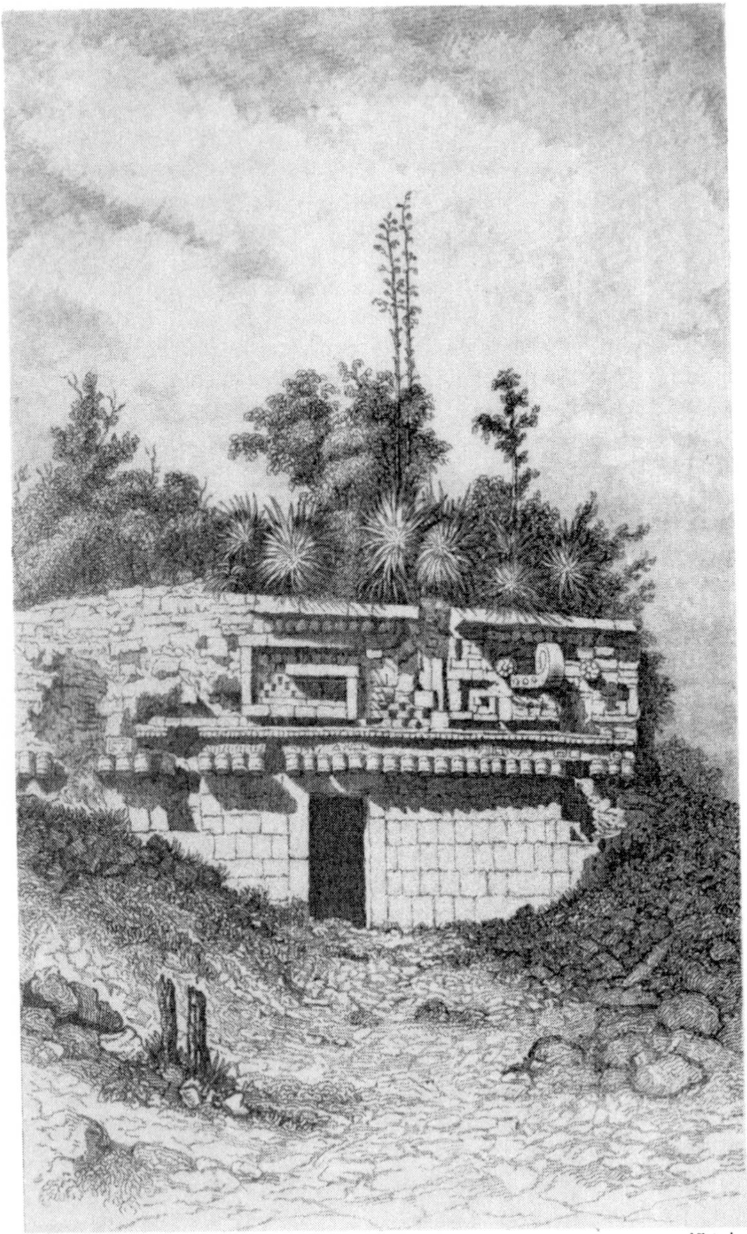

F. Catherwood del

SABACHTSCHÉ

or more modern; and I now learned, what I might have done before by a little asking, that all they meant by their description of it was, that it was the *newest* known to them, having been discovered but twelve years before, accidentally, on clearing the ground for a milpa, until which time it was as much unknown to them as to the rest of the world. This intelligence gave great weight to the consideration which had often suggested itself before, that cities may exist equal to any now known, buried in the woods, overgrown and lost, which will perhaps never be discovered.

On the walls of this desolate edifice were prints of the "mano colorado," or red hand. Often as I saw this print, it never failed to interest me. It was the stamp of the living hand; it always brought me nearer to the builders of these cities, and at times, amid stillness, desolation, and ruin, it seemed as if from behind the curtain that concealed them from view was extended the hand of greeting. These prints were larger than any I had seen. In several places I measured them with my own, opening the fingers to correspond with those on the wall. The Indians said it was the hand of the master of the building.

The mysterious interest which, in my eyes, always attached to this red hand, has assumed a more definite shape. I have been advised that in Mr. Catlin's collection of Indian curiosities, made during a long residence among our North American tribes, was a tent presented to him by the chief of the powerful but now extinct race of Mandans, which exhibits, among other marks, two prints of the red hand; and I have been farther advised that the red hand is seen constantly upon the buffalo robes and skins of wild animals brought in by the hunters on the Rocky Mountains, and, in fact, that it is a symbol recognised and in common use by the North American Indians of the present day. I do not mention these as facts within my own knowledge, but with the hope of attracting the attention of those who have opportunities and facilities for investigation; and I suggest the interesting consideration that, if true, the red hand on the tent and the buffalo robes points back from the wandering tribes in our country to the comparatively polished people who erected the great cities at the south; and if true that it is at this day used as a sign or symbol by our North American Indians, its meaning can be ascertained from living witnesses, and through ages of intervening darkness a ray of light may be thrown back upon the now mysterious and incomprehensible characters which perplex the stranger on the walls of the desolate southern buildings.

On my return to the rancho I learned the cause of the extraordinary attention shown us, which, though we had received it as a matter of course, and no more than what, for some unknown reasons, was justly due to us, had, nevertheless, somewhat surprised us. Our movements in that neighbourhood were matters of some notoriety. Albino's preliminary visit and our intentions had reached the ears of the señora, and the evening before our arrival orders from her had arrived at the rancho for all the Indians to put themselves at our command; and this delicate manner of doing us a service is one of the many acts of kindness I have to acknowledge to the citizens of Yucatan. The old alcalde again waited till he became sleepy, when he asked permission to go to his hut, and four or five Indians again hung up their hammocks under the arbour.

CHAPTER III

The next morning we set out for the ruins of Labnà. Our road lay southeast, among hills, and was more picturesque than any we had seen in the country. At the distance of a mile and a half we reached a field of ruins, which, after all we had seen, created in us new feelings of astonishment. It was one of the circumstances attending our exploration of ruins in this country, that until we arrived on the ground we had no idea of what we were to meet with. The accounts of the Indians were never reliable. When they gave us reason to expect much we found but little, and, on the other hand, when we expected but little a great field presented itself. Of this place even our friend the cura Carillo had never heard. Our first intelligence of ruins in this region was from the brother of the padrecito at Nohcacab, who, however, had never seen them himself. Since our arrival in the country we had not met with anything that excited us more strongly, and now we had mingled feelings of pain and pleasure; of pain, that they had not been discovered before the sentence of irretrievable ruin had gone forth against them; at the same time it was matter of deep congratulation that, before the doom was accomplished, we were permitted to see these decaying, but still proud memorials of a mysterious

people. In a few years, even these will be gone; and as it has
been denied that such things ever were, doubts may again arise
whether they have indeed existed. So strong was this impression
that we determined to fortify in every possible way our proofs.
If anything could have added to the interest of discovering such
a new field of research, it was the satisfaction of having at our
command such an effective force of Indians. No time was lost,
and they began work with a spirit corresponding to their numbers. Many of them had hachas, or small axes, and the crash of
falling trees was like the stirring noise of felling in one of our
own forests.

Plate VI represents a pyramidal mound, holding aloft the
most curious and extraordinary structure we had seen in the
country. It put us on the alert the moment we saw it. We
passed an entire day before it, and, in looking back upon our
journey among ruined cities, no subject of greater interest presents itself to my mind. The mound is forty-five feet high. The
steps had fallen; trees were growing out of the place where they
stood, and we reached the top by clinging to the branches; when
these were cleared away, it was extremely difficult to ascend and
descend. The maguey plants cut down in making the clearing
appear fallen on the steps.

A narrow platform forms the top of the mound. The building faces the south, and when entire measured forty-three feet
in front and twenty feet in depth. It had three doorways, of
which one, with eight feet of the whole structure, has fallen, and
is now in ruins. The centre doorway opens into two chambers,
each twenty feet long and six feet wide.

Above the cornice of the building rises a gigantic perpendicular wall to the height of thirty feet, once ornamented from
top to bottom, and from one side to the other, with colossal
figures and other designs in stucco, now broken and in fragments, but still presenting a curious and extraordinary appearance, such as the art of no other people ever produced. Along
the top, standing out on the wall, was a row of death's heads;
underneath were two lines of human figures in alto relievo (of
which scattered arms and legs alone remain), the grouping of
which, so far as it could be made out, showed considerable proficiency in that most difficult department of the art of design.
Over the centre doorway, constituting the principal ornament
of the wall, was a colossal figure seated, of which only a large
tippet and girdle, and some other detached portions, have been
preserved. Conspicuous over the head of this principal figure is

Plate VI

LABNAH

a large ball, with a human figure standing up beside it, touching it with his hands, and another below it with one knee on the ground, and one hand thrown up as if in the effort to support the ball, or in the apprehension of its falling upon him. In all our labours in that country we never studied so diligently to make out from the fragments the combinations and significance of these figures and ornaments. Standing in the same position, and looking at them all together, we could not agree.

Mr. Catherwood made two drawings at different hours and under a different position of the sun, and Dr. Cabot and myself worked upon it the whole day with the Daguerreotype. With the full blaze of a vertical sun upon it, the white stone glared with an intensity dazzling and painful to the eyes, and almost realizing the account by Bernal Dias in the expedition to Mexico, of the arrival of the Spaniards at Cempoal. "Our advanced guard having gone to the great square, the buildings of which had been lately whitewashed and plastered, in which art these people are very expert, one of our horsemen was so struck with the splendour of their appearance in the sun, that he came back at full speed to Cortez, to tell him that the walls of the houses were of silver."

Our best view was obtained in the afternoon, when the edifice was in shade, but so broken and confused were the ornaments that a distinct representation could not be made even with the Daguerreotype, and the only way to make out all the details was near approach by means of a ladder; we had all the woods to make one of, but it was difficult for the Indians to make one of the length required; and when made it would have been too heavy and cumbersome to manage on the narrow platform in front. Besides, the wall was tottering and ready to fall. One portion was already gone in a perpendicular line from top to bottom, and the reader will see in the engraving that on a line with the right of the centre doorway the wall is cracked, and above is gaping, and stands apart more than a foot all the way to the top. In a few years it must fall. Its doom is sealed. Human power cannot save it; but in its ruins it gave a grand idea of the scenes of barbaric magnificence which this country must have presented when all her cities were entire. The figures and ornaments on this wall were painted; the remains of bright colours are still visible, defying the action of the elements. If a solitary traveller from the Old World could by some strange accident have visited this aboriginal city when it was yet perfect, his account would have seemed more fanciful than any in Eastern

Plate VII

GATEWAY at LABNA

E. Catherwood.

J. N. Gimbrede.

story, and been considered a subject for the Arabian Nights'
Entertainments.

At the distance of a few hundred feet from this structure,
in sight at the same time as we approached it, is an arched gateway, remarkable for its beauty of proportions and grace of ornament. Plate VII represents this gateway. On the right, running
off at an angle of thirty degrees, is a long building much fallen,
which could not be comprehended in the view. On the left it
forms an angle with another building, and on the return of the
wall there is a doorway, not shown in the engraving, of good
proportions, and more richly ornamented than any other portion of the structure. The effect of the whole combination was
curious and striking, and, familiar as we were with ruins, the
first view, with the great wall towering in front, created an impression that is not easily described.

The gateway is ten feet wide, passing through which we
entered a thick forest, growing so close upon the building that
we were unable to make out even its shape; but, on clearing
away the trees, we discovered that this had been the principal
front, and that these trees were growing in what had once been
the area, or courtyard. The doors of the apartments on both
sides of the gateway, each twelve feet by eight, opened upon this
area. Over each doorway was a square recess, in which were the
remains of a rich ornament in stucco, with marks of paint still
visible, apparently intended to represent the face of the sun
surrounded by its rays, probably once objects of adoration and
worship, but now wilfully destroyed. Plate VIII represents this
front. The buildings around the area formed a great irregular
pile, measuring in all two hundred feet in length. The plan
was different from that of any we had seen, but, having so many
subjects to present, I have not had it engraved.

Northeast from the mound on which the great wall stands,
and about one hundred and fifty yards distant, is a large building, erected on a terrace, and hidden among the trees growing
thereupon, with its front much ruined, and having but few remains of sculptured ornaments. Still farther in the same direction, going through the woods, we reach the grand, and, without
extravagance, the really magnificent building represented in the
frontispiece to this volume. It stands on a gigantic terrace, four
hundred feet long and one hundred and fifty feet deep. The
whole terrace is covered with buildings. The front represented
measures two hundred and eighty-two feet in length. It consisted of three distinct parts, differing in style, and perhaps

Plate VIII

INTERIOR OF GATEWAY AT LAHNA.

erected at different times. At a distance, as seen indistinctly through the trees, we had no idea of its extent. We came upon it at the corner which appears on the right in the engraving. Our guide cut a path along the front wall, and stopping, as we did, to look at the ornaments, and entering the apartments as we went along, the building seemed immense.

The whole long façade was ornamented with sculptured stone, of which, large as the engraving is, the details cannot appear; but, to give some idea of their character, a detached portion is represented in Plate IX, and, I ought at the same time to remark, is perhaps the most curious and interesting of any. It is at the left end of the principal building, and in the angle of the corner are the huge open jaws of an alligator, or some other hideous animal, enclosing a human head.

The reader will form some idea of the overgrown and shrouded condition of this building from the fact that I had been at work nearly the whole day upon the terrace, without knowing that there was another building on the top. In order to take in the whole front at one view, it was necessary to carry the clearing back some distance into the plain, and in doing this I discovered the upper structure. The growth of trees before it was almost equal to that on the terrace, or in any part of the forest. The whole had to be cleared, the trees thrown down upon the terrace, and thence dragged away to the plain. This building consists of single narrow corridors, and the façade is of plain stone, without any ornaments.

The platform in front is the roof of the building underneath, and in this platform was a circular hole, like those we had seen at Uxmal and other places, leading to subterranean chambers. This hole was well known to the Indians, and had a marvellous reputation; and yet they never mentioned it until I climbed up to examine the upper building. They said it was the abode of el dueño de la casa, or the owner of the building. I immediately proposed to descend, but the old Indian begged me not to do so, and said apprehensively to the others, "Who knows but that he will meet with the owner?" I immediately sent for rope, lantern, and matches; and, absurd as it may seem, as I looked upon the wild figures of the Indians standing round the hole, and their earnest faces, it was really exciting to hear them talk of the owner. As there was a difficulty in procuring rope, I had a sapling cut and let down the hole, by means of which I descended with a lantern. The news of my intention and of the preparations going on had spread among the Indians, and all

Plate IX

L ABN A H.

left off work and hurried to the spot. The hole was about four feet deep, and, just as my head sunk below the surface, I was startled by an extraordinary scratching and scampering, and a huge iguana ran along the wall, and escaped through the orifice by which I had entered.

The chamber was entirely different in shape from those I had seen before. The latter were circular, and had dome-shaped ceilings. This had parallel walls and the triangular-arched ceiling; in fact, it was in shape exactly like the apartments above ground. It was eleven feet long, seven wide, and ten high to the centre of the arch. The walls and ceiling were plastered, and the floor was of cement, all hard and in a good state of preservation. A centipede was the only tenant after the evasion of the iguana.

While I was making these measurements, the Indians kept up a low conversation around the hole. A mystery hung around it, transmitted to them by their fathers, and connected with an indefinable sense of apprehension. This mystery might have been solved at any time in five minutes, but none of them had ever thought of doing it, and the old man begged me to come out, saying that if I died they would have to answer for it. Their simplicity and credulity seem hardly credible. They had all sense enough to take their hands out of the fire without being told, but probably to this day they believe that in that hole is the owner of the building. When I came out they looked at me with admiration. They told me that there were other places of the same kind, but they would not show them to me, lest some accident should happen; and as my attempt drew them all from work, and I could not promise myself any satisfactory result, I refrained from insisting.

This chamber was formed in the roof of the lower building. That building contained two corridors, and we had always supposed that the great interval between the arches of the parallel corridors was a solid mass of masonry. The discovery of this chamber brought to light a new feature in the construction of these buildings. Whether the other roofs, or any of them, contained chambers, it is impossible to say. Not suspecting anything of the kind, we had made no search for them, and they may exist, but with the holes covered up and hidden by the growth and decay of vegetation. Heretofore I had inclined to the opinion that the subterraneous chambers I had met with were intended for cisterns or reservoirs of water. The position of this in the roof of a building seemed adverse to such an idea, as, in case of a breach, the water might find its way into the apartment below.

At the foot of the terrace was a tree, hiding part of the building. Though holding trees in some degree of reverence, around these ruined cities it was a great satisfaction to hear them fall. This one was a noble ramon, which I had ordered to be cut down, and being engaged in another direction, I returned, and found that the Indians had not done so, and they said it was so hard that it would break their axes. These little axes seemed hardly capable of making any impression upon the trunk, and I gave them directions, perhaps still more barbarous, to cut away the branches and leave the trunk. They hesitated, and one of them said, in a deprecating tone, that this tree served as food for horses and cattle, and their mistress had always charged them not to cut down such. The poor fellow seemed perplexed between the standing orders of the rancho and the special instructions to do what I required.

The ramon tree was growing out of the mouth of a cave which the Indians said was an ancient well. I should perhaps not have observed it, but for the discussion about cutting down the tree. I had no great disposition for another subterraneous scramble, but descended the cavity or opening for the purpose of taking a bird's-eye view of the mouth. On one side was a great ledge of stone projecting as a roof, and under this was a passage in the rock, choked up by masses of fallen stone. It was impossible to continue if I had been so disposed, but there was every reason to believe that formerly there had been some wild passage through the rocks as at Xcoch and Chack, which led to a subterraneous deposite of water, and that this had been one of the sources from which the ancient inhabitants procured their supply.

From the number of Indians at our command, and their alacrity in working, we had been enabled to accomplish much in a very short time. In three days they finished all that I required of them. When I dismissed them, I gave a half dollar extra to be divided among seventeen, and as I was going away Bernabé exclaimed, "Ave Maria, que gracias dan a vd." "Ave Maria, what thanks they give you."

The evening closed with a general gathering of the Indians under the arbour in front of the casa real. Before setting out in the morning the alcalde asked me whether I wished them to assemble for the purpose of talking with them, and we had provided for their entertainment a sheep and a turkey, to which Bernaldo had devoted the day. At sundown all was ready. We insisted upon seating the old alcalde on a chair. Bernaldo served

out meat and tortillas, and the alcalde presided over the agua
ardiente, which, as it was purchased of himself, and to prove
that it was not bad, he tasted before serving the rest, and took
his share afterward. Supper over, we began our conversation,
which consisted entirely of questions on our part and answers
on theirs, a manner of discourse even in civilized life difficult to
be kept up long. There was no unwillingness to give information, but there was a want of communicativeness which made all
intercourse with them unprofitable and unsatisfactory. In fact,
however, they had nothing to communicate; they had no stories
or traditions; they knew nothing of the origin of the ruined
buildings; these were standing when they were born; had
existed in the time of their fathers; and the old men said that
they had fallen much within their own memory. In one point,
however, they differed from the Indians of Uxmal and Zayi.
They had no superstitious feelings with regard to the ruins,
were not afraid to go to them at night, or to sleep in them; and
when we told them of the music that was heard sounding among
the old buildings of Zayi, they said that if it were heard among
these, they would all go and dance to it.

There were other vestiges and mounds, all, however, in a
ruinous condition. The last day, while Mr. Catherwood was
finishing at Labnà, I rode with Bernaldo to the hacienda of
Tabi, two leagues distant, which, and those of Xcanchakan, already presented in these pages, and Vayalke, belonging to the
Señora Joaquina Peon, where we stopped on our first visit to
Uxmal, were distinguished as the three finest in Yucatan. Before
the gate were some noble seybo trees, and near it a tiendicita, or
small shop, supplied with articles adapted to the wants of the
Indians appertaining to the hacienda. The great yard was lined
with buildings, among which were the church and an enclosure
for a bullfight, prepared for a festival which was to commence
the next day. In the wall of the hacienda were sculptured ornaments from the ruins of ancient buildings. At the foot of the
steps was a double-headed eagle, well carved, holding in his
claws a sort of sceptre, and underneath were the figures of two
tigers four feet high. In the back of the house was a projecting
stone figure, with its mouth open, an uncomfortable expression
of face, arms akimbo, and hands pressing the sides, as if in a
qualmish state. It was used as a water-spout, and a stream was
pouring out of the mouth. The buildings from which these
stones were taken were near the hacienda, but were mere piles

of ruins. They had furnished materials for the construction of the church, walls, and all the edifices on the hacienda.

Besides this there was a great cave, of which I had heard in Merida from the owner, who said he had never visited it, but wished me to do so, and he would read my description of it. The major domo was an intelligent Mestizo, who had been at the cave, and confirmed all the accounts I had heard of it, of sculptured figures of men and animals, pillars, and a chapel of rock under the earth. He furnished me with a vaquero as a guide and a relief horse, and, setting out, a short distance from the hacienda we turned into a tree-encumbered path, so difficult to pass through that, before we had gone far, it seemed quite reasonable in the owner to content himself with reading our description of the cave, without taking the trouble to see it for himself. The vaquero was encased in the equipments with which that class ride into the woods after cattle. His dress was a small, hard, heavy straw hat, cotton shirt, drawers, and sandals; over his body a thick jacket, or overall, made of tanned cowhide, with the sleeves reaching below his hands, and standing out as if made of wood; his saddle had large leather flaps, which folded back and protected his naked legs, and leather stirrup fiaps to protect his feet. Where he dashed through the bushes and briers unharmed, my thin blues got caught and torn; but he knew what garrapatas were, and said with emphasis, "Estos chicos son muy Demonios." "Those little ones are the very d—l."

At the distance of a league we reached the cave, and, tying our horses, descended by a great chasm to the depth of perhaps two hundred feet, when we found ourselves under a great shelf of overhanging rock, the cavern being dark as we advanced, but all at once lighted up from beyond by a perpendicular orifice, and exhibiting in the background magnificent stalactites, picturesque blocks and fragments of rock, which, in the shadows of the background, assumed all manner of fantastic shapes, and, from their fancied resemblance, had been called the figures of men and animals, pillars and chapels. I saw at once that there was another disappointment for me; there were no monuments of art, and had never been anything artificial; but the cave itself, being large and open, and lighted in several places by orifices above, was so magnificent that, notwithstanding the labour and disappointment, I did not regret my visit. I passed two hours in wandering through it, returned to the hacienda to dine, and it was after dark when I reached the rancho, and for the last time had the benefit of its well in the shape of a warm bath. Throughout Yucatan, every Indian, however poor, has, as part of the furniture of his hut, a baño, or sort of bathing-tub; and, next to making tortillas, the great use of a wife is to have warm water ready for him when he returns from his work. We had not the latter convenience, but at this place, for a medio, we had the alcalde's baño every evening. It was a wooden dug-out, flat bottomed, about three feet long, eighteen inches wide, three or four inches deep, and bathing in it was somewhat like bathing in the salver of a tea-table, but, covered as we were constantly with garrapata bites, mere ablution was as grateful as a Turkish or Egyptian bath.

CHAPTER IV

The next morning we resumed our journey in
search of ruined cities. Our next point of destination was the
rancho of Kewick, three leagues distant. Mr. Catherwood set
out with the servants and luggage, Dr. Cabot and myself following in about an hour. The Indians told us there was no difficulty
in finding the road, and we set out alone. About a mile from the
rancho we passed a ruined building on the left, surmounted by
a high wall, with oblong apertures, like that mentioned at Zayi
as resembling a New-England factory. The face of the country
was rolling, and more open than any we had seen. We passed
through two Indian ranchos, and a league beyond came to a
dividing point, where we found ourselves at a loss. Both were
mere Indian footpaths, seldom or never traversed by horsemen,
and, having but one chance against us, we selected that most
directly in line with the one by which we had come. In about
an hour the direction changed so much that we turned back,
and, after a toilsome ride, reached again the dividing point, and
turned into the other path. This led us into a wild savanna surrounded by hills, and very soon we found tracks leading off in
different directions, among which, in a short time, we became
perfectly bewildered. The whole distance to Kewick was but
three leagues; we had been riding hard six hours, and began

to fear that we had made a mistake in turning back, and at every step were going more astray. In the midst of our perplexities we came upon an Indian leading a wild colt, who, without asking any questions, or waiting for any from us, waved us back, and, tying his colt to a bush, led us across the plain into another path, following which some distance, he again struck across, and put us into still another, where he left us, and started to return to his colt. We were loth to lose him, and urged him to continue as our guide; but he was impenetrable until we held

Fig. 4

up a medio, when he again moved on before us. The whole region was so wild that even yet we had doubts, and hardly believed that such a path could lead to a village or rancho; but, withal, there was one interesting circumstance. In our desolate and wandering path we had seen in different places, at a distance, and inaccessible, five high mounds, holding aloft the ruins of ancient buildings; and doubtless there were more buried in the woods. At three o'clock we entered a dense forest, and came suddenly upon the casa real of Kewick, standing alone, almost buried among trees, the only habitation of any kind in sight; and, to increase the wondering interest which attended every step of our journey in that country, it stood on the platform of an ancient terrace, strewed with the relics of a ruined edifice. The steps of the terrace had fallen and been newly laid, but the walls were entire, with all the stones in place. Conspicuous in view was Mr. Catherwood with our servants and luggage, and, as we rode up, it seemed a strange confusion of things past and present, of scenes consecrated by time and those of every-day life, though Mr. Catherwood dispelled the floating visions by his first greeting, which was an assurance that the casa real was full of fleas. We tied our horses at the foot of the terrace, and ascended the steps. The casa real had mud walls and a thatched roof, and in front was an arbour. Sitting down under the arbour, with our hotel on this ancient platform, we had seldom experienced higher satisfaction on reaching a new and unknown field of ruins, though perhaps this was owing somewhat to the circumstances of finding ourselves, after a hot and perplexing ride, safely arrived at our place of destination. We had still two hours of daylight; and, anxious to have a glimpse of the ruins before night, we had some fried eggs and tortillas got ready, and while making a hasty meal, the proprietor of the rancho, attended by a party of Indians, came to pay us a visit.

This proprietor was a full-blooded Indian, the first of this ancient but degraded race whom we had seen in the position of land-owner and master. He was about forty-five years old, and highly respectable in his appearance and manners. He had inherited the land from his fathers, did not know how long it had been transmitted, but believed that it had always been in his family. The Indians on the rancho were his servants, and we had not seen in any village or on any hacienda men of better appearance, or under more excellent discipline. This produced on my mind a strong impression that, indolent, ignorant, and debased as the race is under the dominion of strangers, the Indian even now is not incapable of fulfilling the obligations of a higher station than that in which his destiny has placed him. It is not true that he is fit only to labour with his hands; he has within him that which is capable of directing the labour of others; and as this Indian master sat on the terrace, with his dependants crouching round him, I could imagine him the descendant of a long line of caciques who once reigned in the city, the ruins of which were his inheritance. Involuntarily we treated him with a respect we had never shown to an Indian before; but perhaps we were not free from the influence of feelings which govern in civilized life, and our respect may have proceeded from the discovery that our new acquaintance was a man of property, possessed not merely of acres, and Indians, and unproductive real estate, but also of that great desideratum in these trying times, ready money; for we had given Albino a dollar to purchase eggs with, who objected to it as too large a coin to be available on the rancho, but on his return informed us, with an expression of surprise, that the master had changed it the moment it was offered to him.

Our hasty dinner over, we asked for Indians to guide us to the ruins, and were somewhat startled by the objections they all made on account of the garrapatas. Since we left Uxmal the greatest of our small hardships had been the annoyance of these insects; in fact, it was by no means a small hardship. Frequently we came in contact with a bush covered with them, from which thousands swarmed upon us, like moving grains of sand, and scattered till the body itself seemed crawling. Our horses suffered, perhaps, more than ourselves, and it became a habit, whenever we dismounted, to rasp their sides with a rough stick. During the dry season the little pests are killed off by the heat of the sun, and devoured by birds, but for which I verily believe they would make the country uninhabitable. All along we had been told that the dry season was at hand, and they would soon be over; but we began to despair of any dry season, and had no hopes of getting rid of them. Nevertheless, we were somewhat startled at the warning conveyed by the reluctance of the Indians; and when we insisted upon going, they gave us another alarming intimation by cutting twigs, with which, from the moment of starting, they whipped the bushes on each side, and swept the path before them.

Beyond the woods we came out into a comparatively open field, in which we saw on all sides through the trees the Xlappahk, or old walls, now grown so familiar, a collection of vast remains and of many buildings. We worked our way to all within sight. The façades were not so much ornamented as some we had seen, but the stones were more massive, and the style of architecture was simple, severe, and grand. Nearly every house had fallen, and one long ornamented front lay on the ground cracked and doubled up as if shaken off by the vibrations of an earthquake, and still struggling to retain its upright position, the whole presenting a most picturesque and imposing scene of

Plate X

KEWICK

F Catherwood

J N Gimbmore

ruins, and conveying to the mind a strong image of the besom of destruction sweeping over a city. Night came upon us while gazing at a mysterious painting, and we returned to the casa real to sleep.

Early the next morning we were again on the ground, with our Indian proprietor and a large party of his criados; and as the reader is now somewhat familiar with the general character of these ruins, I select from that great mass around only such as have some peculiarity.

The first is that represented in Plate X. It had been the principal doorway, and was all that now remained of a long line of front, which lay in ruins on the ground. It is remarkable for its simplicity, and, in that style of architecture, for its grandeur of proportions.

The apartment into which this door opened had nothing to distinguish it from hundreds of others we had seen, but in the corner one was the mysterious painting at which we were gazing the evening before, when night overtook us. The end wall had fallen inward; the others remained. The ceiling, as in all the other buildings, was formed by two sides rising to meet each other, and covered within a foot of the point of junction by a flat layer of stones. In all the other arches, without a single exception, the layer was perfectly plain: but this had a single stone distinguished by a painting, which covered the whole surface presented to view. The painting itself was curious; the colours were bright, red and green predominating; the lines clear and distinct, and the whole was more perfect than any painting we had seen. But its position surprised us more than the painting itself; it was in the most out-of-the-way spot in the whole edifice, and but for the Indians we might not have noticed it at all. Why this layer of stones was so adorned, or why this particular stone was distinguished above all others in the same layer, we were unable to discover, but we considered that it was not done capriciously nor without cause; in fact, we had long been of opinion that every stone in those ancient buildings, and every design and ornament that decorated them, had some certain though now inscrutable meaning.

Figure 5 represents this painting. It exhibits a rude human figure, surrounded by hieroglyphics, which doubtless contain the whole of its story. It is 30 inches long by 18 inches wide, and the prevailing colour is red. From its position in the wall, it was impossible to draw it without getting it out and lowering it to the ground, which I was anxious to accom-

Fig. 5

plish, not only for the sake of the drawing, but for the purpose of carrying it away. I had apprehensions that the proprietor would make objections, for both he and the Indians had pointed it out as the most curious part of the ruins; but, fortunately, they had no feeling about it, and were all ready to assist in any way we directed. The only way of getting at it was by digging down through the roof; and, as usual, a friendly tree was at hand to assist us in the ascent. The roof was flat, made of stone and mortar cemented together, and several feet in thickness. The Indians had no crowbar, but loosening the mortar with their machetes, and prying apart the stones by means of hard wood saplings with the points sharpened, they excavated down to the layer on the top of the arch. The stone lapped over about a foot on each side, and was so heavy that it was impossible to hoist it out of the hole; our only way, therefore, was to lower it down into the apartment. The master sent some Indians to the rancho to search for ropes, and, as a measure of precaution, I had branches cut,

and made a bed several feet thick under the stone. Some of the
Indians still at work were preparing to let it fall, when Dr.
Cabot, who was fortunately on the roof at the time, put a stop
to their proceedings.

The Indians returned with the rope, and while lowering
the stone one of the strands broke, and it came thundering down,
but the bed of branches saved the painting from destruction.

The proprietor made no objections to my carrying it away,
but it was too heavy for a mule-load, and the Indians would not
undertake to carry it on their shoulders. The only way of removing it was to have it cut down to a portable size; and when
we left, the proprietor accompanied me to the village to procure
a.stonecutter for that purpose, but there was none in the village,
nor any chance of one within twenty-seven miles. Unable to do
anything with the stone, I engaged the proprietor to place it in
an apartment sheltered from rain; and, if I do not mistake the
character of my Indian friend and inheritor of a ruined city, it
now lies subject to my order; and I hereby authorize the next
American traveller to bring it away at his own expense, and
deposite it in the National Museum at Washington.

I shall present but one more view from the ruins of Kewick.
It is part of the front of a long building, forming a right angle
with the one last referred to. The terraces almost join, and
though all was so overgrown that it was difficult to make out the
plan and juxtaposition, the probability is that they formed two
sides of a grand rectangular area. The whole building measures
two hundred and thirty feet in length. In the centre is a wide
ruined staircase leading to the top. Plate XI represents half of
the building to the line of the staircase, the other half being
exactly similar. The whole could not be drawn without carrying
back the clearing to some distance, and consuming more time
than we thought worth while to devote to it. Below the cornice
the entire edifice is plain; and above it is ornamented the whole
length with small circular shafts set in the wall.

The remaining ruins of Kewick we left as we found them.
Fallen buildings and fragments of sculptured stone strew the
ground in every direction; but it is impossible to give the reader
an idea of the impresson produced by wandering among them.
For a brief space only we broke the stillness of the desolate city,
and left it again to solitude and silence. We had reason to believe that no white man had ever seen it, and probably but few
will ever do so, for every year is hurrying it on to more utter destruction.

Plate XI

CHUNHUHU

The same scarcity of water which we had found all over this region, except at Sabachshé, exists here also. The source which supplied the ancient city had engaged the attention of its Indian proprietor, and while Mr. Catherwood was drawing the last building, the Indians conducted us to a cave, called in their language Actum, which they supposed was an ancient well. The entrance was by a hole under an overhanging rock, passing through which by means of a tree, with branches or crotches to serve as steps, we descended to a large platform of rock. Overhead was an immense rocky roof, and at the brink of the platform was a great cavern, with precipitous sides, thirty or forty feet deep, from which the Indians supposed some passage opened that would lead to water. As we flared our torches over the chasm, it presented a scene of wildness and grandeur which, in an hour of idleness, might have tempted us to explore it; but we had more than enough to occupy our time.

Coming out from the cave, we went on to the aguada, which was nearly a league distant. It was a small, muddy pond, with trees growing on the sides and into the water, which, in any other country, would be considered an unfit watering-place for beasts. The proprietor and all the Indians told us that in the dry season the remains of stone embankments were still visible, made, as they supposed, by the ancient inhabitants. The bank was knee deep with mud; a few poles were laid out on supporters driven into the mud, and along these the Indians walked to dip up water. At the time our horses were brought down to drink; but they had to be watered out of the calabashes or drinking-cups of the Indians.

At two o'clock we returned to the casa real. We had "done up" another ruined city, and were ready to set out again; but we had one serious impediment in the way. I have mentioned that on our arrival at this place we gave Albino a dollar, but I omitted to say that it was our last. On setting out on this journey, we had reduced our personal luggage to hammocks and petaquillas, the latter being oblong straw baskets without fastenings, unsafe to carry money in, and silver, the only available coin, was too heavy to carry about the person. At Sabachshé we discovered that our expenses had overrun our estimates, and sent Albino back to Nohcacab with the keys of our money trunk, and directions to follow us in all haste to this place. The time calculated for his overtaking us had passed, and he did not come. We should have thought nothing of a little delay but for our pressing necessities. Some accident might have happened to him, or the temptation might have been too strong. Our affairs were approaching a crisis, and the barbarism of the people of the country in matters of finance was hurrying it on. If we wanted a fowl, food for horses, or an Indian to work, the money must be ready at the moment. Throughout our journey it was the same; every order for the purchase of an article was null unless the money accompanied it. Brought up under the wings of credit, this system was always odious to us. We could attempt nothing on a liberal and enlightened scale, were always obliged to calculate our means, and could incur no expense unless we had the money to defray it on the spot. This, of course, trammelled enterprise, and now, on a mere miscalculation, we were brought suddenly to a stand still. On counting the scattering medios of private stock, we found that we had enough to pay for transporting our luggage to the village of Xul, but if we tarried over the night and Albino did not come, both ourselves and our horses must go without rations in the morning, and then we should have no means of getting away our luggage. Which of the two to choose? Whether it was better to meet our fate at the rancho, or go on to the village and trust to fortune?

In this delicate posture of affairs, we sat down to one of Bernaldo's best miscellaneous preparations of fowls, rice, and frigoles, and finished the last meal that we were able to pay for. This over, we had recourse to a small paper of Havana cigars, three in number, containing the last of our stock, reserved for some extraordinary occasion. Satisfied that no occasion could offer when we should be more in need of extraneous support, we lighted them and sat down under the arbour, and, as the smoke rolled away, listened for the tread of the trotter. It was really perplexing to know what to do; but it was very certain that if we remained at the rancho, as soon as a medio was not forthcoming the moment it was wanted we were undone. Our chance would be better at the village, and we determined to break up and go on.

Leaving special charge for Albino to follow, at three o'clock we set out. The proprietor accompanied us, and at half past five we made a dashing entry into the village of Xul, with horses, and servants, and carriers, and just one solitary medio left.

The casa real was the poorest we had seen in the country, and, under any circumstances, it was not the place for us, for, immediately on dismounting, it would be necessary to order ramon and maize for the horses, and the money must follow the order. There was a crowd of gaping loungers around the door, and if we stopped at this place we should be obliged to expose ourselves at once, without any opportunity of telling our story to advantage, or of making friends.

On the opposite side of the plaza was one of those buildings which had so often sheltered us in time of trouble, but now I hesitated to approach the convent. The fame of the cura of Xul had reached our ears; report said that he was rich, and a money-making man, and odd. Among his other possessions, he was lord of a ruined city which we proposed to visit, particularly interesting to us from the circumstance that, according to the accounts, it was then inhabited by Indians. We wished to procure from him facilities for exploring this city to advantage, and doubted whether it would be any recommendation to his favour as a rich man to begin our acquaintance by borrowing money of him.

But, although rich, he was a padre. Without dismounting, I rode over to the convent. The padre came out to meet me, and told me that he had been expecting us every day. I dismounted, and he took my horse by the bridle, led him across the corridor, through the sala, and out to the yard. He asked why my companions did not come over, and, at a signal, in a few minutes their horses followed mine through the sala.

Still we were not entirely at ease. In Yucatan, as in Central America, it is the custom for a traveller, whether he alights at the casa real, convent, or the hacienda of a friend, to buy ramon and maize for his horses; and it is no lack of hospitality in the host, after providing a place for the beasts, to pay no more attention to them. This might have brought on a premature explanation; but presently four Indians appeared, each with a great back-load of ramon. We ventured to give a hint about maize, and in a moment all anxiety about our horses was at an end, and we had the whole evening to manage for ourselves.

Don José Gulielmo Roderigues, the cura of Xul, was a Guachapino, or native of Old Spain, of which, like all the old Spaniards in the country, he was somewhat proud. He was educated a Franciscan friar; but thirty years before, on account of the revolutions and the persecution of his order, he fled from Spain, and took refuge in Yucatan. On the destruction of the Franciscan Convent in Merida, and the breaking up of the Franciscan monks, he secularized, and entered the regular church; had been cura of Ticul and Nohcacab; and about ten years before had been appointed to the district of Xul. His curacy was one of those called beneficiaries; *i.e.*, in consideration of building the church, keeping it in repair, and performing the duties and services of a priest, the capitation tax paid by the Indians, and the fees allowed for baptism, marriages, masses, salves, and funeral services, after deducting one seventh for the Church, belonged to himself personally. At the time of his appointment, the place now occupied by the village was a mere Indian rancho. The land comprehended in his district was, in general, good for maize, but, like all the rest of that region, it was destitute of water, or, at least, but badly supplied. His first object had been to remedy this deficiency, to which end he had dug a well two hundred feet deep, at an expense of fifteen hundred dollars. Besides this, he had large and substantial cisterns, equal to any we had seen in the country, for the reception of rain-water; and, by furnishing this necessary of life in abundance, he had drawn around him a population of seven thousand.

But to us there was something more interesting than this creation of a village and a population in the wilderness, for here, again, was the same strange mingling of old things with new. The village stands on the site of an aboriginal city. In the corner of the plaza now occupied by the cura's house, the yard of which contains the well and cisterns, once stood a pyramidal mound with a building upon it. The cura had himself pulled down this mound, and levelled it so that nothing was left to indicate even the place where it stood. With the materials he had built the house and cisterns, and portions of the ancient edifice now formed the walls of the new. With singular good taste, showing his practical turn of mind, and at the same time a vein of antiquarian feeling, he had fixed in conspicuous places, when they answered his purpose, many of the old carved stones. The convent and church occupied one side of the plaza; along the corridor of the former was a long seat of time-polished stones taken from the ruins of an ancient building, and in every quarter might be seen these memorials of the past, connecting links between the living and the dead, and serving to keep alive the memory of the fact, which, but for them, would in a few years be forgotten, that on this spot once stood an ancient Indian city.

But the work upon which the padre prided himself most, and which, perhaps, did him most credit, was the church. It was one of the few the erection of which had been undertaken of late years, when the time had gone by for devoting the labour of a whole village to such works; and it presents a combination of simplicity, convenience, and good taste, in better keeping with the spirit of the age than the gigantic but tottering structures in the other villages, while it is not less attractive in the eyes of the Indians. The cura employed an amanuensis to write out a description of the church, as he said, for me to publish in my work, which, however, I am obliged to omit, mentioning only that over the principal altar were sixteen columns from the ruins at the *rancho* of Nohcacab, which were the next we proposed to visit.

During the evening we had a levée of all the principal white inhabitants, to the number of about six or eight. Among them was the proprietor of the *rancho* and ruins of Nohcacab, to whom we were introduced by the cura, with a tribute to our antiquarian, scientific, and medical attainments, which showed an appreciation of merit it was seldom our good fortune to meet with. The proprietor could give us very little information about the ruins, but undertook to make all the necessary arrangements for our exploration of them, and to accompany us himself.

At that moment we stood upon a giddy height. To ask the loan of a few dollars might lower us materially. The evening was wearing away without any opportunity of entering upon this interesting subject, when, to our great satisfaction, we heard the clattering of horses' hoofs, and Albino made his appearance. The production of a bag of dollars fixed us in our high position, and we were able to order Indians for the rancho of Nohcacab the next day. We finished the evening with a warm bath in a hand-basin, under the personal direction of the cura, which relieved somewhat the burning of garrapata bites, and then retired to our hammocks.

CHAPTER V

Journey to the Rancho of Nohcacab.—A Fountain and Seybo Tree.—Arrival at the Rancho.—Its Appearance.—A sick Trio.—Effects of a good Breakfast.—Visit to the Ruins.—Terrace and Buildings.—Three other Buildings.—Character of these Ruins.—Disappointment.—Return to Xul.—Visit to another ruined City.—Ruined Building.—An Arch, plastered and covered with Painted Figures.—Other Paintings.—Subterranean Well.—Return to the Village.—Journey to Ticul.—Large Mounds.—Passage of the Sierra.—Grand View.—Arrival at Ticul.—A Village Festival.—Ball of the Mestizas.—Costumes.—Dance of the Toros.—Lassoing Cattle.—Ball by Daylight.—The Fiscales.—Ludicrous Scene.—A Dance.—Love in a Phrensy.—A unique Breakfast.—Close of the Ball.

Early the next morning we set out for the rancho of Nohcacab, three leagues distant. The proprietor had gone before daylight, to receive us on the ground. We had not gone far when Mr. C. complained of a slight headache, and wishing to ride moderately, Dr. Cabot and myself went on, leaving him to follow with the luggage. The morning air was fresh and invigorating, and the country rolling, hilly, and picturesque. At the distance of two leagues we reached what was called a hebe, or fountain. It was a large rocky basin, about ninety feet in circumference and ten feet deep, which served as a receptacle for rain-water. In that dry country it was a grateful spectacle, and beside it was a large seybo tree, that seemed inviting the traveller to repose under its branches. We watered our horses from the same waccal, or drinking cup, that we used ourselves, and felt strongly tempted to take a bath, but, with our experience of fever and ague, were afraid to run the risk. This fountain was a league from the rancho to which we were going, and was the only watering-place for its inhabitants.

At nine o'clock we reached the rancho, which showed the truth of the Spanish proverb, "La vista del amo engorda el caballo;" "The sight of the master fattens the horse." The first huts were enclosed by a well-built stone wall, along which appeared, in various places, sculptured fragments from the ruins. Beyond was another wall, enclosing the hut occupied by the master on his visits to the rancho, the entrance to which was by a gateway formed of two sculptured monuments of curious design and excellent workmanship, raising high our expectations in regard to the ruins on this rancho, and sustaining the accounts we had heard of them.

The proprietor was waiting to receive us, and, having taken possession of an empty hut, and disposed of our horses, we accompanied him to look over the rancho. What he regarded as most worth showing was his tobacco crop, lying in some empty huts to dry, which he contemplated with great satisfaction, and the well, which he looked at with as much sorrow. It was three hundred and fifty-four feet deep, and even at this great depth it was dry.

While we were thus engaged, our baggage carriers arrived with intelligence that Mr. Catherwood was taken ill, and they had left him lying in the road. I immediately applied to the proprietor for a coché and Indians, and he, with great alacrity, undertook to get them ready; in the mean time I saddled my horse and hastened back to Mr. Catherwood, whom I found lying on the ground, with Albino by his side, under the shade of the tree by the fountain, with an ague upon him, wrapped up in all·the coverings he could muster, even to the saddlecloths of the horses. While he was in this state, two men came along, bestriding the same horse, and bringing sheets and ponchas to make a covering for the coché; then came a straggling line of Indians, each with a long pole, and withes to lash them together; and it was more than an hour before the coché was ready. The path was narrow, and lined on each side with thorn bushes, the spikes of which stuck in the naked flesh of the Indians as they carried the coché, and they were obliged to stop frequently and disentangle themselves. On reaching the rancho I found Doctor Cabot down with a fever. From the excitement and anxiety of following Mr. Catherwood under the hot sun, and now finding Doctor Cabot down, a cold shivering crept over me, and in a few minutes we were all three in our hammocks. A few hours had made a great change in our condition; and we came near bringing our host down with us. He had been employed in preparing breakfast upon a large scale, and seemed mortified that there was no one to do it justice. Out of pure good feeling toward him, I had it brought to the side of my hammock. My effort made him happy, and I began to think my prostration was merely the reaction from over-excitement; and by degrees what I began to please our host I continued for my own satisfaction. The troubles of my companions no longer disturbed me. My equanimity was perfectly restored, and, breakfast over, I set out to look at the ruins.

Ever since our arrival in Yucatan we had received courtesies and civilities, but none more thorough than those bestowed by our host of Nohcacab. He had come out with the intention of passing a week with us, and the Indians and the whole rancho were at our service as long as we chose to remain.

Passing through one of the huts, we soon came to a hill covered with trees and very steep, up which the proprietor had cut, not a mere Indian path, but a road two or three yards wide, leading to a building standing upon a terrace on the brow of the hill. The façade above the cornice had fallen, and below it was of plain stone. The interior was entire, but without any distinguishing features. Following the brow of this hill, we came to three other buildings, all standing on the same range, and without any important variations in the details, except that in one the arch had no overlapping stone, but the two sides of the ceiling ran up to a point, and formed a complete angle. These, the Indians told us, were the only buildings that remained. That from which the pillars in the church at Xul were taken was a mere mass of ruins. I was extremely disappointed. From the accounts which had induced us to visit this place, we had made larger calculations. It was the first time I had been thoroughly disappointed. There were no subjects for the pencil, and, except the deep and abiding impression of moving among the deserted structures of another ruined and desolate city, there was nothing to carry away. The proprietor seemed mortified that he had not better ruins to show us, but I gave him to understand that it was not his fault, and that he was in nowise to blame. Nevertheless, it was really vexatious, with such good-will on his part, and such a troop of Indians at command, that there was nothing for us to do. The Indians sympathized in the mortification of their master, and, to indemnify me, told me of two other ruined cities, one of which was but two leagues from the village of Xul.

I returned and made my report, and Mr. Catherwood immediately proposed a return to the village. Albino had given him an alarming account of the unhealthiness of the rancho, and he considered it advisable to avoid sleeping there a single night. Doctor Cabot was sitting up in his hammock, dissecting a bird. A recurrence of fever might detain us some time, and we determined on returning immediately to Xul. Our decision was carried into execution as promptly as it was made, and, leaving our luggage to the care of Albino, in half an hour, to the astonishment of the Indians and the mortification of the proprietor, we were on our way to the village.

It was late in the evening when we arrived, but the cura received us as kindly as before. During the evening I made inquiries for the place of which the Indians at the rancho had told me. It was but two leagues distant, but of all who happened to drop in, not one was aware of its existence. The cura, however, sent for a young man who had a rancho in that direction, and who promised to accompany me.

At six o'clock the next morning we started, neither Mr. Catherwood nor Doctor Cabot being able to accompany me. At the distance of about two leagues we reached an Indian rancho, where we learned from an old woman that we had passed the path leading to the ruins. We could not prevail on her to go back and show us the way, but she gave us a direction to another rancho, where she said we could procure a guide. This rancho was situated in a small clearing in the midst of the woods, enclosed by a bush fence, and before the door was an arbour covered with palm leaves, with little hammocks swinging under it, and all together the picture of Indian comfort.

My companion went in, and I dismounted, thinking that this promised a good stopping-place, when, looking down, I saw my pantaloons brown with garrapatas. I laid hold of a twig, intending to switch them off, and hundreds fell upon my hand and arm. Getting rid of those in sight as well as I could, and mounting immediately, I rode off, hoping most earnestly not to find any ruins, nor any necessity of taking up our abode in this comfortable-seeming rancho.

We were fortunate in finding at this place an Indian, who, for reasons known to himself and the wife of the master, was making a visit during the absence of the latter at his milpa; but for which we should not have been able to procure a guide. Retracing our steps, and crossing the camino real, we entered the woods on the other side, and tying our horses, the Indian cut a path up the side of a hill, on the top of which were the ruins of a building. The outer wall had fallen, leaving exposed to view the inner half of the arch, by which, as we approached it, my attention was strongly attracted. This arch was plastered and covered with painted figures in profile, much mutilated, but in one place a row of legs remained, which seemed to have belonged to a procession, and at the first glance brought to my mind the funeral processions on the walls of the tombs at Thebes. In the triangular wall forming the end of the room were three compartments, in which were figures, some having their heads adorned with plumes, others with a sort of steeple cap, and carrying on their heads something like a basket; and two were standing on their hands with their heels in the air. These figures were about a foot high, and painted red. The drawing was good, the attitudes were spirited and life-like, and altogether, even in their mutilated state, they were by far the most interesting paintings we had seen in the country.

Another apartment had been plastered and covered with paintings, the colours of which were in some places still bright and vivid. In this apartment we cornered and killed a snake five feet long, and as I threw it out at the door a strong picture rose up before me of the terrific scenes which must have been enacted in this region; the cries of wo that must have ascended to Heaven when these sculptured and painted edifices were abandoned, to become the dwelling-place of vultures and serpents.

There was one other building, and these two, my guide said, were all, but probably others lie buried in the woods. Returning to our horses, he led me to another extraordinary subterraneous well, which probably furnished water to the ancient inhabitants. I looked into the mouth, and saw that the first descent was by a steep ladder, but had no disposition to explore it.

In a few minutes we mounted to return to the village. Ruins were increasing upon us, to explore which thoroughly would be the work of years; we had but months, and were again arrested by illness. For some days, at least, Mr. Catherwood would not be able to resume work. I was really distressed by the magnitude of what was before us, but, for the present, we could do nothing, and I determined at once to change the scene. The festival of Ticul was at hand, and that night it was to open with el báyle de las Mestizas, or the Mestiza ball. Ticul lay in our return route, nine leagues from the village of Xul, but I determined to reach it that evening. My companion did not sympathize in my humour; his vaquero saddle hurt him, and he could not ride faster than a walk. I had need to economize all my strength; but I took his hard-trotting horse and uneasy saddle, and gave him mine. Pushing on, at eleven o'clock we reached Xul, where I had my horse unsaddled and washed, ordered him a good mess of corn, and two boiled eggs for myself. In the mean time, Mr. Catherwood had a recurrence of fever and ague, and my horse was led away; but the attack proved slight, and I had him brought out again. At two o'clock I resumed my journey, with a sheet, a hammock, and Albino. The heat was scorching, and Albino would have grumbled at setting out at this hour, but he, too, was ripe for the fiesta of Ticul.

In an hour we saw in the woods on our right large mounds, indicating that here, too, had once stood an ancient city. I rode in to look at them, but the buildings which had crowned them were all fallen and ruined, and I only gained an addition to the stock of garrapatas already on hand. We had not heard of these ruins at the village, and, on inquiring afterward, I could find no name for them.

At the distance of three leagues we commenced ascending the sierra, and for two hours the road lay over an immense ledge of solid rock. Next to the Mico Mountain, it was the worst range I ever crossed, but of entirely different character; instead of gullies, and holes, and walls of mud, it consisted of naked, broken rock, the reflection of the sun upon which was intense and extremely painful to the eyes. In some places it was slippery as glass. I had crossed the sierra in two different places before, but they were comparatively like the passage of the Simplon with that of San Bernard or San Gothard across the Alps. My horse's hoofs clattered and rang at every step, and, though strong and sure-footed, he stumbled and slid in a way that was painful and dangerous to both horse and rider; indeed, it would have been an agreeable change to be occasionally stuck in the mud. It was impossible to go faster than a walk, and, afraid that night would overtake us, in which case, as there was no moon, we might lose our way, I dismounted and hurried on, leading my horse.

It was nearly dark when we reached the top of the last range. The view was the grandest I had seen in the country. On the very brink stood the church of La Hermita, below the village of Oxcutzcab, and beyond a boundless wooded plain, dotted in three places with villages. We descended by a steep and stony path, and, winding along the front of La Hermita, came upon a broad pavement of stones from the ruined buildings of an aboriginal town. We passed under an imposing gateway, and, entering the village, stopped at the first house for a draught of water, where, looking back, we saw the shades of night gathering over the sierra, a token of our narrow escape. There were ruined mounds in the neighbourhood, which I intended to look at in passing, but we had still four leagues to make, and pushed on. The road was straight and level, but stony, and very soon it became so dark that we could see nothing. My horse had done a hard day's work, and stumbled so that I could scarcely keep him from falling. We roused the barking dogs of two villages, of which, however, I could distinguish nothing but the outline of their gigantic churches, and at nine o'clock rode into the plaza of Ticul. It was crowded with Indians, blazing with lights, and occupied by a great circular scaffold for a bull-ring, and a long, enclosed arbour, from the latter of which strains of music gave notice that the báyle de las Mestizas had already begun.

Once more I received a cordial welcome from the cura Carillo; but the music from the arbour reminded me that the moments of pleasure were fleeting. Our trunks had been ordered over from Nohcacab, and, making a hurried toilet, I hastened to the ball-room, accompanied by the padre Brizeña; the crowd outside opened a way, Don Philippe Peon beckoned to me as I entered, and in a moment more I was seated in one of the best places at the báyle de las Mestizas. After a month in Indian ranchos, that day toiling among ruins, almost driven to distraction by garrapatas, clambering over a frightful sierra, and making a journey worse than any sixty miles in our country, all at once I settled down at a fancy ball, amid music, lights, and pretty women, in the full enjoyment of an armchair and a cigar. For a moment a shade of regret came over me as I thought of my invalid friends, but I soon forgot them.

The enramada, or enclosure for the ball-room, was an arbour about one hundred and fifty feet long and fifty feet wide, surrounded by a railing of rude lattice-work, covered with costal, or hemp bagging, as a protection against the night air and sun, and lighted by lamps with large glass shades. The floor was of hard cement; along the railing was a row of chairs, all occupied by ladies; gentlemen, boys, and girls, children and nurses, were sitting promiscuously on the floor, and Don Philippe Peon, when he gave me his chair, took a place among them. El báyle de las Mestizas was what might be called a fancy ball, in which the señoritas of the village appeared as las Mestizas, or in the costume of Mestiza women: loose white frock, with red worked border round the neck and skirt, a man's black hat, a blue scarf over the shoulder, gold nekclace and bracelets. The young men figured as vaqueros, or major domos, in shirt and pantaloons of pink striped muslin, yellow buckskin shoes, and low, round-crowned, hard-platted straw hat, with narrow brim rolled up at the sides, and trimmed with gold cord and tassels. Both costumes were fanciful and pretty, but at first the black hat was repulsive.

I had heard of the sombreros negros as part of the Mestiza costume, and had imagined some neat and graceful fabric of straw; but the faces of the girls were so soft and mild that even a man's hat could not divest them of their feminine charm. Altogether the scene was somewhat different from what I expected, more refined, fanciful, and picturesque.

To sustain the fancy character, the only dance was that of the toros. A vaquero stood up, and each Mestiza was called out in order. This dance, as we had seen it among the Indians, was extremely uninteresting, and required a movement of the body, a fling of the arms, and a snapping of the fingers, which were at least inelegant; but with las Mestizas of Ticul it was all graceful and pleasing, and there was something particularly winning in the snapping of the fingers. There were no dashing beauties, and not one who seemed to have any idea of being a belle; but all exhibited a mildness, softness, and amiability of expression that created a feeling of promiscuous tenderness. Sitting at ease in an arm-chair, after my sojourn in Indian ranchos, I was particularly alive to these influences. And there was such a charm about that Mestiza dress. It was so clean, simple, and loose, leaving

> "Every beauty free
> To sink or swell as Nature pleases."

The ball broke up too soon, when I was but beginning to reap the fruit of my hard day's work. There was an irruption of servants to carry home the chairs, and in half an hour, except along a line of tables in front of the audiencia, the village was still. For a little while, in my quiet chamber at the convent, the gentle figures of las Mestizas still haunted me, but, worn down by the fatigues of the day, I very soon forgot them.

At daylight the next morning the ringing of bells and firing of rockets announced the continuance of the fiesta; high mass was performed in the church, and at eight o'clock there was a grand exhibition of lassoing cattle in the plaza by amateur vaqueros. These were now mounted, had large vaquero saddles, spurs to match, and each was provided with a coil of rope in hand; bulls of two years old were let loose in the plaza, with the bull-ring to double round, and every street in the village open to them. The amateurs rode after them like mad, to the great peril of old people, women, and children, who scampered out of the way as well as they could, but all as much pleased with the sport as the bull or the vaqueros. One horse fell and hurt his rider, but there were no necks broken.

This over, all dispersed to prepare for the báyle de dia, or ball by daylight. I sat for an hour in the corridor of the convent, looking out upon the plaza. The sun was beaming with intense heat, and the village was as still as if some great calamity had suddenly overtaken it. At length a group was seen crossing the plaza: a vaquero escorting a Mestiza to the ball, holding over her head a red silk umbrella to protect her from the scorching rays of the sun; then an old lady and gentleman, children, and servants, a complete family group, the females all in white, with bright-coloured scarfs and shawls. Other groups appeared crossing in other directions, forming picturesque and pleasing spectacles in the plaza. I walked over to the arbour. Although in broad daylight, under the glare of a midday sun, and shaded only on one side by hemp bagging, as the Mestizas took their seats they seemed prettier than the night before. No adjustment of curtain light was necessary for the morning after the ball, for the ladies had retired at an early hour. The black hat had lost its repugnant character, and on some it seemed most becoming. The costumes of the vaqueros, too, bore well the light of day. The place was open to all who chose to enter, and the floor was covered with Indian women and children, and real Mestizoes in cotton shirts, drawers, and sandals; the barrier, too, was lined with a dense mass of Indians and Mestizoes, looking on good-humouredly at this personification of themselves and their ways. The whole gathering was more informal and gayer, and seemed more what it was intended to be, a fiesta of the village.

The báyle de dia was intended to give a picture of life at a hacienda, and there were two prominent personages, who did not appear the evening before, called fiscales, being the officers attendant upon the ancient caciques, and representing them in their authority over the Indians. These wore long, loose, dirty camisas hanging off one shoulder, and with the sleeves below the hands; calzoncillos, or drawers, to match, held up by a long cotton sash, the ends of which dangled below the knees; sandals, slouching straw hats, with brims ten or twelve inches wide, and long locks of horse hair hanging behind their ears. One of them wore awry over his shoulder a mantle of faded blue cotton cloth, said to be an heirloom descended from an ancient cacique, and each flourished a leather whip with eight or ten lashes. These were the managers and masters of ceremonies, with absolute and unlimited authority over the whole company, and, as they boasted, they had a right to whip the Mestizas if they pleased.

As each Mestiza arrived they quietly put aside the gentleman escorting her, and conducted the lady to her seat. If the gentleman did not give way readily, they took him by the shoulders, and walked him to the other end of the floor. A crowd followed wherever they moved, and all the time the company was assembling they threw everything into laughter and confusion by their whimsical efforts to preserve order.

At length they undertook to clear a space for dancing, backing the company in a summary way as far as they could go, and then taking the men and boys by the shoulder, and jamming them down upon the floor. While they were thus engaged, a stout gentleman, of respectable appearance, holding some high office in the village, appeared in the doorway, quietly lighting another straw cigar, and as soon as they saw him they desisted from the work they had in hand, and, in the capricious and wanton exercise of their arbitrary power, rushed across, seized him, dragged him to the centre of the floor, hoisted him upon the shoulders of a vaquero, and, pulling apart the skirts of his coat, belaboured him with a mock vigour and earnestness that convulsed the whole company with laughter. The sides of the elevated dignitary shook, the vaquero shook under him, and they were near coming down together.

This over, the rogues came directly upon me. El Ingles had not long escaped their eye. I had with difficulty avoided a scene, and my time seemed now to have come. The one with the cacique's mantle led the way with long strides, lash raised in the air, a loud voice, and his eyes, sparkling with frolic and mischief, fastened upon mine. The crowd followed, and I was a little afraid of an attempt to hoist me too on the shoulders of a vaquero; but all at once he stopped short, and, unexpectedly changing his language, opened upon me with a loud harangue in Maya. All knew that I did not understand a word he said, and the laugh was strong against me. I was a little annoyed at being made such a mark, but, recollecting the achievement of our vernacular at Nohcacab, I answered him with an English oration. The effect was instantaneous. He had never before heard a language that he could not understand, bent his ear earnestly, as if by close attention he could catch the meaning, and looked up with an air of real perplexity that turned the laugh completely against him. He began again, and I answered with a stanza of Greek poetry, which had hung by me in some unaccountable way; this, again, completely silenced him, and he dropped the title Ingles, put his arms around my neck, called me "amigo," and made a covenant not to speak in any language but Castilian.

This over, he ordered the music to commence, planted a vaquero on the floor, and led out a Mestiza to dance, again threw all the bystanders into confusion, and sat down quietly on the floor at my feet. All the Mestizas were again called out in order, presenting the same pretty spectacle I had seen the evening before. And there was one whom I had noticed then, not more than fifteen, delicate and fragile, with eyes so soft and dovelike that it was impossible to look upon them without a feeling of tenderness. She seemed sent into the world to be cherished and cared for, and closeted like the finest china, the very emblem of purity, innocence, and loveliness; and, as I had learned, she was the child of shame, being the crianza, or natural daughter, of a gentleman of the village; perhaps it was that she seemed so ill fitted to buffet with contumely and reproach that gave such an indescribable interest to her appearance; but, fortunately, brought up in her father's house, she may go through life without meeting an averted face, or feeling that a stain rests upon her name.

As may be supposed, the presence of this señorita on the floor did not escape the keen eyes of the mercurial fiscal. All at once he became excited and restless, and, starting to his feet, gazed at her for a moment as if entranced by a vision, and then, as if carried away by his excitement, and utterly unconscious of what he was about, he pushed aside the vaquero who was dancing with her, and, flinging his sombrero on the ground, cried out in a tone of ecstacy, "Voy baylár con vd, mi corazon!" "I am going to dance with you, my heart!" As he danced, his excitement seemed to increase; forgetting everything around him, the expression of his face became rapt, fixed, intense; he tore off his cacique's mantle, and, dancing toward her, spread it at the lady's feet. This seemed only to excite him more; and, as if forgetful of everything else, he seized the collar of his camisa, and, dancing violently all the time, with a nervous grasp, tugged as if he meant to pull it over his head, and throw all that he was worth at her feet. Failing in this, for a moment he seemed to give up in despair, but all at once he thrust his hands under the long garment, seized the sash around his waist, and, still dancing with all his might, unwound it, and, moving up to her with mingled grace, gallantry, and desperation, dropped it at her feet, and danced back to his place. By this time his calzoncillos, kept up by the sash, were giving way. Grasping them furiously, and holding them up with both hands, as if by a great effort, he went on dancing with a desperate expression of face that was irresistibly ludicrous.

During all this time the company was convulsed with laughter, and I could not help remarking the extreme modesty and propriety of the young lady, who never even smiled or looked at him, but, when the dance was ended, bowed and returned to her seat. The poor fiscal stood gazing at the vacant place where she had stood, as if the sun of his existence had set. At length he turned his head and called out "amigo," asked if there were any such Mestizas in my country; if I would like to take her home with me; then said that he could not spare this one, but I might take my choice of the others; insisting loudly upon my making a selection, and promising to deliver any one I liked to me at the convent.

At first I supposed that these fiscales were, like the vaqueros, the principal young men of the village, who, for that day, gave themselves up to frolic and fun, but I learned that these were not willing to assume such a character, but employed others known to them for wit and humour, and, at the same time, for propriety and respectability of behaviour. This was a *matador de cochinos*, or pig butcher, of excellent character, and *muy vivo*, by which may be understood "a fellow of infinite wit and humour." The people of the village seemed to think that the power given him to whip the Mestizas was the extremity of license, but they did consider that, even for the day, they put him on equal terms with those who, in his daily walks, were to him as beings of another sphere; for the time he might pour out his tribute of feeling to beauty and attraction, but it was all to be regarded as a piece of extravagance, to be forgotten by all who heard it, and particularly by her to whom it was addressed. Alas, poor matador de cochinos!

According to the rules, the mantle and sash which he had thrown at the feet of the lady belonged to her, and he was obliged to appeal to the charity of the spectators for money to redeem them. In the mean time the dance continued. The fiscales, having once taken ground as dancers, were continually ordering the vaqueros to step aside, and taking their places. At times, too, under the direction of the fiscales, the idle vaqueros seated themselves on the ground at the head of the arbour, and all joined in the hacienda song of the vaqueria, in alternate lines of Maya and Castilian. The chorus was led by the fiscales, with a noise that drowned every other sound; and while this boisterous merriment was going on, the light figures of the Mestizas were moving in the dance.

At twelve o'clock preparations were made for a déjeûner à la fourchette, dispensing, however, with knives and forks. The centre of the floor was cleared, and an enormous earthen jar, equal in capacity to a barrel, was brought in, containing frigoles, or black beans fried. Another vessel of the same size had a preparation of eggs and meat, and near them was a small mountain of tortillas, with all which it was the business of the Mestizas to serve the company. The fiscal did not neglect his amigo, but led to me one of whom I had expressed my opinion to him in confidence, and who brought in the palm of her hand a layer of tortillas, with frigoles in the centre, and turned up at the sides by means of the fingers, so as to prevent the frigoles from escaping. An attempt to acknowledge the civility was repressed by the fiscal, who crowded my hat over my eyes, saying that they passed no compliments on the haciendas, and we were all Indians together. The tortillas, with the frigoles in them, were not easy to hold without endangering my only pair of white pantaloons. I relieved myself by passing them over the railing, where any number of Indians stood ready to receive them; but I had hardly got rid of this when another Mestiza brought another portion, and while this engaged my one hand a third placed tortillas with eggs in the other, and left me afraid to move; but I contrived to pass both handfuls over the railing. Breakfast over, the dancing was resumed with new spirit. The fiscales were more amusing than ever; all agreed that the ball was muy allégre, or very gay, and I could not but notice that, amid all this motley company and extraordinary license, there was less noise than in a private drawing-room at home. At two o'clock, to my great regret, the ball of las Mestizas broke up. It was something entirely new, and remains engraven on my mind as the best of village balls.

CHAPTER VI

In the afternoon commenced the first bull-fight. The bull-fights of Ticul had a great reputation throughout the country. At the last, a toreador was killed, which gave a promise of something exciting. The young men of the village still appeared in character as vaqueros, and before the fight they had a horse-race, which consisted in riding across the ring, one at a time, in at one door and out at the other, and then racing in the same way through the other two doors. It was a fine opportunity for exhibiting horses and horsemanship, and was a sort of pony scamper.

After these came the toreadores, or bull-fighters, who, to do them justice, were by far the worst-looking men I saw in the country, or anywhere else, except, perhaps, the libellous representatives of the twelve apostles in the feet-washing scene, at which I was once a spectator in Jerusalem. They were of a mixed blood, which makes, perhaps, the worst race known, viz., the cross of the Indian and African, and called Pardos. Their complexion is a black tinge laid upon copper, and, not satisfied with the bountiful share of ugliness which nature had given them, these worthies had done something for themselves in the way of costume, which was a vile caricature of the common European dress, with some touches of their own elegant fancy. Altogether, I could imagine that they had fitted themselves out with the unclaimed wardrobe of deceased hospital patients. Their horses, being borrowed by the committee of arrangements, with the understanding that if killed they were to be paid for, were spavined, foundered, one-eyed, wretched beasts. They had saddles covered with scarlet cloths, enormous spurs, with rowels six inches long, and murderous spears, discoloured with old stains of blood. The combination of colours, particularly the scarlet, was intended to frighten the bull, and all together they were almost enough to frighten el demonio.

The races over, the amateur vaqueros led in the first bull, having two real vaqueros at hand for cases of emergency. The toreadores charged upon him with spears brandished, and presenting a vivid picture of the infernals let loose; after which they dismounted and attacked him on foot. The bull was brought to bay directly under our box, and twice I saw the iron pass between his horns, enter the back of his neck with a dull, grating sound, and come out bloody, leaving a ghastly wound. At the third blow the bull staggered, struggled to sustain himself on his feet, but fell back on his haunches, and, with a feeble bellow, rolled over on his side; blood streamed from his mouth, his tongue hung out on the ground covered with dust, and in a few moments he was dead. The amateurs tied his hind legs, ropes were fastened to the saddles of two horsemen, others took hold, and as the carcase was dragged across the ring, a fair and gentle-voiced neighbour said, in a tone of surprise, "Dos caballos y seis Christianos!" "Two horses and six Christians!"

I omit the rest. From the bull-fight we again went to the ball, which, in the evening, was the báyle del etiquette, no gentleman being admitted without pantaloons. Society in Yucatan stands upon an aristocratic footing. It is divided into two great classes: those who wear pantaloons, and those who do not; the latter, and by far the most numerous body, going in calzoncillos, or drawers. The high-handed regulation of the ball of etiquette was aimed at them, and excluded many of our friends of the morning; but it did not seem to give any offence, the excluded quietly taking their places at the outside of the railing. El matador de cochinos, or the pig butcher, was admitted in drawers, but as assistant to the servants, handing refreshments to the ladies he had danced with in the morning. The whole aspect of things was changed; the vaqueros were in dress suits, or such undress as was not unbecoming at a village ball. The señoritas had thrown aside their simple Mestiza dresses, and appeared in tunicas, or frocks, made to fit the figure, or, rather, to cut the

figure in two. The Indian dances had disappeared, and qua-
drilles and contradances, waltzes and gallopades, supplied their
place. It wanted the piquancy of the báyle de las Mestizas; the
young ladies were not so pretty in their more fashionable costume. Still there was the same gentleness of expression, the
dances were slow, the music low and soft, and, in the quiet and
decorum of all, it was difficult to recognise the gay and tumultuous party of the morning, and yet more difficult to believe
that these gentle and, in some cases, lovely faces, had been but a
few hours before lighted up with the barbarous excitement of
the bull-ring.

At ten the next day there was another bull-fight; then a
horse-race from the plaza down the principal street to the house
of Don Philippe Peon; and in the afternoon yet another bull-
fight, which opened for me under pleasant circumstances. I did
not intend to go, had not secured a seat, and took my place in
a box so full that I was obliged to stand up by the door. In
front was one of the prettiest of the Mestizas of the ball; on her
right was a vacant seat, and next to this sat a padre, who had
just arrived at the village. I was curious to know who could be
the proprietor of the vacant seat, when the gentleman himself
(an acquaintance) entered, and asked me to take it. I did not
require much urging, and, in taking it, turned first to the padre
to acknowledge my good fortune in obtaining it, which communication I thought he did not receive quite as graciously as
he might have done. The corrida opened bravely; bulls were
speared, blood flowed, and men were tumbled over. I had never
taken so much pleasure in the opening scenes; but a storm was
gathering; the heavens put on black; clouds whirled through the
air; the men stood up, seeming anxious and vexed, and the
ladies were uneasy about their mantillas and headdresses. Darkness increased, but man and beast went on fighting in the ring,
and it had a wild and strange effect, with the black clouds scud-
ding above us, to look from the fierce struggle up to the sea of
anxious faces on the other side of the scaffold, and beyond, over
the top, to the brilliant arch of a rainbow illuminating with a
single line the blackness of the sky. I pointed out the rainbow to
the lady as an indication that there would be no rain; but the
sign disappeared, a furious gust of wind swept over the frail
scaffold, the scalloped papers fluttered, shawls and handkerchiefs
flew, a few drops of rain fell, and in three minutes the Plaza de
Toros was empty. I had no umbrella to offer the lady; some ill-
natured person carried her off; and the matador de cochinos ex-

tended his poncha over my head, and escorted me to a house, where I made a great discovery, which everybody in the village knew except myself. The lady, whom I had supposed to be a señorita, was a comprometida, or compromised, or, to speak precisely, she was the compagnera of the padre who sat on the other side of me.

I have omitted to mention that a great change, or, as it is sometimes called in the country, a new reformation, is now going on in Yucatan, not like the reformations got up by disorganizing laymen, which have, at times, convulsed the whole Christian world, but peculiar and local, and touching only the domestic relations of the padres. It may be known to many of my readers that in the early ages of the Catholic Church priests were not forbidden to marry. In process of time the pope, to wean them from worldly ties, enjoined celibacy, and separation where marriage had already taken place. The priests resisted, and the struggle threatened to undermine the whole fabric of church government; but the pope prevailed, and for eight centuries, throughout those countries in which the spiritual domination of Rome is acknowledged, no priest has been allowed to marry. But in Yucatan this burden was found too heavy to be borne. Very early, from the necessity growing out of local position, some special indulgences had been granted to the people of this country, among which was a dispensation for eating meat on fast days; and, under the liberal spirit of this bull, or of some other that I am not aware of, the good padres have relaxed considerably the tightness of the cord that binds them to celibacy.

I am about making a delicate and curious communication. It may be considered an ill-natured attack upon the Catholic Church; but as I feel innocent of any such intention, this does not trouble me. But another consideration does. I have a strong liking to padres. I have received from them nothing but kindness, and wherever I have met with them I have found friends. I mean barely to mention the subject and pass on, though I am afraid that by this preface I am only calling more particular attention to it. I would omit it altogether, but it forms so striking a feature in the state of society in that country, that no picture can be complete without it. Without farther preface, then, I mention, but only for the private ear of the reader, that, except at Merida and Campeachy, where they are more immediately under the eyes of the bishop, the padres throughout Yucatan, to relieve the tedium of convent life, have compagneras, or, as they are sometimes called, *hermanas politicas*, or sisters-in-law; or, to

speak with the precision I particularly aim at, the proportion of
those who have to those who have not is about as the proportion
in a well-regulated community of married to unmarried men.

I have now told the worst; the greatest enemy of the padres
cannot say more. I do not express any opinion of my own upon
this matter, but I may remark that with the people of the country it is no impeachment of a padre's character, and does not
impair his usefulness. Some look upon this arrangement as a
little irregular, but in general it is regarded only as an amiable
weakness, and I am safe in saying that it is considered a recommendation to a village padre, as it is supposed to give him
settled habits, as marriage does with laymen, and, to give my
own honest opinion, which I did not intend to do, it is less
injurious to good morals than the by no means uncommon
consequences of celibacy which are found in some other Catholic
countries. The padre in Yucatan stands in the position of a married man, and performs all the duties pertaining to the head of
a family. Persons of what is considered respectable standing in a
village do not shun left-hand marriage with a padre. Still it was
to us always a matter of regret to meet with individuals of
worth, and whom we could not help esteeming, standing in what
could not but be considered a false position. To return to the
case with which I set out: the padre in question was universally
spoken of as a man of good conduct, a sort of pattern padre for
correct, steady habits; sedate, grave, and middle-aged, and apparently the last man to have had an eye for such a pretty compagnera. The only comment I ever heard made was upon his good
fortune, and on that point he knows my opinion.

The next day Mr. Catherwood and Doctor Cabot arrived.
Both had had a recurrence of fever, and were still very weak. In
the evening was the carnival ball, but before the company had
all arrived. We were again scattered by the rain. All the next day
it was more abundant than we had seen it in the country, and
completely destroyed all the proposed gayeties of the carnival.

We had one clear day, which we devoted to taking Daguerreotype likenesses of the cura and two of the Mestizas; and, besides the great business of balls, bull-fights, Daguerreotyping,
and superintending the morals of the padres, I had some light
reading in a manuscript entitled, "Antigua Chronologia Yucateca," "Ancient Chronology of Yucatan; or, a simple Exposition
of the Method used by the Indians to compute Time." This
essay was presented to me by the author, Don Pio Perez, whom
I had the satisfaction of meeting at this place. I had been ad-

vised that this gentleman was the best Maya scholar in Yucatan, and that he was distinguished in the same degree for the investigation and study of all matters tending to elucidate the history of the ancient Indians. His attention was turned in this direction by the circumstance of holding an office in the department of state, in which old documents in the Maya language were constantly passing under his eyes. Fortunately for the interests of science and his own studious tastes, on account of some political disgust he withdrew from public life, and, during two years of retirement, devoted himself to the study of the ancient chronology of Yucatan. It is a work which no ordinary man would have ventured to undertake; and, if general reputation be any proof, there was no man in the country so competent, or who could bring to it so much learning and research. It adds to the merit of his labours that, in prosecuting them, Don Pio stood alone, had none to sympathize with him, knew that the attainment of the most important results would not be appreciated, and had not even that hope of honourable distinction which, in the absence of all other prospects of reward, cheers the student in the solitary labours of his closet.

The essay explains at large the principles imbodied in the calendar of the ancient Indians. It has been submitted for examination (with other interesting papers furnished me by Don Pio, which will be referred to hereafter) to a distinguished gentleman, known by his researches into Indian languages and antiquities, and I am authorized to say that it furnishes a basis for some interesting comparisons and deductions, and is regarded as a valuable contribution to the cause of science.

The essay of Don Pio contains calculations and details which would not be interesting to the general reader; to some, however, even these cannot fail to be so, and the whole is published in the Appendix.* I shall refer in this place only to the result. From the examination and analysis made by the distinguished gentleman before referred to, I am enabled to state the interesting fact, that the calendar of Yucatan, though differing in some particulars, was substantially the same with that of the Mexicans. It had a similar solar year of three hundred and sixty-five days, divided in the same manner, first, into eighteen months of twenty days each, with five supplementary days; and, secondly, into twenty-eight weeks of thirteen days each, with an additional day. It had the same method of distinguishing the

*See Appendix to vol. i.

days of the year by a combination of those two series, and the same cycle of fifty-two years, in which the years, as in Mexico, are distinguished by a combination of the same series of thirteen, with another of four names or hieroglyphics; but Don Pio acknowledges that in Yucatan there is no certain evidence of the intercalation (similar to our leap year, or to the Mexican secular addition of thirteen days) necessary to correct the error resulting from counting the year as equal to three hundred and sixty-five days only.

It will be seen, by reference to the essay, that, besides the cycle of fifty-two years common to the Yucatecans and Mexicans, and, as Don Pio Perez asserts (on the authority of Veytia), to the Indians of Chiapas, Oaxaca, and Soconusco, those of Yucatan had another age of two hundred and sixty, or of three hundred and twelve years, equal to five or six cycles of fifty-two years, each of which ages consisted of thirteen periods (called Ajau or Ajau Katun) of twenty years each, according to many authorities, but, in Don Pio's opinion, of twenty-four years.

The fact that though the inhabitants of Yucatan and Mexico speak different languages, their calendar is substantially the same, I regard as extremely interesting and important, for this is not like a similarity of habits, which may grow out of natural instincts or identity of position. A calendar is a work of science, founded upon calculations, arbitrary signs, and symbols, and the similarity shows that both nations acknowledged the same starting points, attached the same meaning to the same phenomena and objects, which meaning was sometimes arbitrary, and not such as would suggest itself to the untutored. It shows common sources of knowledge and processes of reasoning, similarity of worship and religious institutions, and, in short, it is a link in a chain of evidence tending to show a common origin in the aboriginal inhabitants of Yucatan and Mexico. For this discovery we are indebted to Don Pio Perez.

CHAPTER VII

On the fourteenth of February we returned to Nohcacab. We had sent Albino before to make all our necessary arrangements, and on the fifteenth we took our final leave of this village. We had no regret; on the contrary, it was pleasant to think that we should not return to it. Our luggage was again reduced to the smallest possible compass: hammocks, a few changes of clothes, and Daguerreotype apparatus, all the rest being forwarded to meet us at Peto. The chief of our Indian carriers was a sexton, who had served out his time, an old neighbour in the convent, whom we had never seen sober, and who was this morning particularly the reverse.

To understand our route it will be necessary for the reader to consult the map. On setting out our direction was again south, and again our road was over the sepulchres of cities. At the distance of two miles we saw "old walls" on an eminence at the right; a little farther three ruined buildings on the same side of the road; and beyond these we came to the ruins of Sacbey. These consist of three buildings, irregularly disposed, one of which is represented in Plate XII. It faces the south, measures fifty-three feet front by twelve feet six inches deep, and has

Plate XII

SACBEY

three small doorways. Another, a little farther south, is about the size of the former, and has three apartments, with two columns in the centre doorway. The third is so ruined that its plan could not be made out.

Near as they were to the village, the padrecito had never seen them. They stand about a hundred feet from the path, but so completely buried among the trees, that, though I had visited them before under the guidance of an Indian, I passed now without observing them.

A short distance beyond is one of the most interesting monuments of antiquity in Yucatan. It is a broken platform or roadway of stone, about eight feet wide and eight or ten inches high, crossing the road, and running off into the woods on both sides. I have before referred to it as called by the Indians Sacbey, which means, in the Maya language, a paved way of pure white stone. The Indians say it traversed the country from Kabah to Uxmal; and that on it couriers travelled, bearing letters to and from the lords of those cities, written on leaves or the bark of trees. It was the only instance in which we had found among the Indians anything like a tradition, and the universality of this legend was illustrated by the circumstances attending our arrival. While we were standing upon the road, an old Indian came up from the other direction, bending under a load, who, in crossing it, stopped, and, striking his stick against the stones, uttered the words Sacbey, and Kabah, and Uxmal. At the same time our carriers came up, the old sexton at their head, who, depositing his burden upon the ancient road, repeated Sacbey, and then favoured us with an oration, in which we could only distinguish Kabah and Uxmal.

It had been my intention to explore thoroughly the route of this ancient road, and, if possible, trace it through the woods to the desolate cities which it once connected, and it was among the vexations of our residence at Nohcacab that we had not been able to do so. The difficulty of procuring Indians to work, and a general recurrence of sickness, rendered it impossible. We could not tell how much time might be required; the whole country was overgrown with trees; in some places the track was but faintly marked, and in others it might be lost altogether. It remains, therefore, an unbroken ground for the future explorer.

Again passing "old walls" on each side of the road, at the distance of two leagues we reached Xampon, where stand the remains of an edifice which, when entire, must have been grand and imposing, and now, but for the world of ruins around, might excite a stranger's wonder. Its form was rectangular, its four sides enclosing a hollow square. It measured from north to south eighty feet, and from east to west one hundred and five. Two angles only remain, one of which is represented in Plate XIII. It stood alone, and an Indian had planted a milpa around it. From this "old walls" were again visible, which the Indians called Kalupok.

Beyond we saw at a distance two other places, called Hioko-witz and Kuepak, ruined and difficult of access, and we did not attempt to reach them.

It added to the effect of the ruins scattered in this region, that they were not on a camino real, but on a little-frequented milpa path, in some places so overgrown that we found it diffi-cult to force a passage. The heat was intense; we exhausted our waccals of water, and as there was no stream or fountain, our only chance of a supply was from a deposite of rain-water in the hollow of some friendly rock.

At two o'clock we reached a small clearing, in which stood an arbour of leaves, and under it a rude cross, facing the road; beyond, on the left, was an overgrown path, which, for the first time in many years, had been opened for me on a former occa-sion, to enable me to visit the ruins of Zekilna.

This place had been the object of one of my bootless visits from Nohcacab. The account I had heard was of an apartment containing an altar for buring copal, with traces of its use as left by the ancient inhabitants. When I had arrived where it was necessary to turn off, it was some time before the Indian could discover any signs of a path; and when found, he had to clear every step of the way. By that time my views on the sub-ject of ruined cities had become practical, and, perceiving the discomfort and hardship that must attend an exploration in so desolate a place, I did most earnestly hope that the path would lead to nothing that might require a second visit. I dismounted, and leading my horse as the Indian cleared the way, we came to a broken, stony ascent, climbing up which I discovered that we were upon the top of an ancient terrace. A fine alamo tree was growing on the terrace, under which I tied my horse, and de-scending on the other side, we crossed a closely-wooded hollow, which, from the excessive heat, I supposed to be between two mounds. In a few moments I found myself ascending the side of a lofty stone structure, on the top of which were the remains of a large building, with its walls fallen, and the whole side of the mound strewed with sculptured stones, a scene of irrecoverable

Plate XIII

XAMPON

ruin. Descending on the other side of this structure, we reached a broad platform, in a good state of preservation, with trees growing upon it, without brush or underwood, but so teeming with insects and large black ants that it was necessary to step from stone to stone, and avoid touching the ground: Running off lengthwise from this terrace was a small building, which the Indian pointed out as containing the altar and copal. Passing the first door, he went on to the second, put his head in cautiously, and, without entering, drew back. Going in, I found an apartment differing in nothing from the most ordinary we had seen in the country. For some time I could not get the Indian to enter, and when he did, standing in the doorway, and looking around cautiously, he waved his finger horizontally, açcording to the manner of the Indians, to indicate that there was nothing. Fortunately, however, I learned that the road we had left led to the ruins of Chunhuhu; and it shows the difficulty I had in ascertaining the juxtaposition of places, that though this was one of the places which I intended to visit, until this man mentioned it I had not been able to learn that it lay in the same neighbourhood. I determined at once to continue on, and it was what I saw on that occasion that now put our whole body in motion in this direction.

To return. It was late in the afternoon when we reached the savanna of Chunhuhu, and rode up to the hut at which I had tied my horse on my former visit.

The hut was built of upright poles, had a steep projecting roof thatched with palm leaves, and the sides protected by the same material; as we stopped in front, we saw a woman within mashing maize for tortillas, which promised a speedy supper. She said her husband was away; but this made no difference to us, and, after a few more words, we all entered, the woman at the moment bolting for the door, and leaving us in exclusive possession. Very soon, however, a little boy, about eight years old, came down and demanded the maize, which we were loth to give up, but did not consider ourselves authorized to retain. Albino followed him, in hopes of persuading the woman to return; but as soon as she caught a glimpse of him she ran into the woods.

The hut of which we thus became the sudden and involuntary masters was furnished with three stones for a fireplace, a wooden horse for kneading maize upon, a comal for baking tortillas, an earthen olla, or pot, for cooking, three or four waccals, or gourds, for drinking-cups, and two small Indian hammocks, which also were demanded and given up. Besides these, there was

a circular dining-table about a foot and a half in diameter, supported by three pegs about eight inches high, and some blocks of
wood about the same height for seats. Overhead, suspended from
the rafters, were three large bundles of corn in the husk and two
of beans in the pod; and on each string, about a foot above these
eatables, was half a calabash or squash, with the rounded side
up, like the shade over a lamp, which, besides being ornamental,
filled the office of a rat-trap; for these vermin, in springing from
the rafters to reach the corn and beans, would strike upon the
calabash, and fall to the ground.

Being provided for ourselves, we next looked to our horses.
There was no difficulty about their food, for a supply of corn
had fallen into our hands, and the grass on the savanna was the
best pasture we had seen in the country; but we learned, to our
dismay, from the little boy, who was the only person we saw,
that there was no water. The place was worse supplied than any
we had yet visited. There was neither well, cueva, nor aguada,
and the inhabitants depended entirely upon the rain-water collected in the hollows of the rocks. As to a supply for four horses,
it was utterly out of the question. Any long stay at this place
was, of course, impossible; but immediate wants were pressing.
Our horses had not touched water since morning, and, after a
long, hot, and toilsome journey, we could not think of their
going without all night.

The little boy was hovering about the rancho in charge of
a naked sister some two years old, and commissioned, as he told
us himself, to watch that we did not take anything from the hut.
For a medio he undertook to show me the place where they
procured water, and, mounting his little sister upon his back, he
led the way up a steep and stony hill. I followed with the bridle
of my horse in my hand, and, without any little girl on my back,
found it difficult to keep up with him. On the top of the hill
were worn and naked rocks, with deep hollows in them, some
holding perhaps as much as one or two pails of water. I led my
horse to one of the largest. He was always an extraordinary water
drinker, and that evening was equal to a whole temperance
society. The little Indian looked on as if he had sold his birth-
right, and I felt strong compunctions; but, letting the morrow
take care of itself, I sent up the other horses, which consumed at
a single drinking what might, perhaps, have sufficed the family a
month.

In the mean time our own wants were not slight. We had
been on the road all day, and had eaten nothing. Unluckily, the

Plate XIV

F. Catherwood.

Jordan & Halpin.

CHUNHUHU.

old sexton had taken for his load the box containing our table furniture and provisions for the road, and we had not seen him since we left him at Sacbey. All the other carriers had arrived. I had hired them to remain with us and work at the ruins, and then carry the luggage to the next village. Part of my contract was to feed them, and, knowing the state of things, they scattered in search of supplies, returning, after a long absence, with some tortillas, eggs, and lard. We had the eggs fried, and would, perhaps, have been content but for our vexation with the sexton. While we were swinging in our hammocks, we heard his voice at a distance, and presently he entered in the best humour possible, and holding up his empty bottle in triumph.

The next morning at daylight we sent Albino with the Indians to begin clearing around the ruins, and after breakfast we followed. The path lay through a savanna covered with long grass, and at the distance of a mile we reached two buildings, which I had seen before, and were the inducement to this visit.

The first is that represented in Plate XIV. It stands on a substantial terrace, but lower than most of the others. The front is one hundred and twelve feet long, and when entire must have presented a grand appearance. The end on the left in the engraving has fallen, carrying with it one doorway, so that now only four appear. The doorway was the largest and most imposing we had seen in the country, but, unfortunately, the ornaments over it were broken and fallen. In the centre apartment the back corridor is raised, and the ascent to it is by three steps.

All the doorways were plain except the centre one (the second to the left in the engraving), which is represented in Plate XV. It is in a dilapidated condition, but still presents bold and striking ornaments. Even on this scale, however, the details of the sitting figures above the cornice do not appear.

While we were engaged in making a clearing in front of this building, two young men came down upon the terrace from the corner that was fallen, and apparently from the top of the building, with long guns, the locks covered with deer-skin, and all the accoutrements of caçadores, or hunters. They were tall, fine-looking fellows, fearless and frank in appearance and manner. Dr. Cabot's gun was the first object that attracted their attention, after which they laid down their guns, and, as if for the mere sport of swinging their machetes, were soon foremost in making the clearing. When this was finished, Mr. C. set up his camera lucida, and though at first all gathered round, in a few minutes he was left with only the two brothers, one of them

Plate XV

F. Catherwood.

CHUNHUHU.

Jordan & Halpin

holding over him an umbrella to protect him from the sun.

Except the little boy and the woman, these were the first persons we had seen within speaking distance. We were so pleased with their appearance that we proposed to one of them to accompany us in our search after ruins. The elder was quite taken with the idea of rambling, but soon said, with a rather disconsolate tone, that he had a wife and children. His herman-ito, or younger brother, however, had no such ties, and would go with us. We made an agreement on the spot; and nothing can show more plainly the sense which we entertained of the security of travelling in Yucatan. In Central America we never dared to take a man into our service without strong recommendations, for he might be a robber or an assassin. These men we had never heard of till they came upon us with their guns. Their manly bearing as hunters inspired confidence, and the only suspicious circumstance was that they were willing to take us without references; but we found afterward that they had both known us at Nohcacab. The one whom we engaged was named Dimas, and he continued with us until we left the country.

On the same line, and but a short distance removed, though on a lower terrace, is another building, measuring eighty-five feet in front, which is represented in Plate XVI. It had a fresh-ness about it that suggested the idea of something more modern than the others. The whole was covered with a coat of plaster but little broken, and it confirmed us in the opinion we had entertained before, that the fronts of all the buildings had been thus covered.

Our meeting with these young men was a fortunate circum-stance for us in exploring these ruins. From boyhood their father had had his rancho on the savanna, and with their guns they had ranged over the whole country for leagues around.

From the terrace of the first building we saw at a distance a high hill, almost a mountain, on the top of which rose a wooded elevation surrounding an ancient building. There was something extraordinary in its position, but the young men told us it was entirely ruined, and, although it was then but eleven o'clock, if we attempted to go to it, we could not return till after dark. They told us, also, of others at the distance of half a league, more extensive, and some of which, they said, were, in finish and preservation, equal to these.

At one o'clock Doctor Cabot and myself, under the guidance of Dimas, set out to look for them. It was desperately hot. We passed several huts, and at one of them asked for some water; but

Plate XVI

J.N Gimbrede.

T Catherwood.

CHUNHUHU.

it was so full of insects that we could barely taste it. Dimas led us to the hut of his mother, and gave us some from a vessel in which the insects had settled to the bottom.

Beyond this we ascended the spur of a high hill, and coming down into a thickly-wooded valley, after the longest half league we ever walked, we saw through the trees a large stone structure. On reaching it, and climbing over a broken terrace, we came to a large mound faced on all sides with stone, which we ascended, and crossing over the top, looked down upon an overgrown area, having on each side a range of ruined buildings, with their white façades peering through the trees; and beyond, at a distance, and seemingly inaccessible, was the high hill with the ruins on the top, which we had seen from the terrace of the first building. Hills rose around us on every side, and, for that country, the scene was picturesque, but all waste and silent. The stillness of the grave rested upon the ruins, and the notes of a little flycatcher were the only sounds we heard.

The ruins in sight were much more extensive than those we had first visited, but in a more ruinous condition. We descended the mound to the area in front, and, bearing down the bushes, passed in the centre an uncouth, upright, circular stone, like that frequently referred to before, called the picote, or whipping-post, and farther on we reached an edifice, which Mr. Catherwood afterward drew, and which is represented in Plate XVII. It is thirty-three feet in front, and has two apartments, each thirteen feet long by eight feet six inches deep, and conspicuous in the façade are representations of three uncouth human figures, in curious dresses, with their hands held up by the side of the head, supporting the cornice.

These ruins, Dimas told us, were called Schoolhoke, but, like the others, they stand on what is called the savanna of Chunhuhu; and the ruined building on the top of the hill, visible from both places, seems towering as a link to connect them together. What the extent of this place has been it is impossible to say. Returning, overtaken by night, and in apprehension of rain, we were an hour and a half, which would make the two, by the path we took, at least five miles apart, though much nearer in a straight line. Supposing the two piles of ruins to have formed part of the same city, there is reason to believe that it once covered as much ground and contained as many inhabitants as any that has yet been presented.

The first intelligence I received of the existence of these ruins was from Cocom, who, the reader may remember, was our

Plate XVII

F. Catherwood.

CHUNJUJII.

S.H. Gimber

guide at Nohpat; and this is all that I am able to communicate in regard to their history.

We returned to the rancho worn down with fatigue, just in time to escape a violent rain. This brought within, as an accompaniment to the fleas of the night before, our carriers and servants, and we had eleven hammocks, in close juxtaposition, and through the night a concert of nasal trombones, with Indian variations. The rain continued all the next day, and as no work could be done, Mr. Catherwood took advantage of the opportunity to have another attack of fever. We were glad of it on another account, for we had kept a man constantly employed in the woods searching for water; our horses had exhausted all the rocky cavities around, and we could not have held out another day. The rain replenished them, and relieved us from some compunctions.

In the afternoon the little boy came down with a message from his mother, desiring to know when we were going away. Perhaps the reader is curious to know the costume of boys at Chunhuhu. It consists of a straw hat and a pair of sandals. This one had, besides, some distinguishable spots of dirt, and Mr. Catherwood made a drawing of him as he stood. Soon afterward the poor woman herself was seen hovering about the house. She considered that it was really time to come. We had made a great inroad upon her provisions; given the corn to our horses, and cooked the frigoles; but the special cause of her coming was to return a medio, which she said was bad. She was mild, amiable, and simple as a child; complained that we said we were only going to remain one night, and now she did not know when we were going away. With great difficulty, we prevailed upon her to enter the hut, and told her she might return whenever she pleased. She laughed good-naturedly, and, after looking round carefully to see that nothing was missing, went away comforted by our promise to depart the next day.

CHAPTER VIII

At daylight the next morning the woman was
on the spot to remind us of our promise. We gave her a cup of
coffee, and with a small present, which amply satisfied her for
our forcible occupation of her hut, left her again in possession.

Our party this morning divided into three parcels. The carriers set out direct for Bolonchen; Mr. Catherwood went, under
the guidance of Dimas, to make a drawing of the last building,
and Doctor Cabot, myself, and Albino to visit another ruined
city, all to meet again at Bolonchen in the evening.

Doctor Cabot and myself were warned that the path we
proposed taking was not passable on horseback. For the first
league our arms and legs were continually scratched and torn
by briers, and only our hats saved us from the fate of Absalom.
In that hot climate, it was always uncomfortable to tie the
sombrero under the chin; and there were few things more annoying than to have it knocked off every five minutes, and be
obliged to dismount and pick it up. Our Indian guide moved

easily on foot, just clearing the branches on each side and over-head. We had one alternative, which was to dismount and lead our horses; but, unused to having favours shown them, they pulled back, so that the labour of dragging them on added greatly to the fatigue of walking.

Emerging from this tangled path, we came out upon a large hacienda, and stopped before an imposing gateway, under the shade of great seybo trees, within which were large and well-filled water-tanks. Our horses had drunk nothing since the after-noon before; we therefore dismounted, loosened the saddle girths, and, as a matter of form, sent Albino to ask permission to water them, who returned with the answer that we might for a real. At Chunhuhu it always cost us more than this in the labour of Indians; but the demand seemed so churlish at the gate of this large hacienda, that we refused to pay, and again mounted. Albino told us that we might save a slight circuit by passing through the cattle-yard; and we rode through, close beside the water-tanks and a group of men, at the head of whom was the master, and, coming out upon the camino real, shook from off our feet the dust of the inhospitable hacienda. Our poor horses bore the brunt of sustaining our dignity.

At one o'clock we came to a rancho of Indians, where we bought some tortillas and procured a guide. Leaving the camino real, we turned again into a milpa path, and in about an hour came in sight of another ruined city, known by the name of Ytsimpte. From the plain on which we approached we saw on the left, on the brow of a hill, a range of buildings, six or eight hundred feet in length, all laid bare to view, the trees having just been felled; and as we drew near we saw Indians engaged in continuing the clearing. On arriving at the foot of the buildings, Albino found that the clearing was made by order of the alcalde of Bolonchen, at the instance and under the direction of the padre, in expectation of our visit and for our benefit!

We had another subject of congratulation on account of our horses. There was an aguada in the neighbourhood, to which we immediately sent them, and, carrying our traps up to the terrace of the nearest building, we sat down before it to meditate and lunch.

This over, we commenced a survey of the ruins. The clearings made by our unknown friends enabled us to form at once a general idea of their character and extent, and to move from place to place with comparative facility. These ruins lie in the village of Bolonchen, and the first apartment we entered showed

the effects of this vicinity. All the smooth stones of the inner wall
had been picked out and carried away for building purposes,
and the sides presented the cavities in the bed of mortar from
which they had been taken. The edifice was about two hundred
feet long. It had one apartment, perhaps sixty feet long, and a
grand staircase twenty feet wide rose in the centre to the top.
This staircase was in a ruinous condition, but the outer stones
of the lower steps remained, richly ornamented with sculpture;
and probably the whole casing on each side had once possessed
the same rich decoration.

Beyond this was another large building, square and peculiar
in its plan. At the extreme end the whole façade lay unbroken
on the ground, held together by the great mass of mortar and
stones, and presenting the entire line of pillars with which it
had been decorated. In the doorway of an inner apartment was
an ornamented pillar, and on the walls was the print of the
mysterious red hand. Turn which way we would, ruin was before us. At right angles with the first building was a line of
ruined walls, following which I passed, lying on the ground,
the headless trunk of a sculptured body; the legs, too, were gone.
At the end was an arch, which seemed, at a distance, to stand
entire and alone, like that named the arch of triumph at Kabah;
but it proved to be only the open and broken arch of a ruined
building. From the extent of these remains, the masses of sculptured stones, and the execution of the carving, this must have
been one of the first class of the aboriginal cities. In moral
influence there was none more powerful. Ruin had been so
complete that we could not profit by the kindness of our
friends, and it was melancholy that when so much had been
done for us, there was so little for us to do. It was but another
witness to the desolation that had swept over the land.

A short ride brought us to the suburbs of the village of
Bolonchen, and we entered a long street, with a line of straggling
houses or huts on each side. It was late in the afternoon. Indian
children were playing in the road, and Indians, returned from
their work, were swinging in hammocks within the huts. As we
advanced, we saw a vecino, with a few neighbours around him,
sitting in the doorway thrumming a guitar. It was, perhaps, a
scene of indolence, but it was one of quiet and contentment, of
comfort and even thrift. Often, in entering the disturbed villages
of Central America, among intoxicated Indians and swaggering
white men, all armed, we felt a degree of uneasiness. The faces
that looked upon us seemed scowling and suspicious; we always

apprehended insult, and frequently were not disappointed. Here all looked at us with curiosity, but without distrust; every face bore a welcome, and, as we rode through, all gave us a friendly greeting. At the head of the street the plaza opened upon us on a slight elevation, with groups of Indian women in the centre drawing water from the well, and relieved against a background of green hills rising above the tops of the houses, which, under the reflection of the setting sun, gave a beauty and picturesqueness of aspect that no other village in the country had exhibited. On the left, on a raised platform, stood the church, and by its side the convent. In consideration of what the cura had already done for us, and that we had a large party—perceiving, also, that the casa real, a long stone building with a broad portico in front, was really inviting in its appearance, we resolved to spare the cura, and rode up to the casa real. Well-dressed Indians, with a portly, well-fed cacique, stood ready to take our horses. We dismounted and entered the principal apartment. On one side were the iron gratings of the prison, and on the other two long beams of wood with holes in them for stocks, and a caution to strangers arriving in the village to be on their good behaviour. Our carriers had arrived. We sent out to buy ramon and corn for the horses, had our hammocks swung, and sat down under the corridor.

We had hardly time to seat ourselves before the vecinos, in their clean afternoon clothes, and some with gold-headed canes, came over to "call upon us." All were profuse in offers of services; and as it was the hour for that refreshment, we had a perplexing number of invitations to go to their houses and take chocolate. Among our visitors was a young man with a fine black beard all over his face, well dressed, and the only one wearing a black hat, whom, as we knew they were about drilling companies in the villages to resist the apprehended invasion of Santa Ana, we supposed to belong to the army, but we afterward learned that he was a member of the church militant, being the ministro, or assistant, of the cura. The cura himself did not come, but one of our visiters, looking over to the convent, and seeing the doors and windows closed, said he was still taking his siesta.

We had time to look at the only objects of interest in the village, and these were the wells, which, after our straits at Chunhuhu, were a refreshing spectacle, and of which our horses had already enjoyed the benefit by a bath.

Bolonchen derives its name from two Maya words: *Bolon,* which signifies nine, and *chen,* wells, and it means the nine wells.

From time immemorial, nine wells formed at this place the centre of a population, and these nine wells are now in the plaza of the village. Their origin is as obscure and unknown as that of the ruined cities which strew the land, and as little thought of.

These wells were circular openings cut through a stratum of rock. The water was at that time ten or twelve feet from the surface, and in all it was at the same level. The source of this water is a mystery to the inhabitants, but there are some facts which seem to make the solution simple. The wells are mere perforations through an irregular stratum of rock, all communicate, and in the dry season a man may descend in one and come out by another at the extreme end of the plaza; it is manifest, therefore, that the water does not proceed from springs. Besides, the wells are all full during the rainy season; when this is over the water begins to disappear, and in the heat of the dry season it fails altogether; from which it would appear that under the surface there is a great rocky cavern, into which the floods of the rainy season find a way by crevices or other openings, which cannot be known without a survey of the country, and, having little or no escape, are retained, and furnish a supply so long as they are augmented by the rains.

The custody and preservation of these wells form a principal part of the business of the village authorities, but, with all their care, the supply lasts but seven or eight months in the year. This year, on account of the long continuance of the rainy season, it had lasted longer than usual, and was still abundant. The time was approaching, however, when these wells would fail, and the inhabitants be driven to an extraordinary cueva at half a league from the village.

At about dark Mr. Catherwood arrived, and we returned to the casa real. In a room fifty feet long, free from fleas, servants, and Indian carriers, and with a full swing for our hammocks, we had a happy change from the hut at Chunhuhu.

During the evening the cura came over to see us, but, finding we had retired, did not disturb us; early in the morning he was rapping at our door, and would not leave us till we promised to come over and take chocolate with him.

As we crossed the plaza he came out to meet us, in black gown and cape, bare-headed, with white hair streaming, and both arms extended; embraced us all, and, with the tone of a man who considered that he had not been treated well, reproached us for not coming directly to the convent; then led us

in, showed us its comforts and conveniences, insisted upon sending for our luggage, and only consented to postpone doing so
while we consulted on our plans.

These were, to leave Bolonchen in the afternoon for the
ruins of San Antonio, four leagues distant. The cura had never
heard of such ruins, and did not believe that any existed, but
he knew the hacienda, and sent out to procure information. In
the mean time it was arranged that we should employ the morning in a visit to the cueva, and return to dine with him. He
reminded us that it was Friday, and, consequently, fast day; but,
knowing the padres as we did, we had no apprehension.

There was one great difficulty in the way of our visiting the
cueva at this time. Since the commencement of the rainy season

FIG. 6

it had not been used; and every year, before having recourse to it, there was a work of several days to be done in repairing the ladders. As this, however, was our only opportunity, we determined to make the attempt.

The cura undertook to make the arrangements, and after breakfast we set out, a large party, including both Indians and vecinos.

At the distance of half a league from the village, on the Campeachy road, we turned off by a well-beaten path, following which we fell into a winding lane, and, descending gradually, reached the foot of a rude, lofty, and abrupt opening, under a bold ledge of overhanging rock, seeming a magnificent entrance to a great temple for the worship of the God of Nature. Figure 6 represents this aperture, an Indian with a lighted torch being seen just entering.

We disencumbered ourselves of superfluous apparel, and, following the Indian, each with a torch in hand, entered a wild cavern, which, as we advanced, became darker. At the distance of sixty paces the descent was precipitous, and we went down by a ladder about twenty feet. Here all light from the mouth of the cavern was lost, but we soon reached the brink of a great perpendicular descent, to the very bottom of which a strong body of light was thrown from a hole in the surface, a perpendicular depth, as we afterward learned by measurement, of two hundred and ten feet. As we stood on the brink of this precipice, under the shelving of an immense mass of rock, seeming darker from the stream of light thrown down the hole, gigantic stalactites and huge blocks of stone assumed all manner of fantastic shapes, and seemed like monstrous animals or deities of a subterranean world.

From the brink on which we stood an enormous ladder, of the rudest possible construction, led to the bottom of the hole. It was between seventy and eighty feet long, and about twelve feet wide, made of the rough trunks of saplings lashed together lengthwise, and supported all the way down by horizontal trunks braced against the face of the precipitous rock. The ladder was double, having two sets or flights of rounds, divided by a middle partition, and the whole fabric was lashed together by withes. It was very steep, seemed precarious and insecure, and confirmed the worst accounts we had heard of the descent into this remarkable well.

Our Indians began the descent, but the foremost had scarcely got his head below the surface before one of the rounds

Plate XVIII

F. Catherwood.

S. H. Gimber

BOLONCHEN

Cueva or Well.

slipped, and he only saved himself by clinging to another. The ladder having been made when the withes were green, these were now dry, cracked, and some of them broken. We attempted a descent with some little misgivings, but, by keeping each hand and foot on a different round, with an occasional crash and slide, we all reached the foot of the ladder; that is, our own party, our Indians, and some three or four of our escort, the rest having disappeared.

Plate XVIII represents the scene at the foot of this ladder. Looking up, the view of its broken sides, with the light thrown down from the orifice above, was the wildest that can be conceived. As yet the reader is only at the mouth of this well; but, to explain to him briefly its extraordinary character, I give its name, which is Xtacumbi Xunan. The Indians understand by this La Señora escondida, or the lady hidden away; and it is derived from a fanciful Indian story that a lady stolen from her mother was concealed by her lover in this cave.

Every year, when the wells in the plaza are about to fail, the ladders are put into a thorough state of repair. A day is appointed by the municipality for closing the wells in the plaza, and repairing to the cueva; and on that day a great village fête is held in the cavern at the foot of this ladder. On the side leading to the wells is a rugged chamber, with a lofty overhanging roof and a level platform; the walls of this rocky chamber are dressed with branches and hung with lights, and the whole village comes out with refreshments and music. The cura is with them, a leader of the mirth; and the day is passed in dancing in the cavern, and rejoicing that when one source of supply fails another is opened to their need.

Figure 7 will give some imperfect idea of a section of this cave from the entrance to the foot of the great ladder, with the orifice through which the light descends from above, and the wild path that leads deeper into the bowels of the rock and down to the water.

On one side of the cavern is an opening in the rock, as shown in the engraving, entering by which, we soon came to an abrupt descent, down which was another long and trying ladder. It was laid against the broken face of the rock, not so steep as the first, but in a much more rickety condition; the rounds were loose, and the upper ones gave way on the first attempt to descend. The cave was damp, and the rock and the ladder were wet and slippery. At this place the rest of our attendants left us, the ministro being the last deserter. It was evident that the

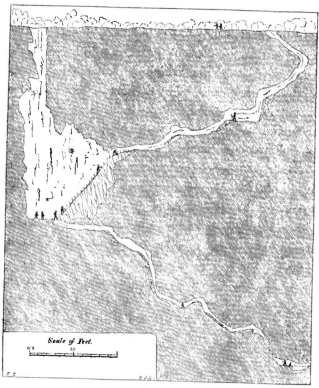

Scale of Feet.

FIG. 7

labour of exploring this cave was to be greatly increased by the state of the ladders, and there might be some danger attending it, but, even after all that we had seen of caves, there was something so wild and grand in this that we could not bring ourselves to give up the attempt. Fortunately, the cura had taken care to provide us with rope, and, fastening one end round a large stone, an Indian carried the other down to the foot of the ladder. We followed, one at a time; holding the rope with one hand, and with the other grasping the side of the ladder, it was impossible to carry a torch, and we were obliged to feel our way in the dark, or with only such light as could reach us from the torches above and below. At the foot of this ladder was a large cavernous chamber, from which irregular passages led off in different directions to deposites or sources of water. Doctor Cabot and myself, attended by Albino, took one of the passages indicated by the Indians, of which some imperfect idea is given in the section.

Moving on by a slight ascent over the rocks, at the distance of about seventy-five feet we came to the foot of a third ladder nine feet long, two or three steps beyond another five feet high, both which we had to go up, and six paces farther a fifth, descending, and eighteen feet in length. A little beyond we descended another ladder eleven feet long, and yet a little farther on we came to one—the seventh—the length and general appearance of which induced us to pause and consider. By this time Albino was the only attendant left. This long ladder was laid on a narrow, sloping face of rock, protected on one side by a perpendicular wall, but at the other open and precipitous. Its aspect was unpropitious, but we determined to go on. Holding by the side of the ladder next the rock, we descended, crashing and carrying down the loose rounds, so that when we got to the bottom we had cut off all communication with Albino; he could not descend, and, what was quite as inconvenient, we could not get back. It was now too late to reflect. We told Albino to throw down our torches, and go back for Indians and rope to haul us out. In the mean time we moved on by a broken, winding passage, and, at the distance of about two hundred feet, came to the top of a ladder eight feet long, at the foot of which we entered a low and stifling passage; and crawling along this on our hands and feet, at the distance of about three hundred feet we came to a rocky basin full of water. Before reaching it one of our torches had gone out, and the other was then expiring. From the best calculation I can make, which is not far out of the way, we were then fourteen hundred feet from the mouth of the cave, and at a perpendicular depth of four hundred and fifty feet. As may be supposed from what the reader already knows of these wells, we were black with smoke, grimed with dirt, and dripping with perspiration. Water was the most pleasant spectacle that could greet our eyes; but it did not satisfy us to drink it only, we wanted a more thorough benefit. Our expiring torch warned us to forbear, for in the dark we might never be able to find our way back to upper earth; but, trusting that if we did not reappear in the course of the week Mr. Catherwood would come to the rescue, we whipped off our scanty covering, and stepped into the pool. It was just large enough to prevent us from interfering with each other, and we achieved a bath which, perhaps, no white man ever before took at that depth under ground.

The Indians call this basin Chacka, which means agua colorada, or red water; but this we did not know at the time, and we did not discover it, for to economize our torch we avoided flaring it, and it lay on the rock like an expiring brand, admonishing us that it was better not to rely wholly upon our friends in the world above, and that it would be safer to look out for ourselves. Hurrying out, we made a rapid toilet, and, groping our way back, with our torch just bidding us farewell, we reached the foot of the broken ladder, and could go no farther. Albino returned with Indians and ropes. We hauled ourselves up, and got back to the open chamber from which the passages diverged; and here the Indians pointed out another, which we followed till it became lower than any we had yet explored; and, according to Doctor Cabot's measurement, at the distance of four hundred and one paces, by mine, three hundred and ninety-seven, we came to another basin of water. This, as we afterward learned, is called Puɔuelha, meaning that it ebbs and flows like the sea. The Indians say that it recedes with the south wind, and increases with the northwest; and they add that when they go to it silently they find water; but when they talk or make a noise the water disappears. Perhaps it is not so capricious with white men, for we found water, and did not approach it with sealed lips. The Indians say, besides, that forty women once fainted in this passage, and that now they do not allow the women to go to it alone. In returning we turned off twice by branching passages, and reached two other basins of water; and when we got back to the foot of the great staircase, exhausted and almost worn out, we had the satisfaction of learning, from friends who were waiting to hear our report, that there were seven in all, and we had missed three. All have names given them by the Indians, two of which I have already mentioned.

The third is called Sallab, which means a spring; the fourth Akahba, on account of its darkness; the fifth Chocohá, from the circumstance of its being always warm; the sixth Oɔiha, from being of a milky colour; and the seventh Chimaisha, because it has insects called ais.

It was a matter of some regret that we were not able to mark such peculiarities or differences as might exist in these waters, and particularly that we were not provided with barometer and thermometer to ascertain the relative heights and temperatures. If we had been at all advised beforehand, we should at least have carried the latter with us, but always in utter ignorance of what we were to encounter, our great object was to be as free as possible from all encumbrances; besides which, to tell the truth, we did some things in that country, among which was the exploring of these caves, for our own satisfaction, and without much regard to the claims of science. The surface of the country is of transition or mountain limestone; and though almost invariably the case in this formation, perhaps here to a greater extent than anywhere else, it abounds in fissures and caverns, in which springs burst forth suddenly, and streams pursue a subterranean course. But the sources of the water and the geological formation of the country were, at the moment, matters of secondary interest to us. The great point was the fact, that from the moment when the wells in the plaza fail, the whole village turns to this cave, and four or five months in the year derives from this source its only supply. It was not, as at Xcoch, the resort of a straggling Indian, nor, as at Chack, of a small and inconsiderable rancho. It was the sole and only watering place of one of the most thriving villages in Yucatan, containing a population of seven thousand souls; and perhaps even this was surpassed in wonder by the fact that, though for an unknown length of time, and through a great portion of the year, files of Indians, men and women, are going out every day with cantaros on their backs, and returning with water, and though the fame of the Cueva of Bolonchen extends throughout Yucatan, from the best information we could procure, not a white man in the village had ever explored it.

We returned to the casa real, made a lavation, which we much needed, and went over to the cura's to dine. If he had not reminded us beforehand that it was Friday and Lent, we should not have discovered it. In fact, we were not used to dainties, and perhaps the good cura thought we had never dined before. It was not in nature to think of moving that afternoon, and, besides, we were somewhat at a loss what to do. The cura had unsettled our plans. He had made inquiries, and been informed that there were no ruins at San Antonio, but only a cueva, and we had had enough of these to last us for some time; moreover, he advised us of other ruins, of which we had not heard before. These were on the rancho of Santa Ana, belonging to his friend Don Antonio Cerbera, the alcalde. Don Antonio had never seen them, but both he and the cura said they intended to visit them; and they spoke particularly of a casa cerrada, or closed house, which, as soon as the dry season came on, they intended to visit con bombas, to blow it up! The cura was so bent upon our visiting this place, that almost in spite of ourselves we were turned in that direction.

CHAPTER IX

Early the next morning we resumed our journey. On leaving the village we were soon again in the wilderness. Albino remained behind to breakfast; we had not gone far before we came to a fork of the road, and took one of the branches, by which we missed our way, and rode on over a great plain covered with bushes above our horses' heads, the path finally becoming so completely choked up that it was impossible to continue. We turned back and took another; and, keeping as near as possible, by the compass, what we understood to be the direction, came out upon a muddy aguada, covered with weeds, and beyond this a sugar rancho, the first we had seen in Yucatan, indicating that we were entering a different section of country. We had escaped the region of eternal stones, and the soil was rich and loamy. A league beyond this we reached the rancho of Santa Rosa. It was a very rare thing in this country to notice any place for its beauty of situation, but we were struck with this, though perhaps its beauty consisted merely in standing upon a slight elevation, and commanding a view of an open country.

The major domo was somewhat surprised at the object of our visit. The ruins were about two leagues distant, but he had never seen them, and had no great opinion of ruins generally. He immediately sent out, however, to notify the Indians to be on the ground in the morning, and during the evening he brought in one who was to be our guide. By way of getting some idea of the ruins, we showed him some of Mr. Catherwood's drawings, and asked him if his bore any resemblance to them. He looked at them all attentively, and pointed to the blanks left for the doorways as the points of resemblance; from his manner we got the impression that we should have to thank the cura for a bootless visit.

The night at this rancho was a memorable one. We were so scourged by fleas that sleep was impossible. Mr. Catherwood and Dr. Cabot resorted to the Central American practice of sewing up the sheets into a bag, and all night we were in a fever.

The next morning we started for the ruins of Labphak, taking care to carry our luggage with us, and not intending, under any circumstances, to return. The major domo accompanied us. It was luxurious to ride on a road free from stones. In an hour we entered a forest of fine trees, and a league beyond found a party of Indians, who pointed us to a narrow path just opened, wilder than anything we had yet travelled. After following this some distance, the Indians stopped, and made signs to us to dismount. Securing the horses, and again following the Indians, in a few minutes we saw peering through the trees the white front of a lofty building, which, in the imperfect view we had of it, seemed the grandest we had seen in the country. It had three stories, the uppermost consisting of a bare dead wall, without any doorways, being, the Indians told us, the casa cerrada, or closed house, which the cura and alcalde intended to open con bombas. The whole building, with all its terraces, was overgrown with gigantic trees. The Indians cutting a path along the front, we moved on from door to door, and wandered through its desolate chambers. For the first time in the country we found interior staircases, one of which was entire, every step being in its place. The stones were worn, and we almost expected to see the foot-prints of the former occupants. With hurried interest we moved on till we reached the top. This commanded an extensive view over a great wooded and desolate plain, to which the appearance of the heavens gave at the moment an air of additional dreariness. The sky was overcast, and portended the coming of another Norte. The wind swept over the ruined building, so that in places we were obliged to cling to the branches of the trees to save ourselves from falling. An eagle stayed his flight through the air and hovered over our heads. At a great height Doctor Cabot recognised it as one of a rare species, the first which he had seen in the country, and stood with his gun ready, hoping to carry it home with him as a memorial of the place; but the proud bird soared away.

It seemed almost sacrilege to disturb the repose in which this building lay, and to remove its burial shroud, but soon, amid the ringing of the axe and machete, and the crash of falling trees, this feeling wore away. We had thirty Indians, who, working under the direction of the major domo, were equal to forty or fifty in our hands, and there was the most glorious excitement I had experienced in walking along these terraces, with Albino and the major domo to convey my directions to the Indians. Indeed, I can hardly imagine a higher excitement than to go through that country with a strong force, time, and means at command, to lay bare the whole region in which so many ruined cities are now buried.

In the mean time Mr. Catherwood, still an invalid, and deprived of sleep the night before, had his hammock slung in an apartment at the top of the building. By afternoon the clearing was finished, and he made his drawing, which appears in Plate XIX.

The lowest range or story is one hundred and forty-five feet in length. The roof and a portion of the façade have fallen, and almost buried the centre doorways. The apartments containing the staircases are indicated hereinafter in Figure 8. Each staircase consists of two flights, with a platform at the head of the first, which forms the foot of the second, and they lead out upon the roof, under the projection which stands like a watchtower in the wall of the second range, and from this range two interior staircases lead out in the same way to the platform of the third.

The reader will observe that in the second and third ranges there are no openings of any kind except those at the head of the staircases, but simply a plain, solid wall. At first sight of this wall we thought we had really at last found a casa cerrada, and almost wished for the cura with his bombas. The major domo, looking up at it, called it so; but it seemed strange that such a character had ever been ascribed to it; for, barely working our way round the platform of the terrace, we found ranges of doorways opening into apartments, and that this was merely what we had often seen before, a back wall without doors or windows. And we made another much more interesting and important discovery. The elevation which we came upon first, facing the west, and shown in the engraving, noble and majestic as it was,

Plate XIX

F Catherwood

J N Gimbrede

LABPHAK.

was acutally the rear of the building, and the front, facing the east, presented the tottering remains of the grandest structure that now rears its ruined head in the forests of Yucatan.

In front was a grand courtyard, with ranges of ruined buildings, forming a hollow square, and in the centre a gigantic staircase rose from the courtyard to the platform of the third story. On the platform of the second terrace, at each end, stood a high square building like a tower, with the remains of rich ornaments in stucco; and on the platform of the third, at the head of the grand staircase, one on each side of it, stood two oblong buildings, their façades adorned with colossal figures and ornaments in stucco, seemingly intended as a portal to the structure on the top. In ascending the grand staircase, cacique, priest, or stranger had before him this gorgeously ornamented portal, and passed through it to enter the centre apartment of the upper story.

This apartment, however, does not correspond with the grandeur of the approach, and, according to our understanding of proprieties, the view of it is attended with disappointment. It is twenty-three feet long, only five feet six inches wide, and perfectly plain, without painting or ornament of any kind. But in this lofty chamber were strange memorials, tokens of recent occupation, indicating, amid the desolation and solitude around, that within a few years this ruined edifice, from which the owners had perhaps fled in terror, or been driven by the sword, had been the refuge and abode of man. In the holes of the archway were poles for the support of hammocks, and at each end were swinging shelves made of twigs and rods. When the cholera swept like a scourge over this isolated country, the inhabitants of the villages and ranchos fled for safety to the mountains and the wilderness. This desolate building was repeopled, this lofty chamber was the abode of some scared and stricken family, and here, amid hardships and privations, they waited till the angel of death passed by.

Figure 8 represents the ground-plan of the lower range. It consists of ranges of narrow apartments on all four of the sides, opening outward, and the reader will see that it has fitness, and uniformity of design and proportion. The grand staircase, forty feet wide, is indicated in the engraving. The interior, represented in black, forms the foundation for the support of the two upper ranges. It is cut off and enclosed on all sides by the inner wall, has no communication with any of the apartments, and is apparently a solid mass. Whether it really is solid or contains apart-

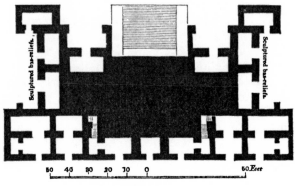

FIG. 8

ments, remains, as in other structures of the same kind, a question for the investigation of future explorers. Under the circumstances attending our visit, we were utterly unable to attempt anything of the kind.

The reader will notice in the plan two places marked "sculptured bas-reliefs." In these places are carved tablets set in the wall, as at Palenque, and, except at Palenque, this was the only place in all our wanderings in which we found bas-reliefs thus disposed. We were now moving in the direction of Palenque, though, of course, at a great distance from it; the face of the country was less stony, and the discovery of these bas-reliefs, and the increase and profusion of stuccoed ornaments, induced the impression that, in getting beyond the great limestone surface, the builders of these cities had adapted their style to the materials at hand, until, at Palenque, instead of putting up great façades of rudely-carved stone, they decorated the exterior with ornaments in stucco, and, having fewer carved ornaments, bestowed upon them more care and skill.

Plate XX represents the bas-reliefs referred to. Though resembling those at Palenque in general character and detail of ornament, they are greatly inferior in design and execution. Standing in the outer wall, they are much defaced and worn; the tablets on the south, both in the drawing and Daguerreotype view, presented a confused appearance. Both were composed of separate stones; but the subjects on the different pieces appeared, in some cases, to want adaptation to each other, and almost suggested the belief that they were fragments of other tablets, put together without much regard to design of any kind.

Night was almost upon us when Albino inquired in what

Plate XX

LABPHAK.
Bas relief in Stone.

F. Catherwood

apartment he should hang up our hammocks. In the interest of our immediate occupations we had not thought of this; a buzzing in the woods gave ominous warning of moschetoes, and we inclined to the highest range; but it was unsafe to carry our things up, or to move about the broken terraces in the dark. We selected, as the most easy of access, the rooms indicated in the engraving by the second doorway on the left, which, as the reader may see, was partly encumbered in front by the ruins of the façade on the right. We secured the doorway against moschetoes with the black muslin used for the Daguerreotype tent. The kitchen was established in the corner room, and as soon as all was arranged we called in the servants, and associated them with us in an interesting and extraordinary sitting, as a committee of ways and means. The horses were well provided for in the way of green food, for many of the trees cut down were noble ramons, but there was neither corn nor water, and we were equally destitute ourselves. Except our staple stock of tea, coffee, chocolate, and a few rolls of Bolonchen bread (like all the bread of that country, sweetened, and only made to be used with chocolate), we had nothing. Morning would break upon us without materials for a breakfast. Summary measures were necessary, and I went out to consult with the major domo and the Indians. They had made a clearing near the horses, had their hammocks swung under the trees, and a large fire in the centre. All vacated their hammocks, and were docile as doves until I mentioned the necessity of sending immediately for provisions. Completely the creatures of habit, used to ending their labours with the sun, and then to gossip and repose, they could not bear to be disturbed. Money was no object to them; and but for the major domo I, should not have been able to accomplish anything. He selected two, each of whom was intrusted with part of the commission, as one could not remember all the items, and a written memorandum would, of course, be of no use. There was one article, the procuring of which was doubtful, and that was an olla, or earthen pot, for cooking; no Indian had more than one in his hut, and that was always in use. Our messengers were instructed to buy, hire, or beg, or get in any other way their ingenuity might suggest, but not to come back without one.

Relieved in this important matter, the encampment under the trees, with the swarthy figures of the Indians lighted by the fire, presented a fine spectacle, and, but for the apprehension of moschetoes, I should have been tempted to hang up my hammock among them. As I returned, the moon was beaming magnificently over the clearing, lighting up the darkness of the woods, and illuminating the great white building from its foundation to the summit.

We had some apprehensions for the night. My hammock was swung in the front apartment. Directly over my head, in the layer of flat stones along the arch, was the dim outline of a faded red painting like that first seen at Kewick. On the walls were the prints of the mysterious red hand, and around were the tokens of recent occupation before referred to, adding strength to the reflection always pressing upon our minds, what tales of fear and wonder these old walls, could they speak, might disclose. We had a large fire built in one corner of the apartment, but we heard no moschetoes, and there were no fleas. During the night we all woke up at the same moment, only to congratulate each other and enjoy the consciousness of feeling ourselves free from these little nuisances.

Our first business the next morning was to send our horses off to drink, and to procure water for ourselves, for the Indians had exhausted all that was found in the hollows of the rocks. At eleven o'clock our emissaries returned with fowls, eggs, tortillas, and an olla, the last of which they had hired for a medio, but for that day only.

Except a small ruined structure which we passed on the way to this building, as yet we had seen only this one with the ranges around the courtyard. It was clear that it did not stand alone; but we were so completely buried in the woods that it was utterly impossible to know which way to turn in search of others. In making our clearing we had stumbled upon two circular holes, like those found at Uxmal, which the Indians called chultunes, or cisterns, and which they said existed in all parts, and Doctor Cabot, in pursuit of a bird, had found a range of buildings at but a short distance, disconnected from each other, and having their façades ornmaented with stucco.

Going out to the path from which we had turned off to reach this edifice, and proceeding upon it a short distance, we saw through the trees the corner of a large building, which proved to be a great parallelogram, enclosing a hollow square. In the centre of the front range a grand but ruined staircase ascended from the ground to the top of the building, and, crossing the flat roof, we found a corresponding staircase leading down into the courtyard. The richest ornaments were on the side facing the courtyard, being of stucco, and on each side of the staircase were some of new and curious design, but, unfor-

tunately, they were all in a ruinous condition. The whole courtyard was overgrown, so that the buildings facing it were but
indistinctly visible, and in some places not at all.

In the afternoon the wind increased to a regular Norther,
and at night all the Indians were driven in by the rain.

The next day the rain continued, and the major domo left
us, taking with him nearly all the Indians. This put an end to
the clearing, Mr. Catherwood had a recurrence of fever, and in
the intervals of sunshine Dr. Cabot and myself worked with the
Daguerreotype.

In the mean time, from the difficulty of procuring water
and necessaries, we found our residence at these ruins uncomfortable. Our Indians, whom we had engaged to carry our luggage, complained of the detention, and, to crown our troubles,
the owner of the olla came, and insisted upon having it returned.
Mr. Catherwood, too, was unable to work, the woods were wet
with the rain, and we considered it advisable to change the
scene. There is no place which we visited that we were so reluctant to leave unfinished, and none that better deserved a month's
exploration. It remains a rich and almost unbroken field for the
future explorer, and, that he may have something to excite his
imagination, and, at the same time, to show that the love of the
marvellous is not confined to any one country, I may add that,
upon the strength of a letter of mine to a friend in the interior,
giving an account of the discovery of this place, and mentioning
the vestiges of six buildings, we found, on our return to Merida,
that these six had gone on accumulating, and had not been
fairly brought to a stop till they had reached six hundred!

CHAPTER X

On Thursday, the twenty-fourth of February, we broke up and left the ruins. A narrow path brought us out into the camino real, along which we passed several small ranchos of sugar-cane. At eleven o'clock we reached the hacienda of Jalasac, the appearance of which, after a few days' burial in the woods, was most attractive and inviting; and here we ventured to ask for water for our horses. The master made us dismount, sent our horses to an aguada, and had some oranges picked from the tree, sliced, and sprinkled with sugar, for ourselves. He told us that his establishment was nothing compared with Señor Trego's, a league distant, whom, he said, we, of course, knew, and would doubtless stop with a few days. Not remembering ever to have heard of Señor Trego before, we had not formed unalterably any such intention, but it was manifest that all the world, and we in particular, ought to know Señor Trego; and we concluded that we would do him the honour of a visit as we passed through. This gentleman had forty criados, or servants, engaged in making sugar. And, on entering the sugar region, I may suggest that Yucatan seems to present some advantages for the cultivation of this necessary; not in the interior, on account of the expense of transportation, but along the coast, the whole line from Campeachy to Tobasco being good for that purpose, and within reach of a foreign market. The advantages are, first, that slave labour is dispensed with, and, secondly and consequently, no outlay of capital is necessary for the purchase of slaves. In Cuba or Louisiana the planter must reckon among his expenses the interest upon the capital invested in the purchase of slaves, and the cost of maintaining them. In Yucatan he has to incur no outlay of capital; Indian labour is considered by those who have examined into the subject in Cuba, as about the same with that of the negroes; and by furnishing them constant employment, Indians can be procured in any numbers at a real per day, which is less than the interest upon the cost of a negro, and less than the expense of maintaining him if he cost nothing.

Resuming our journey, at the distance of a league we reached another rancho, which would have been creditable in any country for its neatness and arrangement. Our road ran through a plaza, or square, with large seybo trees in the centre, and neat white houses on all the sides; and before the door of one of them we saw a horse and cart! an evidence of civilization which we had not seen till that time in the country. This could be no other than Señor Trego's. We stopped in the shade, Señor Trego came out of the principal house, told the servants to take our chances for a dinner, we said nothing. Entering the house, were a little surprised, but, as we were very uncertain about our chances for a dinner, we said nothing. Entering the house, we fell into fine large hammocks; and Señor Trego told us that we were welcome on our own account, even without the recommendation of the padre Rodriguez of Xul. This gave us a key to the mystery. The padre Rodriguez had given us a letter to some one on this road, which we had accidentally left behind, and did not know the name of the person to whom it was addressed; but we now remembered that the cura, in speaking of him, had said deliberately, as if feeling the full import of his words, that he was rich and his friend; and we remembered, too, that the padre had frankly read to us the letter before giving it, in which, not to compromise himself with a rich friend, he had recommended us as worthy of Señor Trego's best offices upon our paying all costs and expenses; but we had reason to believe that the honest padre had reversed the custom of more polished lands, and that his private advices had given a liberal interpretation to his cautious open recommendation. At all events, Señor Trego made us feel at once that there was to be no reserve in his hospitality; and when he ordered some lemonade to be brought in immediately, we did not hesitate to suggest the addition of two fowls boiled, with a little rice thrown in.

While these were in preparation, Señor Trego conducted us round to look at his establishment. He had large sugar-works, and a distillery for the manufacture of habanera; and in the yard of the latter was a collection of enormous black hogs, taking a siesta in a great pool of mud, most of them with their snouts barely above water, a sublime spectacle for one interested in their lard and tallow, and Señor Trego told us that in the evening a hundred more, quite equal to these, would come in to scramble for their share of the bed. To us the principal objects of interest were in the square, being a well, covered over and dry, dug nearly to the depth of six hundred feet without reaching water, and the great seybo trees, which had been planted by Señor Trego himself; the oldest being of but twelve years' growth, and more extraordinary for its rapid luxuriance than that before referred to as existing at Ticul.

At four o'clock we resumed our journey, and toward dark, passing some miserable huts in the suburbs, we reached the new village of Iturbide, standing on the outposts of civilization, the great point to which the tide of emigration was rolling, the Chicago of Yucatan.

The reader may not consider the country through which we have been travelling as over-burdened with population, but in certain parts, particularly in the district of Nohcacab, the people did so consider it. Crowded and oppressed by the large landed proprietors, many of the enterprising yeomanry of this district determined to seek a new home in the wilderness. Bidding farewell to friends and relatives, after a journey of two days and a half they reached the fertile plains of Zibilnocac, from time immemorial an Indian rancho. Here the soil belonged to the government; every man could take up what land he pleased, full scope was offered to enterprise, and an opportunity for development not afforded by the over-peopled region of Nohcacab. Long before reaching it we had heard of this new pueblo and its rapid increase. In five years, from twenty-five inhabitants it had grown into a population of fifteen or sixteen hundred; and, familiar as we were with new countries and the magical springing up of cities in the wilderness, we looked forward to it as a new object of curiosity and interest.

The approach was by a long street, at the head of which, and in the entrance to the plaza, we saw a gathering, which in that country seemed a crowd, giving an indication of life and activity not usual in the older villages; but drawing nearer, we noticed that the crowd was stationary, and, on reaching it, we found that, according to an afternoon custom, all the principal inhabitants were gathered around a card-table, playing monte; rather a bad symptom, but these hardy pioneers exhibited one good trait of character in their close attention to the matter in hand. They gave us a passing glance and continued the game. Hanging on the outskirts of the crowd, however, were some who, not having the wherewithal to join in the stakes, bestowed themselves upon us. Among them was one who claimed us as acquaintances, and said that he had been anxiously looking for us. He had kept the "run" of us as far as Bolonchen, but had then lost us entirely, and was relieved when we accounted for ourselves by mentioning our disappearance in the woods of Labphak. This gentleman was about fifty, dressed in the light costume of the place, with straw hat and sandals, and it was no great recommendation to him when he told us that he had made our acquaintance at Nohcacab. He was an emigrant from that place, and on a visit when he saw us there. He claimed Dr. Cabot more particularly as his friend, and the latter remembered receiving from him some really friendly offices. He apologized for not being able to show us many attentions at that place; it was his pueblo, but he had no house there; this was his home, and here he could make amends. He told us that this was a new village, and had but few accommodations; the casa real had no doors, or they were not yet put on. He undertook to provide for us, however, and conducted us to a house adjoining that of his brother, and belonging to the latter, on the corner of the plaza. It had a thatched roof, and perhaps, by this time, the floor is cemented; but then it was covered with the lime and earth for making the cement, taking a good impression from every footstep, and throwing up some dust. It was, however, already in use as a store-room for the shop on the corner, and had demijohns, water-jars, and bundles of tobacco stowed along the wall; the middle was vacant, but there was no chair, bench, or table; but by an energetic appeal to the lookers-on these were obtained.

Our Nohcacab friend was most efficient in his attentions, and, in fact, constituted himself a committee to receive us; and after repeating frequently that at Nohcacab, though it was his village, he had no house, &c., he came to the point by inviting us forthwith to his house to take chocolate.

Tired of the crowd, and wanting to be alone, we declined, and unluckily assigned as a reason that we had ordered chocolate to be prepared. He went away with the rest, but very soon returned, and said that we had given him a bofetada, or rebuff, and had cheapened him in the estimation of his people. As he seemed really hurt, we directed our preparations to be discontinued, and went with him to his house, where we had a cup of very poor chocolate, which he followed up by telling us that we must eat at his house during the whole of our stay in the village, and that we must not spend a cent for la comida, or food. Our daily expenses at Nohcacab, he said, were enormous; and when we left he escorted us home, carrying with him a little earthen vessel containing castor oil with a wick in it, and said we must not spend any money for candles, and again came to the point by insisting upon our promising to dine at his house the next day.

In the mean time Albino had inquired him out, and we found that we had secured a valuable acquaintance. Don Juan was one of the oldest settlers, and one of the most influential inhabitants. He was not then in public office, but he was highly connected. One of his brothers was first alcalde, and another keeper of the gambling-table.

We considered his attentions for the evening at an end, but in a short time he entered abruptly, and with a crowd at his heels. This time he was really welcome, for he called us out to look at a lunar rainbow, which the people, looking at it in connexion with our visit and its strange objects, considered rather ominous, and Don Juan himself was not entirely at ease; but it did not disturb the gentlemen around the gambling-table, who had, in the mean time, to avoid the night air, moved under the shed of the proprietor, Don Juan's brother and our landlord.

The next morning a short time enabled us to see all the objects of interest in the new village of Iturbide. Five years before the plough had run over the ground now occupied by the plaza, or, more literally, as the plough is not known in Yucatan, the plaza is on the ground formerly occupied by an old milperia, or cornfield. In those ancient days it was probably enclosed by a bush fence; now, at one corner rises a thatched house, with an arbour before it, and a table under the arbour, at which, perhaps, at this moment the principal inhabitants are playing monte. Opposite, on the other corner, stood, and still stands if it has not fallen down, a casa de paja (thatched house) from which the thatching had been blown away, and in which were the undisposed-of remains of an ox for sale. Along the sides were whitewashed huts, and on one corner a large, neat house, belonging

to our friend Señor Trego; then a small edifice with a cross in
the roof, marking it as a church; and, finally, an open casa
publica, very aptly so called, as it had no doors. Such are the
edifices which in five years have sprung up in the new village of
Iturbide; and attached to each house was a muddy yard, where
large black pigs were wallowing in the mire, the special objects
of their owner's care, soon to become large black hogs, and to
bring ten or twelve dollars a piece in the Campeachy market.
But, interesting as it is to watch the march of improvement, it
was not for these we had come to Iturbide. Within the plaza
were memorials of older and better times, indications of a more
ingenious people than the civilized whites by whom it is now
occupied. At one end was a mound of ruins, which had once
supported an ancient building; and in the centre was an ancient
well, unchanged from the time of its construction, and then, as
for an unknown length of time before, supplying water to the
inhabitants. There could be no question about the antiquity of
this well; the people all said that it was a work of the antiguos,
and paid respect to it and valued it highly on that account, for
it had saved them the labour and expense of digging a new one
for themselves.

It was about a yard and a quarter wide at the mouth, and
seven or eight yards in depth, circular, and constructed of stones
laid without plaster or cement of any kind. The stones were all
firmly in their places, and had a polish which, with creases made
by ropes in the platform at the top, indicated the great length
of time that water had been drawn from it.

Besides these memorials, from a street communicating with
the plaza we saw a range of great mounds, the ruins of the ancient city of Zibilnocac, which had brought us to Iturbide.

Don Juan was ready to accompany us to the ruins, and
while he was waiting at our door, one person and another came
along and joined him, until we had an assemblage of all the
respectable citizens, apparently just risen from the gambling-
table, of wan and miserable aspect, and, though they had ponchas wrapped about them, shivering with cold.

On the way to the ruins we passed another ancient well, of
the same construction with that in the plaza, but filled up with
rubbish, and useless. The Indians called it Stu-kum, from a subject familiar to them, and presenting not a bad idea of a useless
well; the word meaning a calabash with the seeds dried up. A
short walk brought us into an open country, and among the
towering ruins of another ancient city. The field was in many

places clear of trees, and covered only with plantations of tobacco, and studding it all over were lofty ranges and mounds, enshrouded in woods, through which white masses of stone were glimmering, and rising in such quick succession, and so many at once, that Mr. Catherwood, in no good condition for work, said, almost despondingly, that the labours of Uxmal were to begin again.

Among them was one long edifice, having at each end what seemed a tower; and, attended by our numerous escort, we approached it first. It was difficult to imagine what could have procured us the honour of their company. They evidently took no interest in the ruins, could give us no information about them, nor even knew the paths that led to them; and we could not flatter ourselves that it was for the pleasure of our society. The building before us was more ruined than it seemed from a distance, but in some respects it differed from all the others we had seen. It required much clearing; and when this was signified to our attendants, we found that among them all there was not a single machete. Generally, on these occasions, there were some who were ready to work, and even on the look-out for a job; but among these thriving people there was not one who cared to labour in any capacity but that of a looker-on. A few, however, were picked out as by general consent the proper persons to work, upon whom all the rest fell and drove them to the village for their machetes. At the same time, many of those who remained took advantage of the opportunity to order their breakfast sent out, and all sat down to wait. Mr. Catherwood, already unwell, worried by their chattering, lay down in his poncha on the ground, and finally became so ill that he returned to the house. In the mean time I went to the foot of the building, where, after loitering more than an hour, I heard a movement overhead, and saw a little boy of about thirteen cutting among the branches of a tree. Half a dozen men placed themselves within his hearing, and gave him directions to such an extent that I was obliged to tell them I was competent to direct one such lad myself. In a little while another lad of about fifteen joined him, and for some time these boys were the only persons at work, while lazy beggars were crouching on every projecting stone, industriously engaged in looking at them. Finally, one man came along with his machete, and then others, until five were at work. They were occupied the greater part of the day, but to the last there were some trees, obstructing the view of particular parts, which I could not get cut down. All this time the spectators remained looking on as if in expectation of some grand finale; toward the last they began to show symptoms of anxiety, and during this time, through the unintentional instrumentality of Don Juan, I had made a discovery. The fame of the Daguerreotype, or la machina, had reached their ears, greatly exaggerated. They, of course, knew but little about it, but had come out with the expectation of seeing its miraculous powers exercised. If the reader be at all malicious, he will sympathize in my satisfaction, when all was cleared and ready to be drawn, in paying the men and walking back to the village, leaving them sitting on the stones.

The untoward circumstances of the morning threw Don Juan into a somewhat anxious state; he had incurred the expense of preparations, and was uncertain whether we intended to do him the honour of dining with him; apprehensive of another bofetada, he was afraid to mention the subject, but on reaching his house he sent to give notice that dinner was ready, and to inquire when he should send it to us. To make amends, and again conciliate, we answered that we would dine at his house, which he acknowledged through Albino as a much higher honour.

His house was on the principal street, but a short distance from the plaza, and one of the first erected, and the best in the place. He had been induced to settle in Iturbide on account of the facilities and privileges offered by the government, and the privilege which he seemed to value most was that of selling out. As he told us himself, when he came he was not worth a medio, and he seemed really to have held his own remarkably well. But appearances were deceitful, for he was a man of property. His house, including doors and a partition at one end, had cost him thirty dollars. The doors and partition his neighbours regarded as a piece of pretension, and he himself supposed that these might have been dispensed with, but he had no children, and did not mind the expense. At one end of the room was a rude frame, supporting the image of a tutelary saint. Near it was a stick thrust into the mud floor, with three prongs at the upper end, in which rested an earthen vessel containing castor oil, with a wick in it, to light up the mansion at night; a sort of bar with bottles containing agua ardiente flavoured with anise, for retailing to the Indians, which, with a small table and three hammocks, constituted the furniture of Don Juan's house. These last served for chairs, but as he had never anticipated the extraordinary event of dining three persons, they could not be brought into right juxtaposition to the table. Consequently, we sent for our two borrowed chairs, and, with the table in front of one of the hammocks, we were all seated except our host, who proposed to wait upon us. There was one aristocratic arrangement in Don Juan's household. His kitchen was on the other side of the street, a rickety old frame of poles, and Don Juan, after running across several times, bare-headed, to watch the progress of the dinner, returned and threw himself into a hammock a little within the doorway, crying out across the street, "Trae la comida, muchacha." "Bring the dinner, girl." The first course included a bowl of soup, a plate of rice, and three spoons; rather an alarming intimation, but at the same time rather grand, and much better than the alternative that sometimes happened, of three plates and one spoon, or none at all; and all apprehension was dissipated by the reappearance of the girl with another bowl and plate. Don Juan himself followed with each hand full, and we had a bowl, plate, and spoon apiece. The contents disposed of, another dish was served, which, by counting the wings and legs, we ascertained to be the substance of two fowls; and while attending to them, we were engaged in the friendly office, which guests but rarely do for their host, of calculating the expense he was incurring. We had too good an opinion of Don Juan's shrewdness to believe that he was making this lavish expenditure in mere wantonness, and wondered what he could expect to get out of us in return. We had hardly begun to speculate upon this when, as if knowing what was passing in our minds, he called in his wife, a respectable-looking elderly person, and disclosed another design upon the Daguerreotype. At Nohcacab he had heard of portraits being taken, and wanted one of his wife, and he was somewhat disappointed, and, perhaps, went over the calculation we had just made, when he learned that, as there were no subjects on which it could be used to advantage, we had determined not to open the apparatus.

But he did not let us off yet. His next attempt was upon Dr. Cabot, and this, too, was in favour of his old wife. Taking her by the hand, he led her before the doctor, and, with an earnestness that gave dignity to his scanty wearing apparel, and ought to have found its way to the depths of medical science, explained the nature of her maladies. It was really a delicate case, and made more so by the length of time that had elapsed since marriage. No such case had ever occurred in my practice, and even Doctor Cabot was at a loss.

While the matter was under discussion several men came in. No doubt they had all received a hint to drop in at that hour. One had an asthma, another a swelling, and there were so many of Don Juan's friends afflicted that we made an abrupt retreat.

In the evening Don Juan's brother, the alcalde, called upon Dr. Cabot for advice for a sick child, which the course he was pursuing would soon have put beyond the reach of medicine. Doctor Cabot made him desist, and in the morning it was so much better that all the people conceived a good opinion of his abilities, and determined to patronise him in earnest.

The condition of the whole country in regard to medical aid is deplorable. Except at Campeachy and Merida there are no regular physicians, nor even apothecaries' shops. In the villages where there are curas, the whole duty of attending the sick devolves upon them. They have, of course, no regular medical education, but practise upon some old treatise or manuscript recipes, and even in their small practice they are trammelled by want of medicines. But in villages where there are no curas, there is no one to prescribe for the sick. The rich go to Campeachy or Merida, and put themselves under the hands of a physician; the poor linger and die, the victims of ignorance and empiricism.

Dr. Cabot's fame as a curer of biscos had spread throughout the country, and whenever we reached a village there was a curiosity, which threw Mr. Catherwood and me into the shade, to see the medico. Frequently we overheard the people say, "Tan joven," "So young;" "Es muchacho," "He is a boy;" for they associated the idea of age with that of a great medico. He was often consulted upon cases for which he could not prescribe with any satisfaction. Treatment which might be proper at the moment might not answer a few days afterward, and the greatest annoyance was that, if our travelling chest could not furnish the medicine, the prescription had to wait an opportunity of beeing sent to Merida; but when the medicine arrived, the case might have altered so much that this medicine had become altogether improper for it. It is gratifying to know that, in general, his practice gave satisfaction, yet, at the same time, it must be admitted that there were complaints. The terms could not well have been made easier, but the ground of dissatisfaction was, that he did not always furnish medicine as well as advice. I do not mention this reproachfully, however; throughout the country he had a fair share of patronage, and the run reached its climax at Iturbide. Unluckily, the day on which the inhabitants resolved to take him up in earnest it rained, and we were kept nearly all the time within doors, and there were so many applications from men, women, and children, many of whom came with Don Juan's recommendation, that the doctor was seriously annoyed. Every latent disease was brought out, and he could even have found business in prescribing for cases that might possibly occur, as well as for those already existing.

The next morning Mr. Catherwood made an effort to visit the ruins. Our numerous escort of the former occasion were all missing, and, except an Indian who had a tobacco patch in the neighbourhood, we were entirely alone. This Indian held an umbrella over Mr. Catherwood's head to protect him from the sun, and, while making the drawing, several times he was obliged by weakness to lie down and rest. I was disheartened by the spectacle. Although, considering the extent of illness in our party, we had in reality not lost much time, we had been so much embarrassed, and it was so disagreeable to be moving along with this constant liability to fever and ague, that here I felt very much disposed to break up the expedition and go home, but Mr. Catherwood persisted.

Plate XXI represents the front of this building. It is one hundred and fifty-four feet in front and twenty feet seven inches in depth. It differed in form from any we had seen, and had square structures rising in the centre and at each end, as seen in ruins in the engraving; these were called towers, and at a distance had that appearance. The façades of the towers were all ornamented with sculptured stone. Several of the apartments had tobacco leaves spread out in them to dry. In the centre, one apartment was encumbered with rubbish, cutting off the light from the door, but in the obscurity we saw on one of the stones, along the layer in the arch, the dim outline of a painting like that at Kewick; in the adjoining apartment were the remains of paintings, the most interesting, except those near the village of Xul, that we had met with in the country, and, like those, in position and general effect reminding me of processions in Egyptian tombs. The colour of the flesh was red, as was always the case with the Egyptians in representing their own people. Unfortunately, they were too much mutilated to be drawn, and seemed surviving the general wreck only to show that these aboriginal builders had possessed more skill in the least enduring branch of the graphic art.

The first accounts we heard of these ruins date back to the

Plate XXI

ITURBIDE.

time of my first visit to Nohpat. Among the Indians there at work was one who, while we were lunching, sitting apart under a tree, mentioned these ruins in exaggerated terms, particularly a row of painted soldiers, as he called them, which, from his imperfect description, I supposed might bear some resemblance to the stuccoed figures on the fronts of the buildings at Palenque; but, on pushing my inquiries, he said these figures carried muskets, and was so pertinacious on this point that I concluded he was either talking entirely at random, or of the remains of old Spanish structures. I noted the place in my memorandum book, and having had it for a long time upon our minds, and received more different accounts of it than of any other, none proved more unlike what we expected to find. We looked for few remains, but these distinguished for their beauty and ornament, and high state of preservation, instead of which we found an immense field, grand, imposing, and interesting from its vastness, but all so ruined that, with the exception of this one building, little of the detail could be discovered.

Back of this building, or, rather, on the other front, was a thriving tobacco patch, the only thriving thing we saw at Iturbide; and on the border another ancient well, now, as in ages past, furnishing water, and from which the Indian attending the tobacco patch gave us to drink. Beyond were towering mounds and vestiges, indicating the existence of a greater city than any we had yet encountered. In wandering among them Dr. Cabot and myself counted thirty-three, all of which had once held buildings aloft. The field was so open that they were all comparatively easy of access, but the mounds themselves were overgrown. I clambered up them till the work became tiresome and unprofitable; they were all, as the Indians said, puras piedras, pure stones; no buildings were left; all had fallen; and though, perhaps, more than at any other place, happy that it was our fortune to wander among these crumbling memorials of a once powerful and mysterious people, we almost mourned that our lot had not been cast a century sooner, when, as we believed, all these edifices were entire.

CHAPTER XI

Our journey in this direction is now ended. We were on the frontier of the inhabited part of Yucatan, and within a few leagues of the last village. Beyond was a wilderness, stretching off to the Lake of Peten, and that region of Lacandones, or unbaptized Indians, in which, according to the suggestion made in my previous volumes, lay that mysterious city never reached by a white man, but still occupied by Indians precisely in the same state as before the discovery of America. During my sojourn in Yucatan, my account of this city was published in one of the Merida papers, and among intelligent persons there was a universal belief that beyond the Lake of Peten there was a region of unconverted Indians of whom nothing was known. We had been moving on in the track of ruined cities. A venerable ecclesiastic in Merida had furnished me with an itinerary of the journey through the wilderness to the Lake of Peten, and I had some hope of being led on from place to place until we should reach a point which might unravel all mystery, and establish a connecting link between the past and present; but this hope was accompanied by a fear, and, perhaps fortunately for us, we did not hear of ruins beyond. If we had, we should not have attempted to go in search of them, and it would have been painful to turn back. I am far from believing, however, that because we did not hear of them none exist. On the contrary, it may well be that wrecks of cities lie buried but a few leagues farther on, the existence of which is entirely unknown at the village of Iturbide, for at that place there was not a single individual who had ever heard of the ruins at Labphak, which we had visited just before, until they heard of them from us.

As yet, however, our face is still set toward the Lake of Peten. In this lake are numerous islands, one of which is called Peten Grande, Peten itself being a Maya word, signifying an island; and before turning back I wish to present this island for one moment to the reader. It now belongs to the government of Guatimala, and is under the ecclesiastical jurisdiction of the Bishop of Yucatan. Formerly it was the principal place of the province of Itza, which province, for one hundred and fifty years after the subjugation of Yucatan, maintained its fierce and native independence. In the year 1608, sixty-six years after the conquest, two Franciscan monks, alone, without arms, and in the spirit of peace, set out to conquer this province by converting the natives to Christianity. The limits of these pages will not permit me to accompany them in their toilsome and dangerous journey, but, according to the account of one of them as given by Cogolludo, at ten o'clock at night they landed on the island, were provided with a house by the king, and the next day preached to the Indians; but the latter told them that the time had not yet come for them to become Christians, and advised the monks to go away and return at some other day. Nevertheless, they carried them round to see the town, and in the middle of one of the temples they saw a great idol of the figure of a horse, made of lime and stone, seated on the ground on his haunches, with his hind legs bent, and raised on his fore feet, being intended as an image of the horse which Cortez left at that place on his great journey from Mexico to Honduras. On that occasion the Indians had seen the Spaniards fire their muskets from the backs of the horses, and supposing that the fire and noise were caused by the animals, they called this image Tzimin Chac, and adored it as the god of thunder and lightning. As the monks saw it, one of them, says the author of the account, seemed as if the Spirit of the Lord had descended upon him; and, carried away by zealous fervour, seized the foot of the horse with his hand, mounted upon the statue, and broke it in pieces. The Indians immediately cried out to kill them; but the king saved them, though they were obliged to leave the island.

In the beginning of October, 1619, the same two monks, undaunted by their previous ill success, again appeared on the island; but the people rose up against them. One of the padres remonstrated; an Indian seized him by the hair, twisted his neck, and hurled him to the ground, tearing out his hair by the roots, and throwing it away. He was picked up senseless, and, with his companion and the accompanying Indians, put on board a bad canoe, without anything to eat, and again sent away. With all their fanaticism and occasional cruelty, there is something soul-stirring in the devotion of these early monks to the business of converting the souls of the Indians.

In the year 1695, Don Martin Ursua obtained the government of Yucatan, and, in pursuance of a proposal previously submitted by him to the king, and approved by the council of the Indies, undertook the great work of opening a road across the whole continent from Campeachy to Guatimala. The opening of this road led to the conquest of Itza, and we have a full and detailed account of this conquest, written by the licenciado, or lawyer, Don Juan Villagutierres, a native of Yucatan. It is entitled, "A History of the Conquest of Itza, reduction and progress of that of Lacandon, and other barbarous Nations of Gentile Indians in the Mediacion of Yucatan and Guatimala." It was published at Madrid in the year 1701, and, what gives it great value, within four years after the events referred to took place.

The work of opening the road was begun in 1695. In prosecuting it, the Spaniards encountered vestiges of ancient buildings raised on terraces, deserted and overgrown, and apparently very ancient. These, it is true, may have been abandoned long before the conquest; but, as the Spaniards had now been in the country one hundred and fifty years, it is not unreasonable to suppose that the terror of their name may have made desolate many places which their arms never reached.

On the twenty-first of January, 1697, Don Martin de Ursua set out from Campeachy to take command of the expedition in person, with a vicar-general and assistant, already nominated by the bishop, for the province of Itza. On the last day of February he had timber cut on the borders of Peten for the construction of vessels which should convey them to the island. He sent before a proclamation, giving notice that the time had come when they should have one cup and one plate with the Spaniards. "If not," says the proclamation, "I will do what the king commands me, but which it is not necessary now to express." The thirteenth of March was appointed for the day of embarcation. Some of the

Spaniards, knowing the immense number of Indians on the island, and the difficulty of conquering it, represented to the general the rashness of his undertaking; but, says the historian, carried away by his zeal, faith, and courage, he answered that, having in view the service of God and the king, and the drawing of miserable souls from the darkness of heathenism, under the favour and protection of the Virgin Mary, whose image he carried on the royal standard, and engraven on his heart, he alone was sufficient for this conquest, even if it were much more difficult.

He embarked with one hundred and eight soldiers, leaving one hundred and twenty, with auxiliary Indians, and two pieces of artillery, as a garrison for the camp. The vicar blessed the vessel, and as the sun rose she got under way for the island, two leagues distant. The vicar offered up a prayer, and the Spaniards cried "Viva la ley de Dios!" Half way across he encountered fleets of canoes filled with warlike Indians; but taking no notice of them, and moving on toward the island, the Spaniards saw assembled immense numbers, prepared for war; Indians crowded the tops of the small islands around; the canoes followed them on the lake, and enclosed them in a half moon between themselves and the shore. As soon as within reach, the Indians, by land and water, poured upon them a shower of arrows. The general, Don Martin Ursua, cried out in a loud voice, "Silence! let no one begin fighting, for God is on our side, and there is nothing to fear." The Spaniards were enraged, but Don Martin still cried out, "Let no one fire, on pain of death!" The arrows from the shore were like thick rain. The Spaniards could scarcely be restrained, and one soldier, wounded in the arm, and enraged by the pain, fired his musket; the rest followed; the general could no longer control them, and, without waiting till they reached the shore, as soon as the oars stopped all threw themselves into the water, Don Martin de Ursua among them. The Indians were thick as if collected at the mouth of a cannon; but at the horrible noise and destruction of the fire-arms they broke and fled in terror. The vessel, with twenty soldiers, attacked the canoes, and those both in the canoes and on the land, from the king to the smallest creature, all leaped into the water, and from the island to the main nothing was to be seen but the heads of Indians, men, women, and children, swimming for life. The Spaniards entered the deserted town, and hoisted the royal standard on the highest point of Peten. With a loud voice they returned thanks to God for his mercies, and Don Martin Ursua took formal possession of the island and the territory of Itza in the name of the king. The vicar claimed it as belonging to the bishopric of Yucatan, and in stole and bonnet blessed the lake. This took place on the thirteenth of March, 1697, one hundred and fifty-five years after the foundation of Merida, and but one hundred and forty-five years ago.

We have, then, accounts of visits by the padres sixty years after the subjugation of Yucatan, and a detailed account of the conquest of Itza, one hundred and fifty-five years afterward; and what did they find on the island? The monks say that, when taken to look over the city, they went to the middle and highest part of the island to see the kues and adoratorios of the heathen idols, and that "there were twelve or more of the size of the largest churches in the villages of the Indians in the province of Yucatan, each one of which was capable of containing more than one thousand persons."

The Spanish soldiers, too, almost before they had time to sheath their blood-stained swords, were seized with holy horror at the number of adoratorios, temples, and houses of idolatry. The idols were so numerous, and of such various forms, that it was impossible to give any description of them, or even to count them; and in the private houses of these barbarous infidels, even on the benches on which they sat, were two or three small idols.

According to the historical account, there were twenty-one adoratorios, or temples. The principal one was that of the great false priest Quin-canek, first cousin of the king Canek. It was of square form, with handsome breastwork, and nine steps, all of wrought stone, and each front was about sixty feet, and very high. It is again mentioned as being in the form of a castillo, and this name, perhaps, makes a stronger impression on my mind from the fact that in the ruined cities of Chichen and Tuloom, which will be presented to the reader hereafter, there is an edifice bearing to this day the name of El Castillo, given to it by the Spaniards, doubtless, from the same resemblance to a castle which induced General Ursua to apply that name to the adoratorio in Peten. On the last step at the entrance was an idol in a squatting position, sitting close to the ground, in human form, but with a very unprepossessing countenance.

Another great adoratorio is described, of the same form and similar construction, and the rest are mentioned only with reference to the number and character of the idols they contained; but, probably, if there had been any material difference in form or construction, it would have been mentioned, and there is reason to believe that they were all alike. These descriptions are brief and general, but, in my opinion, they are sufficient to identify the adoratorios and temples on this island as being of the same general character with all the ruined buildings scattered over this country; and this presumption has great additional interest from another important consideration, for we have clear and authentic historical accounts, perhaps more reliable than any others relating to the aborigines of this country, of the very people by whom and the very time within which these kues, adoratorios, and temples were erected.

According to both Cogolludo and Villagutierres, who drew their conclusions from occurrences of such late date as to leave but little room for error, the Itzites, or people of Itza, were originally from the land of Maya, now Yucatan, and once formed part of that nation. At the time of the insurrection of the caciques of Maya, and the destruction of Mayapan, Canek, one of the rebellious caciques, got possession of the city of Chichen Itza. As it is sometimes said, on account of the foretelling of the arrival of the Spaniards by one of their prophets, but more probably on account of the insecurity of his possessions, he withdrew with his people from the province of Chichen Itza to the most hidden and impenetrable part of the mountains, and took possession of the Lake of Peten, establishing his residence on the large island which now bears that name. This emigration, according to the history, took place but about one hundred years before the arrival of the Spaniards. It follows, therefore, that all the adoratorios and temples which Don Martin Ursua found on the island must have been erected within that time. The conquest took place in March, 1697, and we have the interesting fact, that but about one hundred and forty-five years ago, within the period of two lives, a city existed occupied by unbaptized Indians, precisely in the same state as before the arrival of the Spaniards, having kues, adoratorios, and temples of the same general character with the great structures now scattered in ruins all over that country. This conclusion cannot be resisted except by denying entirely the credit of all the historical accounts existing on the subject.

And where are these kues, adoratorios, and temples now? In both my journeys into that country, it was always my intention to visit the island of Peten, and it has been a matter of deep regret that I was never able to do so; but as the result of my inquiries, particularly from the venerable cura who furnished me with the itinerary, and who lived many years on the island, I am induced to believe that there are no buildings left, but that there are feeble vestiges, not enough in themselves to attract the attention of mere curiosity, but which may possess immense antiquarian interest, as making manifest the hand of the builders of the American cities. But even if these twenty-one kues, adoratorios, or temples have entirely disappeared, not one stone being left upon another, this does not impeach the truth of the historical account that they once existed, for in the history of the Spaniards' first day on the island we have an indication of what the same ruthless spirit might accomplish in one hundred and forty-five years. General Ursua took possession of the island at half past eight o'clock in the morning, and, immediately after returning thanks to God for the victory, the first order he issued was for each captain and officer, with a party of soldiers, to proceed forthwith to different parts of the city to reconnoiter all the temples, and houses of idolaters and of individuals, and to hurl down and break the idols. The general himself set out, accompanied by the vicar and assistant, and we learn incidentally, and only as a means of conveying an idea of the multitude of idols and figures thrown down by the Spaniards, that the taking of the island having been at half past eight in the morning, they were occupied, with but little intermission, in throwing down, breaking, and burning idols and statues, from that hour until half past five in the evening, when the drum called them to eat, which, says the historian, was very necessary after so great labour; and if one day served for destroying the idols, one hundred and forty-five years, in which were erected a fort, churches, and other buildings that now exist, may well have effected the complete destruction of all the native edifices for idol worship.

I have asked where are the adoratorios and temples of Peten, and I am here tempted to ask one other question. Where are the Indians whose heads on that day of carnage and terror covered the water from the island to the main? Where are those unhappy fugitives, and the inhabitants of the other islands and of the territory of Itza? They fled before the terrible Spaniard, plunged deeper into the wilderness, and are dimly connected in my mind with that mysterious city before referred to; in fact, it is not difficult for me to believe that in the wild region beyond the Lake of Peten, never yet penetrated by a white man, Indians are now living as they did before the discovery of America; and it is almost a part of this belief that they are using and occupying adoratorios and temples like those now seen in ruins in the wilderness of Yucatan.

The reader will perhaps think that I have gone quite far enough, and that it is time to come back.

The next on our list were the ruins of Macoba, lying on the rancho of our friend the cura of Xul, and then in the actual occupation of Indians. We learned that the most direct road to this place was an Indian path, but the best way to reach it was to retrace our steps as far as the rancho of Señor Trego; at least, this was so near being the best that the opportunity of passing the night with him determined us to set out immediately by that route. We had our Indian carriers in attendance at the village; but, unluckily, while preparing to set out, Mr. Catherwood was taken with fever, and we were obliged to postpone our departure.

We had another subject of anxiety, but more moderate, in the conduct of Don Juan. He had not been near us all day, and we could not account for his neglect; but toward evening Albino learned that the night before he had lost sixteen dollars at the gaming-table, and had kept his hammock ever since.

The next day it rained. On Sunday the rain still continued. Early in the morning the ministro came over from the village of Hopochen to say mass, and, while lounging about to note the prospect in regard to the weather, I stopped under the shed where the gaming-table remained ready for use, to which, when mass was over, all the better classes came from the church in clean dresses, prepared for business.

It was a matter of some curiosity to me to know how these men lived; none of them worked. Their only regular business seemed to be that of gambling. On taking a seat among them, I learned the secret from themselves. Each man had several outstanding loans of four or five dollars made to Indians, or he had sold agua ardiente or some other trifling commodity, which created an indebtedness. This made the Indian a criado, or servant, and mortgaged his labour to the creditor or master, by the use of which, in milpas or tobacco plantations, the latter lived. By small occasional supplies of cocoa or spirit they keep alive the indebtedness; and as they keep the accounts themselves, the poor Indians, in their ignorance and simplicity, are ground to the earth to support lazy and profligate masters.

We had not formed any very exalted opinion of these people, and they did not rate themselves very high. Don Juan had told us that the Indians were all drunkards, and half the white people; and the other half had occasionally to take to the hammock; he said, too, that they were all gamblers, and the alcalde, as he shuffled the cards, confirmed it, and asked me to join them. He inquired if there was no gambling in my country, or what people did with their money if they did not gamble, and he allowed that to expend it in horses, carriages, dinners, furniture, dress, and other particulars suggested by some of them, was sensible enough; for, as he said very truly, when they died they could not carry it away with them. I mentioned that in my country gambling was forbidden by law, and that for gambling in the street, and on a Sunday, they would all be taken up and punished. This touched the alcalde in his office, and he started up with the cards in his hand, and looking indignantly at the people under his charge, said that there too it was forbidden by law; that any one who gambled, or who connived at it, or who permitted it in his house, was liable to be declared not a citizen; that they had laws, and very good ones; all knew them, but nobody minded them. Everybody gambled, particularly in that village; they had no money, but they gambled corn and tobacco, and he pointed to a man then crossing the plaza, who the night before had gambled away a hog. He admitted that sometimes it was a good way to make money, but he pointed to a miserable-looking young man, not more than two or three-and-twenty, whose father, he said, had ranchos, and Indians, and houses, and ready money, and was close-fisted, and had left all to that son, who was now looking for seven and sixpence to make up a dollar, and the young man himself, with a ghastly smile, confirmed the tale. The alcalde then continued with a running commentary upon the idleness and extravagance of the people in the village; they were all lazy, and having illustrations at hand, he pointed to an Indian just passing with three strings of beef, which, he said, had cost him a medio and a half, and would be consumed at a meal, and that Indian, he knew, had not a medio in the world to pay his capitation tax. One of the gentlemen present then suggested that the government had lately passed an iniquitous law that no Indian should be compelled to work unless he chose; if he refused, he could not be whipped or imprisoned, and what could be expected in such a state of things? Another gentleman interposed with great unction, declaring that the alcalde of a neighbouring village did not mind the law, but went on whipping the same as before. All this time a dozen Indians, by the constitution free and independent as themselves, sat on the ground without saying a word, merely staring from one to the other of the speakers.

After this the conversation turned upon our own party, and

finally settled upon Doctor Cabot. I regretted to find that, in a community which had patronised him so extensively, there was some diversity of opinion as to his qualifications. There was one dissenting voice, and the general discussion settled down into a warm argument between the two brothers of Don Juan, the alcalde and the keeper of the gambling-table, the latter of whom held up an ugly sandalled foot, with a great excrescence upon it, and said, rather depreciatingly, that the doctor did not cure his corns. The alcalde was stanch, and thrust forward his cured child, but his brother shook his head, still holding out his foot, and I am sorry to say that, so far as I could gather the sense of the community, Doctor Cabot's reputation as a medico received somewhat of a shock.

In the afternoon the rain ceased, and we bade farewell to the new village of Iturbide. As we passed, Don Juan left his place at the table to bid us goodby, and a little before dark we reached the rancho Noyaxche of Señor Trego, where we again received a cordial welcome, and in his intelligent society found a relief from the dulness of Iturbide.

CHAPTER XII

Journey resumed.—An Aguada.—The Aguadas artificial, and built by the Aboriginal Inhabitants.—Examination of one by Señor Trego.—Its Construction.—Ancient Wells.—Pits.—A Sugar Rancho.—Rancho of 'Y-a-Walthel.—Rancho of Choop.—Arrival at Macobà.—The Ruins.—Lodgings in a miserable Hut.—Wells.—Ruined Buildings.—Another Aguada.—Pits.—Astonishment of the Indians.—Falling in Love at first Sight.—Interesting Characters.—Departure.—Thick Undergrowth.—Rancho of Puut.—An Incident.—Situation of the Rancho.—Water.—Ruins of Mankeesh.

The next morning after breakfast we again set out. Señor Trego escorted us, and, following a broad wagon road made by him for the passage of the horse and cart, at the distance of a mile and a half we came to a large aguada, which is represented in Plate XXII. It was apparently a mere pond, picturesque, and shaded by trees, and having the surface covered with green water plants, called by the Indians Xicin-chah, which, instead of being regarded as a blot upon the picturesque, were prized as tending to preserve the water from evaporation. Indians were then filling their water-jars, and this aguada was the only watering-place of the rancho. These aguadas had become to us interesting objects of consideration. Ever since our arrival in the country, we had been told that they were artificial, and, like the ruined cities we were visiting, the works of the ancient inhabitants. At first we had considered these accounts unreliable, and so nearly approaching the marvellous that we put but little faith in them; but as we advanced they assumed a more definite character. We were now in a region where the people were entirely dependant upon the aguadas; all considered them the works of the antiguos; and we obtained at length what we had long sought for, certain, precise, and definite information, which would not admit of question or doubt.

Failing in his attempt to procure water from the well, before referred to, in the plaza, in 1835 Señor Trego turned his

Plate XXII

attention to this aguada. He believed that it had been used by the ancients as a reservoir, and took advantage of the dry season to make an examination, which satisfied him that his supposition was correct. For many years it had been abandoned, and it was then covered three or four feet deep with mud. At first he was afraid to undertake with much vigour the work of clearing it out, for the prejudices of the people were against it, and they feared that, by disturbing the aguada, the scanty supply then furnished might be cut off. In 1836 he procured a permission from the government, by great exertions secured the co-operation of all the ranchos and haciendas for leagues around, and at length fairly enlisting them all in the task, at one time he had at work fifteen hundred Indians, with eighty superintendents (major domos). On clearing out the mud, he found an artificial bottom of large flat stones. These were laid upon each other in this form ⌐⌐ , and the interstices were filled in with clay of red and brown colour, of a different character from any in the neighbourhood. The stones were many layers deep, and he did not go down to the bottom, lest by some accident the foundation should be injured, and the fault be imputed to him.

Near the centre, in places which he indicated as we rode along the bank, he discovered four ancient wells. These were five feet in diameter, faced with smooth stone not covered with cement, eight yards deep, and at the time of the discovery were also filled with mud. And, besides these, he found along the margin upward of four hundred casimbas, or pits, being holes into which the water filtered, and which, with the wells, were intended to furnish a supply when the aguada should be dry.

The whole bottom of the aguada, the wells, and pits, were cleared out; Señor Trego portioned off the pits among families, to be preserved and kept in order by them, and the dry basin was then given up to the floods of the rainy season. It so happened that the next year was one of unusual scarcity, and the whole country around was perfectly destitute of water. That year, Señor Trego said, more than a thousand horses and mules came to this aguada, some even from the rancho of Santa Rosa, eighteen miles distant, with barrels on their backs, and carried away water. Families established themselves along the banks; small shops for the sale of necessaries were opened, and the butcher had his shambles with meat; the aguada supplied them all, and when this failed, the wells and the pits held out abundantly till the rainy season came on, and enabled them to return to their several homes.

Throughout our journey we had suffered from the long continuance of the rainy season, and at this place we considered it one of the greatest misfortunes that attended us, that we were unable to see the bottom of this aguada and these ancient wells. Señor Trego told us that usually, at this season, the aguada was dry, and the people were drawing from the wells and pits. This year, happily for them, but unluckily for us, water was still abundant. Still it was a thing of high interest to see this ancient reservoir recovered and restored to its original uses, and, as we rode along the bank, to have indicated to us the particular means and art used to render it available. Hundreds are perhaps now buried in the woods, which once furnished this element of life to the teeming population of Yucatan.

Leaving the aguada, our road lay over a level and wooded plain, then wet and muddy from the recent rains, and at the distance of a league we reached the sugar rancho of a gentleman from Oxcutzcab, who had been a co-worker with Señor Trego in clearing out the aguada, and confirmed all that the latter had told us. A league beyond we came to the rancho of 'Y-a-walthel, inhabited entirely by Indians, and beyond our road opened upon a fine savanna, in which were several aguadas. Beyond this we reached the rancho of Choop, and came into a good road, different from the usual milpa paths, and like a well-beaten camino real, made so by the constant travelling of beasts with water kegs to the aguadas.

In the afternoon we passed the campo santo of Macoba, and very soon, ascending a hill, we saw through the trees the "old walls" of the ancient inhabitants. It was one of the wildest places we had seen; the trees were grander, and we were somewhat excited on approaching it, for we had heard that the old city was repeopled, and that Indians were again living in the buildings. It was almost evening; the Indians had returned from their work; smoke was issuing from the ruins, and, as seen through the trees, the very tops seemed alive with people; but as we approached we almost turned away with sorrow. It was like the wretched Arabs of the Nile swarming around the ruined temples of Thebes, a mournful contrast of present misery and past magnificence. The doors were stopped with leaves and branches; the sculptured ornaments on the façades were blackened by smoke rolling from the doorways, and all around were the confusion and filthiness of Indian housekeeping. As we rode up the Indians stared at us in astonishment, and the scared women snatched up their screaming children and ran away.

Among these ruins a rancho had been erected for the major domo, and as everything we had heretofore seen belonging to the cura of Xul was in fine order, we had no fears about our accommodations; but we found that nothing in this world must be taken for granted. The rancho was thatched, and had a dirty earthen floor, occupied by heaps of corn, beans, eggs, boxes, baskets, fowls, dogs, and pigs. There were two small, dirty hammocks, in one of which was swinging an Indian lad, and from the other had just been taken a dead man, whose new grave we had seen at the campo santo.

The major domo was a short, stupid, well-meaning old man, who apologized for the confusion on account of the death and burial that had just taken place. He was expecting us, had his master's orders to treat us with all due consideration, and we directed the rancho to be swept out. As night approached, we began to feel that our discomforts might be increased, for our carriers did not make their appearance. We had no apprehensions of robbery. Bernaldo was with them, and, knowing his propensities, we supposed that he had stopped at some rancho, where, in waiting to have some tortillas made, he had got belated, and was unable to find the road; but, whatever the cause, we missed the comforts of our travelling equipage. We were without candles, too, and sat in the miserable rancho in utter darkness, listening for the sound of the approaching carriers, until Albino procured a broken vessel of castor oil with a wick in it, which, by faintly illuminating one corner, disclosed more clearly the dreariness and discomfort of the scene.

But worse than all was the prospect of sleeping in the flea-infested hammocks, from one of which the body of a dead man had just been taken. We got the major domo to remove them and hire others, which, perhaps, were in reality not much better. Albino and Dimas had to lie down on the earthen floor, but they could not remain long. Dimas mounted lengthwise upon a log, and Albino doubled himself up in a baño, or bathing-tub, which kept him from the bare ground, but not above the jump of a flea. Fortunately, we suffered excessively from cold, which prevented us from being thrown into a fever, but it was one of the worst nights we had passed in the country.

Early in the morning Bernaldo made his appearance, he and the carriers having had a harder time than our own. They had been lost, and had wandered till ten o'clock, when they came to a rancho, where they learned their mistake, but were too much tired to carry their loads any farther, and, with an Indian from the rancho to guide them, had set out two hours before daylight.

The rancho of Macoba had been established but four years. It was situated in the midst of an immense forest; as yet it had been used only for the cultivation of maize, but the cura intended the ensuing year to commence a plantation of sugar. His inducement to establish a rancho at this place was the existence of the ruined buildings, which saved the expense of erecting huts for his criados; and he was influenced also by the wells and other remains of ancient watering-places. In the immediate vicinity of the buildings, without inquiring or seeking for them, we came across four wells, but all filled up with rubbish, and dry. Indeed, so many were known to exist, and the other means of supply were so abundant, that Señor Trego was about becoming a partner with the cura, under the expectation of clearing out and restoring these ancient reservoirs, furnishing an abundant supply of water, and calling around them a large Indian population.

In the mean time the cura had constructed two large tanks, or cisterns, one of which was twenty-two feet in diameter, and the same in depth, and the other eighteen. Both these were under a large circular roof, or top platform, covered with cement, and sloping toward the centre, which received the great body of rainwater that fell in the rainy season, and transmited it into the cisterns, and these furnished a supply during the whole of the dry season, as the major domo said, for fifty souls, besides fowls, hogs, and one horse.

The ruins at this place were not so extensive as we expected to find them. There were but two buildings occupied by the Indians, both in the immediate neighbourhood of our hut, and much ruined, one of which is represented in Plate XXIII. A noble alamo tree was growing by its side, and holding it up, which, while I was in another direction, the Indians had begun to cut down, but which, fortunately, I returned in time to save. The building is about 120 feet front, and had two stories, with a grand staircase on the other side, now ruined. The upper story was in a ruinous condition, but parts of it were occupied by Indians.

In the afternoon Doctor Cabot and myself set out for a ride to the aguada, induced somewhat by the forest character of the

Plate XXIII

MACOBA.

country, and the accounts the Indians gave us of rare birds, which they said were to be found in that direction. The road lay through a noble piece of woods, entirely different from the usual scrubby growth, with thorny and impenetrable underbrush, being the finest forest we had seen, and abounding in sapote and cedar trees. At the distance of half a league a path turned off to the right, overgrown, and hardly distinguishable, following which we reached the aguada. It was a mere hollow basin, overgrown with high grass. We rode down into it, and, dismounting, my first step from the side of my horse carried me into a hole, being a casimba, or pit, made by the Indians for the purpose of receiving the filtrations of water. We discovered others of the same kind, and to save our horses, backed them out to the edge of the aguada, and moved cautiously around it ourselves. These pits were no doubt of modern date, and we could not discover any indications of ancient wells; nevertheless, such may exist, for the aguada has been disused and neglected for an unknown length of time. Soil had accumulated, without removing which, the character and construction of the bottom could not be ascertained.

I returned from the aguada in time to assist Mr. Catherwood in taking the plan of the buildings. Our appearance in this wilderness had created astonishment among the Indians. All day, whenever we drew near to the buildings, the women and children ran inside, and now, when they found us entering their habitations, they all ran out of doors. The old major domo, unused to such a commotion among the women, followed us close, anxiously, but respectfully, and without uttering a word; and when we closed the book and told him we had finished, he raised both hands, and, with a relieved expression, exclaimed, "Gracias a Dios, la obra es acabada!" "Thank God, the work is done!"

I have nothing to say concerning the history of these ruins. They are the only memorials of a city which, but for them, would be utterly unknown, and I do not find among my notes any memoranda showing how or from whom we first received the intelligence of their existence.

March 2. Early in the morning we were again preparing to move, but, when on the eve of setting out, we learned that Bernaldo wanted to vary the monotony of travelling by getting married. He had met at the well an Indian girl of thirteen, he himself being sixteen. While assisting her to draw water, some tender passages had taken place between them, and he had disclosed to Albino his passion and his wishes; but he was trammelled by that impediment which all over the world keeps asunder those who are born for each other, viz., want of fortune. The girl made no objections on this score, nor did her father. On the contrary, the latter, being a prudent man, who looked to the future well-establishing of his daughter, considered Bernaldo, though not in the actual possession of fortune, a young man of good expectations, by reason of the wages that would be due to him from us; but the great difficulty was to get ready money to pay the padre. Bernaldo was afraid to ask for it, and the matter was not communicated to us until at the moment of setting out. It was entirely against hacienda law to marry off the estate; Don Simon would not like it; and, in the hurry and confusion of setting out, we had no time to deliberate; we therefore sent him on before us, and I am sorry to be obliged to say that this violence to his affections never made it necessary to change the appellation which we had given him very early after he came into our possession, namely, the fat boy.

We found among our carriers another youthful example of blighted affections, but recovering. He was a lad of about Bernaldo's age, to wit, sixteen, but had been married two years before, was a father, a widower, and about to be married again. The story was told us in his hearing, and, from his smiles at different parts of it, it was difficult to judge which he considered the most amusing; and we had still another interesting person, being a runaway Indian, who had been caught and brought back but a few days before, and upon whom the major domo charged all the others to keep a good look-out.

Our road lay through the same great forest in which the ruins stood. At the distance of a league we descended from the high ground, and reached a small aguada. From this place the road for some distance was hilly until we came out upon a great savanna covered with a growth of bushes, which rose above our heads so thick that they met across the path, excluding every breath of air, without shielding us from the sun, and exceedingly difficult and disagreeable to ride through. At one o'clock we reached the suburbs of the rancho of Puut. The settlement was a long line of straggling huts, which, as we rode through them under the blaze of a vertical sun, seemed to have no end. Mr. Catherwood stopped at one of them for a cup of water, and I rode on till I reached an open plain, forming a sort of square with thatched houses, and on one side a thatched church. I inquired of a woman peeping out of a door for the casa real, and was directed to a ruined hut on the same side, at the door, or, rather, at the doorway of which I dismounted, but had hardly crossed the threshold when I saw my white pantaloons speckled with little jumping black insects. I made a hasty retreat, and saw a man at the moment moving across the plaza, who asked me to his house, which was clean and comfortable, and when Mr. Catherwood came up the women of the house were engaged in preparing our dinner. Mr. Catherwood had just experienced the same kind of good feeling at an Indian hut. Water, in the Maya language, is expressed by the word *ha*, but, being that morning rather out of practice, Mr. Catherwood had asked for *ka*, which means fire, and the woman brought him a lighted brand. He motioned that away, but still continued asking for *ka*, fire. The woman went in, sat down, and made him a straw cigar, which she brought out to him. Sitting in the broiling sun, and perishing with thirst, he dropped his Maya, and by signs made her understand what he wanted, when she brought him water.

Our host, who was a Mestizo and ex-alcalde, procured for us another empty hut, which, by the time our carriers arrived, we had swept out and made comfortable.

The situation of this rancho was on a fine open plain; the land was good, and water abundant, though not very near at hand, the supply being derived from an aguada, to which we sent our horses; and they were gone so long that we determined the next morning, as the aguada lay but little out of our road, to ride by it and water them ourselves.

From this place we intended to visit the ruins of Mankeesh, but we learned that it would require a large circuit to reach them, and, at the same time, we received intelligence of other ruins of which we had not heard before, at the rancho of Yakatzib, on the road we had intended taking. We determined for the present to continue on the route we had marked out, and it so happened that we did not reach the ruins of Mankeesh at all, which, according to more particular accounts received afterward, when it was too late to profit by them, merit the attention of the future traveller.

CHAPTER XIII

At seven o'clock the next morning we started, and at the distance of a league reached the rancho of Jalal, from which we turned off to the aguada to water our horses. Plate XXIV represents this aguada. When we first came down upon its banks it presented one of the most beautifully picturesque scenes we met with in the country. It was completely enclosed by a forest, and had large trees growing around the banks and overhanging the water. The surface was covered with water weeds like a carpet of vivid green, and the aguada had a much higher interest than any derived from mere beauty. According to the accounts we had received at the rancho, ten years before it was dry, and the bottom covered with mud several feet deep. The Indians were in the habit of digging pits in it for the purpose of collecting the water which filtered through, and in some of these excavations they struck upon an ancient well, which, on clearing it away, was found to be of singular form and construction. It had a square platform at the top, and beneath was a round well, faced with smooth stones, from twenty to twenty-five feet deep. Below this was another square platform, and under the latter another well of less diameter, and about the same depth. The discovery of this well induced farther excavations, which, as the whole country was interested in the matter, were prosecuted until upward of forty wells were discovered, differing in their character and construction, and some idea of which may

Plate XXIV

be formed from Figure 9. These were all cleared out, and the whole aguada repaired, since which it furnishes a supply during the greater part of the dry season, and when this fails the wells appear, and continue the supply until the rains come on again.

Fig. 9

Leaving this, we continued again upon a plain. Albino had not come up with us, and passing through one Indian rancho, we came to another, in which were many paths, and we were at a loss which to take. The men were all away, and we were obliged to chase the women into their very huts to ask directions. At the last hut we cornered two, who were weaving cotton, and came upon them with our great effort in the Maya language, "Tush y am bé—" "Is this the way to—" adding Yakatzib, the name of the rancho at which we were told there were ruins. We had acquired great facility in asking this question, but if the answer went beyond "yes" or "no," or an indication with the hand, as was the case on this occasion, it was entirely beyond our attainments. The woman gave us a very long, and probably a very civil answer, but we could not understand a word of it; and finding it impossible to bring them to monosyllables, we asked for a draught of water and rode on.

When we had gone some distance beyond the rancho, it occurred to us that this might be Yakatzib itself, and we turned back. Before reaching it, however, we turned off into a grove of large orange trees at one side of the road, dismounted, and tied our horses under the shade to wait for Albino. The trees were loaded and the ground covered with fruit, but the oranges were all of the sour kind. We could not sit down under the trees, for the ground was teeming with garrapatas, ants, and other insects, and while standing we were obliged to switch them off with our riding whips. Soon Albino came thundering along on the trotter, and we learned that we had really passed Yakatzib, as the women had no doubt told us. While we were mounting to go back, a boy passed on a miserable old horse, his bare body perched between two water-kegs, with which he was going to the aguada. For a medio he slipped off, tied his horse to a bush, and ran before us as our guide through the rancho, beyond which, turning off to the right, we soon reached a ruined edifice.

It was small, and the whole front was gone; the door had been ornamented with pillars, which had fallen, and lay on the ground. The boy told us that there were ruined mounds, but no other remains of buildings. We turned back without dismounting, and continued our journey.

At two o'clock we reached the foot of a stony sierra, or mountain range, toilsome and laborious for the horses, but Mr. Catherwood remarked that his pricked up his ears and trod lightly, as if just beginning a journey. From the top of the same sierra we saw at its foot, on the other side, the village of Becanchen, where, on arriving, we rode through the plaza, and up to a large house, the front of which was adorned with a large red painting of a major domo on horseback, leading a bull into the ring. We inquired for the casa real, and were directed to a miserable thatched house, where a gentleman stepped out and recognized Mr. Catherwood's horse, which had belonged to Don Simon Peon, and through the horse he recognised me, having seen me with Don Simon at the fair at Jalacho, on the strength of which he immediately offered his house for a posada, or inn, which offer, on looking at the casa real, we did not hesitate to accept.

We were still on the great burial-ground of ruined cities. In the corridor of the house were sculptured stones, which our host told us were taken from the ancient buildings in the neighbourhood; they had also furnished materials for the foundation of every house on the plaza; and besides these there were other memorials. In the plaza were eight wells, then furnishing an abundant supply of water, and bearing that stamp which could not be mistaken, of the hand of the ancient builders. Below the plaza, on the declivity of the hill, was water gushing from the rocks, filling a clear basin beneath, and running off till it was lost in the woods. It was the first time in our whole journey that we had seen anything like a running stream, and after the parched regions through which we had passed, of almost inaccessible caves, muddy aguadas, and little pools in the hollows of rocks, it was a refreshing and delightful spectacle. Our Indian carriers had taken up their quarters under a brush fence, in sight and within reach of the stream, and to them and the muleteers it was like the fountain to the Arab in the desert, or the rivers of sweet water promised to the faithful in the paradise of Mohammed.

The history of this village has all the wildness of romance, and, indeed, throughout this land of sepulchred cities the genius of romance sits enthroned. Its name is derived from this stream of water, being compounded of the Maya words *Becan*, running, and *chen*, a well. Twenty years ago the country round about was a wilderness of forest. A solitary Indian came into it, and made a clearing for his milpa. In doing so he struck upon the running stream, followed it until he found the water gushing from the rock, and the whole surface now occupied by the plaza pierced with ancient wells. The Indians gathered round the wells, and a village grew up, which now contains six thousand inhabitants; a growth, having regard to the difference in the resources of the country and the character of the people, equal in rapidity to that of the most prosperous towns in ours.

These wells are all mere excavations through a stratum of limestone rock, varying in depth according to the irregularity of the bed, and in general not exceeding four or five feet. The source of the water is considered a mystery by the inhabitants, but it seems manifest that it is derived from the floods of the rainy season. The village is encompassed on three sides by hills. On the upper side of the plaza, near the corner of a street running back to the elevated range, is a large hole or natural opening in the rock, and during the whole of the rainy season a torrent of water collects into a channel, pours down this street, and empties into this hole. As we were told, the body of water is so great that for a week or ten days after the last rains the stream continues to run; and at the time of our visit it was eighteen inches in diameter. The water in the wells is always at the same level with that in the hole. They rise and fall together; and there is another conclusive proof of direct connexion, for, as we were told, a small dog that had been swept into the hole appeared some days afterward dead in one of the most distant wells.

Doctor Cabot and I descended into one of the wells, and found it a rude, irregular cavern, about twenty-five feet in diameter; the roof had some degree of regularity, and perhaps, to a certain extent, was artificial. Directly under the mouth the water was not more than eighteen inches deep, but the bottom was uneven, and a step or two beyond the water was so deep that we could not examine it thoroughly. By the light of a candle we could see no channel of communication with the other wells, but on one side the water ran deep under a shelving of the rock, and here there were probably some crevices through which it passed; indeed, this must have been the case, for this was the well in which the dog had come to light.

When we emerged from this well other business offered. Having little or no intercourse with the capital, this village was the first which Doctor Cabot's fame had not reached, and our host took me aside to ask me in confidence whether Doctor Cabot was a real medico; which fact being easily established by my evidence, he wanted the medico to visit a young Indian whose hand had been mangled by a sugar-mill. Doctor Cabot made some inquiries, the answers to which led to the conclusion that it would be necessary to cut off the hand; but, unluckily, at the last reduction of our luggage he had left his amputating instruments behind. He had a hand-saw for miscellaneous uses, which would serve in part, and Mr. Catherwood had a large spring-knife of admirable temper, which Doctor Cabot said would do, but the former flatly objected to its conversion into a surgical instrument. It had been purchased at Rome twenty years before, and in all his journeyings had been his travelling companion; but after such an operation he would never be able to use it again. Strong arguments were urged on both sides, and it became tolerably manifest that, unless amputation was necessary to save the boy from dying, the doctor would not get the knife.

Reaching the house, we saw the Indian sitting in the sala, the hand torn off to within about an inch of the wrist, and the stump swollen into a great ball six inches in diameter, perfectly black, and literally alive with vermin. At the first glance I retreated into the yard, and thence into the kitchen, when a woman engaged in cooking ran out, leaving her vessels boiling over the fire. I superintended her cooking, and dried my damp clothes, determined to avoid having anything to do with the operation; but, fortunately for me and Mr. Catherwood's knife, Doctor Cabot considered that it was not advisable to amputate. It was ten days since the accident happened, and the wound seemed to be healing. Doctor Cabot ascribed the lad's preservation to the sound and healthy state of the blood, arising from the simple diet of the Indian.

At this place we determined to separate; Mr. Catherwood to go on direct to Peto, a day and a half's journey distant, and lie by a few days to recruit, while Doctor Cabot and I made a retrograde and circuitous movement to the village of Mani. While speaking of our intention, a by-stander, Don Joaquin Sais, a gentleman of the village, told us of ruins on his hacienda of Zaccacal, eight leagues distant by a milpa road, and said that if we would wait a day, he would accompany us to visit them; but as we could not, he gave us a letter to the major domo.

Early the next morning Doctor Cabot and I set out with Albino and a single Indian, the latter carrying a petaquilla and hammocks. We left the village by the running stream, and rode for some time along a deep gully made by the great body of water which rushes through it in the rainy season. At half past nine we reached a large aguada, the banks of which were so muddy that it was impossible to get down to it to drink. A league beyond we reached another, surrounded by fine shade trees, with a few ducks floating quietly upon its surface. As we rode up Dr. Cabot shot a trogan, one of the rare birds of that country, adorning by its brilliant plumage the branches of an overhanging teee. We lost an hour of hard riding by mistaking our road among the several diverging tracks that led from the aguada. It was very hot; the country was desolate, and, suffering from thirst, we passed some Indians under the shade of a large seybo tree eating tortillas and chili, to whom we rode up, confident of procuring water; but they either had none, or, as Albino supposed, hid it away as we approached. At one o'clock we came to another aguada, but the bank was so muddy that it was impossible to get to the water without miring our horses or ourselves, and we were obliged to turn away without relief from our distressing thirst. Beyond this we turned off to the left, and, unusually fatigued with the heat and hard riding, although we had come but eight leagues, to our great satisfaction we reached the hacienda of Zaccacal.

Toward evening, escorted by the major domo and a vaquero to show the way, I set out for the ruins. At the distance of half a mile on the road to Tekax, we turned off into the woods to the left, and very soon reached the foot of a stone terrace. The vaquero led the way up it on horseback, and we followed, dismounting at the top. On this terrace was a circular hole like those before referred to at Uxmal and other places, but much larger; and, looking down into it till my eyes became accustomed to the darkness, I saw a large chamber with three recesses in different parts of the wall, which the major domo said were doors opening to passages that went under ground to an extent entirely unknown. By means of a pole with a crotch I descended, and found the chamber of an oblong form. The doors, as the major domo called them, were merely recesses about two feet deep. Touching one of them with my feet, I told him that the end of his passage was there, but he said it was tapado, or closed up, and persisted in asserting that it led to an indefinite extent. It was difficult to say what these recesses were intended for. They threw a mystery around the character of these subterranean chambers, and unsettled the idea of their being all intended for wells.

Beyond this, on a higher terrace, among many remains, were two buildings, one of which was in a good state of preservation, and the exterior was ornamented all around with pillars set in the wall, somewhat different from those in the façades of other buildings, and more fanciful. The interior consisted of but a single apartment, fifteen feet long and nine feet wide. The ceiling was high, and in the layer of flat stones along the centre of the arch was a single stone, like that seen for the first time at Kewick, ornamented with painting.

This building stood in front of another more overgrown and ruined, which had been an imposing and important edifice. The plan was complicated, and the exterior of one part was rounded, but the rounded part was a solid mass, and within the wall was straight. In the back wall was a recess, once occupied, perhaps, by a statue. Altogether, there was much about this edifice that was new and curious; and there were other cerros, or mounds, of undistinguishable ruins.

Short as my visit was, there were few considerations that could have tempted me to remain longer. The garrapatas would soon be over, but they continued with the rainy season, and, in fact, increased and multiplied. I discovered them the moment I dismounted, and at first attempted to whip them off, but wishing to get through before night, I hurried round this building, creeping under branches and tearing aside bushes, and, actually covered with the abominable insects, started for the road.

In hurrying forward I unwittingly crossed the track of a procession of large black ants. These processions are among the extraordinary spectacles of that country, darkening the ground for an hour at a time; and the insect has a sting equal to that of hornets, as I quickly learned on this occasion. When I reached the road I was almost numbed with pain, and when I mounted I felt that nothing could tempt me to live in such a country. The hacienda was in an unusually pretty situation. Opposite was a long line of hills; the sun was setting, and it was precisely the hour and the scene for a country ramble; but the owner of thousands of acres could never diverge from the beaten path without bringing these pests upon him.

I returned to the house, where the major domo kindly provided me with warm water for a bath, which cooled the fever of my blood. At night, for the first time in the country, we had at one end of the room the hammocks of the women, but this was not so bad as ants or garrapatas.

CHAPTER XIV

March 5. Early the next morning we set out
for the ruins of San José. At seven o'clock we reached the pueb-
locito, or little village, of that name, pleasantly situated between
a range of hills and a sierra, containing about two hundred inhabitants, among whom, as we rode into the plaza, we saw
several white men. At the casa real we found a cacique of respectable appearance, who told us that there were no "old walls"
in that village, which report of his, other Indians standing round
confirmed. We were not much disappointed, nor at all anxious
to find anything that would make it necessary to change our
plans; to lose no time, we determined to push on to Mani, eight
leagues distant, and applied for an Indian to carry our hammocks, which the cacique undertook to provide.

On the opposite side of the square was a thatched church,
the bell of which was tolling for morning mass, and before the
door was a group of men, surrounding a portly old gentleman
in a round jacket, who I knew must be the padre. They all confirmed the accounts we had received at the casa real, that there
were no ruins; but the cura, enforcing his words with an Ave
Maria, said that at Ticul, the head of his curacy, there were
bastante, or enough of them. He intended to return immediately
after mass, and wanted us to go with him to see them, and write
a description of them. I felt a strong disposition to do so, if it

was only to pass a day with him at the convent; but, on inquiring, I learned that the "old walls" were entirely in ruins; they had furnished materials for that church and convent, and all the stone houses of the village.

While this was going on at the door of the church, an Indian sexton was pulling lustily at the bell-rope, ringing for mass, and, as if indignant that his warning was not attended to, he made it so deafening that it was really a labour for us to hear each other. The cura seemed in no hurry, but I had some scruples about keeping the congregation waiting, and returned to the casa real.

Here a scene had just taken place, of which nothing but the noise of the bell prevented my having some previous knowledge. The cacique had sent for an Indian to carry our load, but the latter refused to obey, and was insolent to the cacique, who, in a rage, ordered him to be put into the stocks. When I entered, the recusant, sullen and silent, was waiting the execution of his sentence, and in a few minutes he was lying on his back on the ground, with both legs secured in the stocks above his knees. The cacique sent for another, and in the mean time an old woman came in with a roll of tortillas, and a piteous expression of face. She was the mother of the prisoner, and took her seat on the stocks to remain with him and comfort him; and, as the man rolled his head on the ground, and the woman looked wonderingly at us, we reproached ourselves as the cause of his disaster, and endeavoured to procure his release, but the cacique would not listen to us. He said that the man was punished, not for refusing to go with us, although bound to do so on account of indebtedness to the village, but for insolence to himself. He was evidently one who would not allow his authority to be trifled with; and seeing that, without helping the Indian, we might lose the benefit of the cacique's good dispositions in our favour, we were fain to desist. At length, though evidently with some difficulty, he procured another Indian. As we mounted, we made a final effort in behalf of the poor fellow in the stocks; and, though apparently unable to comprehend why we should take any interest in the matter, the cacique promised to release him.

This over, we found that we had thrown another family into confusion. The wife and a little daughter of our carrier accompanied him to the top of a hill beyond the village, where they bade him farewell as if he was setting out on a long and dangerous journey. The attachment of the Indian to his home is a striking feature of his character. The affection which grows up between the sexes was supposed by the early writers upon the character of the Indians not to exist among them, and probably the sentiment and refinement of it do not; but circumstances and habit bind together the Indian man and woman as strongly as any known ties. When the Indian grows up to manhood he requires a woman to make him tortillas, and to provide him warm water for his bath at night. He procures one, sometimes by the providence of the master, without much regard to similarity of tastes or parity of age; and though a young man is mated to an old woman, they live comfortably together. If he finds her guilty of any great offence, he brings her up before the master or the alcalde, gets her a whipping, and then takes her under his arm and goes quietly home with her. The Indian husband is rarely harsh to his wife, and the devotion of the wife to her husband is always a subject of remark. They share their pleasures as well as their labours; go up together with all their children to some village fiesta, and one of the most afflicting incidents in their lot is a necessity that takes the husband from his home.

In the suburbs of the village we commenced ascending the sierra, from the top of which we saw at the foot the hacienda of Santa Maria. Behind it rose a high mound, surrounded by trees, indicating that here too were the ruins of an ancient city.

Descending the sierra, we rode up to the hacienda, and saw three gentlemen sitting under a shed breakfasting. One of them had on a fur hat, a mark of civilization which we had not seen for a long time; an indication that he was from the city of Tekax, and had merely come out for a morning ride.

The proprietor came out to receive us, and, pointing to the mound, we made some inquiry about the building, but he did not comprehend us, and, supposing that we meant some old ranchos in that direction, said that they were for the servants. Albino explained that we were travelling over the country in search of ruins, and the gentleman looked at him perhaps somewhat as the inn-keeper looked at Sancho Panza when he explained that his master was a knight-errant travelling to redress grievances. We succeeded, however, in coming to an understanding about the mound, and the master told us that he had never been to it; that there was no path; that if we attempted to go to it we should be eaten up by garrapatas, and he called some Indians, who said that it was entirely in ruins. This was satisfactory, for the idea of being loaded with garrapatas to carry about till night had almost made me recoil. At the same time, the other gentlemen told us of other ruins at a league's distance from Tekax, on the hacienda of Señor Calera. I felt strongly disposed to turn off and visit the latter, but our carrier had gone on, and the little difficulties of overtaking him, procuring another for a change of route, and perhaps losing a day, were now serious objections; besides, there was no end to the ruins.

Leaving the hacienda, we entered, with a satisfaction that can hardly be described, upon a broad road for carretas and calesas. We had emerged from the narrow and tangled path of milpas and ranchos, and were once more on a camino real. We had accomplished a journey which we were assured, on setting out, was impracticable; and now we were coming upon the finest portion of the state, famed for its rich sugar plantations. We met heavy, lumbering vehicles drawn by oxen and horses, carrying sugar from the haciendas. Very soon we reached Tekax, one of the four places in Yucatan bearing the name of a city, and I must confess that I felt some degree of excitement. Throughout Yucatan our journey had been so quiet, so free from danger or interruption of any kind, that, after my Central American experience, it seemed unnatural. Yucatan was in a state of open rebellion against Mexico; we had heard of negotiations, but there had been no tumult, confusion, or bloodshed. Tekax alone had broken the general stillness, and while the rest of the country was perfectly quiet, this interior city had got up a small revolution on its own account, and for the benefit of whom it might concern.

According to the current reports, this revolution was got up by three patriotic individuals, whose names, unfortunately, I have lost. They belonged to the party called Los Independientes, in favour of declaring independence of Mexico. The elections had gone against their party, and alcaldes in favour of a reannexation to Mexico were installed in office. In the mean time commissioners arrived from Santa Ana to negotiate with the government of Yucatan, urging it not to make any open declaration, but to continue quietly in its state of independence de facto until the internal difficulties of Mexico were settled, when its complaints would be attended to and its grievances redressed. Afraid of the influence which these commissioners might exercise, the three patriots of Tekax resolved to strike for liberty, went round among the ranchos of the sierra, and collected a band of more than half-naked Indians, who, armed with machetes, a few old muskets, and those primitive weapons with which David slew Goliath, descended upon Tekax, and, to the great alarm of the women and children, took possession of the plaza, set up the figure of Santa Ana, pelted him with stones, put some bullets into him, burned him to ashes, and shouted "Viva la independencia." But few of them had ever heard of Santa Ana, but this was no reason why they should not pelt him with stones and burn him in effigy. They knew nothing of the relations between Yucatan and Mexico, and by the cry of independencia they meant a release from tribute to the government and debts to masters. With but little practice in revolutions, they made a fair start by turning out the alcaldes and levying contributions upon political opponents, and threw out the formidable threat that they would march three hundred men against the capital, and compel a declaration of independence. Intelligence of these movements soon reached Merida, and fearful menaces of war were bandied from one city to the other. Each waited for the other to make the first demonstration, but at length the capital sent forth its army, which reached Ticul the day after I left at the conclusion of my first visit, and while Doctor Cabot was still there. It was then within one day's march of the seat of rebellion, but halted to rest, and to let the moral effect of its approach go on before. The reader has perhaps never before heard of Tekax; nevertheless, a year has not elapsed since the patriotic, half-naked band in arms for independence thought that the eyes of the whole world were upon them. In three days the regular army resumed its march, with cannon in front, colours flying, drums beating, and the women of Ticul laughing, sure that there would be no bloodshed. The same day it reached Tekax, and the next morning, instead of falling upon each other like so many wild beasts, the officers and the three patriot leaders were seen walking arm in arm together in the plaza. The former promised good offices to their new friends, two reales apiece to the Indians, and the revolution was crushed. All dispersed, ready to take up arms again upon the same terms whenever their country's good should so require.

Such were the accounts we had received, always coupled with sweeping denunciations of the population of Tekax as revolutionary and radical, and the rabble of Yucatan. Having somewhat of a leaning to revolutions in the abstract, I was happy to find that, with such a bad reputation, its appearance was finer, and more promising than that of any town I had seen, and I could not but think it would be well for Yucatan if many of her dead-and-alive villages had more such rabble.

The city stands at the foot of the sierra. Riding up the

street, we had in full view the church of La Hermita, with a broad flight of stone steps scaling the side of the mountain. The streets were wide, the houses large and in fine order, and one had three stories, with balconies overhanging the street; and there was an appearance of life and business, which, coming as we did from Indian ranchos, and so long away from anything that looked like a city and the comforts and elegances of living, was really exciting.

As we rode along a gay calesa approached us, occupied by a gentleman and lady, well dressed and handsome, and, to our surprise, in the lady we recognised the fair subject upon whom we had begun business as Daguerreotype portrait takers, and whose gift of a cake had penetrated the very leather of my sad-dle-bags. A few short weeks had made a great change in her condition; she was now riding by the side of her lawful pro-prietor. We attempted, by the courtesy of our salute, to with-draw attention from our wearing apparel. Unluckily, Doctor Cabot's sombrero was tied under his chin, so that he could not get it off. Mine, with one of the strings carried away, described a circle in the air, and, as the doctor maliciously said, disap-peared under my horse. The gentleman nodded condescendingly, but it was flattering ourselves to believe that the lady took any notice of us whatever.

But though old friends forgot us, we were not unnoticed by the citizens of Tekax. As we rode along all eyes were turned upon us. We stopped in the plaza, which, with its great church and the buildings around it, was the finest we had seen in the country, and all the people ran out to the corridors to gaze at us. It was an unprecedented thing for strangers to pass through this place. European saddles, holsters, and arms were strange, and, in-cluding Albino, we made the cabalistic number of three which got up the late revolution. Knowing the curiosity we excited, and that all were anxious to speak to us, without dismounting or ex-changing a word with an inhabitant, we passed through the plaza and continued our journey. The people were bewildered, as if the ragged tail of a comet had passed over their heads; and afterward, at a distant village, we heard the report that we had passed through Tekax *vestidos como Moros,* or dressed like Moors. The good people, having never seen a Moor, and not being very familiar with Moorish costume, had taken our blouzes for such. The strange guise in which we appeared to them alleviated somewhat the mortification of not being recog-nised by the fair lady of Merida.

Our road lay for some distance along the sierra. It was broad, open, and the sun beat fiercely upon us. At half past ten we reached Akil, and rode up to the casa real. At the door was a stone hollowed out like those often before referred to, called pilas. In the steps and foundation were sculptured stones from ruined mounds in the immediate neighbourhood, and the road along the yard of the church ran through a mound, leaving part on each side, and the excavated mass forming on one side the wall of the convent yard. The rest of the wall, the church, and the convent were built with stones from the ancient buildings. We were on the site of another ruined city, of which we had never heard, and might never have known, but for the telltale memorials at the door of the casa real.

At a quarter before three we resumed our journey. The sun was still very hot; the road was straight, stony, and uninteresting, a great part of the way through overgrown milpas. At half past five we reached Mani, again finding over the door and along the sides of the casa real sculptured stones, some of them of new and curious designs; in one compartment was a seated figure, with what might seem a crown and sceptre, and the figures of the sun and moon on either side of his head, curious and interesting in themselves, independent of the admonition that we were again on the site of an aboriginal city.

In all our journey through this country there were no associations. Day after day we rode into places unknown beyond the boundaries of Yucatan, with no history attached to them, and touching no chord of feeling. Mani, however, rises above the rest, and, compared with the profound obscurity or the dim twilight in which other places are enveloped, its history is plainly written.

When the haughty caciques of Maya rebelled against the supreme lord, and destroyed the city of Mayapan, the reigning monarch was left with only the territory of Mani, the people of which had not joined in the rebellion. Here, reduced in power to the level of the other caciques, the race of the ancient lords of Maya ruled undisturbed until the time of the Spanish invasion; but the shadow of the throne rested over it; it was consecrated in the affections of the Indians, and long after the conquest it bore the proud name of la Corona real de Mani.

It has been mentioned that on their arrival at Tihoo the Spaniards encamped on a cerro, or mound, which stood on the site now occupied by the plaza of Merida. While in this position, surrounded by hostile Indians, their supplies cut off and straitened for provisions, one day the scouts brought intelligence to Don Francisco Montejo of a great body of Indians, apparently warlike, advancing toward them. From the top of the cerro they discovered the multitude, and among them one borne on the shoulders of men, as if extended on a bier. Supposing that a battle was certain, the Spaniards recommended themselves to God, the chaplain held up a holy cross, and, prostrating themselves before it, they took up their arms. As the Indians drew near to the cerro, they lowered to the ground the person whom they carried on their shoulders, who approached alone, threw down his bow and arrow, and, raising both hands, made a signal that he came in peace. Immediately all the Indians laid their bows and arrows on the ground, and, touching their fingers to the earth, kissed them, also in token of good-will.

The chief advanced to the foot of the mound, and began to ascend it. Don Francisco stepped forward to meet him, and the Indian made him a profound reverence; Don Francisco received him with cordiality, and, taking him by the hand, conducted him to his quarters.

This Indian was Tutul Xiu, the greatest lord in all that country, the lineal descendant of the royal house which once ruled over the whole land of Maya, and then cacique of Mani. He said that, moved by the valour and perseverance of the Spaniards, he had come voluntarily to render obedience, and to offer his aid and that of his subjects for the pacification of the rest; and he brought a large present of turkeys, fruits, and other provisions. He had come to be their friend; he desired, also, to be a Christian, and asked the adelantado to go through some Christian ceremonies. The latter made a most solemn adoration to the holy cross, and Tutul Xiu, watching attentively, imitated the Spaniard as well as he could until, with many demonstrations of joy, he came to kiss the cross on his knees. The Spaniards were delighted, and, the adoration over, they remarked that this fortunate day for them was that of the glorious San Ildefonso, whom they immediately elected for their patron saint.

Tutul Xiu was accompanied by other caciques, whose names, as found in an Indian manuscript, have been handed down. They remained with the Spaniards seventy days, and on taking leave, Tutul Xiu promised to send ambassadors to solicit the other chiefs, though they were not his vassals, to render obedience to the Spaniards; when, leaving them a great supply of provisions and many Indian servants, he returned to Mani.

He convoked all his Indians, and gave them notice of his

intentions, and of the agreement he had made with the Spaniards; to which they all assented.

Afterward he despatched the caciques who went with him to render submission to the Spaniards, as ambassadors to the Lords of Zotuta, called the Cocomes, and the other nations to the east as far as the region where now stands the city of Valladolid, making known to them his resolution, and the friendship he had contracted with the Spaniards, and beseeching them to do the same; representing that the Spaniards were determined to remain in the land, had established themselves in Campeachy, and were preparing to do so in Tihoo; reminding them how many battles they had fought, and how many lives of the natives had been lost; and informing them that he had experienced from the Spaniards while he remained with them good-will, and that he held it better for all his countrymen to follow his example, considering the dangers of the opposite course.

The ambassadors proceeded to the district of Zotuta, and made known their embassy to Nachi Cocom, the principal lord of that territory. The latter requested them to wait four or five days for their answer, and in the mean time convoked all his dependant caciques, who, in concert with this chief, determined to make a great wild-boar hunt, ostensibly to fête the ambassadors. Under this pretext, they enticed them from the inhabited parts of the country into a dense forest, and feasted them three days. On the fourth they assembled to eat beneath a large sapote tree, and the last act of the feast was to cut the throats of the ambassadors, sparing but one, whom they charged to inform Tutul Xiu of their reception of his embassy, and to reproach him with his cowardice; but though they spared the life of this one, they put out his eyes with an arrow, and sent him, under the charge of four captains, to the territory of Tutul Xiu, where they left him and returned to their own country.

Such were the unfortunate circumstances under which Mani became known to the Spaniards. It was the first interior town that submitted to their power, and by referring to the map, the reader will see that after our long, irregular, and devious route, we are at this moment but four leagues from Ticul, and but eleven from Uxmal by the road of the country, while the distance is much less in a straight line.

Among the wonders unfolded by the discovery of these ruined cities, what made the strongest impression on our minds was the fact that their immense population existed in a region so scantily supplied with water. Throughout the whole country there is no stream, or spring, or living fountain, and, but for the extraordinary caves and hollows in the rocks from which the inhabitants at this day drink, they must have been entirely dependant upon artificial fountains, and literally upon the rain that came down from heaven. But on this point there is one important consideration. The aborigines of this country had no horses, or cattle, or large domestic animals, and the supply required for the use of man only was comparatively small. Perhaps at this day, with different wants and habits, the same country would not support the same amount of population. And, besides, the Indian now inhabiting that dry and thirsty region illustrates the effect of continual scarcity, habit, and training, in subduing the appetites. Water is to him, as to the Arab of the Desert, a scarce and precious commodity. When he puts down the load from his back, his body streaming with perspiration, a few sips of water dipped up in the palm of his hand from a hollow rock suffice to quench his thirst. Still, under any circumstances, the sources of supply present one of the most interesting features connected with the discovery of these ruined cities, and go to confirm belief in the vast numbers and power, as well as the laborious industry of the ancient inhabitants.

It was late on Saturday afternoon when we reached Mani. The guarda of Indians had served their term of a week in attendance at the casa real, and were now retiring from office, as usual all intoxicated, but we got a large room swept out, had it furnished with chairs and tables, and our hammocks hung up; and here, amid the wrecks of cities, we were almost in ruins ourselves. Before resorting to our hammocks we made an important and touching discovery, which was that we had but one clean camisa between us; and if the reader knew the extent of our travelling wardrobe, he would, perhaps, be somewhat astonished that we had that. Nevertheless, the discovery perplexed us. The next day was Sunday; all the village would appear in clean clothes; it was mortifying that we could not do so too, and, besides, we had some little feeling on the score of personal comfort. In Europe, with a frock-coat buttoned tight across the breast, black stock, and one pair of pantaloons, hat, and boots, the traveller is independent of the world, but not so under the hot sun of Yucatan. We sent Albino out to look for supplies, but he returned unsuccessful, though he did succeed in making a bargain with a woman to wash an entire change for us the next day; but she could hardly be made to understand that stockings and sheets were included in a change.

CHAPTER XV

Early in the morning Albino was in quest of some gentleman who might have a spare camisa and pantaloons which he would be willing to part with, and, by one of those rare pieces of good luck that sometimes illuminate the path of a traveller, he procured both, the latter having an elegantly embroidered bosom, which fell to Doctor Cabot; and, with my castoff blouse, which was in better condition than his, and a thin frock-coat, that considered itself cast-off some time before, for myself, we were able to make a dashing appearance in the streets.

Notwithstanding our perplexities, I had an uncommon degree of satisfaction at waking up in Mani. I had heard of this place on my first visit to Uxmal, of relics and heirlooms in the hands of the cacique, and of ruins, which, however, we were advised were not worth visiting. The morning, nevertheless, did not open with much promise. On first emerging we found about the door of the casa real a crowd of loungers, of that mixed race who might trace their ancestry to the subjects of Tutul Xiu and the conquerors, possessing all the bad qualities of both, and but few of the good traits of either. Some of them were intoxicated, and there were many half-grown, impudent boys, who kept close to us, watching every movement, and turning aside to laugh when they could do so unobserved.

We set out to look at the ruins, and the crowd followed at our heels. At the end of a street leading to the well we saw a long building, pierced in the middle by the street, and part still standing on each side. We saw at a glance that it was not the work of the antiguos, but had been erected by the Spaniards since the conquest, and yet we were conducted to it as one of the same class with those we had found all over the country; though we did meet with one intelligent person, who smiled at the ignorance of the people, and said that it was a palace of *El Rey,* or the *king,* Montejo. Its true history is perhaps as much unknown as that of the more ancient buildings. In its tottering front were interspersed sculptured stones taken from the aboriginal edifices, and thus, in its own decay, it publishes the sad story that it had risen upon the ruins of another race.

Near this building, and at the corner of the street, is the well referred to in the conclusion of my legend of the House of the Dwarf at Uxmal. "The old woman (the mother of the Dwarf) then died, but at the Indian village of Mani there is a deep well, from which opens a cave that leads under ground an immense distance to Merida. In this cave, on the bank of a stream, under the shade of a large tree, sits an old woman, with a serpent by her side, who sells water in small quantities, not for money, but only for a criatura, or baby, to give the serpent to eat; and this old woman is the mother of the Dwarf." The entrance to the well was under a great shelf of overhanging rock, forming the mouth of a magnificent cavern, wild enough to sustain the legend. The roof was high, and the villagers had constructed steps, by which, walking erect, we reached a large pool of water, whence women were filling their cantaros. At one side was an opening in the rock above, which should have been, and was intended to be, made directly over the water, for the purpose of drawing it up in buckets; and as this mistake occurred in a cave where the water is but a short distance from the mouth, and the passage is wide, it shows the difficulty, without any knowledge of the use of instruments, of fixing on the surface the precise point over the water in the other caves, which have long, narrow, and winding passages.

In the yards of some houses on a street at the rear of the casa real were the remains of large mounds. In the wall round the square of the church was a large circular upright stone, like those heretofore called picotes, or whipping-posts, and our guide told us that in the suburbs there were other mounds; but, without leaving the streets, we saw enough to satisfy us that Mani stood on the site of an ancient town of the same general character with all the others.

Returning to the casa real, we found a new guarda, who came into office rather more intoxicated than their predecessors in going out. Albino had inquired of the cacique for the ancient relics of which we had heard accounts, and the Indians brought a copy of Cogolludo, wrapped up and treasured with great care in the casa real. This did not astonish us much, and they opened the book and pointed out a picture, the only one in it, being a representation of the murder of the ambassadors of Tutul Xiu; and while we were looking at it they brought out and unrolled on the floor an old painting on cotton cloth, being the original from which Cogolludo had the engraving made. The design was a coat of arms bordered with the heads of the murdered ambassadors, one of which has an arrow fixed in the temple, intended to represent the ambassador who had his eyes put out with this weapon. In the centre is a tree growing out of a box, representing the sapote tree at Zotuta, under which the murder was committed, and which, the Indians say, is still standing. This tree I shall have occasion to mention again hereafter. The painting had evidently been executed by an Indian, and probably very near the time of the occurrence which it was intended to commemorate. Cogolludo refers to it as an ancient and interesting relic in his time, and, of course, it is much more so now. It is an object of great reverence among the Indians of Mani. In fact, throughout our whole journeyings, either in Central America or Yucatan, it was the first and only instance in which we met with any memorial in the hands of the Indians, tending to keep alive the memory of any event in their history; but this must not be imputed to them as a reproach. History, dark as it is on other points, shows clearly enough that this now abject and degraded race did cling with desperate and fatal tenacity to the memory of those ancestors whom they know not now; the records of their conquerors show the ruthless and savage policy pursued by the Spaniards to root this memory from their minds; and here, in this very town of Mani, we have a dark and memorable instance.

In 1571, twenty-nine years after the foundation of Merida, some Indians of Mani relapsed and became idolaters, practising in secret their ancient rites.

Intelligence of their backsliding reached the ears of the provincial in Merida, who came to Mani in person, and forthwith established himself as inquisitor. Some who had died obstinately in the secret practice of idolatrous rites had been buried in sacred ground; he ordered their bodies to be dug up, and their bones thrown into the fields; and, in order to strike terror into the minds of the Indians, and root out the memory of their ancient rites, on a day appointed for that purpose, attended by the principal of the Spanish nobility, and in the presence of a great multitude of Indians, he made them bring together all their books and ancient characters, and publicly burned them, thus destroying at once the history of their antiquities. Those envious of the blessed father, says the historian, gave him the title of cruel; but very differently thought of the action the Doctor Don Pedro Sanchez de Aguilar, in his information against the idolaters of this country.

The sight of this painting made me more earnest in pushing my inquiries for other memorials, but this was all; the Indians had no more to show, and I then inquired of the alcalde for ancient archives. He knew nothing about them, but said we could examine for ourselves, and the key of the apartment in which they were kept was with the second alcalde.

The schoolmaster of the village, who had received a letter in our behalf from our friend the cura Carillo of Ticul, accompanied me to look for the second alcalde, and, after tracing him to several places, we procured the keys, and returned to the casa real, and when we unlocked the door we had thirty or forty persons to enter with us. The books and archives of the municipality were in the back room, and among them was one large volume which had an ancient and venerable appearance, being bound in parchment, tattered, and worm-eaten, and having a flap to close like that of a pocket-book. Unhappily, it was written in the Maya language, and perfectly unintelligible. The dates, however, showed that these venerable pages were a record of events which had taken place within a very few years after the entry of the Spaniards into the country; and as I pored over them, I was strongly impressed with the belief that directly, or in some incidental expressions, they contained matter which might throw some light upon the subject of my investigations.

Being Sunday, a crowd of curious and lazy lookers-on surrounded the table, but they could not distract my attention. I found that, though all could speak the Maya, none could read it. Nevertheless, I continued to turn over the pages. On the 157th page, in a document which bore the date of 1557, I saw the word *Vxmal*. Here I stopped, and called upon the by-standers. The schoolmaster was the only one who could even attempt to give me any assistance, but he was not familiar with the Maya as a written tongue, and said that this, having been written nearly three hundred years before, differed somewhat from that of the present day, and was more difficult to comprehend. Other places were referred to in the document, the names of which were familiar to me, and I observed that the words immediately preceding Vxmal were different from those preceding the other names. The presumption was that Uxmal was referred to in some different sense.

In turning to the end of the document I found a sheet of foolscap paper, which had been secured in the book, but was then loose; and upon it was a curious map, also dated in 1557, of which Mani was the centre. Vxmal was laid down upon it, and indicated by a peculiar sign, different from that of all the other places named. On the back of the map was endorsed a long instrument of the same date, in which the word *Vxmal* again occurred, and which, beyond doubt, contained matter relating to other places named in the map, and to their condition or state of being at that time. With the assistance of the schoolmaster I compared this with the one written in the book, and ascertained that the latter was a recorded copy of the other.

A few pages beyond was another document, bearing date in 1556, one year earlier, and in this, again, the word Vxmal appeared. The schoolmaster was able to give me some general idea of the contents, but he could not translate with facility, nor, as he said, very accurately. The alcalde sent for an Indian escribano, or clerk, of the municipality; but he was not in the village, and an old Indian was brought who had formerly served in that capacity; but, after staring stupidly at the pages as if looking at a row of machetes, he said he had grown so old that he had forgotten how to read. My only course was to have copies made, which the schoolmaster set about immediately, and late in the afternoon he placed them in my hands. In the evening, by the permission of the alcalde, I took the book to my quarters, and looked over every page, running my finger along every line, in search of the word Uxmal, but I did not meet with it in any other place, and probably the documents referred to are the most ancient, if not the only ones in existence of ancient date, in which that name is mentioned.

The copies I carried with me to my friend Don Pio Perez, who discovered some errors, and, at his instance, my good friend the cura Carillo went over to Mani, and made exact copies of the map and documents. He also made diligent search through the Maya archives for other papers mentioning Uxmal, or refer-

ring to it in any way, but found none. He added to his copies a
translation, which was revised by Don Pio, and it is from his
version that what follows is prepared.

Plate XXV is a copy of the ancient map, the original of
which covers one side of a sheet of foolscap paper.

The instrument endorsed on the back, as translated, reads
as follows:

"Memorandum of having divided the lands by D. Francisco
Montejo Xiu, governor of this pueblo of Mani, and the governors of the pueblos who are under him.

"There met together Don Francisco Montejo Xiu, governor
of this pueblo, and of the jurisdiction of Tutul Xiu; Don Francisco Che, governor of Ticul, Don Francisco Pacab, governor of
Oxcutzcab, Don Diego Vs, governor of Tekax, Don Alonzo
Pacab, governor of Jan-monal, Don Juan Che, governor of
Mama, Don Alonzo Xiu, governor of Tekit, and the other governors within the jurisdiction of Mani, together with the regidores, for the purpose of regulating the landmarks, and
maintaining the right of each village respecting the felling of
trees, and to fix and settle with crosses the boundaries of the
milpas of their respective villages, dividing them into parts according to their situation, showing the lands pertaining to each.
The people of Canul, those of Acanceh, of Ticoh, those of Cosuma, those of Zotuta and its jurisdiction, those of Tixcacab, a
part of those of Peto, Colotmul, and Zuccacab, after having
conferred together, declared it necessary to cite the governors of
the villages, and we answered that they should come to this
audiencia of Mani, each one bringing with him two regidores to
be present at the division of the lands. Don Juan Canul, governor of Nunkini, and Francisco Ci, his colleague; D. Juan
Cocom, governor of Ticoh, D. Gaspar Tun of Cosuma, Don
Juan Cocom, governor of Zotuta, D. Gonzalo Tuyn, governor of
Tixcacab, D. Juan Han of Yaxcacab; these received the donation
on the fifth day from Merida, consisting of one hundred 'paties'
of fine sheets, each pati or cotton cloth, and thus they continued
receiving by twenties for a beginning, being rolled up by Juan
Nic, Pedro May, and Pedro Coba, assembled in the house of Don
Francisco Montejo Xiu, governor of the village of Mani; three
arrobas of wax, which were sold by them, Don Juan Cocom of
Zotuta having first received them. In Talchaquillo, on the road
to Merida, toward the north of said village, the cross was
planted, and called Hoal. In Sacmuyalna they put a cross; this
is the limit of the lands of those of Ticoh. In Kochilha a cross

Plate XXV

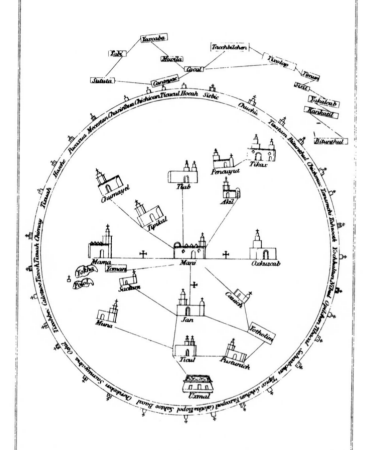

INDIAN MAP

Charles Copley, Sc. N.Y.

was placed. In Cisinil, Toyotha, Chulul Ytza, Ocansip, and Tiphal, crosses were placed; this is the boundary of the milpas and the lands of those of Maxcanú-al Canules. In Kaxabceh Chacnocac, Calam, Sactos, are the limits of the fields of the Canules, and there crosses were placed. In Zemesahal and in Opal were planted crosses: these are the limits of the grounds of the villagers of Kilhini and Becal. In Yaxche Sucilha Xcalchen, Tehico Sahcabchen Xbacal, Opichen, crosses were planted. Twenty-two is the number of the places marked, and they returned to raise new landmarks, by the command of the judge, Felipe Manriques, specially commissioned by his excellency the governor, when he arrived at *Uxmal,* accompanied by his interpreter, Gaspar Antonio," &c. The rest of this document I omit.

The other document begins as follows: "On the tenth of August, in the year one thousand five hundred and fifty-six, the special judge arrived with his interpreter, Gaspar Antonio, *from Vxmal,* when they reached this chief village of Mani, with the other caciques that followed them, Don Francisco Che, governor of Ticul, Don Francisco Pacab, governor of Tekax, Don Alonzo Pacab, governor of Jan, Don Juan Che, governor of Mama, Don Alonzo Xiu, governor of Tekit, with the other governors of his suite, Don Juan Cacom, governor of Tekoh, with Don Gaspar Fun, Don Juan Camal, governor of Nunhini, Don Francisco Ciz, other governor of Cosuma, Don Juan Cocom, governor of Zotuta, Don Gonzalo Fuyú, governor of Tixcacaltuyú, Don Juan Han, governor of Yaxcaba; those were brought to this chief village of Mani *from Vxmal,* with the others named, and the judge Felipe Manrique, with Gaspar Antonio, commissioned interpreter." Of this, too, the rest is omitted, not being relevant to this subject.

The reader will observe that, fifteen or sixteen years after the foundation of Merida, Mani had the same pre-eminence of position as when Tutul Xiu went up with his dependant caciques to make submission to the Spaniards. It was the "chief village," the central point for meeting and settling the boundaries of villages; but it appears, on the face of these documents, that great changes had already occurred. In fact, even at that early date we see the entering wedge, which, since driven to its mark, has overturned all the institutions and destroyed forever the national character of the aboriginal inhabitants. The Indians are still rulers over their villages, and meet to settle their boundary lines, but they meet under the direction of Don Felipe Manriques, a Spanish officer, specially commissioned for that purpose; they establish their boundaries by planting *crosses,* symbols introduced by the Spaniards; they have lost their proud and independent national title of cacique, and are styled *Dons* and *Gobernadores*; under the gentle patting of the hand destined soon to crush their race, they have abandoned even the names received from their fathers, and have adopted, either voluntarily or by coercion, the Christian names of the Spaniards; and the Lord of Mani himself, the lineal descendant of the royal house of Maya, either that same Tutul Xiu who first submitted himself and his vassals to the dominion of Don Francisco Montejo, or his immediate descendant, in compliment to the conqueror and destroyer of his race, appears meekly and ingloriously under the name of *Don Francisco* Xiu.

But it is not for the sake of this melancholy tale that I have introduced these documents; they have another and a more important bearing. By this act of partition it appears that, in 1557, "the judge *arrived at Uxmal,* accompanied by his interpreter Don Antonio Gaspar." And by the agreement it appears that in 1556, one year previous, the special judge *arrived* with his interpreter, Gaspar Antonio, *from Uxmal,* when they reached the chief village of Mani with the other caciques who followed them. The names are all given, and it is said these *"were brought to this* chief village of Mani *from Uxmal,* with the others named, and the judge Felipe Manrique and Gaspar Antonio, commissioned interpreter."

Now what was Uxmal? It is clear, beyond all question, that it was a place at which persons could arrive, at which they could be, and from which they could come. I am safe in supposing that it was not a mere hacienda, for at that early period of the conquest haciendas had not begun to be established; and, besides, the title papers of Don Simon Peon show that the first grant of it was made for the purposes of a hacienda one hundred and forty-four or one hundred and forty-five years afterward, at which time the land was waste and belonged to the crown, and had small settlements of Indians upon it, who were publicly and notoriously worshipping the devil in the ancient buildings. It was not, then, a hacienda. Was it a Spanish town? If so, some remains would have been visible at the time of the grant, and the great object of driving away the Indians and breaking up their idolatrous worship would already have been accomplished. There is no indication, record, or tradition that a Spanish town was ever established at Uxmal; the general belief is that there never was any; Don Simon is sure of it, and in that confidence I fully participate. But as the strongest proof on this point, I call in this ancient map. It is a fact perhaps more clearly established than any other in the history of the conquest, that in every Indian village in which the Spaniards made a settlement, with that strong religious enthusiasm which formed so remarkable a feature in their daring and unscrupulous character, their first act was the erection of a church. Now it will be remarked that nearly all the places laid down on the map are indicated by the sign of a church; most of them now exist, all have aboriginal names, and the inference is that they were at that time existing aboriginal towns, in which the Spaniards had erected churches, or had taken the preliminary steps for doing so. Several of these places we had visited; we had seen their churches reared upon the ruins of ancient buildings, and in their immediate vicinity vestiges and extensive ruins of the same general character with those at Uxmal.

But Uxmal, it will be seen, is not indicated by the sign of a church. This I consider evidence that no church was erected there, and that while the Spaniards were establishing settlements in other Indian towns, for some reason, now unknown, perhaps on account of its unhealthiness, at Uxmal they made none. But it will be seen farther, that Uxmal not only is not indicated by the sign of a church, but is indicated by one entirely different, of a peculiar and striking character, which was manifestly never adopted from caprice or without cause. In my opinion, this sign was intended to represent what would most clearly distinguish a large place without a church from those in which churches had been erected, the characteristic ornaments on the fronts of the aboriginal buildings, as now seen at Uxmal. It is the same obvious character or symbol which might serve at this day to indicate on a map a city like Uxmal, and to my mind the conclusion is irresistible that at the time when the Judge Don Felipe Manriques arrived *at* Uxmal and arrived *from* Uxmal, it was an existing inhabited aboriginal town. Farther, in the scanty light that we have on this subject, the slightest incidental circumstance is not to be disregarded. In each reference to his arrival at or from Uxmal, it is mentioned that he was accompanied by his interpreter. He would not need an interpreter if the place was desolate, or if it was a hacienda, or a Spanish town. He could need an interpreter only when the place was occupied by the aborigines, whose language he did not understand, and such, I cannot help believing, was actually the case. I can easily believe, too, that its depopulation and desolation within the hundred and forty years preceding the royal grant for the purposes of a hacienda, were the inevitable consequence of the policy pursued by the Spaniards in their subjugation of the country. I would remark that there is no doubt of the authenticity of these documents. They are true records of events which occurred at that early period of the conquest. To this day the map and act of partition are good evidence in all legal proceedings affecting the title to lands in that neighbourhood, and I afterward saw them enrolled as proofs and forming part of the record in a contested and protracted lawsuit.

I make no apology for dwelling so long upon this ancient map. Perhaps, however, it will not interest the reader so much as it did ourselves and the half-breeds of Mani. These ascribed our curiosity to a much less innocent motive than that of investigating the history of ancient cities. In consequence of some recent difficulties, los Ingleses were somewhat objects of suspicion; the idlers of Mani made close inquiries of Albino touching our reasons for wanting the map, and, not being able to comprehend his explanations, which were, perhaps, not very clear, they said that we intended to seek out and seize the strong points for fortifications; and, with a spirit unlike that of their warlike sires, Spanish or Indian, quietly made up their minds that we intended to reduce the country and make slaves of them.

Toward evening we strolled over to the church and convent, which are among the grandest of these early structures erected in Yucatan, proud monuments of the zeal and labour of the Franciscan friars. They were built under the direction of Friar Juan of Merida, distinguished as a warrior and conqueror, but who threw aside the sword and put on the habit of a monk. According to Cogolludo, they were both finished in the short space of seven months, the cacique who had been lord of that country furnishing six thousand Indians. Built upon the ruins of another race, they are now themselves tottering and going to decay.

The convent had two stories, with a great corridor all round; but the doors were broken and the windows wide open, rain beat into the rooms, and grass grew on the floor.

The roof of the church formed a grand promenade, commanding an almost boundless view of the great region of country of which it was once the chief place and centre. Far as the eye could reach was visible the great sierra, running from east to west, a dark line along the plain. All the rest was plain, dotted only by small clearings for villages. My guide pointed out and named Tekax, Akil, Oxcutzcab, Schochnoche, Pusto-nich, Ticul, Jan, Chapap, Mama, Tipika, Teab, the same villages laid down in the ancient map, whose caciques came up, three hundred years before, to settle the boundaries of their lands; and he told me that, under a clearer atmosphere, more were visible. Some I had visited, and had seen the crumbling remains of the ancient town; and looking at them from the roof of the church, the old map gave them a vividness, reality, and life, as they had been three hundred years before, more exciting than the wildest speculations in regard to lost and unknown races. The sun went down, and the gloom of night gathered over the great plain, emblematic of the fortunes and the fate of its ancient inhabitants.

CHAPTER XVI

Monday, March 7. Before daylight the next morning we left Mani.

Our present mode of travelling favoured Doctor Cabot's particular objects. His best chance for procuring birds was always on the road, the time passed at ruins, on account of the density of the woods and underbrush, being in a great measure lost to him. Yucatan had never before been explored ornithologically; or, to speak more correctly, the only person who had given any attention to that branch of its natural history, a German, died in the country; his collections were scattered and his notes lost. Doctor Cabot's field of operations, therefore, was, like our own, entirely new; and our attention being constantly directed to the brilliant plumage of the birds and their interesting habits, they became identified with the purposes of our journey. It was my intention to obtain from Doctor Cabot, and publish in this work, a full essay on the ornithology of the country, but I find my materials so abundant and my volumes growing to such a bulk that compression has become a work of serious necessity.

Doctor Cabot has published, in the Boston Journal of Natural History, an account of his observations upon one rare and splendid bird, the ocellated turkey, of which one stuffed specimen at the Jardin des Plantes, and another in the collection of the Earl of Derby, are the only two known to exist, and of which, besides obtaining a stuffed specimen, we succeeded in transporting two living birds from the interior, and embarking them for home, but lost them overboard on the voyage. I have hopes that he may be induced to publish a full account of his observations upon the ornithology of Yucatan. In the mean time I give in the Appendix a memorandum of about one hundred birds observed by him in that country, which are also found within the United States, and have been figured and described by Wilson, Bonaparte, Audubon, and Nuttall; of others, which are well known to the scientific world for their striking brilliancy of plumage, having been observed in different parts of South and Central America, but are known only by skins prepared and sold in the country, and whose habits have never been described; and a third class, more important to the naturalist than either of the others, comprising birds entirely unknown until discovered by him in Yucatan. The memorandum is accompanied by a few notes referring to the places and circumstances under which they were procured; and in referring to them in the Appendix, I would take occasion to say that some of the most really important matter in this work is to be found in that place, for the sake of which I have considered it expedient materially to abridge my narrative.

But to resume. We stopped that night at Tixmeach, eight leagues distant, a neat village with a well one hundred and forty-four feet deep, at which every woman drawing from it left a handful of maize for a cantaro of water, and we paid a medio for watering our horses; and setting out before daylight the next morning, at half past nine we reached Peto, where we found Mr. Catherwood and our luggage on the hands of our friend Don Pio Perez.

Peto is the head of a department, of which Don Pio Perez was gefe politico. It was a well-built town, with streets indicated, as at Merida, by figures on the tops of the houses. The church and convent were large and imposing edifices, and the living of the cura one of the most valuable in the church, being worth six or seven thousand dollars per annum.

At this place we found letters and packets of newspapers from home, forwarded to us from Merida, and, except attending to them, our time was devoted almost exclusively to long and interesting conversations with Don Pio on matters connected with the antiquities of the country. I cannot sufficiently express my obligations to this gentleman for the warm interest he took in facilitating our pursuits, and for the labour he bestowed ungrudgingly in our behalf. Besides preparing a series of verbal forms and other illustrations of the grammar of the Maya language, according to memoranda made by the same distinguished gentleman before referred to, he gave me a vocabulary in manuscript, containing more than four thousand Maya words, and an almanac, prepared by himself, according to the Indian system of computation, for the year from the 16th of July, 1841, to the 15th of July, 1842, a translation of which is published in the Appendix, as a key or supplement to his calendar.*

Besides these, he furnished me with the copy of one other document, which, if genuine and authentic, throws more light upon aborginal history than any other known to be in existence. It is a fragment of a Maya manuscript, written from memory by an Indian, at some time not designated, and entitled "Principal epochs of the ancient history of Yucatan."

It purports to give the series of "katunes," or epochs, from the time of the departure of the Toltecs from the country of Tulapan until their arrival at this, as it is called, island of Chacno-uitan, occupying, according to Don Pio's computation of katunes, the lapse of time corresponding with that between the years 144 and 217 of the Christian era.

It assigns dates to the discovery of Bacalar and then of Chichen Itza, both within the three epochs corresponding with the time between A.D. 360 and A.D. 432; the colonization of Champoton, and its destruction; the times of wandering through the uninhabited forests, and establishing themselves a second time at Chichen Itza, within epochs corresponding with the lapse between A.D. 888 and A.D. 936.

The epoch of the colonization of Uxmal, corresponding with the years between A.D. 936 and 1176 A.D.; the epochs of wars between the governors of Chichen Itza and Mayapan; the destruction of the latter city by the Uitzes of the Sierras, or highlanders; and the arrival of the Spaniards, adding that "Holy men from the East came with them;" and the manuscript terminates with the epoch of the first baptism and the arrival of the first bishop.

I shall make no comment upon the subject matter of this manuscript. How far it is to be regarded as authentic I am not able to say, but as the only known manuscript in existence that purports to be written by an Indian in his native language, giving an account of the events in the ancient history of this country, I publish it entire in the Appendix. It may conflict in

*See Appendix to vol. i.

some particulars with opinions expressed by me, but I consider the discovery of the truth on this subject as far more important than the confirmation of any theory of my own; and I may add that, in general, it bears out and sustains the views presented in these pages.

On the afternoon of the 11th of March we bade farewell to Don Pio Perez, and set out for Chichen. Ever since we left home we had had our eyes upon this place. We had become eager to reach it, and the increasing bulk of these volumes warns me that I must not now linger on the road. I shall therefore barely say that the first night we stopped at the village of Taihxiu, the second at Yaxcaba, and at noon of the third day we reached Pisté, about two miles distant from Chichen. We had heard some unpropitious accounts concerning the hospitality of the proprietor of the hacienda, and thought it safer not to alarm him by going upon him with appetites sharpened by a hard day's ride, but first to lay the village under a moderate contribution.

At four o'clock we left Pisté, and very soon we saw rising high above the plain the Castillo of Chichen. In half an hour we were among the ruins of this ancient city, with all the great buildings in full view, casting prodigious shadows over the plain, and presenting a spectacle which, even after all that we had seen, once more excited in us emotions of wonder. The camino real ran through the midst of them, and the field was so open that, without dismounting, we rode close in to some of the principal edifices. Involuntarily we lingered, but night was approaching, and, fairly dragging ourselves away, we rode on, and in a few minutes reached the hacienda. Vaqueros were shouting, and a large drove of cattle was pouring in at the gate. We were about following, but a crowd of men and women on the steps of the hacienda shouted to us not to come in, and a man ran toward us, throwing up both hands, and shut the gate directly in our faces. This promised us another Don Gregorio welcome; but this ominous demonstration did not mean anything churlish; on the contrary, all was done out of kindness. We had been expected for three months. Through the agency of friends the proprietor had advised the major domo of our intended visit, directing him to do all in his power to make us comfortable, and it was for this reason that the latter had ordered the gate to be shut upon us, for, as the man who did it told us, the hacienda was overrun with women and children, and there was no room for another hammock. He conducted us to the church, standing in a fine situation, and offered us the sacristia, or vestry-room, which was new, clean, and had plastered walls, but it was small, and had only knobs for two hammocks. It had a door of communication with the church, and he said we might swing a third hammock in the latter, but it was toward the end of a fiesta, the Indians might want to use the altar, and we had some scruples.

Our alternative was a house directly opposite the gate of the hacienda, to which there was no objection on the score of size, for as yet its dimensions were unlimited, as it was merely a frame of poles supporting a thatched roof, with a great pile of lime and sand in the centre, intended to be made into walls. The proprietor was erecting it expressly for the accommodation of travellers. While we resided in it, the pile of lime and sand was converted to its destined purpose, and we were plastered in; so that the next visiter to these ruins will find a good house ready for his reception. The major domo wished us to take our meals at the hacienda, but as we had all our travelling equipage, we again organized for housekeeping, and to that end we had an unusual proportion of comforts. Besides the resources of the hacienda, we had the village of Pisté at command, and Valladolid being but six hours' distance, we prepared an order for supplies to be sent off the next day.

The next morning, under the guidance of an Indian of the hacienda, we prepared for a preliminary survey. The ruins of Chichen lie on a hacienda, called by the name of the ancient city. It is the property of Don Juan Sosa, and was set off to him, on the decease of his father and an apportionment of his estate, with cattle, horses, and mules, at a valuation of between five and six thousand dollars. As with most of the lands in that neighbourhood, the fee is in the government, and the proprietor is entitled only to the majores, or improvements.

The ruins are nine leagues from Valladolid, the camino real to which passes directly through the field. The great buildings tower on both sides of the road in full sight of all passers-by, and from the fact that the road is much travelled, the ruins of Chichen are perhaps more generally known to the people of the country than any other in Yucatan. It is an interesting fact, however, that the first stranger who ever visited them was a native of New-York, whom we afterward met at Valladolid, and who is now again residing in this city.

Immediately on our arrival at Chichen we heard of a pay-sanno, or countryman, Don Juan Burque, enginero en la machina de Valladolid, the English of which is, Mr. John Burke, engineer in the factory. In 1838 Mr. Burke came from Valladolid to the village of Cawa, six leagues distant from Chichen. While making excursions in the neighbourhood, one of the young men told him of old buildings on this hacienda, from one of which Valladolid was visible. Mr. Burke rode over, and on the fourth of July stood on the top of the Castillo, spyglass in hand, looking out for Valladolid. Two years afterward, in 1840, they were visited by the Baron Frederichstahl, and by him first brought to the notice of the public, both in Europe and this country; and I take occasion to say that this visit was made in the prosecution of a route recommended to him by me after my return from my former interrupted journey of exploration among the ruins of Yucatan.

But to return. From the door of our hut some of the principal buildings were in sight. We went first to those on the opposite side of the camino real. The path led through the cattle-yard of the hacienda, from which we passed out at one end by a range of bars into the field of ruins, partially wooded, but the greater part open and intersected by cattle-paths. Garrapatas were as abundant as ever, and perhaps more so from the numerous cattle running over the plain, but the luxuries of an open country, and the facility of moving from place to place, were so great, that these could not mar our satisfaction, which was raised to the highest pitch by the ruins themselves. These were, indeed, magnificent. The buildings were large, and some were in good preservation; in general, the façades were not so elaborately ornamented as some we had seen, seemed of an older date, and the sculpture was ruder, but the interior apartments contained decorations and devices that were new to us, and powerfully interesting. All the principal buildings were within a comparatively small compass; in fact, they were in such proximity, and the facilities for moving among them were so great, that by one o'clock we had visited every building, examined every apartment, and arranged the whole plan and order of work. This over, we went to join Doctor Cabot, who was in the mean time pursuing an independent occupation, but on joint account, and for joint benefit.

The name of Chichen is another instance added to those already given, showing the importance attached in that dry country to the possession of water. It is compounded of the two Maya words *chi*, mouth, and *chen*, well, and signifies the mouth of the well. Among the ruins are two great senotes, which, beyond doubt, furnished water to the inhabitants of the ancient city. Since the establishment of a hacienda and the construction of a well, these had fallen into disuse. Doctor Cabot had undertaken to open a path in one of them down to the water, for the purpose of bathing, which, in that hot climate, was as refreshing as food. We came upon him just as he had finished, and, besides his Indian workmen, he had the company of a large party of Mestizo boys from the village of Pisté, who were already taking advantage of his labours, and were then swimming, diving, and perched all about in the hollows of the rocks.

On our journey from Peto, the particulars of which I was obliged to omit, we had entered a region where the sources of the supply of water again formed a new and distinctive feature in the face of the country, wilder, and, at first sight, perhaps creating a stronger feeling of admiration and wonder than even the extraordinary cuevas, aguadas, and senotes we had formerly encountered. These, too, are called senotes, but they differ materially from those before presented, being immense circular holes, from sixty to two hundred feet in diameter, with broken, rocky, perpendicular sides from fifty to one hundred feet deep, and having at the bottom a great body of water, of an unknown depth, always about the same level, supposed to be supplied by subterranean rivers. We had seen ranchos of Indians established near these senotes, with a railing on one side, over which Indian women were drawing up water in little bark buckets; probably the two great senotes at this place were the inducements to the foundation of the ancient city.

Figure 10 represents this senote among the ruins of Chichen. Though wild enough in its appearance, it had less of that extraordinary regularity than the others we had seen. Those were all circular, and it was impossible to get access to the water except by means of a rope. This was oblong, about three hundred and fifty feet in length and one hundred and fifty wide. The sides were between sixty and seventy feet high, and perpendicular, except in one place, which was broken so as to form a steep, winding descent to the water. The view is taken from the edge of the water. The path is evidently, to a certain extent, artificial, as we saw in one place the vestiges of a stone wall along the brink. On this side Doctor Cabot had erected a railing for protection, which the mischievous boys of Pisté afterward pulled down; we tempted them with a reward of two reales apiece for the discovery of the offenders, but none of them ever accepted the offer. These boys, by-the-way, with the inhabitants

FIG. 10

of Pisté generally, both men and women, seemed to consider
that the opening of this path was for their especial benefit, and
at first they made it a point to be on the spot at the same hour
with us. Upon one occasion we were so annoyed by the presence
of two ladies of that village, who seemed determined not to go
away, that we were obliged to come to an amicable understanding by means of a peremptory notice that all persons must give
us the benefit of their absence at that hour; and every day, when
the sun was vertical and scarcely endurable on the surface of the
earth, we bathed in this deep senote.

We returned to the hut well satisfied with our first day at
Chichen; and there was another circumstance which, though
painful in itself, added materially to the spirit with which we

commenced our labours at this place. The danger apprehended from the rainy season was coming to pass, and under the anticipation of a failure of the next crop, corn had risen from two reales to a dollar the load. The distress occasioned in this country by the failure of the corn crop cannot well be imagined. In 1836 this calamity occurred, and from the same cause that threatened to produce it now. Along the coast a supply was furnished from the United States, but it would not bear the expense of transportation into the interior, and in this region corn rose to four dollars a load, which put the staff of life completely beyond the reach of the Indians. Famine ensued, and the poor Indians died of starvation. At the time of our arrival, the criados, or servants, of the hacienda, always improvident, had consumed their small stock, and, with no hope from their milpas, with the permission of the master were about moving away to regions where the pressure would be less severe. Our arrival, as the major domo told us, arrested this movement; instead of our being obliged to hunt them up, the poor Indians crowded round the door of our hut, begging employment, and scrambling for the reales which Albino distributed among them; but all the relief we could afford them was of short duration, and it may not be amiss to mention that at the moment of writing the calamity apprehended has come to pass; the ports of Yucatan are thrown open and begging for bread, and that country in which, but a few short months since, we were moving so quietly and experiencing continual acts of kindness, is now groaning under famine superadded to the horrors of war.

CHAPTER XVII

Plate XXVI represents the general plan of the
ruins of Chichen. This plan is made from bearings taken with
the compass, and the distances were all measured with a line.
The buildings are laid down on the plan according to their
exterior form. All now standing are comprehended, and the
whole circumference occupied by them is about two miles, which
is equal to the diameter of two thirds of a mile, though ruined
buildings appear beyond these limits.

By referring to the plan the reader will see the position of
the hut in which we lived, and, following the path from our
door through the cattle-yard of the hacienda, at the distance of
two hundred and fifty yards he will reach the building represented in Plate XXVII. It does not stand on an artificial terrace,
but the earth seems to have been excavated for some distance
before it, so as to give it elevation of position. It faces the east,
and measures one hundred and forty-nine feet in front by forty-

Plate XXVI

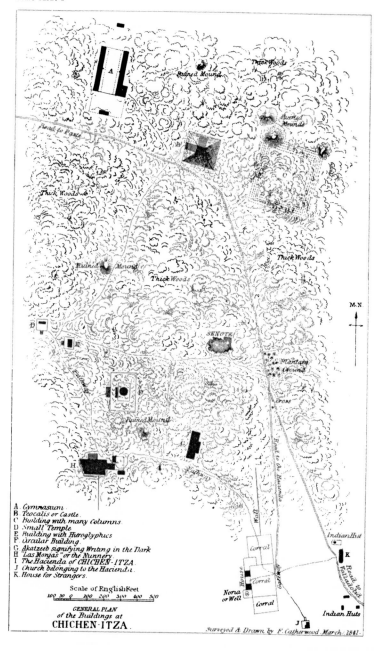

A. Gymnasum.
B. Teocalis or Castle.
C. Building with many Columns.
D. Small Temple.
E. Building with Hieroglyphics.
F. Circular Building.
G. Akatzeeb signifying Writing in the Dark.
H. "Las Monjas" or the Nunnery.
I. The Hacienda of CHICHEN-ITZA.
J. Church belonging to the Hacienda.
K. House for Strangers.

Scale of English Feet
100 50 0   100   200   300   400   500

GENERAL PLAN
of the Buildings at
CHICHEN-ITZA.

Surveyed & Drawn by F. Catherwood March 1842.

Plate XXVII

CHICHEN
building called AKATZEEB

eight feet deep. The whole exterior is rude, and without ornament of any kind. A grand staircase, forty-five feet wide, now
entirely in ruins, rises in the centre to the roof of the building.
On each side of the staircase are two doorways; at each end is a
single doorway, and the front facing the west has seven. The
whole number of apartments is eighteen. The west front opens
upon a large hollow surface, whether natural or artificial it is
not easy to say, and in the centre of this is one of those features
before referred to, a solid mass of masonry, forty-four feet by
thirty-four, standing out from the wall, high as the roof, and
corresponding, in position and dimensions, with the ruined
staircase on the eastern front. This projection is not necessary for
the support of the building; it is not an ornament, but, on the
contrary, a deformity; and whether it be really a solid mass, or
contain interior chambers, remains to be ascertained by the future explorer.

At the south end the doorway opens into a chamber, round
which hangs a greater and more impenetrable mystery. This
chamber is nineteen feet wide by eight feet six inches deep, and
in the back wall a low, narrow doorway communicates with another chamber in the rear, of the same dimensions, but having
its floor one step higher. The lintel of this doorway is of stone,
and on the soffite, or under part, is sculptured the subject represented in Plate XXVIII. This tablet, and the position in which it
exists, have given the name to the building, which the Indians
call Akatzeeb, signifying the writing in the dark; for, as no light
enters except from the single doorway, the chamber was so dark
that the drawing could with difficulty be copied. It was the first
time in Yucatan that we had found hieroglyphics sculptured on
stone, which, beyond all question, bore the same type with those
at Copan and Palenque. The sitting figure seems performing
some act of incantation, or some religious or idolatrous rite,
which the "writing in the dark" undoubtedly explains, if one
could but read it. Physical force may raze these buildings to the
ground, and lay bare all the secrets they contain, but physical
force can never unravel the mystery that involves this sculptured
tablet.

Leaving this building, and following the path indicated in
the map, at the distance of one hundred and fifty yards westward
we reach a modern stone fence, dividing the cattle-field of the
hacienda, on the other side of which appears through the trees,
between two other buildings, the end façade of a long, majestic
pile, called, like one of the principal edifices at Uxmal, the

Plate XXVIII

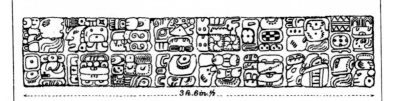

Drawing on Soffite or under side of Doorway

Sculptured Figure and Hieroglyphics in low relief on the Soffite and upper part of a Doorway of a Building called AKATZEEB. at CHICHEN-ITZA

Step

DOORWAY

This Building is of Stone well put together and the Sculpture has been painted. Red. Blue and Yellow. are still visible.

Level of Floor

F. Catherwood.

J. N. Gimbrede

Monjas, or Nuns; it is remarkable for its good state of preservation, and the richness and beauty of its ornaments, as represented in Plate XXIX. The view comprehends the corner of a building on the right, at a short distance, called the Eglesia, or Church. The height of this façade is twenty-five feet, and its width thirty-five. It has two cornices of tasteful and elaborate design. Over the doorway are twenty small cartouches of hieroglyphics in four rows, five in a row, barely indicated in the engraving, and to make room for which the lower cornice is carried up. Over these stand out in a line six bold projecting curved ornaments, like that presented from the House of the Governor at Uxmal, resembling an elephant's trunk, and the upper centre space over the doorway is an irregular circular niche, in which portions of a seated figure, with a head-dress of feathers, still remain. The rest of the ornaments are of that distinctive stamp, characteristic of the ancient American cities, and unlike the designs of any other people, with which the reader must now be familiar. The tropical plants and shrubs growing on the roof, which, when we first saw it, hung over the cornice like a fringe-work, added greatly to the picturesque effect of this elegant façade.

Plate XXX represents the front of the same building. It is composed of two structures entirely different from each other, one of which forms a sort of wing to the principal edifice, and has at the end the façade before presented. The whole length is two hundred and twenty-eight feet, and the depth of the principal structure is one hundred and twelve feet. The only portion containing interior chambers is that which I have called the wing. This has two doorways opening into chambers twenty-six feet long and eight feet deep, behind each of which is another of corresponding dimensions, now filled up several feet with mortar and stones, and appearing to have been originally filled up solid to the ceiling, making again casas cerradas, or closed houses. The whole number of chambers in this wing is nine, and these are all the apartments on the ground floor. The great structure to which the wing adjoins is apparently a solid mass of masonry, erected only to hold up the two ranges of buildings upon it. A grand staircase fifty-six feet wide, the largest we saw in the country, rises to the top. On one side of the staircase a huge breach, twenty or thirty feet deep, has been made by the proprietor, for the purpose of getting out building stone, which discloses only solid masonry. The grand staircase is thirty-two feet high, and has thirty-nine steps. On the top of

Plate XXIX

F. Catherwood.

Gambrede.

MONJAS. CHICHEN ITZA.

Plate XXX

CASA DE LAS MONJAS . CHICHEN.

the structure stands a range of buildings, with a platform of fourteen feet in front extending all round.

From the back of this platform the grand staircase rises again, having the same width, fifteen steps to the roof of the second range, which forms a platform in front of the third range; this last is, unfortunately, in a ruinous condition, and it is to be observed that in this, as in all the other cases, these ancient architects never placed an upper building on the roof of a lower one, but always back, so as to rest on a structure solid from the ground, the roof of the lower range being merely a platform in front of the upper one.

The circumference of this building is six hundred and thirty-eight feet, and its height, when entire, was sixty-five feet. It seems to have been constructed only with reference to the second range of apartments, upon which the art and skill of the builders have been lavishly expended. It is one hundred and four feet long and thirty feet wide, and the broad platform around it, though overgrown with grass several feet high, formed a noble promenade, commanding a magnificent view of the whole surrounding country.

On the side of the staircase are five doorways, of which the three centre ones are what are usually called false doors, appearing to be merely recesses in the wall. The compartments between the doorways contained combinations of ornaments of unusual taste and elegance, both in arrangement and design. The two extreme doorways open into chambers, in each of which are three long recesses in the back wall, extending from the floor to the ceiling, all of which, from the remains still visible, were once ornamented with paintings. At each end of the building was another chamber, with three niches or recesses, and on the other side, facing the south, the three centre doorways, corresponding with the false doors on the north side, opened into an apartment forty-seven feet long and nine deep, having nine long niches in the back wall; all the walls from the floor to the peak of the arch had been covered with painted designs, now wantonly defaced, but the remains of which present colours in some places still bright and vivid; and among these remains detached portions of human figures continually recur, well drawn, the heads adorned with plumes of feathers, and the hands bearing shields and spears. All attempt at description would fail, and much more would an attempt to describe the strange interest of walking along the overgrown platform of this gigantic and desolate building.

Plate XXXI

EGLESIA, CHICHEN ITZA

Descending again to the ground, at the end of the wing stands what is called the Eglesia, or Church, a corner of which was comprehended in a previous view, and the front of which is represented in Plate XXXI. It is twenty-six feet long, fourteen deep, and thirty-one high, its comparatively great height adding very much to the effect of its appearance. It has three cornices, and the spaces between are richly ornamented. The sculpture is rude but grand. The principal ornament is over the doorway, and on each side are two human figures in a sitting posture, but, unfortunately, much mutilated. The portion of the façade above the second cornice is merely an ornamented wall, like those before mentioned at Zayi and Labnà.

The whole of this building is in a good state of preservation. The interior consists of a single apartment, once covered with plaster, and along the top of the wall under the arch are seen the traces of a line of medallions or cartouches in plaster, which once contained hieroglyphics. The Indians have no superstitious feelings about these ruins, except in regard to this building; and in this they say that on Good Friday of every year music is heard sounding; but this illusion, brought with us from Santa Cruz del Quiché, was here destined to be broken. In this chamber we opened our Daguerreotype apparatus, and on Good Friday were at work all day, but heard no music. This chamber, by-the-way, was the best we had found for our Daguerreotype operations. Having but one door, it was easily darkened; we were not obliged to pack up and carry away; the only danger was of cattle getting in and breaking; and there was no difficulty in getting an Indian to pass the night in the room and guard against this peril.

South of the end of the Monjas, and twenty-two feet distant, is another building, measuring thirty-eight feet by thirteen, having the exterior above the cornice decorated in the usual manner, but which I do not think it worth while to present.

Leaving this pile of buildings, and passing on northward from the Monjas, at the distance of four hundred feet we reach the edifice represented in Plate XXXII, conspicuous among the ruins of Chichen for its picturesque appearance, and unlike any other we had seen, except one at Mayapan much ruined. It is circular in form, and is known by the name of the Caracol, or winding staircase, on account of its interior arrangements. It stands on the upper of two terraces. The lower one measures in front from north to south two hundred and twenty-three feet, and in depth from east to west one hundred and fifty feet, and

Plate XXXII

Catherwood.

Jeavons

CHICHEN
Circular Building.

is still in good preservation. A grand staircase forty-five feet wide, and containing twenty steps, rises to the platform of this terrace. On each side of this staircase, forming a sort of balustrade, were the entwined bodies of two gigantic serpents, three feet wide, portions of which are still in place; and among the ruins of the staircase we saw a gigantic head, which had terminated at one side the foot of the steps.

The platform of the second terrace measures eighty feet in front and fifty-five in depth, and is reached by another staircase forty-two feet wide, and having sixteen steps. In the centre of the steps, and against the wall of the terrace, are the remains of a pedestal six feet high, on which probably once stood an idol. On the platform, fifteen feet from the last step, stands the building. It is twenty-two feet in diameter, and has four small doorways facing the cardinal points. A great portion of the upper part and one of the sides have fallen. Above the cornice the roof sloped so as almost to form an apex. The height, including the terraces, is little short of sixty feet, and, when entire, even among the great buildings around, this structure must have presented a striking appearance. The doorways give entrance to a circular corridor five feet wide. The inner wall has also four doorways, smaller than the others, and standing at intermediate points of the compass, facing northeast, northwest, southwest, and southeast. These doors give entrance to a second circular corridor, four feet wide; and in the centre is a circular mass, apparently of solid stone, seven feet six inches in diameter; but in one place, at the height of eight feet from the ground, was a small square opening choked up with stones, which I endeavoured to clear out; but the stones falling into the narrow corridor made it dangerous to continue. The roof was so tottering that I could not discover to what this opening led. It was about large enough to admit the figure of a man in a standing position, to look out from the top. The walls of both corridors were plastered and ornamented with paintings, and both were covered with the triangular arch. The plan of the building was new, but, instead of unfolding secrets, it drew closer the curtain that already shrouded, with almost impenetrable folds, these mysterious structures.

At the distance of four hundred and twenty feet northwest from the Caracol stands the building represented in Figure 11. It is called by the Indians Chichanchob, meaning in Spanish, Casa Colorada, and in English, Red House. The terrace is sixty-two feet long and fifty-five wide, and is still in good

preservation; the staircase is twenty feet wide, and as we approached it on our first visit, a cow was coming quietly down the
steps.

Fig. 11

The building measures forty-three feet front and twenty-
three feet deep, and is still strong and substantial. Above the
cornice it was richly ornamented, but the ornaments are now
much decayed. It has three doorways, which open into a corridor
running the whole width of the building; and along the top of
the back wall was a stone tablet, with a row of hieroglyphics
extending all along the wall. Many of them were defaced, and,
from their height, in an awkward position to copy; but we had
a scaffold erected, and obtained copies of the whole. Plate
XXXIII represents these hieroglyphics, so far as they could be
made out. When not distinct, to avoid misleading they are not
given at all. Under the hieroglyphics, in the plate, is given a
plan of the building, with its terrace and staircase. It has a back
corridor, consisting of three chambers, all of which retain the
marks of painting; and, from the convenience of its arrangements, with the platform of the terrace for a promenade, and
the view of a fine open country in front, but for the greater
convenience of being near the hacienda we should have been
tempted to take up our abode in it.

At the short distance of two hundred feet is the building
represented in Figure 12. The platform of the terrace was sixty-

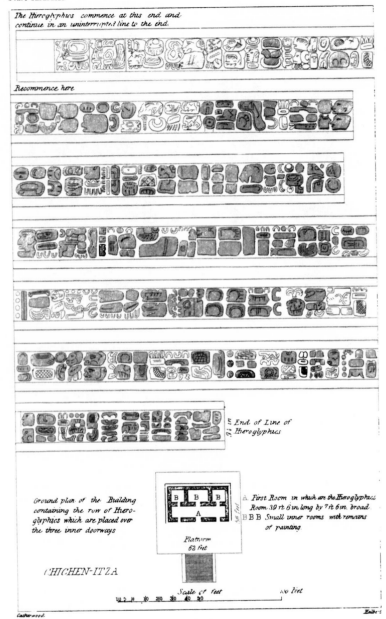

Plate XXXIII

The Hieroglyphics commence at this end and
continue in an uninterrupted line to the end.

Recommence here

End of Line of
Hieroglyphics

Ground plan of the Building
containing the row of Hieroglyphics which are placed over
the three inner doorways

A. First Room in which are the Hieroglyphics
Room 39 ft. 6 in. long by 7 ft. 6 in. broad
BBB Small inner rooms with remains
of painting

Platform
62 feet

CHICHEN-ITZA

Scale of feet   100 feet

Catherwood.   Halbert

four feet square, the building had three rooms, but both terrace
and building are ruined, and the view is presented only because
it was so picturesque that Mr. Catherwood could not resist the
temptation to draw it.

Fig. 12

All these buildings are within three hundred yards of the
staircase of the Monjas; from any intermediate point all are in
full sight; the field is open, and intersected by cattle-paths; the
buildings, staircases, and terraces were overgrown, but Indians
being at hand in sufficient force, they were easily cleared, and
the whole was finished with a despatch that had never before
attended our progress.

These are the only buildings on the west side of the camino
real which are still standing; but great vestiges exist of mounds
with remains of buildings upon them, and colossal stones and
fragments of sculpture at their feet, which it would be impossible to present in detail.

Passing among these vestiges, we come out upon the camino
real, and, crossing it, again enter an open field, containing the
extraordinary edifice represented in Plate XXXIV, which, on

Plate XXXIV

F. Catherwood.

Gandinita.

GYMNASIUM, CHICHEN ITZA

first reaching the field of ruins, we rode in on horseback to examine. It consists of two immense parallel walls, each two hundred and seventy-four feet long, thirty feet thick, and one hundred and twenty feet apart. One hundred feet from the northern extremity, facing the open space between the walls, stands on an elevation a building thirty-five feet long, containing a single chamber, with the front fallen, and, rising among the rubbish, the remains of two columns, elaborately ornamented with sculpture; the whole interior wall being exposed to view, covered from the floor to the peak of the arch with sculptured figures in bas-relief, much worn and faded. The engraving represents the two walls, with this building in the distance. And at the other end, setting back, too, one hundred feet, and commanding the space between the walls, is another building eighty-one feet long, also ruined, but exhibiting the remains of two columns richly ornamented with sculptured figures in bas-relief. The position in which these walls and buildings stand to each other is laid down on the general plan.

In the centre of the great stone walls, exactly opposite each other, and at the height of twenty feet from the ground, are two massive stone rings, four feet in diameter, and one foot one inch thick; the diameter of the hole is one foot seven inches. On the rim and border were two sculptured entwined serpents, one of which is represented in Figure 13.

These walls, at the first glance, we considered identical in their uses and purposes with the parallel structures supporting the rings at Uxmal, of which I have already expressed the opinion that they were intended for the celebration of some public games. I have in all cases adopted the names of buildings which I found assigned to them on the spot, where any existed, and where there were none I have not attempted to give any. At Chichen all the principal buildings have names; this is called an Eglesia, or Church, of the antiguos, which was begun, but not finished, and the great open walls present not a bad idea of one of their gigantic churches before the roof is put on; but as we have already one Eglesia, and there is historical authority which, in my opinion, shows clearly the object and uses of this extraordinary structure, I shall call it, as occasion requires, the Gymnasium or Tennis-court.

In the account of the diversions of Montezuma, given by Herrera, we have the following:

"The King took much Delight in seeing Sport at Ball, which the Spaniards have since prohibited, because of the Mis-

FIG. 13

chief that often hapned at it; and was by them call'd *Tlachtli,*
being like our Tennis. The Ball was made of the Gum of a Tree
that grows in hot Countries, which, having Holes made in it,
distils great white Drops, that soon harden, and, being work'd
and moulded together, turn as black as Pitch.* The Balls made
thereof, tho' hard and heavy to the Hand, did bound and fly as
well as our Foot-balls, there being no need to blow them; nor
did they use Chaces, but vy'd to drive the adverse Party that is
to hit the Wall, the others were to make good, or strike it over.
They struck it with any Part of their Body, as it hapned, or they
could most conveniently; and sometimes he lost that touched it
with any other Part but his Hip, which was look'd upon among
them as the greatest Dexterity; and to this Effect, that the Ball
might rebound the better, they fastned a Piece of stiff Leather
on their Hips. They might strike it every time it rebounded,
which it would do several Times one after another, in so much
that it look'd as if it had been alive. They play'd in Parties, so
many on a Side, for a Load of Mantles, or what the Gamesters
could afford, at so many Scores. They also play'd for Gold, and
Feather-work, and sometimes play'd themselves away, as has been

*Undoubtedly caoutchouc, or India-rubber.

said before. The Place where they play'd was a ground Room, long, narrow, and high, but wider above than below, and higher on the Sides than at the Ends, and they kept it very well plaster'd and smooth, both the Walls and the Floor. *On the side Walls they fix'd certain Stones, like those of a Mill, with a Hole quite through the Middle,* just as big as the Ball, and he that could strike it through there won the Game; and in Token of its being an extraordinary Success, which rarely hapned, he had a Right to the Cloaks of all the Lookers-on, by antient Custom, and Law amongst Gamesters; and it was very pleasant to see, that as soon as ever the Ball was in the Hole, the Standers-by took to their Heels, running away with all their Might to save their Cloaks, laughing and rejoicing, others scouring after them to secure their Cloaks for the Winner, who was oblig'd to offer some Sacrifice to the Idol of the Tennis-court, and the Stone through whose Hole the Ball had pass'd. Every Tennis-court was a Temple, having two Idols, the one of Gaming, and the other of the Ball. On a lucky Day, at Midnight, they perform'd certain Ceremonies and Enchantments on the two lower Walls and on the Midst of the Floor, singing certain Songs, or Ballads; after which a Priest of the great Temple went with some of their Religious Men to bless it; he uttered some Words, threw the Ball about the Tennis-court four Times, and then it was consecrated, and might be play'd in, but not before. The Owner of the Tennis-court, who was always a Lord, never play'd without making some Offering and performing certain Ceremonies to the Idol of Gaming, which shows how superstitious they were, since they had such Regard to their Idols, even in their Diversions. Montezuma carry'd the Spaniards to this Sport, and was well pleas'd to see them play at it, as also at Cards and Dice."

With some slight variation in details, the general features are so identical as to leave no doubt on my mind that this structure was erected for precisely the same object as the Tennis-court in the city of Mexico described by Herrera. The temples are at hand in which sacrifices were offered, and we discover in this something more important than the mere determining of the character of a building; for in the similarity of diversions we see a resemblance in manners and institutions, and trace an affinity between the people who erected the ruined cities of Yucatan and those who inhabited Mexico at the time of the conquest. In the account of Herrera, moreover, we see incidentally the drawing of a funeral pall over the institutions of the natives, for we learn that the sport which "Montezuma took

Plate XXXV

CHICHEN

F. Catherwood.

much delight in seeing," and which, beyond doubt, was a favourite diversion of the people, "the Spaniards have since prohibited."

At the southern extremity of the eastern wall, and on the
outer side, stands the building represented in Plate XXXV, consisting of two ranges, one even with the ground, and the other
about twenty-five feet above it, the latter being in a good state
of preservation, simple, tasteful in its arrangement of ornaments,
and having conspicuous a procession of tigers or lynxes, which
appear on a small scale in the engraving. From its lofty position,
with trees growing around it and on the roof, the effect is beautifully picturesque; but it has, besides, a far higher interest, and
on some considerations may perhaps be regarded as the most
important structure that we met with in our whole exploration
of ruins.

The lower building, standing on the ground, is in a ruinous
condition: the front has fallen, and shows only the remains of
two columns covered with sculptured figures; the fall of the
front has laid bare the entire wall of the chamber, covered from
one end to the other with elaborately-sculptured figures in bas-
relief.

Plate XXXVI represents a portion of these figures. Exposed
for ages to a long succession of winds and rains, the characters
were faded and worn; under the glare of a tropical sun the lines
were confused and indistinct, and the reflection of the heat was
so intense that it was impossible to work before it except for an
hour or two in the afternoon, when the building was in the
shade. The head-dress of the figures is, as usual, a plume of
feathers, and in the upper row each figure carries a bundle of
spears or a quiver of arrows. All these figures were painted, and
the reader may imagine what the effect must have been when all
was entire. The Indians call this chamber Stohl, and say that it
represents a dance of the antiguos; and these bas-reliefs, too,
have a distinct and independent value. In the large work of
Nebel, entitled "Voyage Pittoresque et Archéologique dans le
Mexique," lately published at Paris, is a drawing of the stone
of sacrifice in the Museum of Mexico, and now for the first time
published. It is nine feet in diameter and three feet thick, and
contains a procession of figures in bas-relief, which, though differing in detail, are of the same general character with those
sculptured on the wall of this building. The stone was dug up
in the plaza of Mexico, near the spot on which stood, in the
time of Montezuma, the great teocalis of that city. The resem-

Plate XXXVI

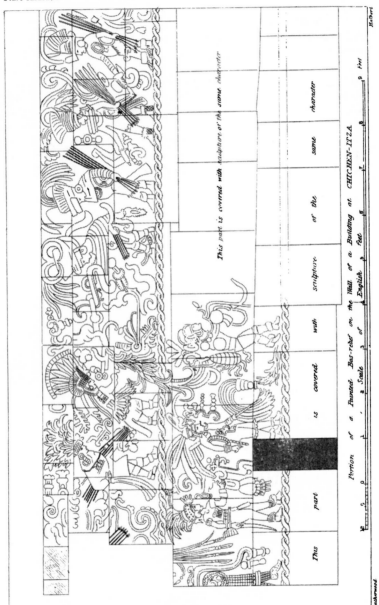

Portion of a Painted Bas-relief on the Wall of a Building at CHICHEN-ITZA.

This part is covered with sculpture of the same character

Catherwood.

Holbert.

blance stands upon a different footing from any which may exist in Mitla, or Xocichalco, or other places, the history of which is unknown, and forms another connecting link with the very people who occupied the city of Mexico at the time of the conquest. And the proofs go on accumulating. In the upper building, the back of which appears in the engraving, is presented a casket containing, though broken and disfigured, perhaps the greatest gem of aboriginal art which on the whole Continent of America now survives.

The steps or other means of access to this building are gone, and we reached it by clambering over fallen stones. The door opens upon the platform of the wall, overlooking the Tennis-court. The front corridor was supported by massive pillars, portions of which still remain, covered with elaborate sculptured ornaments. The lintel of the inner doorway is a beam of sapote richly carved. The jambs are partly buried, and above the rubbish appear sculptured figures with rich head-dresses, which anywhere else we should have considered it necessary to bring to light and copy; but between these jambs we enter an inner chamber, the walls and ceiling of which are covered, from the floor to the peak of the arch, with designs in painting, representing, in bright and vivid colours, human figures, battles, houses, trees, and scenes of domestic life, and conspicuous on one of the walls is a large canoe; but the first feeling of gratified surprise was followed by heavy disappointment, for the whole was mutilated and disfigured. In some places the plaster was broken off; in every part deep and malignant scratches appeared in the walls, and while individual figures were entire, the connexion of the subjects could not be made out. For a long time we had been tantalized with fragments of painting, giving us the strong impression that in this more perishable art these aboriginal builders had made higher attainments than in that of sculpture, and we now had proofs that our impression did them justice. Plate XXXVII represents detached portions of these paintings. The colours are green, yellow, red, blue, and a reddish brown, the last being invariably the colour given to human flesh. Wanting the various tints, the engraving, of course, gives only an imperfect idea of them, though, even in outline, they exhibit a freedom of touch which could only be the result of discipline and training under masters. But they have a higher interest than any that attaches to them as mere specimens of art; for among them are seen designs and figures which call forcibly to mind the well-known picture writings of the Mexicans; and if these

Plate XXXVII

analogies are sustained, this building attached to the walls of the Tennis-court stands an unimpeachable witness that the people who inhabited Mexico at the time of the conquest belonged to the same great race which furnished the builders of the ruined cities in Yucatan.

But to continue. At the distance of five hundred feet southeast from this rises the Castillo, represented in Plate XXXVIII, the first building which we saw, and from every point of view

Fig. 14

the grandest and most conspicuous object that towers above the plain. Every Sunday the ruins are resorted to as a promenade by the villagers of Pisté, and nothing can surpass the picturesque appearance of this lofty building while women, dressed in white, with red shawls, are moving on the platform, and passing in and out at the doors. The mound measures at the base on the north and south sides one hundred and ninety-six feet ten inches, and on the east and west sides two hundred and two feet. It does not face the cardinal points exactly, though probably so intended; and in all the buildings, from some cause not easily accounted for, while one varies ten degrees one way, that immediately adjoining varies twelve or thirteen degrees in another. It is built up apparently solid from the plain to the height of seventy-five feet. On the west side is a staircase thirty-seven feet wide; on the north, being that presented in the engraving, the staircase is forty-four feet wide, and contains ninety steps. On the ground at the foot of the staircase, forming a bold, striking, and well-conceived commencement to this lofty range, are two colossal serpents' heads, ten feet in length, with mouths wide open and tongues protruding, as represented in Figure 14. No doubt they were emblematic of some religious belief, and in the minds of an imaginative people, passing between them to ascend the steps, must have excited feelings of solemn awe.

The platform on the top of the mound measures sixty-one feet from north to south, and sixty-four from east to west; and the building measures in the same directions forty-three feet and forty-nine. Single doorways face the east, south, and west, having massive lintels of sapote wood covered with elaborate carvings, and the jambs are ornamented with sculptured figures, one of which is represented in Plate XXXIX. The sculpture is much worn, but the head-dress, ornamented with a plume of feathers, and portions of the rich attire still remain. The face is well preserved, and has a dignified appearance. It has, too, earrings, and the nose bored, which, according to the historical accounts, was so prevalent a custom in Yucatan, that long after the conquest the Spaniards passed laws for its prohibition.

All the other jambs are decorated with sculpture of the same general character, and all open into a corridor six feet wide, extending round three sides of the building.

The doorway facing the north, represented in the engraving, presents a grander appearance, being twenty feet wide, and having two short massive columns, eight feet eight inches high, with two large projections at the base, entirely covered with elab-

Plate XXXVIII

CASTILLO. CHICHEN ITZA

F. Catherwood.

Gimbrede.

Plate XXXIX

4 feet 8½
Figure in Bas-relief on Stone on one of the Jambs of the
TEOCALLIS at CHICHEN-ITZA.

Catherwood.

orate sculpture. This doorway gives access to a corridor forty feet long by six feet four inches wide and seventeen feet high. In the back wall of this corridor is a single doorway, having sculptured jambs, over which is a richly-carved sapote beam, and giving entrance to an apartment represented in Plate XL, nineteen feet eight inches long, twelve feet nine inches wide, and seventeen feet high. In this apartment are two square pillars nine feet four inches high and one foot ten inches on each side, having sculptured figures on all their sides, and supporting massive sapote beams covered with the most elaborate carving of curious and intricate designs, but so defaced and timeworn that, in the obscurity of the room, lighted only from the door, it was extremely difficult to make them out. The impression produced on entering this lofty chamber, so entirely different from all we had met with before, was perhaps stronger than any we had yet experienced. We passed a whole day within it, from time to time stepping out upon the platform to look down upon the ruined buildings of the ancient city, and an immense field stretching on all sides beyond.

And from this lofty height we saw for the first time groups of small columns, which, on examination, proved to be among the most remarkable and unintelligible remains we had yet met with. They stood in rows of three, four, and five abreast, many rows continuing in the same direction, when they changed and pursued another. They were very low, many of them only three feet high, while the highest were not more than six feet, and consisted of several separate pieces, like millstones. Many of them had fallen, and in some places they lie prostrate in rows, all in the same direction, as if thrown down intentionally. I had a large number of Indians at work clearing them, and endeavouring to trace their direction to the end. In some places they extended to the bases of large mounds, on which were ruins of buildings and colossal fragments of sculpture, while in others they branched off and terminated abruptly. I counted three hundred and eighty, and there were many more; but so many were broken, and they lay so irregularly, that I gave up counting them. They were entirely too low to have supported a roof under which persons could walk. The idea at times suggested itself that they had upheld a raised walk of cement, but there were no remains visible. Plate XLI will give some idea of these columns, with the Castillo and part of the Tennis-court appearing in the background. They enclose an area nearly four hundred feet square; and, incomprehensible as they are in their uses

Plate XL

Plate XLI

and object, add largely to the interest and wonder connected with these ruins.

I have now closed my brief description of the ruins of Chichen, having presented, with as little detail as possible, all the principal buildings of this ancient city. Ruined mounds exist, and detached portions of sculpture strew the ground, exhibiting curious devices, which often arrested us in wandering among them, but which I shall not attempt to give. They were the ruins which we had had longest in prospect, of which we had formed the largest expectations, and these expectations were not disappointed, but more than realized. And they had additional interest in our eyes from the fact that the broad light of day beams upon their history. The first settlement of the Spaniards in the interior was made at this very spot.

The reader may remember that in the early part of these pages he accompanied Don Francisco Montejo to Chichen, or Chichen Itza, as it was called, from the name of the people who occupied the country. The site of this place is identified beyond all peradventure as that now occupied by these ruins; and the reader, perhaps, will expect from Don Francisco Montejo, or the Spanish soldiers, some detailed account of these extraordinary buildings, so different from any to which the Spaniards were accustomed. But, strange as it may appear, no such account exists. The only existing notice of their journey from the coast says, that from a place called Aké they set out, directing their course for Chichen Itza, where they determined to stop and settle, as it appeared a proper place, on account of the strength of the great buildings that were there, for defence against attacks by the Indians. We do not even learn whether these buildings were inhabited or desolate; but Herrera says that the Indians in this region were so numerous, that in making the distribution which the adelantado was allowed by the terms of the royal grant, the least number which fell to the lot of a Spaniard was two thousand.

Having regard, however, to the circumstances of the occupation and abandonment of Chichen by the Spaniards, their silence is perhaps not extraordinary. I have already mentioned that at this place the adelantado made a fatal mistake, and, lured by the glitter of gold in another province, divided his forces, and sent one of his best captains, with fifty men, in search of it. From this time calamities and dangers pressed upon him; altercations and contests began with the Indians; provisions were withheld, the Spaniards were obliged to seek them with the sword, and all that they ate was procured at the price of blood. At length the Indians determined upon their utter destruction. Immense multitudes surrounded the camp of the Spaniards, hemming them in on all sides. The Spaniards, seeing themselves reduced to the necessity of perishing by hunger, determined to die bravely in the field, and went out to give battle. The most sanguinary fight they had ever been engaged in then took place. The Spaniards fought for their lives, and the Indians to remain masters of their own soil. Masses of the latter were killed, but great slaughter was made among the Spaniards, and, to save the lives of those who remained, the adelantado retreated to the fortifications. One hundred and fifty of the conquerors were dead; nearly all the rest were wounded, and if the Indians had attacked them in their retreat they would have perished to a man.

Unable to hold out any longer, they took advantage of a night when the Indians were off their guard, and making sallies in the evening so as to keep them awake, that weariness might afterward overtake them, as soon as all was still they tied a dog to the clapper of a bell-rope, putting some food before him, but out of his reach, and with great silence marched out from the camp. The dog, when he saw them going, pulled the cord in order to go with them, and afterward to get at the food. The Indians, supposing that the Spaniards were sounding the alarm, remained quiet, waiting the result, but a little before daylight, perceiving that the bell did not cease ringing, they drew near the fortification, and found it deserted. In the mean time the Spaniards escaped toward the coast, and in the meager and disconnected accounts of their dangers and escape, it is, perhaps, not surprising that we have none whatever of the buildings, arts, and sciences of the fierce inhabitants of Chichen.

I shall close with one general remark. These cities were, of course, not all built at one time, but are the remains of different epochs. Chichen, though in a better state of preservation than most of the others, has a greater appearance of antiquity; some of the buildings are no doubt older than others, and long intervals may have elapsed between the times of their construction.

The Maya manuscript places the first discovery of Chichen within the epochs corresponding with the time between A.D. 360 and A.D. 432. From the words used, it may be understood that the discovery was then made of an actual existing city, but it is a fair construction of these words to suppose that nothing more is meant than a discovery of what the words Chi-chen import, viz., the mouths of wells, having reference to the two great senotes, the discovery of wells being, among all primitive people, and particularly in the dry region of Yucatan, an event worthy to be noted in their history.

One of these senotes I have already mentioned; the other I did not visit till the afternoon preceding our departure from Chichen. Setting out from the Castillo, at some distance we ascended a wooded elevation, which seemed an artificial causeway leading to the senote. The senote was the largest and wildest we had seen; in the midst of a thick forest, an immense circular hole, with cragged, perpendicular sides, trees growing out of them and overhanging the brink, and still as if the genius of silence reigned within. A hawk was sailing around it, looking down into the water, but without once flapping its wings. The water was of a greenish hue. A mysterious influence seemed to pervade it, in unison with the historical account that the well of Chichen was a place of pilgrimage, and that human victims were thrown into it in sacrifice. In one place, on the very brink, were the remains of a stone structure, probably connected with ancient superstitious rites; perhaps the place from which the victims were thrown into the dark well beneath.

CHAPTER XVIII

On Tuesday, the twenty-ninth of March, we left Chichen. It was still in the gray of the morning when we caught our last view of the great buildings, and as we turned away we felt that the few short months of our journey had been a time of interest and wonder, such as rarely occurs in life. At nine o'clock we reached the village of Kaua, six leagues distant, and at half past eleven the small village of Cuncunul, within an hour's ride of Valladolid, and there we determined to dine, and wait for the servants and carriers.

We remained till four o'clock, and then set out for Valladolid. As far as the suburbs the road was broken and stony. We entered by the great Church of Sisal, with convent and cloisters by its side, and a square in front, which, as we rode across it, sounded hollow under our horses' feet, and underneath was an immense senote. We passed up the Calle de Sisal, a long street with straggling houses on each side, and were directed to the house of Don Pedro Baranda, one of the largest and best in the place. This gentleman had received advices of our intended visit, and had engaged for us a house. As our luggage did not arrive, he furnished us with hammocks, and in an hour we were comfortable as in our house at Merida. About midnight Albino came clattering to the door, accompanied by only one horse, carrying our hammocks, and bringing the disastrous intelligence that the horse carrying the Daguerreotype apparatus had run

223

away, and made a general crash. Hitherto the apparatus had always been carried by an Indian, but the road from Chichen was so good that we were not afraid to trust it on horseback. There was consolation, however, in the thought that we could not lose what we had already done with its assistance.

The next morning we were in no hurry. From Valladolid it was our purpose to prosecute our exploration through a region of which less was known than of any we had yet visited. In our short voyage with Captain Fensley from the Laguna to Sisal, he had told us of stone buildings on the coast, near Cape Catoche, which he called old Spanish forts. These accounts were confirmed by others, and we at length ascertained what we supposed to be the fact, that in two places on the coast called Tancar and Tuloom, what were taken for Spanish forts were aboriginal buildings. Our business at Valladolid was to make arrangements for reaching them, and at the same time for coasting round Cape Catoche, and visiting the Island of Cozumel. We had been told that at Valladolid we should be able to procure all necessary information about the ruins on the coast; but we could not even learn the way to reach them; and by the advice of Don Pedro Baranda we determined to remain a few days, until a person who was expected, and who was familiar with that region, should arrive.

In the mean time, a few days did not hang heavy on our hands in Valladolid. The city, which was founded at an early period of the conquest, contains about fifteen thousand inhabitants, and is distinguished as the residence of the vicar-general of the church of Yucatan.

It was built in a style commensurate with the lofty pretensions of the conquerors, and, like other cities of Spanish America, bears the marks of ancient grandeur, but is now going to decay. The roads leading to it and the very streets are overgrown with bushes. The parochial church still stands, the principal object in the plaza, and the churches of San Servacio, San Juan De Dios, Santa Lucia, Santa Ana, La Virgen de la Candelaria, and the Church of Sisal, the largest buildings in the city, are all more or less dilapidated.

The same melancholy tokens are visible in the private houses. In the principal street stand large buildings, roofless, without windows or doors, and with grass and bushes growing from crevices in the walls; while here and there, as if in mockery of human pride, a tottering front has blazoned upon it the coat of arms of some proud Castilian, distinguished among the daring soldiers of the conquest, whose race is now entirely unknown.

Among these time-shattered buildings stood one in striking contrast, remarkable for its neat, compact, and business-like appearance; and in that country it seemed a phenomenon. It was a cotton factory belonging to Don Pedro Baranda, the first established in the Mexican Republic, and for that reason, as emblematic of the dawn of a great manufacturing system, called the "Aurora de la Industria Yucateca;" and, what gave it a greater interest in our eyes, it was under the direction of that young countryman and fellow-citizen, Don Juan Burque, or Mr. John Burke, to whom I before referred as the first stranger who visited the ruins of Chichen. It seemed strange to meet in this unknown, half-Spanish and half-Indian town a citizen of New-York. It was seven years the day of our arrival since he came to Valladolid. He had almost lost the facility of expressing himself in his native tongue, but in dress, manner, appearance, and feelings he was unchanged, and different from all around him; and it was gratifying to us to know that throughout that neighbourhood it was no small recommendation to be the countryman of "the engineer."

Don Pedro Baranda, the proprietor of the factory, began life in the Spanish navy; at fifteen he was a midshipman on board the flag-ship of the Spanish admiral at the memorable battle of Trafalgar, and, though not unwounded, was one of the few who escaped the terrible slaughter of that day. At the commencement of the war of Mexican independence he was still in the Spanish navy, but, a Mexican by birth, joined the cause of his countrymen, and became admiral of the fleet, which he commanded at the taking of the Castle of San Juan de Ulloa, the closing act of the successful revolution. After this, he resigned and went to Campeachy, his native place, but, being in delicate health, removed to Valladolid, which, in the absence of all other recommendations, was celebrated for the salubrity of its climate. He had held the highest offices of honour and trust in the state, and, although his party was now down and his political influence lost, he had fallen with the respect of all, and, what was a rare thing among the political animosities of that country, the actual government, his successful opponents, gave us letters of introduction to him.

Retired from office, and unable to endure idleness, the spontaneous growth of cotton around Valladolid induced him to undertake the establishment of a cotton factory. He had great difficulties to contend with, and these began with the erec-

tion of the building. He had no architect to consult, and planned
and constructed it himself. Twice the arches gave way, and the
whole building came down. The machinery was imported from
the United States, accompanied by four engineers, two of whom
died in the country. In 1835, when Mr. Burke arrived, the factory had yielded but seventy pieces of cotton, and eighteen yards
had cost eight thousand dollars. At this time the office of acting
governor of the state devolved upon him, but by a political revolution he was deposed; and while his workmen were celebrating
the grito de Dolores, which announced the outbreak of the
Mexican revolution, they were arrested and thrown in prison,
and the factory was stopped for six months. It was afterward
stopped twice by a failure of the cotton crop, and once by
famine; and all the time he had to struggle against the introduction of smuggled goods from Belize; but, in spite of all impediments, it had gone on, and was then in successful operation.

In walking about the yard, Don Pedro led us to the wood-
pile, and showed us that the logs were all split into four pieces.
This wood is brought by the Indians in back-loads at a medio
per load, and Don Pedro told us that at first he had requested
the Indians not to split the logs, as he would rather have them
entire, but they had been used to doing so, and could not alter
their habits; yet these same Indians, by discipline and instruction, had become adequate to all the business of the factory.

The city of Valladolid had some notoriety, as being the
place at which the first blow was struck in the revolution now in
progress against the dominion of Mexico, and also as being the
residence of General Iman, under whom that blow was struck.
The immediate consequence was the expulsion of the Mexican
garrison; but there was another, more remote and of more enduring importance. There, for the first time, the Indians were
brought out in arms. Utterly ignorant of the political relations
between Mexico and Yucatan, they came in from their ranchos
and milpas under a promise by General Iman that their capitation tax should be remitted. After the success of the first outbreak the government endeavoured to avoid the fulfilment of
this promise, but was compelled to compromise by remitting
the tax upon women, and the Indians still look forward to
emancipation from the whole. What the consequences may be of
finding themselves, after ages of servitude, once more in the
possession of arms, and in increasing knowledge of their physical
strength, is a question of momentous import to the people of
that country, the solution of which no man can foretell.

And Valladolid had been the theatre of stranger scenes in anicent times. According to historical accounts, it was once haunted by a demonio of the worst kind, called a demonio parlero, a loquacious or talking devil, who held discourse with all that wished at night, speaking like a parrot, answering all questions put to him, touching a guitar, playing the castanets, dancing and laughing, but without suffering himself to be seen.

Afterward he took to throwing stones in garrets, and eggs at the women and girls, and, says the pious doctor Don Sanchez de Aguilar, "an aunt of mine, vexed with him, once said to him, 'Go away from this house, devil,' and gave him a blow in the face which left the nose redder than cochineal." He became so troublesome that the cura went to one of the houses which he frequented to exorcise him, but in the mean time El Demonio went to the cura's house and played him a trick, after which he went to the house where the cura was waiting, and when the latter went away, told the trick he had been playing. After this he began slandering people, and got the whole town at swords' points to such an extent that it reached the ears of the bishop at Merida, who forbade speaking to him under pain of heavy spiritual punishments, in consequence of which the vecinos abstained from any communication with him; at first the demonio fell to weeping and complaining, then made more noise than ever, and finally took to burning houses. The vecinos sought Divine assistance, and the cura, after a severe tussle, drove him out of the town.

Thirty or forty years afterward, "when I," says the doctor Don Sanchez de Aguilar, "was cura of the said city, this demonio returned to infest some of my annexed villages, and in particular one village, Yalcoba, coming at midnight, or at one in the afternoon, with a great whirlwind, dust, and noise, as of a hurricane; stones swept over the whole pueblo; and though the Indians promptly put out the fires of their kitchens, it did not avail them, for from the flames with which this demonio is tormented proceeded flashes like nightly comets or wandering stars, which set fire to two or three houses at once, and spread till there were not people enough to put out the fire, when I, being sent for to come and drive it away, conjured this demon, and, with the faith and zeal that God gave me, commanded him not to enter that village; upon which the fires and the whirlwinds ceased, to the glory and honour of the Divine Majesty, which gave such power to the priests." Driven out here, this demonio returned to infest the village of Valladolid with new burnings; but by putting crosses in all the hills this evil ceased.

For generations this demonio has not been heard of, but it is known that he can take any shape he pleases; and I fear me much that he has at last entered the padres, and, taking advantage of that so-called amiable weakness which I before hinted at in confidence to the reader, is leading them along seeming paths of roses, in which they do not yet feel the thorns.

I have none but kind feelings toward the padres, but, either as a cause or in consequence of the ascendency of this demonio, the people of Valladolid seemed the worst we had met with, being, in general, lazy, gambling, and good for nothing. It is a common expression, "Hay mucho vago en Valladolid," "There are many idlers in Valladolid;" and we saw more gamecocks tied by the leg along the walls of the houses than we had seen in any other place we visited. Part of our business was to repair our wardrobe and procure a pair of shoes, but neither of these undertakings could we accomplish. There were no shoes ready made, and no artist would promise to make a pair in less than a week, which we learned might be interpreted as meaning at least two.

In the mean time we were making inquiries and arrangements for our journey to the coast. It is almost impossible to conceive what difficulty we had in learning anything definite concerning the road we ought to take. Don Pedro Baranda had a manuscript map, made by himself, which, however, he did not represent as very correct; and the place on the coast which we wished to visit was not laid down on it at all. There were but two persons in the town who could give us any information, and what they gave was most unsatisfactory. Our first plan was to go to the Bay of Ascension, where we were advised we could hire a canoa for our coast voyage, but fortunately, by the advice of Don Pedro Baranda, we were saved from this calamitous step, which would have subjected us to a long and bootless journey, and the necessity of returning to Valladolid without accomplishing anything, which might have disheartened us from attempting to reach the coast in another direction. Upon the information we received, we determined on going to the village of Chemax, from which, we were advised, there was a direct road to Tancah, where a boat was on the stocks, and probably then finished, which we could procure for a voyage down the coast.

Before our departure Doctor Cabot performed an operation for strabismus, under circumstances peculiarly gratifying to us, and, with the satisfaction arising from its complete success, on

Saturday, after an early dinner, we mounted for our journey to the coast, going first to the house of Don Pedro Baranda, and to the factory to bid farewell to Mr. Burke. The road was broad, and had been lately opened for carretas and calesas. On the way we met a large straggling party of Indians, returning from a hunting expedition in the forests along the seacoast. Naked, armed with long guns, and with deer and wild boars slung on their backs, their aspect was the most truculent of any people we had seen. They were some of the Indians who had risen at the call of General Iman, and they seemed ready at any moment for battle.

It was some time after dark when we reached the village. The outline of the church was visible through the darkness, and beside it was the convent, with a light streaming from the door. The cura was sitting at a table surrounded by the officials of the village, who started at the clatter of our horses; and when we appeared in the doorway, if a firebrand had been thrown among them they could not have been more astounded. The village was the Ultima Thule of population, the last between Valladolid and Tancah, and the surprise caused by our appearance did not subside when we told them that we were on our way to the latter. They all told us that it was impossible. Tancah was a mere rancho, seventy miles distant, and the whole intermediate country was a dense forest. There was no road to it, and no communication except by an overgrown footpath. It was utterly impossible to get through without sending Indians before to open a road all the way; and, to crown all, we would be obliged to sleep in the woods, exposed to moschetoes, garrapatas, and rain, which last, in our uncertain state, we regarded with real apprehension.

The rancho was established by one Molas, a smuggler and pirate, who, while under sentence of death in Merida, escaped from prison, and established himself at this lonely point, out of the reach of justice. Soldiers had been sent from Merida to arrest him, who, after advancing as far as Chemax, turned back. In consequence of new political excitements, change of government, and lapse of time, the persecution, as it is called, against poor Molas had ceased; and, having an attack of sickness, he ventured up from the coast, and made his appearance in the village, to procure such medical aid as it afforded. No one molested him; and after remaining a while he set out to return on foot with a single Indian, but, worn down by the fatigues of the journey, while yet eight leagues from the rancho he died upon the road.

These accounts came upon us most unexpectedly, and deranged all our plans. And there was nothing that more strikingly exhibited the ignorance prevailing in that country in regard to the roads, than the fact that, after diligent and careful inquiries at Valladolid, we had set out upon positive information that we could ride directly through to Tancah, and had made all our arrangements for doing so, whereas at six leagues' distance we found ourselves brought to a dead stand.

But turning back formed no part of our deliberations. The only question was whether we should undertake the journey on foot. The mere walking none of us regarded; in fact, it would have been a pleasant change, for there was no satisfaction in stumbling on horseback along those stony roads; but our servants foresaw a great accumulation of their labours, and the risk of exposure to rain was a serious consideration; moreover, I had one little difficulty, which, however, was really a serious one, and could not be remedied except by a delay of several days, in the want of shoes, those on my feet being quite incapable of holding out for such a walk. Our alternative was to go to the port of Yalahao, which, the reader will see by the map, is almost at right angles from Tancah, and thence take a canoa. This would subject us to the necessity of two voyages along the coast, going and returning, and would require, perhaps, a fortnight to reach Tancah, which we had expected to arrive at in three days; but there were villages and ranchos on the road, and the chance of a canoa was so much greater that, under the circumstances, we were glad of such an alternative.

In the midst of the vexation attending this derangement of our plan, we were cheered by the comfortable appearance of the convent, and the warm reception given us by the cura Garcia. The sala was furnished with pictures and engravings from Scott's novels, made for the Spanish market, with Spanish lettering; looking-glasses, with gilt frames, from El Norte, and a large hand organ, horribly out of tune, which, in compliment to us, the cura set to grinding out "God save the King!" And, besides all this, the smiling faces of women were peeping at us through the doors, who at length, unable to repress their curiosity, crowded each other into the room. The cura sat with us till a late hour, and when we retired followed us to our room, and stood by us till we got into our hammocks. His curacy extended to the coast. The ruins which we proposed visiting were within it, but he had never visited that part, and now talked seriously of going with us.

The next day Dr. Cabot was taken with a fever, which the cura said he was almost thankful for, and we were glad of an excuse for passing the day with him. It was Sunday, and, dressed in his black gown, I never saw a priest of more respectable appearance. And he was a politician as well as priest. He had been a member of the convention that formed the constitution of the state, had taken a prominent part in the discussions, and distinguished himself by his strong and manly eloquence. The constitution which he had assisted in forming debarred priests from holding civil offices, but through the loophole of his retreat he looked out upon the politics of the world. The relations between Mexico and Texas were at that time most interesting to him; he had received a Merida paper, containing a translation in full of President Houston's inaugural address; and often repeated, "not a dollar in the treasury, and ten to fifteen millions of debt." He predicted the downfall of that republic, and said that the conquering army in Texas would proclaim Santa Ana emperor, march back upon the capital, and place the diadem upon his head!

Amid the distraction and civil war that devastated his own country, he had looked to ours as the model of a republic, and gave us many though not very accurate details; and it seemed strange in this little interior Indian town to hear an account of late proceedings in our own capital, and to find one taking so deep an interest in them.

But the cura had more accurate knowledge in regard to matters nearer home. The village of Chemax contains nearly ten thousand inhabitants, and was in existence at the time of the conquest. Four years after the foundation of Merida the Indians in the neighbourhood of Valladolid formed a conspiracy to destroy the Spaniards, and the first blow was struck at Chemax, where they caught two brothers, whom they put upon crosses, and shot at from a distance till they were covered with arrows. At sunset they took down the bodies, dismembered them, and sent the heads and limbs to different places, to show that vengeance was begun.

The curacy of Chemax comprehended within its jurisdiction all between it and the sea. The cura had drawn up a report, by order of the government, of the condition and character of the region under his charge, and its objects of curiosity and interest, from which I copied the following notice in regard to ruins known by the name of Coba.

"In the eastern part of this village, at eight leagues' distance, and fourteen from the head of the district, near one of the three lagunas, is a building that the indigenes call Monjas. It consists of various ranges of two stories, all covered with arches, closed with masonry of rude stone, and each piece is of six square yards. Its interior pavement is preserved entire, and on the walls of one, in the second story, are some painted figures in different attitudes, showing, without doubt, according to the supposition of the natives, that these are the remains of that detestable worship so commonly found. From this edifice there is a calzada, or paved road, of ten or twelve yards in width, running to the southeast to a limit that has not been discovered with certainty, but some aver that it goes in the direction of Chichen Itza."

The most interesting part of this, in our eyes, was the calzada, or paved road, but the information from others in the village did not increase our interest. The cura himself had never visited these ruins; they were all buried in forest; there was no rancho or other habitation near; and as our time was necessarily to be much prolonged by the change we were obliged to make, we concluded that it would not be advisable to go and see them.

But the cura had much more interesting information. On his own hacienda of Kantunile, sixteen leagues nearer the coast, were several mounds, in one of which, while excavating for stone to be used in building, the Indians had discovered a sepulchre containing three skeletons, which, according to the cura, were those of a man, a woman, and a child, but all, unfortunately, so much decayed that in attempting to remove them they fell to pieces.

At the head of the skeletons were two large vases of terra cotta, with covers of the same material. In one of these was a large collection of Indian ornaments, beads, stones, and two carved shells, which are represented in Figure 15. The carving on the shells is in bas-relief, and very perfect; the subject is the same in both, and the reader will observe that, though differing in detail, it is of the same type with the figure on the Ticul vase, and those sculptured on the wall at Chichen. The other vase was filled nearly to the top with arrow-heads, not of flint, but of obsidian; and as there are no volcanoes in Yucatan from which obsidian can be procured, the discovery of these proves intercourse with the volcanic regions of Mexico. But, besides these,

FIG. 15

and more interesting and important than all, on the top of these arrow-heads lay a *penknife with a horn handle.* All these the cura had in his possession, carefully preserved in a bag, which he emptied on a table for our examination; and, as may be supposed, interesting as the other memorials were, the penknife attracted our particular attention. The horn handle was much decayed, and the iron or steel was worn and rusted. This penknife was never made in the country. How came it in an Indian sepulchre? I answer, when the fabrics of Europe and this country came together, the white man and the red had met. The figures carved on the shells, those little perishable memorials,

accidentally disinterred, identify the crumbling bones in that
sepulchre with the builders of Chichen, of those mysterious cities
that now lie shrouded in the forest; and those bones were laid in
their grave after a penknife had found its way into the country.
Speculation and ingenuity may assign other causes, but, in my
opinion, the inference is reasonable, if not irresistible, that at
the time of the conquest, and afterward, the Indians were actually living in and occupying those very cities on whose great
ruins we now gaze with wonder. A penknife—one of the petty
presents distributed by the Spaniards—reached the hands of a
cacique, who, far removed from the capital, died in his native
town, and was buried with the rites and ceremonies transmitted
by his fathers. A penknife is at this day an object of curiosity
and admiration among the Indians, and, perhaps, in the whole
of Yucatan there is not one in the hands of a native. At the
time of the conquest it was doubtless considered precious, worthy
of being buried with the heirlooms of its owner, and of accompanying him to the world of spirits. I was extremely anxious to
procure these memorials. The cura said, with Spanish courtesy,
that they were mine; but he evidently attached great value to
them, and, much as I desired it, I could not, with any propriety,
take them.

CHAPTER XIX

On Monday, the fourth of April, we took leave of the warm-hearted cura, and set out for our new point of destination, the port of Yalahao.

I am obliged to hurry over our journey to the coast. The road was lonely and rugged, mostly a complete crust of stone, broken and sharp pointed, which severely tried and almost wore out our horses. It was desperately hot; we had no view except the narrow path before us, and we stumbled along, wondering that such a stony surface could support such a teeming vegetation.

In the afternoon of the third day we were approaching the port. When within about a league of it, we came out upon a low, swampy plain, with a grove of cocoanut trees at a long distance before us, the only objects rising above the level surface, indicating, and, at the same time, hiding, the port of Yalahao. The road lay over a causeway, then wet and slippery, with numerous holes, and sometimes completely overflowed. On each side was a sort of creek, and in the plain were large pools of water. With a satisfaction perhaps greater than we had experienced in our whole journey, we reached the port, and, after a long absence, came down once more upon the shore of the sea.

The village was a long, straggling street of huts, elevated a few feet above the washing of the waves. In passing along it, for the first time in the country we came to a bridge crossing a brook, with a fine stream of running water in sight on the left. Our horses seemed as much astonished as ourselves, and we had great difficulty in getting them over the bridge. On the shore was another spring bubbling within reach of the waves.

We rode on to the house of Don Juan Bautista, to whom we had a letter from the cura of Chemax, but he had gone to his rancho. His house and one other were the only two in the place built of stone, and the materials had been obtained from the ruins of Zuza, standing on his rancho, two leagues distant on the coast.

We returned through the village to a house belonging to our friend the cura, better than any except the two stone houses, and in situation finer than these. It stood on the very edge of the bank, so near the sea that the waves had undermined part of the long piazza in front; but the interior was in good condition, and a woman tenant in possession. We were about negotiating with her for the occupation of a part; but wherever we went we seemed to be the terror of the sex, and before we had fairly made a beginning, she abandoned the house and left us in quiet possession. In an hour we were completely domesticated, and toward evening we sat in the doorway and looked out upon the sea. The waves were rolling almost to our door, and Doctor Cabot found a new field opened to him in flocks of large sea-fowl strutting along the shore and screaming over our heads.

Plate XLII represents this place as taken from the shore. Our house appears in the left corner, and at a distance down the coast is seen an ancient mound. Cut off, to a great extent, from communication with the interior, or, at least, connected with it only by a long and toilsome road, its low huts buried among the cocoanut trees, but few people moving about it, canoas in the offing, and a cannon half buried on the shore, it seemed, what it was notorious for having been, the haunt of pirates in days gone by.

In our journey to the coast we had entered a region of novel and exciting interest. On the road we had heard of quondam pirates, having small sugar ranchos, and enjoying reputations but little the worse for wear, in fact, much respected, and looked upon with a sort of compassion, as men who had been unfortunate and broken up in business. We had now reached the focus of their operations.

Plate XLII

YALAHAO.

It is not many years since the coast of Cuba and the adjacent continent were infested by bands of desperadoes, the common enemies of mankind, and doomed to be hung and shot without trial, wherever caught. Tales of piracies and murders which make the blood run cold are fresh in the remembrance of many. The sailor still repeats or listens to them with shuddering interest, and in those times of rapine and blood, this port was notorious as a rendezvous for these robbers of the sea.

It commanded a view of many leagues, and of all vessels passing between Cuba and the Spanish Main. A long, low flat extended many miles out; if the vessel was armed, and of superior force, the pirates pulled back into shoal water, and if pursued by boats, scattered and saved themselves in the interior. The plunder brought ashore was spent in gaming and revelry. Doubloons, as one of the inhabitants told us, were then as plentiful as medios are now. The prodigality of the pirates brought many people to the place, who, profiting by their ill-gotten gains, became identified with them, and pirate law prevailed.

Immediately on our arrival we had visiters, some of whom were silent and uncommunicative upon the historical associations of the place; and when they went away their good-natured neighbours spoke of them as los pobres, who had good reason to be silent. All spoke with kindness and good feeling of the leaders, and particularly of one Don Juan, the captain, a dashing, generous fellow, whose death was a great public loss. Individuals were named, then living in the place, and the principal men, who had been notoriously pirates; one had been several years in prison and under sentence of death, and a canoa was pointed out, lying in front of our door, which had been often used in pirate service.

Our house had been the headquarters of the bucaniers. It was the house of Molas, to whose unhappy end I have before referred. He had been sent by the government as commandant to put down these pirates, but, as it was said, entered into collusion with them, received their plunder, and conveyed it to the interior. At night they had revelled together in this house. It was so far from the capital that tidings of his misdoings were slow of transmission thither, and, when they were received, he persuaded the government that these reports proceeded from the malice of his enemies. At length, for his own security, he found it necessary to proceed against the pirates; he knew all their haunts, came upon them by stealth, and killed or drove away the whole band. Don Juan, the captain, was brought in wounded, and placed at night in a room partitioned off at the end of our sala. Molas feared that, if carried up to Merida, Don Juan would betray him, and in the morning the latter was found dead. It was more than whispered that he died by the hand of Molas. It is proper to add, what we heard afterward, that these stories were false, and that Molas was the victim of a malicious and iniquitous persecution. I should add, too, that the character of this place has improved. Broken up as a pirates' haunt, it became the abode of smugglers, whose business being now comparatively unprofitable, they combine with it the embarking of sugar and other products of ranchos along the coast.

We found one great deficiency at this place: there was no ramon for the horses. At night we turned them loose in the village; but the barren plain furnished them no grazing, and they returned to the house. Early in the morning we despatched Dimas to a ramon tree two leagues distant, that being the nearest point at which any could be procured; and in the mean time I set about searching for a canoa, and succeeded in engaging one, but not of the best class, and the patron and sailors could not be ready in less than two or three days.

This over, we had nothing farther to do in Yalahao. I rambled for a little while in the Castillo, a low fortress, with twelve embrazures, built for the suppression of piracy, but the garrison of which, from all accounts, connected themselves somewhat closely with the pirates. It was now garrisoned by a little Mestizo tailor, who had run away from Sisal with his wife to avoid being taken for a soldier. The meekest possible tenants of a fort, they paid no rent, and seemed perfectly happy.

The next morning, when we opened our door, we saw a sloop lying at anchor, which we soon understood was the balandra of Don Vicente Albino. Don Vicente was already on shore, and, before we had time to make many inquiries, he called upon us. We had heard of him before, but never expected to see him in person, for our accounts were that he had established a rancho on the island of Cozumel, and had been murdered by his Indians. The first part of the story was true, but Don Vicente himself assured us that the last was not, though he told us that he had had a narrow escape, and showed us a machete cut in the arm as a token.

Don Vicente was the person of all others whom we wished to see, as he was the only one who could give us any information about the island of Cozumel. While he was with us another vessel came in sight, standing in toward the shore; which, when still two leagues distant, lowered a boat, and then stood off again. Don Vicente recognized her as a Yucatecan brig of war. The commandant came ashore; we had already invited Don Vicente to dine with us, and feeling it incumbent upon us to entertain visitors of distinction, I invited the commandant to join us. This was a rather bold attempt, as we had but one spare plate, knife, and fork, but we had all been in worse straits, and were accommodating.

Amid the excitement in the port caused by the arrival of these strangers, the inhabitants were not suffered to forget us. A large sea-bird, prepared by Doctor Cabot with arsenic, and exposed to the sun to dry, had been carried off and eaten by a hog, and the report got abroad that a hog sold that day had died from eating the bird. This created somewhat of a panic, and at night all who had partaken of the suspicious meat were known throughout the port. A scientific exposition, that even if the hog had died from eating the bird, it did not follow that those would die who had eaten of the hog, was by no means satisfactory.

The next day we completed laying in our stock of provisions, to wit, chocolate, sweetened bread, beef and pork in strings, two turtles, three bushels of corn, and implements for making tortillas. We had one other important arrangement to make, which was the disposition of our horses; and, according to our previous plan, to avoid the long journey back through the interior we determined to send Dimas with them to Valladolid, and thence to the port of Silan, a journey of two hundred and fifty miles, while we should, on our return, continue down the coast with the canoa, and meet him there.

At nine o'clock we were taken off, one at a time, in a small dug-out, and put on board our canoa. We had no leave-takings. The only persons who took any interest in our movements were Dimas, who wanted to go with us, the woman whom we had dispossessed of the house, and the agent of the canoa, who had no desire to see us again.

Our canoa was known in the port of Yalahao by the name of El Sol, or the Sun. It was thirty-five feet long and six feet wide at the top, but curving toward the bottom. It carried two large sails, with the peaks held up by heavy poles secured at the masts; had a space of eight or ten feet clear in the stern, and all the rest was filled with luggage, provisions, and water-casks. We had not been on board till the moment of embarcation, and prospects seemed rather unpromising for a month's cruise. There was no wind; the sails were flapping against the mast; the sun beat down upon us, and we had no mat or awning of any kind, although the agent had promised one. Our captain was a middle-aged Mestizo, a fisherman, hired for the occasion.

Under these circumstances we set out on our voyage. It was one which we had determined upon before leaving home, and to which we had always looked forward with interest; and the precise object we had in view was, in following the track of the Spaniards along this coast, to discover vestiges or remains of the great buildings of lime and stone which, according to the historical accounts, surprised and astonished them.

At eleven o'clock the breeze set in. At twelve the patron asked if he should run ashore for us to dine, and at half past one the breeze was so strong against us that we were obliged to come to anchor under the lee of Point Moscheto. This was an island about two leagues distant from Yalahao, with a projecting point, which we had to double. We could have walked round it in an hour, but, after the experience of a few hours' navigation in El Sol, it seemed to stand out like Cape Horn. Our bark had no keel, and could do nothing against the wind. We went ashore on a barren, sandy beach, bathed, shot, and picked up shells. Toward evening the wind fell, and we crawled round the point, when we came to anchor again, for it was now dark, and El Sol could not travel at night. The patron made all secure; we had a big stone for anchor, and rode in water knee deep. In due time we turned in for sleep; and it might have been consoling to distant friends to know that, exposed as we were on this desolate coast, we made so tight a fit in the canoa that if the bottom had fallen out we could hardly have gone through.

The next morning, with the rising of her great namesake, El Sol was under way. The prevalent wind along the coast was southeast, adverse for us; but, as the captain said, on our return it would be in our favour. At one o'clock another bold point intercepted us. It was a great object to get round it, for the wind would then be fair. El Sol made a vigorous effort, but by this time the breeze had become strong, and we were fain to come to anchor under the lee of Point Frances, which was on the same island with Point Moscheto. The island itself has no name, and is a mere sand-bank covered with scrub bushes, having a passage between it and the mainland, navigable for small canoas. Our anchorage ground was in front of the rancho of a fisherman, the only habitation on the island, built like an Indian's wigwam, thatched with palm leaves close down to the ground, and having both ends open, giving free passage to a current of air, so that while without, a step from the door, the heat was burning, within there were coolness and comfort. The fisherman was swinging in his hammock, and a handsome Indian boy was making tortillas, the two presenting a fine picture of youth and vigorous old age. The former, as he told us, was sixty-five years old, tall and erect, with his face burned black, deep seams on his forehead, but without a single gray hair or other symptom of decay. He had been three months living on this desolate island, and called it amusing himself. Our skipper said he was the best fisherman from Yalahao, that he always went alone, and always made more than the rest, but in a week on shore his money was all gone. He had no milpa, and said that, with his canoe, and the sea, and the whole coast as a building spot for a rancho, he was independent of all the world. The fishing on this coast was for turtle; on one side of the hut were jars of turtle oil, and outside, rather too near when the wind was in certain quarters, were the skeletons of turtles from which he had extracted it.

Toward evening the breeze again died away, we slowly got round the point, and at half past eight came to anchor, having made six leagues on our voyage. Our captain told us that this desolate point was Cape Catoche, the memorable spot on the Continent of America at which the Spaniards first landed, and approaching which, says Bernal Dias, we saw at the distance of two leagues a large town, which, from its size, it exceeding any town in Cuba, we named Grand Cairo. The Spaniards set out for it, and passing by some thick woods, were attacked by Indians in ambuscade. Near the place of this ambuscade, he adds, were three buildings of lime and stone, wherein were idols of clay, with diabolical countenances, &c.

Navigators and geographers, however, have assigned different localities to this memorable point, and its true position is, perhaps, uncertain.

At daylight we were again under way, and soon were opposite Boca Nueva, being the entrance to a passage between the island and the main, better known to the fishermen as the Boca de Iglesia, from the ruins of a church visible at a great distance. This church was one of the objects I intended to visit; and one reason for preferring the canoe, when we had the chance of Don Vicente's sloop, was that we might do so; but our captain told us that even with our draught of water we could not approach nearer than a league; that a long muddy flat intervened; and that we could not reach the shore by wading. He said, too, what we had heard from others, and believed to be the case, that the church was certainly Spanish, and stood among the ruins of a Spanish town destroyed by the bucaniers, or, in his own words, by the English pirates. The wind was ahead, but we could make a good stretch from the coast, and, anxious to lose no advantage, we made sail for the island of Contoy. It was dark when we came to anchor, and we were already distressed for water. Our casks were impregnated with the flavour of agua ardiente, and the water was sickening. Through the darkness we saw the outline of a desolate rancho. Our men went ashore, and, moving round it with torches, made a fine piratical appearance; but they found no water.

Before daylight we were roused by the screaming of sea-birds; in the gray of the morning, the island seemed covered with a moving canopy, and the air was noisy with their clamour; but, unfortunately for Doctor Cabot, we had a fine breeze, and he had no opportunity of getting at their nests. The coast was wild and rugged, indented occasionally by small picturesque bays. Below the point of the island Doctor Cabot shot two pelicans, and getting the canoa about to take them on board was like manœuvring a seventy-four gun-ship.

At eleven o'clock we reached the island of Mugeres, notorious in that region as the resort of Lafitte the pirate. Monsieur Lafitta, as our skipper called him, bore a good character in these parts; he was always good to the fishermen, and paid them well for all he took from them. At a short distance beyond the point we passed a small bay, in which he moored his little navy. The mouth was narrow, and protected by ledges of broken rocks, on which, as the patron told us, he had batteries constantly manned. On the farther point of the island we had a distant view of one of those stone buildings which were our inducement to this voyage along the coast. While looking at it from the prow of the canoa, with the patron by my side, he broke from me, seized a harpoon, and pointing with it to indicate the direction to the helmsman, we came silently upon a large turtle, apparently asleep, which must have been somewhat surprised on waking up with three or four inches of cold steel in his back. The patron and sailors looked upon him as upon a bag of dollars snatched from the deep. There are three kinds of turtles which inhabit these seas; the Cahuamo, the eggs of which serve for food, and which is useful besides only for its oil; the Tortuga, of which the meat as well as the eggs is eaten, which also produces oil,

and of which the shell is worth two reales the pound; and the
Karé, of which the shell is worth ten dollars a pound. It was one
of this kind, being the rarest, that had crossed our path. I would
not make any man unhappy, but the fishermen say that the turtle
which forms the delight of the gourmand is of the commonest
kind, not worth killing for the sake of the shell, and therefore
sent away alive. The karé he has never tasted. It is killed for
the sake of the shell, and eaten by the luxurious fishermen on
the spot. I immediately negotiated with the patron for the purchase of the shell. The outer scales of the back, eight in number,
are all that is valuable. Their weight he estimated at four
pounds, and the price in Campeachy he said was ten dollars
a pound, but he was an honest fellow, and let me have it at two
pounds and a half, for eight dollars a pound; and I had the satisfaction of learning afterward that I had not paid more than
twice as much as it was worth.

In the afternoon we steered for the mainland, passing the
island of Kancune, a barren strip of land, with sand hills and
stone buildings visible upon it. The whole of this coast is lined
with reefs of rocks, having narrow passages which enable a canoa
to enter and find shelter; but it is dangerous to attempt the passage at night. We had a good wind, but as the next harbour was
at some distance, the patron came to anchor at about four
o'clock under the lee of the point of Nesuc. Immediately we went
ashore in search of water, but found only a dirty pool, in which
the water was so salt that we could scarcely drink it, but still it
was an agreeable change from that we had on board.

We had time for a bath, and while preparing to take it
saw two large sharks moving along the shore in water four or five
feet deep, and so clear that their ugly eyes were visible. We hesitated, but, from the heat and confinement of the canoa, we were
in real need; and stationing Albino on the prow to keep a look
out, we accomplished our purpose. Afterward we rambled along
the shore to pick up shells; but toward dark we were all hurrying back, flying before the natives, swarms of moschetoes, which
pursued us with the same bloodthirsty spirit that animated the
Indians along this coast when they pursued the Spaniards. We
heaved upon our cable, hauled up our big stone, and dropped
off to some distance from the shore, with horrible apprehensions
for the night, but, fortunately, we escaped.

At daylight the next morning we were again under way, and,
with a strong and favourable wind, steered from the coast for the
island of Cozumel. Very soon, in the comparatively open sea, we

felt the discomfort and even insecurity of our little vessel. The waves broke over us, wetting our luggage and ourselves, and interfering materially with Bernaldo's cooking. At about four o'clock in the afternoon we were upon the coast of Cozumel, and here for the first time we made a discovery, at the moment sufficiently annoying, viz., that our patron was not familiar with the coast of this island; it was bound with reefs; there were only certain places where it was practicable to run in, and he was afraid to make the attempt.

Our plan was to disembark at the rancho of Don Vicente Albino, and the patron did not know where it was. It was too late to look for it, and, sailing along till he saw a passage among the reefs, he laid the old canoa into it, and then threw out the big stone, but at some distance from the shore. On the outer reef was the wreck of a brig; her naked ribs were above the water, and the fate of her mariners no one knew.

The next morning, after some hours spent in groping about, we discovered the rancho of Don Vicente, distant about three miles. Here we encountered a strong current of perhaps four miles an hour; and, taking the wind close hauled, in a little while found that El Sol was not likely to have a very brilliant career that day. At length we went close in, furled sails, and betook ourselves to poles, by means of which, after two hours' hard work, we reached the little Bay of San Miguel, on which stood the rancho of Don Vicente. The clearing around it was the only one on the island, all the rest being thick woods. This bay had a sandy beach extending some distance to a rocky point, but even here the water was discoloured by sunken reefs. In the case of a norther it was an unsafe anchorage ground; El Sol would be driven upon the rocks, and the captain wished to leave us on shore, and go in search of a better harbour; but to this we objected, and for the present directed him to run her up close; when, standing upon the bow, and leaping with our setting poles, we landed upon the desolate island of Cozumel. (Plate XLIII.)

Above the line of the shore was a fine table of land, on which were several huts, built of poles, and thatched with palm leaves. One was large and commodious, divided into apartments, and contained rude benches and tables, as if prepared for our immediate occupation. Back of the house was an enclosure for a garden, overgrown, but with any quantity of tomatoes, ripe, wasting, and begging to be put into a turtle soup then in preparation on board the canoa.

Plate XLIII

F. Catherwood

SAN MIGUEL, ISLAND OF COZUMEL.

J N Gimbrede

This rancho was established by the pirate Molas, who, escaping from death in Merida, made his way hither. He succeeded in getting to him his wife and children and a few Indians, and for several years nothing was heard of him. In the mean time he laid the keel of a sloop, finished it with his own hands, carried it to Belize, and sold it; new subjects of excitement grew up, and, being in a measure forgotten, he again ventured to the mainland, and left the island to its solitude.

After him Don Vicente Albino undertook to establish upon it a rancho for the cultivation of cotton, which was broken up by the mutiny of his Indians and an attempt to murder him. When we met him at Yalahao he had just returned from his last visit, carrying away his property, and leaving five dogs tenants of the island. After him came a stranger occupant than either, being no other than our old friend Mr. George Fisher, that "citizen of the world" introduced to the reader in the early part of these pages, who, since our separation in Merida, had consummated the history of his wandering life by becoming the purchaser of six leagues, or eighteen miles, of the island, had visited it himself with surveyors, set up his crosses along the shore, and was about undertaking a grand enterprise, that was to make the lonely island of Cozumel known to the commercial world.

Our act of taking possession was unusually exciting. It was an immense relief to escape from the confinement of the canoa. The situation commanded a view of the sea, and, barely distinguishable, in the distance was the coast of Yucatan. On the bank were large forest trees which had been spared in the clearing, and orange and cocoanut trees planted by Molas. The place. had a sort of piratical aspect. In the hut were doors and green blinds from the cabin of some unlucky vessel, and reeving blocks, tar buckets, halliards, drinking gourds, fragments of rope, fishing nets, and two old hatches were scattered on the ground. Above all, the first object we discovered, which would have given a charm to a barren sand bank, was a well of pure and abundant water, which we fell upon at the moment of landing, and were almost like the Spanish soldier in the expedition of Cordova, who drank till he swelled and died. And, besides the relief of a pressing want, this well had a higher interest, for it assured us that our visit was not bootless. We saw in it, at the first glance, the work of the same builders with whose labours on the mainland we were now so familiar, being, like the subterranean chambers at Uxmal, dome shaped, but larger both at the mouth and in the interior.

This well was shaded by a large cocoanut tree. We hauled up under it one of the hatches, and, sitting around it on blocks, had served up the turtle which had been accomplishing its destiny on board the canoa. With our guns resting against the trees, long beards, and canoa costume, we were, perhaps, as piratical-seeming a trio as ever scuttled a ship at sea. In the afternoon we walked over the clearing, which was covered with a fine plantation of cotton, worth, as the patron said, several hundred dollars, with the pods open and blowing away, indicating that the rancho had been abandoned in haste, without regard to the preservation of property. Toward evening we strolled for a great distance along the shore, picking up shells, and at night we had a luxurious swing in our hammocks.

CHAPTER XX

The next morning, while breakfasting on the old hatch, we saw a dog peering at us from a distance, as if wishing, but fearful to approach. The poor beast was crippled, limped badly, and had his fore shoulder horribly mangled, the patron said by an encounter with a wild boar. We endeavoured to entice him to us, but, after looking at us a few moments, he went away, and never came near us again. No doubt he was one of the five left by Don Vicente Albino, and, abandoned once, he had lost all confidence in man. In a few years, if these are not eaten up by stronger beasts, a race of wild dogs may inhabit this deserted island.

The island of Cozumel, as it is now called, was known to the natives by the name of Cuzamil, signifying in their language the Island of Swallows. Before setting out from home I had fixed upon this island as one of the points of our journey. My attention was directed to it by the historical accounts of its condition when it first became known to the Spaniards. It was discovered accidentally in 1518 by Juan de Grijalva, who, in attempting to follow in the track of Cordova, was driven in sight of it. The itinerary of this voyage was kept by the chaplain-in-chief of the fleet, under the direction of Grijalva, and, with a collection of original narratives and memoirs, was published for the first time in 1838 at Paris. The itinerary opens thus:

"Saturday, the first of March of the year 1518, the commandant of the said fleet sailed from the island of Cuba. On the fourth of March we saw upon a promontory a white house. * * * * * All the coast was lined with reefs and shoals. We directed ourselves upon the opposite shore, when we distinguished the house more easily. It was in the form of a small tower, and appeared to be eight palms in length and the height of a man. The fleet came to anchor about six miles from the coast. Two little barks called canoes approached us, each manned by three Indians, which came to within a cannon shot of the vessel. We could not speak to them nor learn anything from them, except that in the morning the cacique, *i. e.,* the chief of that place, would come on board our vessel. The next morning we set sail to reconnoiter a cape which we saw at a distance, and which the pilot told us was the island of Yucatan. Between it and the point of *Cucuniel,* where we were, we found a gulf, into which we entered, and came near the shore of Cuzamil, which we coasted. Besides the tower which we had seen, we discovered fourteen others of the same form. Before leaving the first, the two canoes of Indians returned; the chief of the village was in one of them, and came on board the vessel of the admiral, and spoke to us by means of an interpreter (one of the two Indians carried off from Yucatan on the previous voyage of Cordova), and prayed the commander to come to his village, saying that it would be a great honour to him. * * * *

"We set sail, following the coast at the distance of a stone's throw, for the sea is very deep upon the borders. The country appeared very agreeable; we counted, on leaving this point, *fourteen towers* of the form indicated. At sunset we saw a large white tower, which appeared very high. We approached, and saw near it a multitude of Indians, men and women, who were looking at us, and remained until the fleet stopped within musket shot of the tower. The Indians, who are *very numerous* in this island, made a great noise with their drums.

"On Friday, the sixth of May, the commandant ordered one hundred men to arm themselves. They embarked in the boats, and landed. They were accompanied by a priest, and expected to be attacked by a great number of Indians. Being prepared for defence, they arranged themselves in good order, and came to the tower, where they found no one; and in all the environs they did not see a single man. The commandant mounted upon the tower with the standard bearer, the flag unfurled. He planted this standard upon one of the façades of the tower, took possession in the name of the king, in presence of witnesses, and drew up a declaration of said taking possession.

"The ascent to this tower was by eighteen steps; the base was very massive, one hundred and eighty feet in circumference. At the top rose a small tower of *the height of two men placed* one upon the other. Within were figures, bones, and idols that they adored. From these marks we supposed that they were idolaters. While the commandant was at the top of the tower with many of our people, an Indian, followed by three others who kept the doors, put in the interior a vase with very odoriferous perfumes, which seemed of storax. This Indian was old; he burned many perfumes before the idols which were in the tower, and sang in a loud voice a song, which was always in the same tone. We supposed that he was invoking his idols. * * * * * These Indians carried our commandant with ten or twelve Spaniards, and gave them to eat in a hall constructed of stones very close together, and covered with straw. Before the hall was a large well, from which everybody drank. * * * * They then left us alone, and we entered the village, where all the houses were built of stone. Among others, we saw five very well made, and commanded by small towers. The *base* of these edifices is *very large* and *massive; the building is very small at the top.* They appeared to have been built a long time, but there are also *modern ones.*

"That village, or bourg, was paved with concave stones. The streets, elevated at the sides, descended, inclining toward the middle, which was paved entirely with large stones. The sides were occupied by the houses of the inhabitants. They are constructed of stone from the foundation to half the height of the walls, and covered with straw. To *judge by the edifices and houses, these Indians appear to be very ingenious;* and if we had not seen a number of recent constructions, we should have thought that these buildings were the works of the Spaniards. This island appears to me very handsome. * * * * We penetrated, to the number of ten men, three or four miles in the interior. We saw there edifices and habitations separated one from another, and very well constructed."

On the tenth of February, 1519, the armament of Cortez rendezvoused at this island. Bernal Dias was again a companion, and was an actor in a scene which he describes as follows: "There was on the island of Cozumel a temple containing some hideous idols, to which all the Indians of the neighbouring districts used to go frequently in solemn procession. One morning the courts of this temple were filled with Indians, and curiosity having also drawn many of us thither, we found them burning odoriferous resins like our incense, and shortly after an old man in a large loose mantle ascended to the top of the temple, and harangued or preached to the multitude for a considerable time. Cortez, who was present, at length called to him Melchorejo, an Indian prisoner taken on a previous voyage to Yucatan, to question him concerning the evil doctrines which the old man was delivering. He then summoned all the caciques and chief persons to come before him, and as well as he could, by signs and interpretations, explained to them that the idols which they worshipped were not gods, but evil things, which would draw their souls down to hell, and that, if they wished to remain in brotherly connexion with us, they must pull them down, and place in their stead the crucifix of our Lord, by whose assistance they would obtain good harvests and the salvation of their souls, with many other good and holy reasons, which he expressed very well. The priests and chiefs replied that they worshipped these gods as their ancestors had done, because they were kind to them, and that, if we attempted to molest them, the gods would convince us of their power by destroying us in the sea. Cortez then ordered the idols to be prostrated, which we immediately did, rolling them down some steps. He next sent for lime, of which there was abundance in the place, and Indian masons, by whom, under our direction, a very handsome altar was constructed, whereon we placed an image of the Holy Virgin; and the carpenters having made a crucifix, which was erected in a small chapel close to the altar, mass was said by the reverend father Juan Dias, and listened to by the priests, chiefs, and the rest of the natives with great attention."

These are the accounts given by eyewitnesses of what they saw on the first visits of the Spaniards. The later historians are more explicit, and speak of Cozumel as a place containing many adoratorios and temples, as a principal sanctuary and place of pilgrimage, standing to Yucatan in the same relation as Rome to the Catholic world. Gomarra describes one temple as being "like a square tower, broad at the base, having steps on the sides, and at the top a chamber covered with straw, with four doors or windows, with their breastworks or corridors. In the hollow, which seems like a chapel, they seat or paint their gods. Such was that which stood near the seacoast."

By these accounts I had been induced to visit the island of Cozumel; and an incidental notice in the Modern Traveller, speaking of existing ruins as remains of Spanish buildings, led me to suspect that their character had been mistaken, and that they were really vestiges of the original population; but on the ground we asked ourselves where to look for them. Amid all the devastations that attended the progress of the Spaniards in America, none is more complete than that which has swept over the island of Cozumel. When I resolved to visit it I was not aware that it was uninhabited; and knowing it to be but thirty miles long, I supposed that, without much difficulty, a thorough exploration could be made; but even before landing we saw that it would be impossible to accomplish this, and idle to make the attempt. The whole island was overgrown with trees, and, except along the shore or within the clearing around the hut, it was impossible to move in any direction without cutting a path. We had only our two sailors, and if we should cut by the compass through the heart of the island, we might pass within a few feet of a building without perceiving it. Fortunately, however, on the borders of the clearing there were vestiges of ancient population, which, from the directions of Don Vicente Albino, we had no difficulty in finding. One of them, standing about two hundred feet distant from the sea, and even now visible above the tops of the trees to vessels sailing by, is represented in Figure 16. It stands on a terrace, and has steps on all four of its sides. The building measures sixteen feet square; it had four doors facing the cardinal points, and, as will be seen by the figure of a man sitting on the steps, it is very low. The exterior is of plain stone, but was formerly stuccoed and painted, traces of which are still visible. The doorways open into a narrow corridor only twenty inches wide, which encompasses a small room eight feet six inches long and five feet wide, having a doorway opening to the centre.

South-southeast from this, near an opposite angle of the clearing, and five or six hundred feet from the sea, stands another building raised upon a terrace, consisting of a single apartment, twenty feet front and six feet ten inches deep, having two doorways and a back wall seven feet thick. The height is ten feet, the arch is triangular, and on the walls are the remains of paintings.

These were the only buildings in the clearing, and though,

Fig. 16

doubtless, many more lie buried in the woods, we saw no other
on the island; but to us these were pregnant with instruction.
The building presented in the engraving, standing close to the
sea, answers, in all its general features, the description of the
"towers" seen by Grijalva and his companions as they sailed
along the coast. The *ascent is by steps,* the *base is very massive,*
the *building is small at the top,* it is *about the height of two men
placed one above the other,* and at this day we may say, as the
Spaniards did, that, *to judge by their edifices, these Indians appear to be very ingenious.* It is an interesting fact, moreover,
that not only our patron and sailors called this building a
"tower," but in a late article published in the proceedings of
the Royal Geographical Society at London, entitled "Sketch of
the Eastern Coast of Central America, compiled from Notes
of Captain Richard Owen and the Officers of her Majesty's Ship
Thunder and Schooner Lark," this building, with others of the

same general character, is indicated by the name of a "tower." So far as the route of Grijalva can be traced with certainty, there is strong reason to believe that the Spaniards landed for the first time in the bay on the shore of which this building stands, and there is no violence in the supposition that the building presented is the very tower in which the Spaniards saw the performance of idolatrous rites; perhaps it is the same temple from which Bernal Dias and his companions rolled the idols down the steps. And more than this, establishing the great result for which we had visited this island, these buildings were identically the same with those on the mainland; if we had seen hundreds, we could not have been more firmly convinced that they were all erected and occupied by the same people; and if not a single corroborating circumstance existed besides, they afford in themselves abundant and conclusive proof that the ruined cities on the continent, the building of which has been ascribed to races lost, perished, and unknown, were inhabited by the very same Indians who occupied the country at the time of the conquest.

At the rear of the last building, buried in the woods, so that we should never have found it but for our patron, is another memorial, perhaps equal in interest to any now existing on the island of Cozumel. It is the ruins of a Spanish church, sixty or seventy feet front and two hundred deep. The front wall has almost wholly fallen, but the side walls are standing to the height of about twenty feet. The plastering remains, and along the base is a line of painted ornaments. The interior is encumbered with the ruins of the fallen roof, overgrown with bushes; a tree is growing out of the great altar, and the whole is a scene of irrecoverable destruction. The history of this church is as obscure as that of the ruined temples whose worship it supplanted. When it was built or why it was abandoned, and, indeed, its very existence, are utterly unknown to the inhabitants of New Spain. There is no record or tradition in regard to it, and, doubtless, any attempt at this day to investigate its history would be fruitless. In the obscurity that now envelops it we read a lesson upon the vanity of human expectations, showing the ignorance of the conquerors in regard to the value of the newly-discovered countries in America. Benito Perez, a priest who accompanied the expedition of Grijalva, solicited from the king the bishopric of this island. At the same time, a more distinguished ecclesiastic was asking for that of the island of Cuba. The king advanced the latter to the higher honour of the bishopric of Cozumel, and put off Benito Perez with what was considered the comparatively insignificant see of Culhua. Cozumel is now a desert, and Culhua, or Mexico, is the richest bishopric in New Spain.

But I have a particular reason for presenting to the reader this ruined church. It is a notion, or, rather, a principle, pervading all the old Spanish writers, that at some early day Christianity had been preached to the Indians, and connected with this is the belief that the cross was found by the first conquerors in the province of Yucatan as a symbol of Christian worship. Prophecies are recorded supposed to show a traditionary knowledge of its former existence, and foretelling that from the rising of the sun should come a bearded people and white, who should carry aloft the sign of the cross, which their gods could not reach, and from which they should fly away. The same vague idea exists to this day, and, in general, when the padres pay any attention to the antiquities of the country, they are always quick in discovering some real or imaginary resemblance to the cross. A strong support of this belief is advanced in the "Cozumel Cross" at Merida, found on the island of Cozumel, and in the time of Cogolludo, as at this day, supposed to have been an object of reverence among the Indians before their conversion to Christianity.

Until the destruction of that edifice it stood on a pedestal in the patio of the Franciscan convent, and, as we were told, from the time when it was placed there, no lightning had ever struck the building, as had often happened before. It is now in the Church of the Mejorada, and in looking for it at that place, Mr. Catherwood and myself were invited into the cell of an octogenarian monk then lying in his hammock, for many years unable to cross the threshold of his door, but in the full exercise of his mental powers, who told us, in a tone which seemed to indicate that he had done what would procure him a remission from many sins, that he had himself dug it up from among the ruins, and had it set up where it is now seen. It is fixed in the wall of the first altar on the left, and is almost the first object that arrests the eye of one entering the church. It is of stone, has a venerable appearance of antiquity, and has extended on it in half relief an image of the Saviour, made of plaster, with the hands and feet nailed. At the first glance we were satisfied that, whatever might be the truth in regard to its early history, it was, at least, wrought into its present shape under the direction of the monks. And though, at that time, we did not expect ever to know anything more about it, the ruins of this church cleared up in our minds all possible mystery connected with its existence.

In front of the building is a cemented platform, broken and uprooted by trees, but still preserving its form; and on this stand two square pillars, which, as we supposed on the spot, had once supported crosses, and we were immediately impressed with the belief that one of these missing symbols was that now known as the "Cozumel Cross," and that it had probably been carried away by some pious monk at or about the time when the church became a ruin and the island depopulated. For myself, I have no doubt of the fact; and I regard it as important, for, even though crosses may have been found in Yucatan, the connecting of the "Cozumel Cross" with the ruined church on the island completely invalidates the strongest proof offered at this day that the cross was ever recognised by the Indians as a symbol of worship.

At noon we had finished all our work, but there was a charm about our absolute proprietorship of this desolate island which made us regret that there was not more to give us occupation. Doctor Cabot found in it a rich field for his ornithological pursuits, but he was rather unfortunate. Two specimens of rare birds, which he had dissected and put away to dry, were destroyed by ants. In the clearing was a dead tree, holding on its topmost branches the nest of a hawk of a rare species, the eggs of which were unknown to naturalists. The nest seemed to have been built in apprehension of our visit. The dead branches were barely able to support it, and would evidently bear no additional weight. The patron and sailors cut down the tree, and the eggs were broken, but preserved in fragments.

In the afternoon we picked up shells along the shore, and toward evening we again took a bath; while we were in the water black clouds gathered suddenly, thunder rolled, lightning flashed, and sea-birds flew screaming over our heads. Rain following quickly, we snatched up our clothing and ran for the hut. Looking back for a moment, we saw our canoa under way, with scarcely a yard of mainsail, and seeming like a great bird flying over the water. As she turned the point of the island and disappeared our fears were roused. From our experience of a little rough weather we judged it impossible for her to live through a storm so sudden and violent; and our sense of thankfulness at not being on board made us feel more sensibly the danger of those who were. The patron was not familiar with the coast, there was but one place in which he could find shelter, a narrow

passage, difficult to enter even by daylight, and night was almost
upon him; Mr. Catherwood had timed the precise moment when
he turned the point, and we knew that the canoa would not be
able to reach the cove before dark, but would have to ride
through the storm, and, perhaps, be driven to sea. It was fearful
to think of the danger of the poor patron and sailors; and
mingled with these fears was some little uneasiness on our own
account. All our luggage and provisions were on board, as we
had intended to sail early the next morning. The storm had
come up so suddenly that though Albino stood on the bank entreating, the patron would not wait to put a single thing on
shore. We had only our box of table service, with coffee, sugar,
tea, chocolate, and a few biscuit; even if no accident happened,
several days might elapse before the canoa could return, and if
she never returned we should be five Robinson Crusoes, all alone
on a desert island. We had our guns to look to for provisions,
but, unluckily, we had an unusually small quantity of ammunition on shore. As the storm raged our apprehensions ran high,
and we had got so far as to calculate our chances of reaching the
mainland by a raft, finding some relief in the occupation of
moving our hammocks occasionally to avoid the rain as it beat
through the thatched roof, and at length we fell asleep.

CHAPTER XXI

Very early in the morning we were moving. The rain had ceased, but the wind was still high, and the waves exhibited its power. Albino and Bernaldo were even more interested in the missing canoa than we, for tea and coffee were nothing to them, and our supply of biscuit being exhausted at breakfast, they had literally nothing to eat. At daylight Bernaldo set off along the shore, and soon after I followed with Albino. Passing round the point which had cut off our view of the canoa, we came upon what might well be called an iron-bound coast, being a table of rock rising but a few feet above the level of the sea, washed by every storm, until it had become porous and full of holes, and the edges stuck up like points of rusted iron. The waves were still dashing over them, forming great whirlpools in the hollow spaces, and suggesting a frightful picture of the fate of any unhappy voyagers who might have been thrown upon them; and the rocks were strewed with staves and planks from some wrecked vessel. After walking two hours I became satisfied that the canoa must have taken the brunt of the storm, and my apprehensions were seriously excited when I saw, at a long distance beyond, Bernaldo, whom I at first thought I had overtaken, but discovered that he had a small pyramid on his head, consisting of cooking vessel and provisions. He had met one of the sailors coming to our relief, from whom he had taken his burden, and was then returning. We went on, and after three hours' painful walking reached the cove. It was a wild, abrupt, and narrow opening between the rocks, about fifty feet wide, with perpendicular sides, and leading into a sheltered basin, which, while the sea outside was raging, was calm and quiet as a pond. At the head of this lay the canoa, which came down and took me on board.

From the simple and unaffected account of the patron, his entry into the cove must have been sublime. Night had overtaken him, and he supposed that he had run by, when a flash of lightning disclosed the narrow passage, and he turned the old canoa short into the very middle of it. In passing through he struck upon a sunken rock, lost one man overboard, caught him by the light of another flash, and in a moment was in still water. The cove was imbosomed among noble trees. The water was twenty feet deep, and so clear that the bottom was distinctly visible; and from one end ran a creek, which the patron said was navigable for canoes into the centre of the island, where it expanded into a lake. Sails, luggage, Doctor Cabot's birds, and my copy of Cogolludo, were spread out to dry, and, after dining upon turtles' eggs laid a few minutes on the coals, I set out on my return, gathering on the way an unusual harvest of shells. Ever since we came upon the coast our idle moments had been employed in this pleasant occupation, but nowhere with the same success as on this island. Regularly, after stripping the shore, we returned in a few hours, and found others thrown up, pure and fresh from the sea. I was seldom more fatigued than when I reached the hut.

On the third day, at twelve o'clock, the canoa again hove in sight, working her way round the point, and in a short time was at her old anchorage ground. The wind was still so high that the patron was afraid to remain; we filled our water casks, in an hour were on board, and left, solitary as we found it, the once populous island of Cozumel. A hawk mourning over its mate, which we carried away, was the only living thing that looked upon our departure; but there was no place in our whole journey that we left with more regret.

From the point at which we left the island, the opposite coast of Yucatan was dimly visible, and I would remark, that, from our own observation and from information given to us by others, it is the only point from which the opposite coast can be seen at all, whence it is a conclusion almost unquestionable that it was from this same point Grijalva steered for Yucatan. The wind was high, the sea rough, and a strong current was sweeping us down toward the point of Cape Catoche. About an hour before dark we got across the current, and stood up along the coast, passing three low, square buildings, apparently in a good state of preservation, but the sea was so rough that we could not land to examine them. The account of the expedition of Grijalva says, "After leaving the island of Cozumel we saw three large villages, separated two miles from each other. They contained a great number of stone houses, with high towers, and covered with straw." This *must* have been the very part of the coast where these villages were seen. The whole is now covered with forest, but it is not unreasonable to suppose that the stone buildings visible on the shore are tokens of the buried towns in the interior. We ran on till after dark, and came to anchor under a projecting point, behind a reef of rocks. In the edge of the water was a square enclosure for turtle, and on the shore a deserted fisherman's hut.

At daylight we were again under way. We passed three more square buildings; but as the coast was rocky we could not land without endangering the safety of our precious canoa; and far off, on a high cliff, stood the Castillo of Tuloom, the extreme point at which we were aiming. At twelve o'clock we turned a point, and came upon a long, sandy beach, forming a bay, at the head of which was a small collection of huts, composing the rancho of Tancar. The entrance was difficult, being hemmed in by sunken reefs and rocks. Two women were standing in the doorway of one of the huts, except the old fisherman the only persons we had seen along this desolate coast.

It was this point which we expected to reach by land direct from Chemax. The reader will see the circuit it has cost us to make it, but the first glance satisfied us of our good fortune in not going to it direct, for we saw the frame of the sloop we had heard of still on the stocks, which probably is not yet finished. We should not have been able to get a canoa, and should have been obliged to return by the same road. The moment the stone was thrown out we were in the water, wading ashore. The sun was intensely hot, and the sand burning. In front of the principal hut, beside the sloop, was a thatched arbour to protect the carpenter who occasionally worked upon it. Near by was a ruined hut, which we had cleared out, and for the third time

took up our abode in a habitation erected by Molas. On leaving
the island of Cozumel it was only to this desolate point on the
coast that he dared venture. It was a situation that again suited
his proscribed life, and having no fear of pursuit from the interior, his energy and industry did not desert him. He again
cultivated his milpa, and again laid the keel of a sloop, being
the same which we then saw unfinished. But, finding himself
growing old, in a measure forgotten and afflicted by illness, he
ventured to appear in the village of Chemax, on returning from
which, as before mentioned, with a single Indian, while yet eight
leagues from Tancar he died in the road; as our informant
expressed it, he died like a dog, without aid either human or
divine. We had heard so much of Molas, of his long succession
of calamities, and of the heavy retribution that had been poured
upon his aged head, and we had seen so much of his unbroken
energy, that, in spite of the violence and crimes imputed to him,
our sympathies were excited; and having heard afterward from
other sources the opinion expressed strongly, that during these
long years of proscription he was the victim of an iniquitous and
unrelenting persecution, I draw a veil over his history. It was
but a year since he died, and his two sons were in possession of
the rancho, both young men, who paid us a visit soon after our
arrival. When the old man died the Indian left the body in the
road, and came on to the rancho, whence these young men went
up and buried it on the spot. Afterward they went again, dug it
up, put it in a box, brought it to the rancho, and embarked with
it in a canoa for San Fernando, where some of their kinsmen
lived. On the way they were overtaken by a storm, threw the
body overboard, and, said our informant, that was the last of
poor old Molas. The elder son was said to have been implicated
with his father, and the curse seemed entailed upon him. He had
lost entirely the use of one eye, and the other rolled feebly and
lustreless in a watery orbit. Probably by this time he is perfectly
blind.

Our first inquiries were upon the subject of ruins. A short
path through the woods leads to a milpa, in which are numerous
remains of ancient buildings standing on terraces, but all small
and dilapidated. These buildings once stood erect in full view
from the sea, but now the stranger sails along the coast unconscious that among the trees lie shrouded the ruins of an aboriginal town.

In the afternoon we set out for the ruins of Tuloom, a
league distant on the coast, and with the Castillo on a high cliff

in full sight. Our road lay for a mile and a half along the shore. The beach was sandy, and in some places so yielding that we sank above the ankles, and found it a relief to take off our shoes and stockings, and wade in the edge of the water. At the end of the beach was a high rocky promontory, standing out into the sea, and cutting off all progress along the shore. This we ascended, and continued along the cliff, which sloped toward the sea, in some places forming a perpendicular wall, and on our right rose great masses of rock, cutting off entirely the view of the Castillo. In half an hour we came unexpectedly upon a low building, apparently an adoratorio, or altar, climbing to the top of which, we again saw the Castillo. Beyond the cliff became more rugged and barren, reminding us of the witches' gathering-place in the Hartz Mountains, as described in the Faust of Goëthe; and, amid all its barrenness, from the crevices of the rocks sprang a thick growth of scrubby wild palm called tshike, covering the whole surface of the cliff. Toiling through this, we reached another low building, from the top of which we again saw El Castillo, but with a great chasm between, apparently cutting off all hope of access. By this time it was late, and, afraid of being overtaken by darkness on this wild range, we turned back. Night was upon us when we again reached the shore. The sandy beach was now a welcome relief, and at a late hour we again reached the hut, having come to a rapid conclusion that a frequent repetition of this walk would be neither pleasant nor profitable, and that, in order to get through our work with the celerity we aimed at, it would be necessary again to take up our abode among the ruins.

The next morning we set out for that purpose, escorted by the younger Molas, a fine lad of about twenty, who considered our arrival the greatest incident that had ever occurred at Tancar, and before we reached the end of the beach he wanted to go travelling with us. Ascending the cliff, and passing beyond the two buildings we had seen the day before, we descended from the rear of the last to the head of the chasm which had seemed to cut us off from the principal object of our visit; ascending again at the other end of the ravine, we entered a gloomy forest, and, passing a building on the left, with "old walls" visible in different places indistinctly through the trees, reached the grand staircase of the Castillo. The steps, the platform of the building, and the whole area in front were overgrown with trees, large and principally ramon, which, with their deep green foliage and the mysterious buildings around, presented an image of a grove sacred to Druidical worship.

Our boatmen and Molas cut a path up the steps, and, carrying up their loads, in an hour we were domesticated in the Castillo. We had undertaken our long journey to this place in utter uncertainty as to what we should meet with; impediments and difficulties had accumulated upon us, but already we felt indemnified for all our labour. We were amid the wildest scenery we had yet found in Yucatan; and, besides the deep and exciting interest of the ruins themselves, we had around us what we wanted at all the other places, the magnificence of nature. Clearing away the platform in front, we looked over an immense forest; walking around the moulding of the wall, we looked out upon the boundless ocean, and deep in the clear water at the foot of the cliff we saw gliding quietly by a great fish eight or ten feet long.

Plate XLIV represents the front of the Castillo. A few of the trees which grew around it appear in the engraving, and one is left growing on the top of the lower range, with its gnarled roots binding the front wall and obstructing the doorway, but no words and no drawing could convey a true idea of the solemnity of its living shroud, or of the impression made upon us when the ring of the axe first broke the stillness that had so long prevailed around. The building, including the wings, measures at its base one hundred feet in length. The grand staircase is thirty feet wide, with twenty-four steps, and a substantial balustrade on each side, still in good preservation, gives it an unusually imposing character. In the doorway are two columns, making three entrances, with square recesses above them, all of which once contained ornaments, and in the centre one fragments of a statue still remain. The interior is divided into two corridors, each twenty-six feet long; the one in front is six feet six inches wide, and had at each end a stone bench, or divan; and again on the walls we found the mysterious prints of the red hand.*

A single doorway leads to the back corridor, which is nine feet wide, and has a stone bench extending along the foot of the

---

* While these pages were passing through the press the author had an opportunity of conferring with Mr. Schoolcraft, a gentleman well known for his researches into the character and habits of our North American Indians, and was favoured by him with an interesting communication on the subject of the print of the red hand, which will be found in the Appendix, and for which the author here takes occasion to offer his acknowledgments.

Plate XLIV

T U L O O M.
Front of the Castillo

P. Catherwood.

C. H. Jewiohr.

wall. On each side of the doorway are stone rings, intended for the support of the door, and in the back wall are oblong openings, which admit breezes from the sea. Both apartments have the triangular-arched ceiling, and both had a convenience and pleasantness of arrangement that suited us well as tenants.

The wings are much lower than the principal building. Each consists of two ranges, the lower standing on a low platform, from which are steps leading to the upper. The latter consists of two chambers, of which the one in front is twenty-four feet wide and twenty deep, having two columns in the doorway, and two in the middle of the chamber corresponding with those in the doorway. The centre columns were ornamented with devices in stucco, one of which seemed a masked face, and the other the head of a rabbit. The walls were entire, but the roof had fallen; the rubbish on the floor was less massive than that formed in other places by the remains of the triangular-arched roof, and of different materials, and there were holes along the top of the wall, as if beams had been laid in them, all which induced us to believe that the roofs had been flat, and supported by wooden beams resting upon the two columns in the centre. From this apartment a doorway three feet wide, close to the wall of the principal building, leads to a chamber twenty-four feet wide and nine feet deep, also roofless, and having the same indications that the roof had been flat and supported by wooden beams.

Plate XLV represents the back or sea wall of the Castillo. It rises on the brink of a high, broken, precipitous cliff, commanding a magnificent ocean view, and a picturesque line of coast, being itself visible from a great distance at sea. The wall is solid, and has no doorways or entrances of any kind, nor even a platform around it. At evening, when the work of the day was ended and our men returned to the hut, we sat down on the moulding of the wall, and regretted that the doorways of our lofty habitation had not opened upon the sea. Night, however, wrought a great change in our feelings. An easterly storm came on, and the rain beat heavily against the sea wall. We were obliged to stop up the oblong openings, and congratulated ourselves upon the wisdom of the ancient builders. The darkness, the howling of the winds, the cracking of branches in the forest, and the dashing of angry waves against the cliff, gave a romantic interest, almost a sublimity to our occupation of this desolate building, but we were rather too

Plate XLV

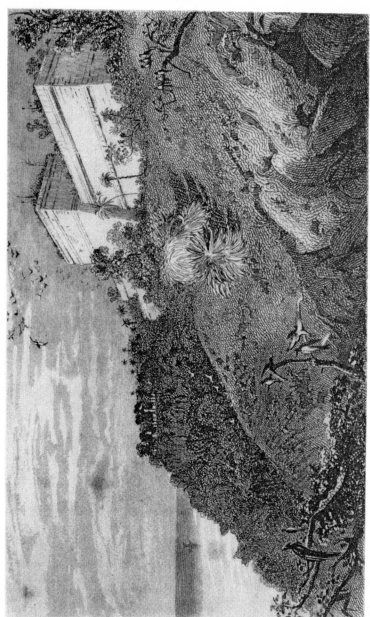

TULOOM

Graham

Catherwood.

hackneyed travellers to enjoy it, and were much annoyed by moschetoes.

Our first day did not suffice to finish the clearing of the area in front of the Castillo. Within this area were several small ruined buildings, which seemed intended for altars. Opposite the foot of the steps was a square terrace, with steps on all four of its sides, but the platform had no structure of any kind upon it, and was overgrown with trees, under the shade of which Mr. Catherwood set up his camera to make his drawing; and, looking down upon him from the door of the Castillo, nothing could be finer than his position, the picturesque effect being greatly heightened by his manner of keeping one hand in his pocket, to save it from the attacks of moschetoes, and by his expedient of tying his pantaloons around his legs to keep ants and other insects from running up.

Adjoining the lower room of the south wing were extensive remains, one of which contained a chamber forty feet wide and nineteen deep, with four columns that had probably supported a flat roof. In another, lying on the ground, were the fragments of two tablets, of the same character with those at Labphak.

On the north side, at the distance of about forty feet from the Castillo, stands a small isolated building, a side view of which is represented in Plate XLVI. It stands on a terrace, and has a staircase eight feet wide, with ten or twelve broken steps. The platform is twenty-four feet front and eighteen deep. The building contains a single room, having, like the Castillo, a triangular-arched roof. Over the doorway is the same curious figure we saw at Sayi, with the head down and the legs and arms spread out; and along the cornice were other curious and peculiar ornaments. The doorway is very low. Throughout the country at times we had heard the building of these cities ascribed to corcubados, or hunchbacks, and the unusual lowness of all the doorways, with the strangeness and desolation of all around, almost gave colour to the most fanciful belief.

The interior of this building consisted of a single chamber, twelve feet by seven, having the triangular-arched ceiling, and at each end a raised step or divan. The wall and ceiling were stuccoed and covered with paintings, the subjects of which were almost entirely effaced.

The day ended without our making any advances beyond this immediate neighbourhood,but the next was made memorable by the unexpected discovery that this forest-buried city was encompassed by a wall, which had resisted all the elements of

Plate XLVI

Gruham

TULOOM

Catherwood

destruction at work upon it, and was still erect and in good preservation. Since the beginning of our exploration we had heard of city walls, but all vestiges of them elsewhere had been uncertain, and our attempts to trace them unsatisfactory. Young Molas had told us of these, and was on the ground early to guide us to them. We set out without much expectation of any decided result, and, following him through the woods, all at once found ourselves confronted by a massive stone structure running at right angles to the sea; and, following its direction, we soon came to a gateway and watch-tower. We passed through the gateway, and followed the wall outside, keeping as close to it as the trees and bushes would permit, down to the sea. The character of this structure could not be mistaken. It was, in the strictest sense, a city wall, the first we had seen that could be identified as such beyond all question, and gave colour to the many stories we had heard of walls, inducing us to believe that many of the vestiges we had seen were parts of continuous lines of enclosure. We immediately set about a thorough exploration, and without once breaking off, measured it from one end to the other.

Figure 17 represents the plan of this wall, as taken from

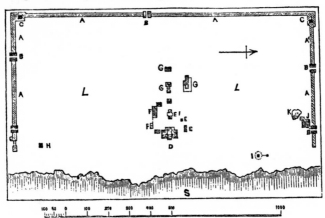

A.A. Walls.	G.G. Buildings last discovered.
B.B. Gateways.	H. Building with wooden roof.
C.C. Watch-towers.	I. Altar.
D. Castillo.	J. Guard house.
E.E. Small adoratorios.	K. Senote of brackish water.
F.F. Casas.	L.L. Thick woods.

Fig. 17

the sea. It forms a parallelogram abutting on the sea, the high, precipitous cliff forming a sea wall 1500 feet in length. We began our survey on the cliff at the southeast angle, where the abutment is much fallen. We attempted to measure along the base, but the close growth of trees and underbrush made it difficult to carry the line, and we mounted to the top. Even then it was no easy matter. Trees growing beside the wall threw their branches across it, thorns, bushes, and vines of every description grew out of it, and at every step we were obliged to cut down the Agave Americana, which pierced us with its long, sharp points; the sun beat upon us, moschetoes, flies, and other insects pestered us, but, under all annoyances, the day employed on the summit of this wall was one of the most interesting we passed among ruins.

The wall is of rude construction, and composed of rough, flat stones, laid upon each other without mortar or cement of any kind, and it varies from eight to thirteen feet in thickness. The south side has two gateways, each about five feet wide. At the distance of six hundred and fifty feet the wall turns at right angles, and runs parallel to the sea. At the angle, elevated so as to give a commanding view, and reached by ascending a few steps, is the watch-tower represented in Figure 18. It is twelve feet square, and has two doorways. The interior is plain, and against the back wall is a small altar, at which the guard might offer up prayers for the preservation of the city. But no guard sits in the watch-tower now; trees are growing around it; within the walls the city is desolate and overgrown, and without is an unbroken forest. The battlements, on which the proud Indian strode with his bow and arrow, and plumes of feathers, are surmounted by immense thorn bushes and overrun by poisonous vines. The city no longer keeps watch; the fiat of destruction has gone out against it, and in solitude it rests, the abode of silence and desolation.

The west line, parallel with the sea, has a single gateway; at the angle is another watch-tower, like that before presented, and the wall then runs straight to the sea. The whole circuit is twenty-eight hundred feet, and the reader may form some idea of its state of preservation from the fact that, except toward the abutments on the sea, we measured the whole length along the top of the wall. The plan is symmetrical, encloses a rectangular area, and, as appears in the engraving, the Castillo occupies the principal and central position. This, however, on account of the

Fig. 18

overgrown state of the area, we were not aware of until the plan was drawn out.

On the north side of the wall, near the east gateway, is a building thirty-six feet in front and thirty-four deep, divided into two principal and two smaller rooms, the ceilings of which had entirely fallen. At one corner is a senote, with the remains of steps leading down to it, and containing brackish water. Near this was a hollow rock, which furnished us with our supply.

Toward the southeast corner of the wall, on the brow of the cliff, stands a building fifteen feet front and ten deep. The interior is about seven feet high, and the ceiling is flat, and discloses an entirely new principle of construction. It has four principal beams of wood, about six inches in diameter, laid on the top of the wall from end to end of the chamber, with smaller beams, about three inches in diameter, laid across the larger so closely as to touch; and on these crossbeams is a thick mass of mortar and large pebbles, which was laid on moist, and now forms a solid crust, being the same materials which we had seen in ruins on the floors of other rooms. Against the back wall was an altar, with a rude triangular stone upon it, which seemed to bear marks of not very distant use. On each side of the doorway were large sea-shells fixed in the wall for the support of the doors.

These were all the buildings to which young Molas conducted us, and he said there were no others within the area of the walls, but there were many vestiges without; and it was our belief that the walls enclosed only the principal, perhaps the sacred buildings, and that ruins existed to a great distance beyond; but, with only young Molas and one boatman, being all that the patron could spare at a time, we did not consider it worth while to attempt any exploration; in fact, our occupation of this walled city was too much disturbed to allow us to think of remaining long. A legion of fierce usurpers, already in possession, were determined to drive us out, and after hard work by day, we had no rest at night;

> "There was never yet philosopher
> That could endure the toothache patiently;"

and I will venture to say that a philosopher would find the moschetoes of Tuloom worse than the toothache. We held our ground against them for two nights, but on the third, one after the other, we crawled out of our hammocks to the platform before the door. The moon was shining magnificently, lighting up the darkness of the forest, and drawing a long silvery line upon the sea. For a time we felt ourselves exalted above the necessity of sleep, but by degrees drowsiness overcame us, and at last we were all stretched at full length on the ground. The onslaught was again terrible; we returned to our hammocks, but found no peace, and emerging again, kindled a large fire, and sat down to smoke till daylight. It was aggravating to look the moon in the face, its expression was so calm and composed. A savage notice to quit was continually buzzing in our ears, and all that we cared for was to get away.

CHAPTER XXII

The next morning we finished what remained
to be done, and, after an early dinner, prepared to leave the
ruins. While the men were arranging their loads I gave Doctor
Cabot a direction to a point in the wall, where, in measuring
around it, Mr. Catherwood and I had started two ocellated turkeys. He set out to cut his way in a straight line with his hunting
knife, and very soon, while sitting on the steps of the Castillo, I
heard him calling to me that he had come upon another building which we had not seen. Having occasion to economize shoe
leather for the walk back over the cliff, I at first hesitated about
going to it, but he insisted. He was so near that we communicated without any particular effort of voice, but I could see
nothing of him or of the building. Following his path, I found
him standing before it; and while working our way around it
we discovered two others near by, almost invisible, so dense was
the foliage of the trees, but the largest, except the Castillo, and
most important of any we had seen. Our plans were all deranged,
for we could not go away without drawings of these buildings.
We returned to the steps of the Castillo, and summoned all
hands to council. The men had their back-loads ready, Bernaldo
reported two tortillas as the stock of provisions on hand, and

Plate XLVII

TULOOM.

Catherwood

Adlard

the idea of another night in the Castillo struck us with dismay. We had been so long accustomed to sleep that it had become part of our nature; a night's rest was indispensable, and we determined to break up and return the next day.

Before daylight the next morning Albino set off with Molas and the sailors, and by the time Mr. Catherwood arrived on the ground the clearing of the first building was made.

Plate XLVII represents the front of this building. It faces the west, measures twenty-seven feet in length and nineteen in depth, and consists of two stories. The exterior had been richly decorated, and above the cornice were fragments of rich ornaments in stucco. The lower story has four columns, making five doorways opening into a narrow corridor, which runs round and encloses on three sides a chamber in the centre. The walls of the corridor on both sides were covered with paintings, but green and mildewed from the rankness of vegetation in which the building is smothered. A small doorway in front opens into the chamber, which measures eleven feet by seven; of this, too, the walls were covered with paintings, decayed and effaced, and against the back wall was an altar for burning copal.

The building on the top stands directly over the lower chamber, and corresponds with it in dimensions, this being the only instance we met with in which one room was placed directly over another. There was no staircase or other visible means of communication between the lower and upper stories.

At the rear of this building were others attached to it, or connected with it, but uprooted and thrown down by trees, and among the ruins were two stone tablets with rounded surfaces, six feet six inches high, two feet four inches wide, and eight inches thick, having upon them worn and indistinct traces of sculpture.

At the short distance of fifty-three feet is the building represented in Plate XLVIII. It stands on a terrace six feet high, with a staircase in the centre, measures forty-five feet by twenty-six, has two pillars in the doorway, and over the centre is the head of a mutilated figure. The interior is divided into two principal and parallel apartments, and at the north extremity of the inner one is a smaller apartment, containing an enclosed altar five feet long, and three feet six inches deep, for burning copal. The roof had fallen, and trees were growing out of the floor.

Near this is another building, larger than the last, constructed on the same plan, but more ruined. These buildings were all within about two hundred feet of the steps of the Cas-

Plate XLVIII

TULOOM

tillo. We were in the very act of leaving before we discovered them, and but for the accidental attempt of Doctor Cabot to cut through in search of birds, or if he had happened to cut a few yards to the right hand or the left, we should have gone away ignorant of their existence.

It will be borne in mind that when this city was inhabited and clear of trees, the buildings were all visible from the sea; the Spaniards are known to have sailed along this coast, and the reader will ask if they have given us no accounts of its existence. The narrative of the expedition of Grijalva, taken up at the point at which we left it, after crossing from Cozumel, continues: "We ran along day and night, and the next day toward sunset we saw a bourg, or village, so large that Seville would not have appeared larger or better. We saw there a very high tower. There was upon the bank a crowd of Indians, who carried two standards, which they raised and lowered as signs to us to come and join them. The same day we arrived at a bay, near which was a tower, the highest we had seen. We remarked a very considerable village; the country was watered by many rivers. We discovered a bay *where a fleet would have been able to enter.*" This account is certainly not so accurate as a coast survey would be at this day, but it is more minute than most accounts of the early voyages of the Spaniards, and, in my opinion, it is all sufficient to identify this now desolate city. After crossing over from Cozumel, twenty-four hours' sailing would bring them to this part of the coast; and the next circumstance mentioned, viz., the discovery of a bay where a fleet would have been able to enter, is still stronger, for at the distance of about eight leagues below Tuloom is the Bay of Ascension, always spoken of by the Spanish writers as a harbour in which the whole Spanish navy might lie at anchor. It is the only bay along the coast from Cape Catoche into which large vessels can enter, and constrains me to the belief that the desolate place now known as Tuloom was that "bourg, or village, so large that Seville would not appear larger or better," and that the Castillo, from which we were driven by the moschetoes, was that "highest tower which the Spaniards had seen."

Farther, it is my firm belief that this city continued to be occupied by its aboriginal inhabitants long after the conquest, for Grijalva turned back from the Bay of Ascension, again passed without landing, and after the disastrous expedition of Don Francisco Montejo, the Spaniards made no attempt upon this part of the coast, so that the aborigines must have remained for a long time in this place unmolested. And the strong impression of a comparatively very recent occupation is derived from the appearance of the buildings themselves, which, though not less ruined, owing to the ranker growth of trees, had in some instances an appearance of freshness and good keeping that, amid the desolation and solitude around, was almost startling.

Outside of the walls are several small buildings, no doubt intended for adoratorios, or altars, one of which is represented in Figure 19. It stands on a terrace, having a circular platform,

Fig. 19

on the brow of the cliff, overlooking the sea, and measures fifteen feet front by twelve deep. The doorway faces the north. The interior consists of a single chamber, and against the back wall is an altar in such a state of preservation as to be fit for its original uses. Near the foot of the steps, overgrown by the scrubby wild palm which covers the whole cliff, is a small altar,

with ornaments in stucco, one of which seems intended to represent a pineapple. These wanted entirely the massive character of
the buildings, and are so slight that they could almost be pushed
over with the foot. They stand in the open air, exposed to strong
easterly winds, and almost to the spray of the sea. It was impossible to believe that the altar had been abandoned three hundred
years; within that time some guardian eye had watched over it,
some pious hand had repaired it, and long since the arrival of
the Spaniards the Indian had performed before it his idolatrous
rites.

Under the circumstances attending our visit to it, we found
this one of the most interesting places we had seen in our whole
exploration of ruins; but I am compelled to omit many details
deserving of description and comment, and shall close with one
remark. The reader knows the difficulty we had in reaching this
place from the interior. The whole triangular region from Valladolid to the Bay of Ascension on one side, and the port of Yalahao on the other, is not traversed by a single road, and the
rancho of Molas is the only settlement along the coast. It is a
region entirely unknown; no white man ever enters it. Ruined
cities no doubt exist, and young Molas told us of a large building
many leagues in the interior, known to an old Indian, covered
with paintings in bright and vivid colours, and the subjects of
which were still perfect. With difficulty we contrived to see this
Indian, but he was extremely uncommunicative; said it was
many years since he saw the building; that he had come upon it
in the dry season while hunting, and should not be able to find
it again. It is my belief that within this region cities like those
we have seen in ruins were kept up and occupied for a long
time, perhaps one or two centuries, after the conquest, and that,
down to a comparatively late period, Indians were living in
them, the same as before the discovery of America. In fact, I
conceive it to be not impossible that within this secluded region
may exist at this day, unknown to white men, a living aboriginal
city, occupied by relics of the ancient race, who still worship in
the temples of their fathers.

The reader will, perhaps, think that I have gone far enough.
We had now finished our voyage along the coast, and the end
which we had in view was fully accomplished. We had seen,
abandoned and in ruins, the same buildings which the Spaniards
saw entire and inhabited by Indians, and we had identified them
beyond question as the works of the same people who created
the great ruined cities over which, when we began our journey,

hung a veil of seemingly impenetrable mystery. At that time, we believed the discovery and comparison of these remains to be the surest, if not the only means, of removing this veil; and though other proofs had accumulated upon us, these were not on that account the less interesting.

Our journey in this direction is now ended, and our course is homeward. We were detained one day at Tancar by a storm, and on Tuesday morning the patron came to us in a hurry with a summons on board; the wind had veered so that he could get out of the harbour; and, bidding good-by to the carpenter and Molas, we were soon under way. The wind was still high, and the sea so rough, and kept the little canoa in such commotion, that in half an hour nearly all our party were sea-sick. The servants were completely disabled, and there was no chance for a dinner. We had a strong wind and fair, passed several small square stone buildings, like those of which representations have been given, but, on account of the rough sea and rocky shore we could not land, and late in the afternoon put in at Nesuc, where we had stopped before, distinguished by its solitary palm tree.

Early in the morning we were again under way, and coasted to the point of Kancune, where we landed in front of a rancho then occupied by a party of fishermen. Near by was another great pile of the skeletons of turtles. The fishermen were busy within the hut mending their nets, and seemed to be leading a hardy, independent, and social life, entirely different from anything seen in the interior. A short walk brought us to the point, on which stood two dilapidated buildings, one entirely fallen, and the other having dimensions like the smallest of those seen at Tuloom. It was so intensely hot, and we were so annoyed by millions of sand-flies, that we did not think it worth while to stay, but returned to the hut, embarked, and, crossing over, in two hours reached the island of Mugeres. Near the shore were immense flocks of sea-birds, sitting on the piles of a turtle enclosure; over our heads was a cloud of white ibises, and, somewhat to the surprise of the fishermen, our coming to anchor was signalized by a discharge of heavy bird artillery, and a splashing into the water to pick up the dead and wounded. In wading ashore we stuck in a mud-bank, and had time to contemplate the picturesque beauty of the scene before us. It was a small sandy beach, with a rocky coast on each side, and trees growing down to the water, broken only by a small clearing opposite the beach, in which were two palm leaf huts, and an arbour covered with palm leaves. Under the arbour hung three small hammocks, and a hardy, sun-dried fisherman sat repairing a net, with two Indian boys engaged in weaving a new one. The old fisherman, without desisting from his work, invited us to the hammocks, and, to satisfy our invariable first want on this coast, sent a boy for water, which, though not good, was better than that on board.

Along the shore, at no great distance, was a funeral pile of the carcasses of turtles, half burned, and covered with countless millions of flies, actually heaving and moving as if alive; and near this hideous pile, as if to contrast beauty and deformity, was a tree, covered to its topmost boughs with the white ibis, its green foliage appearing like an ornamental frame-work to their snowy plumage. We ordered our dinner to be brought to the arbour, and as we were sitting down a canoe came ashore; the fishermen dragged across the beach two large turtles, and leaving the carcasses to swell the funeral pile, brought down to the arbour strings of eggs, and the parts that served for food or oil, and hung them quivering in the sun along the fence, their sudden blackness from swarms of flies disturbing somewhat the satisfaction with which we had first hailed this arbour. We had again stopped to visit ruins, but in the afternoon it rained, and we could not go to them. The arbour was no protection, and we were obliged to go inside the hut, which was snug and comfortable, the oil jars being arranged under the eaves, with turtle-shells tied up carefully in bundles, and on the rafters hung strings of eggs, while nets, old sails, blocks, and other characteristic furniture of a fisherman's hut filled up the corners. It was no hardship to be obliged to pass the afternoon among these fishermen, for their hardy, independent occupation gave manliness to their character, and freedom to their speech and manners.

The island was famed among the fishermen as the rendezvous of Lafitte the pirate, and the patron told us that our host had been his prisoner two years. This man was about fifty-five, tall and thin, and his face was so darkened by the sun that it was hard to say whether he was white or of mixed blood. We remarked that he was not fond of talking of his captivity; he said he did not know how long he was a prisoner nor where he was taken; and as the business of piracy was rather complicated in these parts, we conceived a suspicion that he had not been a prisoner entirely against his will. His fellow-fishermen had no narrow feelings on the subject, and perhaps gave a preference to piracy as a larger business, and one that brought more ounces, than catching turtles. They seemed, however, to have an idea that los Ingleses entertained different views, and the prisoner, el pobre, as our patron called him, said those things were all over, and it was best not to disturb them. He could not, however, help dropping a few words in behalf of Lafitte, or Monsieur Lafitta; he did not know whether it was true what people said of him, but he never hurt the poor fishermen, and, led on by degrees he told us that Lafitte died in his arms, and that his widow, a señora del Norte from Mobile, was then living in great distress at Silan, the port at which we intended to disembark.

Besides piratical associations, this island had been the scene of a strange incident within the last two years. A sailor lay on his death-bed in Cadiz, penniless and friendless, and, to requite the kindness of his host for allowing him to die in his house, he told the latter that, some years before, he had belonged to a band of pirates, and upon one occasion, after taking a rich prize and murdering all on board, he had gone ashore with his companions at the island of Mugeres, and buried a large sum of money in gold. When the piratical hordes were broken up he escaped, and dared not return to regions where he might be recognised. He said his companions were all hanged except one Portuguese, who lived in the island of Antigua, and, as the only means of requiting his host's kindness, he advised him to seek out the Portuguese and recover the money. The host at first thought the story was told only to secure a continuance of good treatment, and paid no attention to it, but the sailor died protesting its truth. The Spaniard made a voyage to the island of Antigua, and found out the Portuguese, who at first denied all knowledge of the transaction, but at length confessed it, and said that he was only waiting for an opportunity to go and dig up the gold. Some arrangement was made between them, and the Spaniard procured a small vessel, and set sail with the Portuguese on board. The vessel became short of provisions and water, and off Yalahao encountered the patron of our canoa, who, as he said, on receiving twenty-five dollars in advance, piloted her into that place for supplies. While there the story of the treasure leaked out; the Portuguese tried to escape, but the Spaniard set sail, carrying him off. The fishermen followed in canoas. The Portuguese, under the influence of threats, indicated a place for the landing, and was carried on shore bound. He protested that in that condition he could not find the spot; he had never been there except at the time of burying the gold, and required time and freedom of movement; but the Spaniard, furious at the notoriety given to the thing, and at the uninvited company of the fishermen, refused to trust him, and set his men to digging, the fishermen joining on their own account. The digging continued two days, during which time the Portuguese was treated with great cruelty, and the sympathy of the fishermen was excited, and increased by the consideration that this island was within their fishing limits, and if they got the Portuguese into their own possession, they could come back at any time and dig up the money quietly, without any wrangle with strangers. In the mean time, our old friend Don Vicente Albino, then living at Cozumel, hearing of treasure on an island belonging to nobody, and so near his own, ran down with his sloop and put in for the Portuguese. The Spanish proprietor was obliged to give him up. Don Vicente could not get hold of him, and the fishermen carried him off to Yalahao, where, finding himself out of the actual grasp of any of them, he set up for himself, and by the first opportunity slipped off in a canoa for Campeachy, since which he had never been heard of.

Early in the morning, under the guidance of two of the fisherman, we set out to visit the ruins. The island of Mugeres is between four and five miles long, half a mile wide, and four miles distant from the mainland. The ruins were at the north end. For a short distance we kept along the shore, and then struck into a path cut straight across the island. About half way across we came to a santa cruz, or holy cross, set up by the fishermen, at which place we heard distinctly the sound of the breakers on the opposite shore. To the right a faint track was perceptible, which soon disappeared altogether; but our guides knew the direction, and, cutting a way with the machete, we came out upon a high, rocky, perpendicular cliff, which commanded an immense expanse of ocean, and against which the waves, roused by the storm of the night before, were dashing grandly. We followed along the brink of the cliff and around the edges of great perpendicular chasms, the ground being bare of trees and covered with a scrubby plant, called the uba, with gnarled roots spreading like the branches of a grape-vine. At the point terminating the island, standing boldly upon the sea, was the lonely edifice represented in Plate XLIX. Below, rocking on the waves, was a small canoa, with our host then in the act of getting on board a turtle. It was the wildest and grandest scene we had looked upon in our whole journey.

The steps which led to the building are in good preservation, and at the foot is a platform, with the ruins of an altar.

Plate XLIX

F. Catherwood.

J. H. Gambrett.

ANCIENT BUILDING, ISLAND OF MUGERES.

The front, on one side of the doorway, has fallen. When entire it measured twenty-eight feet, and it is fifteen feet deep. On the top is a cross, probably erected by the fishermen. The interior is divided into two corridors, and in the wall of that in front are three small doorways leading to the inner corridor. The ceiling had the triangular arch, and throughout the hand of the builders on the mainland could not be mistaken, but on the walls were writings which seemed strangely familiar in an aboriginal building. These inscriptions were,

D. Doyle, 1842.   A. C. Goodall, 1842.
H. M. Ship Blossom.
11th October, 1811. Corsaire Françs (Chebek) le Vengeur,
Capt. Pierre Liovet;

and wafered on the wall on separate cards were the names of the officers of the Texan schooners of war San Bernard and San Antonio.

At the distance of a few hundred feet was another building about fourteen feet square, having four doorways, with steps on three sides, dilapidated, and almost inaccessible on account of the thickets of cactus and thorn bushes growing around it.

In the account given by Bernal Dias of the expedition of Cortez, he says that, after leaving the island of Cozumel, the fleet was separated by a gale of wind, but the next day all the ships joined company except one, which, according to the surmise of the pilot, was found in a certain bay on the coast wind bound. "Here," says Bernal Dias, "several of our companions went on shore, and found in the town hard by, four temples, the idols in which represented human female figures of large size, for which reason we named this place *Punta* de las Mugeres," or the Point of the Women. Gomarra speaks of a *Cape* Mugeres, and says, "At this place there were towers covered with wood and straw, in which, in the best order, were put many idols, that appeared to be representations of women." No mention is made by any of the old historians of the *island* of Mugeres, but there is no point or cape on the mainland; and, considering the ignorance of the coast which must have existed in the early voyages, it is not impossible to believe that the Spaniards gave to the promontory on which these buildings stand the name of point or cape, in which case the building presented in the engraving may be one of the temples or towers referred to by Bernal Dias and Gomarra.

We returned to the hut ready to embark, and at twelve o'clock we took leave of the fishermen, and were again on board our canoa.

The wind was fair and strong, and very soon we reached the point of the island. Toward dark we doubled Catoche, and, for the first time coasting all night, day broke upon us in the harbour of Yalahao. After the desolate regions we had been visiting, the old pirates' haunt seemed a metropolis. We anchored on a mud-bank leg deep, and now discovered that our patron, hired only for the occasion, intended to leave us, and substitute another. Afraid of the men following, and subjecting us to detention, we forwarded a threatening message to the agent, and remained on board.

At seven o'clock we were again under way, with the wind directly astern, and as much as we could carry, the canoa rolling so that we were compelled to take in the mainsail. The coast was low, barren, and monotonous. At three o'clock we passed an ancient mound, towering above the huts that constituted the port of El Cuyo, a landmark for sailors, visible at sea three leagues distant; but our patron told us that there were no buildings or vestiges of ruins.

At four o'clock we saw an old acquaintance in misfortune. It was the brig which had arrived at Sisal a few hours after we did, lying a wreck on the beach, with foremast and bowsprit broken, sails stripped, but the hull still entire; probably long before this the shore is strewed with her fragments.

CHAPTER XXIII

At daylight the next morning we crawled out from the bottom of the canoa, and found her anchored off the port of Silan, which consisted of a few huts built around a sandy square on a low, barren coast. We gave portions of our tattered garments to the waves, and waded ashore. It was three weeks since we had embarked; our coast voyage had been more interesting than we expected, but there was no part of it so agreeable as the end; we were but too happy to get rid of the discomfort and confinement to the canoa. The patron went to find lodgings for us, and I followed with one of the boatmen, carrying a load. A man just opening the door of a sort of warehouse called to me, and offered it for our accommodation, which, on looking within, I did not hesitate to accept. This man had never heard of us nor we of him, and, probably, neither will ever hear of the other again. It was another instance of the universally kind treatment we met with in all parts of the country.

Silan is the port of Izamal, which is eleven leagues distant. According to our arrangement, Dimas was to meet us here with the horses, but he had not arrived or been heard of. We learned, however, that there was no green food to be procured at this place, which Dimas had probably learned at the village, three leagues distant, and had therefore remained at that place; yet we had some uneasiness, as he had to make a journey of two hundred and fifty miles, and our first business was to despatch Albino for information. Next we had a great enterprise in procuring breakfast, and after this in providing for dinner, which we determined should be the best the country afforded, to consist of fish and fowl, each of which had to be bought separately, and, with separate portions of lard, sent to different houses to be cooked.

During the interval of preparation I took a walk along the shore. Toward the end of a sandy beach was a projecting point, on a line with which I noticed on the water what seemed to be a red cloud of singular brilliancy, and, at the same time, delicacy of colour, which, on drawing nearer, I found to be a flat covered with flamingoes. On my return I reported the discovery to Doctor Cabot, when our host gave us such a glowing account of flamingoes, scarlet ibises, and roseate spoonbills at Punta Arenas, about two leagues distant, that my imagination was excited by the idea of such clouds of beautiful plumage. Doctor Cabot was anxious for closer acquaintance with the birds, and we determined, in case our horses arrived, to go thither that same afternoon, and, after a few hours' shooting, overtake Mr. Catherwood the next day at Izamal. In good time our horses arrived with Dimas, in fine order; and as he had had some days' rest, we took him and an Indian procured by our host, and at about four o'clock set out. For the first league our road lay directly along the shore, but farther on there were projecting points, to cut off which a footpath led among mangrove trees, with shoots growing from the branches into the ground, forming what seemed a naked and impenetrable canebrake, surmounted by thick green foliage. In many places it was difficult to advance on horseback; from time to time we came out upon a broken, stony shore, and, considering that we had set out merely for a short ride, we found ourselves travelling on one of the wildest roads we had met with in the country. At dusk we reached a hut in a beautifully picturesque position, imbosomed in a small bay, with a frail bridge, about two feet wide, running out some distance from the shore, and a canoa floating at the end. The hut consisted of two parts, connected by a thatched arbour, empty, and apparently begging for a tenant. A string of fish hung on one of the beams, and on the ground were a few smothered coals. We swung our hammocks, kindled a fire, and when the occupant arrived had a cup of chocolate ready for him, and endeavoured to make him feel himself at home; but this was no easy matter. He was a lad of about sixteen, the son of the proprietor, who had gone away that day, the fishing season being nearly over. He certainly was not expecting us, and was taken somewhat by surprise; he had never seen a foreigner in his life, and was by no means reassured when we told him that we had come to shoot flamingoes and spoonbills. Our Indian gave him some indistinct notion of our object, of which, however, he must have had a very imperfect notion himself; and seeming to intimate that we were beyond his comprehension, or, at all events, entirely too many for him, the boy withdrew to the other division of the hut, and left us in full possession. Instead of a rough night we were well provided for, but, unfortunately, there was no ramon or water for the horses. We made an affecting appeal to our young host, and he spared us part of a small stock of maize, which he had on hand for the making of his own tortillas, but they had to go without water, as none could be procured at night.

In the gray of the morning we heard a loud quacking of ducks, which almost lifted us out of our hammocks, and carried us out of doors. Beyond the point of the little dock was a long sand-bank, covered with immense flocks of these birds. Our host could not go with us till he had examined his fishing nets, and Dimas had to take the horses to water, but we pushed off with our Indian to set the canoe. Very soon we found that he was not familiar with the place, or with the management of a canoe, and, what was worse, we could not understand a word he said. Below us the shore formed a large bay, with the Punta de Arenas, or Point of Sand, projecting toward us, bordered down to the water's edge with trees, and all over the bay were sand-banks, barely appearing above water, and covered with wild fowl of every description known, in numbers almost exceeding the powers of conception. In recurring to them afterward, Doctor Cabot enumerated of ducks, the mallard, pin-tail, blooming teal, widgeon, and gadwall; of bitterns, the American bittern, least bittern, great and lesser egret, blue crane, great blue heron, Louisiana heron, night heron, two kinds of rail, one clapper rail, white ibis, willets, snipes, red-breasted snipe, least snipe, semi-palmated sandpiper, black-breasted plover, marble godwit, long-billed curlew, osprey or fish-hawk, black hawk, and other smaller birds, of which we took no note, and all together, with their brilliant plumage and varied notes, forming, as we passed among them, an animated and exciting scene, but it was no field for sporting. It would have been slaughter to shoot among them. In an hour we could have loaded our canoe with birds, of which one or two brace would be considered a fair morning's work. But we did not know what to do with them, and, besides, these were not what we were looking for. A single flock of flamingoes flew by us, but out of reach, and at the moment we were stuck in the mud. Our Indian made horrible work in setting us, and continued to hit every flat till we reached the head of the bay, and entered a branch like a creek. Unable to hold discourse with him, and supposing that he was setting right, we continued to move slowly up the stream, until we found that we were getting beyond the region of birds; but the scene was so quiet and peaceful that we were loth to return; and still on each bank the snowy plumage of the white ibis appeared among the green of the trees, and the heron stood like a statue in the water, turning his long neck almost imperceptibly, and looking at us. But we had no time for quiet enjoyment, and turned back. Near the mouth of the creek a flock of roseate spoonbills flew over our heads, also out of reach, but we saw where they alighted, and setting toward them till we were stopped by a mud-bank, we took to the water, or rather to the mud, in which we found our lower members moving suddenly downward to parts unknown, and in some danger of descending till our sombreros only remained as monuments of our muddy grave. Extricating ourselves, moving in another direction, and again sinking and drawing back, for two hours we toiled, struggled, floundered, and fired, a laughing stock to the beautiful spoonbills in the free element above. At length Dr. Cabot brought one down, and we parted. In following our separate fortunes along the shore I shot one, which fell at the other side of a stream. As I rushed in, the water rose above all my mud stains, and I fell back, and hastily disencumbered myself of clothing. A high wind was sweeping over the bay; having no stone at hand with which to secure them, my hat and light garments were blown into the water, and at the same moment the roseate bird stood up, opened its large wings, and fluttered along the beach. Distracted between the bird and the fugitive clothing, I let the latter go, and gave chase to the bird, after securing which, and holding it kicking under my arm, I pursued my habiliments, now some distance apart, into the water, and at length got back to dry land with my miscellaneous load, and stood on the beach a picture of an antiquary in distress, doubtless illustrating the proverb to the Indian, who now came to my relief, if he had ever met with it in the course of his reading, that no man can be a hero to his valet de chambre. In honor of the event I determined to make an essay in dissection, and to carry the bird home with me as a memorial of this place.

By this time Doctor Cabot joined me, and it was necessary to return. We had procured but one bird each, and had been disappointed of the grand spectacle of clouds of beautiful plumage, but the account of our host was no doubt true to the letter, for the season was late, and the brilliant birds we were seeking had wended their way north; but even of these, with the knowledge we had acquired of localities, two canoes, and good setters, in another day we could have procured any number we wanted. For mere sporting, such a ground is not often seen, and the idea of a shooting lodge, or rather hut, on the shores of Punta de Arenas for a few months in the season, with a party large enough to consume the game, presented itself almost as attractively as that of exploring ruined cities. On our return, each of us made a single shot, from which we picked up between thirty and forty birds, leaving others crippled and hopping on the beach. We got back to the hut, and tumbled them all into a dry pot (the feathers being, of course, taken off), and sat down ourselves to the business of dissection. With a finishing touch from Doctor Cabot, I prepared a miserable specimen of a beautiful bird, looking upon it, nevertheless, with great satisfaction as the memorial of a remarkable place and an interesting adventure. In the mean time, the birds on the fire were getting on swimmingly, in a literal sense, giving decided evidence touching the richness of their feeding-grounds. We had only tortillas as an accompaniment, but neither we nor the birds had any reason to complain.

At four o'clock we took leave of our young host, and at dark reached the port, and rode across the sandy plaza. The door which had opened to us with so much alacrity was now shut, but not by the hand of inhospitality. Mr. Catherwood and the owner had left for the village, and the house was locked up. Some of the villagers, however, came to us, and conducted us to the quartel, which was garrisoned by two women, who surrendered at discretion, provided us with chocolate, and, although the hut was abundantly large for all of us, unexpectedly bade us good-night, and withdrew to a neighbour's to sleep. If they had remained, not being worn down by fatigue as we were, and, consequently, more wakeful, a sad catastrophe might have been prevented. We laid our birds carefully on a table to dry; during the night a cat entered, and we were awaked to see the fruits of our hard day's labour dragged along the floor, and the cat bounding from them, and escaping through a hole in the side of the hut. It was no consolation to us, but if she had nine lives, the arsenic used for preserving the birds had probably taken them all.

Before daylight the next morning we were again in the saddle. For some distance back from the port the ground had been washed or overflowed by the sea, and was a sandy, barren mangrove brake. Beyond commenced the same broken, stony surface, and before we had proceeded far we discovered that Doctor Cabot's horse was lame. Not to lose time, I rode on to procure another, and at eight o'clock reached the village of Silan. In the suburbs I discovered unexpectedly the towering memorial of another ruined city, and riding into the plaza, saw at one angle, near the wall of the church, the gigantic mound represented in Plate L, the grandest we had seen in the country. Much as we had seen of ruins, the unexpected sight of this added immensely to the interest of our long journeying among the remains of aboriginal grandeur. Leaving my horse at the casa real, and directing the alcalde to see about getting one for Doctor Cabot, I walked over to the mound. At the base, and inside of the wall of the church, were five large orange trees, loaded with fruit. A group of Indians were engaged in getting stone out of the mound to repair the wall, and a young man was superintending them, whom I immediately recognised as the padre. He accompanied me to the top of the mound; it was one of the largest we had seen, being about fifty feet high and four hundred feet long. There was no building or structure of any kind visible; whatever had been upon it had fallen or been pulled down. The church, the wall of the yard, and the few stone houses in the village, had been built of materials taken from it.

In walking along the top we reached a hole, at the bottom of which I discovered the broken arch of a ceiling, and looked through it into an apartment below. This explained the character of the structure. A building had extended the whole length of the mound, the upper part of which had fallen, and the ruins had made the whole a long, confused, and undistinguishable mass. The top commanded an extensive view of a great wooded plain, and near by, rising above the trees, was another mound, which, within a few years, had been crowned with an edifice, called, as at Chichen and Tuloom, El Castillo. The padre, a young man, but little over thirty, remembered when this Castillo stood with its doorways open, pillars in them, and corridors

Plate I.

F. Catherwood.

M. Cohoru

ANCIENT MOUND. VILLAGE OF SILAN.

around. The sight of these ruins was entirely unexpected; if they had been all we had met with in the country, we should have gazed upon them with perplexity and wonder; and they possessed unusual interest from the fact that they existed in a place, the name of which was known and familiar to us as that of an existing aboriginal town at the time of the conquest.

In tracing the disorderly flight of the Spaniards from Chichen Itza, we find them first at Silan, which is described by Herrera as being "Then a fine Town, the Lord whereof was a Youth of the Race of the Cheles, then a Christian, and great Friend to Captain Francis de Montejo, who received and entertained them. Tirrok was near Silan; that and the other Towns along the Coast were subject to the Cheles, who, having been no way disobliged by the Spaniards, did not disturb them, and so they continued some Months, when, seeing no Possibility of being supplied with Men and other Things they wanted, they resolved quite to abandon that Country. In order to it, they were to march to Campeachy, forty Leagues from Silan, which was looked upon as very dangerous, because the Country was very populous; but the Lord of Silan and others bearing them Company, they arrived in Safety, and the Cheles returned to their own Homes." Cogolludo, too, traces the routed Spaniards to Silan, but thence, with more probability, he carries them by sea to Campeachy; for, as he well suggests, the lords of Silan would not have been able to give them safe escort through forty leagues of territory inhabited by different tribes, all hostile to the Spaniards, and some of them hostile to the Cheles themselves. This difference, however, is unimportant; both accounts prove that there was a large town of aboriginal inhabitants in this vicinity, and, as at Ticul and Nohcacab, we must either suppose that these great mounds are the remains of the aboriginal town, or we must believe that another town of the same name existed in this immediate neighbourhood, of which no trace whatever now remains.

The reader may remember that we left the port before daylight. As I stood on the top of the mound, all that I needed to fill up the measure of my satisfaction was the certainty of a breakfast. The padre seemed to divine my thoughts; he relieved me from all uneasiness, and enabled me to contemplate with a tranquil mind the sublimity of these remains of a fallen people. When Doctor Cabot arrived he found a table that surprised him.

Silan was known to us as the scene of a modern and minor

event. Our ambiguous friend on the island of Mugeres had told us that at this place Lafitte died and was buried, and I inquired for his grave. The padre was not in the village at the time, and did not know whether he was buried in the campo santo or the church, but supposed that, as Lafitte was a distinguished man, it was in the latter. We went thither, and examined the graves in the floor, and the padre drew out from amid some rubbish a cross, with a name on it, which he supposed to that of Lafitte, but it was not. The sexton who officiated at the burial was dead; the padre sent for several of the inhabitants, but a cloud hung over the memory of the pirate: all knew of his death and burial, but none knew or cared to tell where he was laid. We had heard, also, that his widow was living in the place, but this was not true. There was, however, a negress who had been a servant to the latter, and who, we were told, spoke English; the cura sent for her, but she was so intoxicated that she could not make her appearance.

The last of the padre's good offices was procuring a horse for Doctor Cabot, which the alcalde had not been able to do. It was the last time we were thrown upon the hospitality of a padre, and in taking leave of him, I do repent me that in my confidential intercourse with the reader I have at times let fall what I might better have kept to myself.

At ten o'clock we set out, and at half past twelve reached Temax, two and a half leagues distant. It had a fine plaza, with a great church and convent, and a stone casa real, with a broad corridor in front, under which the guarda were swinging in hammocks.

We were but six leagues from Izamal, at which place, we learned, a fiesta was then going on, and there was to be a ball in the evening; but we could neither push our horses through, nor procure a calesa, though the road was good for wheel carriages.

Early in the evening we took to our hammocks, but had hardly lain down, when one of the guarda came to inform us that a caricoche had just arrived from Izamal, and wanted a return freight. We had it brought down to the casa real, and at two o'clock, by a bright moonlight, we started, leaving Dimas to follow with the horses. The caricoche was drawn by three mules, and had in it a bed, on which we reclined at full length.

At nine o'clock we entered the suburbs of Izamal, but fifteen leagues from Merida. The streets had lamps, and were designated by visible objects, as at Merida. Peeping through the curtain, we rode into the plaza, which was alive with people.

dressed in clean clothes for the fiesta. There was an unusual proportion of gentlemen with black hats and canes, and some with military coats, bright and flashing to such a degree that we congratulated ourselves upon not having made our entry on horseback. We had on our shooting-clothes, with the mud stains from Punta Arenas, and by computation our beards were of twenty-eight days' growth. In the centre of the plaza our driver stopped for instructions. We directed him to the casa real, and as we were moving on, our English saddles, strapped on behind, caught the eye of Albino, who conducted us to the house in which Mr. Catherwood was already domiciled. This house was a short distance from the plaza, built of stone, and about sixty feet front, divided into two large salas, with rooms adjoining, a broad corridor behind, and a large yard for horses, for all which the rent was three reales per day, being, as we were advised, but two more than anybody else would have been obliged to pay. In a few moments we had done all that our scanty wardrobe would allow, and were again in the street.

It was the last day of the fiesta of Santa Cruz. By the grace of a beneficent government, the village of Izamal had been erected into a city, and the jubilee on account of this accession of political dignity was added to the festival of the holy cross. The bull-fights were over, but the bull-ring, fancifully ornamented, still remained in the centre of the plaza, and two bulls stood under one of the corridors, pierced with wounds and streaming with blood, as memorials of the fight. Amid a crowd of Indians were parties of vecinos, or white people, gay and well dressed in the style and costume of the capital, and under the corridor of a corner house, with an arbour projecting into the plaza, music was sounding to summon the people to a ball. From desolation and solitude we had come into the midst of gayeties, festivities, and rejoicings. But amid this gay scene the eye turned involuntarily to immense mounds rising grandly above the tops of the houses, from which the whole city had been built, without seeming to diminish their colossal proportions, proclaiming the power of those who reared them, and destined, apparently, to stand, when the feebler structures of their more civilized conquerors shall have crumbled into dust.

One of these great mounds, having at that time benches upon it, commanding a view of the bull-fight in the plaza, blocked up the yard of the house we occupied, and extended into the adjoining yard of the Señora Mendez, who was the owner of both. It is, perhaps, two hundred feet long and thirty

high. The part in our yard was entirely ruined, but in that of
the señora it appeared that its vast sides had been covered from
one end to the other with colossal ornaments in stucco, most of
which had fallen, but among the fragments is the gigantic head
represented in Plate LI. It is seven feet eight inches in height
and seven feet in width. The ground-work is of projecting
stones, which are covered with stucco. A stone one foot six inches
long protrudes from the chin, intended, perhaps, for burning
copal on, as a sort of altar. It was the first time we had seen an
ornament of this kind upon the exterior of any of these structures. In sternness and harshness of expression it reminded us
of the idols at Copan, and its colossal proportions, with the
corresponding dimensions of the mound, gave an unusual impression of grandeur.

Two or three streets distant from the plaza, but visible in
all its huge proportions, was the most stupendous mound we
had seen in the country, being, perhaps, six or seven hundred
feet long and sixty feet high, which, we ascertained beyond all
doubt, had interior chambers.

Turning from these memorials of former power to the degraded race that now lingers round them, the stranger might
run wild with speculation and conjecture, but on the north side
of the plaza is a monument that recalls his roving thoughts, and
holds up to his gaze a leaf in history. It is the great church and
convent of Franciscan monks, standing on an elevation, and giving a character to the plaza that no other in Yucatan possesses.
Two flights of stone steps lead up to it, and the area upon
which they open is probably two hundred feet square; on three
sides is a colonnade, forming a noble promenade, overlooking the
city and the surrounding country to a great distance. This great
elevation was evidently artificial, and not the work of the
Spaniards.

At the earliest period of the conquest we have accounts of
the large aboriginal town of Izamal, and, fortunately, in the
pious care of the early monks to record the erection of their
church and convent, the only memorials which, to the exclusive
and absorbing spirit of the times, seemed worth preserving, we
have authentic records which incidentally dispel all uncertainty
respecting the origin of these ancient mounds.

According to the account of the padre Lizana, in the year
1553, at the second chapter held in the province, the padre
Fr. Diego de Landa was elected guardian of the convent of Izamal, and charged to erect the building, the monks having lived

Plate LI

IZAMAL.

Gigantic Head

until that time in houses of straw. He selected as the place for the foundation one of the cerros, or mounds, which then existed, "made by hand," and called by the natives Phapphol-chac, which, says the padre Lizana, "signifies the habitation or residence of the priests of the gods; this place was selected in order that the devil might be driven away by the divine presence of Christ sacrificed, and that the place in which the priests of the idol lived, and which had been the place of abomination and idolatry, might become that of sanctification, where the ministers of the true God should offer sacrifices and adoration due to his Divine Majesty."

This is clear and unmistakeable testimony as to the original use and occupation of the mound on which the church and convent of Izamal now stand; and the same account goes on farther, and says: "At another mound, on which was the idol called Kinick Kakmo, he founded a village or settlement, calling it San Ildefonzo, and to the other cerro, called Humpictok, where falls the village of Izamal, he gave for patron San Antonio de Padua, demolishing the temple which was there; and where was the idol called Haboc he founded a village called Santa Maria, by which means he sought to sweep away the memory of so great idolatry."

It is unnecessary to comment upon these accounts. Testimony, never intended for that purpose, proves, beyond the shadow of a doubt, that these great mounds had upon them temples and idols, and the habitations of priests, in the actual use of the Indians who were found occupying the country at the time of the conquest; and, in my opinion, if it stood alone, unsupported by any other, it is sufficient to dispel every cloud of mystery that hangs over the ruins of Yucatan.

At the present day Izamal is distinguished throughout Yucatan for its fair, but it has a stronger hold upon the feelings of the Indians in the sanctity of its Virgin. From the history of the proceedings of the monks, it appears that the Indians continued to worship El Demonio, and the venerable padre Landa, after severe wrestling with the great enemy, proposed to procure an image of the holy Virgin, offering to go for it himself to Guatimala, in which city there was a skilful sculptor. At the same time, another was wanted for the convent at Merida. The two images were brought in a box, and though there was much rain on the way, it never fell on the box, or on the Indians who carried it, or within some steps of them. At Merida the monks selected for their convent the one which had the most beautiful countenance and seemed most devout; the other, though brought by the Indians of Izamal, and intended for that place, the Spaniards of Valladolid claimed, and said that it ought not to remain in a village of Indians. The Indians of Izamal resisted, the Spaniards attempted to carry their purpose into execution, and when in the suburbs of the village, the image became so heavy that the bearers could not carry it. Divine Majesty interposed on behalf of the Indians of Izamal, and there was not sufficient human force to remove the statue. The devotion of the faithful increased at the sight of these marvels, and in all parts, by land and sea, by means of invocation to this Virgin, innumerable miracles have been wrought, of which, says Cogolludo, a volume might have been written, if proper care had been taken.

But, alas! though this Virgin could save others, herself she could not save. On the left of the door of the church is a square stone set in the wall, with an inscription, which tells the mournful tale, that in the great burning of the church the Santa Virgen was entirely consumed; but the hearts of the faithful are cheered by the assurance that one as good as she has been put in her place.

After our visit to the church we returned to the corridor overlooking the plaza. A young girl whom I had noticed all day sitting in one of the corridors was still there, looking down upon the gay scene in the plaza, but apparently abstracted, pensive, perhaps looking in vain for one who did not appear.

In the evening we went to the ball, which was held in, or rather out of, a house on the corner of the plaza. The sala was opened as a refreshment room. In the corridor was a row of seats for those who did not take part in the dance, and in front was an arbour projecting into the plaza, with a cemented floor for the dancers. The ball had begun at eight o'clock the evening before, and, with an intermission of a few hours toward daylight, had been continued ever since; but it was manifest that there were limits to the capabilities of human nature even in dancing. The room was already less crowded than it had been during the day. Two officers of the army (militia), who had been toiling all day with a determination that promised well for Yucatan under the threatened invasion of Mexico, had danced off their military coats, but still kept the floor in light jackets. One placed a chair for his drooping partner during the intervals of the dance. Another followed his example, and by degrees every lady had her seat of relief. At the last call only four couples appeared on the floor. Ladies, fiddlers, and lights were all wearing out together, and we went away. Before we were in our hammocks a loud

burst of music, as it were a last effort of expiring nature, broke
up the ball.

CHAPTER XXIV

The next morning we started for Merida, with the intention of diverging for the last time to visit the ruins of Aké. The road was one of the best in the country, made for carriages, but rough, stony, and uninteresting. At Cacalchen, five leagues distant, we stopped to dine and procure a guide to Aké.

In the afternoon we proceeded, taking with us only our hammocks, and leaving Dimas to go on direct with the luggage to Merida. Turning off immediately from the main road, we entered the woods, and following a narrow path, a little before dark we reached the hacienda of Aké, and for the last time were among the towering and colossal memorials of an aboriginal city. The hacienda was the property of the Conde Peon, and, contrary to our expectations, it was small, neglected, in a ruinous condition, and entirely destitute of all kinds of supplies. We could not procure even eggs, literally nothing but tortillas. The major domo was away, the principal building locked up, and the only shelter we could obtain was a miserable little hut, full of fleas, which no sweeping could clear out. We had considered all our rough work over, but again, and within a day's journey of Merida, we were in bad straits. By great ingenuity, and giving them the shortest possible tie, Albino contrived to swing our hammocks, and having no other resource, early in the evening we fell into them. At about ten o'clock we heard the tramp of a horse, and the major domo arrived. Surprised to find such unexpected visiters, but glad to see them, he unlocked the hacienda, and walking out in our winding sheets, we took possession; our hammocks followed, and were hung up anew. In the morning he provided us with breakfast, after which, accompanied by him and all the Indians of the hacienda, being only six, we went round to see the ruins.

Plate LII represents a great mound towering in full sight from the door of the hacienda, and called El Palacio, or the Palace. The ascent is on the south side, by an immense staircase, one hundred and thirty-seven feet wide, forming an approach of rude grandeur, perhaps equal to any that ever existed in the country. Each step is four feet five inches long, and one foot five inches in height. The platform on the top is two hundred and twenty-five feet in length, and fifty in breadth. On this great platform stand thirty-six shafts, or columns, in three parallel rows of twelve, about ten feet apart from north to south, and fifteen from east to west. They are from fourteen to sixteen feet in height, four feet on each side, and are comopsed of separate stones, from one to two feet in thickness. But few have fallen, though some have lost their upper layer of stones. There are no remains of any structure or of a roof. If there ever was one, it must have been of wood, which would seem most incongruous and inappropriate for such a solid structure of stones. The whole mound was so overgrown that we could not ascertain the juxtaposition of the pillars till the growth was cleared away, when we made out the whole, but with little or no enlargement of our knowledge as to its uses and purposes. It was a new and extraordinary feature, entirely different from any we had seen, and at the very end of our journey, when we supposed ourselves familiar with the character of American ruins, threw over them a new air of mystery.

In the same vicinity are other mounds of colossal dimensions, one of which is also called the Palace, but of a different construction and without pillars. On another, at the head of the ruined staircase, is an opening under the top of a doorway, nearly filled up, crawling through which, by means of the crotch of a tree I descended into a dark chamber fifteen feet long and ten wide, of rude construction, and of which some of the stones in the wall measured seven feet in length. This is called Akabna,

Plate LII

AKE

Ruined Structure on Mound

casa obscura, or dark house. Near this is a senote, with the remains of steps leading down to water, which once supplied the
ancient city. The ruins cover a great extent, but all were overgrown, and in a condition too ruinous to be presented in a
drawing. They were ruder and more massive than all the others
we had seen, bore the stamp of an older era, and more than any
others, in fact, for the first time in the country, suggested the
idea of Cyclopean remains; but even here we have a gleam of
historic light, faint, it is true, but, in my mind, sufficient to dispel all unsettled and wavering notions.

In the account of the march of Don Francisco Montejo from
the coast, presented in the early part of these pages, it is mentioned that the Spaniards reached a town called Aké, at which
they found themselves confronted by a great multitude of armed
Indians. A desperate battle ensued, which lasted two days, and
in which the Spaniards were victorious, but gained no easy
triumph.

There is no other mention of Aké, and in this there is no
allusion whatever to the buildings, but from its geographical
position, and the direction of the line of march of the Spanish
army from the coast, I have little doubt that their Aké was the
place now known by the same name, and occupied by the ruins
last presented. It is, indeed, strange that no mention is made of
the buildings, but regard must be had to the circumstances of
danger and death which surrounded the Spaniards, and which
were doubtless always uppermost in the minds of the soldiers
who formed that disastrous expedition. At all events, it is not
more strange than the want of any description of the great buildings of Chichen, and we have the strongest possible proof that
no correct inference is to be drawn from the silence of the Spaniards, for in the comparatively minute account of the conquest
of Mexico, we find that the Spanish army marched under the
very shadow of the great pyramids of Otumba, and yet not the
slightest mention whatever is made of their existence.

I have now finished my journey among ruined cities. I
know that it is impossible by any narrative to convey to the
reader a true idea of the powerful and exciting interest of wandering among them, and I have avoided as much as possible all
detailed descriptions, but I trust that these pages will serve to
give some general idea of the appearance which this country
once presented. In our long, irregular, and devious route we
have discovered the crumbling remains of forty-four ancient
cities, most of them but a short distance apart, though, from the

great change that has taken place in the country, and the breaking up of the old roads, having no direct communication with each other; with but few exceptions, all were lost, buried, and unknown, never before visited by a stranger, and some of them, perhaps, never looked upon by the eyes of a white man. Involuntarily we turn for a moment to the frightful scenes of which this now desolate region must have been the theatre; the scenes of blood, agony, and wo which preceded the desolation or abandonment of these cities. But, leaving the boundless space in which imagination might rove, I confine myself to the consideration of facts. If I may be permitted to say so, in the whole history of discoveries there is nothing to be compared with those here presented. They give an entirely new aspect to the great Continent on which we live, and bring up with more force than ever the question which I once, with some hesitation, undertook to consider: Who were the builders of these American cities?

My opinion on this question has been fully and freely expressed, "that they are not the works of people who have passed away, and whose history is lost, but of the same races who inhabited the country at the time of the Spanish conquest, or of some not very distant progenitors." Some were probably in ruins, but in general I believe that they were occupied by the Indians at the time of the Spanish invasion. The grounds of this belief are interspersed throughout these pages; they are interwoven with so many facts and circumstances that I do not recapitulate them; and in conclusion I shall only refer briefly to those arguments which I consider the strongest that are urged against this belief.

The first is the entire absence of all traditions. But I would ask, may not this be accounted for by the unparalleled circumstances which attended the conquest and subjugation of Spanish America? Every captain or discoverer, on first planting the royal standard on the shores of a new country, made proclamation according to a form drawn up by the most eminent divines and lawyers in Spain, the most extraordinary that ever appeared in the history of mankind; entreating and requiring the inhabitants to acknowledge and obey the church as the superior and guide of the universe, the holy father called the pope, and his majesty as king and sovereign lord of these islands, and of the terra firma; and concluding, "But if you will not comply, or maliciously delay to obey my injunction, then, with the help of God, I will enter your country by force; I will carry on war against you with the utmost violence; I will subject you to the yoke of obedience, to the church and king; I will take your wives and children, and make them slaves, and sell or dispose of them according to his majesty's pleasure. I will seize your goods, and do you all the mischief in my power, as rebellious subjects, who will not acknowledge or submit to their lawful sovereign; and I protest that all the bloodshed and calamities which shall follow are to be imputed to you, and not to his majesty, or to me, or the gentlemen who serve under me."

The conquest and subjugation of the country were carried out in the unscrupulous spirit of this proclamation. The pages of the historians are dyed with blood; and sailing on the crimson stream, with a master pilot at the helm, appears the leading, stern, and steady policy of the Spaniards, surer and more fatal than the sword, to subvert all the institutions of the natives, and to break up and utterly destroy all the rites, customs, and associations that might keep alive the memory of their fathers and their ancient condition. One sad instance shows the effects of this policy. Before the destruction of Mayapan, the capital of the kingdom of Maya, all the nobles of the country had houses in that city, and were exempted from tribute; according to the account from which Cogolludo derives his authority, in the year 1582, forty years after the conquest, all who held themselves for lords and nobles still claimed their solares (sites for mansions) as tokens of their rank; but now, he says, "from the change of government and the little estimation in which they are held, it does not appear that they care to preserve nobility for their posterity, for at this day the descendants of Tutul Xiu, who was the king and natural lord by right of the land of Maya, if they do not work with their own hands in manual offices, have nothing to eat." And if at that early date nobles no longer cared for their titles, and the descendants of the royal house had nothing to eat but what they earned with their own hands, it is not strange that the present inhabitants, nine generations removed, without any written language, borne down by three centuries of servitude, and toiling daily for a scanty subsistence, are alike ignorant and indifferent concerning the history of their ancestors, and the great cities lying in ruins under their eyes. And strange or not, no argument can be drawn from it, for this ignorance is not confined to ruined cities or to events before the conquest. It is my belief, that among the whole mass of what are called Christianized Indians, there is not at this day one solitary tradition which can shed a ray of light upon any event in their history that occurred one hundred and fifty years from the present time; in fact, I believe it would be almost impossible to procure any information of any kind whatever beyond the memory of the oldest living Indian.

Besides, the want of traditionary knowledge is not peculiar to these American ruins. Two thousand years ago the Pyramids towered on the borders of the African Desert without any certain tradition of the time when they were founded; and so long back as the first century of the Christian era, Pliny cites various older authors who disagreed concerning the persons who built them, and even concerning the use and object for which they were erected. No traditions hang round the ruins of Greece and Rome; the temples of Pæstum, lost until within the last half century, have no traditions to identify their builders; the "holy city" has only weak inventions of modern monks. But for written records, Egyptian, Grecian, and Roman remains would be as mysterious as the ruins of America; and to come down to later times and countries comparatively familiar, tradition sheds no light upon the round towers of Ireland, and the ruins of Stonehenge stand on Salisbury plain without a tradition to carry us back to the age or nation of their builders.

The second argument I shall notice is, that a people possessing the power, art, and skill to erect such cities, never could have fallen so low as the miserable Indians who now linger about their ruins. To this, too, it might be sufficient to answer that their present condition is the natural and inevitable consequence of the same ruthless policy which laid the axe at the root of all ancient recollections, and cut off forever all traditionary knowledge. But waiving this ground, the pages of written history are burdened with changes in national character quite equal to that here exhibited. And again, leaving entirely out of the question all the analogous examples which might be drawn from those pages, we have close at hand, and under our very eyes, an illustration in point. The Indians who inhabit that country now are not more changed than their Spanish masters. Whether debased, and but little above the grade of brutes, as it was the policy of the Spaniards to represent them, or not, we know that at the time of the conquest they were at least proud, fierce, and warlike, and poured out their blood like water to save their inheritance from the grasp of strangers. Crushed, humbled, and bowed down as they are now by generations of bitter servitude, even yet they are not more changed than the descendants of those terrible Spaniards who invaded and conquered their country. In both, all traces of the daring and warlike character of their ancestors are entirely gone. The change is radical, in feelings and instincts, inborn and transmitted, in a measure, with the blood; and in contemplating this change in the Indian, the loss of mere mechanical skill and art seems comparatively nothing; in fact, these perish of themselves, when, as in the case of the Indians, the school for their exercise is entirely broken up. Degraded as the Indians are now, they are not lower in the scale of intellect than the serfs of Russia, while it is a well-known fact that the greatest architect in that country, the builder of the Cazan Church at St. Petersburgh, was taken from that abject class, and by education became what he is. In my opinion, teaching might again lift up the Indian, might impart to him the skill to sculpture stone and carve wood; and if restored to freedom, and the unshackled exercise of his powers of mind, there might again appear a capacity to originate and construct, equal to that exhibited in the ruined monuments of his ancestors.

The last argument, and that upon which most stress has been laid, against the hypothesis that the cities were constructed by the ancestors of the present Indians, is the alleged absence of historical accounts in regard to the discovery or knowledge of such cities by the conquerors. But it is manifest that even if this allegation were true, the argument would be unsound, for it goes to deny that such cities ever existed at all. Now there can be no doubt as to the fact of their existence; and as it is never pretended that they were erected since the conquest, they must be allowed to have been standing at that time. Whether erected by the Indians or by races perished and unknown, whether desolate or inhabited, beyond all question the great buildings were there; if not entire, they must at least have been far more so than they are now; if desolate, perhaps more calculated to excite wonder than if inhabited; and in either case the alleged silence of the historian would be equally inexplicable.

But the allegation is untrue. The old historians are not silent. On the contrary, we have the glowing accounts of Cortez and his companions, of soldiers, priests, and civilians, all concurring in representations of existing cities, then in the actual use and occupation of the Indians, with buildings and temples, in style and character like those presented in these pages. Indeed, these accounts are so glowing that modern historians, at the head of whom stands Robertson, have for that reason thrown discredit over them, and ascribed them to a heated imagination. To my mind, they bear on the face of them the stamp of truth, and it seems strange that they have been deemed worthy of so little reliance. But Robertson wrote upon the authority of correspondents in New Spain, one of whom, long resident in that country, and professing to have visited every part of it, says that "at this day there does not remain the smallest vestige of any Indian building, public or private, either in Mexico or any province of New Spain." Robertson's informants were probably foreign merchants resident in the city of Mexico, whose travels had been confined to the beaten road, and to places occupied by the Spaniards; and at that time the white inhabitants were in utter ignorance of the great cities, desolate and in ruins, that lay buried in the forests. But at this day better information exists; vast remains have been brought to light, and the discoveries prove incontestably that those histories which make no mention of these great buildings are imperfect, those which deny their existence are untrue. The graves cry out for the old historians, and the mouldering skeletons of cities confirm Herrera's account of Yucatan, that "there were so many and such stately Stone Buildings that it was Amazing; and the greatest Wonder was that, having no Use of any Metal, they were able to raise such Structures, which seem to have been Temples, for their Houses were all of Timber, and thatched." And again, he says, that "for the Space of twenty Years there was such Plenty throughout the Country, and the People multiplied so much that Men said the whole Province looked like one Town."

These arguments then—the want of tradition, the degeneracy of the people, and the alleged absence of historical accounts—are not sufficient to disturb my belief, that the great cities now lying in ruins were the works of the same races who inhabited the country at the time of the conquest.

Who these people were, whence they came, and who were their progenitors, are questions that involve too many considerations to be entered upon at the conclusion of these pages; but all the light that history sheds upon them is dim and faint, and may be summed up in a few words.

According to traditions, picture writings, and Mexican manuscripts written after the conquest, the Toltecs, or Toltecans, were the first inhabitants of the land of Anahuac, now known as New Spain or Mexico, and they are the oldest nations on the continent of America of which we have any knowledge. Banished, according to their own history, from their native country, which was situated to the northwest of Mexico, in the year 596 of our era, they proceeded southward under the directions of their chiefs, and, after sojourning at various places on the way for the space of one hundred and twenty-four years, arrived at the banks of a river in the vale of Mexico, where they built the city of Tula, the capital of the Toltecan kingdom, near the site of the present city of Mexico.

Their monarchy lasted nearly four centuries, during which they multiplied, extended their population, and built numerous and large cities; but direful calamities hung over them. For several years Heaven denied them rain; the earth refused them food; the air, infected with mortal contagion, filled the graves with dead; a great part of the nation perished of famine or sickness; the last king was among the number, and in the year 1052 the monarchy ended. The wretched remains of the nation took refuge, some in Yucatan and other in Guatimala, while some lingered around the graves of their kindred in the great vale where Mexico was afterward founded. For a century the land of Anahuac lay waste and depopulated. The Chechemecas, following in the track of their ruined cities, reoccupied it, and after them the Acolhuans, the Tlastaltecs, and the Aztecs, which last were the subjects of Montezuma at the time of the invasion by the Spaniards.

The history of all these tribes or nations is misty, confused, and indistinct. The Toltecans, represented to have been the most ancient, are said to have been also the most polished. Probably they were the originators of that peculiar style of architecture found in Guatimala and Yucatan, which was adopted by all the subsequent inhabitants; and as, according to their own annals, they did not set out on their emigration to those countries from the vale of Mexico until the year 1052 of our era, the oldest cities erected by them in those countries could have been in existence but from four to five hundred years at the time of the Spanish conquest. This gives them a very modern date compared with the Pyramids and temples of Egypt, and the other ruined monuments of the Old World; it gives them a much less antiquity than that claimed by the Maya manuscript, and, in fact, much less than I should ascribe to them myself. In identifying them as the works of the ancestors of the present Indians, the cloud which hung over their origin is not removed; the time when and the circumstances under which they were built, the rise, progress, and full development of the power, art, and skill required for their construction, are all mysteries which will not easily be unravelled. They rise like skeletons from the grave, wrapped in their burial shrouds; claiming no affinity with the works of any known people, but a distinct, independent, and separate existence. They stand alone, absolutely and entirely anomalous, perhaps the most interesting subject which at this day presents itself to the inquiring mind. I leave them with all their mystery around them; and in the feeble hope that these imperfect pages may in some way throw a glimmer of light upon the great and long vainly mooted question, who were the peoplers of America? I will now bid farewell to ruins.

CHAPTER XXV

At two o'clock we mounted for Merida, nine leagues distant. We did not expect to reach it till night, and, from the unfortunate condition of our travelling costume, did not care to enter the capital by daylight; but, pushing on, and miscalculating the pace of our horses, we found ourselves in the suburbs at that unlucky hour when, the excessive heat being over, the inhabitants, in full dress, were sitting in the doorways or along the side-walks, talking over the news of the day, and particularly alive to the appearance of such a spectacle as our party presented. We rode the whole length of the principal street, running the gauntlet between long rows of eyes, and conscious that we were not looked upon as making a very triumphal entry. Approaching the plaza, an old aquaintance greeted us, and accompanied us to the Casa de las Diligencias, a new establishment, opened since our departure, opposite the convent, one of the largest and finest in the city, and equal to a good hotel in Italy. Very soon we had the best apartments, and were sitting down to *thé du China*, in English, tea, and *pan Françes*, or bread without sweetening. After our hard journey among Indian ranchos and unwholesome haciendas, at times all prostrated by illness, we had returned to Merida, successful beyond our utmost hopes. Our rough work was all over, and our satisfaction cannot easily be described.

While lingering over the table, we heard the loud ringing of the porter's bell, followed by landlord and servants running and tumbling along the corridor, all crying out "La Diligencia," and presently we heard the tramp of horses and the rattling of the post-coach from Campeachy, into the court-yard. The passengers came up, and among them we greeted with lively satisfaction our old friend Mr. Fisher, that citizen of the world, the last traces of whom we had seen on the desolate island of Cozumel. Another passenger, whose voice we had heard rising in English from the court-yard above the jargon of Spanish and Indian, as if entirely on private account, and indifferent whether it was understood or not, immediately accosted me as an acquaintance; said that I had been the cause of his coming to that place, and if he did not succeed, should come upon me for damages; but I soon learned that I had nothing to fear. Mr. Clayton had already created, perhaps, a greater sensation than any stranger who ever visited that country; he had obtained a hold upon the feelings of the people that no explorers could ever win, and will be remembered long after we are forgotten. He had brought from the United States an entire circus company, with spotted horses, a portable theatre, containing seats for a thousand persons, riders, clowns, and monkeys, all complete. No such thing had ever been seen before; it threw far into the shade Daguerreotype and curing biscos. He had turned Campeachy upside down, and leaving his company there to soothe the excitement and pick up the pesos, he had come up to make arrangements for opening in Merida. And this was by no means Mr. Clayton's first enterprise. He had brought the first giraffes into the United States from the Cape of Good Hope, and his accounts of penetrating fifteen hundred miles into the interior of Africa, of his adventures among the Caffres, of shooting lions, and his high excitement when, on a fleet horse, he ran down and shot his first giraffe, made the exploration of ruins seem a rather tame business. He reached the Cape with four giraffes, but two died after their arrival, and with the others he embarked for New-York, where he expected to deliver them over to the parties interested; but from the great care required in their treatment, it became indispensable for him to travel with them while they were exhibited. In one of the Western states he encountered a travelling circus company, which undertook to run an opposition on the same line of travel. The giraffes were rather too strong for the horses, and a proposition was made to him to unite the two and become director of both, which he accepted. He afterward bought the latter out, and so became the manager of a strolling circus company. With it he travelled all over the United States, but in

Canada his last giraffe died, and left him with a stock of horses and a company on hand. He returned to New-York, chartered a brig, and after touching and exhibiting at several West India Islands, sailed for Campeachy, where he was received with such enthusiasm, that among the benefits conferred upon mankind by authors, I rank high that of having been the means of introducing a circus company into Yucatan, in the belief that it may prove the first step toward breaking up the popular taste for bull-fights.

The next morning we advertised for sale our horses and equipments, and sallied out to visit our friends. Great changes had taken place since our departure. Abroad the political horizon was stormy. News had been received of increased difficulties, complicated and uncertain negotiations, and apprehensions of war between our own country and England; also of the failure of the Santa Fé expedition, the capture and imprisonment of American citizens, and that Texas and the whole valley of the Mississippi were in arms to carry the war into Mexico. And black clouds were lowering, also, over Yucatan. The governor had lost his popularity. The great question opened by the revolution two years before was not yet decided. Independence was not declared; on the contrary, during our absence a commissioner had arrived from Mexico, and had negotiated a treaty for the return of Yucatan to the Mexican confederacy, subject to the approval or disapproval of the Mexican government. In the mean while, electors were called to nominate deputies to the Mexican Congress, as if the treaty was approved, and at the same time the Legislature was summoned in extraordinary session, to provide for the protection of the state against invasion, in case the treaty should be rejected. Both bodies were then sitting. Three days after our return, a vessel arrived at Sisal, having on board a special envoy, bearing Santa Ana's ultimatum. He was detained one day at the port, while the government considered the expediency of permitting him to visit the capital. Apartments were prepared for him at our hotel, but he was taken to the house of the secretary of war, ostensibly to save him from insult and violence by the populace, who were represented as highly excited against Mexico, but in reality to prevent him from holding communication with the partisans in favour of reunion. Great dissensions had grown up. The revolution had been almost unanimous, but two years of quasi independence had produced a great change of feeling. The rich complained of profligate expenditures, merchants of the breaking up of trade by the closing of the Mexican ports, and while many asked what they had gained by a separation, a strong "independent" party was more clamorous than ever for breaking the last link that bound them to Mexico. I was in the Senate Chamber when the ultimatum of Santa Ana was read. A smile of derision flitted over the faces of senators, and it was manifest that the terms would not be accepted, yet no man rose to offer a declaration of independence. In the lobby, however, an open threat was made to proclaim it *viva voce* in the plaza on the coming Sunday, and at the mouth of the cannon. The condition of the state was pitiable in the extreme. It was a melancholy comment upon republican government, and the most melancholy feature was that this condition did not proceed from the ignorant and uneducated masses. The Indians were all quiet, and, though doomed to fight the battles, knew nothing of the questions involved. It is my firm conviction that the constant and unceasing convulsions of the southern republics more than from any other cause grow out of the non-recognition or the violation of that great saving principle known among us as state rights. The general government aims constantly at dominion over the states. Far removed by position, ignorant of the wants of the people, and regardless of their feelings, it sends from the capital its military commandant, places him above the local authorities, cripples the strength of the state, and drains its coffers to support a strong, consolidated power. Such were the circumstances which had placed Yucatan in arms against the general government, and such, ere this, might have been the condition of our own republic, but for the triumphant assertion of the great republican principal that the states are sovereign, and their rights sacred.

While the clouds were becoming darker and more portentous, we were preparing for our departure from the country. A vessel was then at Sisal ready to sail. It was one which we had hoped never to be on board of again, being the old Alexandre, in which we made our former unlucky voyage, but we had now no alternative, being advised that if we lost that opportunity, it was entirely uncertain when another would present itself. At the request of the governor, we delayed our departure a few days, that he might communicate with a relative in Campeachy, who wished a surgical operation performed by Doctor Cabot, and had passed two months in Merida awaiting our return. In the mean time the governor procured the detention of the vessel.

On Sunday, the sixteenth of May, early in the morning, we sent off our luggage for the port, and in the afternoon we joined

for the last time in a paseo. All day we had received intimations
that an outbreak was apprehended; a volcano was burning and
heaving with inward fires, but there was the same cheerfulness,
gayety, and prettiness as before, producing on our minds the
same pleasing impression, making us hope that these scenes
might be long continued, and, above all, that they might not
be transformed into scenes of blood. Alas! before these pages
were concluded, that country which we had looked upon as
a picture of peace, and in which we had met with so much
kindness, was torn and distracted by internal dissensions, the
blast of civil war was sounding through its borders, and an exas-
perated, hostile army had landed upon its shores.

In the evening we rode to the house of Doña Joaquina
Peon, said farewell to our first, last, and best friends in Merida,
and at ten o'clock started for the port.

On Tuesday, the eighteenth, we embarked for Havana. The
old Alexandre had been altered and improved in her sailing,
but not in her accommodations. In fact, having on board eleven
passengers, among whom were three women and two children,
these could not well have been worse, and at one time our voyage threatened to be as long as the other of unfortunate memory,
but the captain, a surviver of the battle of Trafalgar, was the
same excellent fellow as before. On the second of June we anchored under the walls of the Moro Castle. Before obtaining
passports to land, a barque entered, which we immediately
recognised as an American, and on landing, learned that she was
the Ann Louisa, Captain Clifford, one of a line of packets from
Vera Cruz, had put in short of water, and was to sail the next
day for New-York. The yellow fever had already broken out;
there was no other vessel in port, and we determined, if possible,
to get on board, but we were met with a difficulty, which at first
threatened to be insuperable. By the regulations of the port, it
was necessary for all luggage to be carried to the custom-house
for inspection, and a list furnished beforehand of every article.
The last was utterly impossible, as we had on board the whole
miscellaneous collection made on our journey, with no such
thing as a memorandum of the items. But by the active kindness
of our late consul, Mr. Calhoun, and the courtesy of his excellency the governor, a special order was procured for transferring
the whole without inspection from one vessel to the other. The
next day was occupied in the details of this business, and in the
afternoon we joined in a paseo, the style and show of which, for
the moment, made us think slightingly of the simple exhibition

at Merida; and after dark, by the light of a single candle, with heads uncovered, we stood before the marble slab enclosing the bones of Columbus.

On the fourth we embarked on board the Ann Louisa. She was full of passengers, principally Spaniards escaping from the convulsions of Mexico, but Captain Clifford contrived to give us accommodations much better than we were used to, and we found on board the comforts and conveniences of Atlantic packets. On the seventeenth we reached New-York. The reader and I must again part, and trusting that he will find nothing in these pages to disturb the friendship that has hitherto existed between us, I again return him my thanks for his kindness, and bid him farewell.

APPENDIX

A MANUSCRIPT WRITTEN IN THE MAYA LANGUAGE, TREATING OF THE PRINCI-
PAL EPOCHS OF THE HISTORY OF THE PENINSULA OF YUCATAN BEFORE THE
CONQUEST. WITH COMMENTS BY DON PIO PEREZ.

Principal Epochs of the Ancient History of Yucatan.

Maya.	Translation.

Maya.

Lai u tzolan Katun lukci ti cab ti yotoch Nonoual cánte anílo Tutul Xiu ti chikin Zuina; u luumil u talelob Tulapan chiconahthan. Cante bin ti Katun lic u ximbalob ca uliob uaye yetel Holon Chantepeuh yetel u cuchulob: ca hokiob ti petene uaxac Ahau bin yan cuchi, uac Ahau, can Ahau cabil Ajau, cankal haab catac hunppel haab; tumen hun piztun oxlahun Ahau cuchie ca uliob uay ti petene cankal haab catac hunppel haab tu pakteil yete cu xinbalob lukci tu luumilob ca talob uay ti petene Chacnouitan lae.

Vaxac Ahau, uac Ahau, cabil Ajau kuchci Chacnouitan Ahmekat Tutul Xiu hunppel haab minan ti hokal haab cuchi yanob Chacnouitan lae.

Laitun uchci u chicpahal Tzucubte Ziyan-caan lae Bakhalal, can Ahau, cabil Ahau, oxlahun Ahau oxkal haab cu tepalob Ziyan-caan ca emob uay lae: lai u haabil cu tepalob Bakhalal chuulte laitun chicpahi Chichen Itza lae.

Translation.

This is the series of " Katunes," or epochs, that elapsed from the time of their departure from the land and house of Nonoual, in which were the four Tutul Xiu, lying to the west of Zuina, going out of the country of Tulapan. Four epochs were spent in travelling before they arrived here, with Tolonchantepeuj and his followers. When they began their journey toward this island, it was the 8th Ajau, and the 6th, 4th, and 2d were spent in travelling; because in the first year of the 13th Ajau they arrived at this island, making together eighty-one years they were travelling, between their departure from their country and their arrival at this island of Chacnouitan.

In the 8th Ajau arrived Ajmekat Tutul Xiu, and ninety-nine years they remained in Chacnouitan.

Then took place the discovery of the province of Ziyan-caan, or Bacalar; the 4th Ajau, the 2d, and the 13th, or sixty years, they ruled in Ziyan-caan, when they came here. During these years of their government of the province of Bacalar occurred the discovery of Chichen Itza.

Buluc Ahau, bolon Ajau, uuc Ahau, ho Ahau, ox Ahau, hun Ahau uac kal haab cu tepalob Chichen Itza ca paxi Chichen Itza, ca binob cahtal Chanputun ti yanhi u yotochob ah Ytzoab kuyen uincob lae.

Vac Ahau, chucuc u luumil Chanputun, can Ahau, cabil Ahau, oxlahun Ahau, buluc Ahau, bolon Ahau, uuc Ahau, ho Ahau, ox Ahau, hun Ahau, lahca Ahau, lahun Ajau; uaxac Ahau paxci Chanputun, oxlahun kaal haab cu tepalob Chanputun tumenel Ytza uincob ca talob u tzaclé u yotochob tu caten, laix tun u katunil binciob ah Ytzaob yalan che yalan aban yalan ak ti numyaob lae.

Vac Ahau, can Ahau, ca kal haab catalob u heɔob yotoch tu caten ca tu zatahob Chakanputun.

Lai u katunil cabil Ahau, u heɔci cab Ahcuitok Tutul Xiu Vxmal. Cabil Ahau, oxlahun Ahau, buluc Ahau, bolon Ahau, uuc Ahau, ho Ahau, ox Ahau, hun Ahau, lahca Ahau, lahun Ahau, lahun kal haab cu tepalob yetel u halach uinicil Chichen Itza yetel Mayalpan.

Lai u katunil buluc Ajau, bolon Ahau, uac Ahau, uaxac Ahau, paxci u halach uinicil Chichen Itza tumenel u kebanthan Hunac-eel, ca uch ti Chacxib-chac Chichen Itza tu kebanthan Hunac-eel u halach uinicil Mayalpan ichpac. Cankal haab catac lahun piz haab, tu lahun tun uaxac Ahau cuchie; lai u haabil paxci tumenel Ahzinteyutchan yetel Tzunte-cum, yetel Taxcal, yetel Pantemit, Xuch-ucuet, yetel Ytzcuat, yetel Kakaltecat lay u kaba uinicilob lae nuctulob ahmayapanob lae.

The 11th Ajau, 9th, 7th, 5th, 3d, and 1st Ajau, or 120 years, they ruled in Chichen Itza, when it was abandoned, and they emigrated to Champoton, where the Ytzaes, holy men, had houses.

The 6th Ajau they took possession of the territory of Champoton; the 4th Ajau, 2d, 13th, 11th, 9th, 7th, 5th, 3d, 1st, 12th, 10th, and the 8th, Champoton was destroyed or abandoned. Two hundred and sixty years reigned the Ytzaes in Champoton, when they returned in search of their homes, and then they lived for several epochs under the uninhabited mountains.

The 6th Ajau, 4th Ajau, after 40 years, they returned to their homes once more, and Champoton was lost to them.

In this Katun of 2d Ajau, Ajcuitok Tutul Xiu established himself in Uxmal; the 2d Ajau, the 13th, 11th, 9th, 7th, 5th, 3d, 1st, the 12th and the 10th Ajau, equal to 200 years, they governed and reigned in Uxmal, with the governors of Chichen Itza and of Mayapan.

After the lapse of the Ajau Katunes of 11th, 9th, 6th Ajau, in the 8th the Governor of Chichen Itza was deposed, because he murmured disrespectfully against Tunac-eel; this happened to Chacxibchac of Chichen Itza, who had spoken against Tunac-eel, governor of the fortress of Mayalpan. Ninety years had elapsed, but the 10th of the 8th Ajau was the year in which he was overthrown by Ajzinte-yutchan, with Tzuntecum, Taxcal, Pantemit, Xuch-ucuet, Ytzcuat, and Kakaltecat; these are the names of the 7 Mayalpanes.

Laili u katunil uaxac Ahau, lai ca binob u pâ ah Vlmil Ahau tumenel u uahal-uahob yetel ah Ytzmal Vlil Ahau lae Oxlahun uuɔ u katunilob ca paxob tumen Hunac-eel tumenel u ɔabal u naátob; uac Ahau ca ɔoci: hunkal haab catac can lahun pizí.

Vac Ahau, can Ahau, cabil Ahau, oxlahun Ahau, buluc ahau, chucuc u luumil ich pâ Mayalpan, tumenel u pach tulum, tumenel multepal ich cah Mayalpan, tumenel Ytza uinicob yetel ah Vlmil Ahau lae, can kaal haab catac oxppel haab: yocol buluc Ahau cuchie paxci Mayalpan tumenel ahuitzil ɔul, tan cah Mayalpan.

Vaxac Ahau lay paxci Mayalpan lai u katunil uac Ahau, can Ahau, cabil Ahau, lai haab ca yax mani upañoles u yaxilci caa luumi Yucatan tzucubte lae, oxkal haab páxac ich pâ cuchie.

Oxlahun Ahau, buluc Ahau, uchci mayacimil ich pâ yetel nohkakil: oxlahun Ahau cimci Ahpulá uacppel haab u binel ma ɔococ u xocol oxlahun Ahau cuchie, ti yanil u xocol haab ti lakin cuchie, canil kan cumlahi pop, tu holhun Zip catac oxppeli, bolon Ymix u kinil lai cimi Ahpulá; laitun año cu ximbal cuchi lae ca oheltabac lay u xoc numeroil años lae 1536 años cuchie, oxkal haab paaxac ich pâ cuchi lae.

Laili ma ɔococ u xocol buluc Ahau lae lai ulci erpañoles kul uincob ti lakin u talob ca uliob uay tac hurmil lae bolon Ahau hoppci cristianoil uchci caputzihil: laili ichil u

In this same period, or Katun, of the 8th Ajau, they attacked King Ulmil, in consequence of his quarrel with Ulil, king of Yzamal; thirteen divisions of troops had he when he was routed by Tunac-eel; in the 6th Ajau the war was over, after 34 years.

In the 6th Ajau, 4th Ajau, 2d Ajau, 13th Ajau, 11th Ajau, the fortified territory of Mayalpan was invaded by the men of Ytza, under their King Ulmil, because they had walls, and governed in common the people of Mayalpan; eighty-three years elapsed after this event, and at the beginning of the 11th Ajau Mayalpan was destroyed by strangers of the Uitzes, or Highlanders, as was also Tancaj of Mayalpan.

In the 6th Ajau Mayalpan was destroyed; the epochs of 6th Ajau, 4th and 2d Ajau, elapsed, and at this period the Spaniards, for the first time, arrived, and gave the name of *Yucatan* to this province, sixty years after the destruction of the fortress.

The 13th Ajau, 11th Ajau, pestilence and smallpox were in the castles. In the 13th Ajau Ajpula died; six years were wanting to the completion of the 13th Ajau; this year was counted toward the east of the wheel, and began on the 4th "Kan." Ajpula died on the 18th day of the month Zip, in the 9th Ymix; and that it may be known in numbers, it was the year 1536, sixty years after the demolition of the fortress.

Before the termination of the 11th Ajau the Spaniards arrived; holy men from the East came with them when they reached this land. The 9th Ajau was the commencement of

katunil lae ulci yax obispo Toroba	baptism and Christianity; and in
u kaba.	this year was the arrival of Toral,
	the first bishop.

Thus far only from the Maya manuscript, because the other events cited are posterior to the conquest, and of little historical interest. Although this manuscript may contain some errors which should be rectified, still, as these are committed in the numeration of the epochs, or Ajaues, which do not keep a correlative numerical order, it was very easy for the author, who wrote from memory, to transpose them; preserving solely the number of periods which· elapsed between the occurrence of one and the other event, without designating correctly the sign of the period. I repeat that the writer of this epitome did it from memory, because it was done long after the conquest: the histories, paintings, and hieroglyphics of the Indians had about this period been collected by order of Bishop Landa, as is related by Cogolludo in his history; and likewise because his historical narrative is so succinct, that it appears rather a list than a circumstantial detail of the events. But, notwithstanding these defects, as the manuscript is the only one which has been found treating of this matter, it is well worthy the trouble of correcting and analyzing it, on account of the ideas which it communicates respecting the ancient history and establishment of the principal peoples of that time, whose ruins are admired at the present day, such as those of Chichen and Uxmal; deducing from these, what were the others which the traveller encounters, and whose origin is unknown.

The manuscript may be abridged in the following manner: " Four epochs were expended by the Toltecos between their departure from their city under the direction of Tolonchante Peech, and their arrival at Chacnouitan.* They arrived at this province of Chacnouitan in the first year of the following epoch, and remained in the same place with their captain Ajmekat Tutul Xiu during the space of four epochs more.† They discovered Ziyancan, or Bacalar, and governed in it three epochs, until they came to Chichen Itza.‡ They remained here until their departure to colonize Champoton, a period of six epochs.§ From the discovery of Champoton, where they settled and reigned until it was destroyed, and they lost it, thirteen epochs elapsed.‖ They were wanderers among the hills during two epochs, when they established themselves for the second time at Chichen Itza.¶ In the following epoch, Ajcuitok Tutul Xiu colonized Uxmal, and reigned with the governor of Mayapan during ten epochs.** After a farther lapse of three epochs, and on the tenth year of the one following, Chacxibchac, governor of Chichen Itza, was defeated by Tunac-eel, gov-

---

* From the year 144 of the vulgar era up to 217. † From 218 until 360.
‡ From 360 until 432.   ◊ From 432 until 576.   ‖ From 576 until 888.
¶ From 888 until 936.   ** From 936 until 1176.

ernor of Mayapan, and his seven generals.* In this same epoch of the defeat of the Governor of Chichen, they marched to attack Ulmil, king of Chichen, because he had made war against Ulil, king of Yzamal, and the object was effected by Tunac-eel in the following epoch.† After this epoch, Ulmil, king of Chichen, recovering from his defeat, invaded the territory of Mayapan in the following epoch, and, after the lapse of two more, and in the third year of the one following, Mayapan was destroyed by the strangers, inhabitants of the hills.‡ After the lapse of three more epochs, the Spaniards arrived for the first time, and gave to this province the name of Yucatan.§ In the following epoch occurred the plague, which visited even the temples and castles; and in its sixth year Ajpula died, on the 11th of September, 1493.‖ In the eleventh epoch, and the last of this record, was the arrival of the conquerors; this happened in 1527.¶ In the following epoch the conquest was finished, and the first bishop reached the province: the first occurred in January, 1541, and the other in 1560."

MEMORANDUM FOR THE ORNITHOLOGY OF YUCATAN.

The genus Accipitres, including eagles, falcons, buzzards, &c., is very numerous, and of these three or four new varieties were obtained. One, a beautiful hawk, resembling in its markings the goshawk (Falco Atricapillus), differing, however, in its form, in the bill, colour of its eyes (dark brown), in not having the white line over the eyes, and in the bands on the tail. The first specimen was killed at Uxmal, but afterward many others were procured, and two were brought home. Another new and beautiful species is a falcon of a very noble character in the form of its bill and head, and in its habits; of which two specimens were obtained at Chichen Itza, the male being shot over the senoté during a heavy shower. No others but this pair were seen. Another is undescribed, or, if described, imperfectly so, under the name of the mingled buzzard of Latham (La Busc Mixté Noire. Voy. d'Azara, vol. iii., No. 20). It is a large black hawk, and was obtained, the female at Punta Française, and the male at the island of Cozumel, where a nest also was found, but was destroyed, together with the eggs, in consequence of Dr. Cabot's being obliged to have the tree felled. He afterward procured an egg from a nest between Silan and Las Bockas de Silan. Another very beautiful hawk is shaped much like the little corporal of Audubon, and belongs to the same division of hawks as the hobby falcon of Europe. It is a bold hawk, and is met with about

---

* From 1176 until 1258, in which was the defeat.　　　† From 1258 until 1272.

‡ From 1272 until 1368, the date of the destruction of Mayapan. And the following, from 1368 to 1392.　　　§ From 1392 until 1488.　　　‖ From 1488 until 1512.

¶ From 1512 until 1536, which concluded the eleventh epoch; the following one beginning in 1536, and concluding in the year 1560.

the ruins and on the tops of the churches. It is quite abundant in Yucatan, though only one specimen was obtained, which was shot from the top of the cross over the gateway at the hacienda of the senoté (Mucuyché), as we rode up on our way to Uxmal. There does not appear to be any published description of this hawk. Still another hawk was procured, which also seems not to have been described; but, as it appears to be in immature plumage, it may be the young of some known bird. Besides these, among the specimens is the laughing falcon (Falco Cachinnans of Lin.). It is called by the natives koss, and was shot at Chichen Itza near the Castillo, and was stuffed. Another specimen of the same bird was procured on the way from Nohcacab to Uxmal, after our first attack of sickness. These birds are quite numerous throughout Yucatan.

Of the genus Strix but three varieties were seen, and of those two were preserved, both of which are believed to be undescribed. The first, a little owl, about six inches and a half long, of a tawny colour, lighter beneath, which was shot near Merida. The second is about six inches long, of a brown above and lighter beneath, called by the natives tiquim thohca. Several specimens of both these owls were seen. The third was caught in one of the ruined buildings, and kept alive for a little while, but afterward escaped. It resembled somewhat the Strix Aluco of Europe. One was afterward shot at Sabachshé, but was so much injured that it could not be stuffed.

Of the genus Corvus were procured three species, two of which are apparently not described. The first is a very beautiful jay, the head and belly black; back, wings, and tail of a beautiful blue; the bill of the male is yellow, and of the female black; the legs yellow. It was first seen and shot near Sisal, on the way up to Merida, and afterward several other specimens were obtained in different parts of the country, for they are numerous throughout Yucatan. The other was first met with at Uxmal, where a female was shot, and afterward two males. They are of a dark brown on the head, neck, back, and tail; belly white; bill of male black, and female yellow; they have a most singular formation of the trachea, there being a sort of membranous sack or bag coming off in front of the trachea at about the middle of its length, and intimately connected with the skin of the neck; this formation, together with the great muscularity of the larynx, may account for their excessively loud and disagreeable cry. The other jay is the Corvus Peruvianus, Peruvian jay. (Shaw, vol. viii., plate 27.) This most beautiful bird is found in great abundance in almost all parts of Yucatan, which is probably its native country, as it is mentioned as rare in Peru.

Of the genus Psittacus were procured four species, three of which have been described, and perhaps the fourth also; but, as the specimen is bad, it is not easy to ascertain positively whether it has or not. One, the Psittacus Albifrons (Ind. Orn., vol. i., p. 119), white-crowned parrot (Shaw, vol. viii., p. 519), is very numerous throughout Yucatan. It is a beautiful bird, coloured with green, blue, red, white, and yellow. Another, supposed to be the Psittacus Guianensis (Gen. Lil., vol. i., p. 323), the green parrot of Guiana (Gen. Syn., i., 231), is not so abundant as the last, but still quite numerous. The specimens were procured at Ticul, and some were afterward shot near Iturbide. The third species was not seen in the wild state, the only specimen procured being given to Dr. Cabot, alive, by the padre Curillo, of Ticul. It is the Psittacus Macao (Ind. Orn., vol. i., p. 82), red and blue macaw (Gen. Syn., i., 199).

Of the genus Ramphastos one specimen was procured, the yellow-breasted toucan (Gen. Syn., vol. i., p. 326), Ramphastos Tucanus (Ind. Orn., vol. i., p. 136). This specimen does not agree with the description in Latham, but is the same as the one described by Mr. Edwards from a living specimen in Lord Spencer's collection. It was procured at Uxmal on the day when Dr. Cabot went down to the hacienda to operate on an Indian's leg. Two or three different species were afterward seen at Macobà, but Dr. C. did not succeed in killing any of them.

Of the genus Momotus were obtained two species: the first, the common Brazilian or blue-headed motmot; this was quite common in Yucatan, but not so common as the other, as to which it is doubtful whether it has been described. It is about the same length as the blue-headed, but the tail is longer in proportion to the body. The markings on the plumage are very different from those of the Brazilian; there is a black stripe extending down from the chin to the middle of the breast, bordered on each side with light blue; a broad, light blue, almost white, stripe extends over the eye from the base of the bill almost to the hind head. The general colour is a sort of greenish bay; primaries and tail light green, tipped with black; the two central feathers of the tail much longer than in the Brazilian, having the shaft bare to a much greater degree, and the feather at the tip is bright pale green, tipped broadly with black.

Of the genus Crotophaga one species was procured, the lesser ani (Crotophagi Ani. Ind. Orn., vol. i., p. 448). These were very abundant in all parts of the country.

Of the genus Oriolus, including under this denomination Icterus and Cassicus, were procured five species, one of which is supposed to be new, three doubtful, and one known. The male of the new species is nine inches and a half long; head, neck, cheeks, breast, belly, rump, tertiaries, and nearly the whole length of the outer tail feathers and the lower part of the third, and occasionally a stripe on the fourth, bright chrome yellow; face, throat, primaries, secondaries, back, and four, and sometimes six tail feathers, black; legs bluish; bill black, except the base of lower mandible, which is bluish; sings finely. Female eight inches and seventh eighths long; marked like the male, but not so brilliant; irides hazel. One of the doubtful comes very near to Latham's description of the lesser Bonana bird

(Oriolus Xanthornus. Ind. Orn., vol. i., p. 181), but is an Icterus, and differs in some particulars of plumage. Another of the doubtful resembles closely the black oriole, and another the black cassican, but is smaller. The known species is the St. Domingo oriole (Oriolus Dominicensis. Ind. Orn., vol. i., p. 182). Two specimens of this bird were procured, being the only two that were seen.

Of the genus Cuculus, including Polophilus, were procured two species. One resembles somewhat the bird described by Latham as the variegated coucal (Polophilus Variegatus); the other the Cayenne cuckoo (Cuculus Cayanus. Ind. Orn., vol. i., p. 221). These were both quite abundant throughout the country.

Of the genus Picus were procured three species, two of which are perhaps new. One of these resembles the little woodpecker of Europe (Picus Minor) very closely. The other resembles Latham's description of the Brazilian woodpecker (Picus Braziliensis). The known one is the lineated woodpecker (Picus Lineatus. Ind. Orn., vol. i., p. 226).

Of the genus Certhia were obtained two species, of one of which no description has been found, though Dr. Cabot was under the impression that he had seen specimens of it in some of the cabinets of Europe. It is three inches and seven eighths long; top of head, neck, and back, dark brown, each feather having a light, buff-coloured, pear-shaped mark in the centre; chin light buff colour; breast and belly light brown, each feather having also a light buff-coloured mark down the centre; primaries, secondaries, tertiaries, and tail dun-coloured ; bill one inch and three eighths along the ridge, and one inch and five eighths along the gap, bent in its whole length, and horn-coloured. They were not numerous. The other species is the yellow-bellied nectarinia (Nectarinia Flaveola. Vieill., Ois. Dor. Certh., plate 51, p. 102). They were quite numerous at Cozumel, where two specimens were procured. They were not seen in any other part of the country.

Of the genus Trochilus were procured two or three species, one of which is undescribed; another is probably the young of the same, and one is described. The undescribed, male, is four inches long; bill six eighths of an inch, yellowish, tipped with black; upper parts of head and back dull green; throat and upper part of breast bright emerald green in scales, with metallic lustre; lower part of breast, belly, and tail dun or bay colour; the feathers of the tail fringed and tipped with black; primaries dark brown, with some purplish reflections. The four middle tail feathers have greenish reflections on them. The female is rather less, and wants the bright emerald throat, the whole under parts being bay-coloured; the male has some white about the thighs. The known species is the Ourissia humming-bird (Trochilus Maugeri. Lesson.).

Of the genus Turdus were procured two species, thought to be new. One agrees very nearly with Le Merle de Paraguai, or Calandra, as described in Vieillot, but it wants the white on the wings. The other is a good deal like the Turdus Plumbeus, as described by the same author. The first is quite common throughout Yucatan, but the second is rather rare.

Of the genus Loxia were obtained four species, three of which are in immature plumage, and cannot, therefore, be placed with certainty. The other does not appear to have been described, though there are some descriptions which come near it. The male is nearly ten inches long; head and chin, extending down the sides of the neck, and in a crescent across the upper part of the breast, black; cheeks very dark steel gray; a white line extending from the bill over the eye almost to the hind head; hind head, back, secondaries, outer edge of the primaries, yellow olive; also the tail; the shafts of the feathers are black; part of the chin and throat pure white; breast, belly, and thighs cinereous; vent, and under the tail coverts, light bay; bill quite stout, nearly an inch long, and black; the female is about nine inches long, having dark cinereous brown in place of the olive; the other markings much the same as the male, but not so vivid. They are very common throughout Yucatan, and said to be very destructive in the fields and gardens: called by the Indians *tsapin*.

Of the genus Emberiza one was procured, in immature plumage; probably the painted bunting.

Of the genus Pipra one: the blue and yellow manakin, not common in Yucatan.

Of the genus Tanagra were procured two species, one of which is the red-crested tanager of Latham. But one pair was seen. The other is believed to be undescribed. The specimen was a male, six inches and a quarter long; bill inflated, and strongly toothed; at about the middle of the upper mandible, six eighths of an inch along the gap, top of the head, wings, and tail, of a deep raspberry, approaching maroon colour; back cinereous, tinged with red; chin and throat bright rose colour; breast and belly light cinereous; vent and under tail coverts light rosy red.

Of the genus Fringilla was procured one species, believed to be described in Latham as the cinereous finch (Fringilla Cinerea); they were quite common about Merida in the latter part of May.

Of the genus Lanius three species were obtained, all of which have been described. They are the Cayenne shrike (L. Cayanus. Ind. Orn., vol. i., p. 80), the rusty shrike (L. Rubiginosus), and the gray-headed shrike (Tanagra Guianensis. Ind. Orn., vol. i., p. 427), more properly the Lanius G. This bird sings quite prettily, and is rather common in Yucatan. The other two were rarer, especially the second.

Of the genus Muscicapa were obtained five species, four of which have been described. The specimen procured of the fifth was a male. It is six inches and a half long; bill one inch along the gap quite stout and broad; top of the head and nape black; back, wings, and tail very dark, slaty brown; breast, belly, cheeks, and chin light cinereous; throat and upper part of the breast bright rose colour; legs black. This was the only specimen seen in the country. The others were Muscicapa Coronata (round-crested flycatcher. Shaw, vol. v., pl. 13). This is quite common throughout Yucatan. Muscicapa Sulphuratus, not rare; M. Barbata, quite common; M. Ferox, very common.

Of the genus Sylvia one was obtained, in young plumage, and, therefore, uncertain whether new or not.

Of the genus Caprimulgus one species was obtained; the specimen so poor that nothing can be made of it.

Of the genus Columba were procured two species, one of which is in such imperfect plumage that its character cannot be made out. The other agrees very nearly with the blue pigeon (Columba Cærulea. Ind. Orn., vol. ii., p. 601). Both are common in Yucatan.

Of the genus Meleagris was procured one species (Meleagris Ocellata), the ocellated turkey, Cuv. This most magnificent bird is common throughout Yucatan.

Of the genus Penelope were procured two species; one the crested guan (P. Crestata. Ind. Orn., vol. ii., p. 619). These are called kosh by the natives; the only specimen seen was given to Dr. Cabot by the brother of the padrecito at Ticul, and was still alive in November, 1842. The other is the Penelope, or Phasianus Paragua (Ind. Orn., vol. ii., p. 632). They are common in all parts of Yucatan, where they are called chachalacha, from the noise they make, which is perfectly astounding, and also bach by the Indians. They have a most remarkable arrangement of the trachea, which passes down on the external surface of the muscles, between them and the skin, in a long loop as low as the pubis, and then passes up on the other side, and enters the thorax.

Of the genus Crax two species were obtained; the red curassow (Crax Rubra, Lin., vol. i., p. 270), and C. Globicera (globose curassow). They are found throughout the country, and are called by the natives kambool.

Of the genus Tinamus one species was obtained, the variegated tinamou (T. Variegatus). They are quite common throughout Yucatan, where they are called by the natives partridges. They are kept tame in many of the houses, being very useful in destroying scorpions, &c.

Of the genus Ortyx one species was obtained, which, as far as the plumage and size go, is undescribed, but it has the same note, habits, &c., as our quail or partridge. It is smaller; the throat of the male is jet black, and most of the markings are different, though having a general resemblance to the Ortyx or Perdix Virginianus. They are very numerous in all parts of Yucatan.

Of the genus Cancroma one specimen was procured, the cinereous boat-bill, which was killed at the senoté at Chichen.

Of the genus Jacana also one species was obtained, the variable jacana

(Parra or Jacana Variabilis. Ind. Orn., vol. i., p. 763). It was killed at Uxmal, at one of the small aguadas, and was the only one seen in the country.

Of the genus Gallinula Dr. Cabot procured two species, the Cayenne gallinule (G. Cayanensis. Ind. Orn., vol. ii., p. 767) and the black-bellied gallinule (G. Ruficollis. Ind. Orn., vol. ii., p. 767).

Of the long-billed wren one specimen only was seen. The violet-headed trogon was more common, several having been procured in different places.

Besides the birds enumerated above, the following list comprises those which were procured in Yucatan, and which are found also in the United States, and have been well described by different naturalists.

Birds observed in Yucatan during the winter of 1841, '2, between the months of October and June, which are also found in the United States, and have been figured and described by Wilson, Audubon, Bonaparte, and Nuttall.

Cathartes Jota, all parts.
Cathartes Papa, at Labphak.
Cathartes Aura, all parts; less numerous than the C. Jota.
Aquila (?) Caracara, all parts.
Falco Pennsylvanicus.
Falco Haliætos.
Falco Cyaneus.
Falco Sparverius.
Icterus Spurius.
Quiscalus Major.
Quiscalus Versicolor.
Muscicapa Crinita.
Muscicapa Virens.
Muscicapa Atra.
Muscicapa Ruticilla.
Muscicapa Verticatis. (?)
Turdus Polyglottus.
Turdus Noveboracensis.
Turdus Lividus, Felisox.
Sylvia Virens.
Sylvia Mitrata.
Sylvia Trichas.
Sylvia Protonotarius.
Sylvia Maculosa. (?)
Sylvia Æstiva.
Sylvia Americana.
Sylvia Coronata.

Tanagra Æstiva.
Tanagra Rubra.
Fringilla Ludoviciana.
Fringilla Ciris.
Fringilla Cyanea.
Loxia Cœrulea.
Loxia Cardinalis.
Picus Carolinensis.
Trochilus Colubris.
Trochilus Mango.
Alcedo Alcyon.
Hirundo Rufa.
Hirundo Lunifrons. (?)
Hirundo Riparia.
Cypselus Pelasgius.
Caprimulgus Carolinensis.
Columba Passerina.
Columba Leucocephala.
Columba Zenaida.
Calidris Arenaria.
Himantopus Nigricollis.
Hæmatopus Ostralagus.
Charadrius Melodus.
Charadrius Wilsonius. (?)
Charadrius Semipalmatus. (?)
Charadrius Helveticus.
Strepsilus Interpres.
Ardea Herodias.

Ardea Rufescens.
Ardea Egretta.
Ardea Candidissima.
Ardea Ludoviciana. (?)
Ardea Nycticorax.
Ardea Cœrulea.
Ardea Lentiginosa.
Ardea Virescens.
Ardea Exilis.
Aramus Scolopaceus.
Phœnicopterus Ruber.
Platalea Ajaja.
Ibis Alba.
Numenius Longirostris.
Tringa Wilsonii.
Tringa Semipalmata.
Totanus Semipalmatus.
Totanus Vociferus.
Totanus Flavipes.
Totanus Chloropygius.
Totanus Macularius.

Totanus Bartramius.
Limosa Fedoa.
Scolopax Grisea.
Scolopax Wilsonii.
Gallinula Martinica.
Podiceps Minor.
Sterna Cayana.
Sterna Boysii.
Larus Atricilla.
Thalassidroma Wilsonii.
Anas Boschas.
Anas Strepera.
Anas Acuta.
Anas Americana.
Anas Discors.
Pelecanus Onocrotalus.
Phalacrocorax Carbo.
Phalacrocorax Graculus.
Trachypetes Aquilus.
Phæton Æthereus. (?)

COMMUNICATION FROM MR. SCHOOLCRAFT.

THE RED HAND.

The figure of the human hand is used by the North American Indians to denote supplication to the Deity or Great Spirit; and it stands in the system of picture writing as the symbol for strength, power, or mastery, thus derived. In a great number of instances which I have met with of its being employed, both in the ceremonial observances of their dances and in their pictorial records, I do not recollect a single one in which this sacred character is not assigned to it. Their priests are usually drawn with outstretched and uplifted hands. Sometimes one hand and one arm, but more commonly both are uplifted. It is not uncommon for those among them who profess the arts of medicine, magic, and prophecy (the three are sometimes united and sometimes not) to draw or depict a series of representative or symbolical figures on bark, skins of animals, or even tabular pieces of wood, which are a kind of notation, and the characters are intended to aid the memory in singing the sacred songs and choruses. When the inscriptions are found to be on wood, as they often are in the region of Lake Superior and the sources of the Mississippi, they have been sometimes called "music boards." I induced a noted meta, or priest, to part with one of these figured boards, many years ago, and afterward obtained impressions from it in this city by passing it through Mr. Maverick's rolling press.   It was covered with figures on both sides, one side containing forty principal figures; six embrace the symbol of the uplifted hand, four of which had also the arm, but no other part of the body, attached.   Their import, which the man also imparted to me, is given in the general remark above.   On the reverse of this board, consisting of thirty eight characters, nine embrace the uplifted hand, in one case from a headless trunk, but in the eight others connected with the whole frame.

The design of the hand is uniformly the same with our tribes, whether it be used disjunctively or alone, or connected with the arm alone, or with the whole body.   In the latter cases it is a compound symbol, and reveals some farther particular or associated idea of the action.   The former is the most mysterious use of it, precisely because there are no accessories to help out the meaning, and it is, I think, in such isolated cases, to be regarded as a general sign of devotion.

In the course of many years' residence on the frontiers, including various journeyings among the tribes, I have had frequent occasion to remark the use of the *hand alone* as a symbol, but it has generally been a symbol applied to the naked body after its preparation and decoration for sacred or festive dances.   And the fact deserves farther consideration, from these preparations being generally made in the arcanum of the medicine, or secret lodge, or some other private place, and with all the skill of the priest's, the medicine man's, or the juggler's art.   The mode of applying it in these cases is by smearing the hand of the operator with white or coloured clay, and impressing it on the breast, the shoulder, or other part of the body.   The idea is thus conveyed, that a secret influence, a charm, a mystic power is given to the dancer, arising from his sanctity or his proficiency in the occult arts.   This use of the hand is not confined to a single tribe or people.   I have noticed it alike among the Dacotahs, the Winnebagoes, and other Western tribes, as among the numerous branches of the red race still located east of the Mississippi River, above the latitude of 42°, who speak dialects of the Algonquin language.

A single additional fact appears to me to be pertinent to your inquiry. In an excursion which I made in the year 1831 into the more unfrequented and interior parts of the Chippewa country, lying between the group of the Twelve Apostles' Islands in Lake Superior and the Falls of St. Anthony, I came to a curious edifice, situated in the edge of the forest, on the elevated banks of a fine lake, which was exclusively used as the village temple.   It was built of stout posts, describing a circle, firmly and well sheathed with thick bark, fastened on transverse pieces.   It constituted a peculiarity in this structure that there was a circular building within, or, rather, it was arranged after the manner of the whorls of a sea-shell, so that a person could, as it were, involve himself in a labyrinth.   It had a single door, subject to the entrance of the priest only.   As this person was the political chief of the band, and a man of more than ordinary intellect, he appeared to have adopted this mode of exhibiting his skill and securing and extending his power. He permitted me to inspect the building. Drums, rattles, and other insignia of the priest's art, were hung up on the wall. Heads of men were rudely carved or inscribed, and numerous marks of the hand, as in the case of naked dancers, were impressed on the involutions of the inner walls.

I have expressed the opinion that the human hand denotes strength, or power, or mastery arising from devotional acts. The want or absence of the hand or arm, therefore, in these symbolical figures, should imply impotence, weakness, or cowardice, arising from fright, subjugation, or other causes; and such is found to be the import of the armless figure of the human body in two of the symbols of the ancient hieroglyphic inscription on the Assonet, or Dighton Rock, as explained by the well-known American chief Chingerauk.

THE END.

CPSIA information can be obtained at www.ICGtesting.com
Printed in the USA
BVOW03*0053200816

459563BV00002B/14/P